AF361505

A LEARNER'S GRAMMAR OF LEVANTINE ARABIC

A Learner's Grammar
of Levantine Arabic

CHRISTOPHER HITCHCOCK

Thoroughly reviewed by Elias Shakkour

GEORGETOWN UNIVERSITY PRESS / WASHINGTON, DC

The publisher is not responsible for third-party websites or their content. URL links were active at time of publication.

Library of Congress Cataloging-in-Publication Data

Names: Hitchcock, Chris (Translator), author. | Shakkour, Elias, editor.
Title: A learner's grammar of Levantine Arabic / Christopher Hitchcock; thoroughly reviewed by Elias Shakkour.
Description: Washington, DC : Georgetown University Press, 2024. | Includes index.
Identifiers: LCCN 2023052682 (print) | LCCN 2023052683 (ebook) | ISBN 9781647124854 (hardcover) | ISBN 9781647124861 (paperback) | ISBN 9781647124878 (ebook)
Subjects: LCSH: Arabic language—Grammar. | Arabic language—Dialects—Middle East. | Arabic language—Spoken Arabic. | Arabic language—Textbooks for foreign speakers—English.
Classification: LCC PJ6307 .H54 2024 (print) | LCC PJ6307 (ebook) | DDC 492.7/82421--dc23/eng /20231201
LC record available at https://lccn.loc.gov/2023052682
LC ebook record available at https://lccn.loc.gov/2023052683

∞ This paper meets the requirements of ANSI/NISO Z39.48-1992 (Permanence of Paper).
25 24   9 8 7 6 5 4 3 2   First printing

Printed in the United States of America
Cover design by Martyn Schmoll
Interior design by Matthew Williams

CONTENTS

ACKNOWLEDGMENTS

I would like to take the opportunity to thank everyone who has contributed to this book. In the absolute first place are Elias Shakkour, for whose help and insights I owe some huge percentage of my knowledge of Levantine Arabic and of this book, and to Barakat Abi Hanna and Nick Lobo, who took on the grueling task of reading the entire manuscript from beginning to end and providing me with crucial feedback. I would also like to thank Charlie Lawrie, Amr Mashlah, Benedikt Römer, Nerouz Satik, and Ruth O'Connell Brown, who have all contributed extensively to this book becoming a reality; Wasim Al Khatib, Majeed Jaafar, Sofia Hanezla, Ahmad Tahhan, Eyad Hamid, Fuad Isa, and Muhammad Amir, who have all helped me enormously; Amal Marogy, Nadira Auty and Rachael Harris, who were my first teachers of Arabic; and Hope LeGro, who has overseen this project from its long-ago beginnings through to its publication. And, of course, I also thank all the other informants and native speakers, too numerous to list, who have provided material or explanations to me over the years.

INTRODUCTION

This book is the product of several years of research and writing. What follows is an explanation of how it came together and what it is supposed to do as well as the reasoning behind some of the choices I have made that are likely to be controversial. This introduction is aimed primarily at teachers and linguists concerned with the general approach of the book. Learners who are more interested in getting straight into the nitty-gritty of grammar are encouraged to skip straight to the next section on how to use this book.

What Is This Book?

This is a grammar of Levantine Arabic, which is to say the group of dialects spoken in Jordan, Palestine, Lebanon, and western areas of Syria as well as limited areas of Turkey and Egypt. More specifically, it is a *learner's* grammar, meaning that it is designed for use by learners of spoken Levantine Arabic.

There are many possible ways of writing a learners' grammar. Works with this sort of title often restrict themselves to the key points or most common structures in order to avoid information overload and to prioritise the things that learners most need to know. They sometimes avoid more complex linguistic points because of the difficulty of explaining them in a way that is accessible to students without a linguistic background or because of a broader pedagogical commitment to natural or functional acquisition. Having this kind of resource available is crucial. My own previous attempts to produce learning materials for Levantine Arabic have been of this kind. But this book is intended to fill a different niche.

What I mean when I say that this book is a "learner's grammar" is that it is supposed to serve the needs, first and foremost, of learners of this set of dialects and not of, for example, academic linguists. This means a focus on semantics and usage from the perspective of an English speaker rather than typological or cross-linguistic points. It means avoiding, as far as is possible, linguistic terms of art and making sure to clearly define those terms that do appear. It means at times a more relaxed style than you might expect in a reference grammar in an attempt to make the material more accessible (as quixotic a quest as this may seem when writing about, for example, the properties of a transitive verb). And it means focusing on the "standard" forms of the dialects in question at the expense of regional variation.

I know that resources of this kind are needed because of my own experience learning Arabic and other languages. In recent years there has been an explosion of new material for learning Levantine and Arabic more broadly. Most of this material, however, targets the absolute basics or takes learners to an intermediate level where they learn useful expressions and vocabulary. Where does a learner without much of a linguistic background go to find an explanation of such forms as شمسات *shamsaat* "sun" or how exactly the dual is used in spoken Arabic? Where can they find a detailed explanation of how participles work in practice? This book is intended to address these sorts of questions and do so in a way that prioritises the needs of *learners*. Some parts began life as materials I produced for my own students. Others are old enough to have originated in my attempts to answer these questions for myself early on in the learning process.

The fact that this grammar is intended for learners and avoids much of the terminology used in the academic literature does not mean that this literature has not played a major role in the development of my analysis. In fact, one of the main aims of this book was to take some of the insights developed in seminal papers and books and make them a central part of how Arabic is described for nonnative speakers. Nobody would write a grammar of Chinese without reference to "topic," for example, but despite many linguists analysing Arabic through the lens of topic prominence, this idea is largely absent from teaching material. The influence of these ideas should be clear in the text.

Dialects Presented

Anyone who has a passing familiarity with Arabic dialectology will already be aware that the Levantine area is linguistically diverse. Putting exact borders on where this area begins and ends is difficult because of the quite fluid transitions between areas, but the borders can probably be said to extend from the Sinai (where it transitions into Egyptian) and southern Jordan (where it transitions into Hijazi) to Jazira and Deir ez-Zor in eastern Syria (where Mesopotamian begins) up into the Turkish province of Hatay. Even if we put aside the famous differences between rural, urban, and Bedouin dialects and focus exclusively on cities, there are isoglosses dividing Jerusalem from Bethlehem (twenty-six minutes by car), Beirut from Sidon (thirty-nine minutes by car), or Banias from Latakia (forty-five minutes by car), to give just a handful of examples. And there is no such thing as a "standard" or geographically neutral form of Syrian, Lebanese, Palestinian, or Jordanian Arabic.

When I set out to write this book, it seemed to me that there were two possible ways of addressing this diversity. The first would have been to try to detail as many of the different variants as possible without prejudice to their geographical scope. The second was to choose one dialect or a selection of dialects to prioritise. In the interest of both accessibility and brevity, this seemed like the better option for learners. After some thought, I decided to follow the well-established tradition of using the dialects of the respective national capitals as the pedagogical standard. I have played down features not present in one of these four dialects and largely consigned them to the additional note boxes scattered throughout the text.

This choice has its downsides. The capital dialects do not have the cachet of a standard language, and a learner who spends any time with native speakers at all is likely to encounter speakers with some features not described in this book. But these capital dialects *do* dominate the media, which these days is an indispensable resource for learning. There is some evidence that a process of dialect levelling is taking place within all four countries, and it is certainly true that speakers will often adopt more capital-like features in particular contexts. You are also most likely to visit one of the capital cities when travelling to a Levantine country. And speaking a capital dialect will allow you to make yourself understood wherever you go in the Levantine region.

On top of this four-way distinction, I have also followed the well-established convention of grouping Jordanian and Palestinian into South Levantine and Syrian and Lebanese into North Levantine. On purely dialectological grounds, this is not very precise: no matter what isogloss we choose as the basis for the distinction, the line between the northern and southern groups does not correspond to modern political borders. But Beirut and Damascus are firmly within the northern area while Amman and Jerusalem are within the southern area. As a result, the similarities between each pair mean that it is often possible to give only one form for each.

Sources

The analysis presented in this book is the product of observation, discussions with native speakers, and engagement with the academic literature. I owe most of the insights here to long discussions with friends and colleagues based on either observed usage in real life or academic analysis by scholars. I have not made any use of formal dialect corpora (although of course some of my sources drew on corpus studies). But this elicitation-based approach has its advantages. For one thing, it has allowed me to prioritise more common usages. For another, it has allowed me to select example sentences that are far more amenable to use by learners.

Early drafts of this book used many example sentences taken unmodified from media sources or social media platforms. While this sometimes provided amusing content, it had the unfortunate effect of filling the book with unusual vocabulary and in many cases with examples that exhibited properties that were not relevant to the point at hand (fronting or complex causative constructions in a section about demonstratives, for example). In this final version, most of the example sentences have been deliberately modified or elicited in order to avoid any distractions of this kind. While this has probably made them less exciting—and there are certainly a lot more references to bookcases in this version than there were in the original—it should make the book easier to use.

Any reference to modifying the example sentences is cause for legitimate alarm in a book that seeks to present native usage of a language as accurately as possible. In the vast majority of cases, all I have done to modify sentences is to remove additional material not central to the meaning of the sentence (adverbs, particles, extra clauses, and so on). More importantly, I have checked all the example sentences for correctness and naturalness with native speakers.

Arabic Script and Transliteration

This is the first grammar of *spoken* Arabic I am aware of that makes full use of Arabic script. In the past, this was understandable. Until first text messaging and then social media became major platforms for dialect writing, there were comparatively few contexts in which the spoken language had its own written form. But today dialect is dominant all over the internet and in personal communications. Even without learners' frequent opposition to studying Arabic in transliteration, this would be sufficient to make Arabic script indispensable in presenting dialect. More likely to be controversial is my decision to transliterate (or transcribe) every word in Latin script.

When first planning out the book, I considered—and discussed at length with colleagues—the possibility of minimising transliteration in favour of Arabic script. But despite its advantages, I decided that some kind of Latin script could not be dispensed with. For one thing, this allows those who cannot read Arabic to access the text. But more importantly, the Arabic script itself presents many obstacles to unambiguous transcription of dialect. The most obvious of these obstacles is the lack of sufficient characters and diacritics to represent all the phonemes used by Levantine Arabic. There is no straightforward way to write the sounds *g, v, oo,* and *ee* in ways distinct from *k, f, aw,* and *ay;* to discriminate between the various pronunciations of ق (*q, 2, g*); or to distinguish *Z* from *DH.*

Of course, there are ways of getting around this particular problem. Some writers have innovated new diacritics or put additional characters from other languages' orthographies to expand the inventory of the Arabic script. But this raises what is arguably a far more significant problem: how far these approaches take us from the way dialect is written in real life. It is not very useful to write dialect exclusively in a version of Arabic script that most native speakers would struggle to interpret. It is much more straightforward to write it *as it is usually written* and provide a Latin script transcription underneath. This is an approach taken by many other textbooks and grammars for Arabic, both written and spoken.

Rather than one of the diacritic-heavy transliteration systems often used in academic settings, I have chosen to use a system based on the conventions of so-called Arabizi (a full transliteration table is given in unit 1). This was motivated in part by my teaching experience: students often have a real antipathy for dots and hooks that does not seem to extend to numbers and capital letters. My choice for this system was also motivated by the fact that this system is akin to the usage of native speakers writing in the Latin alphabet, even if native use is less precise. This system reflects all the distinct phonemes of the different dialects, although I have taken some small liberties in the interest of economy of space. These liberties are addressed in the unit on sounds.

HOW TO USE THIS BOOK

This is a grammar of Levantine Arabic, which is to say the group of dialects spoken in Jordan, Palestine, Lebanon, and western areas of Syria as well as parts of Turkey and perhaps Egypt. The book is also meant to be a *learners'* grammar, which is to say that it aims at providing useful information not primarily to typological linguists or dialectologists but instead for those who are learning these dialects. As a result, this book comes with a few usage warnings.

The first has to do with the dialects covered. Dialectal diversity is generally far greater in the Levant than in English-speaking countries. For this reason, the book covers only four of the many Levantine dialects: those of the four capital cities of Damascus, Beirut, Jerusalem, and Amman. These dialects are the closest thing each country has to a media standard. They are also conveniently similar to one another, particularly the dialects of Damascus and Beirut (North Levantine) and Jerusalem and Amman (South Levantine).

The second point is related to the first. This book is *not* a dictionary. Although the dialects are structurally very similar, they often use quite different vocabulary for the same thing. Where words are used in example sentences, they are (hopefully) current in whatever dialect the sentence is given in. But the sentences are primarily there to demonstrate points of grammar and structure, and you use them as a source of vocabulary at your own risk.

To make the information as digestible as possible, I have divided most of the book into units, each at most two thousand words long. Although this may strike some readers as artificial, and while some bigger topics are covered in several units, each unit is intended to be fairly self-contained and a manageable single-session read. I would not recommend attempting to read and absorb multiple units at a time. Some topics do not lend themselves to this sort of structure (no matter how hard I have tried to crowbar them in). Those that are relatively peripheral to the main topics of the book I have placed at the end as appendices.

It is a much-repeated cliché, but nonetheless true, that grammars are always incomplete. This grammar is no exception. Despite its length—and it is longer than anyone, including me, expected it would be—there are plenty of topics that are not covered in as much detail as they deserve, and there are probably many structures that do not appear at all or only in passing. All I can say on this subject is that I hope you enjoy discovering these structures for yourself as much as I have enjoyed discovering those that have made it into the book.

You should note that the tables given in this book are generally intended to be read right to left. At first this might seem counterintuitive, but it follows the natural direction in which Arabic script is read. In many cases I have used the arrow sign (←) to remind readers of the right way to read.

Navigating the Dialects

Before plunging into the main body of the book, it is worth quickly discussing the dialect point in slightly more detail. As noted, this book approaches all of Levantine Arabic as a single dialect. I (obviously) think this is reasonable: with a few important differences, the dialects share the same basic system. When choosing examples, I have tacked heavily toward forms that are the same or similar across the region.

That being said, there clearly are some important differences between different dialects within the Levantine area. Most of those that we will be discussing here conveniently align with the distinction between North and South Levantine, that is, between Syrian and Lebanese on the one hand and Palestinian and Jordanian on the other. For this reason, it has often been enough to give two forms, divided by a slash. In these cases, unless otherwise noted, the first form will be North Levantine and the second form will be South Levantine.

In order to make navigating the examples as simple as possible, it is worth summarising the most important differences between northern and southern dialects that might trip you up or confuse you when you encounter them in example sentences. Firstly and perhaps most noticeably, North Levantine speakers typically collapse many short *u* sounds into *i*, resulting in divergent pronunciations such as the following (see unit 3):

North Levantine		South Levantine	
كنت	كم	كنت	كم
kint	*kimm*	*kunt*	*kumm*
I was	sleeve	I was	sleeve
قدام	مستشفى	قدام	مستشفى
2iddaam	*mistashfa*	*2uddaam*	*mustashfa*
in front of	hospital	in front of	hospital

There are various small differences in verb forms. The third-person feminine singular perfective suffix ـت "she -ed" is pronounced *-et* in the north and *-at* in the south (see unit 25):

North Levantine		South Levantine	
كتبت	اشتغلت	كتبت	اشتغلت
katb-et	*shtaghl-et*	*katb-at*	*shtaghl-at*
she wrote	she worked	she wrote	she worked

The biggest source of confusion is perhaps the imperfective (see units 26–27). The first-person imperfective prefix "I" is either ا *2i-* or nothing at all in the north, depending on context, but is أ *2a-* consistently in the south:

North Levantine		South Levantine	
اكتب	طير	أكتب	أطير
2i-ktob	*Tiir*	*2a-ktob*	*2a-Tiir*
I write	I fly	I write	I fly

When the *b-* prefix is added to the imperfective, southern speakers often contract *b-yi-* to *bi-*. For northern speakers, this is the form for "I":

North Levantine		South Levantine	
بمسك	بيمسك	بمسك	بمسك
b-i-msek	*b-yi-msek*	*b-a-msek*	*b-(y)i-msek*
I grab	he grabs	I grab	he grabs

Southern speakers also have a set of imperfective prefixes, with *u* used when the stem vowel is *o*, which northern speakers do not have:

North Levantine		South Levantine	
تمسك	تكتب	تمسك	تكتب
ti-msek	*ti-ktob*	*ti-msek*	*tu-ktob*
you grab	you write	you grab	you write
يمسك	يكتب	يمسك	يكتب
yi-msek	*yi-ktob*	*yi-msek*	*yu-ktob*
he grabs	he writes	he grabs	he writes

Where North Levantine speakers have only one verbal negator, ما *maa*, southern speakers can also negate verbs with the forms *ma-sh* and *-sh* (see unit 76):

North Levantine		South Levantine	
ما بكتب	ما رحت	بكتبش	مرحتش
maa biktob	*maa ri7et*	*baktub-esh*	*ma-ru7t-esh*
I don't write	I didn't go	I don't write	I didn't go

There are various other small differences in the forms of pronoun suffixes and common grammatical words, although these often differ from country to country:

North Levantine		South Levantine	
ـكن	ـهن	ـكم	ـهم
-kon	*-hon*	*-kom*	*-hom*
you [P]	them	you [P]	them
هونيك		هناك	
huniik		*hunaak*	
there		there	

Although these differences may seem very significant—and there are others, as we will see—they are dwarfed by the similarities that the dialects share.

PART 1

Sounds

The Sounds of Levantine Arabic

In this unit I will introduce the consonants and vowels that are used in Levantine Arabic. Since it is difficult to describe exact pronunciation except using very specialised linguistic terminology and since there is so much regional variation, I won't be going into very much detail on the exact "realisations" of each sound.

Instead, I will focus mainly on what linguists call the different *phonemes*—the specific units of sound, differentiated from one another, that make up words. These units themselves are largely consistent across the four dialects, although their exact pronunciation is not. In order to develop a good accent, the only option is to listen to and imitate native speakers. But it will help, as a first step, to know what sounds you are supposed to be distinguishing.

A Note on Spelling and Transliteration

Because spoken Arabic is not standardised, colloquial words can be written in a variety of different ways. This ranges from slightly modified fuS7a spelling (قايل *2aayel*) to the very phonetic and simply incorrect by fuS7a standards (ئايل *2aayel*). Most speakers lean toward the former, and since this is both the most common and the most straightforward way of writing dialect, I have largely stuck to it in this book.

Since this spelling lacks ways of distinguishing many of the sounds that appear in dialect—especially vowels but also some consonants—I have also used a transcription/transliteration system to indicate pronunciation. This system is idiosyncratic and based on the (increasingly obsolete) *3arabiizi* conventions used to write Arabic when no Arabic script provision is available. This has the downside of involving capital letters and numbers in places that seem quite unnatural to an English speaker. But it also has the advantage of clearly signposting distinctions that can easily be lost when relying on small hooks and subscript dots, as more scientific transliterations do.

Consonants

There are twenty-eight distinct consonants that all speakers use. Five of these are so-called "emphatic" versions of other consonants, which are distinguished by the exact positioning of the tongue as they are pronounced:

Transliteration	Normal	Transliteration	Emphatic
2	بقول *bi2uul* he says		
3	عيلة *3eele* family		
7	حط *7aTT* put		
b	باع *baa3* sell		
d	داق *daa2* taste	D	ضرب *Darab* hit
f	فات *faat* enter		
g	أركيلة *2argiile* shisha pipe		
gh	غار *ghaar* be jealous		
h	هيك *heek* like that		

Transliteration	Normal	Transliteration	Emphatic
j	جاب *jaab* bring		
k	كتب *katab* to write		
kh	خايف *khaayef* afraid		
l	لبق *libe2* to suit	*L*	الله *2aLLaa* God
m	مكتبة *maktabe* bookcase		
n	مناخ *manaakh* climate		
q	موسيقى *musiiqa* music		
r	رقص *ra2eS* dancing		
s	سؤال *su2aal* question	*S*	صلى *SaLLa* to pray
sh	اشترى *shtara* to buy		

Transliteration	Normal	Transliteration	Emphatic
t	إنتي *2inti* you [F]	*T*	طار *Taar* to fly
w	واطي *waaTi* low		
y	يأس *ya2s* despair		
z	زيد *ziid* add!	*Z*	الظاهر *'ZZaaher* it seems that

There are also three consonants used by only some speakers, primarily but not exclusively South Levantine speakers:

OPTIONAL CONSONANTS (INTERDENTALS)			
Nonemphatic		**Emphatic**	
th	ثورة *thawra* revolution	—	—
dh	مذاق *madhaaq* taste	*DH*	ظل *DHill* shadow

Finally, there are two consonants that appear only in a handful of loanwords and that are pronounced as *p* and *v*, respectively, in some cases:

Nonemphatic		**Emphatic**	
p	أوروبا *2uruppa* Europe	—	—

Nonemphatic		Emphatic	
v	فيديو *viidyo* video	—	—

Note that unlike in English, consonants can be doubled even at the beginning or end of a word. The following pairs are distinguished by the length of the consonant:

Short	Long
درس *daras* to study	درس *darras* to teach
لمح *lama7* to catch a glimpse of	لمح *lamma7* to hint
توب *tuub* repent!	تتوب *ttuub* you repent
حكي *7aki* speaking	حكي *7akki* talk to … !

Vowels

All Levantine dialects have the following long and short vowels. Vowel length is very important to distinguish and is often difficult for native English speakers. Note the distinctions:

Transliteration	Short	Transliteration	Long
a	كتب *katab* to write	*aa*	قال *2aal* to say
e	نومة *noome* sleep	*ee*	غير *gheer* other than

Transliteration	Short	Transliteration	Long
i	دب *dibb* bear	*ii*	ديب *diib* wolf
o	إيدو *2iido* his hand	*oo*	سودا *sooda* black [F]
u	مظاهرة *muZaahara* demonstration	*uu*	قول *2uul* say!

There are also two short diphthongs shared by all speakers:

ay	بيروت *bayruut* Beirut	*aw*	دورة *dawra* course

And one long diphthong that exists primarily in South Levantine because of deletion of final *-e* (see unit 8):

aay	كنباي *kanabaay* sofa

Many vowels are pronounced differently when adjacent to emphatic consonants, *q* and sometimes *r*.[1] Imitating native speakers is the only good way of acquiring this, but note, for example, that the *a* in one set is "light," similar to the vowel in "cat," and in the other is "dark," similar to the vowel in "father":

Dark		Light	
حط *7aTT* to put	طار *Taar* to fly	كتب *katab* to write	ناس *naas* people

Similarly, *i* is often pronounced in a way that approaches the "schwa" sound in English (the sound in "banana") when it appears in the vicinity of these consonants.

In a few other common examples, the vowel is dark with other consonants:

ألمانيا	بابا	ماما	رب
2almaanya	*baaba*	*maama*	*rabb*
Germany	dad	mum	lord

Emphatic Consonants

The emphatic consonants are *S*, *T*, *D*, *Z*, and *DH*, as well as the less common *L*. Exactly what differentiates emphatic consonants from their nonemphatic equivalents is controversial, but the main thing is that the back of the tongue is raised and tensed. The following pairs are all distinct:

ظاهر	زاهر	عض	عد	طار	تار
Zaaher	*zaaher*	*3aDD*	*3add*	*Taar*	*taar*
apparent	flowering	to bite	to count	to fly	vendetta
		عصير	عسير	قصر	أثر
		3aSiir	*3asiir*	*2aSSar*	*2assar*
		juice	hard	to fall short	to affect

For English speakers, the most obvious indicator of an emphatic consonant will probably be their effect on the pronunciation of the surrounding vowels.

In transcription I have generally written only the "main" emphatic consonant (the consonant written as emphatic in the Arabic script) with a capital letter. But in fact emphasis tends to spread throughout the word, affecting all other consonants and vowels.[2] In the following examples I have put a more precise phonetic transcription between the slashes:

اتصل	شلوط	صوت	انبسطتو
^{i}*ttaSal*	*shalluuT*	*Soot*	^{i}*nbasaTtu*
/TTaSaL/	/shaLLuụT/	/SooT/	/imbaSaTTu/
to phone	kick	voice	you [P] enjoyed

Note that there are a few words that are commonly written with emphatic consonants but are not pronounced emphatic. This is particularly common with *S*:

صدق	صندوق
sadda2	*sanduu2*
to believe	box

In other cases, two variants exist in different regions or among different speakers. De-emphasis of this kind is particularly common in Lebanon.

Assimilation

Assimilation is the process by which one sound comes into contact with another sound and becomes *more like it* in terms of how it is pronounced. Some assimilations occur for almost everybody, while some occur for some speakers only.

One very common form of assimilation is between *r*, *n*, and *l*, which when clustered together often merge into a doubled version of the second consonant:

يكنلك	يكون	نروح	تروح
ykun-lak	*ykuun*	*nruu7*	*truu7*
/ykullak/	/ikuun/	/rruu7/	/truu7/
he is to you	he is	we go	you go

An assimilation of this kind is universal in the form صارل *SaLL-* "has been doing" (see unit 40) and is reasonably common elsewhere in rapid speech.

It is also common for voiceless consonants to be voiced when they come into contact with other voiced consonants. Voiced consonants are those where the vocal cords vibrate when you're saying them. The relevant consonants here are:

Voiceless		Voiced	
—		*b*	ب
t	ت	*d*	د
k	ك	*k*	ك
f	ف	*v*	ف
x	خ	*gh*	غ
s	س	*z*	ز
th	ث	*dh*	ذ
T	ط	*D*	ض
S	ص	*DH*	ظ

When consonants from the left column come into contact with consonants from the right column, they often become voiced themselves. I don't usually indicate this in my transliteration, but here are some examples from a Syrian speaker:

قصدي	قصد	بكذب	كذب
2aSdi	*2aS^ed*	*bikzob*	*kazab*
/2aZdi/	/2aSed/	/bigzob/	/kazab/
my intention	intention	I lie	to lie

نسبة	نسب	رافضة	رافض
nisbe	*nasab*	*raafDa*	*raafeD*
/nizbe/	/nasab/	/raavDa/	/raafeD/
attribution	to attribute	refusing [F]	refusing [M]

In Jordanian and Palestinian, 3 sometimes assimilates to 7 when preceding *h*:

معهد	معهم
ma3had	*ma3hom*
/ma77ad/	/ma77om/
institute	with them

Note also that some assimilations have become standardised as part of the root to the extent that they are carried over into other forms of the word. One universal example of this is صغير *zghiir*, from which we get the forms صغر *zigher* "get smaller" and زغرة *zighra/zughra* "insult."

Notes

1. This list may vary from area to area.

2. The exact workings of this system are difficult to study and probably differ considerably from region to region. Some papers claim that emphasis spreading (at least rightward spreading) is blocked by *y* and short *i*. At least one MRI study on a Lebanese dialect found no evidence for this, and my very much not scientific tests of natives from several areas seem to bear out the idea that emphasis spreads throughout the word with no exception. In any case, the best thing for a learner to do is try to imitate natives. See A. Israel et al., "Emphatic Segments and Emphasis Spread in Lebanese Arabic: A Real-Time Magnetic Resonance Imaging Study," *Interspeech* 13, no. 3 (2012); and Ruben Van de Vijver, "Emphasis Spread in Two Dialects of Palestinian," *Linguistics in the Netherlands* (1996): 245–55.

Stress and the Helping Vowel

In this unit, we will discuss two key elements of Levantine phonology that are best considered together: the placement of stress and the use of the helping vowel.

Stress

The position of stress in Levantine Arabic is almost entirely predictable, with a small number of exceptions. The general system is the same across the Levantine area and is nearly identical to the system normally described for fuS7a:

1. If the final syllable has a long vowel, it is stressed: وراه *wa.__raa__,* مباراة *mu.baa.__raa__,* بتحكيه *bti7.__kii__,* مفتاح *mif.__taa7__.*
2. If the second-to-last syllable has a long vowel or ends in a consonant, it is stressed: مكاتب *ma.__kaa__.teb,* كتبنا *ka.__tab__.na.*
3. If neither of these two conditions applies, the stress is on the third-to-last syllable or, in a word with only two syllables, the second-to-last syllable: كتبو *__ka__.ta.bu,* طلبة *__Ta__.la.be,* كتب *__ka__.tab,* مشي *__mi__.shi.*

There are two main cases of irregular stress in North Levantine, occurring with the suffix ـت *-et* (see unit 25) and in the imperfective of *fta3al* and *nfa3al* verbs (see unit 27). Compare the (irregular) northern forms with their southern counterparts:

North Levantine	South Levantine
كتبتو	كتبتو
kat__bi__to	kat__ba__to
she wrote it	she wrote it

North Levantine	**South Levantine**
بتتصل	بتتصل
btitt**i**Sel	btittSel
you phone	you phone

Note that some speakers shorten long vowels in unstressed open syllables. This is discussed further in unit 3.

Helping Vowel

There are many consonant clusters that Levantine speakers find difficult to pronounce. Within words, these clusters are typically broken up with a helping vowel inserted after the first consonant in the cluster. I write helping vowels in superscript:[1]

ضرب	شربت	جملتو	بتكتبي
Dar^{e}b	*shrib^{e}t*	*jum^{i}lto*	*btuk^{u}tbi*
hitting	I drank	his sentence	you [F] write

A helping vowel may also occur at the beginning of a word, either after a pause—with words that begin with difficult clusters—or to smooth the transition between two words that would otherwise produce a complex cluster:

انمسك	جيب قلام	كتب كتابو	كبير العيلة
^{i}nmasak	*jiib ^{i}2laam*	*katab ^{i}ktaabo*	*kbiir ^{i}l3eele*
he got caught	get some pens!	he got engaged	the oldest child

Note that where two words coming together would produce a four-consonant cluster, the helping vowel appears between the second and third consonants (i.e., between the two words):

مسكت المجرم	كتبت كتابي	خوفت كلابي
masakt ^{i}lmujrem	*katabt ^{i}ktaabi*	*khawwaft ^{i}klaabi*
I've caught the criminal	I got engaged	you scared my dogs

Doubled consonants (see unit 1) generally cannot be broken up with a helping vowel. The only exception to this rule is a final *-tt* produced by the addition of the suffix ـت *-t*. Here, the two *t*s can be broken up with the helping vowel as with any other cluster. Note that the suffix is often written with a separate ـت in Arabic script:

بعتت	بعتتو
ba3at-ᵉt	*ba3at-t-o*
I sent	I sent it

The helping vowel is pronounced like its nonhelping counterpart but cannot be stressed and is ignored for the purposes of stress placement. The stress in the following words falls exactly where it would if the helping vowel were not there:

مشكلة	بتكتبي	جملتو	خوفتني
mish*ᶦkle*	**btu**kᵘtbi	**ju**mᶦlto	khaw**waf**ᶦtni
problem	you [F] write	his sentence	you scared me

The helping vowel is pronounced differently in different regions. In North Levantine, it is *e* in final syllables and *i* everywhere else:

Final	Midword	Initial
عذر	جملتو	صغار
3iz{ᵉ}r	*jim{ᶦ}lto*	*ᶦzghaar*
excuse	his sentence	small [P]
خبز	بتمسكي	كتبت كتابي
khib{ᵉ}z	*btim{ᶦ}ski*	*katabt ᶦktaabi*
bread	you [F] grab	I got engaged
درب	بتدرسي	اضطريتي
dar{ᵉ}b	*btid{ᶦ}rsi*	*ᶦDTarreeti*
road	you [F] study	you [F] had to

In South Levantine, the system is more complicated. The default is still *i* (or *e* in final syllables). But when the helping vowel is adjacent to *2, 3, h, 7, gh, k, g, q,* or *r and* where the preceding syllable has a *u*, it is pronounced *u* (*o* in final syllables):

u/o		i/e	
شرب	عذر	جملتو	خبز
shur{ᵒ}b	*3uz{ᵒ}r*	*jum{ᶦ}lto*	*khub{ᵉ}z*
drinking	excuse	his sentence	bread

u/o		i/e	
مهلتو	بكلتي	صغار	درب
*muh**ᵘlto*	*buk**ᵘlti*	*ⁱzghaar*	*dar**ᵉb*
his deadline	my hairclip	small [P]	road
بتضربي	بتكتبو	بتدرسي	بتمسكي
*btuD**ᵘrbi*	*btuk**ᵘtbu*	*btid**ⁱrsi*	*btim**ⁱski*
you [F] hit	you [P] write	you [F] study	you [F] grab

A handful of words, exceptionally, may also have *a*: بحر *ba7ᵃr* "sea."

Note

1. Following the Georgetown University Press transliteration of Syrian and the similar convention followed for Palestinian in Yohanan Elihay, *The Olive Tree Dictionary: A Transliterated Dictionary of Conversational Eastern Arabic* (Minerva Publishing, 2007).

Regional Variation

In this unit we will discuss some of the main differences in pronunciation between different Levantine dialects. As above, we will not be focusing on the specifics of how each sound is produced in the mouth. We will be looking only at changes that make a difference to meaning.

Inherited and Borrowed Vocabulary

Before looking at regional variation, we need to be familiar with the distinction between *inherited* and *borrowed* vocabulary. On the one hand—assuming for the sake of simplicity that classical Arabic is the ancestor of both fus7a and modern Arabic dialects[1]—we can identify various correspondences between fuS7a and Levantine words. These words are assumed to be inherited from an older form of the language because they exhibit all the natural sound changes that have taken place over time:

FuS7a		Levantine	
th	ثلاثة *thalaatha* three	*t*	تلاتة *tlaate* three
dh	ذاب *dhaaba* to melt	*d*	داب *daab* to melt
DH	ظهر *DHahr* back	*D*	ضهر *Daher* back

FuS7a		Levantine	
q	قال *qaala* to say	*2*	قال *2aal* to say
2	رأس *ra2s* head	(dropped with vowel lengthening)	راس *raas* head
U	معلم *mu3allim* teacher	(dropped in some contexts)	معلم *m3allem* teacher

At the same time, spoken Arabic has—for want of a better word—borrowed extensively from fuS7a. These borrowings are adapted to some extent to the structure of Levantine. But as you can see, they do *not* show evidence of the various historical sound changes that their inherited counterparts display:

FuS7a		Levantine			
th	ثورة *thawra* revolution	*th*	ثورة *thawra* revolution	*s*	ثورة *sawra* revolution
dh	نفذ *naffadha* implement	*dh*	نفذ *naffadh* implement	*z*	نفذ *naffaz* implement
DH	مظاهرة *muDHaahara* demonstration	*DH*	مظاهرة *muDHaahara* demonstration	*Z*	مظاهرة *muZaahara* demonstration
q	مقالة *maqaala* article	*q*	مقالة *maqaale* article		
2	رأسا *ra2san* straight away	*2*	رأسا *ra2san* straight away		

FuS7a		Levantine		
u	سرور *suruur* happiness	*u*	سرور *suruur* happiness	

This distinction between inherited and borrowed vocabulary exists for all speakers to a greater or lesser extent, although Lebanese speakers are considerably more likely to adapt fuS7a vocabulary to inherited norms, as we will see. Unfortunately for learners with prior knowledge of the written language, there is no strict rule that will allow you to identify which words fall into each category 100 percent of the time. A decent rule of thumb is that more everyday or lower-register words are likely to be inherited, while higher-register (technical, political, academic) terms and modern coinages are likely to be borrowed.

q, *2*, and *g*

The letter ق *qaaf* has two possible pronunciations for most speakers of Levantine Arabic. In inherited words, it is most commonly pronounced as a glottal stop *2*:

قال	بقي	قبر	داق
2aal	*bi2i*	*2abᵉr*	*daa2*
to say	to stay	grave	to taste

In borrowed vocabulary, it is typically pronounced as *q*:

ديمقراطية	مقالة	قيادة	استقلال
dimuqraaTiyye	*maqaale*	*qiyaade*	*2istiqlaal*
democracy	article	leadership	independence

There are two important regional variations to bear in mind, however. First, Lebanese speakers are much more likely to use *2* even here. The following pronunciations are all common in Lebanon alongside those with *q*:

ديمقراطية	مقالة	قيادة	استقلال
dimu2raaTiyye	*ma2aale*	*2iyaade*	*2isti2laal*
democracy	article	leadership	independence

The other caveat concerns Jordanian speakers. Jordanians maintain the distinction between *q* words and *2* words discussed above. But for male speakers in particular, *g* commonly alternates with *2* in at least some social contexts:

قال	بقي	قبر	داق
gaal	*bigi*	*gab*ᵉ*r*	*daag*
to say	to stay	grave	to taste

Unlike in other regions—where the *g* pronunciation is distinctly rural and likely to sound inappropriate from a nonnative—learners might be expected to imitate this feature in appropriate social situations, particularly male learners.[2]

The Interdentals (*th*, *dh*, and *DH*)

The sounds *th*, *dh*, and *DH* occur only in borrowed vocabulary, and only then for some speakers. In particular, South Levantine speakers are likely to produce interdentals in words such as the following:

ظاهرة	ذروة	ثورة
DHaahira	*dhurwa*	*thawra*
phenomenon	apogee	revolution

> For urban speakers, lower-register vocabulary has *t, d, D*, whereas *fuS7a* would have interdental sounds: ثلاثة *tlaate* "three," داق *daa2* "taste." Some rural dialects retain the interdentals here, producing forms such as ثلاثة *thlaathe*.

This pronunciation also occurs for some people in North Levantine. But northern speakers are much more likely to pronounce these sounds identically to *s, z*, and *Z*, respectively:

ظاهرة	ذروة	ثورة
Zaahira	*zurwe*	*sawra*
phenomenon	apogee	revolution

These pronunciations also occur in a few common words even for many South Levantine speakers (عذر *3uz*ᵒ*r* "excuse," تذكر *tzakkar* "remember").

The Vowels *i* and *u* (North Levantine)

One of the most immediately noticeable differences between North and South Levantine
is in the distribution of *u* and *i*. For North Levantine speakers, short *u* historically collapsed
into *i* in all but final syllables. Consider the following pairs:

North Levantine		South Levantine	
كنت	كتب	كنت	كتب
kin^et	kitob	kun^et	kutob
I was	books	I was	books
دق	دب	دق	دب
di22	dibb	du22	dubb
tap!	bear	tap!	bear

Note, however, that this merger does not necessarily apply to all words. Particularly in
Syrian, many nouns and adjectives have restored the *u* under the influence of fuS7a. Pairs
such as the following exist across North Levantine, with Lebanese speakers more likely overall to use the *i* forms:

مسلم	مسلم	لغة	لغة	حب	حب
mislem	*muslem*	*lugha*	*ligha*	*7ubb*	*7ibb*
Muslim	Muslim	language	language	love	love

The vowel *u* is also normal in words borrowed from fuS7a:

متغير	مدرب	مرور	حضور
mutaghayyer	*mudarreb*	*muruur*	*7uDuur*
variable	trainer	traffic	presence

Vowel Shortening

South Levantine speakers systematically shorten long vowels in unstressed open syllables
(i.e., those that do not end with a consonant). Compare the transcription and the pronunciations below. Note that shortened *ee* and *oo* are generally pronounced *i* and *u*:

كنبايات	معليهوش	جوعان
kanabaayaat	*ma3aleehoosh*	*joo3aan*
/kanabayaat/	/ma3alihoosh/	/ju3aan/
sofas	is not on him	hungry

فيران

fiiraan

/firaan/

mice

بقولولك

bi2uuluulak

/bi2uluulak/

they say to you

Because the effect is predictable (whereas long vowels are not), I generally give words with long vowels except in specifically South Levantine examples.

> This rule does not apply to the plural pattern مفاعيل *mafa3iil* (see unit 12), whose second vowel is pronounced short by all speakers: مكاتيب *makatiib* "letters." Nor does it apply to the feminine past forms of فاعل *faa3al* verbs (see unit 23), whose long vowel is always pronounced long: كاتبتني *kaatabatni* "she wrote to me."

Since this rule applies to unstressed syllables and the addition of suffixes can sometimes lead to a stress shift, this rule has implications for the behaviour of suffixes (see unit 4).

Diphthongs

A diphthong is a combination of a vowel and a semivowel (*y* or *w*). There are two common diphthongs shared by most speakers: *ay* and *aw*.

For most speakers, *aw* is a counterpart of inherited *oo* appearing in words borrowed from fuS7a. For these speakers, pairs such as the following are common:

دورة	دورة	دولة	دولة
dawra	*doora*	*dawle*	*doole*
course	spin	state	coffee pot

The combination *ay* is less common and seems to occur largely in unstressed open syllables (those not ending in a consonant) as a variant of *ee*:

بيروت	صيدلية	بيتوتي	فيروز
bayruut	*sayDaliyye*	*baytuuti*	*fayruuz*
Beirut	pharmacy	homebody	Feyrouz

For Lebanese speakers, however, diphthongs operate quite differently. In inherited vocabulary, they diphthongise the long vowels *oo* and *ee* when the syllable does not end with a consonant. Compare the following:

ميلة	ميل	صوتي	صوت
may.li	*meel*	*Saw.ti*	*Soot*
side	bending	my voice	voice

South Levantine speakers have an additional long diphthong, *-aay*, which results from the deletion of the feminine suffix *-e* (see unit 8) from various words. Compare the following pairs:

North Levantine		South Levantine	
كنباية	مراية	كنباي	مراي
kanabaaye	*mraaye*	*kanabaay*	*mraay*
sofa	mirror	sofa	mirror
جايه		جاي	
jaaye		*jaay*	
coming		coming	

Notes

1. The broad consensus in historical linguistics is, of course, that this is not the case, although there are various accounts of the exact genealogy of the dialects.

2. Whole studies have been written on the sociolinguistic implications of how ق is pronounced. In short, *g* and *2* were originally associated with "native" Jordanians and Palestinian Jordanians, respectively. Today, however, there is also a gender element: women tend to use *2* invariably, while men use both (macho, vernacular) *g* and (educated, refined) *2* in different contexts. Enam El-Wer and Bruno Herin, "The Lifecycle of Qaf in Jordan," *Langage et societé* 2011/4, no. 138 (2011): 59–76.

Sound Changes

In this unit, we will look at some of the sound changes that occur when suffixes are added. There are three major changes that occur with almost all suffixes:

- Stress shifts and lengthening,
- Changes to and deletion of the vowels *e* and *o*, and
- Shifts to semivowels at the end of the word.

There is a fourth change that occurs for some speakers, vowel shortening, which we will discuss last.

Stress Shifts and Lengthening

As we saw in unit 2, stress in Arabic is overwhelmingly predictable from the shape and syllable structure of the word. Since adding suffixes by definition changes word shape, it can also change the stress.

Recall that a final syllable can only be stressed if it contains a long vowel. A second to last syllable, however, only needs to end in a consonant in order to attract stress. Suffixes beginning with consonants generally add an extra syllable to the word. This means that the original final syllable will be stressed:

مكتب + ـنا ← مكتبنا

*mak**tab**-na*	*-na*	***mak**tab*
our office	our	office

درس + ـتو ← درستو

*da**ras**-tu*	*-tu*	***da**ras*
you [P] studied	you [P]	he studied

خلص + ـت ← خلصت

khallaS-ᵉt	-ᵉt	**khallaS**
I finished	I	he finished

When a suffix beginning with a consonant is added to a final short vowel, it triggers lengthening of that vowel. This will also attract stress according to the normal rules:

بتنسى + ـني ← بتنساني

btin**saa**-ni	-ni	**btin**sa
you [M] forget me	me	you [M] forget

تشربي + ـها ← تشربيها

tishra**bii**-ha	-ha	**tish**rabi
you [F] drink it	it	you [F] drink

بعتنا + ـكي ← بعتناكي

ba3at**naa**-ki	-ki	ba**3at**na
we sent you [F]	you [F]	we sent

> For those speakers who regularly shorten unstressed long vowels in open syllables (see unit 3), a stress change can lead to a shortening of a vowel: كاتبها **kaa**teb /kaa.teb/ "has written" → كاتبها kaa**tib**ha /ka.**tib**.ha/ "has written it." But as noted above, this does not apply to *faa3al* verbs: مارست **maa**rasat "she practiced" → مارستو **maa**rasat-o /**maa**.ra.sa.to/ "she practiced it."

A vowel-initial suffix does not generally lead to shifts in stress:

مكتب + ـو ← مكتبو

maktab-o	-o	**mak**tab
his office	his	office

درس + ـو ← درسو

darasu	-u	**da**ras
they studied	they	he studied

Some suffixes are superheavy syllables in themselves and shift the stress out of the original word entirely:

مفوض + ـين ← مفوضين

mufawwa**D-iin**	-iin	mu**faww**aD
commissioners	-s	commissioner

رجيم + ـات ← رجيمات

*rejii**m-aat***   -aat   *re**jii**m*

diets   -s   diet

e/*i* and *o*/*u*

For most speakers, the short vowels *e* and *o* can only appear in unstressed final syllables. When adding a suffix means that this syllable ceases to be unstressed or is no longer word-final, the pronunciation of these vowels changes as a result. In North Levantine all such vowels become *i*, while in South Levantine *o* becomes *u* and *e* becomes *i*:

North Levantine		South Levantine	
بتمسكها ← بتمسك		بتمسكها ← بتمسك	
*btim**sik**-ha* **btim**sek		*btim**sik**-ha* **btim**sek	
you grab it you grab		you grab it you grab	
مجربها ← مجرب		مجربها ← مجرب	
*mjar**rib**-ha* **mjar**reb		*mjar**rib**-ha* **mjar**reb	
have tried it have tried		have tried it have tried	
بتضربها ← بتضرب		بتضربها ← بتضرب	
*bti**Drib**-ha* **bti**Drob		*btu**Drub**-ha* **btu**Drob	
you hit it you hit		you hit it you hit	

> Lebanese speakers in particular may not have this rule, using *i* and *u* everywhere. Some also allow deletion of short *a* in the same contexts as *i* and *u*.

There is a general principle that an unstressed *i*, *u*, *e*, or *o* in a nonfinal open syllable (one not ending in a consonant) is dropped. When a *vowel-initial suffix* is added, the application of this rule leads to predictable changes of the following kind:

مجرب + ـو ← مجربو

***mjarr**b-o*   -o   ***mjar**reb*

have tried it   it   have tried

معلم + ـين ← معلمين

*m3all**m-iin***   -iin   ***m3all**em*

teachers   -s   boss

كتب + ـي ← كتبي

kutb-i   -i   **ku**tob

my books   my   books

In some case, this can produce a difficult consonant cluster, in which case a helping vowel is inserted. Remember that the helping vowel is ignored for the purposes of stress:

بتمسك + ـو ← بتمسكو

btimˈsk-o   -o   **btim**sek

you grab it   it   you grab

بتضرب + ـو ← بتضربو

btuDⁿrb-u   -u   **btu**Drob

you [P] hit   [plural]   you hit

مشمش + ـة ← مشمشة

mishˈmshe   -e   **mish**mesh

an apricot   [singulative]   apricots

This rule has serious implications for the North Levantine feminine perfective suffix ـت *-et* (see unit 52). South Levantine, which has *-at* instead, does not suffer from these problems.

This rule does *not* apply where it would result in three of the same consonants coming together. In these cases, the normal vowel shift (*o > u* and *e > i*) is the only change that occurs:

بتكرر + ـو ← بتكررو

bit**karr**ir-u   -u   bit**karr**er

you [P] repeat   [plural]   you repeat

مصمم + ـين ← مصممين

mSammim-**iin**   -iin   **mSam**mem

set on [P]   [plural]   set on

The rule also does not apply to words borrowed from fuS7a, which never delete these vowels:

متغير + ـات ← متغيرات

mutaghayyir-**aat**   -aat   muta**ghayy**er

variables   -s   variable

مختلف　+　ـة　←　مختلفة

*mukh**talef***　　*-e*　　*mukh**talif*-e*

different [M]　[feminine]　different [F]

Semivowels

The final set of changes we have to be aware of concern semivowels (*y* and *w*). A word-final -*u* or -*i* generally becomes -*w*- or -*y*- when suffixes are added:

شاري　+　ـين　←　شاريين

shaari　*-iin*　*shaary-iin*

has bought　[plural]　have bought

حلو　+　ـة　←　حلوة

7ilu　*-e*　*7ilw-e*

nice [M]　[feminine]　nice [F]

There are a few exceptions to this rule with final -*i*. The most common are simple weak passive participles and the various -*i* suffixes discussed in unit 9, which become -*iyy*:

محكي　+　ـة　←　محكية

ma7ki　*-e*　*ma7kiyy-e*

spoken [M]　[feminine]　spoken [F]

أردني　+　ـة　←　أردنية

2urduni　*-e*　*2urduniyy-e*

Jordanian [M]　[feminine]　Jordanian [F]

Final -*a* is more idiosyncratic, with different suffixes causing different changes. The most common change, however, is a shift to -*aay*-:

مخبى　+　ـين　←　مخباين

mkhabba　*-iin*　*mkhabbaay-iin*

hidden [S]　[plural]　hidden [P]

Stress Shifts and Shortening

We noted in the last unit that South Levantine speakers systematically shorten long vowels in unstressed open syllables (syllables that do not end with a vowel). I gave the following examples of differences between spelling and pronunciation:

جوعان	معليهوش	كنبايات
joo3aan	*ma3aleehoosh*	*kanabaayaat*
/ju3aan/	/ma3alihoosh/	/kanabayaat/
hungry	is not on him	sofas

بقولولك	فيران
bi2uuluulak	*fiiraan*
/bi2uluulak/	/firaan/
they say to you	mice

Since suffixes can cause stress shifts, and since one of the main criteria for shortening is that the syllable is unstressed, adding a suffix can sometimes cause a previously long vowel to become short:

بقولولك	←	ـلك	+	بقولو
bi2uuluu-lak		*-lak*		*bi2uulu*
/bi2uluu-lak/		/lak/		/bi2uulu/
they say to you		to you		they say

كنبايات	←	ـات	+	كنباي
kanabayaat		*-aat*		*kanabaay*
/kanabayaat/		/aat/		/kanabaay/
sofas		-s		sofa

عينين	←	ـين	+	عين
3eeneen		*-een*		*3een*
/3ineen/		/een/		/3een/
eyes		-s		eye

I sometimes indicate this process in my transcriptions, especially in explicitly South Levantine examples.

Introduction to Roots and Patterns

In the last unit we looked at what happens when you add suffixes to a word. For an English speaker, this is a very intuitive way of inflecting words (pluralising them, for example) or deriving new words. But Arabic has another very important tool that it uses for similar ends. It is this tool—*roots and patterns*—that we will be looking at in this unit.

Compared to suffixes, root-and-pattern morphology is much more idiosyncratic, and the rules described here do not always apply. If it all starts to feel a bit overwhelming, don't worry. After all, you're unlikely to need to coin many new words yourself, and it is often safer to learn things such as plural forms along with their nouns than to try to memorise all the underlying rules. But an awareness of how these patterns work in practice and what sorts of changes commonly occur within words will help you learn new vocabulary and make educated guesses as to the meanings of new words.

Roots and Patterns

Anyone who has studied Arabic will be familiar with pairs of words such as those in the table below. The semantic relationships between the items on the left and those on the right are straightforward and correspond closely to the English suffixes that I've used to gloss them. But the actual process by which we get the output word from the base word is very different from just adding a suffix:

Output		Base
كتب	←	كتاب
kitob	-s	*ktaab*
books		book
فتاحة	←	فتح
fattaa7a	-er	*fata7*
opener		open

Output		Base
تجديد	←	جدد
tajdiid -ing		*jaddad*
renewing		renew

So, what is going on here? The easiest way of conceptualising it is to think of it as a two-step process:

1. A root is extracted from the base word, usually comprising three or four consonants and no vowels.
2. The root is then inserted into the gaps in a pattern, a broad "word shape" that generally derives an output word with a specific broad meaning (plural, agent noun, participle, etc.).

Patterns are conventionally written using the dummy root *f-3-l*. Following this convention, we can plot the process involved in the words above as follows:

Output		Pattern		Root		Base
كتب	←	فعل	+	كتب	←	كتاب
kitob		*fi3ol*		*k-t-b*		*ktaab*
books		-s				book
فتاحة	←	فعالة	+	فتح	←	فتح
fattaa⁊a		*fa33aale*		*f-t-7*		*fata⁊*
opener		-er				to open
تجديد	←	تفعيل	+	جدد	←	جدد
tajdiid		*taf3iil*		*j-d-d*		*jaddad*
renewing		-ing				to renew

In unit 6 we will look at some more difficult roots. In this unit, however, we will be looking exclusively at sound roots: those with three or four normal consonants.

> Even English acts like this occasionally. It might help to think of pattern changes as a (much more widespread) version of the process by which "write" becomes "wrote."

Extracting the Root

How do native speakers identify the root of a word? For words with sound roots of the kind we're talking about in this unit, the process is quite straightforward. The root will simply consist of all three distinct consonants:

Output		Pattern		Root		Base
كتابة	←	فعالة	+	كتب	←	كتب
ktaabe		*f3aale*		*k-t-b*		*katab*
writing		-ing				to write
قلام	←	فعال	+	قلم	←	قلم
2laam		*f3aal*		*2-l-m*		*2alam*
pens		-s				pen
أجدد	←	أفعل	+	جدد	←	جديد
2ajdad		*2af3al*		*j-d-d*		*jdiid*
newer		-er				new

Some words have four root consonants:

Output		Pattern		Root		Base
أركل	←	فعلل	+	أركل	←	أركيلة
2argal		*fa3lal*		*2-r-g-l*		*2argiile*
to smoke shisha		[verb]				shisha pipe
بهدلة	←	فعللة	+	بهدل	←	بهدل
bahdale		*fa3lale*		*b-h-d-l*		*bahdal*
telling off		-ing				to tell off
متلفن	←	مفعلل	+	تلفن	←	تلفن
mtalfen		*mfa3lel*		*t-l-f-n*		*talfan*
has phoned		[participle]				to phone

Consonants that are part of a word's pattern (prefixes, suffixes, infixes) are not, as a rule, treated as part of the root. In the following examples, the doubling of the middle consonant in *dakhkhal*, the participle prefix *m-* on *m7ammad*, and the inserted *t* in *ghtarab* are all ignored for the purposes of root identification:

Output		Pattern		Root		Base
تدخيل ←		تفعيل +		دخل ←		دخل
tadkhiil		*taf3iil*		*d-kh-l*		*dakhkhal*
letting in		-ing				to let in
حمادة ←		فعالة +		حمد ←		محمد
7amaade		*fa33aale*		*7-m-d*		*m7ammad*
Hammadeh		[nickname]				Muhammad
غربة ←		فعلة +		غرب ←		اغترب
ghirbe		*fi3le*		*gh-r-b*		*ghtarab*
being abroad		[verbal noun]				to move abroad

As we will see, there are some types of patterns that do carry over additional consonants. But the root itself is still important. In many dictionaries, it is by root (and not, say, by the first letter of a given word) that entries are organised. It is probably best thought of as equivalent to "w-r-t" in groups of English words such as the following:

مكتوب	كتابة	كاتب	كتب
maktuub	*ktaabe*	*kaateb*	*katab*
written	writing	writer	to write

Derivational Patterns

In the last unit, we distinguished two common types of suffixes: *derivational* and *inflectional*. The same distinction can be made with patterns:

- Derivational patterns create new words with new (albeit related) meanings: "dance-r" from "dance," "re-new" from "new," and so on.
- Inflectional patterns produce distinct forms of the same word used in different grammatical contexts: plurals, tense forms, and so on.

These two types of patterns often work differently in terms of what they carry over from a base word. Derivational patterns are more straightforward in this regard. Some examples of common derivational patterns include:

Output		Pattern		Base
مدرسة	←	مفعلة	+	درس
madrase		*maf3ale*		*daras*
school		[noun of place]		to study
فتاحة	←	فعالة	+	فتح
fattaa7a		*fa33aale*		*fata7*
opener		[noun of		to open
		instrument]		
كاتب	←	فاعل	+	كتب
kaateb		*faa3el*		*katab*
writer		[agent noun]		to write
نزل	←	فعل	+	نزل
nazzal		*fa33al*		*nizel*
to lower, take down		[causative]		to go down
		(make s.o. X)		
انمسك	←	انفعل	+	مسك
nmasak		*nfa3al*		*misek*
to be caught		[passive]		to catch
		(be X-ed)		

These patterns tend to operate using the basic root, as we saw in the examples above. They do not generally carry over any extra consonants from the pattern of the base word:

Output		Pattern		Root		Base
شرب	←	فعل	+	شرب	←	شرب
sha*rr*a*b*		*fa33al*		sh-r-b		**shi*r*e*b***
to give to drink		[causative]				to drink
تجربة	←	تفعلة	+	جرب	←	جرب
*ta*j*ri*b*e*		*taf3ile*		j-r-b		***ja*rr*a*b****
experiment		[noun]				to try

One common exception to this rule is that the *m-* that features in various patterns is sometimes carried over to new derivations from a base word:

Output	Pattern	Root	Base
تمركز ←	تفعلل +	مركز ←	مركز
tmarkaz	*tfa3lal*	*(m)-r-k-z*	*markaz*
to centre on	[verb]		centre

Otherwise, there is generally no evidence in the output word of which base word it is derived from. The output word مكتبة *maktabe* "bookcase" is clearly derived from كتاب *ktaab* "book," but there is no *structural* indication of this. We know it only from the meaning.

Inflectional Patterns

If derivational patterns derive new words, inflectional patterns derive additional forms of the same word. The most common inflectional pattern changes produce plurals of nouns and adjectives and perfective/imperfective stems of verbs:

Output		Pattern		Base
ولاد ←		فعال +		ولد
wlaad		*f3aal*		*walad*
boys		-s		boy
دروس ←		فعول +		درس
druus		*f3uul*		*darᶜs*
classes		-s		class
مدارس ←		فعالل +		مدرسة
madaares		*fa3aalel*		*madrase*
schools		-s		school
يتعب ←		يفعل +		تعب
yi-t3ab		*yi-f3al*		*ti3eb*
he gets tired		[imperfective]		he got tired
يعلم ←		يفعل +		علم
y-3allem		*y-fa33el*		*3allam*
he teaches		[imperfective]		he taught

Unlike derivational patterns, inflectional patterns are much more sensitive to the shape of the base word. They commonly carry over consonants from the base word's pattern. The *m-*, the *t-*, and the second *r* in the following examples are all part of the base word's pattern but are nonetheless carried over to the output word:

Output		Pattern		Root		Base
مكاتب	←	فعالل	+	مكتب	←	مكتب
ma<u>k</u>aa<u>t</u>eb		*fa3aalel*		*(m)-k-t-b*		*<u>m</u>ak<u>t</u>a<u>b</u>*
offices		-s				office
تمارين	←	فعاليل	+	تمرن	←	تمرين
<u>t</u>ama<u>r</u>i<u>i</u>n		*fa3aliil*		*(t)-m-r-n*		*<u>t</u>am<u>r</u>i<u>i</u>n*
exercises		-s				exercise
يدرس	←	يفعل	+	دررس	←	درس
y-<u>d</u>a<u>rr</u>es		*y-fa33el*		*d-r-(r)-s*		*<u>d</u>a<u>rr</u>as*
he teaches		[imperfective]				he taught

Plurals, in particular, are sensitive even to concerns such as the length of vowels in the base word. Although Arabic plurals may appear as totally irregular, this is not quite true. As we will see, many different choices of plural pattern are motivated in part by the shape of the root (see unit 12).

Weak Roots

In the last unit, we looked at the basic process by which roots are extracted from words and inserted into patterns to form new words. The roots we used as examples there were all straightforward. Some had three consonants and some had four. But the consonants in question were all well-behaved. In this unit, we will be looking at less well-behaved roots, known in Arabic grammar as *weak* roots.

The characteristic feature of most weak roots is that one of their consonants is a semi-vowel (*y* or *w*). In particular contexts, these consonants act anomalously, either combining with surrounding vowels or disappearing entirely. Consider the following examples:

Output	Pattern	Root	Base
قول ←	فعل +	قول ←	قال
2oo<u>l</u>	*fa3l*	2-w-l	*<u>2aal</u>*
saying	-ing		to say
عصي ←	فعل +	عصي ←	عصاية
3u<u>S</u>i	*fu3ol*	3-S-y	*<u>3</u>a<u>S</u>aa<u>y</u>e*
sticks	-s		stick
أدق ←	أفعل +	دقق ←	دقيق
2a<u>d</u>a<u>22</u>	*2af3al*	d-2-2	*<u>d</u>a<u>2</u>ii<u>2</u>*
more precise	[comparative]		precise

Another way of conceptualising this is to say that the idea of a weak root provides a way of extracting roots from words that don't have the right constellation of consonants. The relevance of this becomes clear when we consider loanwords. The loanword تكسي *taksi* "taxi" obviously has no Arabic root in the traditional sense, but that hasn't stopped speakers from extracting one (*t-k-s-y*) and using it to form a plural تكاسي *takaasi* "taxis."

These examples represent the four basic kinds of weak roots:

1. *Assimilating* roots, whose first consonant is a *w* or a *y*.
2. *Hollow* roots, whose second consonant is a *w* or a *y*.
3. *Defective* roots, whose third consonant is a *w* or a *y*.
4. *Doubled* roots, whose second and third consonant are identical.

Assimilating Roots

Assimilating roots are those roots whose first consonant is a semivowel (*y* or *w*). In Levantine these roots are largely well behaved, but in a handful of fuS7a borrowings they lose their initial consonant, resulting in pairs like the following:

Output		Pattern		Root		Base
صفة ←		فعلة +		وصف ←		وصف
_Si_fa		*fa3le*		*w-S-f*		_waS_af
trait		[noun]				to describe
يثق ←		يفعل +		وثق ←		وثق
*yi-_seq_*		*yi-f3al*		*w-s-q*		_wasaq_
he trusts		[imperfective]				he trusted

For more on some of the complications of conjugating assimilating verbs, see unit 26.

Hollow Roots

Hollow roots are those roots whose second consonant is a semivowel. In this section we will identify some of the very common deviations from normal patterns that these sorts of roots cause. Note that while these rules apply quite broadly, some patterns have their own idiosyncrasies, in particular the conjugation of hollow verbs. We will look at these idiosyncrasies in units 25–30.

Where inserting a hollow root into a pattern produces a sequence of -*ay*- or -*aw*- in a closed syllable (a syllable ending with a consonant), these sequences usually become, respectively, -*ee*- or -*oo*-:

Output		Pattern		Root		Base
موت	←	فعل	+	موت	←	مات
moo**t**		fa3ᵉl		m-w-t		**m**aa**t**
dying		-ing				to die
(**m**a**wt**)						
شيب	←	فعل	+	شيب	←	شاب
shee**b**		fa3ᵉl		sh-y-b		**sh**aa**b**
going grey		-ing				to go grey
(**sh**a**yb**)						

Note, however, that many fuS7a borrowings retain the diphthong *aw* (see unit 1):

Output		Pattern		Root		Base
دورية	←	فعلية	+	دور	←	دار
da**wr**iyye		fa3liyye		d-w-r		**d**aa**r**
patrol		[noun]				to turn

An *iw* or an *iy* becomes *ii*:

Output		Pattern		Root		Base
جيزة	←	فعلة	+	جوز	←	تجوز
jii**z**e		fi3le		j-w-z		tja**ww**a**z**
marriage		[noun]				to get married
(**j**i**wz**e)						

While *uw* or *uy* resolves to *uu*:

Output		Pattern		Root		Base
صورة	←	فعلة	+	صور	←	صور
Suu**r**a		fi3le		S-w-r		**S**a**ww**a**r**
picture		[noun]				to take a picture
(**S**i**wr**a)						

Where the semivowel is doubled or appears between two vowels, on the other hand, it is generally retained straightforwardly as a semivowel:

Output	Pattern	Root	Base
دوق ←	فعل +	دوق ←	داق
dawwa2	*fa33al*	d-w-2	*daa2*
to make s.o. taste	make s.o. X		to taste
دوام ←	فعال +	دوم ←	داوم
dawaam	*fa3aal*	d-w-m	*daawam*
working hours	[noun]		to go to work
طير ←	فعل +	طير ←	طار
Tayyar	*fa33al*	T-y-r	*Taar*
to send flying	make s.o. X		to fly
ساير ←	فاعل +	سير ←	سار
saayar	*faa3al*	s-y-r	*saar*
to humour	[causative]		to move

Defective Roots

Defective roots are those roots whose third consonant is a semivowel (*y* or *w*). These semivowels, like those in hollow roots, tend to collapse into surrounding vowels under specific circumstances. As with hollow roots, we will be trying here to identify general rules that apply to most derivations. The conjugation of defective verbs is idiosyncratic, and we will look at it in detail in units 25–30.

The rules governing defective roots are fairly straightforward. In a final consonant cluster, *y* becomes *i* and *w* becomes *u*:

Output	Pattern	Root	Base
حكي ←	فعل +	حكي ←	حكى
7aki	*fa3ᵉl*	7-k-y	*7aka*
speaking	-ing		said
(*7aky*)			
حشو ←	فعل +	حشو ←	حشى
7ashu	*fa3ᵉl*	7-sh-w	*7asha*
stuffing	-ing		stuffed
(*7ashw*)			

The consonant -*w* can also resolve to -*i*. Many speakers have forms such as حشي *7ashi* "stuffing" or مشي *mashi* "walking" instead of حشو or مشو.

A final -*ey* or -*ew* becomes -*i*:

Output	Pattern	Root	Base
كاوي ← *kaawi* has ironed (*kaawey*)	فاعل + *faa3el* has X-ed	كوي ← *k-w-y*	كوى *kawa* to iron
ثواني ← *sawaani* seconds (*sawaanew*)	فواعل + *fawaa3el* -s	ثني ← *s-n-w*	ثانية *saanye* second

A final -*ay* or -*aw* becomes -*a*:

Output	Pattern	Root	Base
مجرى ← *majra* channel (*majray*)	مفعل + *maf3al* [noun of place]	جري ← *j-r-y*	جرى *jara* to run
ممشى ← *mamsha* walkway (*mamshaw*)	مفعل + *maf3al* [noun of place]	مشو ← *m-sh-w*	مشي *mishi* to walk

Elsewhere—before or between vowels and when doubled—a *y* or *w* is usually retained:

Output	Pattern	Root	Base
مليان ← *malyaan* full	فعلان + *fi3laan* [participle]	ملي ← *m-l-y*	ملي *mili* to get full

Output	Pattern	Root	Base
شروة ←	فعلة +	شرو ←	اشترى
sharwe	*fa3le*	*sh-r-w*	***shtara***
[a] purchase	[noun of instance]		to buy

Doubled Roots

Doubled roots are those roots whose second and third consonants are identical. These roots are generally quite straightforward to identify. Their three consonants are generally clearly identifiable, and in many contexts they operate more or less identically to sound roots:

Output	Pattern	Root	Base
مرور ←	فعول +	مرر ←	مر
muruur	*fu3uul*	*m-r-r*	***marr***
passing	-ing		to pass
تكرار ←	تفعال +	كرر ←	كرر
tikraar	*tif3aal*	*k-r-r*	***karrar***
repetition	-ition		to repeat

When the second and third consonants are separated only by a short vowel, however, they have a tendency to move together and form a doubled consonant. The vowel that would separate them generally shifts earlier in the word or is deleted entirely:

Output	Pattern	Root	Base
مطب ←	مفعل +	طبب ←	طب
maTabb	*maf3al*	*T-b-b*	***Tabb***
speed bump	[noun of place]		to jump
(*maTbab*)			
انكب ←	انفعل +	كبب ←	كب
nkabb	*nfa3al*	*k-b-b*	***kabb***
to be thrown out	[passive]		to throw out
(*nkabab*)			

This is not a universal rule, and individual patterns can be quite idiosyncratic, as can individual words. But the rule is worth being aware of because it explains many of the variations in patterns we will encounter.

Identifying Ambiguous Roots

You will probably have noticed a fundamental problem facing learners of Arabic here. How are you supposed to tell that طار *Taar* "he flew" has the root *T-y-r* while شار *shaar* "he advised" has the root *sh-w-r*? How can you tell whether the root of a word such as مشي *mishi* ends in *y* or *w*?

The answer, unfortunately, is that there simply is no way to know from looking at this individual word. When they need to identify a root, speakers draw on their knowledge of other related words where the root consonants are clear (طير *Teer* "bird" and طيران *Tayaraan* "flying," for example). And in many cases, of course, they will simply have learned the usual form as an exception while acquiring language as children (just as English speakers do with "mouse" → "mice" or "pronounce" → "pronunciation"). Most of the time, the best route for a nonnative speaker is to try to do the same.

Still, just like English speakers who say "pronounciation," Arabic speakers sometimes "misidentify" the root. All four of the following occur, even though you will find only two of the possible roots in a dictionary:

Output	Pattern	Root	Base
نوم ←	فعل +	نوم ←	نام
nawwam	*fa33al*	*n-w-m*	*naam*
to put to sleep	make s.o. X		to sleep
نيم ←	فعل +	نيم ←	نام
nayyam	*fa33al*	*n-y-m*	*naam*
to put to sleep	make s.o. X		to sleep
مشي ←	فعل +	مشي ←	مشي
mashi	*fa3ᵉl*	*m-sh-y*	*mishi*
walking	-ing		to walk
مشو ←	فعل +	مشو ←	مشي
mashu	*fa3ᵉl*	*m-sh-w*	*mishi*
walking	-ing		to walk

PART 2

Word Types

Derived Nouns

In this unit we will look briefly at some very common noun derivations you are likely to encounter: agent nouns, nouns of place and instrument, and nouns derived from participles and *maSdar*s (gerunds). As with the other derivational processes we have been looking at, the importance of these patterns for a learner is not so much knowing how to use them as knowing how to recognise them. This is very helpful for both understanding and learning new words.

> This last point is worth reiterating. Arabic students are often taught this kind of derivation as if it is a straightforward, logical process they can put into practice themselves. But just like in English—and, presumably, in any natural language—derivation involves a great deal of idiom and idiosyncrasy. Knowing the noun of place pattern doesn't mean that applying it to the root for "punch" will generate an understandable word for "boxing ring."

Nouns of Place

Nouns of place, as the name suggests, refer to places associated with the base word. Almost all nouns of place have the pattern *maf3al(e)*:

مطحنة ←	طحن	مكتب ←	كتب
maT7ane	*Ta7an*	*maktab*	*katab*
mill	to grind	office	to write
محمصة ←	حمص	ملعب ←	لعب
ma7maSa	*7ammaS*	*mal3ab*	*li3eb*
roastery	to roast	stadium	to play

Some nouns of place have the meaning "subject of" or "experiencer of":

ملطشة	←	لطش		مضحكة	←	ضحك
maLTashe		*laTash*		*maD7ake*		*Di7ek*
punching bag		to hit		laughing stock		to laugh

Nouns of Instrument

Nouns of instrument generally refer to tools with which you carry out the action expressed by the underlying verb. The most common patterns are فعالة *fa33aale/fi33aale* and مفعلة *maf3ale*, followed by مفعال *muf3aal/mif3aal* and فعول *fa33uul(e)*:

فتاحة	←	فتح		طيارة	←	طار
fattaa7a		*fata7*		*Tayyaara*		*Taar*
opener		to open		plane		to fly

مبشرة	←	بشر		مشربة	←	شرب
mabshara		*bashar*		*mashrabe*		*shireb*
cheesegrater		to grate		cigarette holder		to smoke [a cigarette]

زمور	←	زمر		مفتاح	←	فتح
zammuur		*zammar*		*muftaa7*		*fata7*
car horn		to honk		key		to open

> The nouns of instrument *fa33aale* and *fi33aale* are regional variants. The form with *i* is the norm in Lebanon and is common, to a lesser extent, in Syria as well.

Agent Nouns

Agent nouns denote the person who performs the action of a verb. These are most commonly formed in English with "-er" and in Arabic with فعال *fa33aal* or less commonly with فعيل *fa33iil/fi33iil*:

لحام	←	لحم		طيار	←	طار
la77aam		*la7°m*		*Tayyaar*		*Taar*
butcher		meat		pilot		to fly

لعيب	←	لعب		خريج	←	تخرج
la33iib		*li3eb*		*kharriij*		*tkharraj*
player		to play		[a] graduate		to graduate

Nouns Derived from Participles

Many everyday nouns are derived from participles. Participles are a form of the verb that usually have the meaning "has X-ed" or "X-ing." We will discuss their semantics in more detail in unit 37. All you need to know here is that as well as this meaning, participles are often used as nouns. Nouns derived from participles in this way typically have agent noun meaning ("X-er"):

شاهد ← شاهد		كاتب ← كاتب	
shaahed	*shaahed*	*kaateb*	*kaateb*
witness	has witnessed	writer	has written
مندوب ← مندوب		معلم ← معلم	
manduub	*manduub*	*m3allem*	*m3allem*
commissioner	has been commissioned	teacher	has taught

It might seem odd to use the term "derived from" here, given that the base word and result words are identical in form. But the meaning is clearly quite different, just as in English examples such as "to cook" and "the cook." Thinking of this process as derivation is also useful because these nouns often have the form not of normal participles but instead of their fuS7a counterparts:

مؤلف BUT	مؤلف	محرك BUT	محرك
mu2allef	*m2allef*	*mu7arrek*	*m7arrek*
author	has composed	motor, engine	has moved
مغني BUT	مغني	مقدم BUT	مقدم
mughanni	*mghanni*	*muqaddam*	*m2addam*
singer	has sung	colonel	has been advanced

> Here as in other places (see unit 3), Lebanese speakers are more likely to have typically colloquial forms: *mdarreb, m7arrek,* and so on.

In some cases, these nouns also have distinct broken plurals (see unit 12):

Derived noun		Participle	
كتاب ← كاتب		كاتبين ← كاتب	
kittaab/kuttaab	*kaateb*	*kaatbiin*	*kaateb*
authors	author	have written	has written

Derived noun		Participle	
طلاب ←	طالب	طالبين ←	طالب
Tillaab/Tullaab	*Taaleb*	*Taalbiin*	*Taaleb*
students	student	have requested	has requested

A full table of participle shapes is given in units 29 and 30.

Nouns Derived from *maSdar*s

Another category it is useful to be aware of is nouns derived from *maSdar*s. A verb's *maSdar* is an abstract noun referring to the act of performing that verb. In this sense, *maSdar*s (see unit 31) are very similar to English gerunds formed with "-ing" ("walking," "running," etc.). For our purposes here, however, this is not important. As with participles, the important thing to know is that almost all verbs have a *maSdar* and that the *maSdar* is largely predictable from the shape of the base verb.

Just as with participles, the derived noun and the underlying *maSdar* have the same form, but their meanings are different. The most common relationship between the derived noun and the *maSdar* is for the former to express a specific instance of the overall action described by the latter:[1]

استدعاء ←	استدعاء	تعديل ←	تعديل
2istid3aa2	*2istid3aa2*	*ta3diil*	*ta3diil*
a summons	summoning	amendment	amending
دراسة ←	دراسة	تدريب ←	تدريب
diraase	*diraase*	*tadriib*	*tadriib*
a study	studying	a training [course]	training

Another common relationship is for the derived meaning to be the *product* of the action described by the base *maSdar*:

تصميم ←	تصميم	ترجمة ←	ترجمة
taSmiim	*taSmiim*	*tarjame*	*tarjame*
a design	designing	[a] translation	translating
خسارة ←	خسارة	اقتصاد ←	اقتصاد
khsaara	*khsaara*	*2iqtiSaad*	*2iqtiSaad*
a loss, something lost	losing	[an] economy	being economical

Again, it might seem strange to see this as a derivational relationship, given that the base form and the derived form appear to be identical. But the meanings of the base and derived forms here are clearly distinct, just as in English examples such as "reading" and "a reading." And unlike a normal *maSdar*, these forms can be pluralised, often with broken plural patterns:

خسائر	←	خسارة		دراسات	←	دراسة
khasaa2er		*khsaara*		*diraasaat*		*diraase*
losses		a loss		studies		a study

تمارين	←	تمرين		اقتصادات	←	اقتصاد
tamariin		*tamriin*		*2iqtiSaadaat*		*2iqtiSaad*
exercises		an exercise		economies		an economy

Moreover, the derived noun often actually uses a fuS7a *maSdar* pattern, although this distinction is less clear than it is with participles because most of the *maSdar* patterns are shared by Levantine and fuS7a:

تربية	BUT	ترباية		قراءة	BUT	قراية
tarbiye		*tirbaaye*		*qiraa2a*		*2raaye*
pedagogy		raising		a reading		reading
		[children]				

> As elsewhere, Lebanese speakers are more likely to use typically Levantine forms for the derived noun meanings as well.

The formation of *maSdar*s is described in detail in unit 31.

Diminutives and Nicknames

One final category of noun it is useful to be able to identify with is a *diminutive*. Diminutive forms literally express smallness. By extension, they can also express affection or cuteness. The usual Levantine diminutive patterns are all variants on فعلول *fa3luul* or فعّول *fa33uul*:

بنوتة	←	بنت		دبدوب	←	دب
bannuute		**_bint_**		**_dabduub_**		**_dibb_**
little girly		girl		teddy bear		bear

Sometimes the meaning is difficult to capture in a single-word translation. The meaning of the diminutives here is essentially the same as the nondiminutive form, but the diminutive forms might be used, for example, with children:

شطور	←	شاطر		قمورة	←	قمر
*sha**T**Tuu**r***		*shaa**T**er*		*2a**mm**uu**r**a*		*2a**m**a**r***
smart person		smart		beautiful		beautiful
[= little …]		person		[= little moon]		[= moon]

One kind of nickname (see appendix D) can also be generated using these patterns as well as the alternative pattern فعال *fa33aal* and its variants. We've already seen some examples of these patterns in unit 5:

بشورة	←	بشرة		حمودة	←	محمد
*ba**sh**shuu**r**a*		*bu**sh**r**a***		*7a**mm**uu**d**e*		*m**7**a**mm**a**d***
Bashoura		Bushra		Hammoudeh		Muhammad

Note

1. Mark Cowell, *A Reference Grammar of Syrian Arabic* (Georgetown University Press, 1964), 284–85.

The Feminine Suffix *-a/e*

Perhaps the most common suffix in Arabic is ة *-a/e*. This suffix has a whole range of functions, with the only common thread being that nouns ending in it are almost invariably feminine. Most typically, it is used to create feminine forms of nouns and adjectives (see units 10 and 16) and occasionally plurals (see unit 12):

صغيرة	صغير	كاتبة	كاتب
zghiir-e	*zghiir*	*kaatb-e*	*kaateb*
small [F]	small [M]	writer [F]	writer [M]

مضرة	مضر	ممرضة	ممرض
muDirr-a	*muDirr*	*mumarriD-a*	*mumarreD*
harmful [F]	harmful [M]	nurse [F]	nurse [M]

نجارة	نجار	مسيحية	مسيحي
najjaar-a	*najjaar*	*masii7iyy-e*	*masii7i*
carpenters	carpenter	Christians	Christian

This suffix also forms so-called singulatives from mass nouns, which are nouns referring to individual items (see unit 11):

جزرة	جزر	غيمة	غيم
jazar-a	*jazar*	*gheem-e*	*gheem*
a carrot	carrots	a cloud	clouds

It also occurs, largely arbitrarily, as part of many patterns and pattern variants as well as in many other words:

مكتبة	ضربة	سفرة	مسبحة
maktab-e	*Darb-e*	*safr-a*	*masba7-a*
bookcase	a blow	a trip	prayer beads

إبرة	شفرة	مروحة	طيارة
2ibr-e	*shafr-a*	*marwa7-a*	*Tayyaar-a*
needle	razor	fan	plane

We will look at these uses in more detail in the relevant sections below. This unit will focus mainly on the form and pronunciation of this suffix in different contexts.

Form

The form of the suffix differs depending on the sounds that precede it. The general rule is that after any of the consonants *2, h, 3, 7, q, gh, kh, S, Z, T, D,* or *DH*, it is *-a,* and everywhere else it is *-e:*

ملعونة	دبدوبة	طريقة	بيضة
mal3uun-e	*dabduub-e*	*Tarii2-a*	*beeD-a*
naughty [F]	teddy bear	way	egg

حلوة	مساوية	مزبوطة	وسخة
7ilw-e	*msaawy-e*	*mazbuuT-a*	*wiskh-a*
nice [F]	has done [F]	correct [F]	dirty [F]

كاتبة	متلبكة	سايقة	طاخة
kaatb-e	*mitlabbk-e*	*saay2-a*	*Taakhkh-a*
writer [F]	confused [F]	driving [F]	has shot [F]

After *r*, there is variation. In adjectives of the form *f3iil* and *fa3iil* (see unit 16), it is pronounced *-e:*

صغيرة	كبيرة	أخيرة
zghiir-e	*kbiir-e*	*2akhiir-e*
small [F]	big [F]	last [F]

In short words with the shape *fi3r-* and *fa3r-,* both pronunciations occur, sometimes with the same word, and *-e* is definitely more common:

إبرة	شفرة	شفرة	بزرة
2ibr-e	*shafr-a*	*shafr-e*	*bizr-e*
needle	razor	razor	seed

For North Levantine speakers it is otherwise consistently *-a* after *-r,* whereas for South Levantine speakers it varies by word:

North Levantine		South Levantine	
متأخرة *mit2akhkhr-a* late [F]	شاطرة *shaaTr-a* clever [F]	متأخرة *mit2akhkhr-e* late [F]	شاطرة *shaaTr-a* clever [F]
أميرة *2amiir-a* princess	مخدرة *mkhaddar-a* numbed [F]	أميرة *2amiir-e* princess	مخدرة *mkhaddar-a* numbed [F]
صايرة *Saayr-a* has become [F]	إسوارة *2iswaar-a* wristband	صايرة *Saayr-e* has become [F]	إسوارة *2iswaar-a* wristband

In short words with the shape *fi3a* and *fu3a*, it is invariably pronounced *-a*:

صفة *Sif-a* adjective	لغة *lugh-a* language	صلة *Sil-a* connection	جهة *jih-a* side

There are a few other irregularities. When added to a word ending in *-a*, the suffix typically inserts a *-y-* and triggers vowel lengthening (see unit 4). For South Levantine speakers, it is usually then deleted, leaving the *-y* as the only indication of its presence:

North Levantine		South Levantine	
كنباية *kanabaa-ye* sofa	مخباية *mkhabbaa-ye* hidden [F]	كنباي *kanabaa-y* sofa	مخباي *mkhabbaa-y* hidden [F]

In a handful of words the suffix appears directly after *-aa*, with no *-y*. In these cases, it is either silent or pronounced as *-t*, depending on the speaker. The *-t* is probably more North Levantine:

Silent		-t	
حياة *7ayaa* life	مباراة *mubaaraa* match	حياة *7ayaat* life	مباراة *mubaaraat* match

Transformation to -*t*

In *2iDaafe* constructions (see unit 15), ة is pronounced with a final -*t*, although note that it is generally still written in Arabic with the same letter. The typical form in these cases is -*et*, irrespective of whether the base form is pronounced with -*e* or -*a*:

كاتبة ← كاتبة الكتاب

kaatb-e   *kaatb-et lᵻktaab*

author [F]   the book's author

مكتبة ← مكتبة بابا

maktab-e   *maktab-et baaba*

bookcase   dad's bookcase

سيارة ← سيارة سامي

sayyaar-a   *sayyaar-et saami*

car   Sami's car

بطة ← بطة أسعد

baTT-a   *baTT-et 2as3ad*

duck   Asad's duck

> Some words with a final -*a* that does not represent ة are occasionally treated as if they did. Although generally stigmatised, it is not uncommon to hear forms such as *mistashfet ᴵ3yuun* for مستشفى عيون *mistashfa 3yuun* "eye hospital."

Note that South Levantine speakers with the deletion of -*e* after -*aay* restore it in these contexts:

كنباي ← كنباية ريم

kanabaay   *kanabaay-et riim*

sofa   Reem's sofa

The word مرة *mara* "woman, wife" has the irregular form *mart*:

مرة ← مرة أحمد

mar-a   *mar-t 2a7mad*

woman   Ahmad's wife

For most speakers, short words with the form *fi3a* or *fu3a* retain the -*a*. These are mostly fuS7a loans:

لغة الأم ← لغة

lugh-at ʾl2umm   *lugh-a*

mother tongue   language

جهة العمل ← جهة

jih-at ʾl3amal   *jih-a*

employer   authority

صفة المبالغة ← صفة

Sif-at ʾlmubaalagha   *Sif-a*

emphatic adjective   adjective

Note, however, that Lebanese speakers in particular—who have a tendency to assimilate fuS7a words more to the norms of inherited vocabulary (see unit 3)—have *-et* here:

Lebanese Forms

لغة الإم ← لغة
ligh-et ʾl2imm   *ligh-a*
mother tongue   language
جهة العمل ← جهة
jih-et ʾl3amal   *jih-a*
employer   authority
صغة المبالغة ← صفة
Sif-et ʾlmubaalagha   *Sif-a*
emphatic adjective   adjective

With Suffixes

The shift to *-et* (or *-at*) also occurs when suffixes are added, and in this case the Arabic spelling changes to reflect it (ـة). The forms produced are predictable. As we would expect (see unit 4), suffixes beginning with consonants trigger a stress shift, and *-et* becomes *-it*:

طابتي ← طابتـ ← طابة

*Taab-**it**-na*   *Taab-t-*   *Taabe*

our ball   ball

مكتبتنا ← مكتبتـ ← مكتبة

*maktab-**it**-na*   *maktab-et-*   *maktab-e*

our bookcase   bookcase

سيارتنا   ←   سيارتـ   ←   سيارة

sayyaar-__it__-na   *sayyaar-et-*   *sayyaar-a*

our car   car

بطتنا   ←   بط   ←   بطة

baTT-__it__-na   *baTT-et-*   *baTT-a*

our duck   duck

Similarly, suffixes beginning with vowels generally trigger the deletion of *i* except where this would result in a cluster of three identical consonants (as in the last example below):

طابتي   ←   طابتـ   ←   طابة

__Taab__-t-i   *Taab-t-*   *Taabe*

my ball   ball

مكتبتي   ←   مكتبتـ   ←   مكتبة

mak__tab__-t-i   *maktab-et-*   *maktab-e*

my bookcase   bookcase

سيارتي   ←   سيارتـ   ←   سيارة

sayy__aar__-t-i   *sayyaar-et-*   *sayyaar-a*

my car   car

بطتي   ←   بطتـ   ←   بطة

__baTT__-it-i   *baTT-et-*   *baTT-a*

my duck   duck

Things get slightly more complicated in forms where the addition of *-e* has already caused the deletion of a vowel in the original (masculine) root word. In these cases, the most common strategy is to restore the original vowel from the masculine form:

كاتبتي   ←   كاتبتـ   ←   كاتبة

kaa__tib__-t-i   *kaatb-et-*   *kaatb-e*

my author [F]   author [F]

                                             (← *kaateb*)

معلمتي   ←   معلمتـ   ←   معلمة

m3al__lim__-t-i   *m3allm-et-*   *m3allm-e*

my teacher [F]   teacher [F]

                                             (← *m3allem*)

In order to maintain consistency between the shape of the base feminine form and the feminine form with suffixes, some speakers use a different strategy, shifting stress into the *-it* to avoid deletion:

With Stress Shift		
كاتبتي	←	كاتبة
kaatb-it-i		*kaatb-e*
my author [F]		author [F]
		(← *kaateb*)
معلمتي	←	معلمة
m3allm-it-i		*m3allme*
my teacher		teacher [F]
		(← *m3allem*)

Another common strategy is to stress and lengthen the *i*:

With Lengthened *i*		
كاتبيتي	←	كاتبة
*kaatb-**iit**-i*		*kaatb-e*
my author [F]		author [F]
		(← *kaateb*)
معلميتي	←	معلمة
*m3allm-**iit**-i*		*m3allme*
my teacher		teacher [F]
		(← *m3allem*)

Those forms that retain *-at* are subject to stress change but obviously not to deletion:

صفتنا	←	صفتـ	←	صفة
*Sif-**at**-na*		*Sif-at-*		*Sif-a*
our capacity				capacity
لغتك	←	لغتـ	←	لغة
***lu**gh-at-ak*		*lugh-at-*		*lugh-a*
your language				language

> Remember that Lebanese speakers generally treat these words regularly and shift *-a* to *-et*. The Lebanese forms here would be صفتك *Sif-t-ak* and لغتك *ligh-t-ak*.

Finally, note that for some speakers, various feminine words that have no ة *-a/e* nonetheless insert a *-t-* when suffixes are attached. The following forms co-occur with forms without *-t*:

إجرتين	←	إجر
2ijᵉr-t-een		*2ijᵉr*
legs [dual]		leg
دكانتي	←	دكان
dikkaan-t-i		*dikkaan*
my shop		shop
كروزتك	←	كروز
krooz-t-ak		*krooz*
your carton		carton

This is particularly common with feminine place-names in constructions such as the following:

شامتي	←	الشام
shaam-t-i		*ᵢsh-shaam*
my Damascus		Damascus

Nouns with *-i*

In this unit, we will be looking at a family of suffixes that share some important common behaviours: the *nisbe* (relational) suffix ـي *-i*, its feminine and plural variants ـية *-iyye* and ـيات *-iyyaat*, the Turkish suffix ـجي *-ji*, and the adjective suffix ـاني *-aani*. All of these suffixes derive nouns and adjectives.

-i (the *nisbe* suffix)

The suffix *-i*, known as the نسبة *nisbe* or relational suffix, is a remarkably diverse suffix used to form all sorts of words. Perhaps its oldest function is to produce demonyms (names for people from particular places) and language names. Note that many demonym forms are slightly irregular and cannot be predicted even by native speakers:

أردني	← الأردن	قدسي	← القدس
2urdun-i	*'l2urdon*	*2uds-i*	*'l2uds*
Jordanian	Jordan	Jerusalemite	Jerusalem
طلياني	← إطاليا	درعاوي	← درعا
Tilyaan-i	*2iTaalya*	*dar3aa-wi*	*dar3a*
Italian	Italy	person from Deraa	Deraa
إنكليزي	← إنكلترا	لادقاني	← اللادقية
2ingliiz-i	*2ingiltira*	*laad2aan-i*	*'llaad2iyye*
English	England	Latakian	Latakia

More broadly, it is a highly productive all-purpose adjective suffix. Note that the *-i* replaces rather than attaches to the feminine ending ـة *-a/e*:

دراسي	← دراسة	عسكري	← عسكر
diraas-i	*diraase*	*3askar-i*	*3askar*
academic	study	military	soldiers

طب ← طبي   آلة ← آلي

Tibb   *Tibb-i*   *2aale*   *2aal-i*

medicine   medical   instrument   mechanical

أدب ← أدبي   دورة ← دوري

2adab   *2adab-i*   *dawra*   *dawr-i*

literature   literary   cycle   cyclical

After final *-a*, *-i* usually becomes *-wi*:

دنيا ← دنيوي   سما ← سماوي

dunya   *dunya-wi*   *sama*   *samaa-wi*

world   worldly   sky   celestial

Similarly, a handful of words with only two obvious root consonant suffixes take the suffix *-awi* instead:

لغة ← لغوي   أخ ← أخوي

lugha   *lugh-awi*   *2akhkh*   *2akh-awi*

language   linguistic   brother   brotherly

When suffixes are added to *-i*, it becomes ـيّ *-iyy-*:

عسكري ← عسكرية   سوري ← سوريين

3askar-i   *3askar-iyy-e*   *suur-i*   *suur-iyy-iin*

military [M]   military [F]   Syrian [M]   Syrian [P]

شيوعي ← شيوعيات

shuyuu3-i   *shuyuu3-iyy-aat*

Communist [M]   Communists [F]

Note that a handful of *-i* forms are actually formed using a specific pattern, *fa3ali*, and not simply by adding a suffix. This is not very common but accounts for forms such as:

مدينة ← مدني   شتى ← شتوي

madiine   *madani*   *shita*   *shatawi*

city   urban   winter   winter [ADJ]

Other than the internal vowel changes, however, these forms act exactly like other *-i* forms.

-*iyye* and -*iyyaat*

The suffix ـية -*iyye*, in addition to being the normal feminine of words in -*i*, is used to form abstract nouns from those words. Often this corresponds to "-ism" or "-ness":

قومية	←	قومي		اشتراكية	←	اشتراكي
qawm-iyye		*qawm-i*		*2ishtiraak-iyye*		*2ishtiraak-i*
nationalism		nationalist		socialism		socialist

سورية	←	سوري
suur-iyye		*suur-i*
Syrianness		Syrian

Some -*iyye* forms have more idiosyncratic meanings:[1]

يومية	←	يوم		مديرية	←	مدير
yoom-iyye		*yoom*		*mudiir-iyye*		*mudiir*
daily wage		day		directorate		director

The feminine plural ـيات -*iyyaat* produces plural words meaning "things having to do with," usually with no corresponding singular:

وطنيات	←	وطني		إسلاميات	←	إسلامي
waTan-iyyaat		*waTan-i*		*2islaam-iyyaat*		*2islaam-i*
patriotic rhetoric		patriotic		Islamica		Islamic

لغويات	←	لغوي
lughaw-iyyaat		*lughaw-i*
linguistics		linguistic

-*ji*

The suffix -*ji*, which is very productive and is borrowed from Turkish, derives terms for professions:

مواسرجي	←	مواسير		دكنجي	←	دكان
mawasir-ji		*mawasiir*		*dikkan-ji*		*dikkaan*
plumber		pipes		shopkeeper		shop

More broadly and productively, the suffix -*ji* derives adjectives and nouns expressing that something is someone's "thing," often derisively:

نسوان ← نسونجي   ثورة ← ثورجي

niswaan *niswan-ji*   *thawra* *thawra-ji*

women womaniser   revolution so-called revolutionary

In many respects, this suffix does not act like other suffixes. It does not cause lengthening of a final vowel (see unit 4) or cause *-a/e* to become *-t* (see unit 8). Uniquely, in fact, it causes *shortening* of a long vowel in a final syllable. But when suffixes are added, it is exactly like *-i*, becoming *-iyy-*:

ثورجي ← ثورجيين   دكنجي ← دكنجية

thawra-jiyy-iin *thawra-ji*   *dikkan-jiyy-e* *dikkan-ji*

so-called revolutionaries so-called revolutionary   shopkeeper [F] shopkeeper [M]

Note

1. Many of these words are probably borrowings (or perhaps reborrowings) from Turkish, where the suffix *-iye* is used much more broadly than its Arabic counterpart. Many words in Levantine were originally coined in (Ottoman-era) Turkish using classical Arabic morphology and then adopted in Arabic, where their origin is obscured by the familiarity of the components.

Gender of Nouns

Nouns are either *masculine* or *feminine*. Nouns referring to people generally have distinct masculine and feminine forms, with the feminine created by adding the suffix ‫ة‬ -*a/e* (see unit 8):

كاتبة	كاتب	دكتورة	دكتور
kaatb-e	*kaateb*	*duktoor-a*	*duktoor*
writer [F]	writer [M]	doctor [F]	doctor [M]
معلمة	معلم	طباخة	طباخ
m3allm-e	*m3allem*	*Tabbaakh-a*	*Tabbaakh*
teacher [F]	teacher [M]	cook [F]	cook [M]

These forms are similar to English pairs such as "prince" and "princess," but unlike English, making the distinction is generally obligatory, and feminine forms exist for almost every relevant word. Similar pairs exist for many animals:

فارة	فار	عنكبوتة	عنكبوت
faara	*faar*	*3ankabuute*	*3ankabuut*
mouse [F]	mouse [M]	spider [F]	spider [M]

A small number of relatively unusual nouns ending in ‫ة‬ actually refer to men. These include ‫خليفة‬ *khaliife* "caliph," ‫علامة‬ *3allaame* "great religious scholar," and ‫عمدة‬ *3imde/3umde* "mayor."

For all other nouns, gender is essentially arbitrary and has more to do with the word's pattern (see unit 5) than anything else. The good news, however, is that it is overwhelmingly predictable. Inanimate nouns ending in ‫ة‬ -*a/e* are overwhelmingly feminine. The following are all feminine:

دراسة	شغلة	صحة	مرة
diraase	*shaghle*	*Si77a*	*marra*
study	thing	health	time

Note that for many South Levantine speakers, the *-a/e* drops after *-aay* (see unit 8), but the resulting forms are still feminine:

North Levantine		South Levantine	
مراية	كنباية	مراي	كنباي
mraaye	*kanabaaye*	*mraay*	*kanabaay*
mirror	sofa	mirror	sofa

A handful of other words ending in *-a* or *-e* are also generally feminine:

بطاطا	بندورة	دنيا	ذكرا	سما
baTaaTa	*bandoora*	*dinye/dinya*	*zikra*	*sama*
potatoes	tomatoes	world	memory	sky

> In general, an *-a* which represents a root letter does not make the noun feminine, but some speakers do treat words like مشفى *mashfa* "hospital" or معنى *ma3na* "meaning" as feminine nouns.

Finally, there are several nouns that are simply always feminine, despite not being marked as such. This list varies from place to place and speaker to speaker, and quite a few words can be either masculine or feminine depending on personal preference. But the following words are *always* feminine for all speakers:

إيد	شمس	حرب	أرض	دان
2iid	*shams*	*7arb*	*2arD*	*daan*
hand, arm	sun	war	land	ear

إدن	عين	طيز	سكين	دكان
2id^en	*3een*	*Tiiz*	*sikkiin*	*dukkaan*
ear	eye	arse	knife	store, shop

رجل	إجر			
rij^el	*2ij^r*			
leg, foot	leg, foot			

Other words that are commonly feminine for some speakers include:

طريق	درب	بلد	كرسي
Tarii2	*darb*	*balad*	*kirsi*
way, road	way, road	town, country	chair

Place-names are generally feminine unless they are definite and have no feminine ending, in which case they are normally masculine:

الأردن	السودان	القدس	اليمن
ˈl2urdon	*ˈssuudaan*	*ˈl2uds*	*ˈlyaman*
Jordan	Sudan	Jerusalem	Yemen

> The gender of many place-names varies regionally. For example, لبنان *lubnaan/ libnaan* is feminine for some speakers and masculine for others.

Finally, words *as words* are always feminine. It is easiest to see what I mean by comparing the two sentences below. On the right, الأكل *ˈl2akᵉl* refers to the concept of food, whereas on the left we are talking about the choice of word, not about food per se:

الأكل هون مش منيحة	الأكل هون مش منيح
ˈl2akᵉl hoon mish ˈmnii7a	*ˈl2akᵉl hoon mish ˈmnii7*
[the word] "*ˈl2akᵉl*" here isn't good	the food here isn't good

Some other examples are:

هاي هدي مش رح تزبط معي	وين بتنصرف هاي آسف؟
haay haddi mish ra7 tuzboT ma3i	*ween ˈbtinSiref haay 2aasef?*
[saying] "calm down" isn't going	what good is "sorry"?
to work with me	[= where can one spend this "sorry"?]

Singular, Plural, Count, and Mass Nouns

In this unit we will look briefly at how count nouns and mass nouns work in Arabic and at the all-important distinction between singular and plural. These categories should be broadly familiar from English, although there are some small differences in the details in terms of how they function. We will then look at the false plural form in *-aat*, a distinct category that English has no counterpart to.

Count Nouns

Count nouns are nouns that have a singular and a plural. In Levantine as in English, the singular refers to one thing, while the plural refers to two or more things. Arabic is infamous for the sheer number of strategies it uses to form plurals, and Levantine is no exception here. There are four different suffixes used to produce plurals:

سمانة	سمان	معلمين	معلم
sammaan-e	*sammaan*	*m3allm-iin*	*m3allem*
grocers	grocer	teachers	teacher

عينين	عين	معلمات	معلم
3een-een	*3een*	*m3allm-aat*	*m3allm-e*
eyes	eye	teachers [F]	teacher [F]

> In fuS7a, the dual form is supposed to be used whenever two things are mentioned, while the plural is reserved for three or more things. This rule does not hold in Levantine: plurals can be used for two things (see unit 82). Some nouns, such as *3een* here, have a plural that looks dual. But it behaves differently, as we will see below.

There are also twelve common plural patterns and many other irregular or less common patterns. Plurals formed using root-and-pattern processes are known as *broken plurals*:

بيوت	بيت	كلاب	كلب	مدارس	مدرسة
byuut	*beet*	*klaab*	*kalb*	*madaares*	*madrase*
houses	house	dogs	dog	schools	school

حمير	حمار	أضرار	ضرر	كتب	كتاب
7amiir	*7maar*	*2aDraar*	*Darar*	*kitob/kutob*	*ktaab*
donkeys	donkey	losses	loss	books	book

The various ways of forming the plural are explored in more detail in unit 12.

Note that just as nouns referring to people have distinct masculine and feminine singulars, they usually have distinct feminine plurals formed with *-aat*. Mixed groups, however, default to the masculine plural. The words on the left can only refer to groups of women, whereas the words on the right can refer to a group of any gender makeup so long as there is at least one man:

Feminine Plural		Masculine Plural	
دكتورات	مدرسات	دكاترة	مدرسين
duktooraat	*mdarrs-aat*	*dakaatra*	*mdarrs-iin*
doctors [F]	teachers [F]	doctors [M]	teachers [M]
	مطربات		مطربين
	muTrib-aat		*muTrib-iin*
	singers [F]		singers [M]

Count nouns also generally have a dual, which is formed with the suffix ـين *-een*. This refers specifically to "two" of something. Its uses are discussed in more detail at unit 82.

Mass Nouns

Mass nouns are a familiar concept from English. They refer to indeterminate quantities of something. They cannot generally be pluralised or made dual:

تلج	رمل	مي	جبنة
tal^ej	*ram^el*	*mayy*	*jibne*
snow, ice	sand	water	cheese

A handful of words that are mass nouns in English are count nouns in Arabic:

نصايح	نصيحة	أخبار	خبر
naSaaye7	*naSii7a*	*2akhbaar*	*khabar*
[pieces of] advice	[piece of] advice	[pieces of] news	[piece of] news

		معلومات	معلومة
		ma3luumaat	*ma3luume*
		[pieces of] information	[piece of] information

More significantly, there are many words that are count nouns in English but mass nouns in Arabic. This includes almost all foodstuffs and many animals:

شجر	سمك	بطاطا	جزر
shajar	*samak*	*baTaaTa*	*jazar*
trees	fish [P]	potatoes	carrots

نجاص	بقر	خيار	موز
njaaS	*ba2ar*	*khyaar*	*mooz*
pears	cows	cucumbers	bananas

This is not just an academic distinction. Although the mass noun words are frequently used in the same place as English plurals, the meanings do not overlap perfectly. The Arabic words refer to an undifferentiated mass and take singular agreement (see unit 50), not plural as an English speaker will be tempted to use:

شجر طويل	سمك صغير	بطاطا حرة	جزر مخلل
shajar Tawiil	*samak 'zghiir*	*baTaaTa 7arra*	*jazar 'mkhallal*
tall trees	small fish [P]	spicy potatoes	pickled carrots

Mass nouns can be counted with the special "full" form of the number (see unit 82). The meaning then becomes something like "X measures of." Counterintuitively for an English speaker, the mass noun is not itself pluralised in this construction:

تلاتة بيرا	خمسة سمك
tlaate biira	*khamse samak*
three beers	five [portions of] fish

أربعة قهوة	سبعة جوز
2arba3a 2ahwe	*sab3a jooz*
four coffees	seven [portions, kilos] of walnuts

Many mass nouns have a so-called singulative formed by adding ـة *-a/e*. This form denotes *one unit* of the mass noun and often corresponds to an English singular:

شجر	شجرة	تلج	تلجة
shajar	*shajar-a*	*tal*ᵉ*j*	*talj-e*
trees	a tree	ice	ice cube

سمك	سمكة	جزر	جزرة
samak	*samak-e*	*jazar*	*jazar-a*
fish [P]	a fish	carrots	a carrot

An alternative construction with حبة *7abbet* can also be used to form singulatives. This is particularly useful for those nouns that can't easily form a singulative with *-a/e* but can be used otherwise:

بطاطا	حبة بطاطا	بندورة	حبة بندورة
baTaaTa	*7abbet baTaaTa*	*bandoora*	*7abbet bandoora*
potatoes	a potato	tomatoes	a tomato

Singulatives can generally be pluralised themselves with ـات *-aat* and counted:

أربع حبات بطاطا	تلت جزرات
2arba3 7abb-aat baTaaTa	*tlett jazar-aat*
four potatoes	three carrots

Note the distinction between the counted mass noun and the counted singulative. While the counted mass noun refers to broad measures, the counted singulative is a straightforward plural of the singulative form:

Singulative	Mass
تلت حبات بطاطا	تلاتة بطاطا
tlett 7abbaat baTaaTa	*tlaate baTaaTa*
three potatoes	three portions of fries
سبع جوزات	سبعة جوز
*sab*ᵉ*3 joozaat*	*sab3a jooz*
seven walnuts	seven kilos of walnuts

False Plural in -*aat*

Many mass nouns—and some count nouns—have a form ending in -*aat* that looks like a plural. Close attention, however, shows that it has the same basic meaning as the underlying noun. We might call it a "false plural" in this sense:

تلجات	تلج	تومات	توم
talj-aat	*tal*ᵉ*j*	*toom-aat*	*toom*
ice	ice	garlic	garlic
جزرات	جزر	سمكات	سمك
jazar-aat	*jazar*	*samak-aat*	*samak*
carrots	carrots	fish	fish

In fact, these words can be derived from words that logically have no singulative:

بردات	برد	شمسات	شمس
bard-aat	*bard*	*shams-aat*	*shams*
cold	cold	sunshine	sunshine

These words are used to indicate *specificity*. It is easiest to see what this means in context. In all these examples the -*aat* form refers to a *specific* "batch":

كيف اللحمات اليوم؟	←	لحم
kiif ᶦ*lla7maat* ᶦ*lyoom?*		*la7*ᵉ*m*
how is the meat today?		meat
[the specific meat you have in your shop]		

شو بدنا نساوي تحت هالشمسات؟	←	شمس
shuu baddna nsaawi ta7t ha-shshamsaat?		*sham*ᵉ*s*
what are we going to do in this sunshine?		sun
[this specific kind/amount of sunshine]		

دق التومات	←	توم
di22 ᶦ*ttoomaat*		*toom*
crush the garlic		garlic
[the particular garlic you have]		

In the following contexts, the -*aat* forms refer to the specific product "created by" or associated with a person. Note as well that despite the meaning, they take plural adjectives (see unit 50):

قهوة   ←   قهواتك كتير طيبين

2ahwe — *2ahwaatak ᵢktiir Tayybiin*

coffee — your coffee [the coffee you make] is very tasty

حليب   ←   حلياتها مش كتير مناح

7aliib — *7aliibaatha mish ᵢktiir mnaa7*

milk — its milk [the sheep's] isn't very good

In South Levantine, these forms are used with languages when the meaning is "X's command of," although this is not common in North Levantine:

عربياتو كتير مناح   إنجليزياتو ضعاف

3arabiyyaato ktiir mnaa7   *2ingliziyyaato D3aaf*

his Arabic is very good   his English is poor

These forms can also sometimes have an affectionate or dismissive meaning. This is less easy to give a full account of in brief.[1] But consider the following examples:

بلدي   ←   إنت بلدياتنا

baladi — *2inte baladiyyaatna*

person from a — you're from around our way

town/country — [= you're a fellow countryman]

عقل   ←   مش فاهمة عقلاتك!

3a2ᵉl — *mish faahme 3a2laatak!*

mind — I can't understand the [bizarre] way you think!

Note

1. See the detailed study of this phenomenon in Kristen Brustad, "Drink Your Milks! *āt* as Individuation Marker in Levantine Arabic," in *Classical Arabic Humanities in Their Own Terms*, ed. Beatrice Gruendler and Michael Cooperson (Brill, 2008).

Plural Formation

In this unit we will look in slightly more detail at the different ways of forming plurals. It is sometimes claimed that Arabic plurals are entirely unpredictable. This isn't quite true. Which plural strategies are possible is mostly determined by the shape of the singular noun. It is, however, true that any given singular could usually plausibly form one of two or three plurals. It is also true that many words have irregular plurals with uncommon, unexpected, or unique patterns.

For this reason, I won't be trying to come up with a sophisticated typology of plural forms. Instead, we'll take a whistle-stop tour of the "broken" plural patterns that commonly correspond to particular singular shapes. Ultimately, you will probably have to learn the plural form of a given noun alongside its singular, at least at first. But being aware of these underlying tendencies is still very useful.

Patterns and Suffixes

Singulars with the shape فعل *fi3ᵉl*, *fu3ᵉl*, *fa3ᵉl*, or *fa3al* commonly form their plural on the pattern فعال *f3aal* or its fuS7a counterpart أفعال *2af3aal*:

كلاب ← كلب		ولاد ← ولد	
klaab *kalb*		*wlaad* *walad*	
dogs dog		boys boy	

أحزاب ← حزب		أفلام ← فيلم	
2a7zaab *7izᵉb*		*2aflaam* *filᵉm*	
parties [political] party		films, movies film, movie	

Another common alternative for *fi3ᵉl*, *fu3ᵉl*, *fa3ᵉl* is *f3uul(e)* or its fuS7a counterpart *fu3uul*:

بنوكة ← بنك		قبور ← قبر	
bnuuke *bank*		*2buur* *2abᵉr*	
banks bank		graves grave	

طقوس	←	طقس		حدود	←	حد
Tuquus		**_Taqᶜs_**		**_7uduud_**		**_7add_**
rituals		ritual		borders		border

Singulars with the shape فعلة *fi3le, fu3le* generally take plurals on *fi3al* and *fu3al*, respectively, retaining the vowel they have in the singular:

طوش	←	طوشة		علب	←	علبة
Tuwash		**_Tooshe_**		**_3ilab/3ulab_**		**_3ilbe/3ulbe_**
fights		fight		boxes		box

Nonhuman singulars with the shape فعالة *f3aale* or فعيلة *fa3iile* tend to take plurals on فعايل *fa3aayel* or its fuS7a counterpart فعائل *fa3aa2el*:

خسائر	←	خسارة		جرايد	←	جريدة
khasaa2er		**_khsaara_**		**_jaraayed_**		**_jariide_**
losses		loss		newspapers		newspaper

Human singulars with these shapes tend to take the plural فعلاء *fi3ala/fu3ala*:

زملا	←	زميل		غربا	←	غريب
zimala/zumala		**_zamiil_**		**_ghiraba/ghuraba_**		**_ghariib_**
colleagues		colleague, classmate		strangers		stranger

Four-consonant singulars without a long vowel (primarily فعلل *fa3lal, fa3lel* and فعللة *fa3lale, fa3lile*) tend to take the plural فعالل *fa3aalel*:

مدافي	←	مدفا		مكاتب	←	مكتب
madaafi		**_madfa_**		**_makaateb_**		**_maktab_**
fireplaces		fireplace		offices		office

The same is true for four-consonant singulars with a long vowel followed by a *-y* (those ending in *-aay(e)* and *-iyye*):

صرامي	←	صرماية		أغاني	←	أغنية
Saraami		**_Sirmaaye/Surmaay_**		**_2aghaani_**		**_2ughniyye_**
slippers		slipper		songs		song

Nonhuman four-consonant singulars with a long vowel in the second syllable tend to take the pattern فعاليل *fa3aliil*. Note that this is spelled with a long middle vowel but pronounced, by all speakers, with a short vowel:

مكاتيب ← مكتوب	مفاتيح ← مفتاح
makatiib *maktuub*	*mafatii7* *miftaa7*
letters letter	keys key

فناجين ← فنجان	كراكيب ← كركوبة
fanajiin *finjaan*	*karakiib* *karkuube*
coffee cups coffee cup	bits of junk pieces of junk

Human four-consonant singulars with a long vowel in the second syllable often take the pattern فعاللة *fa3aalle* instead:

أساتذة ← أستاذ	دكاترة ← دكتور
2asaatze *2istaaz*	*dakaatra* *duktoor*
gentlemen gentleman	doctor doctor

The same is true for many *nisbe* nouns, mostly referring to inhabitants of particular cities and countries. Often this involves inserting (essentially random) additional consonants:

توانسة ← تونسي	مصاروة ← مصري
tawaanse *tuunsi*	*maSaarwe* *maSri*
Tunisians Tunisian	Egyptians Egyptian

Agent nouns with the pattern فاعل *faa3el*—largely nouns derived from participles (see unit 29)—generally take the plural فعال *fi33aal/fu33aal* or its weak counterpart *fi3aa(t)/fu3aa(t)*:

كتاب ← كاتب	طلاب ← طالب
kittaab/kuttaab *kaateb*	*Tillaab/Tullaab* *Taaleb*
authors author	students student

هواة ← هاوي	قضاة ← قاضي
huwaa(t) *haawi*	*2uDaa(t)* *2aaDi*
amateurs amateur	judges judge

Nonagent nouns with this shape tend to take the pattern فواعل *fawaa3el* instead:

ثانية	←	ثواني		كارثة	←	كوارث
saanye		*sawaani*		*kaarithe*		*kawaareth*
second		seconds		disaster		disasters

Almost all other agent nouns derived from participles (see unit 29) take the suffix ـين *-iin*:

مجرم	←	مجرمين		مدرب	←	مدربين
mujrem		*mujrim-iin*		*mudarreb*		*mudarrib-iin*
criminal		criminals		coach		coaches

مغترب	←	مغتربين		مقاول	←	مقاولين
mughtareb		*mughtarib-iin*		*m2aawel*		*m2aawl-iin*
expat		expats		contractor		contractors

The suffix *-iin* is also used, alongside ـة *-e*, to pluralise nouns ending in *-i* and *-ji* (see unit 9) and agent nouns on فعيل *fa33iil/fi33iil* and فعّال *fa33aal* (see unit 7). Which of *-iin* and *-e* is used varies regionally and by word, with *-e* slightly more common in North Levantine:

فلسطيني	←	فلسطينية	OR	فلسطينيين
falasTiini		*falasTiiniyy-e*		*falasTiiniyy-iin*
Palestinian		Palestinians		Palestinians

نسونجي	←	نسونجية	OR	نسونجيين
niswanji		*niswanjiyy-e*		*niswanjiyy-iin*
womaniser		womanisers		womanisers

نجار	←	نجارة	OR	نجارين
najjaar		*najjaar-a*		*najjaar-iin*
carpenter		carpenters		carpenters

لعيب	←	لعيبة	OR	لعيبين
la33iib		*la33iib-e*		*la33iib-iin*
player		players		players

A handful of *-i* nouns form their plural by deleting the *-i*:

عربي	←	عرب		روسي	←	روس
3arab-i		*3arab*		*ruus-i*		*ruus*
Arab		Arabs		Russian		Russians

Some words referring to body parts that come in pairs have plurals formed with ـين ‎-een. This looks like a dual form (see unit 82) but is actually a full plural:

عين	←	عينين	
إجر	←	إجرين	

3een	3een-een	2ij⁽e⁾r	2ijr-een
eye	eyes	leg	legs

إيد	←	إيدين	
إدن	←	إدنين	

2iid	2iid-een	2id⁽e⁾n	2idn-een
arm, hand	arms, hands	ear	ears

> This "false dual" suffix behaves unusually when additional suffixes are attached (see unit 18).

Almost all other kinds of singular form their plural with ـات ‎-aat, the least constrained plural ending. As we saw above, this is the default feminine plural equivalent to -iin. But it also occurs with many other words. Note that it replaces ـة ‎-a/e and that nouns ending in ـو ‎-o insert an h:

اقتصاد	←	اقتصادات	باشا	←	باشوات
2iqtiSaad	2iqtiSaad-aat	baasha	baasha-waat		
economy	economies	pasha	pashas		

حفلة	←	حفلات	راديو	←	راديوهات
7afl-e	7afl-aat	raadyo	raadyo-haat		
party	parties	radio	radios		

Finally, there are a number of other unusual or unique plurals, including patterns shared by only a handful of nouns that have no single associated singular shape:

شب	←	شباب	حمار	←	حمير
shabb	shabaab	7maar	7amiir		
guy	guys	donkey	donkeys		

مرة	←	نسوان	إنسان	←	ناس
mara	niswaan	2insaan	naas		
woman	women	person	people		

بير	←	بيارة	شهر	←	إشهر
biir	byaara	shah⁽e⁾r	2ishhor		
well	wells	month	months (North Levantine)		

زلم ← زلمة		سنين ← سنة	
*zil*ᵉ*m* *zalame*		*sn-iin* *sine/sane*	
guys (North Levantine) guy		years year	
فيران ← فار		كتب ← كتاب	
fiiraan *faar*		*kitob/kutob* *ktaab*	
mice mouse		books book	
دببة ← دب		إدوية ← دوا	
dababe *dibb*		*2idwiye* *dawa*	
bears (North Levantine) bear		medicines medicine	

In these cases, there is nothing to do but learn the plurals and singulars together.

> Some words have a "double" plural that looks like a plural of a plural. For many speakers, for example, the plural of فحص *fa7ᵉS* is فحوصات *f7uuS-aat*. Although occasionally these plurals have a different meaning from the normal plural, they are usually just variants.

Definiteness

As in English, Arabic nouns can be definite or indefinite, but a definite noun in Arabic sometimes corresponds to an indefinite noun in English and vice versa. In this unit we will look
first at how nouns are made definite. We will then consider the ways that Arabic uses the
definite article differently from English.

Note that in this unit, we will only discuss the general rules for nouns. For definiteness on
adjectives, see unit 16. For objects that break these rules, see unit 52.

The Definite Article

Arabic's equivalent of the definite article "the" is the prefix الـ *l-*, which takes various forms
depending on the kind of word it is attached to. When a word begins with a consonant cluster, a helping vowel (see unit 2) is normally inserted after the *l-*:

الولاد	ولاد	الكتاب	كتاب
lⁱ-wlaad	*wlaad*	*lⁱ-ktaab*	*ktaab*
the boys	boys	the book	book

When a word begins with one of *t, d, T, D, th, dh, DH, s, z, S, Z, r, n,* or *sh,* the *l* of the article
assimilates to that consonant, becoming identical to it. The word is still spelled as though the
l- were present. Note that this usually results in a consonant cluster and requires a helping
vowel:

الدرب	درب	التلج	تلج
ⁱd-darᵉb	*darᵉb*	*ⁱt-talᵉj*	*talᵉj*
the way	way	the snow	snow

الضرر	ضرر	الطلب	طلب
ⁱD-Darar	*Darar*	*ⁱT-Talab*	*Talab*
the harm	harm	the request	request

الزيارة	زيارة		السبب	سبب
ⁱz-zyaara	zyaara		ⁱs-sabab	sabab
the visit	a visit		the reason	a reason
الظلم	ظلم		الصدفة	صدفة
ⁱZ-Zulᵉm	Zulᵉm		ⁱS-Sadafe	Sadafe
the injustice	injustice		the seashell	seashell
الناس	ناس		الرقص	رقص
ⁱn-naas	naas		ⁱr-ra2ᵉS	ra2ᵉS
the people	people		the dance	a dance
الثقافة	ثقافة		الشروة	شروة
ⁱth-thaqaafe	thaqaafe		ⁱsh-sharwe	sharwe
the culture	culture		the purchase	a purchase
الظهور	ظهور		الذوق	ذوق
ⁱDH-DHuhuur	DHuhuur		ⁱdh-dhawq	dhawq
the appearance	an appearance		the taste	taste

The consonant *j* generally assimilates as well, although not for all speakers:

الجوز	OR	الجوز	←	جوز
ⁱl-jooz		ⁱj-jooz		jooz
the husband		the husband		husband

Before consonant clusters beginning with one of these consonants, speakers have a choice between assimilation and using the helping vowel. North Levantine speakers are more likely to use a helping vowel, but both behaviours occur in all four regions:

الدروس	OR	الدروس	←	دروس
ⁱd-druus		lⁱ-druus		druus
the lessons		the lessons		lessons

الصغير	OR	الصغير	←	صغير
ⁱz-zghiir		lⁱ-zghiir		zghiir
the child		the child		child

For the most part, the definite article attaches to the noun directly. It also attaches to any adjectives directly modifying the noun. But there are a few structures that can appear between the article and its noun, notably:

1. Numbers: التلت رجال *l*ᵗlett *ᵗrjaal* "the three men"; الاتنعشر قطة *l*ᵗTna3shar qiTTa* "the twelve cats."

2. The negative particles غير *gheer* and مو *muu* or مش *mish* "not" (see units 77–78): المو منيح *lmuu mnii7* "the not good [thing]," الغير مواطنين *lgheer muwaaTiniin* "noncitizens."

> Some speakers allow the quantifiers كتير *ktiir* and قليل *2aliil* (see unit 84) to occur between the definite article and the noun as well.

Uses of the Definite

All English definites correspond to Arabic definites, but not all Arabic definites correspond to English definites: the Arabic definite article is used in many places that the English article is not. Since the uses of the English article will probably be reasonably familiar to you, we will concentrate here on the ways Arabic usage differs.

> These rules hold generally for the definite article. But they become slightly confused in object position. For definite and indefinite objects, see unit 52.

Almost all the uses of the definite in Arabic that do not correspond to English are rooted in one basic principle: that the definite is used to express *genericness*. This is most obvious in sentences such as the following, where English tends to use an indefinite plural or (sometimes) an indefinite singular:

<table>
<tr><td align="center">السوريين بحبو يوكلو
ᵗssuuriyyiin bi7ibbu yooklu
Syrians like to eat</td><td align="center">الكتب مفيدة
ᵗlkutob mufiide
books are useful</td></tr>
<tr><td align="center">المرة بتعرف شو بدها
ᵗlmara bti3raf shuu biddha
a woman knows what she wants</td><td align="center">الفلسطيني شغيل
ᵗlfalisTiini shaghghiil
Palestinians are hard-working</td></tr>
<tr><td align="center">بياكل من المطاعم
byaakol mn ᵗlmaTaa3em
he eats from restaurants
[i.e., restaurant food]</td><td align="center">البيضة ما بتنكب
ᵗlbeeDa maa btinkabb
you shouldn't throw eggs out</td></tr>
</table>

The same applies to mass nouns (see unit 11) and abstract nouns, which in English typically take no article at all. Note that this includes *maSdar*s ("X-ing" type forms), discussed in more detail in unit 31:

بحبش الرمل

ᵢba7ibbᵉsh ᵢrramᵉl

I don't like sand

الدهب بجي سبايك

ᵢddahab biji sabaayek

gold comes in ingots

القتل حرام

ᵢl2atᵉl 7araam

killing is wrong

السعادة هي أهم شي

ᵢssa3aade hiyye 2ahamm shi

happiness is the most important thing

There are various other categories of nouns that generally pattern with abstract nouns in this regard. It would be difficult to give an exhaustive list, but some very common examples follow.

Language names:

بتحبي الإنجليزي؟

bit7ibbi l2inglizi?

do you like English?

العربي مش سهل

ᵢl3arabi mish sahᵉl

Arabic isn't easy

Academic disciplines and school subjects:

مالي بالكيميا

maali bilkiimya

chemistry's not really my thing

بموت بالهندسة!

bamuut bilhandase!

I just love engineering!

Seasons and holidays:

العيد الكبير ع الأبواب

ᵢl3iid lᵢkbiir 3al ᵢbwaab

Easter/Eid is just round the corner

أحسن فصل هو الربيع

2a7san faSᵉl huwwe rrabii3

the best season is spring

Days of the week:

هلا بالخميس!

hala bilkhamiis!

thank God it's Thursday!

الجمعة أصعب يوم

ᵢljim3a 2aS3ab yoom

Fridays are the hardest

Illnesses:

السل معدي؟

ᵢssill mu3di?

is TB infectious?

السكري مرض خطير

ᵢssukkari maraD khaTiir

diabetes is a dangerous illness

Numbers standing alone and representing specific quantities:

إلك منو الربع

ما بيسرع فوق العشرين

2ilak minno ᶦrribᵉ3

maa byisra3 foo2 ᶦl3ishriin

a quarter of it is yours

he doesn't go above twenty [kph]

Numbers meaning "all three [of them]," "both," and so on in constructions such as the following:

رحنا التلاتة

شو عم تساوو إنتو التنين؟

ru7na lᶦtlaate

shuu 3am ᶦtsaawu 2intu lᶦtneen?

the three of us went

what are you two doing?

There are various other kinds of expression in which Arabic uses these generic definites where they may not be intuitive to an English speaker. For example, expressions meaning "like" and "similar to" are often followed by a generic definite:

بحكم المتأكد

متل الولد الصغير

b7ukm ᶦlmit2akked

mitl ᶦlwalad lᶦzghiir

as good as certain

like a little child

بمثابة الأخ

زي العصفور

bimathaabet ᶦl2akhkh

zayy ᶦl3aSfuur

like a brother

like a bird

Note in particular expressions describing instruments or means of transport, where English has "with a" (or "by" + a bare noun) but Arabic usually uses a definite article:

جيت بالباص

بتقطعو بالسكينة

jiit bilbaaS

bti2Ta3o bissikkiine

I came by bus

you cut it with a knife

Likewise, expressions meaning "per" and similar words:

خمسين ع الساعة

مرة بالأسبوع

khamsiin 3a ssaa3a

marra bi-l2usbuu3

fifty per hour

once a week

Locational expressions consisting of a preposition and a noun in English ("at home," "to school," etc.):

رحت ع الجامع

ru7ᵉt 3a ljaame3

I went to mosque

أنا بالبيت

2ana bilbeet

I'm at home

Expressions with "last" and "next":

الشهر الجاي

ⁱshshahᵉr ⁱjjaay

next month

المرة الماضية

ⁱlmarra lmaaDye

last time

> A very common alternative with "last" and "next" is to use an *2iDaafe* (see unit 15): سنة الجايه *sint ⁱjjaaye* "next year."

Proper Nouns and Definiteness

A *proper noun* is the name of a particular place, person, entity, and so on. Proper nouns are automatically definite in terms of meaning, but in Arabic—unlike in English—some of them also take a definite article. This is largely arbitrary and has to be learnt. Many place-names have definite articles:

المكسيك

ⁱl-maksiik

Mexico

الصين

ⁱS-Siin

China

القدس

ⁱl-2uds

Jerusalem

الشام

ⁱsh-shaam

Damascus

The Arabic names for heavenly bodies and signs of the zodiac take definite articles:

الدلو

ⁱd-dalu

Aquarius

الجدي

ⁱl-jadi

Capricorn

الأرض

ⁱl-2arD

Earth

المريخ

ⁱl-mariikh

Mars

Various company and organisation names also take definite articles:

السورية

ⁱs-suuriyye

Syrian Air

اليونسكو

ⁱl-yuunisko

UNESCO

العفو الدولي

ⁱl-3afu ⁱd-duwali

Amnesty International

For similar reasons, most titles—when attached to personal names—take a definite article:

السيد الرئيس	الست جمانا	الأب صالح	الرئيس عون
ᵢs-sayyed ᵢr-ra2iis	*ᵢs-sitt jumaana*	*ᵢl-2abb Saale7*	*ᵢr-ra2iis 3oon*
Mr President	Mrs Jomana	Father Saleh	President Aoun

> The titles of education professionals—مس *miss* "Miss" (for female school-teachers), استاذ *2istaaz/2ustaaz* "Mr" (for male schoolteachers), and (ة)دكتور *duktuur(a)* (for academics)—sometimes do not take definite articles.

Proper nouns are very occasionally used in an indefinite sense, just as in English:

بدي سوريا يعيش فيها جميع

biddi suurya y3iish fiiha ᵢjjamii3

I want a Syria everyone can live in

Similarly, there are a few cases where we can use a definite article with a proper noun in English, as in the sentence below. In Arabic the article is possible here but optional:

هادا هو (الـ)حسن اللي بعرفو!

haada huwwe (l-)7asan ᵢlli ba3ᵢrfo!

that's the Hasan I know!

Indefinite Markers

Generally speaking, indefiniteness in Arabic is marked simply by the absence of the article:

كتاب	مدرسة	بنت	بيت
ktaab	*madrase*	*bint*	*beet*
a book	a school	a girl	house

There is, however, an optional indefinite marker, شي *shii*. This gives a sense of nonspecificity very similar to the English word "some":

إذا شي مرة حبيت تجي . . .	روح شفلك شي دكتور
2iza shii marra 7abbeet tiji . . .	*ruu7 shuflak shii duktoor*
if you ever [= on some occasion] feel like coming . . .	go and see some doctor [i.e., any one willing to test you]

In higher-register language, you may occasionally encounter the fuS7a ما *-ma*: أحيانا بجيك حدس ما *2a7yaanan bijiik 7adᵉs ma* "sometimes you get a certain intuition."

The word حيالله *7ayaLLa* gives a sense of "any old" or "just any":

حيالله بيت بكفيني

7ayyaLLa beet bikaffiini

any old house would be fine for me

هادا مش حيالله حدا

haada mish 7ayaLLa 7ada

he isn't just anyone

Demonstratives

In this unit we will be looking at *demonstratives*. A demonstrative is a word that indicates the actual or emotional proximity of a noun to the speaker: "this (one)," "that (one)," "these (ones)," and "those (ones)," which can either stand on their own replacing a noun phrase ("this is difficult") or appear alongside a noun ("this book is difficult"). While overall the demonstrative system in Arabic is fairly similar to that of English, there are some important differences.

We will start by looking at the six basic demonstrative pronouns (the equivalent of English "this," "these," "that," "those"). We will then look at a seventh demonstrative word that English has no direct equivalent to: the omnipresent هيك *heek*. After this, we will consider how these structures combine with nouns ("this house," "that woman"). Finally, we will look at some common idiomatic uses of the demonstratives and some more unusual demonstrative structures.

Basic Demonstratives

The demonstrative pronouns are used in place of a noun. All four dialects have six pronouns of this kind: three referring to things nearby ("this" and "these") and three referring to things farther away ("that" and "those"). The singulars agree with the gender of the noun they are referring to. Note that while the forms are more or less the same in Syrian and South Levantine, the Lebanese forms are quite distinct:

Lebanese	Syrian	South Levantine
هيدا	هادا OR هاد	
hayda	*haada* OR *haad*	
this one [M]	this one [M]	

Lebanese	Syrian	South Levantine
هيدي *haydi* this one [F]	هي *hayy* this one [F]	هاي *haay* this one [F]
هول *hool* these ones		هدول *hadool* these ones
هيداك *haydaak* that one [M]		هداك *hadaak* that one [M]
هيديك *haydiik* that one [F]		هديك *hadiik* that one [F]
هوليك *hawliik* those ones	هدوك *hadook* those ones	هدلاك *had(o)laak* those ones

Additional regional variants include forms with ض in Jordan (e.g., هاضا *haaDa*), هودي *hawdi* and هوديك *hawdiik* for the plural forms in Lebanon, هي *hayy* "this [F]," هدنك *hadink* and هدوليك *hadoliik* "those" in Syrian, and هادي *haadi* "this [F]" as a general variant of هاي *haay*.

You are also likely to encounter variants with a final vowel added. What vowel is used varies by region but is most commonly -*a* in Southern Levantine (هدولا *hadool-a* "these"), -*i* in Lebanese (هولي *hawl-i* "these"), and -*e* in Syrian (هدوله *hadool-e* "these"). The meaning of these forms is exactly the same.

Demonstratives are commonly used in place of a noun:

هاي بقديش؟

haay ᵢb2addeesh?

how much is this one?

هاد أحسن من هداك

haad 2a7san min hadaak

this one is better than that one

ما بدي هيدي

maa baddi haydi

I don't want this one

هدوله قصار عليي

hadoole 2Saar 3aliyyi

these ones are too short for me

Although in English it is not very common to refer to people with "this one" or "that one," the Arabic forms are very common and neutral with people. The English translation usually requires a noun ("this guy," "that woman"):

هودي مصيبة!	هديك مشكلة!	هداك صرصري
hawdi mSiibe!	*hadiik mushkile!*	*hadaak SarSari*
these guys are a disaster!	that woman's trouble!	that guy's a ruffian

As in English, demonstratives can also refer to abstract situations. But unlike English, it is always the "this" forms that are used here:

كلو إلا هاد!	هيدي مصيبة!	شو هاد؟!
killo 2illa haad!	*haydi mSiibe!*	*shuu haad?!*
anything but that!	this is a catastrophe!	what's going on?!

In many such cases, however, it is another demonstrative that provides the idiomatic choice: هيك *heek.*

heek

The word هيك *heek* is used across the Levantine area, although like the normal demonstratives it has local variants formed by addition of a final vowel:

Lebanese	Syrian	South Levantine
هيكي	هيكه	هيكا
heyk-i	*heek-e*	*heek-a*

The word *heek* most commonly translates "like this" or "like that." Rather than replacing nouns, it stands in for a *description.* This is easiest to show by comparison. The descriptions in the sentences on the left have been replaced by *heek* on the sentences on the right:

ارفع إيدك هيك	←	ارفع إيدك شوي شوي
2irfa3 2iidak heek		*2irfa3 2iidak shwayy 'shwayy*
raise your hand like this		raise your hand slowly

لا تشربي هيك	←	لا تشربي بهالسرعة
laa tishrabi heek		*laa tishrabi bhassir3a*
don't drink like that!		don't drink so quickly!

بتحسو غريب؟   ←   بتحسو هيك؟

bit7isso ghariib?   *bit7isso heek?*

you think he's weird?   you think he's like that?

الدنيا صغيرة   ←   الدنيا هيك

ᵢddinye zghiire   *ᵢddinye heek*

the world's a small place   that's how the world is

There is another construction corresponding to English "like this": متل هاد *mitᵉl haad* or زي هاد *zayy haad* "like this (one)." Learners have to be careful to distinguish these structures from *heek*, because although the English translation is the same, the two meanings are distinct in Arabic. The word *mitᵉl* or *zayy* plus a normal demonstrative pronoun usually refers to a specific noun, whereas *heek*, as we have seen, refers more broadly to a description:

سيارتي متل هديك   سيارتي هيك

sayyaarti mitᵉl hadiik   *sayyaarti heek*

my car is like that one   my car is like that

[over there]   [= has the quality just referred to]

في حدا زي هاد؟   في حدا هيك؟

fii 7ada zayy haad?   *fii 7ada heek?*

is anyone like this guy?   is there anyone like that

[= meeting this description]?

Relatedly, *heek* is also commonly used in the sense of "just because" and in the very common structure إذا هيك *2iza heek* "in that case," "if that's how it is," etc.:

هيك!   إذا هيك ما بعرف

heek!   *2iza heek maa ba3ref*

just because!   In that case [= if that's

how it is], I don't know

There are also many cases in which *heek* idiomatically corresponds to a simple "that" or "this" in English. In these sentences, *heek* refers to an overall situation. You could plausibly restructure these examples (albeit not very naturally) with "[a situation] like that" (for more examples with comparatives, see unit 79):

هيك بكون كتير منيح   شو بدك أحسن من هيك؟

heek bikuun ktiir ᵢmnii7   *shuu baddak 2a7san min heek?*

that would be very good   what could be better than that?

This is the idiomatic option for a handful of verbs, including عمل *3imel* "do" and قال *2aal* "say":

ليش قلت هيك؟   ليش هيك عملت؟

leesh 2ul^et heek?   *leesh heek ^i3mil^et?*

why did you say that?   why did you do that?

With Nouns

We can also combine a demonstrative with a noun: "this box," "that man." There are two ways of doing this: with the prefix هالـ *hal-* and with a full demonstrative.

Hal- consists historically of the *ha-* of the demonstrative and the *l-* of the definite prefix (see unit 13) and assimilates to initial consonants in exactly the same way as the definite prefix does:

هالـ   +   شمس   ←   هالشمس

hal-   *shams*   *hash-shams*

     sun   this sun

هالـ   +   ناس   ←   هالناس

hal-   *naas*   *han-naas*

     people   these people

هالـ   +   حدود   ←   هالحدود

hal-   *7duud*   *hal-^i7duud*

     borders   these borders

The normal usage of *hal-* corresponds directly to English "this," "that," "these," and "those" with a noun; it does not distinguish between the different types of demonstrative. Note that a noun with *hal-* is considered definite for adjective agreement purposes (see unit 50):

مالو هالجو التعيس؟   اكسر هالحدود!

maalo hajjaww ^itta3iis?   *2ikser hal^i7duud!*

what's up with this awful weather?   break those borders!

هالسنة بدي ادرس منيح   بتعرف هالزلمة؟

hassine biddi 2idros ^imnii7   *bta3ref hazzalame?*

this year I'm going to study hard   do you know that guy?

It is also possible to simply place a demonstrative pronoun before or after a definite noun. In this case, of course, the pronoun has to agree with the noun:

هاي السنة أطول من هديك

hayy ⁱ*ssine 2aTwal min hadiik*

this year is longer than that one

البيت هاد مش كتير مريح

ⁱ*lbeet haad mish* ⁱ*ktiir murii7*

this house isn't very comfortable

There isn't much difference between these two structures, and different speakers use one or the other more frequently. The two can be combined for emphasis:

قصدي هالسنة هاي!

2aZdi hassine haay!

I mean *this* year!

Some speakers feel uncomfortable using *hal-* in *2iDaafe* structures (see unit 15). For these speakers, a full demonstrative pronoun placed after the *2iDaafe* provides a way of avoiding *hal-*, while other speakers either place *hal-* at the beginning of a definite *2iDaafe* or put it where the definite article would otherwise be:

North Levantine	**South Levantine**
هالبيت المخدة *halbeet l*ⁱ*mkhadde* this pillowcase	بيت المخدة هاد *beet l*ⁱ*mkhadde haad* this pillowcase
هالمكنسة الكهربا *hal*ⁱ*mkannst* ⁱ*lkahraba* this hoover	مكنسة الكهربا هاي *mkannst* ⁱ*lkahraba haay* this hoover
هالشوية المي *hashshwayyt* ⁱ*lmayy* this small amount of water	شوية المي هاي *shwayyt* ⁱ*lmayy haay* this small amount of water

Heek can also be placed before or (less commonly) after indefinite nouns. This gives the literal meaning "such [a]," although the idiomatic translation is usually "an X/Xs like that":

ايش بدك بهيك واحد؟

shuu biddak bheek waa7ad?

what do you want with someone like that?

هيك ناس ما بتنطاق

heek naas maa btinTaa2

people like that are insufferable

بعرف ناس هيك

ba3ref naas heek

I know people like that

Idiomatic Uses

For the most part, *hal-* and a full demonstrative pronoun are interchangeable in meaning. But *hal-* also has an idiomatic use that has no immediate equivalent in English and cannot be replaced with a full demonstrative. In the following examples *hal-* gives a sort of extra narrative flavour, drawing the listener in:

بدي أرتاح بهالصالون

biddi 2artaa7 bhaSSaaloon

I'm about to chill out in
the [= this] living room

طول نهاري قاعد ورا هالدركسيون

Tool ⁱnhaari 2aa3ed wara haddirkⁱsyoon

[I spend] my whole day sitting behind
the [= this] steering wheel

The forms *hadaak/haydaak* and *hadiik/haydiik* "that one" also have a distinctive idiomatic use that (correspondingly) is not interchangeable with *hal-*. In the following sentence, *hadaak* does not refer necessarily to a person who has already been mentioned, as you would expect with "that." Instead, *hadaak* invokes a sort of platonic ideal of a special specific person:

قديش بغير حياتك هداك الشخص!

2addeesh bighayyer 7ayaatak hadaak ⁱshshakhᵉS!

How much that [one special] person [can] change your life!

By extension it can be used to refer euphemistically to things, particularly in the famous expression هداك المرض *hadaak ⁱlmaraD* "that [particular] illness" (cancer). It can also be combined with time expressions in a similar way: هديك المرة *hadiik ⁱlmarra* "this one time," هداك اليوم *hadaak ⁱlyoom* "the other day."

> For some speakers, *hadaak* is used in these constructions even when the noun is feminine: هداك المرة *hadaak ⁱlmarra* "this one time . . ."

hashshi and *hal2ishi*

The words هالشي *hashshi* and هالإشي *hal2ishi* "this thing" occasionally translate "this" or "that" with reference to abstract situations:

هالإشي خلاني أكمل

hal2ishi khallaani 2akammel

that kept me going

عن جد صار هالشي؟

3an jadd Saar hashshi?

did this really happen?

hal7aki and *halkalaam*

The words هالحكي *hal7aki* and هالكلام *halkalaam,* both meaning "this speech," translate "this" when referring to events that are being or have just been recounted to you:

صحيح هالكلام؟   هالحكي من ست سنين

hal7aki min sitt ⁱsniin   *Sa7ii7 halkalaam?*

this was six years ago   is this true?

The *2iDaafe*

In this unit we will be looking at the *2iDaafe* (literally "addition" or "annexation"), a distinctively Arabic construction involving the juxtaposition of two nouns. This structure corresponds to a range of English counterparts expressing association and possession.

We will start by looking at exactly how *2iDaafes* are formed. We will then look at how they are used to express possession and to form certain kinds of compound expression. Finally, we will look at some idiomatic uses of *2iDaafe* constructions with the particle تبع *taba3* and with expletive expressions.

Form of the *2iDaafe*

An *2iDaafe* construction consists of two nouns placed alongside one another. The "modifying" noun—the possessor or the noun that provides more information about the main noun—comes second, the opposite order compared to English:

بيت طارق ← طارق + بيت

beet Taare2　　*Taare2*　　*beet*

Tariq's house　　Tariq　　house

طريق عمان ← عمان + طريق

Tarii2 3ammaan　　*3ammaan*　　*Tarii2*

the Amman road　　Amman　　way

The first complication here is that a final ة -a/e in the first word becomes -et in this sort of construction (see unit 8 for some exceptions):

بطة رامي ← رامي + بطة

baTT-et raami　　*raami*　　*baTTa*

Rami's duck　　Rami　　duck

معلمة   +   سامي   ←   معلمة سامي

m3allm-et saami   *saami*   *m3allme*

Sami's teacher   Sami   teacher

The words أخ *2akhkh* "brother" and أب *2abb* "father" also have distinct forms in *2iDaafe*, typically becoming أخو *2akhu* and أبو *2abu*, respectively:

أب   +   مريم   ←   أبو مريم

2abu maryam   *maryam*   *2abb*

Maryam's dad   Maryam   father

أخ   +   رامي   ←   أخو رامي

2akhu raami   *raami*   *2akhkh*

Rami's brother   Rami   brother

The second complication is that as a general rule, only the final word in an *2iDaafe* can take the definite article (see unit 13). Making this word definite makes the whole structure definite:

Definite		Indefinite
بيت المخدة ←		بيت مخدة
beet lⁱ-mkhadde		*beet ⁱmkhadde*
the pillowcase		pillowcase
غرفة النوم ←		غرفة نوم
ghirfet ⁱn-noom		*ghirfet noom*
the bedroom		bedroom

This means that a separate structure is required when the first noun needs to be indefinite and the second definite ("an X of Y's"). This is generally achieved using لـ *la-* "for" (see appendix B):

غنية   +   فيروز   ←   غنية لفيروز

ghinniyye lafeyruuz   *feyruuz*   *ghinniyye*

a song of Feyrouz's   Fayrouz   song

بيت   +   محمد   ←   بيت لمحمد

beet lam7ammad   *m7ammad*   *beet*

a house of Muhammad's   Muhammad   house

A third general complication is that as a rule, nothing can "break" the *2iDaafe* by appearing between the two nouns. Most obviously, adjectives—although agreeing with the first noun—will follow the *2iDaafe* as a unit:

بيت مخدة كبير	←	كبير +	بيت مخدة
beet ᶦmkhadde kbiir		kbiir	beet ᶦmkhadde
a big pillowcase		big	pillowcase
غرفة عادل الصغيرة	←	صغير +	غرفة عادل
ghirfet 3aadel lᶦzghiire		zghiir	ghirfet 3aadel
Adel's small room		small	Adel's room

This also creates problems for the prefix هال *hal-* "this" (see unit 14), which normally replaces the definite article. Some speakers allow this in *2iDaafe* constructions as well (column 1). But many feel uncomfortable using it like this when it involves breaking an *2iDaafe* and either attach it to the beginning of an already definite *2iDaafe* (column 2) or use a full demonstrative pronoun after the structure instead to avoid using *hal-* at all (column 3):

3 No *hal-*	2 *hal-* **Prefixes to** **Definite *2iDaafe***	1 *hal-* **Replaces** *ᶦl-*
كاسة المي هاي	هالكاسة المي	كاسة هالمي
kaaset ᶦlmayy haay	halkaaset ᶦlmayy	kaaset halmayy
this cup of water	this cup of water	this cup of water
بيت المخدة هاد	هالبيت المخدة	بيت هالمخدة
beet lᶦmkhadde haad	halbeet lᶦmkhadde	beet halᶦmkhadde
this pillowcase	this pillowcase	this pillowcase

All three of these forms occur. The paraphrase in column 3 seems to be favoured in South Levantine, but there is considerable regional and personal variation.

Meanings of the *2iDaafe*

The *2iDaafe* basically corresponds to four types of English construction. The first, expressing basic possession or association, is the apostrophe "s":

بيت محمد	←	محمد +	بيت
beet ᶦm7ammad		ᶦm7ammad	beet
Muhammad's house		Muhammad	house

راس + لينا ← راس لينا

raas   *liina*   *raas liina*

head   Lina   Lina's head

فكرة + اليوم ← فكرة اليوم

fikra   *ᵉlyoom*   *fikret ᵉlyoom*

idea   today   today's idea

The second construction is "of," which is used for quantity/container expressions (see unit 84), part-and-whole relationships, and various other associations:

آخر + الشارع ← آخر الشارع

2aakher   *ᵉshshaare3*   *2aakher ᵉshshaare3*

end   the street   the end of the street

أول + الشهر ← أول الشهر

2awwal   *ᵉshshahᵉr*   *2awwal ᵉshshahᵉr*

start   the month   the start of the month

شوية + مصاري ← شوية مصاري

shwayye   *maSaari*   *shwayyet maSaari*

a bit   money   a bit of money

كاسة + مي ← كاسة مي

kaase   *mayy*   *kaaset mayy*

cup   water   a cup of water

جمهورية + مصر ← جمهورية مصر

jumhuuriyye   *maSᵉr*   *jumhuuriyyet maSᵉr*

republic   Egypt   the Republic of Egypt

The third is the so-called attributive noun or adjectival noun construction, where a noun is used to provide more information about another noun, for example, the material it is made from:

كتاب + تاريخ ← كتاب تاريخ

ktaab   *taariikh*   *ktaab taariikh*

book   history   history book

معرض + كتاب ← معرض كتاب

ma3raD   *ktaab*   *ma3raD ᵉktaab*

exhibition   book   book fair

كيس + نايلون → كيس نايلون

kiis	naaylon	kiis naaylon
bag	plastic	plastic bag

خاتم + دهب → خاتم الدهب

khaatem	dahab	khaatem 'ddahab
ring	gold	gold ring

Finally and relatedly, the *2iDaafe* is often used to produce compound nouns:

بيت + مخدة → بيت مخدة

beet	mkhadde	beet 'mkhadde
house	pillow	pillowcase

غزل + بنات → غزل بنات

ghaz*ᵉ*l	banaat	ghaz*ᵉ*l banaat
spinning	girls	candyfloss

غرفة + نوم → غرفة نوم

ghirfe	noom	ghirfet noom
room	sleep	bedroom

خلاطة + كهربا → خلاطة كهربا

khallaaTa	kahraba	khallaaTet kahraba
mixer	electricity	blender

As a rule, anything expressed in any of these four ways in English can be expressed with an *2iDaafe* in Arabic.

Stacking *2iDaafes*

It is possible to have an *2iDaafe* with more than two parts. A chain of possession and/or association, for example, can be expressed as follows:

لون + جرابات + سامي → لون جرابات سامي

loon	jraabaat	saami	loon 'jraabaat saami
colour	socks	Sami	the colour of Sami's socks

بيت + أب + علاء → بيت أبو علاء

beet	2abb	3alaa2	beet 2abu 3alaa2
house	dad	Ala	Ala's dad's house

نهاية عطلة العيد ←   العيد + عطلة + نهاية

nihaayet 3uTlet ᶦl3iid	*ᶦl3iid*	*3uTle*	*nihaaye*
the end of the Eid holiday	Eid	holiday	end

There is, however, a complication. Speakers tend to find these constructions unacceptable when there is no direct relationship of association or possession between each pair of adjacent nouns. This causes problems when it comes to compound or attributive noun structures such as خلاطة كهربا *khallaaTet kahraba* "blender" ("electricity mixer") and خاتم دهب *khaatem dahab* "gold ring." If Sami owns a blender, he obviously owns the *khallaaTa*, but does he have a straightforward relationship with the *kahraba*? Many Arabic speakers feel that he does not.

> Different speakers disagree on where to draw the line between more and less "possession-like" relationships here. While one speaker provided "Rami's driving licence" as an example where "driving" clearly "belongs to" Rami, allowing us to add the possessor to the end of the *2iDaafe*, another used the exact same example as a case where a lack of a clear relationship of possession made this kind of structure incorrect!

The safest option in these cases is generally to use the particle تبع *taba3* or تاع *taa3*, which follows a definite *2iDaafe* (see the next section for more on this particle):

خلاطة الكهربا تبعت سامي	خاتم الدهب تبع مروة
khallaaTet ᶦlkahraba taba3et saami	*khaatem ᶦddahab taba3 marwa*
Sami's blender	Marwa's gold ring

Some but not all speakers permit the possessor to be inserted into the middle of the *2iDaafe*:

خلاطة سامي الكهربا	خاتم مروة الدهب
khallaaTet saami lkahraba	*khaatem marwa ddahab*
Sami's blender	Marwa's gold ring

The correctness and even existence of this structure are highly contested by those speakers who do not use it, however. It is probably safest for learners to avoid it.

2iDaafe with *taba3*

The particle تبع *taba3* or تع *ta3* stands in for the first noun of a *2iDaafe*. It has a range of feminine and plural forms, but the most common sets are as follows. Note that many speakers do not have a distinct feminine plural (see unit 17):

Feminine Plural	Plural	Feminine	Masculine
تبعات	تبعون	تبعت	تبع
taba3aat	*taba3uun*	*taba3et/tab3at*	*taba3*
تعات	تعون	تاعت	تع
ta3aat	*ta3uun*	*taa3et/taa3at*	*ta3*

Alternative feminines include تبعيت *taba3iit* and تعيت *ta3iit*. Alternative plurals include تبعول *taba3uul* and تبعوت *taba3uut*.

Standing alone, a definite *2iDaafe* with *taba3* most commonly expresses a loose association. These examples could refer to objects or to people and can be used in almost every conceivable context that the English equivalents can be used:

تبع المي	تبعت المصاري	تبعون الفيلا
taba3 ⁱlmayy	*taba3et ⁱlmaSaari*	*taba3uun ⁱlvilla*
the water one	the money one	the ones from the villa
the water guy	the money woman	the villa guys

This construction can also, less commonly, form an equivalent to English structures such as "Ahmed's [one]" and "mine." Note, however, that this structure is sometimes used as a euphemism for genitalia, so it should be deployed with caution:

تبع الضابط	تبعت سمير
taba3 ⁱDDaabeT	*taba3et samiir*
the officer's [one]	Samir's [one]

With an indefinite noun, the construction can express "the sort of person who would," "given to," and "inclined toward":

تبع مصاري	تبعون حركات
taba3 maSaari	*taba3uun 7arakaat*
money-grubbing [M]	tricksy [P]
	[= given to manoeuvres]

An *2iDaafe* structure with *taba3* can also be attached to a noun. Here it usually gives the same sense as it does when it stands alone:

ناس تبع جماعات خيرية

naas taba3 jamaa3aat kheyriyye

people from charity organisations

ناس تعون مصاري

naas ta3uïn maSaari

people only interested in money

> Note that for North Levantine speakers, agreement is optional and uncommon when a *taba3* expression is used after a noun. In these contexts, *taba3* is generally used invariably for masculine, feminine, and plural nouns alike.

taba3 is also used to avoid uncomfortable structures. As we saw above, many speakers use it to add a possessor to an *2iDaafe* that would otherwise not be able to take one. It is also sometimes used to avoid applying pronoun suffixes to foreign words or words that aren't easily suffixed. For more on possessive pronouns, see unit 18.

Expletive *2iDaafe*

One common idiomatic use of the *2iDaafe* is to form emphatic and (mildly to very) obscene expressions for intensity. Sensitive nouns such as دين *diin* "religion," سما *sama* "heavens," رب *rabb* "Lord," إخت *2ikht* "sister," and إم *2imm* "mother" are combined with a possessor, giving an effect quite like the use of "the hell" or other rude adjectives in English:

شو بعرف إختي؟

shuu bi3arref 2ikht-i?

how the hell should I know?

[= how should *my sister* know?]

صارت عز دين الصبح!

Saarat 3izz diin ˈSSubº7!

we're halfway through the bloody morning!

[= it's the height *of the religion* of the morning]

> These examples use attached pronouns (see unit 18).

It goes without saying that as a learner, it is safest for you not to try to use these expressions yourself.

Adjectives

In this unit we will be looking at *adjectives*. This is a word class that should be fairly familiar to English speakers: "describing words" that typically provide additional information about a noun (traits, colours, etc.). While in this sense Arabic adjectives are much like their English counterparts, their behaviour differs. They have a lot in common with nouns, having distinct feminine, plural, and definite forms.

We will begin by looking at some common types of adjective. We will then see how adjectives are used in practice and how this differs from English. Finally, we will look at how adjectives form their feminine and plural.

Common Types of Adjectives

Most adjectives have one of a handful of basic shapes. In this section we will give a quick overview of these shapes and—in those cases where they are clearly derivational—look quickly at their meanings.

> Remember: Derivational processes are those that derive new words from other words, and inflectional processes are those that derive new forms of existing words.

The most common adjectives mostly have the form *fa3iil* or *f3iil* or its defective counterpart *fa3i*:

كبير	صغير	غريب	سميك
kbiir	***zghiir***	***ghariib***	***smiik***
big	small	strange	thick

تقيل	خفيف	غبي	غني
t2iil	*khafiif*	*ghabi*	*ghani*
heavy	light	stupid	rich

Some have the form *fi3el* or (very occasionally) its fuS7a counterpart *fa3el*:

وسخ	وقح	حلو	وقح
wisekh	*wi2e7*	*7ilu*	*waqe7*
dirty	rude	nice	rude

There are many common adjectives that express characteristic behaviours or features. These largely have the forms *fa33iil/fi33iil* or (for four-letter roots) *fa3luul*:

خويف ← خاف	صريف ← صرف
khawwiif *khaaf*	*Sarriif* *Saraf*
scaredy-cat to be scared	spendthrift to spend

شريب ← شرب	بريد ← برد
sharriib *shireb*	*barriid* *barad*
drinks a lot to drink	sensitive to cold to get cold

فركوش ← فركش	كركوب ← كركب
farkuush *farkash*	*karkuub* *karkab*
clumsy to trip over	messy to mess up

The suffix *-i* (see unit 9), which we have already encountered with nouns, is very common in adjectives. As with nouns, *-i* produces adjectives referring to ideologies, nationalities, and so on. But it also has far broader scope, acting as a sort of general-purpose adjective former:

اشتراكي ←	الاشتراكية	صيني ←	الصين
2ishtiraak-i	*'l2ishtiraakiyye*	*Siini*	*'SSiin*
socialist	socialism	Chinese	China

جزئي ←	جزء	احتياطي ←	احتياط
jiz2-i	*jizᶜ2*	*2i7tiyaaT-i*	*2i7tiyaaT*
partial	part	precautionary	caution

ثقافي ←	ثقافة	دراسي ←	دراسة
thaqaaf-i	*thaqaafe*	*diraas-i*	*diraase*
cultural	culture	academic	study

A few very common adjectives end in اني- *-aani*, which behaves identically to *-i*:

فوقاني	←	فوق		براني	←	برا
foo2-aani		*foo2*		*barr-aani*		*barra*
upper		above		exterior		outside
وراني	←	ورا		تحتاني	←	تحت
warr-aani		*wara*		*ta7t-aani*		*ta7ᵉt*
rear		behind		lower		below

Most other common adjectives are either *passive* or *active* participles, both of which we've already encountered as a source of nouns (see unit 7). The passive participle expresses the state of "having been X-ed"—the state of the *object* of a verb after the action described by the verb is completed. It corresponds very closely to the English past participle (the "X-ed" form):

مترجم	←	ترجم		مكتوب	←	كتب
mtarjam		*tarjam*		*maktuub*		*katab*
translated		to translate		written		to write
مشغول	←	شغل		منسي	←	نسي
mashghuul		*shaghal*		*minsi/mansi*		*nisi*
occupied, busy		to occupy		forgotten		to forget

Note that a handful of passive participles can have the meaning "-able":

مقروء	←	قرأ		مقبول	←	قبل
maqruu2		*qara2*		*ma2buul*		*2ibel*
legible		to read		acceptable		to accept

Active participles occupy a more complex position as part of the verbal system, as we will see, and their usual meanings vary depending on the underlying verb (see unit 37). Nonetheless, many active participles are used as simple adjectives, corresponding with English adjectives:

تافه	عابر	ناقص	نادر
taafeh	*3aaber*	*naa2eS*	*naader*
petty	passing, ephemeral	missing, lacking	rare

In both cases some fuS7a loans are also used in Levantine, although they are less common than their noun counterparts, and as elsewhere Lebanese speakers are more likely to use the more "Levantine" patterns (see unit 3). Some examples:

متخلف	مستمر	متبادل	ممتاز
mutakhallef	*mustamirr*	*mutabaadal*	*mumtaaz*
backward	continuous	mutual	outstanding, excellent

See unit 29 for a table of participle forms.

Using Adjectives

As in English, an adjective can modify a noun directly. Unlike in English, however, an Arabic adjective follows its noun and agrees with that noun for gender and number. We will look in more detail at how feminine and plural adjectives are formed below, but the strategies are very similar to those in nouns, as you can see:

بيت كبير ← كبير + بيت

beet ⁱkbiir	*kbiir*	*beet*
a big house	big	a house [M]

بنت طويلة ← طويل + بنت

bint Tawiil-e	*Tawiil*	*bint*
a tall girl	tall	girl [F]

مدرا ممتازين ← ممتاز + مدرا

mudara mumtaaz-iin	*mumtaaz*	*mudara*
outstanding managers	outstanding	managers

> Agreement is a bit more complex than the examples here suggest. See unit 50 for more detail.

Adjectives also have to agree with their noun in definiteness. An adjective is made definite by addition of the definite article الـ *ⁱl-* (see unit 13), just like a noun:

البيت الكبير ← كبير + البيت

ⁱlbeet l-ⁱkbiir	*kbiir*	*ⁱlbeet*
the big house	big	the house

البنت طويلة ← طويل + البنت

ⁱlbint ⁱT-Tawiile	*Tawiil*	*ⁱlbint*
the tall girl	tall	the girl

المدرا الممتازين ← ممتاز + المدرا

'lmudara 'l-mumtaaziin	mumtaaz	'lmudara
the outstanding managers	outstanding	the managers

Unlike in English, the definite adjective can stand alone in the meaning "the X one(s)." In this case, the definite adjective still agrees for number and gender with the *implicit* noun to which it refers:

الكبار   الكبيرة   الكبير

l'kbaar	l'kbiire	l'kbiir
the big ones	the big one [something feminine]	the big one [something masculine]

الممتازين   الممتازة   الممتاز

'lmumtaaziin	'lmumtaaze	'lmumtaaz
the outstanding ones	the outstanding one [something feminine]	the outstanding one [something masculine]

The indefinite counterpart of this—"a(n) X one"—requires واحد *waa7ed/ waa7ad* or its feminine counterpart وحدة *wa7de*: واحد ممتاز *waa7ad mumtaaz* "an outstanding one," وحدة كبيرة *wa7de kbiire* "a big one."

With reference to situations, this construction sometimes gives the sense of "the X thing":

المنيح إنو . . .   الصعب إنو . . .

l'mnii7 2inno . . .	'SSa3'b 2inno . . .
the good thing is that . . .	the difficult thing is that . . .

In all other contexts, adjectives still have to agree for gender and number but do not agree for definiteness. The most common context where this occurs is in "to be" sentences (see unit 49). Since there is no word for "is" or "are" in the following sentences, the presence or absence of the definite prefix produces quite different meanings. Compare the following:

البنت طويلة   بنت طويلة   البيت كبير   البيت الكبير

'lbint Tawiile	'lbint 'T-Tawiile	'lbeet 'kbiir	'lbeet l-'kbiir
the girl is tall	the tall girl	the house is big	the big house

المدرا ممتازين   المدرا الممتازين

'lmudara mumtaaziin	'lmudara 'l-mumtaaziin
the managers are outstanding	the outstanding managers

Forms of the Adjective

Unlike their English counterparts, adjectives have masculine, feminine, and plural forms. Luckily, these are considerably more straightforward than their counterparts in nouns. Almost without exception, feminine adjectives are formed by adding the suffix *-a/e* (see unit 8):

صغيرة ←	صغير	كبيرة ←	كبير
zghiir-e	*zghiir*	*kbiir-e*	*kbiir*
small [F]	small [M]	big [F]	big [M]

تافهة ←	تافه	وسخة ←	وسخ
taafh-a	*taafeh*	*wiskh-a*	*wisekh*
petty [F]	petty [M]	dirty [F]	dirty [M]

مقابلة ←	مقابل	متبادلة ←	متبادل
muqaabil-e	*muqaabel*	*mutabaadal-e*	*mutabaadal*
corresponding [F]	corresponding [M]	mutual [F]	mutual [M]

Plurals are slightly more complicated although nowhere near as complicated as they are in nouns. Adjectives on the pattern *f3iil/fa3iil* generally have a plural on *f3aal*:

خفاف	خفيف	كبار	كبير
khfaaf	**khafiif**	**kbaar**	**kbiir**
light [P]	light [S]	big [P]	big [S]

قصار	قصير	صغار	صغير
2Saar	**2aSiir**	**zghaar**	**zghiir**
short [P]	short [S]	small [P]	small [S]

طوال	طويل	تقال	تقيل
Twaal	**Tawiil**	**t2aal**	**t2iil**
long	long [S]	heavy [P]	heavy [S]

A handful of common adjectives have irregular plurals that have to be learned. In many cases these coexist with more regular plurals:

أغبيا	غبي	اغنيا	غني
2aghbiya	**ghabi**	**2ighniya/2aghniya**	**ghani**
stupid [P]	stupid [S]	rich [P]	rich [S]

قلايل	قليل	قدما	قديم
2alaayel	*2aliil*	*2idama/2udama*	*2adiim*
few [P]	few [S]		old

Otherwise, the vast majority of adjective plurals are formed using ‍ين -*iin*. In fact, even many of the adjectives discussed above can form plurals using -*iin*:

شاطرين	شاطر	وسخين	وسخ
shaaTr-iin	*shaaTer*	*wiskh-iin*	*wisekh*
clever [P]	clever [S]	dirty [P]	dirty [S]

مشتركين	مشترك	قديمين	قديم
mushtarak-iin	*mushtarak*	*2adiim-iin*	*2adiim*
shared [P]	shared [S]	old [P]	old [S]

Note that this plural is generally all-purpose and can be used for feminine plurals as well as mixed groups. However, a distinct feminine plural does exist—on paper at least—for all adjectives, formed with the suffix ات -*aat*. For more on this, see unit 17.

A handful of adjectives are invariable, which is to say they have no feminine or plural forms. Most are either originally nouns or are more or less recent loanwords:

تازة	وسط	صح	غلط
taaza	*wasaT*	*Sa77*	*ghalaT*
fresh	medium	true, right	wrong

سادة	اوفر	تركواز	تمام
saada	*2oover*	*tirkwaaz*	*tamaam*
black [coffee]	exaggerated, over-the-top	turquoise	fine, good

Note as well حامل *7aamel* "pregnant," which is invariable for gender.

More on Adjectives

In the last unit we looked at the basic form and function of adjectives. In this unit, we will consider some slightly more complicated forms and types of adjective: the feminine plural -*aat*, the invariable suffix -*i*, adjectives of colour and quality, and compound adjectives formed with the *2iDaafe*.

The Feminine Plural -*aat*

In unit 16, we saw how adjectives form feminines and general-purpose plurals. You will probably have noticed that there seems to be something missing here. Nouns have a distinct feminine plural formed with ات -*aat*. This form also exists—on paper at least—in those adjectives that do not have a broken plural:

شاطرات	شاطر	وسخات	وسخ
shaaTr-aat	*shaaTer*	*wiskh-aat*	*wisekh*
clever [FP]	clever [S]	dirty [FP]	dirty [S]
مشتركات	مشترك	قديمات	قديم
mushtarak-aat	*mushtarak*	*2adiim-aat*	*2adiim*
shared [FP]	shared [S]	old [FP]	old [S]

For some South Levantine speakers, these forms provide an entirely idiomatic feminine plural alternative to the masculine or mixed plural forms we saw above. While these speakers tend to accept the structures on the right, they also produce the structures on the left:

Feminine Plural	Normal Plural
نسوان شاطرات	نسوان شاطرين
niswaan shaaTraat	*niswaan shaaTriin*
clever women	clever women

Feminine Plural	Normal Plural
الهويات المطبوعات	الهويات المطبوعين
ʾlhawiyyaat ʾlmaTbuu3aat	ʾlhawiyyaat ʾlmaTbuu3iin
the printed ID cards	the printed ID cards

Most speakers, however, only use the structures on the right, and *-aat* plurals are very uncommon with adjectives. The most common context in which they occur is with *-i* adjectives referring to people, perhaps because these words are perceived as very similar to nouns (and can also be used as nouns). Even here, alternative constructions with normal plurals are available:

Feminine Plural	Normal Plural
بنات لبنانيات	بنات لبنانية
banaat libnaaniyy-aat	*banaat libnaaniyye*
Lebanese girls	Lebanese girls
نسوان اشتراكيات	نسوان اشتراكيين
niswaan 2ishtiraakiyy-aat	*niswaan 2ishtiraakiyyiin*
socialist women	socialist women

Beyond this, Syrian and South Levantine speakers—but not, usually, Lebanese speakers—may use the feminine plural in a handful of idiomatic contexts. The most common examples of this are in agreement with the false *-aat* plural (see unit 11) and/or in some time expressions:

قهواتك طيبات	قهواتك طيبين
2ahwaatak Tayyb-aat	*2ahwaatak Tayybiin*
your coffee is tasty	your coffee is tasty
تلت ساعات تانيات	تلت ساعات تانيين
tlett saa3aat taany-aat	*tlett saa3aat taanyiin*
another three hours	another three hours

Overall, there is considerable regional variation on which form is preferred. The best solution is to imitate what you hear around you.

Invariable -*i*

In the previous unit, we looked briefly at adjectives with the suffix -*i*. For some speakers, these adjectives behave normally. But for many speakers, they do not form a distinct feminine in many contexts:

No Feminine	Regular Form	Adjective		Noun
سيارة ألماني	سيارة ألمانية	←	ألماني +	سيارة
sayyaara 2almaani	*sayyaara 2almaaniyye*		*2almaani*	*sayyaara*
German car	German car		German	car
قهوة عربي	قهوة عربية	←	عربي +	قهوة
2ahwe 3arabi	*2ahwe 3arabiyye*		*3arabi*	*2ahwe*
Arabic coffee	Arabic coffee		Arabic	coffee

This also applies to تاني *taani* "(an)other," "second":

مرة تاني	مرة تانية	←	تاني +	مرة
marra taani	*marra taanye*		*taani*	*marra*
again	again		second	time

Not forming feminines from at least some of these adjectives is common in Lebanon, Jordan and Palestine, and seems to be less common than Syria. Note, however, that these forms still take normal *plurals* where required.

Adjectives of Colour and Quality (*2af3al*)

> Although these words have the basic shape *2af3al*, they should not be confused with comparative/superlative adjectives, which have no feminine or plural forms (see units 79–80).

There is one set of nouns that breaks the general rule that feminines are formed by suffixation, the nouns of colour and quality.[1] This category has distinct masculine, feminine, and plural patterns, and it consists of most of the primary colours and a range of human qualities. The masculine has the shape *2af3al*, the feminine *fa3la*, and the plural *fi3ᵉl/fu3ºl*:

Plural	Feminine	Masculine
خضر _khi**D**ᵉr/khu**D**ᵒr_ green	خضرا _kha**D**ra_ green	أخضر _2a**khD**ar_ green
بيض _bii**D**_ white	بيضا _bee**D**a_ white	أبيض _2a**by**a**D**_ white
سود _suu**d**_ black	سودا _soo**d**a_ black	أسود _2a**sw**a**d**_ black
عمي _3im**i**/3um**i**_ blind	عميا _3a**my**a_ blind	أعمى _2a**3m**a_ blind
هبل _hib**ᵉl**/hub**ᵒl**_ stupid	هبلا _ha**bl**a_ stupid	أهبل _2a**hb**a**l**_ stupid
سمر _sim**ᵉr**/sum**ᵒr**_ dark-skinned	سمرا _sa**mr**a_ dark-skinned	أسمر _2a**sm**a**r**_ dark-skinned

For at least some speakers and in at least some words, the ‎ﻟ‎ -*a* of the feminine can also be pronounced -*e*. Note as well that for Lebanese speakers with the diphthong alternation described in unit 3, the feminine form with hollow roots will have a diphthong: سودا *sawda* "black," بيضا *bayDa* "white."

Some of these adjectives have alternative plurals: أعمى *2a3ma* can pluralise as عميان *3imyaan/3umyaan*, for example, and أهبل *2ahbal* as أهابل *2ahaabel* or هبلان *hiblaan/hublaan*. These vary from area to area, but in most cases they alternate with the regular plural.

Comparative Adjectives

Arabic has an adjective that corresponds to both English "-er" and "-est": the comparative adjective. Most simple adjectives and many complex adjectives have comparative forms. But this is far from predictable; many adjectives have to use a workaround rather than having their own distinct comparative. In this section we will look very briefly at how these forms are generated and at their behaviour, leaving a more detailed analysis for the section on comparative constructions below (see unit 79).

Comparative adjectives are generally formed using the pattern *2af3al*:

أكتر	←	كتير		أكبر	←	كبير
2aktar		*ktiir*		*2akbar*		*kbiir*
more		a lot		bigger		big

أتفه	←	تافه		أوسخ	←	وسخ
2atfah		*taafeh*		*2awsakh*		*wisekh*
stupider		stupid		dirtier		dirty

أوفى	←	وفي		أجدد	←	جديد
2awfa		*wafi*		*2ajdad*		*jdiid*
more loyal		loyal		newer		new

Note the comparative adjectives from منيح *mnii7* "good," which like their English counterparts are irregular:

أفضل	←	منيح		أحسن	←	منيح
2afDal		*mnii7*		*2a7san*		*mnii7*
better		good		better		good

Many participles also have *2af3al* comparatives:

أدرى	←	دريان		أضرب	←	مضروب
2adra		*diryaan*		*2aDrab*		*maDruub*
knows more		knows		worse		bad

أنسب	←	مناسب		أحوج	←	محتاج
2ansab		*munaaseb*		*2a7waj*		*mi7taaj*
more appropriate		appropriate		more in need		needy

Some words with four-root consonants have comparative adjectives formed on *2afa3lal*:

أشيطن	←	مشيطن		أحيون	←	حيوان
2ashayTan		*mshayTan*		*2a7aywan*		*7ayawaan*
naughtier		naughty		more idiotic		idiotic

Superficially, these adjectives are similar to the adjectives of colour and quality we looked at above in that both have the basic form *2af3al*. But where adjectives of colour and quality have distinct feminine and plural forms, comparative adjectives are invariable:

Plural	Feminine	Masculine
قصور أحسن	شقة أحسن	بيت أحسن
ʼ2Suur 2a7san	*sha22a 2a7san*	*beet 2a7san*
better palaces	a better apartment	a better house

Most adjectives of colour and quality can themselves form comparatives. In the masculine singular, the forms can only be clearly distinguished by context. But in the feminine and plural, the invariability of the comparative makes it unambiguous:

Plural	Feminine	Masculine
قصور بيض	شقة بيضا	بيت أبيض
ʼ2Suur biiD	*sha22a beeDa*	*beet 2abyaD*
white palaces	a white apartment	a white house
قصور أبيض	شقة أبيض	بيت أبيض
ʼ2Suur 2abyaD	*sha22a 2abyaD*	*beet 2abyaD*
whiter palaces	a whiter apartment	a whiter house

The *2iDaafe* with Adjectives

In unit 15 we looked at the *2iDaafe,* which among other things is used to form compound nouns. A similar structure can also be used to form compound *adjectives.* A compound adjective consists of a normal adjective (most often كتير *ktiir* "a lot" or قليل *2aliil* "a little") followed by a noun:

Output		Noun		Adjective
كتير حكي	←	حكي	+	كتير
ktiir 7aki		*7aki*		*ktiir*
talkative		talk		a lot
كتير غلبة	←	غلبة	+	كتير
ktiir ghalabe		*ghalabe*		*ktiir*
troublesome		trouble		a lot
قليل أدب	←	أدب	+	قليل
2aliil 2adab		*2adab*		*2aliil*
impolite		politeness		little

Output	Noun	Adjective
خفيف دم ←	دم +	خفيف
khafiif damm	*damm*	*khafiif*
good company	blood	light

In some cases, the compound adjective comprises a characteristic adjective (see unit 16) derived from a verb and that verb's object:

صريف بنزين ←	بنزين +	صريف
Sarriif banziin	*banziin*	*Sarriif*
gas-guzzling	gas, petrol	consumes a lot

شريب شاي ←	شاي +	شريب
shirriib shaay	*shaay*	*shirriib*
drinks lots of tea	tea	drinks a lot

Only the adjective part of a compound adjective is marked for gender and number. The plural forms are straightforward, but the feminine form—just like in compound nouns—takes the *-t* form (see unit 15):

Plural	Feminine	Masculine
كتيرين حكي	كتيرة حكي	كتير حكي
ktiir-iin 7aki	*ktiir-et 7aki*	*ktiir 7aki*
talkative	talkative	talkative
قليلين أدب	قليلة أدب	قليل أدب
2aliil-iin 2adab	*2aliil-et 2adab*	*2aliil 2adab*
impolite	impolite	impolite
صريفين بنزين	صريفة بنزين	صريف بنزين
Sarriif-iin banziin	*Sarriif-et banziin*	*Sarriif banziin*
gas-guzzling	gas-guzzling	gas-guzzling

Again, definiteness raises complications. The definite article can occur on either part of the compound adjective or on both parts, with no difference in meaning. Personal and regional variation plays a role here, but all of the following forms occur:

الكتير حكي   الكتير الحكي   كتير الحكي

lⁱ-ktiir 7aki	*lⁱ-ktiir ⁱl-7aki*	*ktiir ⁱl-7aki*
the talkative one	the talkative one	the talkative one

القليل أدب   القليل الأدب   قليل الأدب

ⁱl-2aliil 2adab	*ⁱl-2aliil ⁱl-2adab*	*2aliil ⁱl-2adab*
the impolite one	the impolite one	the impolite one

In normal conversational language, constructions such as these are limited to a relatively small number of idiomatic combinations. But a similar construction—borrowed from fuS7a—is sometimes used more productively in higher-register language. The only difference here is that the second element is *always* marked as definite:

مكسور الخاطر   مجهول الاسم

maksuur ⁱlkhaaTer	*majhuul ⁱl2is^em*
broken-hearted	anonymous, of unknown name

سهل التنفيذ   طيب القلب

sahl ⁱttanfiidh	*Tayyeb ⁱlqalb*
easily implemented	good-hearted

Note

1. These nouns are often described as "nouns of colour and *defect*," which apart from being slightly unpleasant is also not very accurate. Although many of the qualities are negative, this is far from universally true.

Pronouns

In this unit we will be discussing pronouns. A pronoun is a word that takes the place of a noun. This is easiest to demonstrate with the so-called third-person pronouns, which generally refer to a noun that has already been mentioned or can be identified from context:

The guy is talking.	→	He's talking.
This woman is amazing.	→	She's amazing.
The people left.	→	They left.

As well as third-person pronouns, there are dedicated counterparts referring to the speaker (or a group that the speaker is part of), known as first-person pronouns ("I" and "we"), and the addressee (or a group that the addressee is part of), known as second-person pronouns ("you").

While in English the main distinction in pronouns is between "subject," "object," and "possessive" pronouns, in Arabic the important division is between *independent* pronouns, words in their own right, and *attached* pronouns, which are suffixes that combine with other words. We will start by looking at the independent pronouns and then go on to discuss their attached counterparts. We will then look at differences in meaning between the Arabic pronouns and their English equivalents.

Independent Pronouns

The independent pronouns are fairly consistent across the four dialect areas:

	North Levantine		South Levantine	
I	2ana	أنا	2ana	أنا
you [M]	2inte 2inta	إنت	2inte 2inta	إنت

	North Levantine		**South Levantine**	
you [F]	*2inti*	إنتي	*2inti*	إنتي
he, it [M]	*huwwe*	هو	*huwwe*	هو
she, it [F]	*hiyye*	هي	*hiyye*	هي
we	*ni7na*	نحنا	*2i7na*	إحنا
you [P]	*2intu*	إنتو	*2intu*	إنتو
they	*hinne*	هنه	*humme*	همه

Even this table gives a stricter sense of division than is really accurate: *hinne* and *ni7na* also occur in Palestinian, for example.

Although you are likely to have encountered these pronouns largely as equivalents of the English subject pronouns ("I," "he," etc.), their function is actually quite different. Subject pronouns per se are mostly dropped in Arabic, and the independent pronouns are largely quite emphatic and mark a contrast (see unit 66), although there are some circumstances in which they are less so (see unit 48):

إنت شو بتحب؟

أنا ما بروح

2inte shuu bit7ibb?

2ana maa bruu7

what would *you* like?

I wouldn't go

They often occur alongside their attached counterparts—which we will discuss below—for emphasis:

راسي أنا اللي انضرب!

احكيلي أنا!

raas-i 2ana lli nDarab!

2i7kiil-i 2ana!

it was *my* head that was hit!

talk to *me*!

They also occur in certain kinds of "to be" sentence as a counterpart to "is" (see unit 49):

السعادة هي أهم شي

أستاذ أحمد هو المدير

ⁱssa3aade hiyye 2ahamm ⁱshii

2ustaaz 2a7mad huwwe lmudiir

happiness is the most important thing

Mr Ahmad is the director

They are also used, as you would expect, when a pronoun is required on its own. Here they correspond to English *object* pronouns:

مين راح؟ أنا

miin raa7? 2ana

who went? Me

لأ مش هو

la2 mish huwwe

no, not him

Attached Pronouns

The attached pronouns are slightly less straightforward. Many of them have different forms depending on whether they follow a vowel or a consonant. There is also more pronounced dialectal variation. The table below gives a set of common forms for North and South Levantine, but note that again, it is a simplification: some Palestinian speakers use *-kon* and *-hon* or *-hen*, and the form كو *-ku* is also common in South Levantine.

	NORTH LEVANTINE				SOUTH LEVANTINE			
	After Consonants		**After Vowels**		**After Consonants**		**After Vowels**	
my, me	ـي	-i	ـي	-yi	ـي	-i	ـي	-y
your, you [M]	ك	-ak	ك	-ek	ك	-ak	ك	-k
your, you [F]	ك	-ek	ـكي	-ki	ك	-ek	ـكي	-ki
his, its [M]	ـو	-o	ـه	-	ـو	-o	ـه	-
her, its [F]			ـها	-(h)a			ـها	-ha
our, us			ـنا	-na			ـنا	-na
your, you [P]			ـكن	-kon			ـكم	-kom
their, them			ـهن	-(h)on			ـهم	-hom

There are two important points to note here. First, the form for "his," "him" used with words ending in consonants, ـو *-o*, is well-behaved, but the form used after vowels is not. Usually written ـه in Arabic, it is nonetheless not pronounced as an *h*. The only thing indicating the presence of this suffix is the lengthening of the final vowel (see unit 4) and the resulting stress shift:

بنتساه   ←   بتنسى

*btin**saa***   ***btin**sa*

you forget him   you forget

فحواه   ←   فحوى

*fa7**waa***   *fa**7**wa*

its content   content

The other point to note is that for many speakers, the *h* of *-ha* and *-hon* (and sometimes *-hom*) can be dropped freely after consonants. This does not typically affect the stress (see unit 3):

معلمهن	←	معلمهن		بعرفها	←	بعرفها
m3allim-on		*m3allim-hon*		*ba3rif-a*		*ba3rif-ha*
their teacher		their teacher		I know her		I know her

> Some speakers occasionally produce forms with regularised stress here; you might encounter, for example, ***ba3ʰrfa*** and ***m3allmon***.

For some speakers, this *h* can also be dropped after *-i* and *-u*, which produces a shift to *-iyy-* and *-uww-* respectively:

بتنسيها	←	بتنسي
btinsiyy-a		*btinsi*
you [F] forget her		you [F] forget

بتنسوها	←	بتنسو
btinsuww-a		*btinsu*
you [P] forget her		you [P] forget

These pronouns occur far more commonly than their independent counterparts. They can be attached to nouns in place of the second portion of an *2iDaafe* (see unit 15):

كتابها	←	كتاب سامية		بيتو	←	بيت محمد
ktaab-ha		*ktaab saamya*		*beet-o*		*beet ʰm7ammad*
her book		Samia's book		his house		Muhammad's house

Note that they trigger the special form of the noun used in *2iDaafe* (see unit 15):

أبوها	←	أبو مريم		مدرستهم	←	مدرسة الولاد
2abuu-ha		*2abu maryam*		*madrasit-hom*		*madraset lʰwlaad*
her dad		Maryam's dad		their school		the kids' school

Note as well that nouns that form their plural with ـين *-een* ("false dual" plurals, see unit 12) usually lose their final *-n* when pronouns are attached:

عينيه	←	عينين		إجريكي	←	إجرين
3een-ee		*3een-een*		*2ijree-ki*		*2ijreen*
his eyes		eyes		your legs		legs

This does not happen to normal duals (see units 12 and 82).

As we will see, they also occur with prepositions (see unit 22):

وراه	←	ورا البيت		معي	←	مع أحمد
waraa		*wara lbeet*		*ma3-i*		*ma3 2a7mad*
behind it		behind the house		with me		with Ahmad

غصبن عنكن	←		غصبن عن إخواتو
ghaSben 3an-kon			*ghaSben 3an 2ikhwaato*
in spite of you [P]			in spite of his sisters

They are also used, as we will see, as the objects of verbs (see unit 52). Note that here, the form for "me" is not -*(y)i* but ـني *-ni*:

صلحتها	←	صلحت الماسورة		شافو	←	شاف سامي
Salla7t-ha		*Salla7t ᵉlmaasuura*		*shaaf-o*		*shaaf saami*
I repaired it		I repaired the pipe		he saw him		he saw Sami

عرفني؟	←		عرف وجهي؟
3irif-ni?			*3iref wijhi?*
did he recognise me?			did he recognise my face?

They also occur in a range of other miscellaneous contexts. Note that -*ni* is used for "me" in many of these contexts, including:

1. Expressions of surprise/delight with *ma2af3al*: ماحلاني *ma7laani* "I look so nice," مأضربني *ma2aDrabni* "I'm so useless."
2. In various regions: كل *kill/kull* "all of" and بعض *ba3ᵉD-* "part of."
3. Various other adverbial constructions: بعد *ba3d-* and لسا *lissa-* "still," "[not] yet" (see unit 40) and حلـ *7all-* "it's about time that . . ."
4. Question words, particularly وين *ween* "where," كيف *kiif* and شلون *shloon* "how," and قديش *2addeesh* "how much!" (in exclamations).
5. For some North Levantine speakers, with the preposition فيـ *fii-* and its derived forms: فيني *fii-ni* "in me" (see unit 22).

Idiomatic Points

For the most part, the pronouns correspond fairly closely with English in their meaning. There are a few points to note, however, which may not be intuitive for an English speaker.

The first is that the third-person pronouns are wrapped up in the agreement system (see unit 50). This means that the forms translated in isolation as "he/him" and "she/her" commonly correspond to English "it," referring to masculine and feminine nouns, respectively:

اشتريتها   ←   اشتريت البلوزة   شفتو   ←   شفت البيت

shtareet-ha   *shtareet ⁱlbluuze*   *shift-o*   *shift ⁱlbeet*

I bought it   I bought the top [F]   I saw it   I saw the house [M]

As we will see in unit 50, the feminine singular forms are also commonly used for certain kinds of plural, thus corresponding to "they/them" in English:

سطوحها   ←   سطوح البيوت

sTuu7-ha   *sTuu7 lⁱbyuut*

their rooves   the houses rooves

The distinct second-person singular forms are used for masculine and feminine referents, respectively, including (on the rare occasions when this is called for) inanimate masculine and feminine nouns. The plural is used for any group of more than one person.

> Very occasionally, the second-person plural is also used to indicate respect. But you should not mistake this for a counterpart to the famous French *vous*, which is much less elevated. For more on politeness, see appendix D.

The plural first-person forms ("we," "us") are commonly used with singular meaning. The exact nuance that this expresses is difficult to pin down, although it often has a slightly familiar tone:

لك فهمنا فهمنا!   مشاغل لفوق راسنا

lak ⁱfhimna ⁱfhimna!   *mashaaghel lafoo2 raas-na*

OK, I get it!   I'm up to my neck in work

تشرفنا   منشوفك

tsharrafna   *minshuufak*

nice to meet you   I'll see you later

[= I'm honoured]

The Carrier *(y)yaa-*

Under some circumstances—largely when a pronoun cannot attach to the main verb
because another pronoun is already attached—the attached pronouns appear on a carrier,
the word يا *(y)yaa-*. As a general rule, the carrier is pronounced *yaa-* after consonants everywhere and *yyaa-* after vowels in South Levantine, although there is variation on this point:

North Levantine	South Levantine
عطيتهن ياها	أعطيتهم ياها
3aTeethon yaaha	*2a3Teethom yaaha*
I gave them it	I gave them it
بدي ياهن	بدي ياهم
biddi yaahon	*biddi yyaahom*
I want them	I want them

This form is also commonly used for the second pronoun in structures such as "me and you,"
"him and her" (see unit 67) in the form ويا‑ *wiyyaa*:

إنتي وياها	أنا وياه
2inti wiyyaaha	*2ana wiyyaa*
you and her	me and him

For more on the contexts in which this structure is used, see units 52–53.

The *-l-* Suffix

In this unit we will look at the special pronoun set produced using the *-l-* suffix. This set has no counterpart in literary Arabic or—broadly speaking—in English. It is subject to a great deal of regional variation in exactly what forms it takes under what circumstances. Moreover, it has a very broad range of uses, from replacing straightforward preposition-noun combinations to various idiomatic combinations. I will begin by trying to make sense of the many different forms that the suffix takes before looking at how it is used.

Form of the Suffix

The *-l-* suffix is one of the more idiosyncratic Arabic suffixes, and its behaviour varies considerably between the different regions of the Levantine area. The basic southern and northern systems are as follows:

NORTH LEVANTINE		SOUTH LEVANTINE	
After a Consonant Cluster	**Basic Form**	**After a Consonant Cluster**	**Basic Form**
لـي	لـي	لـي	لـي
-illi	*-li*	*-illi*	*-li*
to me	to me	to me	to me
لـلك	لـلك	لـلك	لـلك
-illak	*-lak*	*-illak*	*-lak*
to you [M]	to you [M]	to you [M]	to you [M]
لـلك	لـلك	لـلك	لـلك
-illek	*-lek*	*-illek*	*-lek*
to you [F]	to you [F]	to you [F]	to you [F]

NORTH LEVANTINE		SOUTH LEVANTINE	
After a Consonant Cluster	**Basic Form**	**After a Consonant Cluster**	**Basic Form**
ـلو *-illo* to him	ـلو *-lo* to him	ـلو *-illo* to him	ـلو *-lo* to him
ـلها *-ilha* to her	ـلها *-l(h)a* to her	ـلها *-ilha* to her	ـلها *-lha* to her
ـلنا *-ilna* to us	ـلنا *-lna* to us	ـلنا *-ilna* to us	ـلنا *-lna* to us
ـلكن *-ilkon* to you [P]	ـلكن *-lkon* to you [P]	ـلكم *-ilkom* to you [P]	ـلكم *-lkom* to you [P]
ـلهن *-ilhon* to them	ـلهن *-l(h)on* to them	ـلهم *-ilhom* to them	ـلهم *-lhom* to them

In both sets of dialects, the central distinction is that the forms on the right are used after a vowel or a single consonant, while the forms on the left are used after a consonant cluster.

Compare the forms produced by combining *-li* "to me" with the three different verbs below. As you can see, the words ending in a vowel (*7aka*) and a consonant (*katab*), respectively, take a different form from the word ending in a consonant cluster (*katabᵉt*):

حكالي   حكى

*7a**kaa**-li*   *7aka*

he spoke to me   he spoke

كتبلي ← ـلي + كتب

*ka**tab**-li*   *-li*   *katab*

he wrote to me   to me   he wrote

كتبتلي   كتبت

*katab**t-il**li*   *katabᵉt*

you wrote to me   I wrote

Note that where the "basic" form follows a consonant directly and this produces a three-consonant cluster, a helping vowel (see unit 2) is inserted to break the cluster up. This looks superficially like the form used after consonant clusters, but the helping vowel in *katab-'lna* below cannot be stressed, unlike the vowel in *katabt-**il**na*:

حكالنا   حكى

*7a**kaa**-lna*   *7aka*

he spoke to us   he spoke

كتبلنا ← لنا + كتب

*ka**tab**-'lna*   *-lna*   *katab*

he wrote to us   to us   he wrote

كتبتلنا   كتبت

*katab**t-il**na*   *katabᵉt*

you wrote to us   I wrote

Defective verbs ending in ‍يت‍ *-eet* or *-iit* (the "I" or "you [M]" form of the perfective; see unit 33) behave anomalously, triggering the "cluster" form of the pronoun. In South Levantine, moreover, the vowel is shortened to *i*:

North Levantine	South Levantine
حكيتلك	حكيتلك
*7akeet-**il**lak*	*7akit-**il**lak*
I told you [M]	I told you [M]
حكيتلو	حكيتلو
*7akeet-**il**lo*	*7akit-**il**lo*
I told him	I told him

Hollow verbs—those with a long vowel in place of a middle root consonant—also behave oddly with these suffixes. In a hollow verb with no other suffixes, these forms cause the stem vowel to shorten. In North Levantine, this shortening has the additional effect of transforming long *uu* into *i* (in line with the merger described in unit 3). Consider the following examples with *-li*:

North Levantine	South Levantine	Base Word
شفلي	شفلي	شوف
shif-li	*shuf-li*	*shuuf*
see for me!	see for me!	see! [M]

North Levantine	South Levantine	Base Word
جبلي *jib-li* bring me … !		جيب *jiib* bring! [M]
قللي *2al-li* he said to me		قال *2aal* he said

Note as well that with *2aal*, these suffixes are usually not separated from the stem using a helping vowel even where that would normally be the case:

قللنا   بقللكم

2al-lna   *ba2ul-lkom*

he told us   I'm telling you [P]

> There are many further regional variations on this system. Some worth being aware of are the following:
>
> - Many North Levantine speakers treat the helping vowel in forms such as *katab-ᶦlna* as stressable, producing *katab-ilna* instead.
> - Many South Levantine speakers do not have a distinct set of forms used after clusters and happily produce forms such as *katabt-li* or *7akeet-lak*.
> - Lebanese speakers often use forms with *-al-* instead of *-il-* following perfective doubled verbs with no other suffixes: *da22-allak*.
> - Syrian speakers often have an anomalous form for "he told X" with the stem *2il-*: *2il-lak*, *2il-lna*, and so on.

Uses of the -l- Suffix

The most basic use of the *-l-* suffix corresponds to combinations of the preposition لـ *la-* "to," "for" and a noun (see unit 53). Unlike other prepositions—whose more conventional behaviour when combined with pronouns is described in more detail below (see unit 22)—when a pronoun is added to *la-* in place of its normal noun, it tends to transform into the *-l-* suffix and attach to the verb:

اشتريتلهم تياب   ←   اشتريت تياب للولاد

shtareet-ᶦlhom ᶦtyaab   *shtareet ᶦtyaab lalᶦwlaad*

I bought them clothes   I bought clothes for the kids

ساوي شاي لإمي   →   ساويلها شاي

saawii-lha shaay   *saawii shaay la2immi*

make her tea   make tea for my mom

بطالع صورة لأخي   →   بطالعلو صورة

bTaali3-lo Suura   *bTaale3 Suura la2akhi*

I'll get a picture of him up   I'll get a picture of my brother up

عم اسمع غنية لفيروز   →   عم اسمعلها غنية

3am 2isma3-la ghinniyye   *3am 2isma3 ghinniyye lafayruuz*

I'm listening to a song by her   I'm listening to a song by Feyrouz

Note as well that if another pronoun suffix is already present—expressing the direct object, for example (see unit 52)—it is pushed off the verb and onto the carrier يا *(y)yaa-*:

اشتريت تياب للولاد   →   اشتريتلهم ياهم

shtareet-ˈlhom ˈyyaahom   *shtareet ˈtyaab lalˈwlaad*

I bought them them   I bought clothes for the kids

بعت المصاري لأخي   →   بعتلو ياها

ba3att-illo yaaha   *ba3att ˈlmaSaari la2akhi*

I sent him it   I sent the money to my brother

There are many idiomatic uses of these suffixes that cannot be rephrased with a noun; they are exclusively pronominal. Many of these are similar in sense to colloquial English constructions such as "get <u>you</u> a guy who can do both" or "have <u>yourself</u> a nice little holiday" in that they express that the referent of the pronoun is *personally affected* in some way:

اقعدلك يومين تلاتة بهالفندق   بظنلك الطبيعي أحسن

2u23ud-lak yomeen ˈtlaate bhalfundo2   *baZunn-illek ˈTTabii3i 2a7san*

stay at this hotel for a couple of days   I think the natural one would be better

[= stay for yourself]   [= I think for you]

شربتلي كاستين ورجعت ع البيت   كللك لقمة

shribt-ˈlli kaasteen w rji3ᵉt 3 albeet   *kil-lak li2me*

I drank two glasses and went home   have a bite to eat

[= I drank for myself]   [= eat for yourself]

These suffixes are very commonly used when the direct object of a verb is a possessed noun. Here they match the possessor. Again, the logic is that the possessor is personally affected:

سرقولها جزدانها
sara2uu-lha juzdaanha
they stole [for her] her purse

وائل كسرلي رجلي!
waa2el kasar-li rijl-i!
Wael broke [for me] my leg!

ليش دقيتلي بابي؟
leesh da22eet-li baabi?
why did you knock [for me] on my door?

صرعولي راسي
Sara3uu-li raasi
they've driven me crazy
[= maddened for me my head]

"For" usually expresses a positive effect. But as you can see, this is not true of the *-l-* suffixes in Arabic, which are often negative. Note as well constructions like the following:

الزلمة ميتلو أخ
^{i}zzalame mayyit-lo 2akhkh
the guy has had a brother die
[= a brother has died for him/to him]

In narrative, the second person forms ("for you") can be used to draw listeners into the narrative:

لما فتت ما شفتلك غير كلب كبير!
lamma fit^{e}t maa shift-illak gheer kalb ^{i}kbiir!
when I went in, I saw [for you] this *massive dog*!

بنط لقدام وبدوسلك بنزين ع الآخر!
banuTT la2uddaam w baduslak banziin 3a l2aakher!
I jump in the front and absolutely floor it [for you]!

Often the effect is to express that someone's behaviour is strange, ridiculous, or objectionable:

والرئيس قاعدلك عم يلعب بتليفونو!
w^{i}rra2iis 2aa3id-lak 3am yil3ab btilifoono!
While the President is just sitting there
[= sitting for you] playing on his phone!

وهادا الشب كل يوم بجبلك كاسة حليب ع الشغل!
haada shshabb kull yoom bijiblak kaaset 7aliib 3a shshugh^{o}l!
This guy brings [for you] a glass of milk to work every day [how weird]!

Note that occasionally the possessive pseudoverb *2il-* "have" turns into this suffix when combined with framing verbs (see units 38–41), particularly for North Levantine speakers:

المرة السورية كانلها حضور

ʾlmara ssuuriyye kan-la 7uDuur

Syrian women had a presence

بكنلك أخ صغير

bikin-lak 2akhkh ʾzghiir

you would have a little brother

For the use of this suffix with comparatives, see unit 79. For its use in the construction صارل *SaLL-* "has been," see unit 40.

Adverbs

In this unit we will be looking at *adverbs*. The category of adverb is a strange one, as it brings together words that have a very broad range of functions. An English speaker will most likely be familiar with adverbs as words modifying adjectives. But adverbs also commonly modify verbs:

Modifying an adjective: أحمد كتير شاطر

2a7mad ⁱktiir shaaTer

Ahmad is very smart

Modifying a verb: سميرة بتحكي منيح

samiira bti7ki mnii7

Samira speaks well

There is no obvious a priori reason why words modifying adjectives and words modifying verbs should belong to the same broad category. And in some ways, the subcategories of adverb do differ. But they also share some key similarities. In particular, in both English and Arabic, they are often derived using the same strategies ("-ly" in English and ـاً *-an* in Arabic).

You don't need to worry too much about these distinctions, because they will come naturally to you. The point here is just to establish that "adverb" refers to all these different categories of words. Now that we have done that, we can look first at some of the ways that Arabic forms distinct adverbs—that is, words that can only be used adverbially—before examining how adverbs are used to modify adjectives and verbs.

Common Adverb-Forming Strategies

Many adverb structures are formed using a preposition plus a noun. In some cases, these are the adverbial counterpart of an adjective and are formed using the abstract noun derived from that adjective. The combinations are unpredictable and must be learnt, but it is worth noting that the noun is almost always *indefinite*, even though the usual rules of definiteness would lead us to expect the opposite (see unit 13):

سريع	←	بسرعة		آمن	←	بأمن وأمان
sarii3		bsur3a		2aamen		b2amn w2amaan
quick		quickly		safe		safely and securely

قصد	←	عن قصد		حقد	←	عن حقد
2aZd		3an 2aZd		7i2^{e}d		3an 7i2^{e}d
intention		deliberately		spite		out of spite

حسة	←	على حسة		طمعة	←	على طمعة
7isse		3ala 7isse		Tam3a		3ala Tam3a
sensation		quietly		greed		with ulterior motives

In higher-register language, it is common to use the structure بشكل *bshak^{e}l* "in a . . . way" to form adverbs from adjectives:

ودي	←	بشكل ودي		عام	←	بشكل عام
widdi		bshak^{e}l widdi		3aamm		bshak^{e}l 3aamm
amicable		amicably		general		generally

Many adverbial expressions are formed by repeating a word. The following are set phrases:

هيك	هيك هيك		عينك	عينك عينك
heek	heek heek		3eenak	3eenak 3eenak
like that	anyway		your eye	flagrantly

يلا	يلا يلا		معو	معو معو
yaLLa	yaLLa yaLLa		ma3o	ma3o ma3o
come on	barely		with it	with time

Repetition of a noun is also used productively to express "X by X":

كلمة	كلمة كلمة		خطوة	خطوة خطوة
kilme	kilme kilme		khiTwe	khiTwe khiTwe
word	word by word		step	step by step

شوي	شوي شوي		حبة	حبة حبة
shwayy	shwayy 'shwayy		7abbe	7abbe 7abbe
a bit	bit by bit, slowly		piece	bit by bit

-an

Many adverbs are derived with the fuS7a suffix ـ‍ *-an*. This is particularly productive as a way of forming adverbs from adjectives ending in the suffix *-i* (see unit 9):

حاليا ← حالي	تاريخيا ← تاريخي
7aaliyy-an *7aali*	*taariikhiyy-an* *taariikhi*
currently current	historically historical

نظريا ← نظري	نسبيا ← نسبي
naZariyy-an *naZari*	*nisbiyy-an* *nisbi*
theoretically theoretical	relatively relative

There are many common adverbs ending in *-an*, however, that do not meet this criterion:

أصلا ← أصل	تماما ← تمام
2aSl-an *2aS^el*	*tamaam-an* *tamaam*
to start with origin	exactly precise

عمدا ← عمد	طبعا ← طبع
3amd-an *3amd*	*Tab3-an* *Tab^e3*
deliberately intention	of course, naturally nature

> This suffix can be written with a special diacritic, the *tanwiin fat^e7*: ً . But this is unusual in natural writing of Levantine, in part because it can be hard to find on a keyboard.

When attached to final ة *-a/e*, the combination is pronounced *-atan* and is usually written identically to the base word:

خاصة ← خاصة	عادة ← عادة
khaaSSat-an *khaaSSa*	*3aadat-an* *3aade*
especially special	habitually habit

In many cases with final *-a/e*, the bare word can be used as an adverb without *-an*, with the *-an* version existing as a (sometimes higher-register) alternative:

خاصة OR خاصة ← خاصة
khaaSSat-an   *khaaSSa*   *khaaSSa*
especially   especially   special

صراحة   OR   صراحة   ←   صراحة

Saraa7at-an	Saraa7a	Saraa7a
honestly	honestly	honesty

فجأة   OR   فجأة   ←   فجأة

faj2at-an	faj2a	faj2a
suddenly	suddenly	surprise

Note in particular the fuS7a "accusative of purpose," which expresses a motivation. This occurs in a few very common fuS7aisms and is sometimes used more productively in higher-register language:

خوفا من   ←   خوف   محبة بـ   ←   محبة

khawf-an min	khawf	ma7abbat-an b-	ma7abbe
for fear of	fear	out of love for	love

Many of these structures have less high-register counterparts formed with a secondary object with no suffix, for which see unit 54.

Modifying Adjectives

Arabic has relatively few adverbs that can modify adjectives directly. Those that exist generally follow the adjective:

حلو لدرجة   طويلة زيادة   عظيم كتير   كبير بشكل

7ilu ladaraje	Tawiile zyaade	3aZiim ᵢktiir	ᵢkbiir bshakᵉl
so pretty	too long	truly excellent	really big

Exceptions are the very common كتير *ktiir* "very," جدا *jiddan* "very," and فعلا *fi3lan* "truly," which can either precede or follow the adjective:

جدا عظيم   كتير منيح

jiddan 3aZiim	ᵢktiir ᵢmnii7
truly excellent	very good

In English, we can produce new adjective-modifying adverbs quite easily: "he was *extremely* handsome," "I was *unbelievably* upset." In Arabic these are not so easy to generate. The best way is generally to combine لدرجة *ladaraje* "to a degree [that]" or بشكل *bshikᵉl* "in a . . . way" with an adjective or a longer phrase:

شاطرة بشكل مو طبيعي

shaaTra bshik^el muu Tabii3i

uncommonly clever

حلو لدرجة ما بتتصدق

7ilu ladaraje maa btitsadda2

unbelievably handsome

In higher-register language, a special version of the secondary object construction may be used in a similar way (see unit 54):

ذكية ذكاء غريب

zakiyye zakaa2 ghariib

weirdly clever

مريض مرض الموت

mariiD maraD ⁱlmawt

terminally ill

Modifying Verbs

Modifying verbs is easier than modifying adjectives. As a general rule, adverbs modifying verbs come after a verb's objects:

بتحكي معاي كتير

bti7ki ma3aay ⁱktiir

she talks to me <u>a lot</u>

بشرب شاي على طول

bishrab shaay <u>3ala Tool</u>

I'm <u>always</u> drinking tea

As in colloquial English, many adjectives can be used as adverbs without any change:

بيحكي منيح

byi7ki <u>mnii7</u>

he speaks <u>well</u>

بتكتب حلو

btuktob <u>7ilu</u>

you write <u>nicely</u>

قعود آدمي!

ⁱ23ood <u>2aadami</u>!

sit <u>politely</u>!

جايين بكير

jaayiin <u>bakkiir</u>

they're coming <u>early</u>

Again, a way of forming constructions corresponding to more complex adverbs in English is to use بشكل *bshik^el* or لدرجة *ladaraje* or else using some kind of rephrasing with an abstract noun and an adjective:

عم دخن بشكل فظيع

3am dakhkhen <u>bshak^el faZii3</u>

I'm smoking <u>like crazy</u>

[= in an outrageous way]

بكتب إشي بتصدقش

buktob <u>2ishi bitsadda2^esh</u>

he writes <u>unbelievably</u> quickly

[= a thing that cannot be believed]

The secondary object construction also provides an alternative way of expressing many of
the ideas for which adverbs are used in English:

ضربوه ضرب حقيقي

Darabuu <u>Darᵉb 7a2ii2i</u>

they <u>really</u> hit him

تجوزو جوازة عادية

tjawwazu ᵢ<u>jwaaze 3aadiyye</u>

they got married <u>in the normal way</u>

For more on this construction, see unit 54.

Presentatives

In this unit we will discuss *presentatives*, words used to point out or draw attention to ("present") people, objects, or events. This is a class of words that has no direct parallel in English—in the sense of there being a distinct word class—although as we will see it maps closely onto certain English structures with "here" and "there." Presentatives are related to, although distinct from, the demonstratives we looked at in unit 14 and sometimes correspond to demonstrative constructions in English.

There are many different regional demonstratives used throughout the Levantine area. Here, however, we will focus on only two forms, which are characteristic of the capital dialects in which we are most interested in this book. These two forms are هي *hayy* and ليك *leek*.

hayy

The most common presentative is *hayy*, which can translate to either "here is" or "there is." This is used by Syrian, Palestinian, and Jordanian speakers but not by Lebanese speakers:

هي المفتاح   هي أحمد!

hayy ⁱlmuftaa7   *hayy 2a7mad!*

here's the key   and there's Ahmad!

هي أخوي   هي البيت

hayy 2akhuuy   *hayy ⁱlbeet*

this is my brother   here's the house

Note that although *hayy* resembles the feminine "this"—and sometimes "this is" can be an idiomatic translation—it does not change for gender. However, *hayy* can take suffixed pronouns (see unit 18), generally with the meaning "here X is":

هيو

hayyo
here he is

هيني قدامك

hayyni 2iddaamak
I'm right here in front of you
[= here I am in front of you]

For many speakers, هيـ *hayy-* becomes or can become هياتـ *hayyaat-* or هيا *hayyaa-* when a pronoun is attached:

هياتو

hayyaato
here he is

هياتني قدامك

hayyaatni 2iddaamak
I'm right here in front of you
[= here I am in front of you]

As well as being used with nouns, *hayy* can appear before whole sentences. The simplest use of this structure is an idiomatic extension of the use with nouns:

هي أحمد أجا

hayy 2a7mad 2aja
and here's Ahmad arriving
[= here Ahmad's got here]

هي القطار وصل

hayy ʾlqiTaar waSSal
and now the train's arrived
[= here the train has arrived]

The presentative *hayy* can also be used to respond to questions about your location or other people's location at a given time:

هياتها جايه

hayyaatha jaaye
she's on her way
she'll be here in a minute

هيني بالتاكسي

hayyni bittaksi
I'm in a taxi

هيني فوق!

hayyni foo2!
I'm upstairs!

The presentative *hayy* also has various extended uses. The term can be used in contexts such as the following to mean something like "there you go, you've …" or "there, I've …" In this context, *hayy* signals new information or a change:

وهي خلصت المرحلة التانية

w hayy khallaSt ʾlmar7ale ʾttaanye
and now you've finished the second stage
and with that, you're done with the second stage

هيني وقعت عليه

hayyni waqqa3ᵉt 3alee
there, I've signed it
there you go, I've signed

Similarly, *hayy* gives updates:

هيو خلص كل شي

hayyo khallaS kill shii

OK, he's all done

[= here he's finished everything]

اوكي هيني وصلت!

2ooke hayyni waSSal^et!

OK, I'm here!

[= here I've arrived]

The presentative *hayy* can also express a realisation or surprise (and often co-occurs with the "surprise" meaning of the participle here, for which see unit 37):

هيك جالي!

hayyak jaali!

oh, you've done the washing up!

هيك بتعرف تلعب!

hayyak ^ibti3raf til3ab!

so you *do* know how to play!

leek

The other major presentative is ليك *leek*, which is exclusively North Levantine. It tends to refer to objects and events that are farther away, making it more like "look over there." Like *hayy*, *leek* can be followed by a noun or an attached pronoun:

ليكو

leek-o

there it is

ليك البيت

leek ^ilbeet

there's the house

leek differs from *hayy* in that it can optionally take the suffixes *-i* (feminine singular) and *-u* (plural) to agree with the addressee:

ليكو أحمد!

leeku 2a7mad!

there's Ahmad!

[to a group]

ليكي البيت!

leeki lbeet!

there's the house!

[to a woman]

Note, however, that when a pronoun is attached, these suffixes cannot be used, and *leek* is invariable:

ليكي البيت!   ←   ليكو!

leeki lbeet!   *leek-o!*

there's the house!   there it is!

[to a woman]

ليكو!   ←   ليكو البيت!

leek-o!   *leeku lbeet!*

there it is!   there's the house!

[to a group]

Like *hayy*, it can precede full sentences and can also be used to give updates or respond to questions about location:

ليكو فوق   ليكني بالتاكسي

leeko foo2   *leekni bittaksi*

he's upstairs   I'm in a taxi

However, *leek* does not have any of the other idiomatic uses of *hayy*. Unlike *hayy*, *leek* can be used on its own to mean "look" or "listen":

ليكي، في ناس بدها تشوفني

leeki, fii naas biddha tshuufni

listen, there are some people who want to see me

UNIT 22

Prepositions

In this unit we will look briefly at how *prepositions* work. I said in the introduction to this book that we would not be looking too much at the possible meanings of individual words, which is more the function of a dictionary than a grammar. For this reason, I will be focusing here almost entirely on generalities: how prepositions as a class operate and the ways they are different from their English counterparts. For a brief overview of the meanings of the most common prepositions, see appendix B.

Main Points

A preposition is a word that combines with a noun or pronoun in order to express that noun or pronoun's relationship—most commonly a relationship of space or time—with another word in the sentence. As the "pre-" suggests, prepositions typically precede their noun:

with Hani	under the bed	after the party	from Shams

In broad terms, Arabic prepositions are very similar to their English counterparts. They precede their noun:

مع هاني	تحت التخت	بعد الحفلة	من شمس
ma3 haani	*ta7t* ^{i}*ttakh*^{e}*t*	*ba3d* ^{i}*l7afle*	*min shams*
with Hani	under the bed	after the party	from Shams

Note that لـ *la-* "for" and بـ *b-* "in" are generally attached to the following word in writing: لهاني *lahaani* "for Hani," بالبيت *b*^{i}*lbeet* "at home." The same sometimes applies to the shortened form of على *3ala* "on," عـ *3a-*: عالقدس *3al2uds* "to Jerusalem."

But there are two major differences you need to be aware of. The first is that—as we might expect from other Arabic constructions—prepositions take *attached* pronouns (see unit 18). This means that English combinations of preposition and pronoun will typically correspond to a single word in Arabic:

معي	تحتو	بعدها	منها
ma3-i	*ta7t-o*	*ba3d-ha*	*minn-ha*
with me	under it	after it	from her

For the most part, these combinations are predictable. But as we will see below, several prepositions change their form when pronouns are attached.

The second point that needs to be made is that unlike their English counterparts, Arabic prepositions cannot—as a rule—stand on their own. Pedantic style guides aside, English speakers are perfectly happy having prepositions end sentences such as the following (so-called preposition stranding), but Arabic speakers definitely are not:

على شو عم تدوري؟	مع مين عم تحكي؟
3ala shuu 3am ˈtdawwri?	*ma3 miin 3am ti7ki?*
what are you looking for?	who are you talking to?
[= for what . . .]	[= with whom . . .]

المشكلة عم بنبحث فيها	البنت اللي كنت راكض وراها
ˈlmishˈkle 3am yinbi7eth fiiha	*ˈlbint ˈlli kint raakeD waraaha*
that problem's being looked at	the girl you were chasing after
[= looked at it]	[= after her]

As you can see, question words drag prepositions with them to the beginning of the sentence (see unit 73), while in other contexts they must be combined with a pronoun (see unit 63).

Form

As noted, most prepositions combine with the attached pronouns straightforwardly. A preposition such as متل *mit**ᵉl* "like," for example, has the following forms:

As usual, this list of forms is simplified for ease of use. Not all North Levantine speakers drop *h* in *-ha* and *-hon*; many Palestinian speakers have *-hon* and *-kon* or *-hen* and *-ken*, among other forms. See unit 18 for more on attached pronoun forms.

متل *mitᵉl* "LIKE"			
North Levantine		**South Levantine**	
متلي *mitli* like me		متلي *mitli* like me	
متلك *mitlek* like you [F]	متلك *mitlak* like you [M]	متلك *mitlek* like you [F]	متلك *mitlak* like you [M]
متلها *mitla* like her	متلو *mitlo* like him	متلها *mitᵉlha* like her	متلو *mitlo* like him
متلنا *mitᵉlna* like us		متلنا *mitᵉlna* like us	
متلكن *mitᵉlkon* like you [P]		متلكم *mitᵉlkom* like you [P]	
متلهن *mitlon* like them		متلهم *mitᵉlhom* like them	

Many of the most common prepositions, however, change form when pronouns are added. على *3ala* "on" takes the form عليـ (pronounced *3alee-* except in the first person singular):

على *3ala* "ON"	
North Levantine	**South Levantine**
عليي *3aliyyi* on me	علي *3alayy* on me

على 3ala "ON"			
North Levantine		**South Levantine**	
عليكي 3aleeki on you [F]	عليك 3aleek on you [M]	عليكي 3aleeki on you [F]	عليك 3aleek on you [M]
عليها 3aleyya on her	عليه 3alee on him	عليها 3aleeha on her	عليه 3alee on him
علينا 3aleena on us		علينا 3aleena on us	
عليكن 3aleekon on you [P]		عليكم 3aleekom on you [P]	
عليهن 3aleyyon on them		عليهم 3aleehom on them	

The word عند *3and/3ind* "by" is regular except in the first person plural, where the *d* is often dropped:

عند 3and/3ind "BY"			
North Levantine		**South Levantine**	
عندي 3andi by me		عندي 3indi by me	
عندك 3andek by you [F]	عندك 3andak by you [M]	عندك 3indek by you [F]	عندك 3indak by you [M]

عند 3and/3ind "BY"			
North Levantine		**South Levantine**	
عندها *3anda* by her	عندو *3ando* by him	عندها *3indha* by her	عندو *3indo* by him
عننا *3anna* by us		عننا *3inna* by us	
عندكن *3andkon* by you [P]		عندكم *3indkom* by you [P]	
عندهن *3andon* by them		عندهم *3indhom* by them	

When suffixes are added, من *min* "from" and عن *3an* "about" both double their final *n*.

من *min* "FROM"			
North Levantine		**South Levantine**	
مني *minni* from me		مني *minni* from me	
منك *minnek* from you [F]	منك *minnak* from you [M]	منك *minnek* from you [F]	منك *minnak* from you [M]
منها *minna* from her	منو *minno* from him	منها *minnha* from her	منو *minno* from him
مننا *minna* OR *minn'na* from us		مننا *minna* from us	

min من "FROM"	
North Levantine	**South Levantine**
منكن *minnkon* from you [P]	منكم *minnkom* from you [P]
منهن *minnon* from them	منهم *minnhom* from them

3an عن "ABOUT"			
North Levantine		**South Levantine**	
عني *3anni* about me		عني *3anni* about me	
عنك *3annek* about you [F]	عنك *3annak* about you [M]	عنك *3annek* about you [F]	عنك *3annak* about you [M]
عنها *3anna* about her	عنو *3anno* about him	عنها *3annha* about her	عنو *3anno* about him
عننا *3anna* OR *3annᵢna* about us		عننا *3anna* about us	
عنكن *3annkon* about you [P]		عنكم *3annkom* about you [P]	
عنهن *3annon* about them		عنهم *3annhom* about them	

The word مع *ma3* "with" can be entirely regular but for many South Levantine speakers has an irregular form معا *ma3aa-*:

<table>
<tr><td colspan="4" align="center">مع ma3
"WITH"</td></tr>
<tr><td colspan="2" align="center">North Levantine</td><td colspan="2" align="center">South Levantine</td></tr>
<tr><td colspan="2" align="center">معي
ma3i
with me</td><td colspan="2" align="center">معاي
ma3aay
with me</td></tr>
<tr><td align="center">معاك
ma3ek
with you [F]</td><td align="center">معك
ma3ak
with you [M]</td><td align="center">معاكي
ma3aaki
by you [F]</td><td align="center">معاك
ma3aak
by you [M]</td></tr>
<tr><td align="center">معاها
ma3a
with her</td><td align="center">معو
ma3o
with him</td><td align="center">معاها
ma3aaha
by her</td><td align="center">معاه
ma3aa
by him</td></tr>
<tr><td colspan="2" align="center">معنا
ma3na
with us</td><td colspan="2" align="center">معانا
ma3aana
with us</td></tr>
<tr><td colspan="2" align="center">معكن
ma3kon
with you [P]</td><td colspan="2" align="center">معاكم
ma3aakom
with you [P]</td></tr>
<tr><td colspan="2" align="center">معهن
ma3on
with them</td><td colspan="2" align="center">معاهم
ma3aahom
with them</td></tr>
</table>

When pronouns are attached, بـ *b-* "in" uses the stem في *fii-*:

<table>
<tr><td colspan="2" align="center">بـ b-
"IN"</td></tr>
<tr><td align="center">North Levantine</td><td align="center">South Levantine</td></tr>
<tr><td align="center">فيي OR فيني
fiyyi OR fiini
in me</td><td align="center">في
fiyyi OR fiyy
in me</td></tr>
</table>

ب -*b* "IN"			
North Levantine		**South Levantine**	
فيكي *fiiki* in you [F]	فيك *fiik* in you [M]	فيكي *fiiki* in you [F]	فيك *fiik* in you [M]
فيها *fiyya* in her	فيه OR فيو *fii* OR *fiyyo* in him	فيها *fiiha* in her	فيه OR فيو *fii* OR *fiyyo* in him
فينا *fiina* in us		فينا *fiina* in us	
فيكن *fiikon* in you [P]		فيكم *fiikom* in you [P]	
فيهن *fiyyon* in them		فيهم *fiihom* in them	

The word ل *la-* "for" generally uses the stem إل *2il-* (sometimes لإ *la2il-*). Note that *la-* is unusual, however, in that it often becomes a special verbal suffix when combined with pronouns (see unit 19):

la- ل "FOR"			
North Levantine		**South Levantine**	
إلي *2ili* for me		إلي *2ili* for me	
إلك *2ilek* for you [F]	إلك *2ilak* for you [M]	إلك *2ilek* for you [F]	إلك *2ilak* for you [M]

<table>
<tr><td colspan="4" align="center">la- لـ
"FOR"</td></tr>
<tr><td colspan="2" align="center">North Levantine</td><td colspan="2" align="center">South Levantine</td></tr>
<tr><td align="center">إلها
2ila
for her</td><td align="center">إلو
2ilo
for him</td><td align="center">إلها
2ilha
for her</td><td align="center">إلو
2ilo
for him</td></tr>
<tr><td colspan="2" align="center">إلنا
2ilna
for us</td><td colspan="2" align="center">إلنا
2ilna
for us</td></tr>
<tr><td colspan="2" align="center">إلكن
2ilkon
for you [P]</td><td colspan="2" align="center">إلكم
2ilkom
for you [P]</td></tr>
<tr><td colspan="2" align="center">إلهن
2ilon
for them</td><td colspan="2" align="center">إلهم
2ilhom
for them</td></tr>
</table>

When pronouns are attached, حوالين *7awaleen* "around" loses its *-n*:

<table>
<tr><td colspan="4" align="center">حولين 7awaleen
"AROUND"</td></tr>
<tr><td colspan="2" align="center">North Levantine</td><td colspan="2" align="center">South Levantine</td></tr>
<tr><td colspan="2" align="center">حولي
7awaliyyi
around me</td><td colspan="2" align="center">حولي
7awalayyi OR 7awalayy
around me</td></tr>
<tr><td align="center">حوليكي
7awaleeki
around you [F]</td><td align="center">حوليك
7awaleek
around you [M]</td><td align="center">حوليكي
7awaleeki
around you [F]</td><td align="center">حوليك
7awaleek
around you [M]</td></tr>
<tr><td align="center">حوليها
7awaleyya
around her</td><td align="center">حوليه
7awalee
around him</td><td align="center">حوليها
7awaleeha
around her</td><td align="center">حوليه
7awalee
around him</td></tr>
<tr><td colspan="2" align="center">حولينا
7awaleena
around us</td><td colspan="2" align="center">حولينا
7awaleena
around us</td></tr>
</table>

7awaleen حولين "AROUND"	
North Levantine	**South Levantine**
حوليكن *7awaleekon* around you [P]	حوليكم *7awaleekom* around you [P]
حوليهن *7awaleyyon* around them	حوليهم *7awaleehom* around them

When the attached pronoun is plural, بين *been* "between" can become بيناتـ *beenaat-*:

been بين "BETWEEN"	
North Levantine	**South Levantine**
بيناتنا *beenaatna* between us	بيناتنا *binaatna* between us
بيناتكن *beenaatkon* between you [P]	بيناتكم *binaatkom* between you [P]
بيناتهن *beenaaton* between them	بيناتهم *binaathom* between them

For South Levantine speakers, بعد *ba3ᵉd* "after," قبل *2abᵉl* "before," فوق *foo2* "above," and تحت *ta7t* "underneath" have an alternative form ending in *-ii* that is used when (some) pronouns are attached. All four patterns with the examples with *ba3ᵉd* are given below. Note that the North Levantine forms are regular:

بعد *ba3d* "AFTER"			
North Levantine		**South Levantine**	
بعدي *ba3di* after me		بعدي *ba3di* after me	
بعدك *ba3dek* after you [F]	بعدك *ba3dak* after you [M]	بعديكي *ba3diiki* after you [F]	بعديك *ba3diik* after you [M]
بعدها *ba3da* after her	بعدو *ba3do* after him	بعديها *ba3diiha* after her	بعديه *ba3dii* after him
بعدنا *ba3ᵢdna* after us		بعدينا *ba3diina* after us	
بعدكن *ba3ᵢdkon* after you [P]		بعديكم *ba3diikom* after you [P]	
بعدهن *ba3don* after them		بعديهم *ba3diihom* after them	

Note that for some North Levantine speakers, most prepositions can avoid taking pronouns directly by attaching the suffix *-en* and using من *min* as a stand-in: تحتن منا *ta7ten minnᵢna* "underneath us," بعدن منك *ba3den minnak* "after you."

Verb Derivation

In previous units we have looked at the common derivational patterns and word shapes associated with nouns (see unit 7) and adjectives (see unit 16). In this unit we will be looking at the corresponding patterns and shapes for verbs. Unlike nouns in particular, verbs are quite constrained in the shapes they can have. As a result, it is feasible to draw up a relatively short list of all or almost all the possible verb shapes, which is what we'll be doing here.

Note that where English uses the infinitive as the citation form given in dictionary entries for verbs ("[to] go" as opposed to "goes" or "went," for example), Arabic often uses the third-person singular masculine ("he") form of the perfective, which is identical to what I call the perfective stem. We will discuss stems and the formation of the perfective and imperfective in more detail in units 25–27. For now, we will be focusing primarily on the meanings of the different shapes.

Simple Verbs

Simple verbs—"Form I" in the schema sometimes adopted in Arabic textbooks—are the most basic kind of verb. Unlike the other patterns discussed in this unit, the word shapes described here are not usually used to derive new words. But quickly reviewing the patterns is worthwhile anyway.

There are two basic simple verb shapes: *fi3el* and *fa3al.* These combine with different types of roots (see units 5–6) in predictable ways to produce six distinct shapes:

Root type	Shape	Example	Shape	Example
Sound	*fa3al*	كتب *katab* to write	*fi3el*	شرب *shireb* to drink

Root type	Shape	Example	Shape	Example
Hollow	*faal*	قال *2aal* to say		
Defective	*fa3a*	حكى *7aka* to speak	*fi3i*	دري *diri* to find out
Doubled	*fa33*	دق *da22* to tap		

fa33al

fa33al is probably the most common of all the derivational patterns. It is the default way of deriving verbs from nouns, as the following examples show:

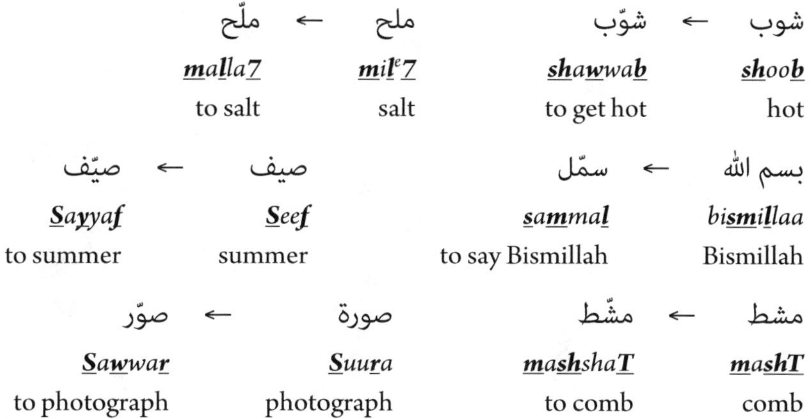

It is also used to derive verbs from other verbs. Here the most common output is a causative, a form meaning "make" or "let" explored in detail in unit 56. In some cases, however, it is either a more or less intense version of the underlying verb, sometimes with a sense of repeated action:

وطّى ← وطي   درّس ← درس
waTTa   *wiTi*   *darras*   *daras*
to lower   to become low   to teach   to study

كبّس ← كبس   فوّت ← فات
kabbas   *kabas*   *fawwat*   *faat*
to press repeatedly   to press   to let in   to enter

نقّش ← نقش   قطّع ← قطع
na22ash   *na2ash*   *2aTTa3*   *2aTa3*
to score [pastry]   to carve   to chop up into   to cut
                                   multiple pieces

> In a few cases, a *fa33al* verb may also act as its own causative: وقف *wa22af* can mean either "stand/stop" or "cause to stand/stop."

Often a *fa33al* verb forms a pair with an simple or *tfa33al* verb corresponding to a single verb in English. In this case, the *fa33al* verb will be transitive—that is, take an object—and the other verb will be its intransitive counterpart (see unit 24):

طوّل ←   طول   تغيّر ←   غيّر
Tawwal   *Tiwel*   *tghayyar*   *ghayyar*
to lengthen   to lengthen   to change   to change
[to make longer]   [to get longer]   [to be changed]   [s.th.]

In other cases, a *fa33al* verb has more or less the same broad meaning as its simple counterpart—and both correspond to the same verb in English—but the *fa33al* verb is used in a more specific context. In particular:

شطّف ←   شطف   غسّل ←   غسل
shaTTaf   *shaTaf*   *ghassal*   *ghasal*
to rinse   to rinse   to wash   to wash
[a body part]   [a body part]

faa3al

It is more difficult to identify clear derivational logic with *faa3al* verbs than with *fa33al*s. Some are equivalent to a simple verb plus a preposition:

كاتب ←   كتب لـ   حاكى ←   حكى مع
kaatab   *katab* la-   *7aaka*   *7aka ma3*
to correspond with   to write to   to speak to   to speak to

Some express something such as "try to X" or "seek to X." Most of the examples of this are metaphorical or extended, however, and it is probably not worth making too much effort trying to understand the process:

خنق ← خانق	قتل ← قاتل مع
khana2 *khaana2*	*2atal* *2aatal ma3*
to strangle to fight, argue with	to kill to fight with

سبق ← سابق	شارك ← شريك
saba2 *saaba2*	*shariik* *shaarak*
to precede, beat [in a race] to race	partner to partner with

2af3al

2af3al is a largely *fuS7a* pattern that is used with only a relatively small number of verbs in Levantine. Its semantics are broadly similar to those of *fa33al*:

هدية ← أهدى	علن ← أعلن
hdiyye *2ahda*	*3alan* *2a3lan*
gift to gift to	public to announce

tfa33al

tfaa3al is the normal way of forming passive verbs (see unit 57) from *fa33al*s:

غيّر ← تغيّر	صوّر ← تصوّر
ghayyar *tghayyar*	*Sawwar* *tSawwar*
to change [s.th.] to change [to be changed]	to photograph to be photographed

درّب ← تدرّب	هوّى ← تهوّى
darrab *tdarrab*	*hawwa* *thawwa*
to train [s.o.] to be trained	to blow air, ventilate to be ventilated

faa3al occasionally produces verbs meaning "act like" from nouns or adjectives, although these are more common for *tfaa3al*:

فن ← تفنّن	أهبل ← تهبل
fann *tfannan*	*2ahbal* *thabbal*
art to be artful, artistic	silly to act silly

tfaa3al

tfaa3al is the normal way of forming passive verbs (see unit 57) from *faa3al*s:

تعارض ← عارض		تحاكى ← حاكى	
t3aaraD *3aaraD*		*t7aaka* *7aaka*	
to be opposed to oppose		to be spoken to to speak to	

tfaa3al also forms verbs expressing reciprocal action ("with one another"). These structures are discussed in more detail in unit 55.

توافق ← وافق		تسابق مع ← سابق	
twaafa2 *waafa2*		*tsaaba2 ma3* *saaba2*	
to agree with to agree		to race with to race	
one another [for your own part]			

Finally, *tfaa3al* commonly derives verbs from adjectives expressing "act X," "act like X," or occasionally "pretend to be X":

تقاوى على قوي		تشاطر على شاطر	
t2aawa 3ala *2awi*		*tshaaTar 3ala* *shaaTer*	
to lord it over strong		to outsmart clever	
تبالد بليد		تناسى نسي	
tbaalad *baliid*		*tnaasa* *nisi*	
to act irritatingly irritating		to pretend to have forgotten to forget	

nfa3al

nfa3al verbs are almost exclusively passive counterparts of simple verbs:

انكوى كوى		انكتب كتب	
ⁱ*nkawa* *kawa*		ⁱ*nkatab* *katab*	
to be ironed to iron		to be written to write	
انقال قال		انضب ضب	
n2aal *2aal*		ⁱ*nDabb* *Dabb*	
to be said to say		to be put away to put away	

fta3al

fta3al is commonly used to form passives of simple or other verbs:

استلم ← سلّم		نسي ← انتسى	
s_talam	**sa_llam**	**n_tasa**	**n_isi**
to receive,	to hand over	to be forgotten	to forget
take possession of			

		اقتنع ← قنع	
		qtana3	**qana3**
		to be convinced	to convince

fta3al also derives more abstract senses from underlying verbs, often in a way that corresponds to the same English word:

اعترف بـ ← عرف		افتتح ← فتح	
3taraf b-	**3iref**	**ftata7**	**fata7**
to recognise	to know,	to open	to open
[formally],	recognise	[a new business]	
give recognition to	[a person]		

fta3al is perhaps the most idiosyncratic of the derivational patterns. The *t* of the pattern assimilates to similar consonants, becoming *d* next to *z* and *T* next to *D* or *T*. Unlike other assimilated forms of the kind we discussed above (unit 4), these are usually written as follows:

اضطر ← ضروري		ازدهر ← زهرة	
D_Tarr	**D_aruuri**	**zdahar**	**zahra**
to have to	obligatory	to flourish	flower

A root-initial *w* assimilates to *t*, as do some instances of 2:

اتّخذ ← أخذ		اتّكل ← وكّل	
ttakhadh	**2akhadh**	**ttakal**	**wakkal**
to take [a decision]	to take (fuS7a)	to rely	to entrust

Note, however, the forms for *2akal* and *2akhad*, which have a long vowel as well as assimilation:

اتّاخد ← أخد		اتّاكل ← أكل	
ttaakhad	**2akhad**	**ttaakal**	**2akal**
to be taken	to take	to be eaten	to eat

f3all

f3all is a fairly unusual form that is very closely associated with adjectives of colour and quality of the shape *2af3al* (see unit 17) and derives verbs of becoming, often with the meaning of gradual change:

ابيضّ	←	أبيض		احمرّ	←	أحمر
byaDD		*2abyaD*		*7marr*		*2a7mar*
to turn		white		to turn		red
[gradually] white				[gradually] red		

staf3al

Many common examples of *staf3al* are derived from adjectives and express "consider something X":

استغرب	←	غريب		استغلى	←	غالي
staghrab		*ghariib*		*staghla*		*ghaali*
to think X		strange		to think X		expensive
is strange				is expensive		

Some express "act like" or "act in accordance with," similar to *tfaa3al*:

استرجل	←	رجّال		استعرب	←	عربي
starjal		*rijjaal*		*sta3rab*		*3arabi*
to act macho		man		to act like an Arab,		Arab
				become Arabised		

Some have a meaning similar to "get X to do Y," where Y is the underlying verb, although usually with metaphorical extension:

استقال	←	أقال		استرجع	←	رجع
staqaal		*2aqaal*		*starja3*		*rije3*
to resign		to fire, release		to restore, regain		to return
		from a job				

Perhaps more than any other form, however, it is often very difficult to identify a clear derivational relationship between *staf3al* verbs and their underlying counterparts.

fa3lal

fa3lal is the basic pattern for four-letter roots. Like *fa33al* for three-letter roots, *fa3lal* is a fairly all-purpose verb deriver, used most commonly with foreign loans:

بستر ← بستور	سشور ← سشوار
bastar *bastuur*	*sashwar* *sishwaar*
to pasteurise Pasteur	to blow-dry hairdryer

أركل ← أركيلة	هستر ← هستيريا
2argal *2argiile*	*hastar* *histirya*
to smoke shisha shisha pipe	to go hysterical hysteria

Some *fa3lal* verbs are in fact from three-letter roots, modified by insertion of another root consonant. These forms express either a less intense or a more repetitive version of the underlying verb (or sometimes both). The most common patterns are repetition of a syllable or insertion of a *w* before the final root consonant:

بكبك ← بكي	شخوط ← شخط
bakbak *biki*	*shakhwaT* *shakhaT*
to snivel to cry	to scribble to draw a line

طخطخ ← طخّ	نكوش ← نكش
TakhTakh *Takhkh*	*nakwash* *nakash*
to shoot in every direction to shoot	to root around to dig up

Onomatopoeic words are commonly formed on these patterns:

طقطق ← طقّ	بسبس ← سّ
Ta2Ta2 *Ta22*	*basbas* *bass*
to pop, crack to burst	to keep saying "but," find excuses but

tfa3lal

tfa3lal is used to form passives of *fa3lal* verbs:

تتلفن ← تلفن	تسشور ← سشور
ttalfan *talfan*	*tsashwar* *sashwar*
to be phoned to phone	to be blow-dried to blow-dry

In some cases, *tfa3lal* is also used to form reciprocal counterparts (see unit 55), similar to *tfaa3al,* and is also used to produce intransitive verbs in general, including ones meaning "act like" even when there is no equivalent without *t-*:

شنكل   ←   تشنكل   شيطان   ←   تشيطن

shangal   *tshangal*   *sheeTaan*   *tsheeTan*

to link arms with   to link arms   devil   to act naughty
                with one another

As noted elsewhere, *tfa3lal* commonly allows the *m-* of nouns of instance, place, and so on (see unit 7) to be carried over into verb forms:

مقطع   ←   تمقطع   مركز   ←   تمركز على

maqTa3   *tmaqTa3*   *markaz*   *tmarkaz 3ala*

scene   to act   centre   to centre on
            melodramatic

Some Unexpected Verb Types

In many respects, Arabic verbs behave much like their counterparts in English or other European languages you may be familiar with. They express the same sorts of categories (tense, mood, person, number), take objects and indirect objects straightforwardly, and can overall be relied on to be recognisably "verbal" in many other respects. In this unit, however, we will be looking at some less intuitive types of Arabic verb (at least for English speakers). These verb types are important because they have significant implications for some of the other questions and phenomena that we will be discussing later, particularly tense.

We will start by looking at change-of-state verbs: verbs that express a shift from one state to another and often correspond to more complex English constructions with "become" or "get." We will then look at double-meaning verbs: verbs that have both a state and a change-of-state meaning and often map onto multiple verbs in English. Finally, we will look at English ergative verbs and how they translate to Arabic.

Change-of-State Verbs

The first point to note is that Arabic has many verbs that are derived from adjectives or nouns and express a change of state. These typically correspond to "get" or "become" plus an adjective, although in some cases they have slightly different translations:

طول	طويل		صغر	صغير
Tiwel	*Tawiil*		*zigher*	*zghiir*
to get long[er]	long		to get small[er]	small

صيف	صيف		كبر	كبير
Sayyaf	*Seef*		*kiber*	*kbiir*
to get summery	summer		to get big[ger]	big

رشح	رشح		شوب	شوب
rashsha7	*rash^e7*		*shawwab*	*shoob*
to develop a cold	cold		to get hot	heat, hot weather

جوعان	جاع	تعبان	تعب
joo3aan	*jaa3*	*ta3baan*	*ti3eb*
[have got] hungry	get hungry	[have got] tired	get tired

Using these verbs is typically more idiomatic than صار *Saar* "become" plus an adjective. As we will see, they generally form their participle (see unit 29) with the pattern *-aan*, which often corresponds to a basic adjective in English:

جوعان	جاع	تعبان	تعب
joo3aan	*jaa3*	*ta3baan*	*ti3eb*
[have got] hungry	to get hungry	[have got] tired	to get tired

In some cases—where there is an underlying adjective—the participle and adjective express slightly different ideas:

صغران	صغير	طولان	طويل
zaghraan	*zghiir*	*Toolaan*	*Tawiil*
has got small[er]	small	has got long[er]	long

Double-Meaning Verbs

There is a related category of verbs that I call double-meaning verbs. These are verbs that can have both a state meaning and a change-of-state meaning, depending on context. Consider the following pairs:

Change-of-State	State
ركب الباص عند أول موقف	ركب الباص ساعة بعدين نزل
rikeb 'lbaaS 3ind 2awwal maw2ef	*rikeb 'lbaaS saa3teen ba3deen nizel*
he got on the bus at the first stop	he rode the bus for an hour then got off
عرفت إنو . . .	كانت تعرف إنو . . .
3irfat 2inno . . .	*kaanat ti3raf 2inno . . .*
she found out that . . .	she knew that . . .
نامو دغري	نامو ساعتين
naamu dighri	*naamu saa3teen*
they went to sleep straight away	they slept for two hours

The meanings of each pair are obviously clearly related, but there is a crucial difference: "Ride," "know," and "sleep" all express a whole state from (ill-defined) beginning to end. "Get on," "find out," and "go to sleep," on the other hand, express the action that "begins" that state, that is, the action that moves you from "not being on" the bus to "being on" it, from "not knowing" to "knowing," or from "awake" to "asleep."

I chose the examples above because English distinguishes them whereas Arabic does not. But it is important to be able to identify this distinction elsewhere too. Consider these pairs:

Change-of-State	State
قعدت دغري *2a3ad^et dughri* I <u>sat down</u> straight away	قعدت ساعة *2a3ad^et saa3a* I <u>sat</u> for an hour
بس فات وقفت قراية *bass faat <u>wa22aft</u> ˈ2raaye* as soon as he came in <u>I stopped</u> reading	وقفت قراية نهار كامل *<u>wa22aft</u> ˈ2raaye ˈnhaar kaamel* <u>I stopped</u> reading for a whole day

In the right column, "sat" expresses the state of being seated, and "stopped" expresses the state of not reading. In the left column, on the other hand, "sat down" expresses the action of moving into a sitting position, and "stopped" expresses the act of ceasing to read.

Why are these distinctions important? It is useful to know that Arabic often has a single verb corresponding to two verbs in English. Moreover, these distinctions are of broader relevance to the way the tense system works. In particular, the English continuous is translated into Arabic in different ways—with the participle (see unit 37) or with the *3am* form (see unit 35)—depending on whether the verb has a whole-state or change-of-state meaning:

Change-of-State	State
عم تلبس جاكيت *3am tilbes jakeet* she's putting a jacket on	لابسة جاكيت *laabse jakeet* she's wearing a jacket
عم اقعد! *3am 2i23od!* I'm sitting, I'm sitting! [in response to an order]	قاعد جوا *2aa3ed juwwa* he's sitting inside

There are other implications too, as we will see below.

Ergative Verbs

Remember that the *subject* is the "doer" of the verb, the thing it agrees with. The *object* is the thing that is being "verbed," the thing that is being acted on. See units 51–53.

A peculiar feature of English is its ergative verbs. Ergative verbs can be either intransitive (not have an object) or transitive (have an object), but they behave differently in each case: when they are used *intransitively*, their subject is the "experiencer" or "undergoer" of the action, but when they are used *transitively*, it is the object that plays this role. This is easiest to demonstrate with examples:

Subject Undergoes Action	Object Undergoes Action
The house burned down.	Sami burned the house down.
The sugar melted.	You melted the sugar.
Everything changed.	We changed everything.

In each case, the semantic relationship between the underlined noun and the verb is the same. The house is still being destroyed by fire, the sugar is still dissolving, and everything is still changing, whether they are the subject or the object. The only difference is how the English verbs in question decide what is a subject and what is an object.

If Arabic worked in the same way, there would be no need for this section. But as you have probably guessed, it does not work the same way. Most English verbs of this kind correspond to pairs of distinct verbs in Arabic:

<table>
<tr><td align="center">سامي حرق البيت
saami 7ara2 ʾlbeet
Sami burned the house down</td><td align="center">احترق البيت
7tara2 ʾlbeet
the house burned down</td></tr>
<tr><td align="center">دوبتي السكر
dawwabti ssikkaar
you melted the sugar</td><td align="center">داب السكر
daab ʾssikkaar
the sugar melted</td></tr>
<tr><td align="center">غيرنا كل إشي
ghayyarna kull 2ishi
we changed everything</td><td align="center">تغير كل إشي
tghayyar kull 2ishi
everything changed</td></tr>
</table>

As you can see, in all three examples the words on the right have different patterns than those on the left. In the first pair, the transitive form (*7ara2*) is a simple verb, and its intransitive counterpart is derived using the pattern *fta3al* (*7tara2*). In the second pair, the intransitive form (*daab*) is a simple verb, and its transitive counterpart (*dawwab*) is derived using the pattern *fa33al* (which commonly forms causatives, for which see unit 56). In the third pair, both the intransitive form (*tghayyar*) and the transitive form (*ghayyar*) are on derivational patterns, *tfa33al* and *fa33al*, respectively.

Pairs of this kind are very common, but there is no way to be absolutely certain of which correspondence applies to a particular word. These pairs, like passive/active pairs, have to be learned as you encounter them.

> There are a few pairs that both seem to be underived verbs and differ only in their vowelling: شفى *shafa* "heal" versus شفي *shifi* "recover," "be healed"; خلق *khile2* "be born" versus خلق *khala2* "create"; and يدور *yduur* "turn (intransitive)" versus يدير *ydiir* "turn (transitive)." This is not productive or common, however.

Note that some verbs work exactly like their English counterparts and can be used both transitively and intransitively:

<table>
<tr><td align="center">فتحت الباب</td><td align="center">فتح الباب</td></tr>
<tr><td align="center">fat7at ᵢlbaab</td><td align="center">fata7 ᵢlbaab</td></tr>
<tr><td align="center">she opened the door</td><td align="center">the door opened</td></tr>
<tr><td align="center"></td><td align="center">he opened the door</td></tr>
<tr><td align="center">وقفتهن قدام المحل</td><td align="center">وقفو قدام المحل</td></tr>
<tr><td align="center">wa22afton 2iddaam ᵢlma7all</td><td align="center">wa22afu 2iddaam ᵢlma7all</td></tr>
<tr><td align="center">I stopped them in front of the shop</td><td align="center">they stopped in front of the shop</td></tr>
</table>

The Perfective

The Arabic tense system is built around two main sets of forms, the *perfective* and the *imperfective*. We will be looking in more detail at the semantics of these two forms and their subforms below. For now, however, I will be glossing the perfective with the English past and the imperfective with the English present. In this unit we will look at the perfective suffixes and how they combine with different types of stem.

Suffixes and Stems

The perfective is formed using suffixes. These suffixes mark the gender (masculine, feminine) number (singular, plural) and person (first, second, third) of the verb's subject:

ـنا -na we	ـت -*e*t I	
ـتو -tu you [P]	ـتي -ti you [F]	ـت -*e*t you [M]
ـو -u they	ـت -et/-at she	[no suffix] he

The only regional variation is that the third-person singular feminine ("she") form is *-et* in North Levantine and *-at* in South Levantine. They are attached to the perfective *stem,* which as we have seen is identical to the dictionary form.

These suffixes are the same for all perfective verbs. Although they themselves do not change, they do cause various changes in the stem itself depending on its shape. In the sections below we will look very quickly at how they combine with different stem shapes: *sound, hollow, defective,* and *doubled.*

For a recap of the different kinds of roots, see units 5–6.

Sound Stems

Sound stems are, broadly speaking, those that have three or four root consonants that are not semivowels. We saw in unit 23 that there are basically two shapes that simple verbs in this category can have. The first, *fa3al*, is fairly straightforward. The only unexpected feature is that *-et/-at* "she" tends to trigger deletion of the preceding unstressed *a* as though it were an *i* or a *u* (see unit 4):

كتبنا	كتبت
katab-na	*katab-ᵉt*
we wrote	I wrote

كتبتو	كتبتي	كتبت
katab-tu	*katab-ti*	*katab-ᵉt*
you [P] wrote	you [F] wrote	you [M] wrote

كتبو	كتبت	كتب
katab-u	*katb-et/katb-at*	*katab*
they wrote	she wrote	he wrote

Not all speakers drop the *a* here.

Most derived verbs pattern very similarly. The patterns *fta3al* and *nfa3al*, which have an almost identical overall shape (the initial consonant cluster aside), have identical conjugation, including the dropping of *a* before *-et/at*:

انشغلنا	انشغلت
nshaghal-na	*nshaghal-ᵉt*
we got busy	I got busy

انشغلتو	انشغلتي	انشغلت
nshaghal-tu	nshaghal-ti	nshaghal-ᵉt
you [P] got busy	you [F] got busy	you [M] got busy
انشغلو	انشغلت	انشغل
nshaghal-u	nshaghl-et/nshaghl-at	nshaghal
they got busy	she got busy	he got busy

Other derived verbs are even simpler, not even undergoing *a*-deletion:

تعلمنا	تعلمت	
t3allam-na	t3allam-ᵉt	
we learnt	I learnt	
تعلمتو	تعلمتي	تعلمت
t3allam-tu	t3allam-ti	t3allam-ᵉt
you [P] learnt	you [F] learnt	you [M] learnt
تعلمو	تعلمت	تعلم
t3allam-u	t3allam-et/t3allam-at	t3allam
they learnt	she learnt	he learnt

The other kind of simple stem, *fi3el*, is slightly more complicated, although the changes it undergoes are largely predictable from the general rules (see unit 4). The first vowel of the stem (*i*) is deleted when a consonant-initial suffix is added (shifting the stress to the second syllable), and the second (*i/e*) is deleted when a vowel-initial suffix is added:

تعبنا	تعبت	
t3ib-na	t3ib-ᵉt	
we got tired	I got tired	
تعبتو	تعبتي	تعبت
t3ib-tu	t3ib-ti	t3ib-ᵉt
you got [P] tired	you [F] got tired	you [M] got tired
تعبو	تعبت	تعب
ti3b-u	ti3b-et/ti3b-at	ti3eb
they got tired	she got tired	he got tired

Hollow Stems

Hollow verbs—those with a semivowel as their middle root letter—have two perfective stems, one with a long vowel and one with a short vowel. The short stem is used when suffixes beginning with consonants are added, and the long stem is used elsewhere. For most simple verbs, the vowel in the short stem is *i*:

شلنا *shil-na* we picked up		شلت *shil-ᵉt* I picked up
شلتو *shil-tu* you [P] picked up	شلتي *shil-ti* you [F] picked up	شلت *shil-ᵉt* you [M] picked up
شالو *shaal-u* they picked up	شالت *shaal-et/shaal-at* she picked up	شال *shaal* he picked up

In derived verbs, the short stem has an *a*:

اخترنا *khtar-na* we chose		اخترت *khtar-ᵉt* I chose
اخترتو *khtar-tu* you [P] chose	اخترتي *khtar-ti* you [F] chose	اخترت *khtar-ᵉt* you [M] chose
اختارو *khtaar-u* they chose	اختارت *khtaar-et/khtaar-at* she chose	اختار *khtaar* he chose

> Some speakers, especially Syrian speakers, have *i* instead of *a* in derived forms: اخترت *khtir-ᵉt* "I chose."

For South Levantine speakers, a handful of simple verbs have a *u* in their short stem. These are largely verbs that have a *uu* in their imperfective stem (see unit 26) and are thus perceived as having a root with *w* as its middle letter. Compare:

North Levantine		South Levantine	
قلت *2il-ᵉt* I said		قلت *2ul-ᵉt* I said	
قلتي *2il-ti* you [F] said	قلت *2il-ᵉt* you [M] said	قلتي *2ul-ti* you [F] said	قلت *2ul-ᵉt* you [M] said
قالت *2aal-et* she said	قال *2aal* he said	قالت *2aal-at* she said	قال *2aal* he said
قلنا *2il-na* we said		قلنا *2ul-na* we said	
قلتو *2il-tu* you [P] said		قلتو *2ul-tu* you [P] said	
قالو *2aal-u* they said		قالو *2aal-u* they said	

For North Levantine speakers—who have collapsed short *u* in these positions into *i* (see unit 3)—*all* simple verbs have *i* in their short stem.

Defective Stems

Defective verbs are those whose stem ends with a vowel. For the vast majority of verbs, both derived and simple, this vowel is *-a*. A suffix beginning with a consonant causes it to shift to *-ee-*, while a suffix beginning with a vowel simply deletes it. A simple example:

حكينا *7akee-na* we spoke	حكيت *7akee-t* I spoke

حكيتو	حكيتي	حكيت
7akee-tu	*7akee-ti*	*7akee-t*
you [P] spoke	you [F] spoke	you [M] spoke
حكو	حكت	حكى
7ak-u	*7ak-et/7ak-at*	*7aka*
they spoke	she spoke	he spoke

Derived verbs work in exactly the same way:

اشترينا	اشتريت	
shtaree-na	*shtaree-t*	
we bought	I bought	
اشتريتو	اشتريتي	اشتريت
shtaree-tu	*shtaree-ti*	*shtaree-t*
you [P] bought	you [F] bought	you [M] bought
اشترو	اشترت	اشترى
shtar-u	*shtar-et/shtar-at*	*shtara*
they bought	she bought	he bought

Some nonderived verbs have the shape *fi3i* instead, the counterpart to the sound *fi3el*. The final *-i* here becomes *-ii-* before a consonant-initial suffix but is not usually deleted before vowel-initial suffixes, becoming *y* instead (see unit 4):

درينا	دريت	
drii-na	*drii-t*	
we found out	I found out	
دريتو	دريتي	دريت
drii-tu	*drii-ti*	*drii-t*
you [P] found out	you [F] found out	you [M] found out
دريو	دريت	دري
diry-u	*diry-et/diry-at*	*diri*
they found out	she found out	he found out

> Some speakers may delete the *y* before vowel-initial suffixes: درت *diret* "she found out," درو *diru* "they found out."

Doubled Stems

Doubled verbs—those whose stem ends with a doubled consonant—mostly behave as expected. When suffixes beginning with a consonant are added, however, an *-ee-* is added in order to separate them from the stem, making them resemble defective verbs:

زتينا	زتيت
zattee-na	*zattee-t*
we tossed	I tossed

زتيتو	زتيتي	زتيت
zattee-tu	*zattee-ti*	*zattee-t*
you [P] tossed	you [F] tossed	you [M] tossed

زتو	زتت	زت
zatt-u	*zatt-et/zatt-at*	*zatt*
they tossed	she tossed	he tossed

The same applies to derived verbs:

استمرينا	استمريت
stamarree-na	*stamarree-t*
we continued	I continued

استمريتو	استمريتي	استمريت
stamarree-tu	*stamarree-ti*	*stamarree-t*
you [P] continued	you [F] continued	you [M] continued

استمرو	استمرت	استمر
stamarr-u	*stamarr-et/stamarr-at*	*stamarr*
they continued	she continued	he continued

In most cases, having a doubled *stem* is the same as having a doubled *root*; that is, the root under which the word would be listed in a dictionary has identical second and third consonants. But verbs on the unusual derived form افعلّ *f3all* (see unit 23) have a doubled stem (i.e., ending with a double consonant) despite not having a doubled root:

احمرينا	احمريت	
7marree-na	*7marree-t*	
we turned red	I turned red	
احمريتو	احمريتي	احمريت
7marree-tu	*7marree-ti*	*7marree-t*
you [P] turned red	you [F] turned red	you [M] turned red
احمرو	احمرت	احمر
7marr-u	*7marr-et/7marr-at*	*7marr*
they turned red	she turned red	he turned red

The Imperfective: Simple Verbs

The second major verb form—and the form from which most other common constructions are derived—is the *imperfective*, which for the time being we will be glossing using the English simple present. The imperfective is conjugated using a combination of prefixes and suffixes, which are attached to the imperfective stem:

Imperfective of *shireb* "Drink"		
نشرب	اشرب	
ni-shrab	*2i-shrab/2a-shrab*	
we drink	I drink	
تشربو	تشربي	تشرب
ti-shrab-u	*ti-shrab-i*	*ti-shrab*
you [P] drink	you [F] drink	you [M] drink
يشربو	تشرب	يشرب
yi-shrab-u	*ti-shrab*	*yi-shrab*
they drink	she drinks	he drinks

For most verbs, the imperfective stem is different from the perfective stem. The main difficulty—beginning from the dictionary form—is working out what this stem should be, particularly in simple verbs. In this unit we will be looking at the various possibilities for imperfective stems and how they correspond to perfective stems. We will then look at how the prefixes and suffixes interact with these stems.

The information in this unit may seem overwhelming. There is so much irregularity in the relationship between (simple) perfective and imperfective stems that a description of the correspondences inevitably ends up running to several pages. But don't worry! The easiest solution is simply to learn the imperfective stem alongside the dictionary form of the verb. If you have already decided to do this, you can skip straight to the later sections on prefixes and suffixes.

Stems

There are three basic stem shapes in the imperfective, one for each of the short vowels *a*, *e*, and *o*. These combine with the various kinds of root (sound, hollow, defective, doubled) to produce a maximum of twelve possible imperfective stem shapes:

Sound	*-f3el*	*-f3ol*		*-f3al*
Hollow	*-fiil*	*-fuul*		*-faal*
Defective	*-f3i*	*(-f3u)*		*-f3a*
Doubled	*-fi33*	*-fu33* (South Levantine only)		*-fa33*

The forms with *o* and the forms with *e* have a tendency to become confused across the Levantine area as a whole. Any verb that has *e* in one region is likely to have *o* in another region and vice versa. For many North Levantine speakers, especially Lebanese speakers, the *-f3el* form is practically nonexistent; all the verbs given here as *-f3el* forms have *-f3ol* instead.

The perfective has only seven possible stem shapes. For any given (simple) perfective, there are thus multiple plausible imperfectives. It is impossible to know with certainty what the imperfective of an simple verb will be just by looking at its perfective.

That said, it is sometimes possible to make an educated guess. In particular, the perfective stems *fi3el* and *fi3i* are closely associated with imperfectives on *-f3al* and *-f3a*, respectively, while *fa3al* and *fa3a* are closely associated with imperfectives on *-f3el* and *-f3ol*:

Imperfective			**Perfective**	
يلمس	*-f3el*	←	لمس	*fa3al*
yi-lmes			*lamas*	
touches			touched	
يقتل	*-f3ol*	←	قتل	*fa3al*
yi-2tol/yu-2tol			*2atal*	
kills			killed	
يشرب	*-f3al*	←	شرب	*fi3el*
yi-shrab			*shireb*	
drinks			drank	

Imperfective			Perfective	
يحكي	-f3i	←	حكى	fa3a
yi-7ki			7aka	
speaks			spoke	
يدرى	-f3a	←	دري	fi3i
yi-dra			diri	
finds out			found out	

There are many exceptions to this general rule, however:

Imperfective			Perfective	
يمسح	-f3al	←	مسح	fa3al
yi-msa7			masa7	
wipes			wiped	
يمسك	-f3el	←	مسك	fi3el
yi-msek			misek	
grabs			grabbed	
يقرا	-f3a	←	قرا	fa3a
yi-2ra			2ara	
reads			read	
يبكي	-f3i	←	بكي	fi3i
yi-bki			biki	
cries			cried	

Moreover, for hollow verbs—where there is only one basic perfective stem shape—we usually have no similar way of making an educated guess. You simply have to learn what imperfective corresponds to what perfective:

يدير	-fiil	←	دار	faal
y-diir			daar	
runs, manages			ran, managed	
يقول	-fuul	←	قال	faal
y-2uul			2aal	
says			said	

ينام *-faal* ← نام *faal*

y-naam   *naam*

sleeps   slept

> For South Levantine speakers who have a distinct short stem in *ful-* (see unit 25), there is a small clue: many verbs that have *ful-* in the perfective have *-fuul-* in the imperfective.

The same applies to doubled verbs:

يزت *-fi33* ← زت *fa33*

y-zitt   *zatt*

tosses   tossed

يضل *-fa33* ← ضل *fa33*

y-Dall   *Dall*

stays   stayed

Note that for doubled verbs, South Levantine speakers distinguish an additional imperfective stem to which there is no counterpart in North Levantine: *y-fu33*. The northern merger of *u* and *i* in these circumstances (see unit 3) means that for North Levantine speakers, these verbs have the same imperfective stem as *y-fi33* verbs:

North Levantine			South Levantine
بزت		←	زت
bi-zitt			*zatt*
he tosses			toss
بدق	بدق	←	دق
bi-di22	*bi-du22*		*da22*
he taps	he taps		tap

A handful of high-register defective verbs have two options for their imperfective stem, at least for some speakers. These forms do not exist for everyone:

يسطي *-f3i* ← سطا *fa3a*

yi-sTi   *saTa*

burgles   burgle

OR

←   -f3u   يسطو

yi-sTu

burgles

Similarly, some verbs whose stems begin with *w*—so-called assimilating verbs—have an alternative imperfective stem that drops the initial consonant entirely. This often has a different vowelling:

fa3al وثق   ←   -f3al   يوثق

wathaq   *yu-wthaq/yi-wthaq*

trust   trusts

OR

←   -3el   يثق

yi-theq

trusts

Complications with Prefixes

The most complicated part of forming the imperfective is generally finding the stem. Most stems interact much more straightforwardly with the prefixes and suffixes than do their perfective counterparts.

The main point to note is that the shape of the imperfective prefixes is variable. There are two sets, one used with stems beginning with a consonant cluster and one with stems beginning with a single consonant. As you can see, the first-person singular ("I") forms also differ by region: South Levantine has *2a-* throughout, while North Levantine has *2i-* before clusters and no prefix elsewhere:

SINGLE CONSONANT		CLUSTER	
North Levantine	**South Levantine**	**North Levantine**	**South Levantine**
دور	أدور	امسك	أمسك
duur	*2a-duur*	*2i-msek*	*2a-msek*
I turn	I turn	I grab	I grab
تدور		تمسك	
t-duur		*ti-msek*	
you [M] turn		you [M] grab	

SINGLE CONSONANT		CLUSTER	
North Levantine	**South Levantine**	**North Levantine**	**South Levantine**
يدور		يمسك	
y-duur		*yi-msek*	
he turns		he grabs	
ندور		نمسك	
n-duur		*ni-msek*	
we turn		we grab	

In South Levantine, the *i* of the consonant cluster set becomes *u* when attached to a stem with the shape *-ʃ3ol*:

North Levantine		**South Levantine**	
اكتب		أكتب	
2i-ktob		*2a-ktob*	
I write		I write	
تكتبي	تكتب	تكتبي	تكتب
ti-kⁱtb-i	*ti-ktob*	*tu-kᵘtb-i*	*tu-ktob*
you [F] write	you [M] write	you [F] write	you [M] write
تكتب	يكتب	تكتب	يكتب
ti-ktob	*yi-ktob*	*tu-ktob*	*yu-ktob*
she writes	he writes	she writes	he writes
نكتب		نكتب	
ni-ktob		*nu-ktob*	
we write		we write	
تكتبو		تكتبو	
ti-kⁱtb-u		*tu-kᵘtb-u*	
you [P] write		you [P] write	
يكتبو		يكتبو	
yi-kⁱtb-u		*yu-kᵘtb-u*	
they write		they write	

Otherwise, the complications are largely confined to small groups of verbs. In North Levantine, the prefix vowel *i* shifts to *a* with the verbs عطى *3aTa* "give," عرف *3iref* "know," and عمل *3imel* "do," although not before other initial 3s. The South Levantine forms are regular:

North Levantine		South Levantine	
أعمل *2a-3mel* I do		أعمل *2a-3mel* I do	
تعملي *ta-3ᶦml-i* you [F] do	تعمل *ta-3mel* you [M] do	تعملي *ti-3ᶦml-i* you [F] do	تعمل *ti-3mel* you [M] do
تعمل *ta-3mel* she does	يعمل *ya-3mel* he does	تعمل *ti-3mel* she does	يعمل *yi-3mel* he does
نعمل *ni-3mel* we do		نعمل *ni-3mel* we do	
تعملو *ta-3ᶦml-u* you [P] do		تعملو *ti-3ᶦml-u* you [P] do	
يعملو *ya-3ᶦml-u* they do		يعملو *yi-3ᶦml-u* they do	

Also in North Levantine, the prefix vowel *i* shifts to *u* before a stem beginning with *w-*. The South Levantine forms are regular:

North Levantine	South Levantine
اوصل *2u-wSal* I arrive	أوصل *2a-wSal* I arrive

North Levantine		South Levantine	
توصلي *tu-wSal-i* you [F] arrive	توصل *tu-wSal* you [M] arrive	توصلي *ti-wSal-i* you [F] arrive	توصل *ti-wSal* you [M] arrive
توصل *tu-wSal* she arrives	يوصل *yu-wSal* he arrives	توصل *ti-wSal* she arrives	يوصل *yi-wSal* he arrives
نوصل *nu-wSal* we arrive		نوصل *ni-wSal* we arrive	
توصلو *tu-wSal-u* you [P] arrive		توصلو *ti-wSal-u* you [P] arrive	
يوصلو *yu-wSal-u* they arrive		يوصلو *yi-wSal-u* they arrive	

We saw above that some of these verbs have alternative imperfective stems that lose the initial consonant. Here both North and South Levantine have *2a-* in the first-person singular ("I") form, where we would otherwise expect *2i-*:

North Levantine	South Levantine
أثق *2a-theq* I trust	أثق *2a-theq* I trust

There are two verbs whose perfective stems begin with 2, أكل *2akal* "eat" and أخد *2akhad* "take," which lose this 2 in the imperfective. This produces a conjugation not unlike that of assimilating verbs. The exact outcomes are slightly different in North and South Levantine:

North Levantine	South Levantine
آخد *2-aakhod* I take	آخد *2-aakhod* I take

North Levantine		South Levantine	
تاخدي *taa-khd-i* you [F] take	تاخد *taa-khod* you [M] take	تاخدي *too-khd-i* you [F] take	تاخد *too-khod* you [M] take
تاخد *t-aakhod* she takes	ياخد *y-aakhod* he takes	تاخد *t-ookhod* she takes	ياخد *y-ookhod* he takes
ناخد *n-aakhod* we take		ناخد *n-ookhod* we take	
تاخدو *t-aakhd-u* you [P] take		تاخدو *t-ookhd-u* you [P] take	
ياخدو *y-aakhd-u* he takes		ياخدو *y-ookhd-u* he takes	

You may also encounter أوخد *2ookhed* "I take" in South Levantine, with the rest of the paradigm as we would expect: *tookhed, yookhed,* and so on.

Complications with Suffixes

The suffixes are consistent across the Levantine area. They occur only in the second-person feminine (-*i*) and the second- and third-person plural (-*u*). In sound verbs, they often cause the expected deletion of the short stem vowel (see unit 4):

With *daar* "Turn"	With *misek* "Grab"
تدوري *t-duur-i* you [F] turn	تمسكي *ti-m^{i}sk-i* you [F] grab
تدورو *t-duur-u* you [P] turn	تمسكو *ti-m^{i}sk-u* you [P] grab

With *daar* "Turn"	With *misek* "Grab"
تدورو	يمسكو
y-duur-u	*yi-mˈsk-u*
they turn	they grab

> Note that many speakers can retain the stem vowel, producing more straight-forward forms such as يكتبو *yuktubu* "they write" and تمسكي *timsiki* "you [F] grab." Since the forms with deletion are more complex, I have presented them as the default here.

In defective verbs, the suffixes always cause deletion of final stem vowels (i.e. a final *-a, -i* or *-u*):

With *diri* "Find Out"		With *7aka* "Talk"	
ادرى		احكي	
2i-dra/2a-dra		*2i-7ki/2a-7ki*	
I find out		I talk	
تدري	تدرى	تحكي	تحكي
ti-dr-i	*ti-dra*	*ti-7k-i*	*ti-7ki*
you [F] find out	you [M] find out	you [F] talk	you [M] talk
تدرى	يدرى	تحكي	يحكي
ti-dra	*yi-dra*	*ti-7ki*	*yi-7ki*
she finds out	he finds out	she talks	he talks
ندرى		نحكي	
ni-dra		*ni-7ki*	
we find out		we talk	
تدرو		تحكو	
ti-dr-u		*ti-7k-u*	
you [P] find out		you [P] talk	
يدرو		يحكو	
yi-dr-u		*yi-7k-u*	
they find out		they talk	

The Imperfective: Derived Verbs

In unit 26 we looked at how to conjugate various simple verbs in the imperfective. In this unit we will be taking up the task of forming imperfectives from *derived* verbs, those verbs that have a clear derivational pattern (see unit 23). Luckily, derived verbs tend to only have one possible imperfective stem, making their conjugation simpler than that of their simple counterparts. Nonetheless, there are still some complications to be aware of.

The vast majority of derived verbs form their imperfective in a way that closely parallels the *fa3al-yif3el* pairs we saw in the simple verbs section. We will first look at relatively unproblematic examples of this (*fa33al, faa3al, fa3lal, staf3al,* and *2af3al*). We will then consider the even more straightforward *t-* forms (*tfa33al, tfaa3al,* and *tfa3lal*), which parallel *fa3al-yif3al* pairs. Finally, we will analyse the more complicated *nfa3al* and *fta3al* patterns, which have multiple possible imperfectives.

fa33al, faa3al, fa3lal

Verbs of the forms *fa33al, faa3al,* and *fa3lal* form their imperfective straightforwardly by shifting their second stem vowel from *a* to *e.*

Imperfective			Perfective	
يدرس	*-fa33el*	←	درس	*fa33al*
y-darres			*darras*	
teaches			taught	
يعلي	*-fa33i*	←	علّى	*fa33a*
y-3alli			*3alla*	
raises			raised	

Imperfective			Perfective	
يقاتل *y-2aatel* fights	*-faa3el*	←	قاتل *2aatal* fought	*faa3al*
يعاني *y-3aani* suffers	*-faa3i*	←	عانى *3aana* suffered	*faa3a*
يسشور *y-sashwer* blow-dries	*-fa3lel*	←	سشور *sashwar* blow-dried	*fa3lal*
يفرجي *y-farji* shows	*-fa3lel*	→	فرجى *farja* showed	*fa3la*

staf3al, 2af3al

The forms *staf3al* and *2af3al* are similar in that the main shift is from *a* to *e*. The only difference here is that there are also doubled and hollow stems on these patterns. Again, the pattern is very similar to the *fa3al-yif3el* pairs. Note that the distinctive feature of *2af3al* is the loss of *2a-* in the imperfective stem, making it identical to a simple verb:

Imperfective			Perfective	
يعلن *yi-3len* announces	*-f3el*	←	أعلن *2a3lan* announced	*2af3al*
يقيل *y-qiil* dismisses	*-fiil*	←	أقال *2aqaal* dismissed	*2afaal*
يغري *yi-ghri* seduces	*-f3i*	←	أغرى *2aghra* seduced	*2af3a*
يقر *y-qirr* acknowledges	*-fi33*	←	أقر *2aqarr* acknowledged	*2afall*

Imperfective				Perfective	
يسترجع	*-staf3el*	←		استرجع	*staf3al*
yi-starje3				*starja3*	
retrieves				retrieved	
يستشير	*-stafiil*	←		استشار	*stafaal*
yi-stashiir				*stashaar*	
consults				consulted	
يستولي على	*-staf3i*	←		استولى على	*staf3a*
yi-stawli 3ala				*stawla 3ala*	
takes over				took over	
يستقر	*-stafi33*	←		استقر	*stafall*
yi-staqirr				*staqarr*	
settles				settled	

tfa33al, tfaa3al, tfa3lal

The patterns prefixed with *t-* (*tfa33al, tfaa3al, tfa3lal*) have the same stem in the imperfective as in the perfective:

Imperfective				Perfective	
يتعلم	*-tfa33al*	←		تعلم	*tfa33al*
yi-t3allam				*t3allam*	
learns				learnt	
يتعبى	*-tfa33a*	←		تعبى	*tfa33a*
yi-t3abba				*t3abba*	
is filled				was filled	
يتقارن مع	*-tfaa3al*	←		تقارن	*tfaa3al*
yitqaaran				*tqaaran*	
is compared				was compared	
يتداوى	*-tfaa3a*	←		تداوى	*tfaa3a*
yi-tdaawa				*tdaawa*	
is doctored				was doctored	

Imperfective			Perfective	
يتبهدل	-tfa3lal	←	تبهدل	tfa3lal
yi-tbahdal			*tbahdal*	
gets told off			got told off	
يتفرشى	-tfa3la	←	تفرشى	tfa3la
yi-tfarsha			*tfarsha*	
gets brushed			got brushed	

nfa3al, fta3al

The imperfective of the patterns *nfa3al* and *fta3al* is more complex than that of the other derived verbs. For *sound* and *defective* stem shapes, the most common way of forming the imperfective is to change the two stem vowels to *i* and *e,* respectively. In the absence of suffixes, this creates the kind of environment that normally leads to deletion of short *i* (see unit 4). For many South Levantine and Lebanese speakers, this produces forms such as the following, with or without insertion of a helping vowel [i] (see unit 2):

Imperfective			Perfective	
يشتغل	-ft3el	←	اشتغل	fta3al
yi-shtghel			*shtaghal*	
works			worked	
يلتقي	-ft3i	←	التقى	fta3a
yi-lt2i			*lta2a*	
meets			met	
ينكتب	-n[i]f3el	←	انكتب	nfa3al
yi-n[i]kteb			*nkatab*	
is written			was written	
ينشري	-n[i]f3i	←	انشرى	nfa3a
yi-n[i]shri			*nshara*	
gets bought			got bought	

Once suffixes are added to the sound forms, however, the preconditions for deletion of the first vowel are no longer present. In fact, it is now the *second* vowel that is in the right environment for deletion. This produces pairs such as the following:

يشتغلو   ←   ـو   +   يشتغل

yi-shtighl-u   -u   *yi-shtghel*

they work   [plural]   he works

تتصلي   ←   ـي   +   تتصل

ti-ttiSl-i   -i   *ti-ttSel*

you [F] phone   [feminine]   you [M] phone

In order to maintain consistency throughout the paradigm, some North Levantine speakers—especially Syrian speakers—stress the first syllable of the stem consistently, in violation of the normal stress rules (see unit 2). This removes the need to delete the *i* in this syllable and produces stems such as the following:

Imperfective			Perfective	
يشتغل *-fti3el*	←	اشتغل *fta3al*		
yi-shtighel		*shtaghal*		
works		worked		
يلتقي *-fti3i*	←	التقى *fta3a*		
yi-lti2i		*lta2a*		
meets		met		
ينكتب *-nfi3el*	←	انكتب *nfa3al*		
yi-nkiteb		*nkatab*		
is written		was written		
ينشري *-nfi3i*	←	انشرى *nfa3a*		
yi-nshiri		*nshara*		
gets bought		got bought		

A few verbs whose perfective stem is *fta3a* have the same stem in the imperfective. The most common is التقى *lta2a* "be found" or "meet":

يلتقى *-fta3a*   ←   التقى *fta3a*

yi-lta2a   *lta2a*

gets found   got found

Both *nfa3al* and *nfa3a* can similarly form imperfectives with the same stem as the perfective. This is particularly common in Lebanon, but you may hear it elsewhere with some verbs:

ينكتب   *-nfa3al*   ←   انكتب   *nfa3al*

yi-nkatab   *nkatab*

is written   was written

ينشرى   *-nfa3a*   ←   انشرى   *nfa3a*

yi-nshara   *nshara*

gets bought   got bought

> Note that for those speakers who stress the first syllable of the stem with *-fti3el* and *-fti3i*, the middle syllable is generally stressed here as well.

The hollow and doubled stem shapes on these patterns invariably form their imperfective on the same stem as the perfective. There is no *i-e* stem available for these verbs:

Imperfective		Perfective	
يحتار *-ftaal*	←	احتار	*ftaal*
yi-7taar		*7taar*	
gets confused		got confused	
يحتل *-fta33*	←	احتل	*fta33*
yi-7tall		*7tall*	
occupies		occupied	
ينشال *-nfaal*	←	انشال	*nfaal*
yi-nshaal		*nshaal*	
gets removed		got removed	
ينكب *-nfa33*	←	انكب	*nfa33*
yi-nkabb		*nkabb*	
gets thrown out		got thrown out	

Complications with Prefixes and Suffixes

The most difficult part of forming the imperfective from derived verbs is indisputably identifying the stem. The prefixes and suffixes are much better behaved than the perfective suffixes are, and the complications that present with different kinds of simple stems are totally absent.

Derived verbs use the same two sets of prefixes as simple verbs: one set for stems beginning with a single consonant and one set for stems beginning with a cluster:

SINGLE-CONSONANT		CLUSTER	
North Levantine	**South Levantine**	**North Levantine**	**South Levantine**
قاتل *2aatel* I fight	أقاتل *2a-2aatel* I fight	استقيل *2i-staqiil* I resign	أستقيل *2a-staqiil* I resign
تقاتل *t-2aatel* you [M] fight		تستقيل *ti-staqiil* you [M] resign	
يقاتل *y-2aatel* he fights		يستقيل *yi-staqiil* he resigns	
نقاتل *n-2aatel* we fight		نستقيل *ni-staqiil* we resign	

The suffixes (*-i* and *-u*) are likewise identical to those used with simple verbs. These cause deletion of a stem-final vowel (i.e., *a* or *i* in defective stems):

Stem Ends in *-i*		**Stem Ends in *-a***	
استرجي *2i-starji/2a-starji* I dare		اتقاوى على *2i-t2aawa/2a-t2aawa 3ala* I lord it over	
تسترجي *ti-starj-i* you [F] dare	تسترجي *ti-starji* you [M] dare	تتقاوي على *ti-t2aaw-i 3ala* you [F] lord it over	تتقاوى على *ti-t2aawa 3ala* you [M] lord it over
تسترجي *ti-starji* she dares	يسترجي *yi-starji* he dares	تتقاوى على *ti-t2aawa 3ala* she lords it over	يتقاوى على *yi-t2aawa 3ala* he lords it over
نسترجي *ni-starji* we dare		نتقاوى على *ni-t2aawa 3ala* we lord it over	

Stem Ends in *-i*	Stem Ends in *-a*
تسترجو *ti-starj-u* you [P] dare	تتقاوو على *ti-t2aaw-u 3ala* you [P] lord it over
يسترجو *yi-starj-u* they dare	يتقاوو على *yi-t2aaw-u 3ala* they lord it over

Other than this, the only notable complication is for those speakers who have regular *i*-deletion in *fta3al/nfa3al* verbs. These speakers alternate between forms with the first stem vowel deleted (without suffixes) and forms with the second stem vowel deleted (with suffixes). Compare with the forms on the left, which are distinctively North Levantine:

Irregular Stress		i-Deletion	
التزم *2i-ltizem* I commit		التزم *2i-ltzem/2a-ltzem* I commit	
تلتزمي *ti-ltizm-i* you [F] commit	تلتزم *ti-ltizem* you [M] commit	تلتزمي *ti-ltizm-i* you [F] commit	تلتزم *ti-ltzem* you [M] commit
تلتزم *ti-ltizem* she commits	يلتزم *yi-ltizem* he commits	تلتزم *ti-ltzem* she commits	يلتزم *yi-ltzem* he commits
نلتزم *ni-ltizem* we commit		نلتزم *ni-ltzem* we commit	
تلتزمو *ti-ltizm-u* you [P] commit		تلتزمو *ti-ltizm-u* you [P] commit	
يلتزمو *yi-ltizm-u* they commit		يلتزمو *yi-ltizm-u* they commit	

UNIT 28

The Imperative

The last major set of verbal forms that we need to be familiar with is the *imperative*. The imperative is used for giving orders or instructions:

بعدي هيك!	نضف البيت!
ba33di heek!	*naDDef ⁱlbeet!*
get out of my way!	clean the house!

As with the corresponding English form, the imperative is quite a direct way of achieving this end. There are many other ways of telling people what to do (or asking them to do something). In this unit, however, we will be looking mainly at how to *form* the imperative rather than its usage. We will discuss its usage in more detail in unit 43.

We will begin by giving a brief overview of the imperative suffixes. We will then look at how these interact with different types of verb stem.

The Imperative Suffixes

Unlike the perfective and the imperfective, the imperative has only three distinct forms: masculine singular, feminine singular, and plural. All of these have explicitly *second-person* reference (i.e., they refer to the addressee). The masculine has no suffix, the feminine has the suffix *-i*, and the plural has the suffix *-u*. As you can see, these forms correspond exactly to the equivalent imperfective forms:

Imperative		Imperfective
تذكر	←	تتذكر
tzakkar		*ti-tzakkar*
remember [M]!		you [M] remember

Imperative	Imperfective
تذكري ←	تتذكري
tzakkar-i	*ti-tzakkar-i*
remember [F]!	you [F] remember
تذكرو ←	تتذكرو
tzakkar-u	*ti-tzakkar-u*
remember [P]!	you [P] remember

Since these suffixes are fairly well behaved and since we have already looked at how they combine with different types of stems in unit 26, we won't go into any more detail here except to note again that these suffixes cause all the general changes discussed in unit 4 (deletion of final vowels, deletion of short *i/e* and *u/o*, etc.).

Simple Verbs

Simple verbs—that is, "nonderived" verbs—are, as usual, more complicated than their derived counterparts.

With sound-simple verbs, there is major regional variation. In North Levantine, the stem is used on its own, with the vowel lengthened in the masculine singular. Note that the addition of the suffixes *-i* and *-u* causes the normal shift from *e/o* to *i*:

Imperative (North Levantine)				Stem
شربو	شربي	شراب ←		يشرب
shrab-u	*shrab-i*	*shraab*		*yi-shrab*
drink [P]!	drink [F]!	drink [M]!		drinks
مسكو	مسكي	مسيك ←		يمسك
msik-u	*msik-i*	*mseek*		*yi-msek*
grab [P]!	grab [F]!	grab [M]!		grabs
كتبو	كتبي	كتوب ←		يكتب
ktib-u	*ktib-i*	*ktoob*		*yi-ktob*
write [P]!	write [F]!	write [M]!		writes

In South Levantine, on the other hand, these forms take the prefix ا, whose pronunciation depends on the stem vowel: *2i-* if the stem vowel is *e* or *a* and *2u-* if it is *o*. This is the same behaviour as the imperfective prefix (see unit 26):

Imperative (South Levantine)				Stem
اشربو	اشربي	اشرب	←	يشرب
2i-shrab-u	*2i-shrab-i*	*2i-shrab*		*yi-shrab*
drink [P]!	drink [F]!	drink [M]!		drinks
امسكو	امسكي	امسك	←	يمسك
2i-msik-u	*2i-msik-i*	*2i-msek*		*yi-msek*
grab [P]!	grab [F]!	grab [M]!		grabs
اكتبو	اكتبي	اكتب	←	يكتب
2u-ktub-u	*2u-ktub-i*	*2u-ktob*		*yu-ktob*
write [P]!	write [F]!	write [M]!		writes

For many Palestinian speakers, an alternative prefix ـه *hi/hu-* is used with stems beginning with a glottal stop in order to avoid two glottal stops appearing in close succession: هقعد *hu-23od* "sit!"

Defective verbs—those ending in a vowel—exhibit similar variation. As in the imperfective, however, the stem vowel is deleted when suffixes are added. As a result, the lengthening is transferred to the *suffix* vowel:

Imperative (North Levantine)				Stem
نسو	نسي	نسا	←	ينسى
ns-uu	*ns-ii*	*nsaa*		*yi-nsa*
forget [P]!	forget [F]!	forget [M]!		forgets
حكو	حكي	حكي	←	يحكي
7k-uu	*7k-ii*	*7kii*		*yi-7ki*
speak [P]!	speak [F]!	speak [M]!		speaks

The prefix forms, on the other hand, are straightforward. Note that these forms are commonly used by many North Levantine speakers as well, especially Syrians:

Imperative (South Levantine)				Stem
انسو	انسي	انسا	←	ينسى
2i-ns-u	*2i-ns-i*	*2i-nsa*		*yi-nsa*
forget [P]!	forget [F]!	forget [M]!		forgets

Imperative (South Levantine)				Stem
احكو	احكي	احكي	←	يحكي
2i-7k-u	*2i-7k-i*	*2i-7ki*		*yi-7ki*
speak [P]!	speak [F]!	speak [M]!		speaks

Hollow verbs are more straightforward. In this case, the imperfective stem is simply used on its own without any prefix:

Imperative Forms				Stem
قولو	قولي	قول	←	يقول
2uul-u	*2uul-i*	*2uul*		*y-2uul*
say [P]!	say [F]!	say [M]!		says
شيلو	شيلي	شيل	←	يشيل
shiil-u	*shiil-i*	*shiil*		*y-shiil*
remove [P]!	remove [F]!	remove [M]!		removes
نامو	نامي	نام	←	ينام
naam-u	*naam-i*	*naam*		*y-naam*
go to sleep [P]!	go to sleep [F]!	go to sleep [M]!		sleeps

The verbs أخد *2akhad* "take" and أكل *2akal* "eat"—which also have irregular imperfectives (see unit 26)—have unusual imperatives that drop the initial glottal stop. Both South and North Levantine speakers have lengthening in the masculine singular here. Note the vowel shift to *i* for North Levantine speakers (see unit 4):

أكل		أخد	
2akal		*2akhad*	
eat		take	
كلي	كول	خدي	خود
kil-i/kul-i	*kool*	*khid-i/khud-i*	*khood*
eat [F]!	eat [M]!	take [F]!	take [M]!
كلو		خدو	
kil-u/kul-u		*khid-u/khud-u*	
eat [P]!		take [P]!	

For many Syrian speakers, قعد *2a3ad* "sit" patterns with these verbs: عود *3ood* "sit [M]!"

The verb اجا/اجا *2ija/2aja* "come," a highly irregular verb, has the imperative stem تعال *ta3aal*, تع *ta3*, or تعا *ta3a*, which form masculines and feminines regularly:

تعي	تع	تعالي	تعال
ta3-i	*ta3*	*ta3aal-i*	*ta3aal*
come [F]!	come [M]!	come [F]!	come [M]!
تعو		تعالو	
ta3-u		*ta3aal-u*	
come [P]!		come [P]!	

Derived Verbs

Derived verbs are much more straightforward. For North Levantine speakers, the imperfective stem is simply used as is, with the feminine and plural suffixes added as you would expect. A few examples should be enough to demonstrate the point:

North Levantine			
تعاملو ←	يتعامل	درس ←	يدرس
t3aamal-u	*yi-t3aamal*	*darres*	*y-darres*
deal with [P]!	deal with	teach [M]!	teaches
افتعل ←	يفتعل	قاتلي ←	يقاتل
fti3el	*yi-fti3el*	*2aatl-i*	*y-2aatel*
fabricate [M]!	fabricates	fight [F]!	fights
استمري ←	يستمر	قوو ←	يقوي
stamirr-i	*yi-stamirr*	*2aww-u*	*y-2awwi*
continue [F]!	continues	strengthen [P]	strengthen

For South Levantine speakers, stems beginning with a single consonant behave similarly, as do the forms *tfa33al* and *tfaa3al*. But *fta3al*, *nfa3al*, and *staf3al* verbs take the prefix ا *2i-*:

South Levantine			
تعاملو ← يتعامل *t3aamal-u* — *yi-t3aamal* deal with [P]! — deal with		درس ← يدرس *darres* — *y-darres* teach [M]! — teaches	
افتعل ← يفتعل *2i-ft3el* — *yi-ft3el* fabricate [M]! — fabricates		قاتلي ← يقاتل *2aatl-i* — *y-2aatel* fight [F]! — fights	
استمري ← يستمر *2i-stamirr-i* — *yi-stamirr* continue [F] — continues		قوو ← يقوي *2aww-u* — *y-2awwi* strengthen [P]! — strengthen	

The Active Participle

In this unit we will be looking at the *active participle*. Although derived from verbs, active participles occupy an ambiguous middle ground between verb and adjective/noun. While having subjects and taking objects—and often translating an English verb—they are "conjugated" using the same set of suffixes that adjectives are.

The active participle has a range of different meanings that we will look at in more detail below. In this unit, however, we will be looking mainly at how it is formed.

Active Participles from Simple Verbs

Most simple verbs' active participles are formed on the pattern *faa3el*, which has the predictable hollow and defective counterparts *faayel* and *faa3i*:

ضارب	← ضرب		كاتب	← كتب
Daareb	*Darab*		*kaateb*	*katab*
has hit	to hit		has written	to write

ساطي	← سطا		حاكي	← حكى
saaTi	*saTa*		*7aaki*	*7aka*
has burgled	to burgle		has spoken	to speak

صاير	← صار		قايل	← قال
Saayer	*Saar*		*2aayel*	*2aal*
has become	to become		has said	to say

Note that the hollow form is *faayel* even if the middle root letter is *w*. There are no participles with the form *faawel*.

For most speakers, doubled roots act exactly like sound roots. But an occasional alternative, especially in Jordanian, is to delete the *i*, producing clusters such as the following:

حاس   OR   حاسس   ←   حس
7aass   *7aases*   *7ass*
feels   feels   to feel

كاب   OR   كابب   ←   كب
kaabb   *kaabeb*   *kabb*
has thrown away   has thrown away   to throw away

Note that for many speakers, the verb ضل *Dall* "to stay" (see unit 40) has an irregular participle:

ضايل   OR   ضالل   ←   ضل
Daayel   *Daalel*   *Dall*
staying   staying   to stay

> For a refresher on the various types of root, see units 5–6.

Some simple participles are formed on a different pattern altogether: *fa3laan*.

طولان   ←   طول   نعسان   ←   نعس
Tawlaan   *Tiwel*   *na3saan*   *ni3es*
has got long[er]   to get long[er]   sleepy   to get sleepy

غليان   ←   غلي   غيران   ←   غار
ghalyaan   *ghili*   *ghayraan*   *ghaar*
has got [more]   to get [more]   jealous   to feel jealous
expensive   expensive

This is particularly common with change-of-state verbs. Examples such as those above have participles on *fa3laan* throughout the Levantine area. But North Levantine and particularly Syrian have extended the pattern further. With North Levantine speakers, you are likely to encounter forms such as those on the left alongside those on the right:

General		North Levantine	
شارب	قابل	شربان	قبلان
shaareb	*2aabel*	*sharbaan*	*2ablaan*
has drunk	accepts	has drunk	accepts

General		North Levantine	
عارف *3aaref* knows		عرفان *3arfaan* knows	

Participles from Derived Verbs

Derived verbs largely have predictable active participles. For the most part, they are formed from the imperfective stem by addition of the prefix ـم *mi-* (before consonant clusters) or *m-* (before a single consonant):

Participle	Imperfective	Perfective
معلم ← *m-3allem* has taught	يعلم ← *y-3allem* teaches	علم *3allam* taught
مقوي ← *m-2awwi* has strengthened	يقوي ← *y-2awwi* strengthens	قوى *2awwa* strengthened
مشارك ← *m-shaarek* has partnered with	يشارك ← *y-shaarek* partners with	شارك *shaarak* partnered with
محاكي ← *m-7aaki* has talked to	يحاكي ← *y-7aaki* talks to	حاكى *7aaka* talked to
معلن ← *mi-3len* has announced	يعلن ← *yi-3len* announces	أعلن *2a3lan* announced
مغري ← *mi-ghri* has seduced	يغري ← *yi-ghri* tempts, seduces	أغرى *2aghra* tempted, seduced
محمر ← *mi-7marr* has turned red	يحمر ← *yi-7marr* turns red	احمر *7marr* turned red

Participle	Imperfective	Perfective
مستخدم ←	← يستخدم	استخدم
mi-stakhdem	*yi-stakhdem*	*stakhdam*
has used	uses	used
مستغلي ←	← يستغلي	استغلى
mi-staghli	*yi-staghli*	*staghla*
has deemed expensive	deems expensive	deemed expensive
مستقيل ←	← يستقيل	استقال
mi-staqiil	*yi-staqiil*	*staqaal*
has resigned	resigns	resigned
مستمر ←	← يستمر	استمر
mi-stamirr	*yi-stamirr*	*stamarr*
continuing	continues	continued
مسشور ←	← يسشور	سشور
m-sashwer	*y-sashwer*	*sashwar*
has blow-dried	blow-dries	blow-dried
مفرشي ←	← يفرشي	فرشى
m-farshi	*y-farshi*	*farsha*
has brushed	brushes	brushed

Some North Levantine speakers use what appear to be passive participle forms as active participles with some words: مسافر *msaafar* "travelling," مغير *mghayyar* "having changed," and so on.

The patterns *tfa33al*, *tfaa3al*, and *tfa3lal* behave slightly differently. Because vowellings in *a* are associated with the *passive* participle (see unit 30), they cannot use the unmodified imperfective stem. To form their participle, they change the last *a* to *e* and then use the prefix *mi-*:

Participle	Imperfective	Perfective
متعلم ←	← يتعلم	تعلم
mi-t3allem	*yi-t3allam*	*t3allam*
has learned	learns	learnt

Participle		Imperfective		Perfective
متقوي	←	يتقوى	←	تقوى
mi-t2awwi		yi-t2awwa		t2awwa
has been strengthened		is strengthened		was strengthened
متعامل	←	يتعامل	←	تعامل
mi-t3aamel		yi-t3aamal		t3aamal
has dealt [with]		deals [with]		dealt [with]
متداوي	←	يتداوى	←	تداوى
mi-tdaawi		yi-tdaawa		tdaawa
has been doctored		is doctored		was doctored
متسشور	←	يتسشور	←	تسشور
mi-tsashwer		yi-tsashwar		tsashwar
has been blow-dried		is blow-dried		was blow-dried
متفرشي	←	يتفرشى	←	تفرشى
mi-tfarshi		yi-tfarsha		tfarsha
has been brushed		is brushed		was brushed

The active participles of *nfa3al* and *fta3al* verbs deserve special attention. These verbs form their participle straightforwardly from the imperfective stem by prefixing *mi-*. But because there is some variation in how these stems are formed (see unit 27), there is also variation in the exact form of the participle. The variation, between speakers who apply regular vowel deletion and speakers who do not, is carried over into the participle:

Participle		Imperfective		Perfective
منكتب	←	ينكتب	←	انكتب
mi-nⁱkteb		yi-nⁱkteb		nkatab
has been written		is written		was written
منكتب	←	ينكتب	←	
mi-n**ki**teb		yi-n**ki**teb		
has been written		is written		
ملتزم	←	يلتزم	←	التزم
mi-ltzem		yi-ltzem		ltazam
has committed		commits		commited

Participle	Imperfective	Perfective
ملتزم ←	يلتزم ←	
mi-ltizem	*yi-ltizem*	
has committed	commits	

Hollow and doubled verbs on these patterns (*nfaal, ftaal, nfa33,* and *fta33*) do not exhibit this variation. Their imperfective stems, and thus their active participles, all have *a*:

Participle	Imperfective	Perfective
محتار ←	يحتار ←	احتار
mi-7taar	*yi-7taar*	*7taar*
confused	gets confused	was confused
محتل ←	يحتل ←	احتل
mi-7tall	*yi-7tall*	*7tall*
occupying	occupies	occupied
منشال ←	ينشال ←	انشال
mi-nshaal	*yi-nshaal*	*nshaal*
has got removed	gets removed	got removed
منكب ←	ينكب ←	انكب
mi-nkabb	*yi-nkabb*	*nkabb*
has got thrown out	gets thrown out	got thrown out

Feminine and Plural Forms

All participles form their feminine and plural forms regularly using the suffixes ـة *-a/e* (see unit 8) and ـين *-iin,* respectively. These suffixes cause the usual expected changes (see unit 4). A few examples should demonstrate the point:

كاتبين	كاتبة	كاتب
kaatb-iin	*kaatb-e*	*kaateb*
have written	has written [F]	has written [M]

شايفين	شايفة	شايف
shaayf-iin	*shaayf-e*	*shaayef*
have seen	has seen [F]	has seen [M]

مشارطين	مشارطة	مشارط
mshaarT-iin	*mshaarT-a*	*mshaareT*
have bet	has bet [F]	has bet [M]

متقويين	متقوية	متقوي
mit2awwy-iin	*mit2awwy-e*	*mit2awwi*
have been strengthened	has been strengthened [F]	has been strengthened [M]

> Some South Levantine speakers also have an optional feminine plural in ات -aat (see unit 50): كاتبات *kaatb-aat* and so on.

Objects and Object Pronouns

One of the ways in which active participles are like verbs is that they can take objects straight-forwardly (see unit 52):

كاتب مقالة	←	مقالة	+	كاتب
kaateb maqaale		*maqaale*		*kaateb*
has written [M] an article		article		has written [M]

ضاربة أخوها	←	أخوها	+	ضاربة
Daarbe 2akhuuha		*2akhuuha*		*Daarb-e*
has hit [F] her brother		her brother		has hit [F]

شايفين الولد	←	الولد	+	شايفين
shaayfiin ᵢlwalad		*ᵢlwalad*		*shaayf-iin*
have seen [P] the boy		the boy		have seen

When a participle takes a *pronoun* object, however, there are complications to be aware of. A pronoun object is expressed using the attached pronouns (see unit 18), as we would expect. With the plural and the masculine singular, these behave more or less predictably. Note that *-ni* is used for "me":

كاتبو	←	ـو	+	كاتب
kaatb-o		*-o*		*kaateb*
has written it		it		has written [M]

شايفينها ← ـها + شايفين

shaayf-iin-ha   *-ha*   *shaayf-iin*

have seen her   her   have seen

معلمك ← ـك + معلم

m3allm-ak   *-ak*   *m3allem*

has taught you   you [M]   has taught [M]

مشاركينني ← ـني + مشاركين

mshaarkiin-ni   *-ni*   *mshaark-iin*

have partnered with me   me   have partnered with

With feminine forms, however, there are two major complications. First, as you might expect, ـة *-a/e* takes a form with *-t-* when pronoun suffixes are added (see units 8 and 18). But exactly what forms are used varies from region to region and speaker to speaker.

The most straightforward pattern is to treat this *-e* like any other, resulting in a different set of forms depending on whether the pronoun suffix begins with a consonant or a vowel. Suffixes beginning with vowels attach to the form *faa3il-t-*, and suffixes beginning with consonants attach to the form *faa3l-it-*:

ضاربتنا *Daarb-it-na* she's hit us	ضاربتني *Daarb-it-ni* she's hit me

ضاربتكن *Daarb-it-kon* she's hit you [P]	ضاربتك *Daarib-t-ek* she's hit you [F]	ضاربتك *Daarib-t-ak* she's hit you [M]
ضاربتهن *Daarb-it-(h)on* she's hit them	ضاربتها *Daarb-it-(h)a* she's hit her	ضاربتو *Daarib-t-o* she's hit him

> I use "she" here in the gloss for the sake of simplicity. These forms can have a range of meanings, including "I've hit" and "they've hit."

Forms such as these can be found across the Levantine area, with the relevant changes to the form of the pronoun (*-kom* for *-kon*, *-hom* for *-hon*, etc.). But there has been a tendency in many areas to regularise the form of the participle so that it stays consistent no matter what suffixes are applied. One possibility, common in Syria and South Levantine, is to use the *faa3ilt-* form (i.e., with *-t-*, not *-it-*) consistently even when this produces an unusual cluster:

ضاربتنا *Daarib-t-na* she's hit us		ضاربتني *Daarib-t-ni* she's hit me	
ضاربتكم *Daarib-t-kom* she's hit you [P]	ضاربتك *Daarib-t-ek* she's hit you [F]	ضاربتك *Daarib-t-ak* she's hit you [M]	
ضاربتهم *Daarib-t-hom* she's hit them	ضاربتها *Daarib-t-ha* she's hit her	ضاربتو *Daarib-t-o* she's hit him	

Another possibility is to use the form *faa3l-it-* everywhere, keeping irregular stress on the *i* where a suffix beginning with a vowel is added:

ضاربتنا *Daarb-it-na* she's hit us		ضاربتني *Daarb-it-ni* she's hit me	
ضاربتكن *Daarb-it-kon* she's hit you [P]	ضاربتك *Daarb-__it__-ek* she's hit you [F]	ضاربتك *Daarb-__it__-ak* she's hit you [M]	
ضاربتهن *Daarb-it-(h)on* she's hit them	ضاربتها *Daarb-it-(h)a* she's hit her	ضاربتو *Daarb-__it__-o* she's hit him	

A variation on this is to use a form with a long vowel (*-iit*) everywhere:

ضاربيتنا *Daarb-iit-na* she's hit us		ضاربيتني *Daarb-iit-ni* she's hit me	
ضاربيتكن *Daarb-iit-kon* she's hit you [P]	ضاربيتك *Daarb-iit-ek* she's hit you [F]	ضاربيتك *Daarb-iit-ak* she's hit you [M]	

ضاربيتهن	ضاربيتها	ضاربيتو
Daarb-iit-(h)on	*Daarb-iit-(h)a*	*Daarb-iit-o*
she's hit them	she's hit her	she's hit him

One final alternative—found among some South Levantine speakers—is to consistently use the form *-faa3l-aa-* with suffixes, dispensing with the *-t-* entirely:

ضاربانا		ضارباني
Darb-aa-na		*Darb-aa-ni*
she's hit us		she's hit me
ضارباكم	ضارباكي	ضارباك
Darb-aa-kom	*Darb-aa-ki*	*Darb-aa-k*
she's hit you [P]	she's hit you [F]	she's hit you [M]
ضارباهم	ضارباها	ضاربا
Darb-aa-hom	*Darb-aa-(h)a*	*Darb-aa*
she's hit them	she's hit her	she's hit him

You are likely to encounter all of these forms at some point. Imitate what you hear around you.

The other complication is that when a feminine participle with an object suffix has second-person singular reference ("you [F]"), the form is invariably *faa3il-**tii**-*, with an *-ii-* inserted between the *-t* and the pronoun suffix. This produces a person contrast:

ضاربتيني BUT	ضاربتني
Daaribt-ii-ni	*Daarbit-ni*
you [F] have hit me	she's hit me
معلمتيها BUT	معلمتها
m3allimt-ii-ha	*m3allmit-ha*
you [F] have taught her	she's taught her

The Passive Participle

In unit 29 we looked at how to form the active participle, which plays a key role in the Arabic tense system. In this unit we will look at its less significant cousin, the *passive participle*. This is basically an adjective similar to the adjective use of the English past participle ("X-ed") and has none of the verbal qualities of its active counterpart. The passive participle is also simpler to form. We will start with simple verbs' participles before moving on to the participles of derived verbs. We will then consider a few important points about structure.

Simple Verbs

Simple (underived) verbs are the most complicated. Sound and doubled verbs form their passive participle on *maf3uul:*

معروف ← عرف		مكتوب ← كتب	
ma3ruuf 3iref		*maktuub* katab	
known to know		written to write	
مسموم ← سم		مغشوش ← غش	
masmuum samm		*maghshuush* ghashsh	
poisoned to poison		adulterated to adulterate	
مأكول ← أكل		مأخود ← أخد	
ma2kuul 2akal		*ma2khuud* 2akhad	
eaten to eat		taken to take	

Defective simple verbs have slightly different forms in North and South Levantine. The patterns are مفعي *mif3i* and مفعي *maf3i,* respectively:

North Levantine	South Levantine		Verb
محكي *mi7ki* spoken	محكي *ma7ki* spoken	←	حكى *7aka* to speak
منسي *minsi* forgotten	منسي *mansi* forgotten	←	نسي *nisi* to forget
مسطي *misTi* burgled	مسطي *masTi* burgled	←	سطا *saTa* to burgle

Note that when suffixes are added, the *-i* here becomes *-iyy* (see unit 9):

منسيين   منسية ← منسي

mansiyy-iin   *mansiyy-e*   *mansi*

forgotten [P]   forgotten [F]   forgotten [M]

محكيين   محكية ← محكي

mi7kiyy-iin   *mi7kiyy-e*   *mi7ki*

spoken [P]   spoken [F]   spoken [M]

Hollow simple verbs vary. For many speakers they simply cannot form a passive participle, and a form derived from their passive verb counterpart (generally *minfaal*, see units 23 and 57) is used instead. But for those speakers who do allow a participle, the pattern is generally *mafyuul*:

مزيود ← زاد   مبيوع ← باع

mazyuud   *zaad*   *mabyuu3*   *baa3*

increased   to increase   sold   to sell

Derived Verbs

There are a few complications with derived verbs. Those stems that begin with a single consonant basically correspond to the active participle (see unit 29), with the vowel in the final syllable changed to *a* where necessary:

Passive Participle		Active Participle	Verb
مدرس *m-darras* [has been] taught	←	مدرس *m-darres* has taught	درس *darras* teach
مخبى *m-khabba* [has been] hidden	←	مخبي *m-khabbi* has hidden	خبى *khabba* hide
مشارك *m-shaarak* [has been] partnered with	←	مشارك *m-shaarek* has partnered with	شارك *shaarak* partner with
محاكى *m7aaka* [has been] spoken to	←	محاكي *m7aaki* has spoken to	حاكى *7aaka* speak to
مسشور *m-sashwar* [has been] blow-dried	←	مسشور *m-sashwer* has blow-dried	سشور *sashwar* blow-dry
مفرشى *m-farsha* [has been] brushed	←	مفرشي *m-farshi* has brushed	فرشى *farsha* brush

Stems that begin with a consonant cluster, however, behave differently in North and South Levantine. Although both sets of dialects show the same final vowel shift to *a*, North Levantine uses the prefix *mi-* (as in the active participle), while South Levantine uses the prefix *mu-*:

North Levantine	South Levantine	Verb
معلن *mi-3lan* [has been] announced	معلن *mu-3lan* [has been] announced	أعلن *2a3lan* to announce
مغرى *mi-ghra* [has been] seduced	مغرى *mu-ghra* [has been] seduced	أغرى *2aghra* to tempt, to seduce

North Levantine	South Levantine	Verb
مستخدم *mi-stakhdam* [has been] used	مستخدم *mu-stakhdam* [has been] used	استخدم *stakhdam* to use
مستغنى (عنو) *mi-staghna (3anno)* [has been] dispensed with	مستغنى (عنو) *mu-staghna (3anno)* [has been] dispensed with	استغنى عن *staghna 3an* to dispense with
مستشار *mi-stashaar* [has been] consulted	مستشار *mu-stashaar* [has been] consulted	استشار *stashaar* to consult
مستمر *mi-stamarr* [has been] continued	مستمر *mu-stamarr* [has been] continued	استمر *stamarr* to continue
متعربط *mi-t3arbaT* [has been] clambered on	متعربط *mi-t3arbaT* [has been] clambered on	تعربط *t3arbaT* to clamber

The participles of sound and defective *fta3al* verbs, which you will remember caused us problems in the active participle, have *a-a* in the last two syllables:

North Levantine	South Levantine		Verb
مفتعل *mi-fta3al* fabricated	مفتعل *mu-fta3al* fabricated	←	افتعل *fta3al* to fabricate
مشترى *mi-shtara* bought	مشترى *mu-shtara* bought	←	اشترى *shtara* to buy

The patterns *tfa33al*, *tfaa3al*, and *nfa3al*, which are overwhelmingly passive or intransitive (see unit 29) in meaning, do not generally have passive participles. If forced to use them, speakers will often fall back on the fuS7a forms (*mutafa33al, mutafaa3al, munfa3al*). FuS7a passive participles are also commonly found in use as adjectives (see unit 16).

In parts of Syria and Lebanon, some participles with apparently passive shapes are used as active participles: مغيّر *mghayyar* "has changed," مسافر *msaafar* "is travelling," and so on.

Notes on Structure

You might imagine that verbs that cannot take an object would not be able to form a passive participle. But this is not quite true, because participles can also refer to nondirect objects in (slightly elaborate) constructions such as the following:

الملف المستشار فيه ← استشرتو بالملف

'lmalaff 'lmustashaar fii ← *stasharto bilmalaff*

the file [that was] consulted on ← I asked him about the file

الشارع الممشي فيه ← بمشي بالشارع

'shshaare3 'lmamshi fii ← *bimshi bishshaare3*

the street [that is] walked in ← I walk in the street

Note that in these circumstances the participle itself defaults to masculine, and the "agreement," such as it is, is provided by a pronoun on the preposition:

القضية محكوم فيها ← حكمو بالقضية

'l2aDiyye ma7kuum fiiha ← *7akamu bil2aDiyye*

the case has been judged ← they judged the case

الشباب المحكي عنهم ← حكو عن الشباب

'shshabaab 'lma7ki 3anhom ← *7aku 3an 'shshabaab*

the guys [who were] spoken about ← they talked about the guys

For more on this, see unit 57.

Note that passive participles can take the *-l-* suffix (see unit 19) and that this results in shortening of the vowel in *maf3uul* forms:

مسمحلي أروح ← سمحولي أروح

masmu7-li 2aruu7 ← *sama7uuli 2aruu7*

I'm allowed to go ← they allowed me to go

maSdars

In this unit we will look at the *maSdar* and (briefly) the noun of instance. These are noun forms derived from verbs and refer, broadly speaking, to the action expressed by the verb from which they are derived. The closest equivalent to the *maSdar* in English is generally a gerund, the "-ing" form we see in constructions such as "dancing is good for you." As we will see, it also—to a lesser extent—is used as a counterpart to the English infinitive.

I will begin by explaining how the *maSdar* and the noun of instance are derived. We will then consider how they are used, first as a translation of the English gerund and then of the infinitive.

Derivation of the *maSdar*

As noted above, almost all verbs have a *maSdar*, which corresponds to the English gerund form in "-ing." Unfortunately for learners, *maSdar*s are formed using a range of patterns (see unit 5), and which pattern a given verb uses is generally not predictable and to some extent varies from region to region. This means that as a rule, you will have to learn a verb with its *maSdar*.

As usual, "simple" (underived) verbs present the most complications, and all we can do here is give a very broad sense of the patterns that are used. The most common pattern is *fa3l* or *fi3l/fu3l*:

ضرب ← ضرب		نوم ← نام	
Dar^e b *Darab*		*noom* *naam*	
hitting to hit		sleeping to sleep	
فت ← فت		مشي ← مشي	
fatt *fatt*		*mashi* *mishi*	
dealing to deal [cards]		walking to walk	
شرب ← شرب		شيب ← شاب	
shir^e b/shur^o b *shireb*		*sheeb* *shaab*	
drinking to drink		going grey to go grey	

Some other common-ish possibilities include *fa3aal, fa3al, f3uul, fa3alaan, fa3iil/f3iil,* and *f(i)3aale*:

عطا ← أعطى	نجاح ← نجح
3aTa 2a3Ta	najaa7 nije7
giving to give	succeeding to succeed
فشل ← فشل	طلب ← طلب
fashal fishel	Talab Talab
failure to fail	requesting to request
طلوع ← طلع	نزول ← نزل
Tluu3 Tile3	nzuul nizel
going up to go up	going down to go down
دوران ← دار	طيران ← طار
dawaraan daar	Tayaraan Taar
turning to turn	flying to fly
الرحيل ← رحل	ركيض ← ركض
ʾrra7iil ra7al	rkiiD rakaD
leaving to leave	running to run
قراية ← قرى	دراسة ← درس
2raaye 2ara	diraase daras
reading to read	studying to study

> The pattern *fa3al* is relatively uncommon as a *maSdar* but is quite common as a noun pattern: عرق *3ara2* "sweat," طلب *Talab* "a request," "a form."

For derived verbs, the *maSdar* is generally more predictable. Most of the derivational patterns have one or two associated *maSdar* patterns, shown in the following table. Note that for the most part, passive and reciprocal verbs (see unit 23)—that is, *tfa33al, tfaa3al,* and *nfa3al* in particular—use the *maSdar*s of their nonpassive counterpart, meaning that forms like *tafaa3ol, tafa33ol,* and *2infi3aal* are more common as fuS7aisms.

تغيير ← تغير	تعليم ← تعلم
taghyiir tghayyar	ta3liim t3allam
change to be changed	learning to learn

انفتح	←	فتح		تفاوض	←	مفاوضة
nfata7		*fat⁶7*		*tfaawaD*		*mfaawaDa*
to be opened		opening		to negotiate		negotiating

maSdar		Verb Type
FuS7a Form	**Inherited Form**	**Verb Type**
تفعيل *taf3iil*		فعّل *fa33al*
تفعية *taf3iye*	تفعاية *tif3aaye*	فعّل *fa33al*
مفاعلة *mufaa3ale*	مفاعلة *mfaa3ale*	فاعل *faa3al*
إفعال *2if3aal*		أفعل *2af3al*
تفعل *tafa33ol*		تفعل *tfa33al*
تفاعل *tafaa3ol*		تفاعل *tfaa3al*
انفعال *2infi3aal*		انفعل *nfa3al*
افتعال *2ifti3aal*		افتعل *fta3al*
افعلال *2if3ilaal*		افعل *f3all*
استفعال *2istif3aal*		استفعل *staf3al*
فعللة *fa3lale*		فعلل *fa3lal*
N/A	تفعلي *tfi3li*	فعلى *fa3la*
تفعلل *tafa3lol*		تفعلل *tfa3lal*

Derivation of the Noun of Instance

Some verbs also have a distinct "noun of instance." This refers generally to a *single instance* of the action described by the verb. This distinction is most common with simple (underived) verbs, where the pattern is overwhelmingly فعلة *fa3le*:

خطوة ←	خطا	ضربة ←	ضرب
khaTwe	*khaTa*	*Darbe*	*Darab*
step	to take a step	a blow	to hit
نومة ←	نام	شيلة ←	شال
noome	*naam*	*sheele*	*shaal*
a sleep	to sleep	picking up	to pick up

> Some nouns of instance may be formed on *fi3le* for some speakers: نزلة *nizle*, طلعة *Til3a*.

Some derived verbs can also form distinct nouns of instance by adding an ـة *-a/e* to their normal *maSdar*. This is particularly common with *maSdars* on *taf3iil*:

ترجيعة ←	رجع
tarjii3a	*rajja3*
a return	to send back

For other verbs the *maSdar* itself can also be used in a noun of instance meaning.

As an Abstract Noun

The most basic use of a *maSdar* is as a sort of abstract noun referring to an action. In this context it is usually definite (see unit 13) and generic. Consider the following examples:

المشي مفيد	الشرب بضر
ⁱlmashi mufiid	*ⁱshshirᵉb biDirr*
walking is good for you	drinking is bad for you
بحب الركض	مليت من الرسم
ba7ibb ⁱrrakᵉD	*malleet mn ⁱrrasᵉm*
I like running	I'm bored of drawing

Like a verb, however, a *maSdar* can also have a subject, objects, and adverbials. Note that both objects and subjects are added using the *2iDaafe* structure (see unit 15):

أكل التفاح منيح

2akl ⁱttuffaa7 ⁱmnii7

eating apples is good

جيتو لعندي بهلوقت غريبة

jayyto la3indi bhalwa2ᵉt ghariibe

his coming here just at this moment is strange

بهون عليك تعبي؟

bihuun 3aleek ta3bi?

is me working so hard so unimportant to you?

شيلتها سهلة

sheelitha sahle

it's easy to pick up

[= picking it up is easy]

If a *maSdar* has both a subject and an object, then the subject takes priority, and the object is added with the preposition ل *la-*:

حبي لإلك كان خطأ

7ubbi la2ilak kaan khaTa2

my loving you was a mistake

شوفتي لمايا زعلتو

shoofti lamaaya za33alito

me seeing Maya upset him

An English gerund structure can easily be negated with "not": "you not going," "her not saying anything." It is possible to negate a *maSdar* structure by placing it in *2iDaafe* with عدم *3adam*, a masculine noun:

عدم التنازل طبع مش منيح   ←

3adam ⁱttanaazol Tabᵉ3 mish mnii7

not compromising is not a good trait

التنازل طبع منيح

ⁱttanaazol Tabᵉ3 mnii7

compromise is a good trait

But these structures are fairly unusual in practice, and speakers tend to paraphrase in order to avoid them.

You may have noticed that several of these examples actually use what appear to be nouns of instance (*roo7a, sheele, shoofe,* etc.). For many simple verbs, the noun of instance is more idiomatic in these sentences than the *maSdar*. But there are examples of idiomatic structures where only the noun of instance works:

فوتاتها ع المحل كترانة

footaatha 3 alma7all katraane

she's been coming into the shop a lot more

[= her comings into the shop
have increased]

إنت مالك فوتة!

2inte maalak foote!

you are not coming in!

[= you do not have a coming in!]

These structures overlap a great deal with subordinate clauses (see part 5). In many cases, which to use is a stylistic or personal choice, since both express more or less the same meaning. But clauses with a subject and an object and clauses with a negative are more likely to be expressed with a full verb.

Both the *maSdar* and the noun of instance are very commonly used in secondary object structures, which are covered in detail in unit 54.

Indefinite *maSdar* as Object

In the examples above, the *maSdar*s have mostly been definite, as we would expect from abstract nouns (see unit 13). Some verbs, however, can take an indefinite *maSdar* object. Consider the following examples:

> The lack of definiteness marking on the *maSdar* is related to the general complications surrounding definiteness in objects. See unit 52.

حاج بكي!	بلشت حكي	بطل قراية
7aaj buki!	*ballashat 7aki*	*baTTal ʾ2raaye*
stop crying!	she started talking	he stopped reading

مليت كتابة	خلصنا أكل	منكمل مشي
malleet kitaabe	*khallaSna 2akᵉl*	*minkammel mashi*
I'm bored of reading	we finished eating	we'll keep walking

قضيناها ضحك	شبعنا نق	زهقت قعود
2aDDeenaaha Du7ᵒk	*shbi3na na22*	*zhi2t ʾ23uud*
we spent the whole time laughing	we've had enough nagging	I'm sick of sitting

It is worth noting that some verbs of this kind carry a sort of adverbial meaning that they pass on to the main verb, making them difficult to translate directly:

خففت شرب	بكترو حكي
khaffafᵉt shirᵉb	*bikattru 7aki*
I stopped drinking so much	they talk too much
[= lightened drinking]	[= do a lot of talking]

Like other *maSdar* constructions, these structures allow an object to be attached using a *2iDaafe* (although with objects it is probably more common to use a zero-imperfective clause):

حاج شرب ماي!	خلص قراية الجريدة؟
7aaj shurᵒb mayy!	*khallaS ʾ2raayt ʾjjariide?*
stop drinking water!	has he finished reading the newspaper?

بلشنا أكل لوز

ballashna 2akl looz

we started eating almonds

مليت كتابة مقالات

malleet kitaabet maqaalaat

I'm sick of writing articles

This structure is tantalisingly similar to the natural phrasing in English. But it should not be taken as a direct equivalent of English gerund structures. All of the verbs given above can also take normal bare clause objects (see unit 59), and most verbs that require a gerund in English cannot naturally take a *maSdar* object in Arabic at all.

> In very high-register language, you may occasionally encounter constructions with a definite *maSdar*. This mimics fuS7a usage, where all zero-imperfective clauses can be replaced by definite *maSdars*: بحاول الكتاب الإجابة عن أكتر من سؤال *bi7aawel l²ktaab ˈl2ijaabe 3an 2aktar min su2aal* "the book tries to answer more than one question." This is unusual language, however, and is unlikely to be used in everyday conversation.

Tense

Introduction to Tense

In this unit I will be providing a brief overview of how Levantine Arabic expresses *tense*. This is intended to serve as a quick and broad description of the Arabic tense system as a whole, sketching out the broad contours without going into too much detail about the particularities of the individual forms and structures. These will be the subject of the subsequent units.

Since "tense" is both a technical term with a specialised meaning and a fairly common term with a much looser meaning, I will start by defining exactly what I mean by tense. After this we will look very broadly at the distinctions expressed by the different Arabic forms and how they fit together.

What Is Tense?

The term "tense" is commonly used in everyday discussions of language to refer to different sets of verb forms. In European languages, these sets of forms typically express some combination of the *time* that an event took place (relative to the present), the general *time structure* of the event (repeated, lasting, continuous), and sometimes the *speaker's view* on the event (hoped-for, nonreal, etc.). In specialised linguistic language, however, tense usually refers only to the first of these (time relative to the present), and the terms "aspect" and "mood" are used for the second and third categories, respectively. You may have encountered pedantic comments insisting, for example, that the zero-imperfective is a mood and not a tense. This sort of assertion is rooted in these specialist definitions.

In this and the following units, we will largely be talking about how Arabic expresses the first two categories: tense and aspect. We will be looking, for example, at how to express an ongoing action in the past (a past continuous) or a repeated action in the present. We will not—and this is the important part—be looking at how it expresses commands, requests, wishes, possibilities, hopes, or other more mood-like distinctions. These will be the subject of part 4.

For brevity and because this largely corresponds with a familiar use of the word "tense," I will largely be referring to this combination of tense and aspect as "tense" alone. I hope linguists will forgive me.

How Does the Arabic Tense System Work?

The Arabic tense system is built around three central forms. The first two, the perfective and the imperfective, consist of sets of suffixes and prefix-suffix combinations, respectively. We have already looked at how to generate these forms in units 25–27:

Imperfective		Perfective	
اكتب		كتبت	
2ikteb/2akteb		katab^et	
I write		I wrote	
تكتبي	تكتب	كتبتي	كتبت
tikⁱtbi	tikteb	katabti	katab^et
you [F] write	you [M] write	you [F] wrote	you [M] wrote
تكتب	يكتب	كتبت	كتب
tikteb	yikteb	katbet/katbat	katab
she writes	he writes	she wrote	he wrote
نكتب		كتبنا	
nikteb		katabna	
we write		we wrote	
تكتبو		كتبتو	
tikⁱtbu		katabtu	
you [P] write		you [P] wrote	
يكتبو		كتبو	
yikⁱtbu		katabu	
they write		they wrote	

The third, the active participle, more closely resembles a noun or an adjective. We saw how to form participles in unit 37:

Active Participle		
كاتبين	كاتبة	كاتب
kaatbiin	*kaatbe*	*kaateb*
have written	has written [F]	has written [M]

The perfective, which will be covered in unit 33, typically corresponds to the English past but does not overlap entirely with it, since the perfective can only express actions that are fairly narrowly delineated in time. The perfective cannot express, for example, past states or past repeated actions:

رحت مرة   عرفتو

ru7ᵉt marra   *ᶦ3rifto*

I went once   I recognised him

Unit 34 will look at imperfective forms. The bare imperfective forms given above rarely occur in a specifically *tense* context; they are largely confined to the expression of wishes, commands, and the like. (see units 43–44) and to some kinds of subordinate clause (see part 5). In order to express simple tense, an imperfective form usually has to be combined with the prefix *b-*. By default, this gives the meaning of a repeated or habitual present or of a future:

بحكي معاه   بشوفو

b-a7ki ma3aa   *b-shuufo*

I talk to him [every day]   I see him [regularly]

I'll talk to him   I'll see him

Units 35 and 36 will consider the particles عم *3am* and رح *ra7* (and a range of local variants), which are combined with the bare imperfective to give a continuous and a future meaning, respectively:

رح شوفو بكرا   عم يحكي معاك

ra7 shuufo bukra   *3am yi7ki ma3aak*

I'm going to see him tomorrow   he's talking to you

Finally, the participle—the subject of unit 37—can give either a sort of ongoing state meaning or a resulting state meaning, corresponding most often to the English continuous and present perfect, respectively:

فاتحة محل

faat7a ma7all

she's opened a shop

رايح لعندو

raaye7 la3indo

I'm going to his house

In many respects, these distinctions are similar to English: we have two future forms (glossed as "will" and "going to"), a structure for repeated action, a present perfect, a past, and a continuous form. As we will see, these forms do not correspond exactly with their English counterparts. But nor are they entirely alien to an English speaker. Careful examination, however, reveals a few holes in our system. How, for example, do we express past continuous action or a past state?

Here English and Arabic diverge somewhat. The answer you are most likely to be familiar with is that adding some form of كان *kaan* "to be" allows you to project the meaning of otherwise present forms back into the past:

كنت عم أحكي معاه

kunt 3am 2a7ki ma3aa

I was talking to him

كان يحبني كتير

kaan y7ibbni ktiir

he loved me a lot

This is true, as these examples show. But it isn't the whole story. The word *kaan* is just one of a number of framing verbs that can be used to achieve this effect (units 38–41):

رجعت اكتب شعر

rji3ᵉt 2iktob shi3ᵉr

I started writing poetry again

صرت أروح معاه كل مرة

Surᵉt 2aruu7 ma3aa kull marra

[after that] I went with him every time

Moreover, the focus on *kaan* (and to a lesser extent on all framing verbs) draws attention away from the fact that there are many other structures and contexts that can provide additional tense information without us needing to change the verb itself, including subordinate clauses (see part 5) and sometimes simply narrative flow:

شافت إني عم أكتب

shaafat 2inni 3am 2akteb

she saw that was [= am] writing

شفت واحد بتدرب معو

shifᵉt waa7ed bitdarrab ma3o

I saw a guy I trained with
[= that I train with]

In each of these cases, the Arabic verb has no explicit past marking but nonetheless has to be translated with an English past tense. The verb form itself provides information only about the "aspect" properties of the action (continuous, regular action, etc.). It is the overall context of the sentence or of the narrative that situates it in *time*.[1] We will explore how this works in practice in unit 42.

Note

1. This feature of Arabic, among others, has been the grounds for a long debate about whether to classify Arabic as an aspect-prominent language (i.e., a language in which the marking of *aspectual* distinctions such as continuousness or iterative action is more significant than the marking of *tense* distinctions in the formal sense).

The Perfective

The first of the tense structures that we need to look at is the *perfective*. We looked at how to form the perfective in unit 25. As you will recall, the perfective is conjugated by adding suffixes to the perfective stem (the dictionary form):

كتبنا *katab-na* we wrote	كتبت *katab-ᵉt* I wrote	
كتبتو *katab-tu* you [P] wrote	كتبتي *katab-ti* you [F] wrote	كتبت *katab-ᵉt* you [M] wrote
كتبو *katab-u* they wrote	كتبت *katb-et/katb-at* she wrote	كتب *katab* he wrote

In the previous units, I have generally glossed the perfective as an English past or (sometimes) a present perfect. These two forms translate the majority of Arabic perfectives. But the perfective does not correspond perfectly to either of them. We will look first of all at the basic uses of the perfective before looking at the ways in which it differs from these two forms.

Basic Use

Most instances of the perfective correspond to the English simple past or present perfect. The distinction made in English has no direct counterpart in Arabic, and so depending on context, both translations of the following sentences are possible:

رحت معاه

ru7ᵉt ma3aa

I went with him

I've gone with him

شربت قهوة

shribᵉt 2ahwe

I drank some coffee

I've drunk some coffee

كتبت كتاب

katbat ⁱktaab

she wrote a book

she's written a book

ساوينالو كل شي

saweenaalo kill shii

we did everything for him

we've done everything for him

خلصت قراية؟

khallaSt ⁱ2raaye?

did you finish reading?

have you finished reading?

حكيت معو؟

7akeet ma3o?

did you talk to him?

have you talked to him?

أكلت

2akalᵉt

I ate

I've eaten

أعطيتها المصاري

2a3Teetha lmaSaari

I gave her the money

I've given her the money

The perfective is negated with ما *maa*. For South Levantine speakers, it can also be negated with مـ ـش *ma-sh*:

North Levantine	South Levantine
ما شربت قهوة	مشربتش قهوة
maa shribᵉt 2ahwe	*ma-shribt-ᵉsh 2ahwe*
I didn't drink any coffee	I didn't drink any coffee
I haven't drunk any coffee	I haven't drunk any coffee

For more on negation, see part 9.

The Perfective with Verbs of Becoming

We noted in unit 24 that Arabic has many single verbs that express a change of state or an act of becoming. These verbs are commonly used in the perfective in a way that is best translated in English using the corresponding *adjective*. This can be thought of as an extension of the present perfect meaning of the perfective:

شوبت

shawwab^et

I'm [too] hot

[= I've got hot]

نعست

n3is^et

I'm sleepy

[= I've got sleepy]

شبعت

shbi3^et?

are you full?

[= have you got full?]

جعنا

ji3na

we're hungry

[= we've got hungry]

Similarly, the "beginning-state" meanings of double-meaning verbs (see unit 24) can be used in ways that are often not quite idiomatic in English if translated literally. Again, here the verb expresses a change of state (from not-loving to loving, from not-hating to realising you hate), and the structure has a sort of present perfect meaning:

حبيتها؟

7abbeetha?

do you like it?

[= did you like it?]

خلص كرهت الجامعة

khalaS ᶦkriht ᶦjjaam3a

that's it, I hate university

[= I've hated university]

فهمت

fhim^et

I get it

[= I have understood]

آه عرفتو!

2aa ᶦ3rifto!

oh, I know who you mean!

[= I've known him]

The Perfective Is Not the English Past

While almost all perfectives can be translated into English pasts, the opposite does not hold. Not all pasts can be translated as perfectives. This is because the perfective is confined to what we might call "snapshot" descriptions of events. Compare the following examples:

أيام المدرسة كان يضحكني بشكل

2iyyaam ᶦlmadrase kaan yDa77ikni bshak^el

when we were at school he made me laugh so much

هديك المرة ضحكني بشكل

hadiik ᶦlmarra Da77akni bshak^el

the other day he made me laugh so much

كنت اكتبلو مكتوب كل يوم

kint 2iktiblo maktuub kill yoom

I would write him a letter every day

اليوم كتبتلو مكتوب

ᶦlyoom katabtillo maktuub

I wrote him a letter today

من زمان كنت اقدر ميز بيناتهن

min zamaan kint 2i2der mayyez baynaaton

in the old days, I was able to distinguish
between them

بالنهاي قدرت أقنعو

binnihaay 2dir^et 2aqni3o

in the end, I was able to convince
him

The sentences on the right describe a sort of single snapshot in time, a single event. This snapshot might be longer or shorter in actual temporal terms. But it is definitely more constrained than the sentences on the left, which give much broader, wide-angle descriptions of events, often over a longer period. While snapshot descriptions are the territory of the perfective, wide-angle descriptions are more the jurisdiction of the imperfective, a form that we will look at in more detail in unit 34.

> English has ways of making a similar distinction in the past. The auxiliaries "would" and "used to," in particular, always correspond to imperfective forms plus an auxiliary: "I would go every day," "I used to go every day." But it is much less sensitive to this distinction than Arabic is, and the English past can serve both functions.

Note in particular عرف *3iref*, which as we have noted has both a state meaning ("know") and a change-of-state meaning ("find out"). It is possible to come up with contexts where the state meaning appears in a snapshot context. But overall, most cases of *3iref* in the perfective will be interpreted as having the change-of-state meaning, and the usual translation for "knew" requires *kaan* and an imperfective form:

كنت أعرف شو لازم أعمل

kint 2a3ref shuu laazem 2a3mol

I knew [in those days] what I had to do

وقتها عرفت شو لازم أعمل

wa2ta 3rif^et shuu laazem 2a3mol

I knew then what I had to do
I realised then what I had to do

The Perfective Is Not the Present Perfect

It is also true, although less importantly so, that not all English present perfects correspond to perfective forms in Arabic. In this case, the only major point of difference is that the English present perfect can appear (with some verbs) in constructions with "for." In Arabic, the imperfective is the only choice here. Note the translation of the perfective form on the left:

عرفتو من سنين

ⁱ3rifto mn ⁱsniin

I knew him years ago

بعرفو من سنين

ba3ⁱrfo mn ⁱsniin

I've known him for years

Note as well that while the present perfect is not clearly distinguished from the past in Arabic, there are optional ways of capturing some of its nuances, in particular the resultative participle (see unit 37).

Secondary Uses of the Perfective

The perfective also appears in other contexts. It is used in conditional constructions (see part 7):

إذا شفتو خبرني

2iza shufto khabbirni

if you see him, tell me

لو مشي كنتي انتبهتي

law mishi kinti ntabahti

if he'd gone you would have noticed

The perfective is also used after certain other particles, often with future meaning. We will discuss these particles in unit 44 (wishes), unit 68 (subordinating conjunctions), units 69–71 (conditional structures), and appendix C (overview of conjunctions):

بلكي عرف؟

balki 3iref?

what if he finds out?

بس إجت بحاكيك

bass 2ijet b7aakiik

as soon as she gets here I'll call you

The perfective is also used in many set phrases as a marker of wishes or prayers (see unit 44):

حياك الله

7ayyaak 2aLLa

greetings

[= may God give you life]

العمى ضربك

l3ama Darabak

damn you

[= blindness strike you]

Note that in all these contexts, the perfective retains its *snapshot* meaning; that is, it cannot be used to express repeated action or states. We will explore the relevance of this in more detail in units 69–71, which cover conditional structures.

The Imperfective

In this unit we will be looking at the imperfective. In previous units, we've tended to look at the imperfective in isolation, without any additional prefixes or particles. I've presented forms that look something like the following:

نشرب *ni-shrab* we drink	اشرب *2i-shrab/2a-shrab* I drink
تشربو *ti-shrab-u* you [P] drink	تشربي *ti-shrab-i* you [F] drink	تشرب *ti-shrab* you [M] drink
يشربو *yi-shrab-u* they drink	تشرب *ti-shrab* she drinks	يشرب *yi-shrab* he drinks

I did this because these forms are easily recognisable for those who have studied fuS7a and because they are the foundation on which a number of other structures are built. But this set of forms—which I will be calling the *zero-imperfective*—is not much used in a straight-forward tense context. Their most common use in isolation is to express wishes and other similar meanings (see unit 44). To express repeated or characteristic action, on the other hand (the meaning of English present simple forms such as "runs" or "sits"), they require the prefix *b-*:

تشربي شاي   بتشرب شاي

tishrabi shaay   *b-tishrab shaay*

[I hope you] drink tea   you drink tea

يفوت

y-fuut

let him come in

بفوت

b-ifuut

he comes in

Since the *b-* form does most of the heavy lifting in tense terms, we will be focusing on this form in this unit. But this is not to say that the bare imperfective has no tense uses whatsoever. After considering the main uses of the *b-*imperfective, we will briefly look at some of these uses as well.

The Prefix *b-*

The prefix *b-* is attached directly to the imperfective prefix. As you will recall, there are two sets of imperfective prefixes, one used before stems beginning with a single consonant and the other used before stems beginning with a cluster (see unit 26). The *b-* prefix combines with these two sets in a way that is largely but not entirely predictable:

SINGLE CONSONANT		CLUSTER	
North Levantine	**South Levantine**	**North Levantine**	**South Levantine**
بقول *b-2uul* I say	بقول *ba-2uul* I say	بمسك *bi-msek* I grab	بمسك *ba-msek* I grab
بتقول *bi-t-2uul* you [M] say		بتمسك *b-ti-msek* you [M] grab	
بقول *b-i-2uul* he says		بيمسك *b-yi-msek* he grabs	بمسك *b-i-msek* he grabs
منقول *mi-n-2uul* we say		منمسك *m-ni-msek* we grab	

The regional differences in the first person are as we would expect, but note that South Levantine speakers often contract *b-yi-* to *b-i-*. This makes their third-person singular masculine ("he") form identical to the North Levantine first-person singular ("I") form. Recall as well that South Levantine speakers shift the prefix vowel to *u* in simple sound verbs with a *u* as the stem vowel (see unit 26). This form combines with *b-* exactly like its *i* counterpart does:

يكتب   +   بـ   ←   بكتب

bu-ktob	*b-*	*yu-ktob*
he writes		he writes

تضربي   +   بـ   ←   بتضربي

btu-D^urb-i	*b-*	*tu-D^urb-i*
you [F] hit		you [F] hit

Note as well the assimilation of *b-* to *m-* before the first-person plural ("we") suffixes. Not all speakers have this assimilation, especially South Levantine speakers. You are likely to hear the variants *b-ni-msek* and *bi-n-2uul*.

Use of the *b-* Prefix

The primary use of the *b-*imperfective is to express *repeated or habitual action*. Conveniently, this corresponds very closely to the English present tense form. In the following examples, the meaning is habitual:

بالعادة برقصش	الصبح بشرب قهوة
bil3aade bar2uS^esh	*'SSub^o7 bashrab 2ahwe*
normally I don't dance	in the morning I drink coffee
النمر بياكل بشر	بروح ع الجيم كل يوم
'nnim^er 'byaakol bashar	*bruu7 3a ljim kill yoom*
tigers eat people	I go to the gym every day

A very common idiomatic extension of this is the use of *imperfective* verbs as an equivalent of English adjectives. This is particularly common with passives (see unit 57) and causatives (see unit 56).

There is an obvious parallel here with English sentences such as "makes you laugh" and "annoys you" (with a generic "you"). Note though that there is no equivalent to the generic "you" in these structures. The object is simply dropped:

الفيلم بضحك	المي هون ما بتنشرب
'lfil^em biDa77ek	*'lmayy hoon maa btinshireb*
the film is funny	the water here isn't drinkable
[= makes laugh]	[= isn't drunk]

هادا ما بينمشى معو

haada maa byinmasha ma3o

this guy is intolerable

[= isn't walked with]

تربية القطط بتعذب

tirbaayt 'l2iTaT bit3azzeb

raising cats is bothersome

[= bothers]

For Southern Levantine speakers—but not generally for Northern Levantine speakers—the *b*-imperfective can also express a *continuous* meaning:

بتمزح!

btimza7!

you're joking!

أنا هلق بدرس

2ana halla2 badres

I'm studying right now

In this sense the *b*-imperfective is synonymous with the *3am* continuous, which we will discuss in detail in unit 35.

The *b*-imperfective is negated using ما *maa*. For South Levantine speakers, مـ ـش *ma-sh* and ـش *-sh* are also available:

South Levantine Alternatives		*maa* Form
باكلش لحمة *baakul-ᵉsh la7me* I don't eat meat	مباكلش لحمة *ma-baakul-ᵉsh la7me* I don't eat meat	ما باكل لحمة *maa baakol la7me* I don't eat meat

For more on negation, see part 9.

The *b-* Imperfective with Verbs of Knowledge, Opinion, and Ability

There is a small group of verbs whose imperfective form often expresses not regular action but instead an ongoing and lasting state. The most common verbs in this group are:

- Verbs of knowledge and ability: عرف *3iref* "know," دري *diri* "know," قدر *2ider* "be able to," and حسن *7asan* "be able to."
- Verbs of opinion: حب *7abb* "love, like," كره *kireh* "hate," بغض *baghaD* "loathe," حس *7ass* "feel, consider," اعتقد *3taqad* "believe," ظن *Zann* "think," افتكر *ftakar* "think," and so on.

This should be relatively intuitive to an English speaker, because this group overlaps with a group of verbs that have a similar meaning in English:

بحبك

ba7ibbak

I love you

بعرف عربي

bi3raf 3arabi

he knows Arabic

بعتقد   بتفهم بالسياسة

bi3ti2ed   *btifham bissiyaase*

I think so   she gets politics

> In English, verbs of perception—"feel," "smell," "hear," "see"—pattern like this. But in Arabic, these verbs typically use participles when the meaning is not habitual or repeated: حاسس؟ *7aases?* "can you feel it?"

Note that they can also have the repeated or characteristic action meaning. In the following examples, the adverbs make it clear that the action is taking place repeatedly or habitually:

أوقات بحبها أوقات لأ   الصبح ما بقدر امشي

2aw2aat ba7ibbha, 2aw2aat la2   *ᵉSSibᵉH maa bi2der 2imshi*

sometimes I like it, sometimes I don't   in the mornings, I can't walk

Recall as well that many of these verbs also have change-of-state meanings (see unit 24). Where this is the intended meaning, the *b*-imperfective expresses repeated or characteristic action:

كل سنة بتحب وحدة جديدة   كل يوم بعرف بخبر جديد

kill sine bit7ibb wa7de jdiide   *kull yoom ba3raf ᵉb-khabar ᵉjdiid*

every year you fall in love with a new one   every day I find out about something new

The Zero-Imperfective as a Tense Form

As noted above, the zero-imperfective does occasionally appear as a straightforward tense form. In narrative contexts, it can be used to provide information about what is going on in the background to the main narrative. The meaning here is always *repeated* action, and this form cannot be used with verbs of knowledge and ability or to express other states:

كل أسبوع يجينا تقرير من المديرية

kill 2isbuu3 yijiina taqriir mn ᵉlmudiiriyye

every week we'd get a report from the directorate

نتخانق كتير مع ولاد الحارات التانية

nitkhaana2 ᵉktiir ma3 ᵉwlaad ᵉl7aaraat ᵉttaanye

[in those days] we had a lot of fights with kids from other neighbourhoods

Although these examples are in the past, this form can also be used in present descriptions. This, for example, is a line from the setup to a joke:

كل شوي تمد إيدها وتوخد فستقة

kull ˈshwayy ˈtmidd 2iidha w tookhod fustu2a

every little while, she reaches out her hand and takes a nut

The zero-imperfective can also be triggered by a handful of expressions that appear before the verb. Here the meaning is identical to the *b*-imperfective:

يا دوب أعرف أصحى   بالكاد لحق

yaa doob 2a3raf 2aS7a   *bilkaad la77e2*

I can barely wake up   I barely make it

Finally, as we will see, the zero-imperfective is the normal counterpart to the *b*-imperfective when combined with various framing verbs (see units 38–41):

كنت أعرفو   صرت شوفو كتير

kunt 2a3rafo   *Sirᶜt shuufo ktiir*

I used to know him   I started seeing him a lot

Secondary Uses of the Imperfective

The *b*-imperfective has various secondary idiomatic uses. We will look at these in more detail in later units, but it is worth noting them here for comprehensiveness. First, the *b*-imperfective often has a future sense corresponding (mostly) with the English word "will." This contrasts with various other future constructions and is discussed in unit 36:

بشوفك بكرا   أنا بحكي معها

bashuufek bukra   *2ana bi7ki ma3a*

I'll see you tomorrow   I'll speak to her

Second and relatedly, the *b*-imperfective often gives the sense of the English word "would," either in an explicitly conditional sentence (with an "if" clause attached) or in isolation. We'll look at this usage in more detail in unit 70:

لو عرف بقتلني!   أنا ما بدفع عليها ولا فرانك!

law 3iref bu2tulni!   *2ana maa bidfa3 3aleyya wala fraank!*

if he found out, he'd kill me!   I wouldn't pay a single penny for it!

Third and only for North Levantine speakers, the *b*-imperfective is used to make polite suggestions and offers (see unit 44). For some, it is also used for first-person suggestions (see unit 44):

بتشرب قهوة؟

btishrab 2ahwe?

would you like some coffee?

بعملك شاي؟

ba3millak shaay?

shall I make you some tea?

Fourth, the *b*-imperfective is occasionally used for instructions (see unit 43). This corresponds to a similar use of the simple present in English:

بتروح من بكرا ع النيابة

bitruu7 min bukra 3 anniyaabe…

you go to the Prosecutor's Office tomorrow…

بتكملي لتحت وبتلفي ع اليمين

bitkammli lata7ᵉt w bitliffi 3 alyamiin

you carry on down here and turn right

Finally, as in English, it is not uncommon to recast past events in the present tense, giving a narrative a sort of extra urgency. In this sort of context, we can use the *b*-imperfective as an exact equivalent of the English narrative present:

بيجي أبو عصام بقللي…

biiji 2abu 3iSaam bi2ulli…

so Abu Isam comes and tells me…

وقتها بتجي سامية تسلم عليي…

wa2ta btiji saamiya tsallem 3aliyyi…

then Samia comes over to say hi…

Continuous Constructions

In this unit we will be looking at Arabic *continuous* constructions. These constructions correspond primarily to English structures with "is X-ing," although as we will see, they do not overlap perfectly. The main continuous construction shared by all Levantine dialects is formed using the particle عم *3am*. We will thus be looking at this construction first before considering some regional or more specialised alternatives used in different parts of the Levantine area.

The Particle *3am*

The most common continuous construction uses the particle عم *3am*, which is combined with the imperfective, with or without the *b-* prefix:

عم نشرب	عم اشرب
3am ni-shrab	*3am 2i-shrab/2a-shrab*
we are drinking	I am drinking

عم تشربو	عم تشربي	عم تشرب
3am ti-shrab-u	*3am ti-shrab-i*	*3am ti-shrab*
you [P] are drinking	you [F] are drinking	you [M] are drinking

عم يشربو	عم تشرب	عم يشرب
3am yi-shrab-u	*3am ti-shrab*	*3am yi-shrab*
they are drinking	she is drinking	he is drinking

Note that unlike the *b-* prefix, a single *3am* can give its meaning to multiple closely associated verbs simultaneously. In the left-hand column, both verbs in each pair have continuous meaning, even though *3am* only occurs once:

عم يلف ويدور   ←   بلف وبدور

3am yliff w yduur   *biliff w biduur*

he's beating about the bush   he beats about the bush

[= he's turning and spinning]   [= he turns and spins]

عم تروح وتجي   ←   بتروح وبتجي

3am ᵢtruu7 w tiji   *bitruu7 w btiji*

she's been coming and going   she comes and goes

> There are many regional variants of *3am* you may encounter, including عن *3an*, مـ *m-*, عـ *3a-*, عمّ *3ammi-*, and عمال *3ammaal* (which can occur both with and without an attached pronoun).

Using *3am*

There are two basic uses of *3am*. The first is to express ongoing, in-the-moment action, the meaning we usually associate with the English continuous:

مش عم يكذب عليك   شو عم تعمل هلق؟

mish 3am yikzeb 3aleek   *shuu 3am ta3mel halla2?*

he's not lying to you   what are you doing right now?

عم قللك!   عم بنضف المطبخ

3am 2illak!   *3am banaDDef ᵢlmaTbakh*

I'm telling you!   I'm cleaning the kitchen

The second is to express repeated action that *has been going on* (recently) up to the present:

مش عم أطلع برا   عم شوفو كتير

mish 3am 2aTla3 barra   *3am shuufo ktiir*

I've not been going out much   I've been seeing him a lot

عم تروح لعندها شي؟   ضرسي ما عم ينومني

3am ᵢtruu7 la3indha shii?   *Dirsi maa 3am ynawwimni*

have you been going to her house at all?   my tooth's been keeping me up

The particle *3am* is negated with ما *maa* or مش *mish*:

ما عم أعمل شي
maa 3am 2a3mel shii
I'm not doing anything

مش عم أكذب!
mish 3am 2akzeb!
I'm not lying!

For more on negation, see part 9.

3am Is Narrower Than the English Continuous

As always, however, there are complications. The English and Arabic forms are not totally equivalent. We have just seen that the Arabic forms express not just "is X-ing" but also "has been X-ing." But at the same time, their use is more restricted than their English counterparts: many English "is X-ing" constructions correspond not to *3am* forms but instead to participles (see unit 37).

You may already have encountered this constraint with verbs of motion. While *3am* works here for the "have been X-ing" meaning, the "is X-ing" meaning requires a participle:

Participle	***3am***
وين رايح؟ *ween raaye7?* where are you going?	عم تروح ع الجيم؟ *3am ^{i}truu7 3 aljim?* have you been going to the gym?
طالعة لبرا؟ *Taal3a labarra?* are you going out?	عم تطلعي لبرة؟ *3am tiTla3i labarra?* have you been going out?

The broader principle here is that verbs expressing a *state*—rather than an action—form a continuous participle. This is easiest to see with double-meaning verbs (see unit 24), which have both a state and a change-of-state meaning:

Participle	***3am***
لابس جاكيتي *laabes jakeeti* I'm wearing my jacket	عم البس جاكيتي *3am 2ilbes jakeeti* I'm putting on my jacket
راكب البيسكليت *raakeb ^{i}lbisikleet* I'm on [riding] the bike	عم اركب البيسكليت *3am 2irkab ^{i}lbisikleet* I'm getting on the bike

Participle	*3am*
حاملين الشنطة	عم نحمل الشنطة
7aamliin ᵢshshanTa	*3am ni7mel ᵢshshanTa*
we're carrying the bag	we're picking up the bag

As we would expect, the translation of "is wearing," "is [riding] on," and "are carrying"—the state meaning—requires a participle. These ideas cannot be expressed with *3am*. The translations of "is putting on," "is getting on," and "are picking up," on the other hand—the more "action-like" change-of-state meaning—use an *3am* form.

> This principle applies to verbs of motion as well. On the face of it, "going" or "coming" seem fairly action-like. But the semantic emphasis here is on being in a state of movement. When the emphasis is placed on the action itself—for example, the manner of movement—we can sometimes use a *3am* form.

Bear in mind that this constraint applies only to the "is X-ing" ongoing event meaning. For "has been X-ing," *3am* is acceptable for all kinds of verbs:

عم البس		لابس
3am ilbes		*laabes*
I'm putting on	I've been putting on	I've been wearing	I'm wearing

عم أركب		راكب
3am 2arkab		*raakeb*
I'm getting on	I've been getting on	I've been riding	I'm riding

Note as well that while the English continuous can be used with *future* meaning, this is not true of its Arabic counterpart. The sense of sentences such as "I'm having dinner with him tomorrow" or "he's arriving at six" can only be expressed with a participle or a marked future form, as we will see in unit 36.

3am Is Broader Than the English Continuous

On the other hand, *3am* can occur with verbs that English does not accept in the "is X-ing" construction. The most common examples of this are verbs of ability, almost always in the negative:

مش عم أعرف أفتح الباب

mish 3am 2a3raf 2afta7 'lbaab

I don't seem to be able to open the door

[= I'm not knowing how . . .]

ما عم اقدر امشي

maa 3am 2i2der 2imshi

I don't seem to be able to walk

[= I'm not being able to . . .]

Although English has no way of making the distinction, the meaning here is intuitive and expresses in-the-moment ongoing action, just like other kinds of continuous expressions. For North Levantine speakers, the continuous can also be used with verbs of perception and sense ("see," "hear") in the meaning "can X." This is an alternative to the participle form (see unit 37), which is acceptable for all speakers:

North Levantine	**All Dialects**
مش عم اسمعك	مش سامعتك
mish 3am 2isma3ak	*mish saami3tak*
I can't hear you	I can't hear you
عم تشوفو؟	شايفو؟
3am 'tshuufo?	*shaayfo?*
can you see it?	can you see it?

With the negative, *3am* often gives a sense of frustration; that is, that *despite all the speaker's efforts*, events are not turning out how they'd like. This is similar to English "won't" (for more constructions of this kind, see unit 38):

البنت مش عم ترد!

'lbint mish 3am 'tridd!

The girl won't answer!

The girl isn't answering!

الباب ما عم يفتح

'lbaab maa 3am yifta7

The door won't open

The door isn't opening

لهلق مش عم اترقى

lahalla2 mish 3am 2itra22a

they still won't promote me

I'm still not getting promoted

3am as an Optional Particle

3am is used throughout the Levantine area, and in North Levantine it is more or less compulsory when talking about continuous action, just like English "is X-ing." For South Levantine speakers, however, it is often optional: these speakers can use a *b*-imperfective with continuous meaning. If a South Levantine speaker wants to ask what a friend is doing, both of these sentences are acceptable:

شو عم تعمل؟

shuu 3am ti3mel?

what are you doing?

شو بتعمل؟

shuu bti3mel?

what are you doing?

For North Levantine speakers, only the structure with *3am* would work here. For them, the distinction between "what are you doing?" and "what do you do?" is compulsory, just as it is for English speakers. But for South Levantine speakers, the following examples are quite normal:

بنضف المطبخ

banaDDef ⁱlmaTbakh

I'm cleaning the kitchen

بقللك!

ba2ullak!

I'm telling you!

It is also possible for the *b-* form to have the "have been Xing" meaning of the continuous, although this is much less likely in isolation and is most common in contexts that make the meaning explicit. In the following examples, the time expressions make the meaning clear:

إلي مدة بشوفو كتير

2ili mudde bashuufo ktiir

I've been seeing him a lot for a while

بطلعش برا هاليومين الماضيين

baTla3ᵉsh barra halyomeen ⁱlmaDyiin

I haven't been going out these past two days

Alternative Construction: *2aa3ed*

South Levantine speakers also have a further alternative to *3am* in the participle قاعد *2aa3ed*, literally "sitting," which combines with a zero-imperfective. The participle agrees with its subject as you would expect, including (for some speakers) the feminine plural (see unit 50):

قاعدة أدرس

2aa3de 2adros

I'm studying [F]

قاعد أدرس

2aa3ed 2adros

I'm studying [M]

قاعدات ندرس

2aa3daat nudros

We're studying [F]

قاعدين ندرس

2aa3diin nudros

We're studying

The structure with *2aa3ed* is largely interchangeable with *3am*. Like *3am*, *2aa3ed* can express either ongoing action ("is X-ing") or recent repeated action ("has been X-ing"):

قاعد أنضف المطبخ

2aa3ed 2anaDDef ᵢlmaT'bakh

I'm cleaning the kitchen

قاعدة أكتب شعر

2aa3de 2akteb shi3ᵉr

I'm writing poetry

قاعد أشوفو كتير

2aa3ed 2ashuufo ktiir

I've been seeing him a lot

وين قاعدة تروحي؟

ween 2aa3de truu7i?

where've you been going?

It goes without saying that in the sentences above, the literal meaning of "sitting" has completely disappeared. *2aa3ed* is simply a continuous marker.

Unlike *3am*, *2aa3ed* can be delayed and appear toward the end of a sentence. For more on this, see unit 66:

واضح إنو الكل بمزح قاعد!

waaDe7 2inno lkull bimza7 2aa3ed!

apparently everyone's joking!

Idiomatic Structure: *naazel*

The participle نازل *naazel* can also form a continuous construction with the bare imperfective. Although this looks like the structure with *2aa3ed* described above, it is used throughout the Levantine area. It also has a more specific meaning. *naazel* implies that the action is unreasonable, undesirable, or over the top:

إحنا بالاجتماع وانتي نازلة تغني؟

2i7na bil2ijtimaa3 w2inti naazle tghanni?

we're in the meeting and you're just singing away?

صارلك ساعتين نازل تحكي بالدين!

SaLLak saa3teen naazel ti7ki biddiin!

you've been going on about religion for two hours!

Future Constructions

In this unit we will be looking at ways of talking about the *future*. This will involve a slight divergence from the pattern we have been following in previous units. Instead of focusing on one specific particle or form of the verb, we will be thinking primarily about the differences between two different constructions: the particle *ra7* and the *b*-imperfective.

ra7, *7a-*, and the *b*-Imperfective

There are two very common constructions used for talking about the future: the particle رح *ra7* (or ح *7a-*)—typically combined with the zero-imperfective—and the *b*-imperfective:

بحاكيها بكرا   رح حاكيها بكرا

b7aakiiha bukra   *ra7 7aakiiha bukra*

I'll ring her tomorrow   I'm going to ring her tomorrow

> Regional variants of the particle/prefix include لح *la7*, *la7i-*, and *la7a-* as well as *ra7i-* and *ra7a-*. Some North Levantine speakers, especially Lebanese speakers, allow it to be combined with the *b*-imperfective: بشوفو بكرا *ra7 'bshuufo bukra* "I'm going to see him tomorrow."

As the translations suggest, these constructions are not interchangeable. But the distinction between them, conveniently for an English speaker, corresponds closely to a distinction also made in English.

The *b*-imperfective largely maps onto the English term "will." It is used to express in-the-moment decisions and choices:

خلص باجي عندك   يلا أنا بدبرها

khalaS baaji 3indak   *yaLLa 2ana badabbirha*

OK forget it, I'll come over   OK, I'll sort it out

هيدي بكبها بكرا

heydi bkibbha bukra

I'll get rid of this one tomorrow

قلت باجي بسلم عليك

2ult baaji basallem 3aleek

I thought I'd come and say hi to you

The *b*-imperfective is very commonly appended to an expression of duration. With durations this is equivalent to the English construction "X and ...":

وقتها بتشوف المشكلة

wa2ta bitshuuf ⁱlmishⁱkle

then you'll see the problem

هلق بتعرف

halla2 ⁱbta3ref

you'll find out in a minute

خمس دقايق بكون عندك

khams ⁱd2aaye2 bakuun 3indak

I'll be there in five

دقيقتين وبستوى الأكل

d2ii2teen w bistawa l2akᵉl

two minutes and the food will be done

The (fairly limited) use of the present simple in English to describe scheduled action is also translated by the *b*-imperfective:

الكتاب بيطلع بكرا

lⁱktaab byiTla3 bukra

the book comes out tomorrow

القطار بيوصل ع الستة

ⁱlqiTaar byiwSal 3 assitte

the train gets in at six

The particles *ra7* and *7a-*, on the other hand, usually indicate intentions, plans, or certain predictions. In this respect they are very close to English "going to" or "about to":

رح شوفو بكرا

ra7 shuufo bukra

I'm seeing him tomorrow [anyway]

مش رح يزبط معاك

mish ra7 yuzboT ma3aak

no, you're not going to get it to work

مش رح ساعدك بشي!

mish ra7 saa3dek bshi!

I'm not helping you with anything!

حأنجن!

7a2anjann!

I'm going to go mad!

[if things go on as they are]

ra7 is also used for generalisations about the future. Here, of course, the *b*-imperfective would be understood as a simple (present) generalisation:

كل إنسان بموت

kull 2insaan bimuut

everyone dies

كل إنسان رح يموت

kull 2insaan ra7 ymuut

everyone will [eventually] die

Note as well that for predicted outcomes (where an "if" is implied), *ra7* is interchangeable with *b-*:

ماما بتقتلني!

maama btu2tulni!

mum will kill me!

ماما رح تقتلني!

maama ra7 tu2tulni!

mum will kill me!

[if I do that]

The same applies to assertions about the future of the following kind:

لما يجي البيبيه بصير عليك شغل كتير

lamma yiji lbeebe biSiir 3aleek shighl ᵢktiir

when the baby comes you'll have lots to do

لما يجي البيبيه رح يصير عليك شغل كتير

lamma yiji lbeebe ra7 ySiir 3aleek shighl ᵢktiir

when the baby comes you'll have lots to do

Note that while the *b-*imperfective is negated as we would expect, *ra7* is not necessarily. While Syrians tend to use ما *maa* here, and this form is occasionally found elsewhere, Lebanese and South Levantine speakers are more likely to us مش *mish*:

مش حاتغير!

mish 7aatghayyar!

I'm not going to change!

ما رح ساعدك

maa ra7 saa3dak

I won't help you

For more on negation, see part 9.

Alternative Construction: *bidd-*

The pseudoverb بد *bidd-* or *badd-*, literally "want," is often used as a future marker with the same basic meaning as *ra7*. In rapid speech it is sometimes contracted to *d-* and (very occasionally) written like this as well:

كل إنسان بدو يموت

kull 2insaan biddo ymuut

every person is going to die [eventually]

بدي شوفو بكرا

biddi shuufo bukra

I'm going to see him tomorrow

شودك تساوي؟

shuu dak ᵢtsaawi?

what are you going to do?

وين بدك تروحي؟

ween baddek ᵢtruu7i?

where are you going to go?

Unlike the forms with *ra7*, however, these constructions are ambiguous. As well as literally meaning "want," *bidd-* can also express "should" and other related meanings (see unit 46).

Participles

The last verb form that we need to be aware of in order to understand the Levantine tense system is the *active participle,* whose formation we examined in unit 29. Participles are not like other verb forms. They look like adjectives and take feminine and plural marking like adjectives do:

كاتبين	كاتبة	كاتب
kaatbiin	*kaatbe*	*kaateb*
have written	has written [F]	has written [M]

Unlike adjectives, however, participles take objects. In fact, they generally behave much more like verbs than like adjectives or nouns and typically correspond to English constructions with verbs. Participles have three basic meanings. Most verbs can form a *resultative* participle and a *future* participle, and some verbs can also form a *continuous* participle. In this unit we will look at each of these meanings in turn before considering some more complicated cases and idiomatic uses.

Continuous Participles

I said above that it was unhelpful to think of the participle as straightforwardly equivalent to English "X-ing." This is true. But there are *some* participles for which this is in fact a useful way in:

وين آخدني؟	قاعدين جوا
ween 2aakhidni?	*2aa3diin juwwa*
where are you taking me?	we're sitting inside

Of course, we have already encountered another structure that corresponds to English "is X-ing" structures: the continuous with *3am* (see unit 35). But *3am* and the participle have almost no overlap with one another, because the participle expresses an ongoing *state*, while the *3am* form expresses an ongoing *action*. This is easiest to see by looking at double-meaning verbs (see unit 24) with both state and action meanings. The *3am* form translates the continuous of the "action" meaning ("put on," "get on," "pick up"), while the participle translates the continuous of the state meaning ("wear," "ride," "carry"):

Participle (State Meaning)	3am (Action Meaning)
لابس جاكيتي *laabes jakeeti* I'm wearing my jacket	عم البس جاكيتي *3am 2ilbes jakeeti* I'm putting on my jacket
راكب البيسكليت *raakeb ᵢlbisikleet* I'm on [riding] the bike	عم اركب البيسكليت *3am 2irkab ᵢlbisikleet* I'm getting on the bike
حاملين الشنطة *7aamliin ᵢshshanTa* we're carrying the bag	عم نحمل الشنطة *3am ni7mel ᵢshshanTa* we're picking up the bag

You may have already encountered forms such as this with verbs expressing movement from one place to another, which are some of the first continuous participles that students of colloquial Arabic are taught. On the face of it, "going" or "coming" is more action-like than state-like. But the semantic emphasis here is on being in a state of movement:

طالعة لبرا؟   وين رايح؟

Taal3a labarra?   *ween raaye7?*

are you going outside?   where are you going?

آخدينو ع باريس   فايتة ع الغرفة

2aakhdiino 3a bariis   *faayte 3 alghirfe*

we're taking him to Paris   she's entering the room

But any verb that has a state meaning can form a continuous participle. "Waiting," "standing," "winning," and "lying" are all states more than they are actions:

أنا مستنيك   واقفة برا

2ana mistanniik   *waa2fe barra*

I'm waiting for you   she's standing outside

مين فايز؟

miin faayez?

who's winning?

متسطحة ع التخت

mitsaTT7a 3 attakh^et

she's lying on the bed

In some cases, these continuous participles are most idiomatically translated using a normal adjective or some other expression in English. But the participle still expresses the meaning of an ongoing, continuous state:

هيدا نايم

hayda naayem

this guy's asleep

ساكن هون؟

saaken hoon?

do you live here?

Resultative Participles

The second primary use of the participle is to express a "resultative," which expresses the state that results from a verb being completed. It is probably easiest to get a sense of what this means in practice by provisionally translating the participle using the English present perfect form ("have X-ed"), with which it shares some similarities. Note that unlike the continuous participle, almost any verb can form a resultative:

Result	Action
كاتب كتاب *kaateb ᵢktaab* he has written a book	كتب كتاب *katab ᵢktaab* he wrote a book
ضاربة أخوها *Daarbe 2akhuuha* she's hit her brother	ضربت أخوها *Darbet 2akhuuha* she hit her brother
طالعين من الحارة *Taal3iin mn ᵢl7aara* they've left the neighbourhood	طلعو من الحارة *Til3u mn ᵢl7aara* they left the neighbourhood

Of course, these two sets of translations leave something to be desired, because as we have seen, the perfective often gives the sense of the English present perfect. This means that the perfective and the resultative participle are usually both possible in the same sentence, while the distinction between the English forms is generally more solid. Nonetheless, the participle gives a different nuance, because it tends to place emphasis on the *present relevance of the event* (or the *state resulting from it*) rather than on the action itself:

حاضرة هالفيلم؟

7aaDra halfil^em?

have you seen this film?

كاتبلك كل شي ع ورقة

kaatiblak kill shii 3a wara2a

I've written everything down
for you on a piece of paper

The English present perfect and the Arabic active participle are not identical, however. For one thing, it is possible to combine the participle with expressions of time, which is famously impossible with the present perfect:

متفقين امبارح إنو . . .

mittif2iin ᵉmbaare7 2inno . . .

we agreed yesterday that . . .

[not "we have agreed yesterday that"]

شايفتو من تلت سنين

shaayifto min tlett ᵉsniin

I saw it three years ago

[not "I have seen it three years ago"]

For another, the resultative is broader in meaning than its English counterpart. Situations such as the following tick all the boxes—past action, present relevance—but wouldn't work with the present perfect in English:

دارس أدب إنجليزي

daares 2adab 2ingliizi

I studied English literature

[= I'm an English literature grad]

ربيانة برا

rabyaane barra

I was raised abroad

[= I'm an expat kid]

Moreover, resultative participles are very commonly used with change-of-state verbs (see unit 24) that correspond to English structures with "get" or "become." In these cases the idiomatic translation is often a simple adjective. Note, however, that the *meaning* is the same. The participle expresses the state (being sleepy, being hungry, having a cold) resulting from the action (getting sleepy, getting hungry, getting a cold):

جوعان ← جاع

joo3aan   *jaa3*

He's hungry   He got hungry

نعسانة ← نعست

na3saane   *n3is^et*

I'm sleepy   I got sleepy

عاشقة ← شقت

3aash2a   *3ish2at*

She's in love   She's fallen in love

مرشح ← رشح

mrashshe7   *rashsha7*

He's got a cold   He got a cold

Eagle-eyed readers may have noticed that some of the participles given as examples of *resultative* participles here were also given as *continuous* participles in the previous section. Most verbs that can form a continuous participle can also form a resultative participle. It would be nice if there were a straightforward way of distinguishing these two meanings, but there is not other than context:

Resultative	Continuous
أحمد نايم هون امبارح *2a7mad naayem hoon ˈmbaare7* Ahmad slept here yesterday	أحمد نايم *2a7mad naayem* Ahmad is asleep
فايت لجوا شي من قبل؟ *faayet lajuwwa shii min 2abᵉl?* have you been inside before?	فايت لجوا أنا *faayet lajuwwa 2ana* I'm going inside
في حدا من الجيران راجع *fii 7ada mn ˈjjiiraan raaje3* one of the neighbours has come back	يلا راجعة *yaLLa raaj3a* all right, I'm coming back

These structures may be more common for some speakers than others.

Future Participles

There is one final common use of the participle: referring to the *future*. This use of the participle is deceptively simple for English speakers. Having learnt forms like جايه *jaaye* "coming" and رايحين *raay7iin* "going" as continuous forms, it feels natural to use them in contexts such as the following:

رايحين ع البيت بعدين *raay7iin 3 albeet ba3deen* They're going home afterwards.	جايه بكرا؟ *jaaye bukra?* Are you coming tomorrow?
	نايم عندي اليوم صح؟ *naayem 3indi lyoom Sa77?* You're sleeping at mine today, right?

On closer inspection, it is clear that these forms aren't really continuous in English or in Arabic. The action isn't taking place in the moment. What we are really expressing here is a prescheduled intention or plan for the future. This overlaps very closely with (one use of) the future formed with رح *ra7* (see unit 36):

ra7	Participle
رح تجي بكرا؟ *ra7 tiji bukra?* Are you going to come tomorrow?	جايه بكرا؟ *jaaye bukra?* Are you coming tomorrow?

ra7	Participle
رح يروحو ع البيت بعدين	رايحين ع البيت بعدين
ra7 yruu7u 3a lbeet ba3deen	*raay7iin 3a lbeet ba3deen*
They're going to go home afterwards.	They're going home afterwards.

So far, so good. But it's important to note that even verbs that cannot form a continuous participle can still form a future participle. The following examples can only have a resultative or a future meaning. They absolutely cannot have a continuous meaning:

أنا بكرا الصبح تعبان

2ana bukra SSub°7 ta3baan

I'll be tired tomorrow morning

أنا ماني موقعة!

2ana maani mwaqq3a!

I'm not signing it!

[= I'm not going to sign it!]

مش باعتة حدا!

mish baa3te 7ada!

she's not sending anyone!

[= isn't going to send]

ولله إني قاتلو!

waLLaahi 2inni 2aatlo!

I'm going to kill him!

As these examples show, although most future participles correspond to the English future use of the continuous ("is X-ing"), this is not always true. The participle works with more verbs than the English "X-ing" form does.

Continuous Participle Versus the Imperfective

The continuous participles we looked at above generally correspond to continuous forms in English. There is a fairly large subset of verbs, however, that *cannot* form continuous structures in English but *do* have continuous participles in Arabic. For these verbs, both the imperfective and the participle tend to translate to the English present simple. But the meaning is distinct. While the imperfective expresses a general or repeated situation, the participle—like other continuous participles—generally expresses an ongoing, in-the-moment state.

These verbs include verbs of ability and sense:

Participle	Imperfective
إيدي مش حاسة فيها! *2iidi mish 7aasse fiiha!* I can't feel my hand! [right now]	إيدي ما بحس فيها! *2iidi maa b7iss fiiha!* I can't feel my hand! [as a general rule]
سامع الصوت؟ *saame3 'SSoot?* can you hear that sound? [right now]	بتسمع الصوت *btisma3 'SSoot?* can you hear the sound? [generally]
مش عارف إني طلعت! *mish 3aaref 2inni Tli3et!* he doesn't realise that I went out! [right in this moment]	بعرف إني طلعت *bi3raf 2inni Tli3et* he knows I left [general]
أنا مو قدرانة ابقى *2ana muu 2adraane 2ib2a* I can't stay [right now]	ما بقدر ابقى *maa bi2der 2ib2a* I can't stay [in general or right now]

Note that for North Levantine speakers, these structures can be replaced with continuous structures with *3am* (see unit 35): عم تسمعني؟ *3am tisma3ni?* "can you hear me?"

Verbs of knowledge and understanding:

Participle	Imperfective
عارف شو بدك *3aaref shuu biddak* I know what you want [right now]	بعرف شو بدك *ba3raf shuu biddak* I know what you want [generally or in the moment]
بفهم بالسياسة *bifham bissiyaase* I get politics [in general]	فهمانة عليك *fahmaane 3aleek* I get you [in this moment]

And verbs of feeling ("is afraid to," "would like to," "hates"):

Participle	Imperfective
خايف سوق *khaayef suu2* I'm scared to drive [right now]	بخاف سوق *bkhaaf suu2* I'm scared to drive [in general]
حابة تركض *7aabbe tirkoD* she'd like to go for a run [right now]	بتحب تركض *bit7ibb tirkoD* she likes running [generally]

With Verbs of Deeming

Verbs of deeming—"consider to be," "think that X is," etc.—also commonly appear in participle form. Again, there is a contrast here with the imperfective form. In this case, the imperfective generally expresses *repeated action*, while the participle corresponds to the "general state" meaning of the English present simple. Again, the imperfective and the participle are not interchangeable even though they translate to the same English form:

Participle	Imperfective
مفكرني أهبل *'mfakkirni 2ahbal* he thinks I'm stupid [generally]	أوقات بفكرني أهبل *2aw2aat bifakkirni 2ahbal* sometimes he thinks I'm stupid [repeated action]
محسبينني أردني *m7assbiinni 2urduni* they think I'm Jordanian [right now, generally]	مرات بحسبوني أردني *marraat bi7assbuuni 2urduni* sometimes they take me for a Jordanian [repeated action]
بس هالمرة مستغليه *bass halmarra mistaghlii* but this time he thinks it's too expensive	كل مرة بستغليه *kull marra bistaghlii* every time he thinks it's too expensive [repeated action]

Idiomatic Uses of the Participle

Before ending this unit, it is worth noting some important idiomatic uses of the participle. In the sections above, we largely characterised the participle in purely tense-based terms, that is, what sort of time characteristics it attaches to the action described by a verb. But an additional factor often differentiating a participle from a structure with a straightforward verb is the extra information it gives about the speaker's attitude.

Participles are sometimes used to signal that what is being said is secondhand information, that is, that the speaker did not witness the action firsthand:

<table>
<tr><td align="center">رايحة حاكية مع المدير</td><td align="center">قال في واحد ملاقي تليفونك</td></tr>
<tr><td align="center">raay7a 7aakye ma3 ˈlmudiir</td><td align="center">2aal fii waa7ad ˈmlaa2i telefoonak</td></tr>
<tr><td align="center">[apparently] she went and talked
to the manager</td><td align="center">supposedly someone's found
your phone</td></tr>
</table>

Relatedly, participles can connote surprise, realisation, or sometimes anger:

<table>
<tr><td align="center">كاينة كربوجة أنا وصغيرة!</td><td align="center">بلاقيك قاعد عند أبوك امبارح!</td></tr>
<tr><td align="center">kaayne karbuuje 2ana w ˈzghiire!</td><td align="center">balaa2iik 2aa3ed 3ind 2abuuk ˈmbaare7!</td></tr>
<tr><td align="center">[turns out] I was cute when I was
little!</td><td align="center">so you stayed at your dad's yesterday!</td></tr>
<tr><td align="center">ليش هيك ضاربتيني؟</td><td align="center">كاين داقلي وأنا مش حاسس</td></tr>
<tr><td align="center">leesh heek Daaribtiini?</td><td align="center">kaayen daa2i2li w 2ana mish 7aases</td></tr>
<tr><td align="center">why did you hit me like that?</td><td align="center">[it seems] you rang and I didn't notice</td></tr>
</table>

Framing Constructions: *kaan*

In this unit we will be looking at the framing verb كان *kaan*. The verb *kaan* is only one of a number of framing verbs that play a role in the Arabic tense system. But *kaan* is probably the most common of these verbs as well as the only one whose function is more or less exclusively to provide *tense* framing without adding any extra information. For this reason, *kaan* provides a useful way into understanding the functioning of framing verbs more broadly.

Almost every conceivable form of *kaan* can be combined with other structures in order to frame them differently in time. In order to make this more straightforward, I have divided the forms into past structures (with *kaan*), non–past structures (with *bikuun*, the *b*-imperfective form of *kaan*), and participle structures (with *kaayen*). We will look at each of these in turn and see what sort of effects they have when combined with different kinds of sentence.

Past Structures

The perfective form of *kaan* frames sentences in the past. The simplest examples of this are with nouns, adjectives, locations, and so on in "to be" sentences (see unit 49):

شاطرة ← كانت شاطرة

shaaTra   *kaanat shaaTra*

she's clever   she was clever

الشباب دكاترة ← الشباب كانو دكاترة

'shshabaab dakaatra   *'shshabaab kaanu dakaatra*

the guys are doctors   the guys were doctors

أنا بالبيت ← كنت بالبيت

2ana bilbeet   *kint bilbeet*

I'm at home   I was at home

The same structure can be used to frame other tense constructions of the kind that we have been looking at in the previous units. For example, the *b*-imperfective alone generally expresses repeated action or a state (see unit 34). Combining it with *kaan* produces a structure expressing repeated action or a state *in the past*. Note that this causes deletion of the *b*-prefix:

بضحكني   ←   كان يضحكني

biDa77ikni   *kaan yDa77ikni*

he makes me laugh   he used to make me laugh

he would make me laugh

بتعرفي كل إشي   ←   كنتي تعرفي كل إشي

bti3rafi kull 2ishi   *kunti ti3rafi kull 2ishi*

you know everything   you knew everything

you used to know everything

> Some speakers do not delete the *b-* here, particularly in North Levantine. For most speakers, however, the presence or absence of *b-* here generally marks the structure as past or conditional (see part 7). With verbs that are perceived as particularly "adjectival," however—such as بغار *bighaar* "he's jealous"—constructions retaining the *b-* seem to be more acceptable to all speakers.

Those South Levantine speakers who use the *b*-imperfective on its own as a continuous (see unit 35) can similarly project it back into the past using *kaan*, but in this case the *b-* is not dropped:

بوكلو خبز   ←   كانو بوكلو خبز

booklu khubᵉz   *kaanu booklu khubᵉz*

they're eating bread   they were eating bread

The same applies to other continuous constructions, whether with *3am*, *2aa3ed*, or the continuous participle (see unit 37):

عم يكتب مكتوب   ←   كان عم يكتب مكتوب

3am yiktob maktuub   *kaan 3am yiktob maktuub*

he's writing a letter   he was writing a letter

قاعدين يكولو خبز   ←   كانو قاعدين يوكلو خبز

2aa3diin yooklu khubᵉz   *kaanu 2aa3diin yooklu khubᵉz*

they're eating bread   they were eating bread

رايحين على عمان   ⟵   كنا رايحين على عمان

kunna raay7iin 3ala 3amman   *raay7iin 3ala 3ammaan*

we were going to Amman   we're going to Amman

The *ra7* and *7a-* future forms (see unit 36) can be used to give a future-in-past meaning, as can the alternative structure with *bidd-*. This often gives the meaning "was about to" or "almost X-ed":

ماما رح تقتلني!   ⟵   كانت ماما رح تقتلني!

kaanat maama ra7 tu2tulni!   *maama ra7 tu2tulni!*

Mum was going to kill me!   Mum's going to kill me!

Mum almost killed me!

حشوفها بكرا   ⟵   كنت حشوفها تاني يوم

kint 7ashuufa taani yoom   *7ashuufa bukra*

I was going to see her the next day   I'm going to see her tomorrow

بدي أوقع   ⟵   كان بدي أوقع

kaan baddi 2uu2a3   *baddi 2uu2a3*

I was about to fall   I'm going to fall

I almost fell

Finally, *kaan* can be combined with a resultative participle (see unit 37) to give a pluperfect (past-in-past) meaning corresponding to the English "had X-ed."

شايفها امبارح   ⟵   كان شايفها قبل بيوم

kaan shaayifa 2abl ᵢbyoom   *shaayifa mbaare7*

he'd seen her the day before   he saw her yesterday

You might expect to be able to combine *kaan* with a perfective form as well and produce a similar past-in-past or pluperfect structure. For North Levantine speakers, this absolutely is possible and normal:

فلينا   ⟵   كنا فلينا

kinna falleena   *falleena*

we'd [already] left   we left

This provides a convenient way of disambiguating "we had already gone" (*kinna falleena*) and "we were leaving" (*kinna faalliin*). This is possible in South Levantine as well but requires a different construction, with صار *Saar* (see unit 39).

But for South Levantine speakers, structures of this kind will generally be understood as conditional (see part 7).

Non-Past Structures

The *b*-imperfective form of *kaan*—بكون *bikuun*—acts similarly to its past counterpart. The motivation for this form, however, can be less intuitive to an English speaker. Often it has the present "repeated action" meaning (see unit 34) of the *b*-imperfective. With "to be" sentences, this frames what would otherwise be a *general, current* statement as a *repeated-action* statement:

كل مرة بكون مبسوط ← أنا مبسوط

kull marra bakuun mabsuuT ← *2ana mabsuuT*

every time, I'm happy ← I'm happy

الصبح بكون أحمد بالبيت ← أحمد بالبيت

ᵢSSibᵉ7 bikuun 2a7mad bilbeet ← *2a7mad bilbeet*

in the mornings, Ahmad is at home ← Ahmad is at home

> A *b*-imperfective form of *kaan* is also used by default with family relationships (هادا بكون أخي *haada bikuun 2akhi* "this is my brother") and in some idiomatic contexts (حضرتك مين بتكون؟ *7aDᵢrtak miin bitkuun?* "who do I have the pleasure of speaking to?"). For more, see unit 49.

The same structure can be combined with other tense constructions. The underlying logic here is exactly the same, although the particularities make it slightly more complicated:

لما بيرجع المسا بكون عم اشرب قهوة ← عم اشرب قهوة

lamma byirja3 ᵢlmasa ᵢbkuun 3am 2ishrab 2ahwe ← *3am 2ishrab 2ahwe*

when he gets back in the evenings, I'll be drinking coffee ← I'm drinking coffee

كل يوم لما بتجي بكون أنا مساوي أكل ← مساوي أكل

kill yoom lamma btiji ᵢbkuun ᵢmsaawi 2akᵉl ← *msaawi 2akᵉl*

every day when she arrives I've made food ← I've made food

كل مرة بكون رح أطلع ... ← رح أطلع

kull marra bakuun ra7 2aTla3 ... ← *ra7 2aTla3*

every time, I'll be about to go out [when] ... ← I'm about to go out

عارفة شو بدو   →   كل مرة بكون عارفة شو بدو

kill marra bkuun 3aarfe shuu baddo   *3aarfe shuu baddo*

every time, I know what he wants   I know what he wants

The base forms on the right mark ongoing action (continuous), a completed action (resultative), a planned or anticipated action (future), and an ongoing state (continuous participle), respectively. These meanings are carried over to the scenes described by the sentences on the left. But these sentences—as you can see from the extra context—are also describing scenes that are repeated "in the evenings," "every day," or "every time." Since repeated action is not expressed by the base forms, we introduce *b(a)kuun* to complete the framing.

Of course, the *b*-imperfective also has a future meaning (see unit 36). This works similarly to frame other constructions, in this case pushing them into the future. Note that this form—unlike the past *kaan*—can be combined with perfectives for all speakers straightforwardly, producing a past-in-future meaning:

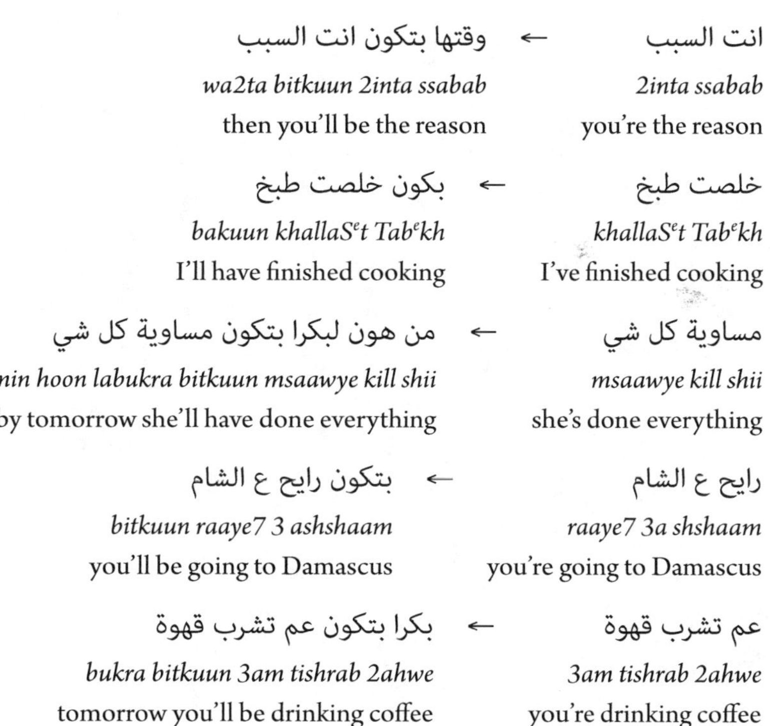

انت السبب   →   وقتها بتكون انت السبب

wa2ta bitkuun 2inta ssabab   *2inta ssabab*

then you'll be the reason   you're the reason

خلصت طبخ   →   بكون خلصت طبخ

bakuun khallaS^et Tab^ekh   *khallaS^et Tab^ekh*

I'll have finished cooking   I've finished cooking

مساوية كل شي   →   من هون لبكرا بتكون مساوية كل شي

min hoon labukra bitkuun msaawye kill shii   *msaawye kill shii*

by tomorrow she'll have done everything   she's done everything

رايح ع الشام   →   بتكون رايح ع الشام

bitkuun raaye7 3 ashshaam   *raaye7 3a shshaam*

you'll be going to Damascus   you're going to Damascus

عم تشرب قهوة   →   بكرا بتكون عم تشرب قهوة

bukra bitkuun 3am tishrab 2ahwe   *3am tishrab 2ahwe*

tomorrow you'll be drinking coffee   you're drinking coffee

These forms also have an important secondary usage marking conjecture, for which see unit 45.

Participle Structures

The participle of *kaan*, كاين *kaayen*, can also be used to frame other verbal constructions. The time semantics of this form are resultative, but its main function is to give the sentence one of the various idiomatic senses of the participle (see unit 37). This form usually implies surprise, anger, or an unexpected discovery:

كاين كربوج أنا وصغير!

kaayen karbuuj 2ana w ˈzghiir!
Seems like I was cute when I
was little!
[looking at a picture and expressing
surprise]

كاينة عم تقبض العالم!

kaayne 3am ti2boD ˈl3aalam!
Apparently [other] people have been
getting paid!
[a nasty discovery after a month
of no pay]

To this end, *kaayen* is quite often combined with another participle, reinforcing the emotive or discovery meaning:

حدا كاين داقئلي

7ada kaayen daa2i2li
apparently someone's rung me
[checking your phone and discovering a missed call you didn't notice]

Idiomatic Construction: *muu/mish kaayen, maa kaan*

The negative of the participle, combined with a present tense verb, expresses repeated effort resulting in failure. In a question, by extension, it means "isn't it about time that . . . ?"

عم دقلها بس مو كاينة ترد

3am di22illa bass muu kaayne tridd
I'm ringing her but she's just not
answering

مش كاينة تنحل هالمشكلة؟

mish kaayne tin7all halmushkile?
isn't it about time this problem was
solved?

For North Levantine speakers, there is a synonymous structure with the past form *maa kaan*:

عم دقلها بس ما كانت ترد

3am di22illa bass maa kaanet ˈtridd
I'm ringing her but she's just not
answering

ما كانت تنحل هلمشكلة؟

maa kaanet tin7all halmishˈkle?
isn't it about time this problem was
solved?

Framing Constructions Indicating a Change of State

In the last unit we looked at the framing verb كان *kaan*, which provides additional tense information to frame an existing sentence or clause. In the next three units, we will be looking at other framing verbs. These work more or less exactly like *kaan*. The main difference is that while *kaan* carries no additional meaning of its own beyond tense, these verbs add something extra on top.

For the verbs we will look at in this unit—صار *Saar*, رجع *rije3*, صفى *Saffa,* and بطل *baT-Tal*—this something extra is a *change of state*, with the specific kind of change varying from verb to verb. We will look at each of these verbs in turn, along with some alternatives.

Saar "Become"

Almost as common as *kaan* is صار *Saar*, which expresses a change of state. This sometimes translates as "become," but often a better choice in English is "start" or "begin" or an expression such as "nowadays" or "now" (implicitly expressing a contrast with "previously," just as *Saar* does). Arabic is much more likely to explicitly indicate changes of state than English is. As a result, many English sentences that leave a change of state implicit will require a *Saar* in the Arabic counterpart:

صرت كاتبة

Sur^et kaatbe

[now] I'm an author

صار كلو عم يتجوز

Saar killo 3am yitjawwaz

[nowadays] everyone's getting married

صرت اشرب قهوة

Sir^et 2ishrab 2ahwe

I drink coffee [now]

صارو بحبو بعض

Saaru bi7ibbu ba3^eD

they're in love [now]

In these examples, the perfective form of *Saar* has a present perfect meaning, referring to an event in the past whose effects are still current. But it can also have a straightforwardly past meaning. Depending on context, the sentences above can also have meanings such as the following:

صرت كاتبة

صار كلو عم يتجوز

Sur͑t kaatbe

Saar killo 3am yitjawwaz

I became an author

everyone started getting married

صرت اشرب قهوة

صارو بحبو بعض

Sir͑t 2ishrab 2ahwe

Saaru bi7ibbu ba3͑D

I started drinking coffee

they came to love one another

Which meaning is intended will only be clear from context.

Saar is often combined with a participle (see unit 37). For all speakers, this can have a straightforward change-of-state meaning:

صرت شايفتو تافه

<u>Sir͑t</u> shaayifto taafeh

I've started to think he's pettyt

[= become to see him as]

Saar can also express frustration at repeated action:

صرت قايللك ميت مرة!

صرتي كاتبة شي ميت مقالة!

Sir͑t 2aayillak miit marra!

Surti kaatbe shii miit maqaale!

I've told you a hundred times

you've written a hundred articles

[and you still won't listen]!

[and it's got you nowhere]!

For South Levantine speakers, *Saar* is more common. It is their default way of expressing "already":

صار الأستاذ طالع

صرت آكل

Saar ͵l2ustaaz Taale3

Sur͑t 2aakel

The boss has already left

I've already eaten

As we have seen, for North Levantine speakers *kaan* + perfective fulfils this function (see unit 38).

rije3, radd "Go Back to Being"

Like *Saar*, رجع *rije3* expresses a change of state. The main difference is that *rije3* implies a return to an old state. Its use is straightforward and uniform, but the lack of a direct counterpart in English means that the translation will vary with context.

<table>
<tr><td align="center">رجعت أكتب شعر</td><td align="center">برجع ولد صغير</td></tr>
<tr><td align="center">rji3ᵉt 2akteb shi3ᵉr</td><td align="center">birja3 walad ᶦzghiir</td></tr>
<tr><td align="center">I'm writing poetry again</td><td align="center">I turn into a kid again</td></tr>
<tr><td align="center">I've started writing poetry again</td><td align="center">[I feel like] I'm a kid again</td></tr>
<tr><td align="center">[= I have returned to writing]</td><td align="center">[= I return to being a kid]</td></tr>
</table>

Like *Saar*, the perfective forms can have both a present meaning or a straightforward past meaning, depending on context:

<table>
<tr><td align="center">رجعت أكتب شعر</td><td align="center">رجعنا نحب بعض</td></tr>
<tr><td align="center">ᶦrji3ᵉt 2akteb shi3ᵉr</td><td align="center">ᶦrji3na n7ibb ba3ᵉD</td></tr>
<tr><td align="center">I'm writing poetry again [now]</td><td align="center">we love one another again [now]</td></tr>
<tr><td align="center">I started writing poetry again [then]</td><td align="center">we came to love one another again
[then]</td></tr>
</table>

Unlike most of the other framing verbs in this section, *rije3* has a causative (see unit 56), رجع *rajja3*. Again, it is difficult to give a single catchall translation, but the basic sense is of "returning" someone to a previous state:

<table>
<tr><td align="center">الحفلة رجعتني ولد صغير</td><td align="center">هالشوفة بترجع الشايب شب</td></tr>
<tr><td align="center">ᶦl7afle rajja3itni walad ᶦzghiir</td><td align="center">hashshoofe bitrajje3 ᶦshshaayeb shabb</td></tr>
<tr><td align="center">the concert made me [feel like] a little
boy again</td><td align="center">that sight would make an old man
young again</td></tr>
</table>

For some North Levantine speakers, both *rije3* and *rajja3* can be replaced by رد *radd*:

<table>
<tr><td align="center">رديت صغيرة</td><td align="center">هالشوفة بترد الشايب شب</td></tr>
<tr><td align="center">raddeet ᶦzghiire</td><td align="center">hashshoofe bitridd ᶦshshaayeb shabb</td></tr>
<tr><td align="center">I [felt like] a kid again</td><td align="center">that sight would make an old man young again</td></tr>
</table>

rije3 and *radd* are also used in the similar-looking—but quite distinct—double verb construction, for which see unit 62.

Saffa, Sifi "End Up"

The word صفى *Saffa*—for some North Levantine speakers صفي *Sifi*—expresses a change of state much like the last two verbs we've looked at. The difference is that *Saffa* generally implies that someone found themselves in an unexpected or unpleasant situation. One common translation is "end up," although this doesn't always work:

صفيت عم بستناكي

Saffeet 3am bastannaaki

I've ended up having to wait for you

I ended up having to wait for you

صفيت أجدب نظامي

Sfiit 2ajdab niZaami

I've been left looking like a real idiot

I was left looking like a real idiot

baTTal, maa 3aad, maa ba2a "No Longer"

Like صار *Saar*, the verb بطل *baTTal* expresses a change of state. But in this case the emphasis is on the end of the previous state and not the beginning of the new one. A less inscrutable way of putting this is to say that it translates as "no longer" or "not . . . anymore":

بطلت أشتغل زي أول

baTTalt 2ashtghel zayy 2awwal

I don't work as much as I did before

I stopped working as much as I had before

بطل ولد صغير

baTTal walad ᵉzghiir

he's not a little boy anymore

he wasn't a little boy anymore

Note the idiomatic usage to mean "I've changed my mind and now I'm not going to":

بطلت بدي!

baTTalᵉt biddi!

I don't want to anymore!

خلص بطلت آكل!

khalaS baTTalᵉt 2aakol!

forget it, I just won't eat anything!

I'm no longer going to eat

> *baTTal* can also act as a normal verb meaning "stop": بطلها لهلعادة *baTTilha lahal3aade* "you need to stop doing this all the time"; بطلت تدخين *baTTalᵉt tadkhiin* "I stopped smoking."

The structures ما عاد *maa 3aad* and ما بقى *maa ba2a* (North Levantine) and معدش *ma3adᵉsh* and مبقاش *maba2aash* (South Levantine) express the same idea. Note that although *3aad* and *ba2a* are historically verbs, they frequently do not conjugate:

North Levantine	**South Levantine**
أنا ما بقى صغير	أنا مبقاش صغير
2ana maa ba2a zghiir	*2ana maba2aash zghiir*
I'm not a kid any more	I'm not a kid any more
ما عاد أعمل شي	معدش أعمل شي
maa 3aad 2a3mel shii	*ma3adᵉsh 2a3mel shii*
I don't do anything anymore	I don't do anything anymore
these days, I don't do anything	these days, I don't do anything

Note that these forms are often combined with a perfective:

ما عاد دخنت

maa 3aad dakhkhanᵉt

I don't smoke any more

I stopped smoking

ما بقى حكيت معاه

maa ba2a 7akeet ma3aa

I don't talk to him any more

I stopped talking to him

They can also give an imperative or future meaning:

خلص أنا ما عاد شوفو!

khalaS 2ana maa 3aad shuufo!

OK, I won't see him again!

ما بقى تحكي معي!

maa ba2a ti7ki ma3o!

don't talk to him again!

Framing Constructions Indicating Duration

In unit 39, we looked at a set of framing constructions that indicated a change of state. In this unit, we will be looking at another set. These constructions indicate not a change of state but rather various kinds of *duration*, that is, that the scene described by the framed verb continues for some period of time. These verbs largely correspond to English constructions with "stay," "keep," or "still," with various additional connotations.

Dall, bi2i, tamm "Stay," "Keep X-ing"

Unlike the other verbs we have looked at so far, these words are used to express that a situation is drawn out or continues. With verbs they usually translate as "keep X-ing" or "carry on X-ing," while with "to be" sentences they typically correspond to "stay," but the meaning is the same:

<table>
<tr><td>بقيت واقفة</td><td>بضل عم حاول</td></tr>
<tr><td>b2iit waa2fe</td><td>bDall 3am 7aawel</td></tr>
<tr><td>I stayed standing</td><td>I'll keep trying</td></tr>
<tr><td>تميت فوق</td><td>ضليت عم بكتب</td></tr>
<tr><td>tammeet foo2</td><td>Dalleet 3am bakteb</td></tr>
<tr><td>I stayed upstairs</td><td>I kept writing</td></tr>
</table>

These verbs often appear with object pronouns (see unit 18) mirroring the subject:

<table>
<tr><td>بقيتني واقفة</td><td>بضلني عم حاول</td></tr>
<tr><td>b2iit-ni waa2fe</td><td>bDall-ni 3am 7aawel</td></tr>
<tr><td>I stayed standing</td><td>I'll keep trying</td></tr>
<tr><td>تميتني فوق</td><td>ضليتني عم بكتب</td></tr>
<tr><td>tammeet-ni foo2</td><td>Dalleet-ni 3am bakteb</td></tr>
<tr><td>I stayed upstairs</td><td>I kept writing</td></tr>
</table>

The behaviour of these pronouns is complicated and varies widely from region to region. The pronouns interact in unpredictable ways with other verb suffixes. The following paradigm is representative of one Syrian speaker:

Imperfective		Perfective	
	بضلني *bDall-ni* I keep		ضليتني *Dalleet-ni* I kept
بتضلك *bitDall-ek* you [F] keep	بتضلك *bitDall-ak* you [M] keep	ضليتك *Dalleet-ek* you [F] kept	ضليتك *Dalleet-ak* you [M] kept
بتضلها *bitDall-ha* she keeps	بضلو *biDall-o* he keeps	ضلها OR ضلتها *Dall-ha OR Dallit-ha* she kept	ضلو *Dall-o* he kept
	منضلنا *minDall-na* we keep		ضلينا *Dalleena* we kept
	بتضلكن *bitDall-kon* you [P] keep		ضليتكن *Dalleet-kon* you [P] kept
	بضلهن OR بضلوهن *biDall-hon OR biDalluu-hon* they keep		ضلهن OR ضلوهن *Dall-hon OR Dalluu-hon* they kept

As you can see, the pronouns sometimes result in deletion of one or another of the existing suffixes, especially when those suffixes are long vowels. It is best to simply copy what you hear. It is never wrong to use a form without the suffix.

Note that *Dall* is the idiomatic translation of "still" in sentences such as the following:

حتى ولو! بضل أبوك!

7atta wlaw! biDall 2abuuk!

even if he did, he's still your dad!

khalla "Stay, Keep"

A partial synonym of the verbs above is خلّى *khalla* "stay," "keep." This word, however, is mainly used in its imperative form, ـخلّي *khallii-*, and is invariably combined with a pronoun. This pronoun marks the subject, with *khallii-* itself generally remaining invariable:

خلّينا *khallii-na* let's stay	خلّيني *khallii-ni* let me stay	
خلّيكم *khallii-kom* (you [P]) stay	خلّيكي *khallii-ki* (you [F]) stay	خلّيك *khallii-k* (you [M]) stay
خلّيهم *khallii-hom* let them stay	خلّيها *khallii-ha* let her stay	خلّيه *khallii* let him stay

As you can see, *khallii-* is largely an imperative counterpart to *Dall, bi2i*, etc. The uses of the first-person and third-person imperatives are explained in more detail in part 4. Given the glosses above, however, structures such as the following should be fairly transparent:

خليكي هون

khalliiki hoon

stay here

خلّينا عم نحاول

khalliina 3am 'n7aawel

let's keep trying

خليك عم تدقلها

khalliik 3am 'tdi22illa

you keep ringing her

خليني ساكتة أحسن

khalliini saakte 2a7san

I'd better just shut up

[= let me stay silent, that's better]

The verb *khalla* is sometimes used in other forms as well:

خليتني عم دقلها

khalleetni 3am di22illa

I kept ringing her

Note that the verb *khalla* has many other uses. For more, see unit 56.

lissa and *ba3ᵉd* "Still"

These two words express that a state remains in place; that is, they translate the English term "still." The term *lissa* sometimes occurs on its own but is more commonly combined with an attached pronoun (see unit 18) that agrees with the subject of the sentence, almost like a pseudoverb. Note that these are among the words that take *-ni* for "me" (see unit 18) despite not being verbs:

أبو أحمد لسا موجود؟   لساتني عم اكتب

2abu 2a7mad lissa mawjuud?   *lissaatni 3am 2iktob*

is Abu Ahmad still here?   I'm still writing

The word *ba3ᵉd* almost invariably appears with pronouns:

بعدني عم آكل   بعدو موجود

ba3dni 3am 2aakol   *ba3do mawjuud*

I'm still eating   it's still around

Note the idiomatic use of *ba3ᵉd* and *lissa* to mean "[is] still here/there," which corresponds to a similar use with *kaan* (see unit 38):

روح ولا لساتو؟

rawwa7 willa lissaato?

has he gone home or is he still here?

With negatives, these words give the meaning of "not . . . yet":

بعدني مأكلتش   لسا ما خلص

ba3dni ma2akaltᵉsh   *lissa maa khileS*

I haven't eaten yet   it hasn't finished yet

بعدو ما إجا   خلصت؟ لسا

ba3ᵉdo ma 2ija   *khallaSᵉt? lissa*

he's not here yet   have you finished? not yet

Some North Levantine speakers allow *ba3ᵉd* to appear without pronouns in negative constructions. For these speakers, it is sometimes only very marginally distinct from بعد ما *ba3ᵉd ma*, the conjunction form of "after" (see unit 68):

بعد ما إجا   بعد ما إجا

ba3ᵉd maa 2ija   *ba3ᵉd ma 2ija*

he's not here yet   after he got here

Combined with a participle (see unit 37), these structures mean "only just":

لسا جاي

بعدني واصلة

lissa jaay

ba3dni waaSle

I've only just got here

I've only just got here

kill/kull maalo "Just Keeps"

Our last framing structure is كل مالو *kill/kull maal-o* "just keeps." Like *lissa* and *ba3ᵉd*, this expression is similar to a pseudoverb in that it never appears without a suffixed pronoun marking the subject:

كل مالو عم يزيد

حياتي كل مالها لورا

kill maalo 3am yziid

7ayaati kull maalha lawara

it just keeps increasing

my life just keeps getting worse

my life just keeps going backwards

SaLLo and 2ilo "Have Been"

The words صارلو *SaLL-o* (occasionally *Sarl-o*) and إلو *2il-o* are pseudoverbs, which is to say that their subject is marked by suffixed pronouns (see unit 18). In every other respect, they function like other framing verbs. Their function is to express how long something has gone on or went on for; that is, they express "have been . . . for." The terms *SaLLo* and *2ilo* are always combined with a time expression:

صارلو سنة عم يتعلم

إلي يومين تعبان

SaLLo sane 3am yit3allam

2ili yoomeen ta3baan

he's been learning for a year

I've been feeling fatigued for a couple of days

قديش صارلك هون؟

إلي من الصبح مشربتش إشي

2addeesh SaLLak hoon?

2ili mn ᶜSSubᵒ7 mashribtᵉsh 2ishi

how long have you been here?

I haven't had anything to drink since this morning

The *r > l* change here is an example of assimilation (see unit 4).

Miscellaneous Framing Structures

In this unit, we will look at two additional framing structures that do not fit into either of the two previous categories. These structures are يا دوب *ya doob* "barely" (and its variants) and هلق *halla2* "just now."

ya doob, doob, bilkaad, yaLLa yaLLa, 2anja2

The framing structures يا دوب *yaa doob* and دوب *doob* mean "barely," "just about." They appear immediately after the topic. Both commonly appear with pronoun suffixes agreeing with the topic, and *doob-* cannot appear without them:

يا دوب عم لحق اشتري غراض

أنا يا دوبني قادر أكتب

yaa doob 3am la77e2 2ishtiri ghraaD

2ana yaa doobni 2aader 2akteb

I can barely afford to buy groceries

I'm barely able to write

With resultative participles these structures express "only just":

يا دوبو جاي من الجامعة

دوبني واصل ع بيروت

yaa doobo jaay mn ⁱljaam3a

doobni waaSel 3a beyruut

he's only just got back from university

I've only just got to Beirut

Note the phrases يلا يلا *yaLLa yaLLa*, أنجق *2anja2*, and بالكاد *bilkaad*, all of which mean "barely" and also appear after the topic but do not take pronoun suffixes:

أنا يلا يلا وصلت ع البيت

بالكاد شايفتو

2ana yaLLa yaLLa waSSalt 3 albeet

bilkaad shaayifto

I'd barely got home

I can barely see it

أنجق عرفت افتح تمي

2anja2 ⁱ3rifⁱt 2ifta7 timmi

I could barely get a word in edgeways

halla2

The word هلق *halla2* "now" can be used in framing position to mean "only just":

أنا هلق وصلت

هلق فهمت

2ana halla2 wSilᵉt · *halla2 fhimᵉt*

I've only just got here · I only just got it

It is sometimes combined with *lissa* or *ba3ᵉd* in this meaning:

أنا هلق بعدني جاي

أنا بعدني هلق بلشت

2ana halla2 ba3dni jaay · *2ana ba3dni halla2 ballashᵉt*

I've only just got here · I've only just started

Note that this is also a meaning of *lissa* and *ba3ᵉd* in some contexts (see unit 40).

Context Framing

In the last few units we looked at how *kaan* and other similar structures frame sentences, adding extra tense information to that which is already provided by the verb itself. Although there are various ways in which framing verbs differ from the corresponding English constructions, you could be forgiven for thinking that I talked up the Arabic system's differences too much: English too uses complex multiword structures to express many of the same ideas even if the details are different. But it is not only explicit structures of this kind that can provide framing. In this final unit of part 3, we will look at two other important kinds of framing: subordinate clause and through-narrative context.

Subordinate Clause Framing

First, *subordinate clauses* are often framed not by any framing construction or expression of tense within the subordinate clause itself but instead by the tense marking on the *main* verb that precedes it. We will look at subordination in detail in Part 6), but in short, a subordinate clause is a sentence that has been made to act as a constituent part of another sentence. This includes relative clauses, "that" clauses, and all sorts of other miscellaneous structures with conjunctions:

شفت الشب اللي حكيت معو

سمعت إنها فاتحة محل

shift ᵢshshabb ᵢlli 7akeet ma3o

smi3ᵉt 2innha faat7a ma7all

I saw the guy <u>who I'd spoken to</u>

I heard <u>that she'd opened a shop</u>

بعرف إني رح أنجح

كنت حبو لإنو بضحكني

ba3raf 2inni ra7 2anja7

kint 7ibbo la2inno biDa77ikni

I know <u>I'm going to succeed</u>

I loved him <u>because he made me laugh</u>

You don't need to worry too much about the definition of subordination at the moment. The point is simply to note that the main verb can frame the structure in the subordinate clause in much the same way that *kaan* frames whatever comes after it. Compare the following examples:

Past		Present
سمعت إنو عم يدرس أدب ←		سامع إنو عم يدرس أدب
smi3ᵉt 2inno 3am yidros 2adab		*saame3 2inno 3am yidros 2adab*
I heard that he was studying literature		I've heard he's studying literature
كنت أعرف إني رح أنجح ←		بعرف إني رح أنجح
kunt 2a3raf 2inni ra7 2anja7		*ba3raf 2inni ra7 2anja7*
I knew I'd succeed		I know I will succeed
شفت السيارة الي اشتريتها ←		شايف السيارة الي اشتريتها
shift ¹ssayyaara lli shtareetha		*shaayef ¹ssayyaara lli shtareetha*
I saw the car that I'd bought		I can see the car that I bought
كنت أحبها لإنها بتضحكني ←		بحبها لإنها بتضحكني
kunt 2a7ibbha la2innha bitDa77ikni		*ba7ibbha la2innha bitDa77ikni*
I loved her because she made me laugh		I love her because she makes me laugh

The only structural difference is that in the sentences on the right, the main verb has *present* meaning, while in those on the left, all the main verbs are in the perfective and have *past* meaning. But note the effect that this has on the English translation of the subordinate clause. In English, we have to explicitly mark the subordinate verbs as past ("is," "will," "bought," and "makes" becomes "was," "would," "had bought," and "made"). But in Arabic the framing effect of the main verb means that this is not necessary. Inserting *kaan* into the subordinate clauses on the right would usually be clunky if not outright ungrammatical.

For more on tense in subordinate clauses, see unit 58.

Narrative Framing

In the cases we've looked at so far, there has always been some explicit indication of the tense of the sentence even if it is not where we would expect it to be in English. In the cases we looked at in previous units, this indication was provided by explicit "framing structures," while in the subordinate clauses we have just looked at it was provided by the tense marking on the main verb. But it is important to be aware of cases where there is *no* explicit indication other than the context.

It is difficult to demonstrate this point with single sentences. Instead, let's look at a couple of examples of extended narrative from genuine natural speech. The following is taken from an interview with the Syrian actor Taim Hasan.[1] He is describing to the interviewer his early educational experiences in Beirut, where he was sent by his family to study law:

1 سجلت . . .

sajjal^et . . .

So I enrolled . . .

2 الوالد والوالدة متفائلين كتير.

ⁱlwaaled w ⁱlwaalde <u>mitfaa2liin</u> ⁱktiir.

Mum and Dad <u>were really hopeful</u>.

3 أساتذة مهمين كانو يدرسو هونيك.

2asaatze muhummiin kaanu ydarrsu huniik.

[There] were some big names teaching there.

4 وكلها كتب. أصغر كتاب هالقد قدو.

w <u>killa kitob</u>. 2azghar ⁱktaab <u>hal2add 2addo</u>.

And it <u>was full of books</u>. The smallest book there <u>would have been at least this big</u>.

5 فأنا الحقيقة لا وفقت ولا حبيت.

fa2ana ⁱl7a2ii2a laa wuffiqt wala 7abbeet.

But the truth is I wasn't very good, and I didn't like it either.

6 اللي حبيتو هو بيروت فترتها.

ⁱlli 7abbeeto huwwe beyruut fatritha.

What I did like, at the time, was Beirut.

7 عم نلفلف ورايحين جايين . . .

3am ⁱnlaflef w <u>raay7iin jaayiin</u> . . .

We were <u>flitting about, coming and going</u> . . .

As you can see, in lines 1, 3, 5, and 6 the tense marking corresponds closely to the English translation. The verbs are either in the perfective form or (in line 3) are framed with *kaan*. But in the other cases, which I have underlined, participles (*mitfaa2liin* "hopeful, optimistic," *raay7iin jaayiin* "coming and going"), "to be" sentences (*killa kitob* "it was full of books" and *2azghar ⁱktaab hal2add 2addo* "the smallest book would have been at least this big"), and a continuous form (*3am ⁱnlaflef* "we were flitting about") have no obvious framing whatsoever, even though the reference is past and so is the English translation. The tense is provided exclusively by the context.

This is a feature of narrative language. You don't need to master it, because using *kaan* in these cases is never wrong. Compare the section above with a similar narrative from the Palestinian-Jordanian businessman Munib al-Masri:[2]

1 حاولت أشتغل بوزارة الاقتصاد.

7aawalt 2ashtghel bi-wazaaret ᶦl2iqtiSaad

I tried to get a job at the Ministry of the Economy.

2 كان في شركة بترول اسمها شركة بولي وصارت شركة فيلبس

kaan fii shariket batrool 2isᶦmha shariket booli w Saarat shariket filibs

There was an oil company called Poly, which [later] became Phillips.

3 وكان الله يرحمو محمد فرحان وكيل وزارة الاقتصاد

w kaan 2aLLa yir7amo m7ammad far7aan wakiil wazaaret ᶦl2iqtiSaad

And the late Muhammad Farhan was the undersecretary at the Economy Ministry.

4 وكنت بحب كتير كتير أشتغل في وزارة الاقتصاد

w kunt ba7ibb ᶦktiir ᶦktiir 2ashtghel fii wazaaret ᶦl2iqtiSaad

I really, really wanted to get a job at the Economy Ministry.

5 فاستنيت شهر شهرين تلاتة، ما كان في بدجت

fa stanneet shahᵉr, shahreen, talaata, maa kaan fii badjet

I waited a month, two months, three months—but there wasn't [money in the] budget.

6 وكان المعاش وقتيها خمسين دينار.

w kaan ᶦlma3aash wa2tiiha khamsiin dinaar.

The salary then was fifty dinar.

7 بس كنت قابل إنو أشتغل بخمسين دينار.

bass kunt qaabel 2inno 2ashtghel b-khamsiin dinaar.

But I was willing to work for that amount.

As you can see, al-Masri uses *kaan* to frame every single sentence that does not have a perfective verb.

In any case, there are a few ways of analysing (and translating) these sentences. You could argue that Taim Hasan is simply switching between past and narrative present in the same way that English speakers sometimes do in the same context. Whatever analysis you adopt, you don't need to master this phenomenon, but you do need to recognise it when you see it.

Notes

1. This transcript is based on "ردة فعل والد تيم حسن عندما علم بفشله دراسيا" ("How Taim Hassan's Father Responded When He Found Out He Had Failed Academically"), interview by Dawood Al-Shirian, posted February 16, 2022, by MBC1, YouTube, https://youtu.be/VxmYGgMDAjI.

2. This transcript is based on "حوار مع كبار" ("Discussion with Great Men"), interview with Munib al-Masri, posted June 2, 2013, by Jordan TV التلفزيون الأردني, YouTube, https://youtu.be/hSdeARSCeOU.

PART 4

Mood

Commands and Instructions

In part 3, we focused on the tense system: how Arabic expresses relationships of time. In the next two units, we will look at *mood*: how it expresses all sorts of ideas that are "tense-adjacent" without being part of the tense system proper. I say "tense-adjacent" because most of these structures make use of the zero-imperfective or imperative forms of the verb, part of the overall set of verb forms that English speakers might be tempted to describe as "tense." But the common thread tying all these types of sentences together is that they do not have primarily temporal meaning.

In this unit we will be looking specifically at how to give commands and instructions. Like English, Arabic has many different ways of doing this that vary in their level of directness and politeness. In the first section of the unit we will be focusing on second-person structures, which should present few problems for English speakers. In the second and third sections, however, we will look at some less intuitive and more idiomatically complex kinds of structure: third-person and first-person imperatives.

Commands

The most straightforward way of telling someone to do something is to use the imperative form of the verb, which differs slightly between North and South Levantine (see unit 28):

كتوب اللي بدك ياه	احكي عربي!
ktoob ʾlli biddak ʾyyaa	*2i7ki 3arabi!*
write whatever you want	speak Arabic!

The negative equivalent is to use a negative zero-imperfective (see unit 26):

ما تكتب اللي بدك ياه	متحكيش عربي!
maa tiktob ʾlli biddak ʾyyaa	*mati7kiish 3arabi!*
don't write whatever you want	don't speak Arabic!

Note that the framing structures ما عاد *maa 3aad* and ما بقى *maa ba2a* "no longer," "never again" (see unit 39) can be used in negative commands:

ما بقى تشوفو

ما عاد تحكي معاه

maa ba2a tshuufo   *maa 3aad ti7ki ma3aa*

never see him again   don't speak to him again

For more on negation, see part 9.

As with the English imperative, commands of this kind are very direct and can sound rude. There are various particles in the general vicinity of "please" that can be used to soften a request and that usually trigger an unmarked zero-imperfective form (دخيلك *dakhiilak,* دخلك *dakhlak,* يا ريت *yaa reet,* أمانة *2amaane*):

يا ريت تشفلي وقت الموعد

أمانة إذا فزت تساعدني

yareet 'tshifli wa2t 'lmaw3ed   *2amaane 2iza fuzᵉt 'tsaa3idni*

please could you find out what time the   If you win, please help me out

appointment is?

Instructions (directions, for example) are sometimes given with the *b*-imperfective (see unit 34), paralleling English usage:

بتروح لآخر الشارع وبتاخد يمينك

bitruu7 la2aakhar 'shshaare3 w btaakhod yamiinak

you go to the end of the street and turn right

ma

The particle ما *ma* (with a short *a*), which is distinguished from the negative *maa* only by the length of the vowel and is often written identically, adds a nuance of frustration or urgency to an imperative. It is generally followed by a zero-imperfective. Compare the following:

ما تجاوب!

ما تجاوب!

maa tjaaweb!   *ma tjaaweb!*

don't answer me!   would you just give me an answer!

     just answer me!

Lebanese speakers instead combine *ma* with a normal imperative:

ما قولي!

ما جاوب!

ma 2uuli!   *ma jaaweb!*

would you just say something!   would you just give me an answer!

Sometimes this particle is written م to signal that the vowel is short.

Warnings

The term اوعى *2oo3a/2iw3a* "careful not to," "careful it doesn't" behaves similarly. Note that while for South Levantine speakers the term conjugates like a normal imperative, for North Levantine speakers this conjugation is optional:

North Levantine	South Levantine
اوعى توقعي!	اوعي توقعي!
2oo3a tuu2a3i!	*2iw3i tiw2a3i!*
be careful [F] not to fall!	be careful [F] not to fall!

The term اوعى can also carry a threatening tone similar to "don't you dare":

اوعى تحكي كلمة تانية!

2oo3a ti7ki kilme taanye!

don't you dare say another word!

اوعى تقرب عليي!

2iw3a ᵒt2arreb 3aliyyi!

don't you dare come near me!

The same applies to two other particles, اسحى *2is7a* and the slightly more elevated إيا *2iyyaa-*. The particle *2is7a* can be combined with pronouns (اسحك *2is7-ak, 2is7-ek*), treated as invariable, or conjugated as a verb (اسحى *2is7a*, اسحي *2is7i*):

إياكي تقولي كلمة تانية!

2iyyaaki t2uuli kilme taanye!

don't you dare say another word!

اسحك تقرب عليي!

2is7ak ᵒt2arreb 3aliyyi!

don't you dare come near me!

The word انتبه *ⁱntibeh* "careful not to," "careful it doesn't," literally "be aware," is a North Levantine alternative. It is followed by a zero-imperfective but is translated with a negative:

انتبه يوقع!

2ntibeh yiw2a3!

careful it doesn't fall!

انتبه تحترق!

ntibeh ti7tire2!

careful you don't burn yourself!

For some speakers, *maa* is also acceptable: انتبهي ما تحترقي *ntibhi maa ti7tir2i* "careful you don't burn yourself."

Nonverbal Imperatives

A handful of nonverbal structures, conjugated with attached possessive pronouns (see unit 18), have imperative meaning:

<table>
<tr><td align="center">إيدك</td><td align="center">ع مهلك</td><td align="center">عندك</td></tr>
<tr><td align="center">2iid-ak</td><td align="center">3a mahl-ak</td><td align="center">3and-ak/3ind-ak</td></tr>
<tr><td align="center">don't touch it</td><td align="center">slow down</td><td align="center">stop right there</td></tr>
<tr><td align="center">[= your hand]</td><td align="center">[= on your time]</td><td align="center"></td></tr>
</table>

<table>
<tr><td align="center">مكانك</td><td align="center">رجلك</td><td align="center">إجرك</td></tr>
<tr><td align="center">makaan-ak</td><td align="center">rijl-ak</td><td align="center">2ijr-ak</td></tr>
<tr><td align="center">stop right there</td><td align="center">hurry up</td><td align="center">hurry up</td></tr>
<tr><td align="center">[= your place]</td><td align="center">[= your leg]</td><td align="center">[= your leg]</td></tr>
</table>

وجهك على

wishsh-ak 3ala

head for . . .

[= your face to . . .]

bala (ma) and *balaash*

The words بلا *bala* and بلاش *balaash* (South Levantine) are both derived from the preposition *bala* "without" (see appendix B). They can both be used with nouns and act like a sort of negative imperative:

<table>
<tr><td align="center">بلاش كيس</td><td align="center">بلاه للكيس</td></tr>
<tr><td align="center">balaash kiis</td><td align="center">balaa lalkiis</td></tr>
<tr><td align="center">forget the bag</td><td align="center">forget the bag</td></tr>
<tr><td align="center">I don't need a bag</td><td align="center">I don't need a bag</td></tr>
</table>

They can also be used with a noun or a *maSdar* to advise someone against doing something, sometimes with the *-l-* suffixes:

<table>
<tr><td align="center">بلا روحتك</td><td align="center">بلالك هالشغلة</td></tr>
<tr><td align="center">bala roo7tak</td><td align="center">balaalak hashshaghle</td></tr>
<tr><td align="center">you're better off not going</td><td align="center">you're better off staying</td></tr>
<tr><td align="center">I wouldn't go if I were you</td><td align="center">away from this thing</td></tr>
</table>

Note that they can also be followed by verbs. While *balaash* can take a verb directly, *bala* needs to be followed by *ma*, just like the conjunction *bala ma* "without" (see appendix C):

لا بلا ما تروح

laa bala ma truu7

you're better off not going

I wouldn't bother going

بلاش تحكي معاه

balaash ti7ki ma3aa

you're better off not talking to him

I wouldn't bother talking to him

Sometimes it is used as a response to someone saying they won't do something:

طيب بلا ما تروحي!

Tayyeb bala maa truu7i!

fine, then don't go!

7aaj and *bikaffi*

The forms حاج *7aaj* (for some speakers حاجة *7aaje*) and بكفي *bikaffi* mean "enough X" or "stop X." They can be followed by a noun or a *maSdar* (see unit 31):

حاج حكي فاضي!

7aaj 7aki faaDi!

stop talking nonsense!

enough nonsense!

بكفي بكا!

bikaffi buka!

stop crying!

enough crying!

They can also be followed by a full verb. The most common option is zero-imperfective:

حاج تحكي حكي فاضي!

7aaj ti7ki 7aki faaDi!

stop talking nonsense!

بكفي تبكي!

bikaffi tibki!

stop crying!

Note, however, that with reference to an ongoing situation, other verbal forms can be used, such as the participle. This is similar to the behaviour of *badaal ma* and *la-* clauses (see appendix C):

حاج قاعد فوق!

7aaj 2aa3ed foo2!

stop sitting around upstairs!

بكفي قالبها محزنة!

bikaffi 2aalibha ma7zane!

enough feeling sorry for yourself!

For some speakers, حاج *7aaj* has a counterpart with pronoun suffixes, formed from the stem حاجتـ *7aajt-*:

حاجتي بكي!

7aajti biki!

enough crying!

حاجتك تاكل!

7aajtak taakol!

stop eating!

Third-Person Imperatives

It is also possible in Arabic to direct a command toward a third person who is not present. In English the closest equivalents ("let him X") are not in normal use, but in Arabic these forms are common. The most neutral constructions of this kind are formed with an invariable verb خليـ *khallii-* plus an object pronoun. Note that despite the literal gloss, a natural English translation requires some restructuring:

آه خليه يجي إذا بدو

2aa khallii yiji 2iza biddo

OK, he can come [= let him come] if he wants to

إذا إجت بكير خليها تفوت من الباب التاني

2iza 2ijet bakkiir khalliiha tfuut mn ⁱlbaab ⁱttaani

If she gets here early, she can get in [= let her come in] through the other door

> The "let" in the English structures is not the normal "allow" but instead is the semi-archaic way of forming imperatives: "let he who is without sin cast the first stone."

It is also possible to form structures of this kind with a simple zero-imperfective. One use of this is in an order to someone who is present but needs to be referred to, formally, with a pronoun or structure that normally takes third-person marking ("everyone," "nobody"). While in English these structures do not seem to differ from normal imperatives, using a second-person imperative here in Arabic is incorrect:

الكل ينبطح!

ⁱlkull yinⁱbTe7!

everyone get down!

ما حدا يلمسني!

maa 7ada yilmisni!

nobody touch me!

Unmarked *imperfectives* can also be used in a more defiant or dismissive way. Consider the following:

اللي مش عاجبو ينساني!

ⁱlli mish 3aajbo, yinsaani!

if you don't like me, forget about me!

[= he who I don't please, let him forget me]

اي يجي يجرب حظو!

2ee yiji yjarreb 7aZZo!

he can come and try his luck [if he thinks he's tough enough]!

[= let him come and try his luck]

وإذا الساعة تلاتة؟ اي تكون الساعة خمسة!

w2iza ssaa3a tlaate! 2ee tkuun ⁱssaa3a khamse!

so what if it's three o'clock? It could be five for all I care!

[= let it be five]

Note the use with questions such as the following in the context of planning. Although the English translation is often "should" or a future, the meaning is again third-person imperative:

مين يكنس البيت؟   شو يساوي بعدين؟

miin ykannes ⁱlbeet?   *shuu ysaawi ba3deen?*

who's going to sweep the house?   what should he do next?

While *khallii-* clauses and clauses with a simple unmarked imperfective do overlap in some contexts, the unmarked imperfective often has a much ruder or more direct feel. If a manager's secretary tells him that there is someone at the door, he could answer with either of the following:

خليه يفوت!   يفوت!

khallii yfuut!   *yfuut!*

But there is a difference. While the utterance on the left is neutral, the one on the right sounds defiant: "I'm not afraid of him!" or "well, who's stopping him from coming in?"

Idiomatic Use: Conditions

A third-person imperative (using the zero-imperfective) can be used to set conditions. For example, if I'm shopping for watches and the watchmaker asks me what kind of watch I want, I can say:

ما بهمني النوع بس تكون كبيرة وقيمتها عالية

maa bihimmni nnoo3 bass ⁱtkuun ⁱkbiire w qiimitha 3aalye

the type doesn't matter, so long as it's big and valuable

Similarly, if a friend is asking me where we should eat today:

ع زوقك بس ما يكون المحل بعيد

3a zoo2ak bass maa ykuun ⁱlma7all ⁱb3iid

wherever you like, as long as it's not too far away

Or if I'm talking about making a salad:

حط بندورة بالسلطة بس تكون طازة

7uTT bandoora bissalaTa, bass ᵢtkuun Taaza

put tomatoes in the salad, but make sure they're fresh

Idiomatic Use: Rhetorical Questions

It is possible to use structures of this kind in a rhetorical question. The sense is again like a command—or like saying "X should do Y"—but the English equivalent is different. The implication here is one of disapproval, defiance, or scoffing:

يروح ع العرس هيك؟

yruu7 3 al3urᵒs heek?

you think he should go to the wedding [dressed like] that?

بكلمة تشلحني؟

ᵢbkilme tishla7ni?

you think you're going to get rid of me with one word?

First-Person Imperatives

The zero-imperfective or a construction with خليـ *khallii-* plus a pronoun is used to make suggestions or give orders to a group that also includes the speaker, just like "let's" in English:

خلينا نلتقي قبل ما تسافر

khalliina nilt2i 2abᵉl ma tsaafer

let's meet up before you leave

يلا ننزل هون

yaLLa ninzel hoon

let's get off here

This structure also works with "I." The meaning here is the same but in English typically corresponds to a simple future with "will" or sometimes with "let me":

خليني أدور ع حد تاني

khalliini 2adawwer 3a 7add taani

let me look for someone else

خليني ساوي الشاي

khalliini saawi shshaay

I'll make the tea

In this sense, North Levantine speakers also accept a structure with *la-/la7atta/ta-* (see appendix C):

إذا هو ما بدو تدور ع حدا تاني

2iza huwwe maa baddo tadawwer 3a 7ada taani

if he doesn't want to do it, I'll look for someone else

لساوي الشاي

lasaawi shshaay

I'll just make the tea

Suggestions, Requests, Wishes, Exclamations, and Oaths

In unit 43 we looked at various kinds of direct and indirect commands. In this unit we will take a whistle-stop tour of five other kinds of "modal" language: *suggestions, requests, wishes, exclamations,* and *oaths.* As in unit 43, many of the constructions we will look at here are associated with the zero-imperfective.

Suggestions

How suggestions are structured varies over the Levantine area. In South Levantine, polite suggestions directed toward someone else use the zero-imperfective, while in North Levantine the *b*-imperfective is used. The usual structure in English here is with "like" or "want":

North Levantine	South Levantine
بتروح معي؟	تروح معي؟
bitruu7 ma3i?	*truu7 ma3i?*
would you like to come with me?	would you like to come with me?
بتشرب شاي؟	تشرب شاي؟
btishrab shaay?	*tishrab shaay?*
would you like some tea?	would you like some tea?

On occasion this structure is more naturally translated into English with some other structure. But note that here as well we are asking, politely, about a preference:

North Levantine	South Levantine
وين بتروحو بكرا؟	وين تروحو بكرا؟
ween bitruu7u bukra?	*ween ʾtruu7u bukra?*
where would you like to go tomorrow?	where would you like to go tomorrow?

North Levantine	South Levantine
ايمتى بتيجي تاخدني؟	ايمتى تيجي توخدني؟
2eemta btiiji taakhidni?	*2eemta tiiji tookhudni?*
when would you like to come and pick me up?	when would you like to come and pick me up?

A similar distinction applies in the first person, where English uses "shall I?" or "should I?" Here South Levantine uses the zero-imperfective and Lebanese uses the *b-* form, with Syrian speakers accepting both:

b-Imperfective (Lebanese, Syrian)	Zero-Imperfective (South Levantine, Syrian)
بعمل شاي؟	أعمل شاي؟
ba3mol shaay?	*2a3mel shaay?*
shall I make some tea?	shall I make some tea?
منروح معك؟	نروح معك؟
minruu7 ma3ak?	*nruu7 ma3ak?*
shall we go with you?	shall we go with you?
شو بعمل؟	شو أعمل؟
shuu ba3mol?	*shuu 2a3mel?*
what shall I do?	what shall I do?

These questions can be used, rhetorically, in a frustrated or resigned way:

بس شو نعمل يعني؟ دنيا   بس ادفع منين؟

bass shuu ni3mel ya3ni? dinya.   *bass 2idfa3 mneen?*

but what can we do? That's life   but how am I supposed to pay?

When discussing possible problems or hypothetical situations, solutions can be suggested using the zero-imperfective or in a structure with خليـ *khallii-* plus a pronoun. This obviously overlaps with the third-person imperatives discussed above. In English this is typically expressed with a simple present or a rhetorical question:

اي يفوت من الباب التاني

2ee yfuut mn ʼlbaab ʼttaani

[If he's lost his key,] why doesn't he get in through the other door?

[If he's lost his key,] he can get in through the other door

ليش ما يروح معاك؟

leesh maa yruu7 ma3aak?

[If he doesn't have his car,] why doesn't he go with you?

آه خليه يدرس طب أحسنلو

2aa khallii yudros Tibb 2a7sanlo

Yes, he should study medicine, that's better

Here there isn't much difference between a zero-imperfective and a structure with *lii-*, although as with third-person commands *khallii-* can sound softer.

Note in particular this sort of aggressive construction with ليش *leesh*, often followed by *la-/la7atta/ta-* (see appendix C):

وليش ليجي معنا؟	وليش أساعدك؟
w leesh layiji ma3na?	*w leesh 2asaa3dak?*
and why should he come with us?	why would I help you?

Note also suggestions introduced by شو رأيك *shuu ra2yak* "how about":

شو رأيك نروح سوا؟	شو رأيك تسكت أحسن؟
shuu ra2yek ⁱnruu7 sawa?	*shuu ra2yak tuskot 2a7san?*
how about we go together?	how about you shut up?

Requests

The words ممكن *mumken* and في مجال *fii majaal* produce polite requests:

في مجال تيجي معاي؟	ممكن تفتح الشباك؟
fii majaal tiiji ma3aay?	*mumken tifta7 ⁱshshubbaak?*
could you come with me?	could you open the window?

The word *mumken* can also mean "could I have":

ممكن قلم؟	ممكن سؤال ع السريع؟
mumken 2alam?	*mumken su2aal 3a ssarii3?*
could I have a pen?	could I ask a quick question?

The words بصير *biSiir* "is it all right if" and معليش *ma3leesh* (North Levantine) or معلش *ma3lishsh* (South Levantine) "do you mind if" have a similar effect:

بصير آخد قلم؟	معليش تفتح الشباك؟
biSiir 2aakhod 2alam?	*ma3leesh tifta7 ⁱshshubbaak?*
is it all right if I take a pen?	would you mind opening the window?

Wishes

There are several possible types of wishes. Wishes referring to events in the past that did not take place ("I wish I had") are expressed using one of various expressions plus the perfective. The most common such expressions are (لو) يا ريت *yareet (law)* "if only," usually combined with object pronouns matching the subject of the following verb; (لو) علواه *3aluwwaa (law),* "if only"; and بتمنى لو *bitmanna/batmanna law* "I wish":

بتمنى لو درست هندسة

batmanna law daras^et handase

I wish I'd studied engineering

يا ريتني رحت ع الجيم بالشتى!

yareetni ri7^et 3a jjim bishshite!

If only I'd gone to the gym in the winter!

law alone can also carry this meaning:

لو درست هندسة بس!

law daras^et handase bass!

If only I'd studied engineering!

If I'd just studied engineering!

Present wishes ("I wish it was true," "if only you were here") are formed with the same set of words plus a past, present, or zero-imperfective:

يا ريتني ذكي متلك

yareetni zaki mitlak

I wish I was as clever as you

بتمنى يكونو كل الناس زيك

batmanna ykuunu kull ⁱnnaas zayyek

I wish everyone was like you

علواه نرجع متل ما كنا

3aluwwaa nirja3 mit^el ma kinna

If only we could go back to the way we were

It is also possible, of course, to wish about things that might happen in the future. This overlaps quite a lot with present wishes, but there are also explicitly future structures. Perhaps the most common of these are with انشالله *nshaLLa/2inshaLLa* "God willing," "hopefully" and يا رب *yaa rabb* "o Lord," "hopefully":

ان شاء الله ياكلو الديب!

nshaLLa yaaklo ddiib!

I hope the wolf eats him!

يا رب ما يزبط!

yaa rabb maa yiZbaT!

Lord, let it not work out!

This obviously also overlaps with the meanings of the zero-imperfective discussed above under suggestions and third-person commands.

Many common set phrases are formed as wishes or invocations to God:

يعطيك العافية

ya3Tiik ⁱl3aafye

excuse me

[= may (God) give you health]

تصبح على خير

tiSba7 3ala kheer

goodnight

[= may you awaken to goodness]

In various fixed expressions the perfective is used to express wishes. This is not productive, however:

العمى ضربك!

l3ama Darabak!

damn you!

[= blindness strike you]

عاش الملك!

3aash ⁱlmalek!

long give the King!

Exclamations

Exclamations are formed in a range of ways. Perhaps the most common is with شو *shuu* (see unit 73) and شو إنو *shuu 2inno*, which can precede adjectives, nouns, and verbs. A single translation is difficult to give, but the meaning in all these examples is more or less the same:

شو حلو!

shuu 7ilu!

how pretty!

شو إنك ذكية!

shuu 2innek zakiyye!

you're so clever!

شو مصيبة!

shuu mSiibe!

what a catastrophe!

شو كنتي تجي لعننا!

shuu kinti tiiji la3anna!

you used to come to our house so much!

Another possibility is قديش *2addeesh* (see units 73–74), often with a pronoun suffix:

قديشك حلوة!

2addeeshek 7ilwe!

you're so pretty!

قديشو وسخ هادا!

2addeesho wisekh haada!

this guy is so nasty!

With nouns, ملا *malla* (North Levantine) and أما *2amma* can be used:

ملا جرصة!

malla jirSa!

what a scandal!

أما مصيبة!

2amma mSiibe!

what a crisis!

These are often preceded by swear words or other expressions of surprise:

يخرب بيتو شو تيس!

yikhreb beeto shuu tees!

he's such a moron!

يا الله شو بكتب!

yaa 2aLLaa shuu bikteb!

my God, he writes so much!

As we have noted, a participle is occasionally used—especially a participle of a framing verb (see units 38–41)—to express surprise. If I find out my son has been skiving off school, I can say:

كاين عامل حالو مريض وراجع ع البيت!

kaayen 3aamel 7aalo mariiD w raaje3 3 albeet!

apparently he pretended to be ill and came home!

Similarly, if I notice five missed calls from you, I can say:

كاين متصل علي وأنا مش حاسس!

kaayen miTTsel 3alayy w 2ana mish 7aases!

it looks like you rang me without me noticing!

Finally, for some speakers it is possible to use a sentence introduced with هي *hayy* (see unit 21), with or without attached pronouns, to express surprise. If we start playing a card game I thought you didn't know and you immediately win, I can say:

هي بتعرف تلعب!

hayy ᵢbti3raf til3ab!

so you know how to play!

so you *do* know how to play!

Oaths

Oaths ("I swear to God that I will . . .") are quite common in Arabic. Some common phrases used to introduce oaths include the following:

قسما بالله

qasaman billaa

I swear to God

أقسم بالله

2uqsem billaah

I swear to God

والله

waLLa

by God

والله

waLLaahi

by God

بشرفي

bsharafi

on my honour

والله العظيم

waLLaaahi l3aZiim

by Almighty God

عليي الطلاق

3aliyyi TTalaa2

may I be divorced

The actual oath itself is sometimes expressed using a normal structure:

قسما بالله رح جن!

qasaman billaa ra7 jann!
I swear to God, I'm going to go mad!

Often, however, a future verb is introduced by لـ *la-* or one of its regional variants (see appendix C), which replaces *ra7* and *b-*:

وﷲ العظيم تتندم!

waLLaahi l3aZiim tatindam!
you're going to regret this!
[= by Almighty God, you'll regret it!]

وﷲ لزورك!

waLLa lazuurak!
I promise I'll visit you!
[= by God, I'll visit you!]

> You may occasionally encounter participles used in these structures: وﷲ أنا *waLLaahi 2ana mwaqqe3 3alee min bukra* موقع عليه من بكرا "I swear to God I'll sign it tomorrow."

Note that when combined with terms of address (see appendix D) and names, oaths trigger the particle يا *yaa*:

وﷲ عظيم يا سيدي ما عملتها!

waLLaahi l3aZiim yaa siidi maa 3milta!
I swear to God, sir, I didn't do it!

وﷲ يا أبو عمار أنا بحبك

waLLaahi yaa 2abu 3ammaar ʾb7ibbak
let me tell you, Abu Ammar, I am very
fond of you

Oaths should be used with caution. Although few people are likely to take seriously non-native speakers swearing that they will divorce their wife if they're wrong, swearing by anything—and especially by God—can be sensitive.

Modal Framing Structures

In units 38–41 we looked at what I call "framing" structures, structures that can be straight-forwardly attached to a sentence of any other kind in order to express a specific time relationship. In this unit we will look at another kind of framing structure. While these behave very similarly to the structures we saw in units 38–41, they do not express relationships of time. Instead, they give extra "modal" meanings to the sentences to which they are attached.

Uses of *kaan*

We have already seen how *kaan* is used as a tense structure (see unit 38). But it also has several modal uses. The *b-* forms and (to a lesser extent) future forms express "must" or "will probably" in inferences. For example:

بدي كون غفيت أنا وعم اقرى

بكون بالشغل

baddi kuun ⁱghfiit 2ana w 3am 2i2ra

bikuun bishshugh°l

I must have fallen asleep while reading

he must be at work

he's probably at work

The form ليكون *laykuun*, which for many speakers is fixed, is used to express shocked conjectures. For example, if you're telling me about a wedding you're planning on attending tomorrow and I notice some unlikely similarities with a wedding *I'm* attending tomorrow, I can say:

أنا ابن عمي عرسو بكرا كمان، ليكون نفسو؟

2ana 2ibᵉn 3ammi 3irso bukra kamaan, laykuun nafso?

it's my cousin's wedding tomorrow, too—could it be the same one?

If we call a restaurant and no one answers, I can say to you:

ليكون مسكرين؟

laykuun ˈmsakkriin?

don't tell me they're closed?

This structure is available to all speakers. But many North Levantine speakers can also use the nonvariable لا يكون *laa ykuun*—presumably the origin of *laykuun*—in the same sense:

لا تكوني راجعة لهون؟
لا يكونو مسكرين؟

laa tkuuni raaj3a lahoon?   *laa ykuunu msakkriin?*

surely you're not coming back?   don't tell me they're closed?

The conditional *kaan* (see unit 70) plus an imperative expresses "you could have" or "you should have," in a chastising tone. This *kaan* is usually invariable for South Levantine speakers:

North Levantine	**South Levantine**
كنت قول!	كان احكيلي!
kint 2uul!	*kaan 2i7kiili!*
you could have said!	you could have told me!
you should have said!	you should have told me!

A similar effect is often achieved with a past conditional (see unit 70):

كنت قلتلي!
كنا أكلنا سوا!

kint 2iltilli!   *kunna 2akalna sawa!*

you could have said!   we could have eaten together!

2akiid "Must"

The term أكيد *2akiid*, literally "sure" or "certain," expresses "must" in the sense of "according to the evidence available to me, you must certainly have":

أكيد شفتو!
أكيد راحت مشي

2akiid shifto!   *2akiid raa7at mashi*

you must have seen it!   she must have gone on foot

الزلمة أكيد هون

ˈzzalame 2akiid hoon

the guy must be here

Tile3 "Turned Out to Be"

Finally, طلع *Tile3* means "turned out (to be)." It is a full verb:

طلع عم يسرقنا!

Tile3 3am yusru2na!

he turned out to be stealing from us!

turns out he was stealing from us!

بيطلع كذاب

byiTla3 kazzaab

he'll turn out to be a liar

The word طلع *Tile3* has a causative, طلع *Talla3*, used in sentences such as the following:

ليش كل مرة بتطلعني كذاب قدام بيك؟

leesh kill marra bitTalli3ni kazzab 2iddaam bayyak?

why do you always make me out to be a liar in front of your dad?

[= make me turn out to be]

3ala 2asaas, 3a 2asaas "Supposedly"

The phrase *3ala 2asaas* and its shortened version *3a 2asaas* imply secondhand knowledge or casts doubt on what you're saying:

بدو يجي بكرا على أساس

biddo yiji bukra 3ala 2asaas

supposedly he's coming tomorrow

مش على أساس جوعانة؟

mish 3ala 2asaas jo3aane?

I thought you were supposed to be hungry?

In rhetorical questions, *3ala 2asaas* expresses "as if":

على أساس ما بتعرف شو مساوي!

3ala 2asaas maa bta3ref shuu msaawi!

as if you don't know what you've done!

ka2inno, kinno "Seems That"

The conjunction كإنو *ka2inno* and its variant كنو *kinno* "as if" (see appendix C) are used independently to frame conclusions or inferences:

كإنو ما عندك؟

ka2inno maa 3indak?

it seems like you don't have any?

كنو في حدا ع الباب

kinno fii 7ada 3 albaab

looks like there's someone at the door

> For some speakers, *kinno* is used in the framing sense and *ka2inno* in the conjunction sense.

mbayyen, baayinto, mbayyinto "It Seems"

The phrase مبين على *mbayyen 3ala* and the derived forms باينتو *baayint-o* and مبينتو *mbayyint-o* most commonly express "seems" or "apparently":

مبينتها ذكية

مبين عليه بدوش ييجي

mbayyintha zakiyye — *mbayyen 3alee biddoosh yiiji*

she seems to be clever — it seems like he doesn't want to come

shiklo "It Seems," "Seems"

The word شكلو *shiklo* (the *-o* is a pronoun) translates as "seems" or "looks":

هالسيارة شكلها كبيرة

شكلو حلو كتير!

hassiyyaara shikla kbiire — *shiklo 7ilw ᶦktiir!*

this car looks big — it looks really nice!

seems like this car is big

The word شكلو *shiklo* can express inferences:

شكلو ما عندك؟

شكلو في حدا ع الباب

shiklo maa 3indak? — *shiklo fii 7ada 3 albaab*

it seems like you don't have any? — looks like there's someone at the door

Miscellaneous Modal Structures

In unit 45 we looked at framing structures with modal (rather than tense) uses. In this unit we will quickly review the most common nonframing structures used to express similar meanings. The majority of these structures are essentially auxiliaries—verbs or pseudoverbs—that trigger zero-imperfective structures, but some are simple adverbs or particles. I've followed a rough-and-ready division based on the sort of semantics that they express: *possibility and probability, ability, obligation,* and *inference.*

Possibility and Probability

The most common structures for expressing possibility and probability are ممكن *mumken* and يمكن *yimken.* These two words are worth considering together because although they are clearly closely related and express similar meanings, they are not interchangeable for the most part. We've already seen ممكن *mumken* being used in requests (see unit 44), where يمكن *yimken* is not possible. But even as auxiliaries of possibility they are not used in the same way.

Generally speaking, *mumken* expresses a judgment of possibility. *mumken* combines straightforwardly with a zero-imperfective clause (see unit 59) like other auxiliaries. In the following sentences *mumken* is probably best translated with "can" (i.e., "is possible"):

الواحد ممكن يطلع خلقو

ᵢlwaa7ad mumken yiTla3 khil2o

sometimes you lose your temper

مش ممكن اليوم يكون عننا هيك رئيس!

mish mumken ᵢlyoom ykuun 3inna heek ra2iis!

we just can't have a president like that today!

In the past, *mumken* usually requires a framing verb (see units 38–41) and gives a counterfactual meaning, as in "could have (but didn't)":

كان ممكن أحكي معاها

kaan mumken 2a7ki ma3aaha

I could have spoken to her

كان ممكن يعمل فتنة بيناتنا

kaan mumken ya3mel fitne beenaatna

it could have caused problems between us

Some speakers allow *mumken* to be combined with a perfective: ممكن رحت *mumken ri7°t* "I might have gone."

The word *yimken*, on the other hand, expresses a judgment of probability: "might," "perhaps," "maybe." The term *yimken* floats around the sentence and does not necessarily trigger zero-imperfective and can freely be combined with the past:

يمكن التلفزيون خربان   يمكن راح يمكن ما راح

yimken raa7 yimken maa raa7	*yimken ᵢttilivizyoon kharbaan*
maybe he went, maybe he didn't	maybe the TV is broken

Note, however, that *yimken* can also be combined with a zero-imperfective clause, just like *mumken*. In these cases, the distinction seems to break down somewhat, with different speakers preferring or rejecting different options in structures such as the following:

ممكن ما يتوفر عندي   يمكن ما يتوفر عندي

yimken maa yitwaffar 3indi	*mumken maa yitwaffar 3indi*
I might not be able to get hold of it	I might not be able to get hold of it

ممكن تشتي بكرا   يمكن تشتي بكرا

yimken ᵢtshatti bukra	*mumken ᵢtshatti bukra*
it might rain tomorrow	it might rain tomorrow

كان ممكن وافق   كان يمكن وافق

kaan yimken waafe2	*kaan mumken waafe2*
I might have agreed	I might have agreed

A less common synonym of *yimken* is بجوز *bijuuz*. Like *yimken*, بجوز *bijuuz* expresses "might," "perhaps," "possibly" and can either float around the sentence or combine with a zero-imperfective clause:

في منهم بجوز من الجنوب   بجوز قلهم بدو يشتكي عليهم

bijuuz 2allhom biddo yishtki 3aleehom	*fii minhom bijuuz mn ᵢljanuub*
maybe he told them he was going to report them	some of them are maybe southerners

بجوز تفكرها مشابهة   بجوز يجي بجوز ما يجي

bijuuz yiji bijuuz maa yiji	*bijuuz ᵢtfakkirha mushaabiha*
he might come, he might not come	maybe you'll think it's similar

> *jaaz* is also a verb, typically meaning "be permissible" in a religious or legal context. The participle of *jaaz* is جايز *jaayez* is also (occasionally) used to mean "possible" as a less common adjective synonym of *mumken* and وارد *waared*.

Similarly, احتمال *2i7timaal* ("possibility") and معقول *ma32uul* (literally "it's reasonable" or "conceivable") express possibility. *ma32uul* often carries an implication of surprise or scepticism on the part of the speaker:

معقول يجي قبل الضو؟

ma32uul yiji 2abl ᵢDDaww?

is there any chance he'll get here
before dawn?

احتمال تشتي بكرا

2i7timaal ᵢtshatti bukra

there's a possibility it might rain tomorrow

The Turkish loan بلكي *balki* or (in North Levantine) بركي *birki* can also express "might" and is sometimes combined with a zero-imperfective but not always:

ياخي بركي تغير!

yakhi berki tghayyar!

maybe he's changed, you never know!

بلكي جبلك كل يوم بيتسا

balki jiblek kill yoom biitsa

maybe I'll bring you pizza every day

The word مستحيل *mista7iil* "impossible" is similarly combined with a zero-imperfective:

مستحيل يجي بكرا

mista7iil yiji bukra

no way is he coming tomorrow

مستحيل أسوي هيك!

mista7iil 2asawwi heek!

I could never do that!

The words إلا *2illa* and (more commonly) إلا ما *2illa ma* are used with zero-imperfectives to express certainties or unbreakable rules:

إلا ينجح!

2illa yinja7!

there's no way he won't succeed!

المجرم إلا ما يرجع لمشهد الجريمة!

ᵢlmujrem 2illa ma yirja3 lamashhad ᵢljariime!

the criminal always returns to the scene
of the crime!

Most other ways of expressing judgments of possibility are normal adverbs or adverbial structures. For example:

فش مشكلة غالبا

fish mushkile ghaaliban

there's probably no problem

ع الأغلب ما في شغل

3 al2aghlab maa fii shighᵉl

most likely there's no work

بدو يجي أكيد

baddo yiji 2akiid

he'll come for sure

For the framing use of *2akiid* meaning "must (have)," see unit 45.

The word بصير *biSiir* is a frozen form of صار *Saar* (see unit 39) that expresses that something is acceptable or possible:

بصير روح يومين وارجع؟	ما بصير تحكي هيك قدام الضيوف!
biSiir ruu7 yoomeen w 2irja3?	*maa biSiir ti7ki heek 2uddaam ᶦDDyuuf!*
would it be all right for me to go for a couple of days then come back?	you can't talk like that in front of the guests!

Ability

The most common words expressing ability are عرف *3iref* "know [how to]" and قدر *2ider* "be able to." There is obviously overlap between the two, but consider:

بتقدر تسوق؟	بتعرف تسوق؟
bti2der ᶦtsuu2?	*bta3ref ᶦtsuu2?*
can you drive?	can you drive?
[will you be able to, in your current state?]	[do you know how?]

Note, however, that *3iref* does extend to some contexts in which "know how to" would seem unnatural:

مش عارف أحكي اليوم	بدي أعرف كمل شغل
mish 3aaref 2a7ki lyoom	*baddi 2a3ref kammel shighᵉl*
I can't talk properly today	I want to be able to keep working
	[and I can't because of the noise you're making]

غدر *ghider* is a South Levantine variant of قدر *2ider* and حسن *7asan*, a Syrian synonym:

مو حسنانة فوت	بغدرش أسوي إشي
muu 7asnaane fuut	*baghdarᵉsh 2asawwi 2ishi*
I can't come in now	I can't do anything

The pseudoverb فيـ *fii-*, sometimes فينـ *fiin-*, is a North Levantine synonym. Note that exceptionally for a nonverb it can take *ra7* in the future (see unit 36):

فيكي تعيشي هيك؟

fiiki t3iishi heek?

could you live like this?

بكرا ما رح فيني

bukra maa ra7 fiini

tomorrow I'm not going to be able to

Obligation

Obligation is most commonly expressed by لازم *laazem*. This can translate as both "should" or "must" and is combined with a zero-imperfective clause:

لازم تجي معي!

laazem tiji ma3i!

you should come!

لازم تكتب كل إشي ع ورقة

laazem tuktob kull 2ishi 3a wara2a

you should write everything down on a piece of paper

Note that *laazem* is often negated with ما *maa* as if it were a verb. The negative usually expresses "shouldn't" rather than "don't have to":

ما لازم تروح!

maa laazem ˈtruu7!

you shouldn't go!

ما لازم تعملي هيك

maa laazem ti3mli heek

you shouldn't do that

> Some speakers allow *laazem* to be combined with a perfective form: لازم حاكيتني *laazem 7aakeetni!* "you should have talked to me!"

In the past *laazem* often has a counterfactual meaning "should have" or "were supposed to":

كان لازم أروح معاه!

kaan laazem 2aruu7 ma3aa!

I should have gone with him!

كان لازم تحاكيني!

kaan laazem ˈt7aakiini!

you should have called me!

The verbs اضطر *Dtarr* and انجبر *njabar* also combine with zero-imperfective clauses and give the meaning "have to," "be obliged to." The equivalent of present "have to" with these verbs is the participle:

اضطريت أرجع ع البيت

DTarreet 2arja3 3a lbeet

I had to go home

انجبرت اترك كل شي عندو

njabarˁt 2itrok kill shii 3indo

I had to leave everything with him

مضطر أخلص!

miDTarr 2akhalleS!

I have to finish!

مجبور احكي عربي

majbuur 2i7ki 3arabi

I have to speak Arabic

The word ضروري *Daruuri* means "compulsory," "obligatory," or "absolutely necessary":

ضروري روح شخصيا؟

Daruuri ruu7 shakhSiyyan?

do I really need to go in person?

مش ضروري تروحي

mish Daruuri truu7i

you don't have to go

It is very commonly used in rhetorical questions:

ضروري تضوج من أول لحظة؟

Daruuri tDuuj min 2awwal la7Za?

do you have to jump straight to being angry?

The word بد *bidd-* or (Lebanese) *badd-* "want" commonly expresses "need" or "should" with *maSdar*s or nouns:

المخدة بدها دعك

ⁱmkhadde bidda da3ᵉk

the pillow needs wringing out

الخاتم بدو تزبيط

ⁱlkhaatem biddo tazbiiT

the ring needs adjusting

For North Levantine speakers it is also reasonably common with verbs in this meaning (see unit 36):

بدي روح لعندها

baddi ruu7 la3andha

I need to go and see her

For all speakers, it is also often used in forceful suggestions as an equivalent of "you need":

بدك تهديلي شوي

biddak ⁱthaddiili shwayy

you're gonna need to calm down a bit

Inference

Most of the ways of expressing inference fall into the category of framing structures (see unit 38) and were discussed in unit 45. However, there are a few counterexamples worth mentioning here for comprehensiveness.

The first of these is مفروض *mafruuD* or المفروض *ⁱlmafruuD*. Like *yimken* and *bijuuz*, المفروض *ⁱlmafruuD* can either be combined with a zero-imperfective or wander around the sentence freely. As you would expect from its literal meaning—"the assumed thing"—it expresses an expectation:

بدو يجي المفروض
biddo yiji lmafruuD
he's supposed to come

المفروض يجي
ilmafruuD yiiji
he's supposed to come

مفروض *mafruuD* can only be combined with a zero-imperfective:

هو مفروض يجي بكرا
huwwe mafruuD yiji bukra
he's supposed to be getting here tomorrow

The particle قال *2aal*, meanwhile, is used to express hearsay. Although قال *2aal* originally means "he said"—and looks like a verb—it is a frozen form and does not conjugate or have a clear subject. It is often combined with participles in their "hearsay" meaning (see unit 37):

قال سارقين البريد!
2aal saar2iin ilbariid!
apparently they've robbed the post office!

قال جايينا ناس من البلدية
2aal jaayiina naas mn ilbaladiyye
apparently there are some people coming from the municipality

2aal can also have a sarcastic meaning ("supposedly") or can express disapproval:

قال طلع أول ع الصف!
2aal Tile3 2awwal 3 aSSaff!
supposedly he came top of his class!
[seems pretty unlikely to me]

قال بدهم يشترو البيت!
2aal biddhom yishtru lbeet!
apparently they're going to buy the house!
[over my dead body]

PART 5

Sentence Structure

Verbal Sentences

In this unit we will look very briefly at the most basic kind of sentence in Arabic: the verbal sentence, or a sentence beginning with a verb. In subsequent units we will look in far more detail at the various constituent parts of this kind of sentence and at other sentences. This unit is intended primarily as a sort of introduction to Arabic sentence structure, an overview of how all these parts fit together. As such, it is not very long and contains many brief summaries whose relevance and content might not be immediately obvious without following the cross-referencing to the relevant units. But don't worry, all will become clear over the course of the next few units. The main thing to take away from this unit is a general sense of how word order functions in verbal sentences.

Overall Structure

Although the exact order is different from English, the makeup of a verbal sentence should be relatively familiar to anyone who has studied the grammar of a European language. The most basic sort of verbal sentence consists of a verb and a subject, in that order. The verb agrees with the subject for number and gender (for more on agreement, see unit 50):

انحلت مشكلتك   طلع أحمد

'n7allat mushkiltak   Tile3 2a7mad

your problem's solved   Ahmad left

روحو سامي ونادرة   أجو الشرطة

rawwa7u saami w naadira   2aju shshurTa

Sami and Nadira went home   the police came

In the examples above, the subject is a noun. In many cases, however, the subject is "implicit"; that is, it is expressed only by the agreement markers on the verb. This applies in most cases where we would use a pronoun subject in English (see unit 51):

عم تغني | شو عم تساوي؟

3am ʾtghanni | *shuu 3am ʾtsaawi?*

she's singing | what are you doing?

بتلبك | روحو

batlabbak | *rawwa7u*

I get confused | they went home

> If you are coming to this unit with prior knowledge of Arabic—or have just been paying close attention to the examples given elsewhere in the book—you may be surprised by the claim that subjects by default follow the verb. It is true that subjects (and other constituents) often precede the verb. But this is the effect of the topic construction, discussed in unit 48.

In some cases, a verbal sentence may not have a real subject at all but instead has a so-called dummy subject. This is a generic pronoun that refers to nothing in particular and cannot be replaced by a noun. In English, a dummy subject is usually "it." In Arabic, it is typically a feminine agreement marker:

عم بتشتي | ما بتفرق

3am bitshatti | *maa btifre2*

it's raining | it doesn't make any difference

> Native English speakers sometimes try to account for this pronoun by saying that it stands in for "the weather," but this is clearly wrong. Nobody would say "the weather is raining." The "it" cannot be replaced with a noun.

A verb can also have one or more objects. By default, these come after the subject. The various kinds of objects are discussed in more detail in unit 52. The most familiar to English speakers will be so-called direct objects (a noun that is "acted on") and indirect objects (usually defined as the "receiver" of the action). Some verbs are connected to their objects by prepositions:

شافو القطة | عم يشرب شاي

shaafu l2iTTa | *3am yishrab shaay*

they saw the cat | he's drinking tea

أعطو المصاري لأخوهم | بعتت المسج لرامي

2a3Tu lmaSaari la2akhuuhom | *ba3att ʾlmasej laraami*

they gave the money to their brother | I sent the message to Rami

اتصل الضابط بمديرو

TTaSal ᵢDDaabet ᵢbmudiiro

the officer rang his boss

دورت ع الوراق

dawwarat 3 a-lᵢwraa2

she looked for the papers

Object nouns, of course, can be replaced by pronouns, generally attached pronouns, which attach either to the verb directly (for direct objects) or to the preposition. Note that combinations of *la-* and a noun are anomalous in that they are usually replaced by the *-l-* suffixes (see unit 53):

عم يشربو

3am yishrab-o

he's drinking it

شافوها

shaafuu-ha

they saw her

بعتتلو المسج

ba3att-ᵢllo lmasej

I sent him the message

أعطوهم لأخوهم

2a3Tuu-hom la-2akhuuhom

they gave it to their brother

اتصل فيه الضابط

ᵢttaSal fii DDaabeT

the officer rang him

دورت عليهم

dawwarat 3aleehom

she looked for them

Note that pronouns and preposition-pronoun combinations tend to be attracted to the verb, often resulting in what looks like verb-object-subject word order. With direct object pronouns, there is no alternative to this; the object pronoun attaches to the verb, and the subject obviously cannot appear between them. But even preposition-pronoun combinations also usually appear adjacent to the verb:

بدو مني مصاري

biddo minni maSaari

he wants money from me

اتصل فيي خيي

ttaSal fiyyi khayyi

my brother phoned me

اشتريت من عندو كتاب

shtareet min 3indo ktaab

I bought a book from him

طلعتو علي إشاعة

Talla3tu 3alayy 2ishaa3a

you started a rumour about me

As well as the sort of objects we are broadly familiar with from English, Arabic has a broad range of "secondary object" constructions (see unit 54) expressing a broad range of additional idiomatic meanings. These generally follow the more common kinds of object:

ضربوني ضرب

Darabuuni Darᶜb

they properly hit me

عطوني ياها هدية

3aTuuni yaaha hdiyye

they gave me it as a gift

حضرناه تسلاية

7aDarnaa tislaaye

we watched it for fun

اشتغلت ساعتين

shtaghal[e]t saa3teen

I worked for two hours

The last constituent part of a verbal sentence and the most optional is a class of words and phrases described in linguistics jargon as "adverbial" (i.e., modifying the verb). This class is usually divided into expressions of time, place, and manner and includes both single-word expressions and structures with prepositions:

بحبني كتير

bi7ibbni ktiir

he loves me a lot

تعلمت بالجامعة

[i]t3allamt bijjaam3a

I learnt (it) at university

بغني منيح

bighanni mnii7

he sings well

بحكي عليي ع الطالعة والنازلة

bi7ki 3aliyyi 3 aTTaal3a w[i]nnaazle

he gossips about me left, right and centre

Note that the verb slot can be occupied by many types of words that are not, strictly speaking, verbs. One obvious example is the active participle, which in many respects is like a verb (see unit 37):

مخلصة أختك القهوة

[i]mkhallSa 2ukhtak [i]l2ahwe

your sister's finished the coffee

كاتبين الجماعة كل شي

kaatbiin [i]jjamaa3a kill shii

the guys have written everything down

Although participles only have agreement marking for number and gender (with the tiniest of exceptions, for which see unit 29), their subjects can also be dropped in the same places that verbs' subjects can:

مخلصة القهوة

[i]mkhallSa [i]l2ahwe

she's finished the coffee

كاتبين كل شي

kaatbiin kill shii

they've written everything down

The other type of word that can take the place of verbs is what I call "pseudoverbs," words such as بدي *baddi/biddi* "I want" that are not verbs etymologically or structurally but still display verbal behaviour:

بدي خبز تازة

baddi khib[e]z taaza

I want fresh bread

نفسي بصحن حمص

nifsi bSa7[e]n 7ummoS

I'm craving a plate of hommous

Topic Sentences

In unit 47 we looked at verbal sentences, which I characterised as the simplest kind of sentence in Arabic. But many sentences that you will encounter either break the verb-initial rule that I set out there (for example, by having the subject appear first) or have no verb at all. These structures are called *topic sentences*,[1] and they represent one of the most significant ways in which Arabic sentence structure differs from its English counterpart. As we will see, a topic is not the same as a subject, although it often corresponds to a subject in English. A topic is part of a sentence—most commonly a noun or pronoun—that the rest of the sentence is *about*.

Although topic-comment structures are common worldwide and even occur in English to some extent, they are not an immediately intuitive way of organising information for English speakers. We will look first at the basic shape of topic sentences and at their constituent parts (topics and comments). We will then consider in greater detail the properties of topics in general and then at structures with multiple topics (double-topic constructions). We will talk briefly about what happens when topics are dropped or left implicit. Finally, we will discuss the basic difference between topic and nontopic constructions where a choice is available.

Topic and Comment

A topic sentence consists of a *topic* and a *comment*. The topic, usually a noun or pronoun, is what the sentence is about. The comment then provides information about the topic. The topic is what we are discussing, while the comment is what we are saying about the topic.

> You may be familiar with the Arabic counterparts to these terms: جملة اسمية *jumla ismiyya* "topic sentence," مبتدأ *mubtada2* "topic," and خبر *khabar* "comment."

It is easiest to see how topic sentences work with "to be" sentences. While in English we require a verb ("is," "are," etc.) to assign a quality, identity, or location to an entity, in Arabic we simply juxtapose that entity (the topic) with the properties we want to assign to it (the comment):

العرس بكرا

الجو حلو

'l3ir‘s bukra

'ljaww 7ilw

the wedding is tomorrow

the weather is nice

جنان دكتورة

محمد بالبيت

jinaan diktoora

m7ammad bilbeet

Jinan is a doctor

Muhammad is at home

The same applies to more complicated sentences, those with verbs, for example. In the following sentences, the topic (a noun) is followed by a verbal clause (the comment). Again, the comment provides information about the noun:

أبوي بدخن

هيك أفلام ما بتنحضر

2abuuy bidakhkhen

heek 2aflaam maa btin7iDer

my dad smokes

films like that are unwatchable

النمر بياكل بشر

جنان بتحكي عربي

'nnimr 'byaakol bashar

jinaan 'bti7ki 3arabi

tigers eat people

Jinan speaks Arabic

At this point you may be thinking that "topic" is just an abstruse way of referring to the *subject*. But this would not be quite right. For one thing, the first set of example sentences in this unit have no verb, and as a result they cannot formally have a subject (see unit 51). But even if you were to dismiss this point as pedantic, you would still have to explain the sentences below:

عمرو ما بيخوفو شي

هالكتاب أعطتني ياه إمي

3am‘r maa bikhawwfo shii

hal'ktaab 2a3Tatni yyaa 2immi

Amr, nothing scares him

this book, my mum gave me it

As you can see, these sentences have both topics (*hal'ktaab* "this book" and *3am‘r* "Amr") and subjects (*2immi* "my mum" and *shii* "thing"). The verb agrees not with the topic but instead with the subject, but the sentences are still *about* the book and Amr, respectively. The default position for the subject, as we have seen, is *after* the verb (see unit 47). The topic, on the other hand, appears at the very beginning of the sentence.

There is, however, a kernel of truth to the intuition that subject and topic are closely related. The same sort of factors that motivate topicalisation of nonsubjects in Arabic—relevance to the conversation, "aboutness," etc.—often cause English speakers to look for ways to make them into subjects. The sentences above could be idiomatically translated into English as follows, keeping topic and subject identical:

هالكتاب أعطتني ياه إمي

hal'ktaab 2a3Tatni yyaa 2immi

this book was given to me by my mum

عمرو ما بيخوفو شي

3am'r maa bikhawwfo shii

Amr isn't afraid of anything

Properties of the Topic

A topic is almost always definite (see unit 13). The main exceptions to this are structures with هيك *heek* "such X-es" (see unit 14) and كل *kill/kull* "every," which although they are not formally definite are certainly generic and thus similar to definites:

المرة بتعرف شو بدها

'lmara bta3ref shuu badda

a woman knows what she wants

أنا اليوم مو فاضي

2ana lyoom muu faaDi

I'm not free *today*

كل شي تمام

kill shii tamaam

everything's fine

هيك ناس ما بتنطاق

heek naas maa btinTaa2

people like that are intolerable

Indefinite nouns in the sense of "a single" or "one" can also be topics:

كلمة واحدة بتسوى الدنيا

kilme wa7de btiswa ddunye

a single word is enough

زر بندورة بكفيني

zirr bandoora bikaffiini

one tomato will be enough

> Generics are sometimes expressed with "a" in English, as in the first example above. But note that the counterpart to this in Arabic is always definite (see unit 13).

The topic appears by default at the very beginning of the sentence, even preceding question words (see units 73–74) and words fronted for emphasis (see unit 66):

سري من شو خايف؟

sari min shuu khaayef?

what's Sari scared of?

أنا اليوم مو فاضي

2ana lyoom muu faaDi

I'm not free *today*

سليم شو بحب؟

saliim shuu bi7ibb?

what does Saleem like?

إختي بصلة ما بتاكل!

2ikhti baSale maa btaakol!

my sister won't even eat an onion!

The only alternative order for a nominal sentence is the comment and topic to be reversed, that is, the topic coming last:

من شو خايف سري؟

min shuu khaayef <u>sari</u>?

what's Sari scared of?

اليوم مو فاضي أنا

'lyoom muu faaDi <u>2ana</u>

I'm not available *today*

شو بحب سليم؟

shuu bi7ibb <u>saliim</u>?

what does Saleem like?

بصلة ما بتاكل إختي!

baSale maa btaakol <u>2ikhti</u>!

my sister won't even eat an onion!

When a topic is a possessor, an object, or the object of a preposition, it must be represented in the comment by a pronoun that agrees with it. Compare the nontopicalised and topicalised versions:

سامي شفنا بيتو   ←   شفنا بيت سامي

saami shifna beeto ← *shifna beet saami*

Sami, we saw his house   we saw Sami's house

الكلاب ما بخوفهم   ←   ما بخوف الكلاب

l'klaab maa bikhawwifhom ← *maa bikhawwef l'klaab*

the dogs, he doesn't scare them   he doesn't scare the dogs

المديرة حكينا معها   ←   حكينا مع المديرة

'lmudiira 7akeena ma3ha ← *7akeena ma3 'lmudiira*

the director, we talked to her   we talked to the director

Note that when a topic that is not the same as the subject—an object, a possessor, etc.—is put in final position, it is often introduced with the ل *la-* construction (see unit 54):

بحبها لساميا

bi7ibbha lasaamiya

he loves Samia

شفنا بيتو لسري

shufna beeto lasari

we saw Sari's house

Sometimes an adverb or an expression of location or time can act as topic:

بالبيت في كل إشي

bilbeet fii kull 2ishi

in the house, there's everything

النهار بتشتغل الناس

l'nhaar btishtighel 'nnaas

during the day, people work

Double-Topic Constructions

The sentences given above all had a single topic. But it is one of the quirks of Arabic syntax that a sentence can have more than one topic or, to put it another way, that a topic's comment can itself be a topic sentence, with its own topic.

أحمد الحكومة ما بتخوفو

2a7mad ˈl7ukuume maa bitkhawwfo

Ahmad isn't scared of the government

[= Ahmad, the government doesn't

scare him]

بنتي كل إشي بصعب عليها

binti kull 2ishi biS3ab 3aleeha

my daughter finds everything difficult

[= my daughter, everything is

difficult for her]

Perhaps the most common motivation for using these sentences is found in cases such as the following, where the second topic is possessed by the first. Insofar as possession implies a close semantic link between the possessor and what is possessed, it makes sense that a statement about what is possessed can also be conceptualised as a statement about the possessor:

أنا أبوي بدخن

2ana 2abuuy bidakhkhen

my dad smokes

[= me, my dad smokes]

إلياس أصحابو بعطيهمش مصاري

ˈlyaas 2aS7aabo bi3Tiihommˤsh maSaari

Elias doesn't give his friends money

[= Elias, his friends, he doesn't give them money]

In the above examples, *2ana* could have been dropped, with *2as7aabo* treated as a straightforward object without much of a change in meaning or idiomaticity. But there is one crucial type of sentence where a double-topic construction is more or less compulsory. When discussing body parts or other inherent qualities of a person, we almost always use a double-topic construction:

أحمد عيونو خضر

2a7mad ˈ3yuuno khuDᵒr

Ahmad has green eyes

[= Ahmad, his eyes are green]

سامي لهجتو غريبة

saami lahˈjto ghariibe

Sami has a funny accent

[= Sami, his accent is funny]

محمد طولو ميتين سنتي

m7ammad Tuulo miiteen santi

Muhammad is 200 cm tall

[= Muhammad, his height is 200 cm]

سامية كنيتها شقور

saamya kinyitha sha22uur

Samia's surname is Shaqqour

[= Samia, her surname is Shaqqour]

سامية عيونها بخوفو

saamya 3yuunha bikhawwfu

Samia has scary eyes

[= Samia, her eyes are scary]

عمرو طولو مو طبيعي

3amˤr Tuulo muu Tabii3i

Amr is unbelievably tall

[= Amr, his height is unbelievable]

We might expect to use a possessive construction here: Samia's eyes are scary. But these sentences are at heart a statement not about Samia's eyes but instead *about Samia*. In English too, Samia is kept as the subject of "Samia has scary eyes" by using a verb ("have").

Using a possessive structure is sometimes possible but produces a different nuance. You can say لهجة فارس غريبة *lahjet faares ghariibe* "Fares's accent is funny," but the topic here is *Fares's accent*. In most cases, we will be making a statement about Fares himself, in which case we have to say فارس لهجتو غريبة *faares lahⁱjto ghariibe* "Fares has a funny accent." These are not important nuances for you to internalise, however.

Implicit (Dropped) Topics

We already know that Arabic subjects can be dropped where they are easily identified from the context (see unit 47). The same applies to topics. Where a topic has already been stated or is obvious from the context, it can be dropped, producing sentences such as those on the left:

غريب	←	هادا غريب
ghariib		*haada ghariib*
he's strange		this guy's strange
متجوزة؟	←	بديعة متجوزة؟
mitjawwze?		*badii3a mitjawwze?*
is she married?		is Badia married?
ما بياكلو سوشي	←	الولاد ما بياكلو سوشي
maa byaaklu suushi		*ⁱlwlaad maa byaaklu suushi*
they don't eat sushi		kids don't eat sushi
بتخوفوش الكلاب	←	سمير بتخوفوش الكلاب
bitkhawwfoosh lⁱklaab		*samiir bitkhawwfoosh lⁱklaab*
he isn't afraid of dogs		Samir isn't afraid of dogs
انباع بيتها	←	لامية انباع بيتها
nbaa3 beetha		*laamiya nbaa3 beetha*
her house has been sold		Lamia's house has been sold

Note, however, that while independent pronouns (see unit 18) are generally fairly emphatic when used as subjects, this is not necessarily the case with topics. Sentences such as the following—where انت *2inte* and هو *huwwe* are occupying the topic slot—are quite normal even when no unusual emphasis is being placed on "you" or "he":

إنت شخص غريب؟	بحب السوشي هو
2inte shakh^eS ghariib?	*bi7ibb ⁱssuushi huwwe*
are you a strange person?	he loves sushi

Choice between Topic and Nontopic Constructions

In many of the sentences we have looked at above, there is no choice as to the internal structure. A "to be" sentence, for example, must always consist of a topic and a comment. With verbal sentences, however, we often have the choice between multiple constructions, one without any identifiable topic and one (or more) with a topic-comment structure:

Topic-Comment	Nontopic
الجماعة إجو ᶦjjamaa3a 2iju the group have arrived	إجو الجماعة 2iju jjamaa3a the group have arrived
البيئة بتتأثر ᶦlbii2a btit2assar the environment is affected	بتتأثر البيئة btit2assar ᶦlbii2a the environment is affected
النمر بياكل ᶦnnimr ᶦbyaakol the tiger eats	بياكل النمر byaakol ᶦnnimᵉr the tiger eats
هداك بيرجع ع البيت hadaak byirja3 3a lbeet that guy goes home	بيرجع هداك ع البيت byirja3 hadaak 3a lbeet that guy goes home

Although both choices are grammatical, this is not to say that they are interchangeable. Topic constructions are used in different contexts from nontopic constructions. The basic difference is as we would expect. Topic sentences are *about the topic*, while sentences without a topic serve generally to move narratives along, placing the focus more on the action described by the verb.

This is not a distinction that can easily be mastered based on a book. These sorts of syntactic nuances are best acquired by internalising the usage you hear from natives. In any case, you will not struggle to make yourself understood if the only error you are making is topicalising (or failing to topicalise) one element of a sentence.

Note

1. I owe the basic substance of my analysis here to Kristen Brustad's excellent *The Syntax of Spoken Arabic* (Georgetown University Press, 2000), which makes a very compelling argument for analysing Arabic as topic-prominent.

"To Be" Sentences and Existential ("There Is") Sentences

In this unit we will look at two specific types of sentences that account for most structures you will encounter in Arabic, focusing on how they are formed and how they interact with the concept of topic introduced in the last unit. These two types of sentence, "to be" sentences and "existential" sentences, are relatively straightforward to characterise and describe: they correspond to English constructions with "to be" and "there is"/"there are," respectively.

"To Be" Sentences

Let's look first of all at "to be" sentences, that is, sentences corresponding to English structures with "be" ("am," "is," "are"). As we saw in unit 48, in most cases the Arabic counterpart to an English "to be" structure is simply to juxtapose a topic and a comment. Adjectives in the comment agree with the topic, as we would expect (see unit 50), as do nouns with masculine and feminine forms (see unit 10):

<table>
<tr><td align="center">أبوي مترجم</td><td align="center">أنا سورية</td></tr>
<tr><td align="center">2abuuy mutarjem</td><td align="center">2ana suuriyye</td></tr>
<tr><td align="center">my dad's a translator</td><td align="center">I'm Syrian</td></tr>
<tr><td align="center">بديعة بالبيت</td><td align="center">أحمد مش هون</td></tr>
<tr><td align="center">badii3a bilbeet</td><td align="center">2a7mad mish hoon</td></tr>
<tr><td align="center">Badia is at home</td><td align="center">Ahmad isn't here</td></tr>
<tr><td align="center">أحمد فوق</td><td align="center">القطة تحت الطاولة</td></tr>
<tr><td align="center">2a7mad foo2</td><td align="center">'l2uTTa ta7t 'TTaawle</td></tr>
<tr><td align="center">Ahmad is upstairs</td><td align="center">the cat is under the table</td></tr>
<tr><td align="center">الجو حلو</td><td align="center">الجنينة حلوة</td></tr>
<tr><td align="center">'ljaww 7ilw</td><td align="center">l'jneene 7ilwe</td></tr>
<tr><td align="center">the weather is nice</td><td align="center">the garden is nice</td></tr>
</table>

أخي كاتب

2akhi kaateb

my brother is a writer

سلمى وجودة كتاب

salma w juude kittaab

Salma and Joudeh are writers

> Where the topic and comment are reversed, some speakers allow neutralisation of adjective agreement here: شاطر بديعة *shaaTer badii3a* "Badia is clever."

Sometimes an independent pronoun (see unit 18) occurs between the topic and the comment, agreeing with one or the other. This is particularly common, although not compulsory, where the comment is definite. Although the pronoun can be stressed for emphasis, as in the last example, it doesn't have to be. It is also fairly common before pauses:

أحمد هو الدكتور

2a7mad huwwe ddoktoor

Ahmad is the doctor

سلمى هي الدكتورة

salma hiyye ddoktoora

Salma is the doctor

الكتاب هو . . . كتاب حلو

lᵉktaab huwwe . . . ktaab 7ilu

the book is . . . a nice book

ميادة هي الشاطرة

mayyaada hiyye shshaaTra

Mayada is the clever one

Otherwise, most "to be" sentences correspond quite straightforwardly to their English counterparts. There are two major exceptions, however. First, recall that "to be" sentences referring to inherent characteristics often have two topics (see unit 49), which makes them quite structurally different from their English translations:

أحمد عيونو خضر

2a7mad ᶦ3yuuno khuDᵒr

Ahmad has green eyes

سامي لهجتو غريبة

saami lahᶦjto ghariibe

Sami has a funny accent

محمد طولو ميتين سنتي

m7ammad Tuulo miiteen santi

Muhammad is 200 cm tall

سامية كنيتها شقور

saamya kinyitha sha22uur

Samia's surname is Shaqqour

Second, Arabic is looser with the sorts of structures it allows as comments than English is with the sorts of structures it allows to follow "to be." While the comments in these sentences are undoubtedly saying something about the topic, they are not expressing the sort of strict relationship implied by "X is Y":

إنتي خبرة

2inti khibra

you're experienced

[= experience]

هاني سنة تالتة

haani sane taalte

Hani is a thirird year

[= third year]

أنا وياه صحبة

2ana wiyyaa Su7be

me and him are friends

[= friendship]

الصبي تربايتك

'SSabi tirbaaytak

the boy's [the product of]

your upbringing

البحر نو

'lba7ᵉr naww

there's a gale

[= the sea is a gale]

الدنيا صيف

'ddinye Seef

it's summer

[= the world is summer]

Sentences of this kind have quite particular tense properties. They can either be "timeless" (in the sense of not specific to any given time) or else can refer to ongoing, current situations. To express a repeated state (see unit 34), we use an imperfective form of the framing verb *kaan* (see unit 38):

الويكند بتكون فاضي

'lwiikend bitkuun faaDye

on weekends she's free

كل جمعة بكون بالبيت

kull jum3a bakuun bilbeet

every Friday I'm at home

We also generally use a form of *kaan* for statements about generic topics. Compare the sentences on the right—which refer to a specific doctor and a specific elephant—with those on the left:

الدكتور شاطر

'ddoktoor shaaTer

the doctor is clever

الدكتور بكون شاطر

'ddoktoor bikuun shaaTer

doctors are clever

الفيل أنفو طويل

'lfiil 2anfo Tawiil

the elephant has a long nose

الفيل بكون أنفو طويل

'lfiil bikuun 2anfo Tawiil

elephants have long noses

For the generic use of the definite singular, see unit 13.

Exceptionally, family relationships are typically expressed with a form of *kaan*:

أحمد بكون أخي

سلمى بتكون بنت عمي

2a7mad bikuun 2akhi

salma bitkuun bint 3ammi

Ahmad is my brother

Salma is my cousin

Finally, *kaan* is sometimes used for distancing, which can be either polite or rude:

ومين بكون حضرة جنابو؟

وحضرتك مين بتكون؟

w miin bikuun 7adret janaabo?

w 7ad'rtak miin bitkuun?

and who might his lordship be?

to whom do I have the pleasure of speaking?

Of course, *kaan* (and other framing verbs) can also be used to add other tense information as with other sentences. See unit 8 for more on this.

Existential Sentences

Now let's look at a type of sentence that generally does *not* have any associated topic. Existential sentences express that something exists (or no longer exists, or existed, etc.). In English, most existential sentences have "there is" or "there are." The Arabic counterpart to this is the pseudoverb في *fii*, typically followed by an indefinite noun:

في شي بالبيت؟

في خبز بالبراد

fii shii bilbeet?

*fii khub*ᵉ*z bilbarraad*

is there anything in the house?

there's bread in the fridge

اليوم في مشكلة

في ناس برا

ⁱlyoom fii mushkile

fii naas barra

today there's a problem

there are people outside

Although unlike "there is/are" *fii* does not change for person or number, it is negated like a verb (see unit 76). The form acceptable everywhere is ما في *maa fii*, but in South Levantine the alternatives مفش *mafish* and فش *fish* are more common:

North Levantine	**South Levantine**
ما في مشكلة	فش مشكلة
maa fii mish'kle	*fish mushkile*
there's no problem	there's no problem
ما في شي بالبراد	مفش إشي بالبراد
maa fii shii bilbarraad	*mafish 2ishi bilbarraad*
there's nothing in the fridge	there's nothing in the fridge

Other structures can also form existential sentences. Three common verbs, ضل, بقي *bi2i,* *Dall* and صفي *Sifi* (North Levantine), are all used to express "there's/there're still …" Like *fii,* in this context they do not change to agree with the subject, although they can take different tense forms:

صفي مي؟

Sifi mayy?

is there any water left?

ضل خبز بالبراد

Dall khub°z bilbarraad

there's still some bread in the fridge

مش رح يبقى خبز بالبراد

mish ra7 yib2a khib°z bilbarraad

there won't be any bread left in the fridge

مش ضايل إشي!

mish Daayel 2ishi!

there's nothing left!

> Note that the perfective forms *Sifi, Dall,* and *bi2i* all express present meaning in these sentences. This is another example of the "result" sense of the perfective, for which see unit 33.

Full preposition structures also sometimes form existential sentences. On their own, these must be combined with *fii.* But with framing constructions (see units 38–41) and relative clauses (see unit 63), it is possible to drop the *fii* and still have a grammatical sentence such as the following:

في بمدرستك هيك ولد

fii bmadrastak heek walad

there's a kid like that in your school

كان بمدرستك هيك ولد

kaan bmadrastak heek walad

there was a kid like that in your school

الطالب في براسو مشروع

ᵢTTaaleb fii braaso mashruu3

the student's got a plan

[in his head]

الطالب اللي براسو مشروع . . .

ᵢTTaaleb ᵢlli braaso mashruu3 . . .

a student who's got a plan

[in their head] . . .

Existential sentences do not, as a rule, have a topic. But some existential-type constructions do have a topic-comment structure. Consider the following examples:

البيت فيو كل إشي

ᵢlbeet fiyyo kull 2ishi

the house has everything

[= the house, there is in it . . .]

الشقة فيها دوش

ᵢshsha22a fiiha doosh

the apartment has a shower

[= the apartment, there is in it . . .]

البيت فوقو سطح

'lbeet foo2o saT'Z'7

the house has a roof on it

[= the house, there is atop it . . .]

سامية معاها مصاري

saamya ma3aaha maSaari

Samia has money on her

[= Samia, there is on her . . .]

In these sentences the comment begins with a preposition and a pronoun (standing in for the topic), which then takes on an existential meaning ("there is in," "there is on," "there is with"). This structure is similar to other topic constructions that we have seen. Note, however, that it is not a topicalised version of the standard existential sentence. It is a distinct structure.

In many cases, sentences of this kind also have idiomatic uses derived from but not identical to their existential uses:

الشب عليه ديون

'shshabb 3alee dyuun

the guy is in debt

[= on him there are debts]

أخوكي فيه شي؟

2akhuuki fii shii?

is there something wrong with your brother?

Note that prepositions used in this sense are negated like verbs (see unit 76):

البيت ما فيو إشي

'lbeet maa fiyyo 2ishi

there's nothing in the house

أخوكي ما فيه شي

2akhuuki maa fii shii

there's nothing wrong with your brother

Note as well that these structures can optionally take في *fii*:

في عليه ديون

fii 3alee dyuun

he has debts

في عندك موعد مع الدكتور

fii 3indak maw3ed ma3 'ddoktoor

you have an appointment with the doctor

> Occasionally you may encounter topic structures such as المسدس ما في رخصة *l'msaddas maa fii rikhSa* "the gun isn't licensed" [= the gun, there isn't a licence]. These are probably comparable to the more unusual "to be" structures discussed above.

Agreement

This unit is about *agreement*. Agreement, broadly speaking, is when words take different forms depending on other words in the same sentence, thereby "agreeing" with them. In English this phenomenon is limited to subject-verb agreement, with certain subjects triggering an "-s" ending ("he run<u>s</u>") and others a zero-ending ("they run"). In Arabic, however it is far more pervasive. We will first consider the basic system of agreement in Arabic before looking at how it operates with some more complicated sorts of nouns.

Basic System

The basic agreement system is fairly straightforward. Adjectives will be marked as masculine, feminine, or plural to match the noun to which they refer:

أواعي نضاف	غرفة نضيفة	بيت نضيف
2awaa3i nDaaf	*ghirfe nDiife*	*beet ⁱnDiif*
clean clothes	a clean room	a clean house

دكاترة جداد	دكتورة جديدة	دكتور جديد
dakaatra jdaad	*doktoora jdiide*	*doktoor ⁱjdiid*
new doctors	a new [female] doctor	a new [male] doctor

> Adjectives directly modifying a noun will also "agree" for definiteness: المكتب الكبير *ⁱl-maktab ḻⁱ-kbiir* "the big office." For more on this, see unit 13.

Similarly, verbs will be marked as masculine, feminine, or plural to match their subject:

راحو الدكاترة	راحت الدكتورة	راح الدكتور
raa7u ddakaatra	*raa7at ⁱddoktoora*	*raa7 ⁱddoktoor*
the doctors went	the [female] doctor went	the [male] doctor went

انكسرو البواب	انكسرت الحنفية	انكسر الباب

nkasaru lⁱbwaab	*nkasret ⁱl7anafiyye*	*nkasar ⁱlbaab*
the doors broke	the tap broke	the door broke

The three sets of pronouns (see unit 18)—the masculine singular, feminine singular, and plural—are likewise used to refer to masculine, feminine, and plural nouns, respectively. This is different from English, in which "he" and "she" are restricted to animate nouns and all inanimate nouns are referenced with "it":

أخدتها	←	أخدت التفاحة		أخدتو	←	أخدت الكتاب
2akhadt-ha		*2akhadt ⁱttuffaa7a*		*2akhadt-o*		*2akhadt lⁱktaab*
I took it		I took the apple		I took it		I took the book
[= her]				[= him]		

أخدتهم	←	أخدت الكتب
2akhadt-hom		*2akhadt ⁱlkitob*
I took them		I took the books

There is a complication, however. Inanimate plurals, in addition to taking plural agreement, can also take feminine singular agreement:

Feminine Agreement		**Plural Agreement**
الكراسي فاضية	OR	الكراسي فاضيين
ⁱlkaraasi faaDy-e		*ⁱlkaraasi faaDy-iin*
the chairs are empty		the chairs are empty
انكسرت البواب	OR	انكسرو البواب
nkasr-et lⁱbwaab		*nkasar-u lⁱbwaab*
the doors broke		the doors broke
أخدتها	OR	أخدتهن
2akhadt-ha		*2akhadt-hon*
I took them (the books)		I took them (the books)

Some speakers are less comfortable than others using feminine singular for plural. The exact boundaries of what is possible vary from speaker to speaker.

Sometimes either feminine singular or plural agreement can be used with little difference in meaning. The plural typically gives the sense of a more internally differentiated group and cannot usually have generic meaning. The feminine singular, on the other hand, focuses the attention more on the group as a group:

الكتب بساعدوك

ᵢlkitob bisaa3duuk
the [specific] books help you

الكتب بتساعدك

ᵢlkitob bitsaa3dak
books help you
the [specific] books help you

الكتب مفيدين

ᵢlkutob mufiidiin
the [specific] books are useful

الكتب مفيدة

ᵢlkutob mufiide
books are useful
the [specific] books are useful

A similar distinction can sometimes be made with animate plurals. Some speakers do not accept sentences such as the following, but they do occur. As with inanimate nouns, using feminine singular here gives a more generic or undifferentiated meaning:

المدرا بتكون مسافرة

ᵢlmudara bitkuun ᵢmsaafra
the managers will [all] be abroad

الولاد ما عم تتعلم

lᵢwlaad maa 3am tit3allam
kids aren't learning

Note that some speakers have a distinct feminine plural form for some adjectives (see unit 17). For these speakers, feminine plural nouns can trigger this form instead of a normal plural:

دكتورات مؤهلات

daktuuraat mu2ahhalaat
qualified [female] doctors

نسوان شاطرات

niswaan shaaTraat
clever women

Note as well that a few other words—أنو *2anu* and أني *2ani* "which" (see unit 73), for example—also agree for gender.

Agreement with Dual Nouns

Dual nouns almost always trigger plural agreement (special dual adjectives are occasionally encountered, for which see unit 17). They cannot take feminine singular agreement:

كتابين حلوين

ktaabeen 7ilwiin
two nice books

غرفتين نضاف

ghurᵘfteen ᵢnDaaf
two clean rooms

سنتين تانيين

sinteen taanyiin
another two years

Agreement with Mass Nouns

A mass noun is a noun that refers to some unspecified quantity of something. As noted in unit 11, many nouns that in English are plural are mass nouns in Arabic. It would be impossible to list all of these words here, although it is worth noting that many foodstuffs (بطاطا *baTaaTa* "potatoes," تفاح *tuffaa7* "apple(s)," etc.) are mass nouns rather than straightforward singular-plural pairs. Mass nouns take singular agreement. Most but not all are masculine:

تفاح زاكي	بطاطا حرة	شجر حلو	هاي البطاطا
tuffaa7 zaaki	*baTaaTa 7arr-a*	*shajar 7ilu*	*haay ᵢlbaTaaTa*
tasty apples	spicy potatoes	pretty trees	these potatoes

Agreement with False Plurals

Words with the false plural suffix *-aat* (see unit 11) trigger plural agreement:

قهواتك بجننو	هالشمسات بدهم شورت
2ahwaatek bijanninu	*hashshamsaat biddhom short*
the coffee you make is delicious	sun like this calls for [wearing] shorts

With adjectives—exceptionally—they trigger a form ending in *-aat* for many non-Lebanese speakers:

قهواتك طيبات	هالشمسات الصيفيات حلوات
2ahwaatek Tayybaat	*hashshamsaat ᶦSSayfiyyaat 7ilwaat*
the coffee you make is tasty	this summer sun is lovely

For Lebanese speakers, however, they invariably trigger normal plural forms:

قهواتك طيبين	هالشمسات الصيفية حلوين
2ahwaatek Tayybiin	*hashshamsaat ᶦSSayfiyye 7ilwiin*
the coffee you make is tasty	this summer sun is lovely

For more on these forms, see unit 17.

Agreement with Quantified Nouns

Note that a noun placed in *iDaafe* with some sort of expression of quantity (see unit 84), even a singular expression, typically triggers agreement as if that expression were not present. Both of the following options treat the expression *nuSS 2afkaari* "half my ideas" as plural:

بكونو نص أفكاري مزبوطين

bikuunu nuSS 2afkaari maZbuuTiin

half my ideas are spot on

[agreement in plural]

بتكون نص أفكاري مزبوطة

bitkuun nuSS 2afkaari maZbuuTa

half my ideas are spot on

[agreement in singular feminine]

Singular words following كذا *kaza* "a few," كام *kamm* "a few," and أكمن *2akammen* "a few" (South Levantine) and or numbers from 11 upward—all of which have plural meaning—can take plural or singular agreement:

كذا واحد ظراف

kaza waa7ad ⁱZraaf

a few nice guys

كذا واحد ظريف

kaza waa7ad Zariif

a few nice guys

أكمن شغلة حلوين

2akammen shaghle 7ilwiin

a few nice things

أكمن شغلة حلوة

2akammen shaghle 7ilwe

a few nice things

Agreement with Nouns Referring to Groups

There are a few words referring to humans that despite *looking* singular can also take plural agreement. What they all have in common is that they refer to groups made up of multiple people. All can take plural agreement as well as singular agreement. Note that the very common words ناس *naas* and عالم *3aalam* "people" are both feminine:

أجو ناس كتير ع الحفلة

2aju naas ⁱktiir 3 al7afle

a lot of people came to the party

أجت ناس كتير ع الحفلة

2ajat naas ⁱktiir 3 al7afle

a lot of people came to the party

فتشو الأمن البيت كلو

fattashu l2amn ⁱlbeet killo

the police searched the whole house

فتش الأمن البيت كلو

fattash ⁱl2amn ⁱlbeet killo

the police searched the whole house

This is quite similar to the plural agreement with singular subjects that occurs in British English ("the bank are phoning me"), although more restricted.

Agreement with Multiple Nouns

Two nouns coordinated with "and" usually trigger agreement as is logical. If a first-person subject is included, it defaults to the "we" form, and if a second-person subject is included, it defaults to the "you" plural form. Otherwise, the "they" form is used.

بتروحو إنت وهاني

bitruu7u 2inte w haani

you and Hani will go

منروح أنا وياك

minruu7 2ana wiyyaak

me and you will go

سارا وميس سوريات

saara w mays suuriyyaat

Sara and Mays are Syrian

بروحو هاني وأحمد

biruu7u haani w 2a7mad

Hani and Ahmad will go

Unlike its English equivalent, لا ... لا *laa ... laa* and its variants ("neither ... nor") trigger plural agreement, just like و *w* (see unit 78):

لا سارا ولا ميس سوريات

laa saara wala mays suriyyaat

neither Sara nor Mays is Syrian

لا أنا ولا إنت منغير إشي

laa 2ana wala 2inta minghayyer 2ishi

neither you or me can change anything

However, especially with independent pronouns (see unit 18), a second subject appearing after the verb may be added almost as an afterthought, and the verb itself agrees only with one subject:

بروح أنا وياك

bruu7 2ana wiyyaak

me and you will go [= I'll go, and you]

Nonagreement

A few structures are invariably masculine singular. In these cases, agreement is not only optional but is also entirely incorrect. The most common examples of this are "existential" expressions that take the place of في *fii* (see unit 49). These always precede their (indefinite) subjects, are always in the masculine singular, and express things such as "be left over":

صفي ماي؟

Sifi maay?

is there still water left?

ضل قهوة إذا بدك

Dall 2ahwe 2iza biddek

there's some coffee left if you want

زاد معك مصاري؟

zaad ma3ak maSaari?

did you have any money left over?

The same applies to the fuS7a يوجد *yuujad*, a formal equivalent to في *fii*. Another example is اجا *2ija/2aja* with indefinite subjects in constructions such as the following:

بكرا بجيك ولاد

bukra bijiik ˈwlaad

someday you'll have children

[= tomorrow children will come to you]

جايه ضيوف

jaaye ˈDyuuf

there are guests coming

[= coming guests]

Certain verbs quite commonly default to masculine singular when their subject follows them (but not when it precedes). All three of the following are possible, despite *maSla7a* being feminine:

مصلحة بلدو بتهمو

maSla7et balado bithimmo

بتهمو مصلحة بلدو

bithimmo maSla7et balado

بهمو مصلحة بلدو

bihimmo maSla7et balado

he has the best interests of his country at heart

[= the good of his country is important to him]

It is difficult to come up with any kind of hard-and-fast rule for these cases, although for a learner it is probably worth noting that making these verbs agree is always correct.

Note as well ما بتفرق *maa btifre2* "makes no difference," which sometimes remains feminine even with masculine subjects.

For South Levantine speakers although not for North Levantine speakers, conditional كان *kaan* (see unit 70) is also invariable:

كان أجيت معاك

kaan 2ajiit ma3aak

I would have come with you

كان أفرقت

kaan 2afra2at

it would have been different

Subjects

____

In this unit we will look briefly at *subjects*. The subject should be a reasonably familiar concept from English grammar. According to one very basic definition, the subject is the *doer* of the verb. This applies as much in Arabic as it does in English. But the positioning of subjects and how they relate to their verbs differs somewhat between the two languages.

What Is a Subject?

The subject of a verb is usually defined as the "doer": the noun or pronoun that *does* the action that the verb expresses. The subjects in the following sentences are underlined:

راحت سميرة   بيطلع أحمد

raa7-at <u>samiira</u>   *b-yi-Tla3 <u>2a7mad</u>*

<u>Samira</u> went   <u>Ahmad</u> leaves

بتفضى الخزانة   روحو الشباب

b-ti-fDa <u>lkhazaane</u>   *rawwa7-u <u>shshabaab</u>*

<u>the wardrobe</u> [F] will be empty   <u>the guys</u> have gone home

As you can see, the subject is the same in English and in Arabic. But in Arabic its default position is *after* the verb, not before it, as in English. Moreover, the form of the verb changes to "agree" with it: the verb reflects (through prefixes and suffixes) the number and gender of the subject. While this happens in English as well—the suffix in "Ahmad leave-s" marks that the subject is singular—the agreement system is much less extensive than in Arabic.

> If you have studied fuS7a, you might expect there to be a different agreement rule depending on whether the verb *precedes* or *follows* its subject. In Levantine, however, there is no such rule. Although there are some complications with agreement, for which see unit 50, it is generally consistent regardless of the relative positioning of subject and verb.

Another difference between English and Arabic subjects is that Arabic can *drop* a subject without making a sentence ungrammatical. In fact, English combinations of subject pronoun and verb usually correspond to a verb alone in Arabic, with the agreement suffixes and prefixes doing the semantic heavy lifting. Here the subject is "implicit":

بشوفك بكرا	رجعو ع البيت	راحت	بيطلع
b-a-shuufak bukra	*rij3-u 3 albeet*	*raa7-at*	*b-yi-Tla3*
I'll see you tomorrow	they went home	she went	he leaves

It is important to note that when we say that the subject is the "doer," we are making a point about its *relationship to the verb*. The energetic connotations of "doer" and "do" in normal language are unhelpful here. A subject is not necessarily actively "doing" anything at all. In these sentences there is no conscious "doing" (in the sense of action), but there are easily identifiable subjects:

خلصت القهوة	نعس القط
khilS-at ^{i}*l2ahwe*	*ni3es* ^{i}*l2iTT*
the coffee's finished	the cat got sleepy

This point bears repeating. Note that the object of a verb—the thing that the verb is "done to"—can be transformed straightforwardly into a subject using the passive (see unit 57). This does not change the nature of the event described by the verb. The coffee is still being acted upon. It could hardly be otherwise, since coffee is an inanimate object. But in the right-hand sentence "coffee" is the object, while in the left-hand sentence it is the subject, as we can see from the agreement on the verb:

شرب القهوة	انشربت القهوة
shireb ^{i}*l2ahwe*	*nsharb-et* ^{i}*l2ahwe*
he drank the coffee	the coffee was drunk

Moreover, some verbs have what is referred to as a "dummy subject," a subject that refers to nothing at all. This is the same as the "dummy 'it'" in English structures such as "it's raining." Usually—although not invariably—this subject is feminine:

بيصعب عليك	عم بتشتي
b-yi-S3ab 3aleek	*3am bi-t-shatti*
it'll be difficult for you	it's raining

ما بتفرق معي

maa b-ti-fre2 ma3i

it makes no difference to me

Although for the most part the subject of a verb in English will correspond to the subject of the corresponding Arabic verb, there are a few cases in which an Arabic verb has the opposite structure. In English the subject here is "I," but in Arabic the subject is "your cleverness," and the whole sentence can be rendered (unidiomatically) as "your cleverness pleased me":

عجبتني شطارتك

3ajbatni shaTaartek

I liked your cleverness

Subject and Topic

I noted above that the default position for a subject is *after* its verb. If you have encountered much Levantine Arabic in real life—or have been paying close attention to the ordering in some of the examples we've already looked at in this book—you may be scratching your head. It is very common for the subject to *not* follow the verb:

أحمد بيطلع

2a7mad byiTla3

Ahmad leaves

سميرة راحت

samiira raa7at

Samira went

الشباب روحو

'ishshabaab rawwa7u

the guys have gone home

الخزانة فضيت

'lkhazaane fiDyet

the wardrobe has emptied

These sentences are what I call *topic* constructions (جمل اسمية *jumal 2ismiyye* "nominal sentences" in Arabic terminology). Their subject has been shifted to the topic position at the very beginning of the sentence. This phenomenon is quite frequently mischaracterised as simply optional subject-verb order for some types of subjects. But it is a bit more complicated than this and dovetails with other topic constructions involving nonsubjects. For more on these topics, see unit 48.

Direct and Prepositional Objects

In this section we will be discussing various kinds of *objects*. By the most basic definition, if the subject is the noun that "does" the verb, then the object is the noun that the verb is "done to." An object that just attaches to the verb straightforwardly is called a *direct object*:

> She reads <u>newspapers</u>.
> I like <u>languages</u>.

An object that is attached to its verb by a preposition, on the other hand, is called a *prepositional object*:

> She looks <u>at me</u>.
> He thinks <u>about the cat</u>.

We will look at these two types of structure in Arabic and how they work.

Direct Objects

Some verbs take a *direct object*. This means that they do not need to be connected to the verb by a preposition. This should be fairly intuitive to an English speaker:

سمعت الصوت

sim3at ˈSSoot

she heard the sound

بيقرى الجريدة

byi2ra ljariide

he reads the paper

بتعرفي أحمد

bta3ˈrfi 2a7mad

you know Ahmad

شافت كلب

shaafat kalb

she's seen a dog

The same applies to pseudoverbs, which in this respect act exactly like normal verbs:

معك المصاري؟

بدي سيارة جديدة

ma3ak ⁱlmaSaari?

baddi sayaara jdiide

do you have the money?

I want a new car

A small number of normal verbs can have two direct objects. Most of these verbs involve transferring something from someone to a recipient, like the English term "give." The most common examples are عطى *3aTa* (North Levantine) / أعطى *2a3Ta* (South Levantine) "give"; سلم *sallam* "hand in/over"; ناول *naawal* "pass," "hand to"; باع *baa3* "sell"; and فرجى *farja,* ورجى *warja,* أرجى *2arja* "show." With these verbs the recipient always comes first, and the object to be transferred comes second:

سلمت لينا التقرير

باعت محمد البيت

*sallam*ᵉ*t liina ttaqriir*

baa3at ⁱ*m7ammad* ⁱ*lbeet*

I gave Lina the report

she sold Muhammad the house

ناول إمك كاسة مي

بعطي أخي هدية

naawel 2immak kaaset mayy

ba3Ti 2akhi hdiyye

pass your mum a glass of water

I'll give my brother a present

Just like their English counterparts, these can be idiomatically rephrased with a single object and *la-* "to":

سلمت التقرير للينا

باعت البيت لمحمد

sallamt ⁱ*ttaqriir laliina*

baa3at ⁱ*lbeet lam7ammad*

I gave the report to Lina

she sold the house to Muhammad

ناول كاسة مي لإمك

بعطي عيدية لأخي

naawel kaaset mayy la2immak

ba3Ti 3iidiyye la2akhi

pass a glass of water to your mum

I'll give a present to my brother

These structures, however, are much more limited than they are in English, where we can form a double-object structure of this kind with many verbs. In examples like the following, only the structure with *la-* works:

عملت شاي لمرتي

ببعت المصاري للخيي

*3mil*ᵉ*t shaay lamarti*

bib3at ⁱ*lmaSaari lakhayyi*

I made my wife some tea

I send my brother the money

I made some tea for my wife

I send the money to my brother

Note that many causative verbs (see unit 56) also require a double-object construction. In these cases, it is the person being made/allowed to do something that comes first and the object of the underlying verb that comes second. Here the structure with *la-* is *not* possible; only a double-object construction is correct:

<table>
<tr><td align="center">بعلم الشب عربي</td><td align="center">كرهو إختي الإنجليزي</td></tr>
<tr><td align="center">bi3allem ᵢshshabb 3arabi</td><td align="center">karrahu 2ikhti l2ingliizi</td></tr>
<tr><td align="center">he's teaching the guy Arabic</td><td align="center">they made my sister hate English</td></tr>
</table>

Direct Objects with Pronouns

Direct objects can of course be replaced by pronouns ("I saw <u>him</u>," "he sold <u>it</u>"). As we saw in unit 18, the relevant set is the *attached pronouns,* which suffix directly onto the verb and cause all the expected changes (see unit 4). Note that the form for "me" is ني‍ *-ni*:

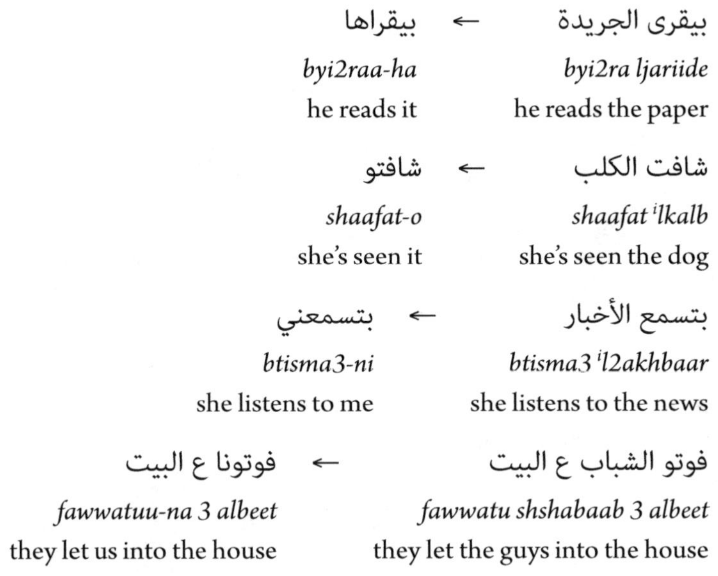

<table>
<tr><td align="center">بيقراها</td><td align="center">←</td><td align="center">بيقرى الجريدة</td></tr>
<tr><td align="center">byi2raa-ha</td><td></td><td align="center">byi2ra ljariide</td></tr>
<tr><td align="center">he reads it</td><td></td><td align="center">he reads the paper</td></tr>
<tr><td align="center">شافتو</td><td align="center">←</td><td align="center">شافت الكلب</td></tr>
<tr><td align="center">shaafat-o</td><td></td><td align="center">shaafat ᵢlkalb</td></tr>
<tr><td align="center">she's seen it</td><td></td><td align="center">she's seen the dog</td></tr>
<tr><td align="center">بتسمعني</td><td align="center">←</td><td align="center">بتسمع الأخبار</td></tr>
<tr><td align="center">btisma3-ni</td><td></td><td align="center">btisma3 ᵢl2akhbaar</td></tr>
<tr><td align="center">she listens to me</td><td></td><td align="center">she listens to the news</td></tr>
<tr><td align="center">فوتونا ع البيت</td><td align="center">←</td><td align="center">فوتو الشباب ع البيت</td></tr>
<tr><td align="center">fawwatuu-na 3 albeet</td><td></td><td align="center">fawwatu shshabaab 3 albeet</td></tr>
<tr><td align="center">they let us into the house</td><td></td><td align="center">they let the guys into the house</td></tr>
</table>

Note that North Levantine speakers' third-person singular feminine ("she") form *-et* has a vowel that, according to the normal rules, should be deleted when a vowel-initial suffix is added (see unit 4). Most speakers avoid this by placing irregular stress on the *-et* in these cases, especially where the deletion would lead to ambiguity:

<table>
<tr><td align="center">شافتو</td><td align="center">عرفتك</td></tr>
<tr><td align="center">shaaf-it-o</td><td align="center">3irf-it-ak</td></tr>
<tr><td align="center">she saw him</td><td align="center">she recognised you</td></tr>
</table>

You may hear regular forms from some Syrian speakers: شافتك *shaaf-t-ak* "she saw you," عرفتك *3ir*ᶦ*f-t-ak* "she recognised you."

Pseudoverbs can also take pronoun objects. There is a slight complication here, however. Since a pseudoverb already carries a pronoun suffix by definition—marking, in this case, its subject—it cannot take another attached pronoun to mark the object. Instead, the carrier word يا *(y)yaa-* (see unit 18) is introduced to carry the object pronoun:

بدي ياها ← بدي سيارة جديدة

baddi yyaaha   *baddi siyyaara jdiide*

I want it   I want a new car

معك ياهن؟ ← معك المصاري؟

ma3ak yaahon?   *ma3ak* ᶦ*lmaSaari?*

do you have it [= them]?   do you have the money?

Double-object verbs exhibit similar complications. If we replace the *first* object with a pronoun, the structure is straightforward:

باعتو البيت ← باعت محمد البيت

baa3at-o lbeet   *baa3at* ᶦ*m7ammad* ᶦ*lbeet*

she sold him the house   she sold Muhammad the house

سلمتها التقرير ← سلمت لينا التقرير

sallamt-ha ttaqriir   *sallam*ᵉ*t liina ttaqriir*

I gave her the report   I gave Lina the report

If we replace the *second* object, however, we can no longer use the double-object construction. Just like in English—where we have to use "to" in the sentences on the right—we have to use a *la-* construction:

باعتو لمحمد ← باعت محمد البيت

baa3at-o lam7ammad   *baa3at* ᶦ*m7ammad* ᶦ*lbeet*

she sold it to Muhammad   she sold Muhammad the house

سلمتو للينا ← سلمت لينا التقرير

sallamt-o liina   *sallam*ᵉ*t liina ttaqriir*

I gave it to Lina   I gave Lina the report

When *both* objects are pronouns, the word *(y)yaa-* is used to carry the second pronoun:

باعتو ياه   ←   باعت محمد البيت

baa3at-o yyaa   *baa3at ⁱm7ammad ⁱlbeet*

she sold him it   she sold Muhammad the house

سلمتها ياه   ←   سلمت لينا التقرير

sallamt-ha yyaa   *sallamᵉt liina ttaqriir*

I gave her it   I gave Lina the report

Definiteness in Direct Objects

In unit 13, we saw that the definite article الـ *l-* is used with all sorts of generic nouns where English uses no article at all:

الحب   الكيميا   السوريين   التلفزيون

ⁱl7ubb   *ⁱlkiimya*   *ⁱssuuriyyiin*   *ⁱttilivizyoon*

love   chemistry   Syrians   television

This rule, however, is largely broken by direct objects. There are a handful of verbs—mainly those expressing *opinions*—that behave as we would expect them to:

بحب القهوة   بكره الكيميا

bi7ibb ⁱl2ahwe   *bakrah ⁱlkiimya*

he likes coffee   I hate chemistry

The majority, however, default to an indefinite form even when the meaning is straight-forwardly something we would think of as "generic":

عم اتعلم عربي   بدرس هندسة

3am 2it3allam 3arabi   *badros handase*

I'm learning Arabic   I'm studying engineering

بطلت قراية   بتحكي فرنساوي؟

baTTalt ⁱ2raaye   *bti7ki faransaawi?*

I've stopped reading   do you speak French?

The same applies to the direct objects of pseudoverbs. Even though السلام *ⁱssalaam* "peace" and السل *ⁱssill* "tuberculosis" are concept names and are typically accompanied by a definite article, as the objects of *baddi* "I want" and *3indo* "he's got" here they are indefinite:

بدي سلام   لك الزلمة عندو سل!

baddi salaam   *lak ⁱzzalame 3indo sill!*

I want peace   come on, the guy's got TB!

When the definite form is used with these verbs, it inevitably refers to something *specific*; that is, it is used where "the" would be used in English. Consider the following pair:

بتشرب القهوة؟   بتشرب قهوة؟

btishrab ⁱl-2ahwe?   *btishrab 2ahwe?*

do you drink the coffee [that I've been bringing you]?   do you drink coffee?

This rule applies only to *direct* objects. Compare these synonyms, one of which takes a direct object and the other a prepositional object. As you can see, even though the meaning is basically identical, the preposition must be followed by a definite form, while the direct object is marked as indefinite:

بتفرج ع التلفزيون   بحضر تلفزيون

bitfarraj 3a ttilivizyoon   *bi7Dar tilivizyoon*

"I watch TV"   "I watch TV"

Prepositional Objects

Many verbs must be connected to their object by a preposition, just as in English:

اطلع بـ   فكر بـ   حكى على   كتب عن

TTalla3 b-   *fakkar b-*   *7aka 3ala*   *katab 3an*

look at   think about   talk about   write about

ركض ورا   بعت ورا   تصفح بـ   استولى على

rakaD wara   *ba3at wara*   *tSaffa7 b-*   *stawla 3ala*

run around after   send for   flick through   take over

Which preposition a verb uses has to be learnt alongside the verb itself. Although there may be some internal logic, it is largely a matter of usage. Some verbs' prepositions differ from region to region, and it is rare that the preposition used in Arabic corresponds directly to the one used in English. Consider the following synonyms, which all use different prepositions (or no preposition at all) corresponding to a direct object in English:

رنيت على جودة   طلبت جودة

ranneet 3ala juude   *Talabᵉt juude*

I called Joudeh   I called Joudeh

اتصلت بجودة

ttaSalt ᵢbjuude

I called Joudeh

دقيت لجودة

da22eet lajuude

I called Joudeh

As you would expect, these objects can be replaced by attached pronouns. For the most part, these combine with prepositions as we would expect from unit 22:

اطلعت فيه   ←   اطلعت بأخي

ᵢTTala3ᵉt fii   *ᵢTTalla3ᵉt b2akhi*

I looked at him   I looked at my brother

حكيت معاها   ←   حكيت مع المس

7akeet ma3aa-ha   *7akeet ma3 ᵢlmiss*

I spoke to her   I spoke to the teacher

دوري عليهن   ←   دوري ع المصاري

dawwri 3aleyy-on   *dawwri 3a lmaSaari*

look for it   look for the money

أنس معي   ←   أنس مع سامي؟

2anas ma3-i   *2anas ma3 saami?*

Anas is with me   is Anas with Sami?

There is a slight complication with the preposition ل *la-*. While pronouns can be combined with *la-* more or less straightforwardly (see unit 22), it is far more common, when it connects a verb to its object, to use a special suffixed form (see unit 19):

دقيتلو   ←   دقيت لجودة

da22eet-illo   *da22eet lajuude*

I rang him   I phoned Joudeh

We will talk more about constructions with *la-* in unit 53.

Dropped Objects

Both English and Arabic can occasionally drop objects. But Arabic allows indefinite objects in particular to be dropped entirely in more contexts than English does. Here the effect is usually similar to using "any" or "some" on their own in English:

اشتريت   ←   اشتريت موز

shtareet   *shtareet mooz*

I bought some   I bought [some] bananas

لقيتي كتب   →   لقيتي

la2eeti   *la2eeti kitob*

you found some   you found [some] books

جبت كولا؟   →   جبت؟

jibᵉt?   *jibᵉt koola?*

did you bring any?   did you bring any coke?

اشتري ساعة!   →   اشتري!

shtiri!   *shtiri saa3a!*

buy one!   buy a watch!

These structures sometimes serve as the equivalents of English constructions with "did" standing in for a main verb ("I did!" and "did you?").

Indirect Objects with *la-* and *3ala*

In unit 52 we looked at direct and prepositional objects, which tend to express the "experiencer" of the action described by a verb. In this unit, we will be thinking about object constructions introduced specifically by the prepositions *la-* and *3ala*. In some respects, *la-* is like other prepositions used to connect verbs to their objects. But *la-* differs in two key ways from these prepositions:

1. The preposition *la-* commonly marks recipients or beneficiaries. In other words, *la-* introduces what in English are sometimes called "indirect objects."
2. When introducing a pronoun instead of a noun, *la-* does not act straightforwardly and typically transforms into a suffix that attaches to the verb.

We will look at how *la-* structures work before considering the parallel uses of *3ala* to mark those harmed by actions.

Structures with *la-*

The word ل *la-* most commonly corresponds to the English words "to" and "for." This means that ل *la-* generally marks either recipients or beneficiaries of actions:

بعطي خبز للمعلم

ba3Ti khubᵒz lalˈm3allem

I'll give some bread to the teacher

I'll give the teacher some bread

بعتت المصاري لأخي

ba3att ˈlmaSaari la2akhi

I sent the money to my brother

I sent my brother the money

ساوي شاي لإمي

saawi shaay la2immi

make tea for my mum

make my mum some tea

اشتريت تياب للولاد

shtareet ˈtyaab lalˈwlaad

I bought clothes for the kids

I bought the kids some clothes

As you can see from the translations, in English it is often possible to transform sentences of this kind into double-object constructions. In Arabic this is generally not possible (although for some exceptions see unit 52 above), and these sentences are the only possible translations of either English phrasing.

As we have seen in units 15 and 19, *la-* plays a role in various possessive constructions. In particular, it can be used to combine an indefinite "possessee" with a definite possessor in structures such as the following. In the following examples, *la-* translates to English "by":

عم اسمع غنية لفيروز

3am 2isma3 ghinniyye lafayruuz

I'm listening to a song of Feyrouz's

I'm listening to a song by Feyrouz

قريت كتاب لنزار قباني

2areet ᵎktaab lanizaar 2abbaani

I read a book of Nizar Qabbani's

I read a book by Nizar Qabbani

This *la-* and the possessor can become detached from the possessee and used in structures such as the following:

عم اسمع لفيروز

3am 2isma3 lafayruuz

I'm listening to some Feyrouz

I'm listening to something by Feyrouz

قريت لنزار قباني؟

2areet lanizaar 2abbaani?

have you read any Nizar Qabbani?

have you read anything by Nizar Qabbani?

When combined with a direct object pronoun, these structures can sometimes end up looking exactly like the repeated object construction (discussed later in this unit), where a pronoun is used to refer to a noun object that is then also explicitly referenced using *la-*. Compare the following:

Repeated Object	**Normal** *la-*
بضربو لأخي	بضربو لأخي
baD"rbo la2akhi	*baD"rbo la2akhi*
I hit my brother	I hit him for my brother
بتشوفها لإختي	بتشوفها لإختي
bitshuufa la2ikhti	*bitshuufa la2ikhti*
you see my sister	you look at it for my sister

With the repeated object construction, the pronoun refers forward to the noun introduced with *la-*, and the English sentence has only one object. In the other construction, the noun with *la-* is entirely separate from the pronoun, and *la-* means "for." In cases such as these, the only way to tell which meaning is intended is context.

Structures with *la-* and a Pronoun

As noted above, when the noun object of *la-* is replaced by a pronoun, this typically triggers a transformation into a suffix that is attached to the verb. The forms of this suffix are discussed in unit 19:

اشتريت تياب للولاد   ←   اشتريتلهم تياب

shtareet ᶦtyaab lalᶦwlaad   *shtareet-ᶦlhom ᶦtyaab*

I bought clothes for the kids   I bought them clothes

بعتت المصاري لأخي   ←   بعتلو المصاري

ba3att ᶦlmaSaari la2akhi   *ba3att-illo lmaSaari*

I sent the money to my brother   I sent him the money

ساوي شاي لإمي   ←   ساويلها شاي

saawii shaay la2immi   *saawii-lha shaay*

make tea for my mum   make her tea

The same applies to the possessive use of *la-*:

بطالع صورة لأخي   ←   بطالعلو صورة

bTaale3 Suura la2akhi   *bTaali3-lo Suura*

I'll get a picture of my brother up   I'll get a picture of him up

عم اسمع غنية لفيروز   ←   عم اسمعلها غنية

3am 2isma3 ghinniyye lafayruuz   *3am 2isma3-la ghinniyye*

I'm listening to a song by Feyrouz   I'm listening to a song by her

قريت لنزار قباني؟   ←   قريتلو؟

2areet lanizaar 2abbaani?   *2areet-lo?*

have you read anything by Nizar Qabbani?   have you read anything by him?

Note that if another pronoun suffix is already present—expressing the direct object, for example (see unit 18)—it is pushed off the verb and onto the carrier يا *(y)yaa-*:

اشتريت تياب للولاد   ←   اشتريتلهم ياهم

shtareet ᶦtyaab lalᶦwlaad   *shtareet-ᶦlhom ᶦyyaahom*

I bought clothes for the kids   I bought them them

بعتت المصاري لأخي   ←   بعتلو ياهم

ba3att ᶦlmaSaari la2akhi   *ba3att-illo yaahom*

I sent the money to my brother   I sent him it

For other uses of this suffix—including those with no corresponding noun construction—
see unit 19. For use of this suffix with comparatives, see unit 79. For use of this suffix in the
construction صارل *SaLL-* "has been," see unit 40.

Repeated Object Construction

The word *la-* is also used in another construction that is characteristic of Levantine Arabic.
This is the so-called repeated object construction in which a definite noun is marked with a
pronoun *and* at the same time is stated explicitly with *la-*. This is easiest to demonstrate with
examples. The most common use is with the direct object of a verb (see unit 52):

شربتها للمي   =   شربت المي

shribt-ha lalmayy   *shribt ⁱlmayy*

I drank the water   I drank the water

خلصتو للكتاب   =   خلصت الكتاب

khallaSt-o lalⁱktaab   *khallaSt lⁱktaab*

I finished the book   I finished the book

شايفهم للصبايا   =   شايف الصبايا

shaayif-hom laSSabaaya   *shaayef ⁱSSabaaya*

I can see the girls   I can see the girls

This also occurs with the second noun of an *2iDaafe* (see unit 15):

بيتو لسامي   =   بيت سامي

beet-o lasaami   *beet saami*

Sami's house   Sami's house

مكتبها لرشا   =   مكتب رشا

maktab-ha larasha   *maktab rasha*

Rasha's office   Rasha's office

كتبهم للشباب   =   كتب الشباب

kutub-hum lashshabaab   *kutob ⁱshshabaab*

the guys' books   the guys' books

For some speakers, at least, this can also occur with the object of a preposition (see unit 22):

معو لسمير   =   مع سمير

ma3-o lasamiir   *ma3 samiir*

with Samir   with Samir

قريبة من المكتبة   =   قريبة منها للمكتبة

2ariibe minn-ha lalmaktabe   *2ariibe mn ⁱlmaktabe*

close to the library   close to the library

This construction is difficult to account for and expresses nuances that are hard to pin down. As the equal signs (=) in the tables suggest, there is no clear difference in meaning between these structures and their more straightforward counterparts. Sometimes the *la-* allows a noun to be reintroduced as a sort of afterthought or clarification of a pronoun. This seems to be more common with animate nouns in North Levantine and among younger speakers. In any case, it is never wrong to use the simpler structure.

Structures with *3ala*

We have encountered على *3ala* as a preposition connecting some verbs to their objects (see unit 52). But like *la-*, *3ala* also appears in other contexts. Its first use is as a negative counterpart to *la-* expressing that someone has been *harmed* by the action. This sometimes has a nice colloquial English counterpart in "on," but the two constructions don't line up perfectly:

أبو أحمد تزوج على مرتو   شو, أطفي الشوفاج ع الولاد؟

2abu 2a7mad tzawwaj 3ala marto   *shuu, 2aTaffi shshoofaaj 3 alⁱwlaad?*

Abu Ahmad married [a second wife]   so I'm supposed to turn the heating

[= he married on his (current) wife]   off and let the kids freeze?

[= turn off the heating on the kids]

Unlike *la-*, replacing *3ala*'s object with a pronoun does not transform it into a suffix. The only significant change—which is to be expected according to the normal rules of sentence structure (see unit 47)—is that the preposition-pronoun combination often comes closer to the verb:

طلعو عليها إشاعات   مسكر عليي الباب

Talla3u 3aleeha 2ishaa3aat   *msakker 3aliyyi lbaab*

they spread rumours about her   he's locked the door

[and I can't get in!]

> It is not always possible to draw a clear distinction between structures of this kind and the use of *3ala* as a preposition used to connect a normal object to a verb.

The other common idiomatic usage is to add destinations or final locations to verbs, often ones that cannot easily take a destination in English. Consider the following examples:

أجا عندي ع البيت

2aja 3indi 3 albeet

he came to my place

[= came chez moi to the house]

تجوز على أميركا

ˈ*tjawwaz 3ala 2ameerka*

he got married to someone in America

and went there

[= married on America]

In the left-hand example, unlike the English translation, there are two destinations: *3indi* "to my place" and *3albeet* "to the house." In the right-hand example, the English translation requires an extra verb to express the movement involved. For more on this use, see appendix B.

Secondary Objects

In units 52 and 53 we looked at a range of direct and indirect object constructions. Although the terminology may have been new—and the precise details may have been a bit different—those constructions largely had clear English counterparts. In this unit, however, we will be considering various types of object that for the most part correspond to nonobject constructions in English. I will be calling these *secondary* objects.

These secondary objects typically appear after direct and indirect objects. The main feature that they all have in common is that—like normal direct objects—they are not accompanied by a preposition or any other indication of what their function is. They are also invariably indefinite, regardless of their translation or whether they are the sort of noun that would normally be definite (see unit 13):

بحضر تسلاي بس

ba7Dar tislaay bass

I only watch it for entertainment

تعبت عليه ساعة

t3ibᵉt 3alee saa3a

I worked hard on it for an hour

As you can see from these examples, the meaning and translation of these objects varies quite a lot. In what follows I will divide them up into different categories depending on how they are used.

Object = "For" (Duration)

This kind of object expresses the duration of an action. These typically correspond to phrases with "for X" in English:

بدي اطلع ربع ساعة

biddi 2iTla3 ribᵉ3 saa3a

I'm going to step outside for fifteen minutes

قعد عندي يومين

2a3ad 3indi yoomeen

he stayed with me for two days

ضلت عم تشتغل فيه شهر كامل	اشتغلت عندو سنة
Dallet 3am tishtighel fii shah^e^r kaamel	*'shtaghal^e^t 3indo sane*
she worked on it for a whole month	I worked for him for a year

Object = "As"

This kind of secondary object provides *extra information* about the direct object or the subject and corresponds to the vast majority of instances of the word "as" in English. Using ک *ka-* (see appendix B) here—the usual dictionary translation for "as"—is not idiomatic. Whether the secondary object refers to the object or the subject is determined by context, just as in structures with "as":

بشتغل مهندسة	جيت على بريطانيا لاجئ
bashtghel muhandise	*jiit 3ala briTaanya laaje2*
I work as an engineer	I came to Britain as a refugee
جبتو مفاجأة	عطيتها الورد هدية
jibto mufaaja2a	*3aTeetha lward ^i^hdiyye*
I got it as a surprise	I gave her the flowers as a gift

Object = "Into" (Result)

Like "as" objects, this kind of object provides extra information about the direct object or subject. In this case, however, it describes the *state* of that direct object or subject once the action described by the verb is completed. This most commonly corresponds to a construction with "into" in English:

قلبنا الصالون غرفة نوم	قسموها قسمين
2alabna SSaaloon ghurfet noom	*2assamuuha 2ismeen*
we made the living room into a bedroom	they divided it into two parts

> Note that some verbs do take a *la-* here, corresponding to English "into": قلب لوحش *2alab lawa7^e^sh* "he turned into a monster."

Most instances of the English term "into," of course, are straightforwardly (or metaphorically) directional. For these, see unit 81.

Same-Verb *maSdar* Object

The *maSdar* of a verb (see unit 31) is often used as its secondary object. When it appears alone, the effect is usually to either make the language more "colourful" or emphasise the meaning of the verb against other possible interpretations:

كاتب اسمي كتابة

kaateb 2ismi ktaabe

I've written my name

[as opposed to typing it]

عم تدور على مشاكل دوارة

3am ᴵtdawwer 3ala mashaakel ᴵdwaara

you're looking for an argument

[deliberately]

ضربني ضرب

Darabni Darᵉb

he properly hit me

ركضت ركيض

rakaDt ᴵrkiiD

I ran [I didn't walk]

> This construction has various names in English-language descriptions of Arabic. It is sometimes called the "cognate accusative" or "cognate object," with "cognate" here meaning "from the same root" (referring to the *maSdar* and the main verb). It is also sometimes referred to by its Arabic name, the مفعول مطلق *maf3uul muTlaq* or "absolute object."

Often, however, the *maSdar* is combined with an adjective or some other kind of noun-modifying construction. This tends to correspond to an adverb in English. The meaning is generally transparent but sometimes requires some restructuring in order to translate idiomatically:

عاملوني معاملة مخزية

3aamaluuni mu3aamale mukhziye

they treated me terribly

[= a terrible treatment]

بعرفها معرفة سطحية بس

ba3rifha ma3rife saT7iyye bass

I only know her superficially

[= a superficial knowledge]

بعرفو عز المعرفة

ba3ᴵrfo 3izz ᴵlma3rife

I know him really well

[= the height of knowledge]

ركضلك أحلى ركيض!

rakaDlak 2a7la rkiiD!

And he ran marvelously!

[= the best running]

بزقلك بزقة أكابر

bazza2lek baz2et 2akaaber

he spat like a real high-class guy

[= a VIP spitting]

مسكوه مسك اليد

masakuu mask ᴵlyad

they caught him red-handed

[= the catching of the hand]

Note that occasionally, particularly in more high-register or idiomatic contexts, adjectives may also take similar constructions with abstract nouns:

مريض مرض الموت

ذكية ذكاء غريب

mariiD maraD ⁱlmawt

zakiyye zakaa2 ghariib

he has a terminal illness

she's clever in a weird way

[= ill the illness of death]

[= intelligent a strange intelligence]

Same-Verb Noun of Instance Object

The noun of instance (see unit 31) of a verb can also be used as its object. This is very similar in usage to the *maSdar* construction but with the additional nuance that it describes a *single instance* of the action:

نمتلي أحلى نومة

صرعتيلك شي صرعة؟

nimtilli 2a7la noome

Sara3tiilek shii Sar3a?

I had a lovely sleep

have you gone crazy?

> Occasionally, something that looks like a noun of instance is actually just serving as its *maSdar*. For more on this, see unit 31.

These instances are countable (see unit 11):

ضربني تلت ضربات على راسي

غبلك غبتين هيك

Darabni tlett Darbaat 3ala raasi

ghabbillak ghabbteen heek

he hit me three times on the head

he took two big gulps

[three hits]

Object = Manner

Sometimes the secondary object describes the *manner* in which the action described by the verb is carried out. There are some words that work in almost all contexts or with all kinds of verbs:

أخدت المصاري غصب

أكلت الصندويشة ركض

2akhadt ⁱlmaSaari ghaSᵉb

2akalt ⁱSSandwiishe rakᵉD

I took the money by force

I ate the sandwich in a hurry

I wolfed down the sandwich

فتحت المحل حرام

fat7et ⁱlma7all 7araam

she opened the shop illegally

غلبني غش

ghalabni ghushsh

he beat me dishonestly

Other examples of this construction are more idiosyncratic to individual verbs. For example, verbs expressing motion from one place to another commonly combine with *maSdars* expressing the *manner* of motion:

رجعت ع السيارة ركيض

rij3et 3 assayyaara rkiiD

she ran back to the car

رحنا ع البيت مشي

ri7na 3 albeet mashi

we walked home

جايبني لهون شحط

jaayibni lahoon sha7ᵉT

you've dragged me

[all the way] here

الرئيس رايح مهمة

ⁱrra2iis raaye7 muhimme

the president's gone

on an [official] mission

> As an English speaker you are likely to be tempted to use the manner verb directly: "I <u>walked</u> there." In Arabic this is unusual, and the common structure uses "go" plus the *maSdar* of "walking," "running," and so on.

It is beyond the scope of a grammar to try to give a comprehensive list of structures of this kind; you will need to learn how individual words work in the wild. But a few examples should be enough to give you the general idea. Verbs meaning "hit" can take an object indicating how or with what (including metaphorical uses):

طرقني سكينة

Tara2ni sikkiine

he stabbed me

[= hit me a knife]

ضربني كوع

Darabni koo3

he elbowed me

[= hit me an elbow]

ندفتني كم

nadfitni kimm

she really got one over on me

[= smacked me a sleeve]

سفقني محاضرة

safa2ni mu7aaDara

he gave me this big lecture

[= slapped me a lecture]

The same goes for certain other similar idiomatic expressions:

هريتنا تضييف

hareetna taDyiif

you've been such a gracious host

[= you wore us out hosting]

حرقت نفسها غسيل

7ara2ᵉt nafsa ghasiil

I washed the living daylights out of it

[= I burnt its soul washing]

فرطت ضحك

faraTᵉt Da7ᵉk

I pissed myself laughing

[= I broke up laughing]

الوجع عم يزداد سوء

ⁱlwajᵉ3 3am yizdaad suu2

the pain is getting worse

[= increasing badness]

There are many other examples. But it is important not to overgeneralise these structures. To take a morbid example, قتل *2atal* "kill" can take a *maSdar* object indicating *how* someone was killed:

قتلوه حرق

2ataluu 7arᵉ2

they burned him to death

[= killed him burning]

You might reasonably conclude from this that it was possible to add *7arᵉ2* to a sentence such as تخلصت من الورقة *tkhallaSt mn ⁱlwara2a* "I got rid of the paper" to express that you had burned it to get rid of it. But this would not be correct. The ability of *2atal* to take a secondary object of this kind—and the meaning that it carries—is idiosyncratic to *2atal* itself.

Object = Purpose

Another common construction with a *maSdar* or abstract noun object is the object of motivation or purpose. These objects basically give a motivation for the action described by the verb. This is not a very *productive* construction; you can't use any word you like in this meaning. But there are many common (semifrozen) examples, including the following:

واجب	خوف من	مزح	تسلاية / تسلاي
waajeb	*khoof min*	*mazᵉ7*	*tislaaye/tislaay*
out of social obligation	for fear of	as a joke	for fun

قصاص	مسايرة	جكارة بـ	نكاية بـ
2aSaaS	*msaayara*	*jakaara b-*	*nikaaye b-*
to punish [s.o.]	to keep [s.o.] happy / to humour [s.o.]	to spite / out of spite	to spite / out of spite

The following are some examples in context:

اشتريت بلوزة جديدة نكاية بإختي

shtareet bluuze jdiide nikaaye b2ikhti

I bought a new top to spite my sister

حضرت الفيلم تسلاية

7aDart ^{i}*lfil*^{e}*m tislaaye*

I watched the film for fun

عملت هيك خوف

3mil^{e}*t heek khoof*

I did it out of fear

قعدتو بالقرنة قصاص

2a33adto bil2urne 2aSaaS

I sat him in the corner to punish him

Some of these forms are synonymous with adverbs in *-an* (see unit 20).

Complement Object

There is a range of other object-like constructions that will be more intuitive to an English speaker. In these constructions, the secondary "object" (a noun or an adjective) provides extra information about the subject or the direct object. I call this a "complement object" (in English it is often called a "subject complement" or "object complement"):

ما خلقت شوفير

maa khli2^{e}*t shofeer*

I wasn't born a driver

اشتريتها جديدة

shtareetha jdiide

I bought it new

ماتت زعلانة

maatat za3laane

she died angry

رجعت مبسوطة

rji3^{e}*t mabsuuTa*

I came back happy

سمى ابنو أحمد

samma 2ibno 2a7mad

he named his son Ahmad

طرش الحيط أحمر

Tarash ^{i}*l7eeT 2a7mar*

he painted the wall red

As you can see, these examples work more or less identically to their English counterparts. But in some ways English and Arabic do differ here. Although English does allow this construction with verbs such as "think," it is very stuffy. The same is not true of the equivalent constructions in Arabic:

حسبت البنت سورية

7assabt ^{i}*lbint suuriyye*

I thought the girl was Syrian

[= thought the girl a Syrian]

مفكرة أحمد أهبل؟

^{i}*mfakkra 2a7mad 2ahbal?*

Do you think Ahmad is an idiot?

[= do you think Ahmad an idiot?]

Object = "What" or "How Much"

One final category of secondary object is worth noting here. The English word "what" can be combined with a noun ("what cars," "what desserts") to ask about a broad category of things. The same effect can be achieved in Arabic, but the counterparts to "what"—شو *shuu* and ايش *2eesh*—cannot be placed before a noun directly. Instead, the noun is phrased as a secondary object:

إنتي شو قارية كتب أجنبية؟

2inti shuu 2aarye kitob 2ajnabiyye?

what foreign books have you read?

ايش عندكم حلو؟

2eesh 3indkom 7ilu?

what desserts have you got?

The same applies to قديش *2addeesh* and كم *kamm* "how much":

كم معك مصاري؟

kamm ma3ek maSaari?

how much money have you got?

قديش معك مصاري؟

2addeesh ma3ak maSaari?

how much money have you got?

For more on these structures, see units 73 and 74.

Reflexive and Reciprocal Constructions

In units 52–54, we looked at various kinds of objects. In this unit, we will look at two special kinds of construction that generally occupy the object slot: *reflexives* and *reciprocals*. Both of these constructions express unusual relationships between the subject and object of a verb. In the case of reflexives, the relationship is one of equivalence: the subject and the object are the same person, thing, or entity. In the case of reciprocals, the relationship is a more complicated one: the different people (or things) making up the (plural) subject are acting on one another at the same time.

As the final sentences of the last paragraph show, it is quite difficult to alight on a clear and succinct definition of "reflexive" or "reciprocal." You don't need to worry too much, though, because both of these structures have very obvious parallels in English. We will begin with reflexives, which correspond to structures with "-self." We will then look at reciprocals, which correspond to structures with "each other" or "one another."

Reflexive Constructions "-self"

Reflexive pronouns are most commonly used to express that the object of a verb is the same as the subject: that the subject is *acting on itself*. In English we use a set of pronouns with the suffix "-self" to achieve this. The corresponding forms in Arabic are derived by suffixing the attached pronouns (see unit 18) to the base word حال 7aal-, literally "situation." This produces paradigms such as the following:

North Levantine	South Levantine
حالي	حالي
7aal-i	7aal-i
myself	myself

North Levantine		South Levantine	
حالك *7aal-ek* yourself [F]	حالك *7aal-ak* yourself [M]	حالك *7aal-ek* yourself [F]	حالك *7aal-ak* yourself [M]
حالها *7aal-(h)a* herself	حالو *7aal-o* himself	حالها *7aal-ha* herself	حالو *7aal-o* himself
حالنا *7aal-na* ourselves		حالنا *7aal-na* ourselves	
حالكن *7aal-kon* yourselves		حالكم *7aal-kom* yourselves	
حالهن *7aal-(h)on* themselves		حالهم *7aal-(h)om* themselves	

> As usual, I have simplified here. Some Palestinian speakers have forms that closely resemble those given for North Levantine speakers or else use the forms حالكو *7aalku* and حالهن *7aalhen* for "yourselves" and "themselves." For more on pronoun variations, see unit 18.

For the most part, these pronouns are used exactly like their English equivalents. Consider the following examples. As you can see, when the object (direct or prepositional) is the same as the subject, we use a *7aal-* form:

ضرب حالو ← ضرب حدا
Darab 7aalo ← *Darab 7ada*
he hit himself ← he hit someone

عم تكذب ع حالها ← عم تكذب عليك
3am tikzob 3a 7aalha ← *3am tikzob 3aleek*
she's lying to herself ← she's lying to you

حكو عني   ←   حكو عن حالهم

7aku 3an 7aalhom   *7aku 3anni*

they talked about themselves   they talked about me

There are, however, a handful of cases in which the Arabic structures may be counterintuitive. A handful of set expressions have "-self" in English but do not in Arabic. More notably, when the "underlying object" of a causative verb (that is, the object of the noncausative verb from which it is derived) is the same as the subject, the reflexive is not used:

ضحكني عليه   ←   ضحكني عليها

Da77akni 3alee   *Da77akni 3aleeha*

he made me laugh at him   he made me laugh at her

[he = him]

كتبو غصبن عنو   ←   كتبو غصبن عني

katabo ghaSben 3anno   *katabo ghaSben 3anni*

he forced himself to write it   he wrote it against my will

[= in spite of himself]   [= in spite of me]

It is easy to overthink the definition of "reflexive" given above and start overusing these pronouns. It is possible to imagine a language where structures such as "he took me to his house" and "he pushed me away from him" would always have to be marked as reflexive if the pronoun referred to the same person as the subject. Languages such as this do exist! But Arabic, conveniently enough, generally patterns with English in its use of the reflexive forms, and English is your best guide to how to deploy them correctly.

Note as well the idiomatic structure لحال *la7aal-*, which translates as "on X's own," "by X-self":

قاعد لحالي   فتح لحالو

2aa3ed la7aali   *fata7 la7aalo*

sitting on my own   it opened on its own

For the emphatic use of "-self" as in "I myself never do that"—which is formed using نفس *nafs*—see unit 66.

Reciprocal Constructions ("One Another," "Each Other")

Reciprocal structures are used to express that two subjects are acting *simultaneously on each other*. The most common way of achieving this in Arabic is to replace the object or prepositional object with the invariable pronoun بعض *ba3ᵉD/ba3ᵃD* "each other":

شافوها

shaafuuha

they saw her

شافو بعض

shaafu ba3ᵃD

they saw each other

عم يكذبو عليه

3am yikⁱzbu 3alee

they're lying to him

عم يكذبو ع بعض

3am yikⁱzbu 3a ba3ᵉD

they're lying to one another

فوقها

foo2ha

they're on top of it

فوق بعض

foo2 ba3ᵉD

they're on top of one another

As with reflexives, these structures work almost identically to their English counterparts, and there is no need to think too hard about their underlying semantics.

> You may occasionally encounter pronouns attached to *ba3ᵉD* referring back to the subject: منساعد بعضنا *minsaa3ed ba3ⁱD-na* "we help each other."

Note that مع بعض *ma3 ba3ᵉD* is also a set expression meaning "together":

قاعدين مع بعض

2aa3diin ma3 ba3ᵉD

they're sitting together

بروحو مع بعض

biruu7u ma3 ba3ᵉD

they go together

Reciprocal Verbs (*tfaa3al*)

Some *tfaa3al* verbs (see unit 23) are inherently reciprocal; that is, they include the sense of simultaneous, mutual action without *ba3ᵉD/ba3ᵃD*. They usually provide a reciprocal counterpart to the (not inherently reciprocal) verb from which they are derived. The structures on the right are more or less synonymous with the verbs on the left:

بشاورو بعض

bishaawru ba3ᵃD

they consult one another

=

بتشاورو

bitshaawaru

they consult one another

عم يسابقو بعض = عم يتسابقو

3am ysaab2u ba3ᵉD   3am yitsaaba2u

they're racing one another   they're racing one another

عم يصارعو بعض = عم يتصارعو

3am ySaar3u ba3ᵉD   3am yitSaara3u

they're wrestling one another   they're wrestling one another

We have to be careful here, though, because some reciprocal verbs can appear in constructions such as the following:

وافقت معو ← توافقت معو

waafa2ᵉt ma3o   twaafa2ᵉt ma3o

I made an agreement with him   I made an agreement with him [and he with me]

خانقو معها ← تخانقو معها

khaana2u ma3ha   tkhaana2u ma3ha

they fought with her   they fought with her [and she with them]

There is a distinction in meaning here. The word *twaafa2* still contains a reciprocal element, implying that the action goes both ways, which *waafa2* does not imply. But unlike a straightforward reciprocal construction, the two actors do not both have to be part of the subject. The subject can be singular.

Note that some reciprocal verbs are used with مع بعض *ma3 ba3ᵉD* even when reciprocity is inherently part of their meaning:

تخانقو مع بعض

tkhaana2u ma3 ba3ᵉD

they fought with one another

توافقو مع بعض

twaafa2u ma3 ba3ᵉD

they agreed with one another

Causative Constructions ("Make" and "Let")

In this unit we will be looking at Arabic's range of *causative* constructions—in short, ways of expressing "make" and "let" in structures such as "I made him come with me" and "she let me write everything down." These structures can basically be divided into two broad categories: derived causatives (those formed with a distinct verb with causative meaning) and causatives with an auxiliary verb (most commonly خلى *khalla*). We will consider these two categories in turn before briefly reviewing a situation in which Arabic does not have a distinct construction ("get X Yed") and what it does instead.

What Is a Causative?

The term "causative" usually refers to constructions expressing that a third party "made" somebody (the subject) do something (the verb). By extension, it sometimes applies to other structurally or semantically similar constructions, such as "allowing" or "letting" someone to do something or "getting" someone to do something. While English has a compulsory distinction between "make," "let," and "get...to," by default Arabic does not, and the most basic forms can be used to express all three:

خليتو يفوت	فوتو ع البيت
khalleeto yfuut	*fawwatto 3 albeet*
I let him in	I let him in
I made him go in	I made him go in
I got him to go in	I got him to go in

As you can see, the basic way of forming causative constructions is to use either a derived form of the verb, *fa33al*, or the auxiliary *khalla*. Forms on *fa33al* are particularly common as causative equivalents of "simple" (underived) verbs, while derived verbs generally (although not exclusively) take *khalla* instead. In this section we will discuss both structures and then look at some alternatives.

Derived Causatives

Causative verbs overwhelmingly have the form *fa33al* (see unit 23), and this is the only productive way of deriving new causatives. Each causative verb has an underlying noncausative verb to which it corresponds. Since the causative can express both direct involvement ("make X do") and noninvolvement ("let X do") and since many underlying verbs have multiple meanings that can all generate causatives, causative verbs often have a bewildering array of idiomatic translations:

فوت ← فات

fawwat   *faat*

to let X in   to go in

to put X in

to take/bring X in

خفف ← خف

khaffaf   *khaff*

to lighten, make lighter   to get lighter

to reduce [the burden of]

to go light(er) on

مشى ← مشي

mashsha   *mishi*

to walk [a dog]   to walk/move

to make X walk

to get X moving

طلع ← طلع

Talla3   *Tile3*

to take/bring X up/out/off   to come/go up/

to let X go up/out/off   out/off

to remove X

A handful of *2af3als* (see unit 23)—fuS7a causatives—are also used, but they are far less common.

Note as well that derived causatives have a tendency to acquire extended meanings (i.e., they not simply straightforward causatives of the underlying verb):

مشى ← مشي   سمك ← سمك

mashsha   *mishi*   *sammak*   *simek*

to cause to walk   to walk   to thicken   to get thicker

to process   to wrap up warm

[paperwork]

The base words given above are all "simple" (underived) verbs. A handful of derived verbs do have causatives, however. As elsewhere, some of the relationships are not exactly straightforwardly causative (see unit 23 for more on this):

غير ← تغير   خير ← اختار

ghayyar   *tghayyar*   *khayyar*   *khtaar*

to [cause to]   to [undergo]   to make   to choose

change   change   choose

علم ← تعلم

3allam   *t3allam*

to teach   to learn

When we make a verb causative, we add a new subject (the causer). The old subject becomes the direct object (see unit 52):

نيمو البيبي ← البيبي نام

nayyamu lbeebi   *ᵢlbeebi naam*

they put the baby to sleep   the baby went to sleep

فيقوني ← فقت أنا

fayya2uuni   *fi2ᵉt 2ana*

they woke me up   I woke up

If the verb already has a direct object, it becomes a double-object verb (see unit 52): the original subject becomes the direct object, and the original object becomes the new second object. All the normal points about double verbs and pronouns apply here, including the use of *yaa* to carry an extra pronoun:

علموني عربي ← تعلمت عربي

3allamuuni 3arabi   *t3allamᵉt 3arabi*

they taught me Arabic   I learnt Arabic

سامي شرب ديبة كولا ← ديبة شربت كولا

saami sharrab diibe koola   *diibe shirbat koola*

Sami gave Dibeh some coke to drink   Dibeh drank some coke

If the verb has a prepositional object, its causative will also have a prepositional object:

فهمت عليه   ←   فهموني عليه

fhim't 3alee   *fahhamuuni 3alee*

I understood him   they got me to understand him

When the new subject (the causer) and the object are the same, you might expect a reflexive form (see unit 55) to be used. But in fact a normal pronoun is used here:

ضحكو عليك   ←   ضحكتهم عليك

Di7ku 3aleek   *Da77akthom 3aleek*

they laughed at you   you made them laugh at you

Causatives with *khalla*

The main alternative to a distinct causative form is to use the auxiliary verb خلى *khalla* (for other uses of this verb, see units 43–44) with a zero-imperfective. Like the causative form, this structure can mean "make," "let," or "get to" depending on context:

سامية نقت الهدية   ←   خلينا سامية تنقي الهدية

saamiya na22at l'hdiyye   *khalleena saamiya tna22i l'hdiyye*

Samia picked the gift   we let Samia pick the gift

رح يندم أسعد   ←   رح نخلي أسعد يندم

ra7 yindam 2as3ad   *ra7 'nkhalli 2as3ad yindam*

Asad is going to regret this   we're going to make Asad regret this

النمر فات ع الغرفة   ←   خليت النمر يفوت ع الغرفة

'nnim'r faat 3 alghurfe   *khalleet 'nnimr yfuut 3 alghurfe*

the tiger came into the room   I got the tiger to come into the room

As you can see, the way this structure works is similar to the English terms "make" and "let." The causer is the subject of *khalla*, and the subject of the noncausative verb also becomes *khalla*'s object, as you can tell by both its positioning and what happens when it is replaced with a pronoun:

نقت الهدية   ←   خليناها تنقي الهدية

na22at l'hdiyye   *khalleenaaha tna22i l'hdiyye*

she picked the gift   we let her choose the gift

رح نخليه يندم   →   رح يندم

ra7 'nkhallii yindam   *ra7 yindam*

we're going to make him regret this   he's going to regret this

Note that even when a separate causative exists, *khalla* can be and often is used.

Causatives with Other Auxiliaries

A few other causative auxiliaries exist that form similar structures to *khalla* but convey more specific meanings. The word ترك *tarak*, literally "leave," is an unambiguous way of saying "let" or "leave X to":

تركو يرجع ع البيت!   →   بيرجع ع البيت

triko yirja3 3 albeet!   *byirja3 3 albeet*

let him go home!   he's going to go home

اتركو يكتب شعر   →   بكتب شعر

2itriko yuktob shi3ᵉr   *buktob shi3ᵉr*

let him write poetry!   he'll write poetry

The term جبر *jabar* is an unambiguous way of saying "force to," "oblige to":

بجبرني أشرحلو كل إشي   →   بشرحلو كل إشي

bujburni 2ashra7lo kull 2ishi   *bashra7lo kull 2ishi*

he'll force me to explain everything   I'll explain everything

جبروها تحكي عربي   →   بتحكي عربي

jabaruuha ti7ki 3arabi   *bti7ki 3arabi*

they made her speak Arabic   she speaks Arabic

"Get My Hair Cut" Constructions

In English we have a construction that allows us to express causative meaning without explicitly mentioning the person who will be doing the action, that is, the "original subject" in the terminology I've been using so far in this section. This construction uses "have" or "get," as in "I need to get the car fixed," "I'm going to get my hair cut," and "we've just had it painted."

Arabic has no corresponding distinct construction. Usually the most idiomatic choice is simply to use a straightforward verb with the *causer* as the subject. This occasionally works in English too but is far more marginal than in Arabic:

قصيت شعري امبارح

2aSSeet sha3ri mbaare7

I got my hair cut yesterday

[= I cut my hair yesterday]

بدي أترجم هاي الورقة

biddi tarjem haay ᴵlwara2a

I want to get this paper translated

[= I want to translate this paper]

Passive and Impersonal Constructions

In this unit we will look at how Arabic forms *passive* and *impersonal* constructions: constructions that either remove entirely or "impersonalise" the subject and, in some cases, "promote" another part of the sentence in its place. Most of these constructions have obvious parallels in English but are more restricted in their application.

We will start by considering the two most basic types of passive construction: the verbal passive and the passive participle. We will then discuss some more specialised or unusual passive structures before discussing impersonal constructions such as الواحد *ˈlwaa7ed/ ˈlwaa7ad* "one" and the impersonal "they."

The Verbal Passive

The passive transforms a verb's object into its subject ("promotes" it in linguistic jargon), generally deleting the original subject. In English this is achieved with a catchall structure with "be" or "get":

he spoke to me	→	I was spoken to
you read the book	→	the book was read
they rob houses	→	houses get robbed

Unlike English, Arabic has distinct passive verbs derived using various verbal patterns (see unit 23). The general rule is that the form of the underlying (nonpassive) verb will determine the shape of the corresponding passive verb.

Simple (underived) verbs generally have passives on *nfa3al* or (irregularly) *fta3al*:

انتشل	←	نشل		انكتب	←	كتب
ntashal		*nashal*		*nkatab*		*katab*
to be picked up		to pick up		to be written		to write

حكى ← انحكى   نسي ← انتسى

7aka   *n7aka*   *nisi*   *ntasa*

to speak   to be spoken   to forget   to be forgotten

The *fa33al* verbs generally have passives on *tfa33al*:

درس ← تدرس   شرف ← تشرف

darras   *tdarras*   *sharraf*   *tsharraf*

to teach   to be taught   to honour   to be honoured

مرن ← تمرن   هوى ← تهوى

marran   *tmarran*   *hawwa*   *thawwa*

to train   to be trained   to ventilate   to be ventilated

The *faa3al* verbs generally have passives on *tfaa3al*:

حاكى ← تحاكى   قاوم ← تقاوم

7aaka   *t7aaka*   *qaawam*   *tqaawam*

to speak to   to be spoken to   to resist   to be resisted

And four-consonant verbs on the pattern *fa3lal* have passives on the pattern *tfa3lal*:

سشور ← تسشور   بهدل ← تبهدل

sashwar   *tsashwar*   *bahdal*   *tbahdal*

to blow-dry   to be blow-dried   to tell off   to be told off

There are a few anomalous cases:

اشترى ← انشرى

shtara   *nshara*

to buy   to be bought

Many of these passive forms are also used as intransitive equivalents of the underlying verb rather than true passives; تغير *tghayyar*, for example, can mean "be changed" but is also often best translated simply as "change." For more, see unit 24.

As noted above, passivising a verb deletes the original subject and replaces it with the object, which is promoted to subject position. With most verbs this will not cause any problems for an English speaker:

انشرى كل شي

nshara kill shii

everything's been bought

انباع البيت

nbaa3 ˈlbeet

the house has been sold

Note, however, that verbs with a prepositional object (see unit 52) do not transform the object into a subject. Instead, the object stays with its preposition, and the verb simply defaults to masculine singular:

انحكى عن لبنان كتير

ˈn7aka 3an libnaan ˈktiir

Lebanon was spoken about a lot

حكيت عن لبنان كتير

7ikyet 3an libnaan ˈktiir

she talked a lot about Lebanon

You will probably have noticed that of the twelve main forms discussed in the derivation section (see unit 23), only four have a consistent way of forming a passive equivalent. This means that many verbs simply have no corresponding passive form. This can be difficult for a native speaker of English, since we're used to being able to passivise any verb we feel like. But this is simply not the case in Arabic.

The most basic use of the passive is similar to English. There are various kinds of situations where we might want to refer only to what would normally be the object of a verb without specifying the subject:

انمسكت

nmasak^et

I was caught

بنحس عليك!

bin7ass 3aleek!

you'll be noticed!

Note, however, that there is no catchall equivalent to the English "by," which allows us to add the original subject back to a sentence that has been passivised. A passive sentence with "by" often corresponds to a nonpassive topic sentence (see unit 48):

هالكتاب عطتني ياه إمي

halˈktaab 3aTitni yaa 2immi

this book was given to me by my mum

[= this book, my mum gave me it]

أنا شافوني

2ana shaafuuni

I was seen by them

[= I, they saw me]

> With some passives, من *min* in the sense of "because of" (see appendix B) sometimes approximates the English "by": انصدمت منو *nSadam^et minno* "I was shocked by it." But this is only with specific verbs.

Perhaps the main use of the Arabic passive is in fact in the imperfective, in the descriptive/generalising sense (see unit 34). Here it generally means that something can or cannot (or should or should not) be done, often translating an adjective with "-able":

المي هون بتنشرب؟

'lmayy hoon 'btinshireb?

can you drink the water here?

[= is it drunk here?]

البيض بنكبش هيك

'lbeeD binkabb°sh heek

eggs shouldn't be thrown out like that

[= aren't thrown out]

مبطلة تتحاكى!

mbaTT'le tit7aaka!

you can't talk to her anymore!

[= she is no longer talked to]

هالضيعة ما بينعاش فيها!

haDDee3a maa byin3aash fiiha!

this village is uninhabitable!

[= isn't lived in]

المدينة بتتنقطع مشي

lmadiine btin'2Te3 mashi

the city can be crossed on foot

[= the city is crossed walking]

البيت كيف بينراح عليه؟

'lbeet kiif 'byinraa7 3alee?

how do you get to the house?

[= how is the house gone to]

The passive is also used in conjunction with مع ma3 "with" to distance the original subject from the action. There is no single obvious English parallel, but the meaning is clear. Consider the following examples:

ما عم تنفتح معي!

maa 3am tinfite7 ma3i!

I can't get it to open!

[= isn't opening with me]

هالحيط ما عم يتعمر معي!

hal7eeT maa 3am yit3ammar ma3i!

I can't get this wall built!

[= isn't being built with me]

Passive Participle

Any verb can in principle form a passive participle (see unit 30). The meaning generally corresponds fairly closely to the English past participle (usually formed with "-ed"). It is usually resultative (see unit 29), describing the state of the object of a verb after the action described by the verb has been completed:

سمح   ←   مسموح

sama7   masmuu7

to allow   allowed

حكى   ←   محكي

7aka   mi7ki/ma7ki

to speak   spoken

غش   ←   مغشوش

ghashsh   maghshuush

to adulterate   adulterated

Note that like the verbal passive, the passive participle of a verb that takes a prepositional object (see unit 22) defaults to masculine singular, and a pronoun takes the place of the object:

حكى عن لبنان كتير   ←   لبنان محكي عنو كتير

7aka 3an libnaan ⁱktiir　　　　　*libnaan mi7ki 3anno ktiir*

he spoke about Lebanon a lot　　　Lebanon has been spoken about a lot

هالقضية سجنو فيها تلت أشخاص   ←   هالقضية مسجون فيها تلت أشخاص

hal2aDiyye sajanu fiiha tlatt 2ashkhaaS　　　*hal2aDiyye masjuun fiyya tlatt 2ashkhaaS*

they imprisoned three people in this case　　　three people were imprisoned in this case

For English speakers, the distinction between a construction with the passive participle and a construction with a passive verb may not be immediately obvious, because (at least superficially) the two structures are the same in English. Note, however, that the participle describes a *state*, while the verb describes *action*:

Verb	**Participle**
اسمها بنكتب عليها	اسمها مكتوب عليها
2isⁱmha binⁱkteb 3aleeha	*2isⁱmha maktuub 3aleeha*
its name is written on it	its name is written on it
[= gets written]	[= has been written]

Passive with *2akal* "Eat"

The verb أكل *2akal* "eat" is used metaphorically with various nouns and *maSdar*s to express negative experience in a way that corresponds to the passive. Its use is more limited than the normal passive but is nonetheless common:

عطاني مخالفة   ←   أكلت مخالفة

3aTaani mukhaalafe　　　　*2akalᵉt mukhaalafe*

he gave me a [speeding] ticket　　I got a [speeding] ticket

أصابوه   ←   أكل إصابة

2aSaabuu　　　　*2akal 2iSaabe*

they injured him　　he got injured

بهدلوني   ←   أكلت بهدلة

bahdaluuni → *2akal^et bahdale*

they told me off   I got a real telling-off

Note that most of these have a de-passivised equivalent formed, logically, with طعمى *Ta3ma* "feed."

> You may encounter fuS7a internal passives (formed by pattern change) in higher-register language: يعتبر *yu3tabar* "can be considered," يرثى له *yurtha lahu* "deplorable." These should generally be considered set phrases and should not be treated as productive counterparts to nonpassive forms. You may also occasionally encounter structures with the auxiliary تم *tamm* plus a *maSdar*: تمت الموافقة *tammet 'lmuwaafaqa* "has been approved." This is also a fuS7aism and is not common in everyday language.

Impersonal Constructions

The simplest construction of this kind for an English speaker is to use the impersonal "you." Note that the Arabic "you" still changes for gender and number according to the gender and number of the addressee:

أحيانا بطلع خلقك   شو بدك تساوي

2a7yaanan biTla3 khil2ak   *shuu biddak 'tsaawi*

sometimes you lose your temper   but what are you gonna do?

The word الواحد *'lwaa7ad* or *'lwaa7ed* (Syrian), literally "the one," is a dedicated impersonal pronoun and functions exactly like the English "one" but is far less stuffy and formal and is used in normal speech:

الواحد أحيانا بيطلع خلقو   شو بدو يحكي الواحد بهيك ظروف؟

'lwaa7ad 2a7yaanan biTla3 khil2o   *shuu biddo yi7ki lwaa7ed 'bheek Zuruuf?*

sometimes you lose your temper   what are you supposed to say under those

[= one loses . . .]   circumstances?

[= what will one say . . .]

Note that when the imaginary person is female, الوحدة *'lwa7de* is also sometimes used:

شو بدا تحكي الوحدة بهيك ظروف؟

shuu bidda ti7ki lwa7de ⁱbheek Zuruuf?

[as a woman,] what are you supposed to say under those circumstances?

The third-person plural form alone with no pronoun is often used in lieu of a more specific subject in a way that sometimes corresponds to a passive. We do this in English as well ("they say that . . ."), but it is more common in Arabic:

كيف بروحو ع حلب؟

kiif biruu7u 3a 7alab?

how do you get to Aleppo?

[= how do they go to Aleppo]

وقفوني ع الحدود

wa22afuuni 3 alⁱ7duud

I was stopped at the border

they stopped me at the border

This can sometimes have the same "moral" or "proper" implication as the normal passive:

هيك بسكرو الباب؟

heek bisakkru lbaab?

is that how you close a door?

مو هيك بيشربو الشاي

muu heek byishrabu shshaay

that's not how you drink tea

Introduction to Subordination

The vast majority of the example sentences we have looked at so far have had at most one verb (or clause); they are what I call "simple" sentences. In the next few units, however, we will be looking at various ways of introducing additional verbs—or, to be more linguistically accurate, additional clauses—into simple sentences, making them complex sentences. These processes are collectively described as *subordination*.

In this unit, we will first introduce subordination in general and set out the key concepts that will allow us to better understand the range of constructions that we will look at in the next few units. We will then look at the two main families of subordination structure into which these constructions will fall: indicative and zero-imperfective.

What Is Subordination?

In grammar terms, "subordination" means taking a sentence—a structure that could stand alone—and making it a subordinate part of another sentence. The first sentence, the subordinate clause, will then act like a subject, object, or adverbial construction of the second sentence, the main clause. This produces a *complex sentence*. Consider the following examples:

Complex		Simple
بتعرف إنو بتحكي عربي	←	بتعرف اسمك
bti3raf <u>2inno bti7ki 3arabi</u>		*bti3raf <u>2ismak</u>*
she knows <u>that you speak Arabic</u>		she knows <u>your name</u>
قللك إنو رح اترك ألشغل؟	←	قللك هالحكي؟
2allak <u>2inno ra7 2atrek ˈshshughᵒl</u>?		*2allak <u>hal7aki</u>?*
did he tell you <u>that I'm quitting</u>?		did he tell you <u>this</u>?

Complex		Simple
حاسس إنو في مشكلة ←		حاسس بالبرد
7aases 2inno fii mushkile		*7aases bilbarᵉd*
I feel <u>that there's a problem</u>		I feel <u>the cold</u>

The sentences on the left are simple sentences: they have a single verb and a straightforward noun object. In the sentences on the right, however, a subordinate clause occupies the object position. There is an obvious parallel between the meanings of the underlined sections on each side. In both cases, the underlined section refers to what is *known*, what was *said*, and what is *felt*, respectively. The only difference is the complexity of the structure.

Although object subordination is perhaps most common, subordinate clauses can also occupy other positions. Here, for example, a clause is combined with an adjective in a construction that parallels the simple "to be" sentence (see unit 49). Apart from the English "dummy 'it'" (see unit 60), the sentences on the left and the right are again straightforwardly parallel:

منيح إنو تعلمت إشي جديد   ←   منيح هالفكرة

mnii7 2inno t3allamᵉt 2ishi jdiid   *mnii7 halfikra*

it's good that you learnt something new   this is a good idea

مش مؤكد إنو هاي صورتو   ←   مش مؤكد التقرير

mish mu2akkad 2inno haay Suurto   *mish mu2akkad ᶦttaqriir*

it's not confirmed that this is a photo of him   the report isn't confirmed

The Arabic examples above correspond relatively straightforwardly to the English forms; there is a word translating "that" followed by a structure that under other circumstances could be a full sentence in itself. I call this an *indicative clause*. Unfortunately for learners, there are other very common cases where the English and Arabic equivalents do not line up so nicely with one another:

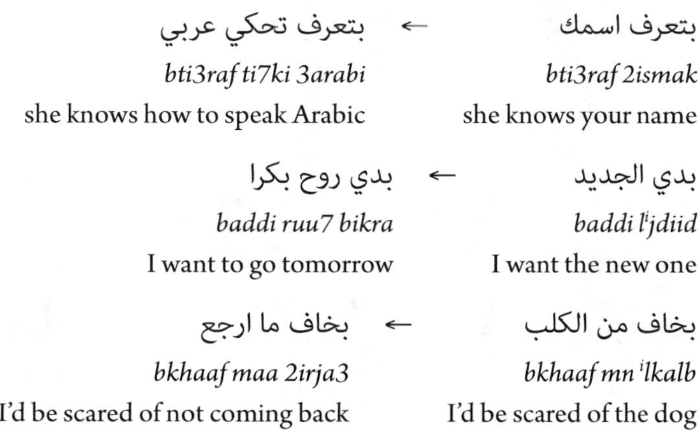

In these examples, the English subordinate clause ("how to speak"), the infinitive ("to go"), and the gerund ("coming back"), respectively, correspond to a single form in Arabic: the zero-imperfective (see unit 26). The zero-imperfective is required in many contexts and is not interchangeable with the indicative. The choice is determined by the main clause, most often by the verb in the main clause.

Between them, zero-imperfective and indicative clauses account for the vast majority of subordination structures in Arabic. Before looking at how they are used in specific positions, let's briefly look at their overall use and meaning.

Indicative Clauses

Indicative clauses closely resemble simple sentences and are commonly introduced by إنو *2inno* "that" and will largely be translated by "that" clauses in English. Verbal sentences (see unit 47), topic sentences (see unit 48), "to be" sentences (see unit 49), and so on can all be used straightforwardly:

متوقعة إنو ما رح يجي   بعرف إنو ما بحبني

mitwaqq3a 2inno maa ra7 yiji   *ba3ref 2inno maa bi7ibbni*

I expect that he won't come   I know that he doesn't love me

Note that unlike English, Arabic does not have what we call "backshifting," "tense agreement," or "the sequence of tenses." What I mean by this should be clear from the following examples:

حاسس إنو أنا مش أنا   حسيت إنو أنا مش أنا

7aases 2inno 2ana mish 2ana   *7asseet 2inno 2ana mish 2ana*

I feel as if I'm not myself   I felt as if I wasn't myself

                                            [= am not myself]

بعرف إنو رح أنجح   كنت أعرف إنو رح أنجح

ba3raf 2inno ra7 2anja7   *kunt 2a3raf 2inno ra7 2anja7*

I know I will succeed   I knew I'd succeed

                                            [= will succeed]

In the examples on the right, the past tense on the English main verb forces the subordinate verb into the past or the pluperfect. But as you can see, the same is not true of Arabic. The Arabic form used in the subordinate clauses on the right is the same as the form used on the left. It has already been situated in the past—"framed" (see unit 42)—by the tense of the main verb. The same principle applies with a past tense verb in the indicative clause:

قلتلها إنو راحت   بقللها إنو راحت

ba2ullha 2inno raa7at	*2ultillha 2inno raa7at*
I'll tell her that she's gone	I told her that she'd gone

كنت أعرف إنو طاب   بعرف إنو طاب

ba3raf 2inno Taab	*kunt 2a3raf 2inno Taab*
I know he got better	I knew he'd got better

Here the combination of two past tense verbs produces a pluperfect (past-in-past) meaning.

Zero-Imperfective Clauses

Zero-imperfective clauses are slightly more complicated than their indicative counterparts. They correspond to a range of structures in English, including gerunds ("X-ing"), infinitives ("to X"), and "that" clauses:

مش قادر أقلك   بحب اتمشى بالليل

b7ibb 2itmashsha billeel	*mish 2aader 2a2ullak*
I like walking around at night	I can't seem to be able to tell you

صحلي شوفو قبل ما يمشي   بخاف ما ارجع

bkhaaf maa 2irja3	*Sa77illi shuufo 2ab^el ma yimshi*
I'd be scared that I wouldn't come back	I got the chance to see him before he left

The structure of a zero-imperfective clause is much more restricted than its indicative counterpart. Naturally enough, there has to be a zero-imperfective verb present. However, the zero-imperfective has particular tense characteristics: it has the same sort of "snapshot" meaning as the perfective (see unit 33) or the future (see unit 36):

خايف يروح ← رح يروح

khaayef yrawwe7	*ra7 yrawwe7*
I'm scared he'll go home	he's going to go go home

وعدني يرجع ع الشغل ← بيرجع ع الشغل

wa3adni yirja3 3 ashshigh^el	*byirja3 3 ashshigh^el*
he promised me he'd go back to work	he'll go back to work

This means that like the past, verbs with state or repeated meaning require a framing verb (see unit 38), most commonly *ykuun*, in order to form zero-imperfective constructions and retain their zero-imperfective meaning:

ما بحبني   خايف يكون ما بحبني ←

khaayef ykuun maa bi7ibbni   *maa bi7ibbni*

I'm worried that he doesn't love me   he doesn't love me

بعرف عربي   بدي يكون بعرف عربي ←

biddi ykuun bi3raf 3arabi   *bi3raf 3arabi*

I want him to know Arabic   he knows Arabic

> Note that خايف يحبني *khaayef y7ibbni* and بدي يعرف *biddi yi3raf* are gram-matical but force the change-of-state meaning (see unit 24) onto the verb: "I'm afraid he'll like me," "I want him to find out."

The same naturally applies to continuous verbs (see unit 35), perfective verbs (see unit 33), and so on:

عم يدرس   خايف يكون عم يدرس ←

khaayef ykuun 3am yidros   *3am yidros*

I'm worried that he's studying   he's studying

رجع ع البيت   خايف يكون رجع ع البيت ←

khaayef ykuun rije3 3 albeet   *rije3 3 albeet*

I'm worried that he's gone home   he's gone home

The same also applies to sentences that in their simple form would have no verb at all, such as "to be" sentences (see unit 49), existential sentences, and so on:

أخوه أستاذ مدرسة   خايف يكون أخوه أستاذ مدرسة ←

khaayef ykuun 2akhuu 2ustaaz madrase   *2akhuu 2ustaaz madrase*

I'm worried his brother's a teacher   his brother's a teacher

في ناس   خايف يكون في ناس ←

khaayef ykuun fii naas   *fii naas*

I'm worried that there are people   there are people

Since the verb always has to be zero-imperfective, the same principle applies to zero-imperfective clauses as to indicative clauses with respect to backshifting. The zero-imperfective remains the same irrespective of the tense of the main verb, unlike in English:

خفت يروح   خايف يروح

khift yrawwe7   *khaayef yrawwe7*

I was worried he'd go home   I'm worried he'll go home

خفت يكون أخوه أستاذ مدرسة

khift ykuun 2akhuu 2ustaaz madrase
I was worried that his brother
was a teacher

خايف يكون أخوه أستاذ مدرسة

khaayef ykuun 2akhuu 2ustaaz madrase
I'm worried that his brother's a teacher

Note that zero-imperfective verbal clauses can have a topic-comment structure (see unit 48); that is, a topic can be shifted to the very beginning of the clause.

أنا كانو مفكرين إني مش طايقو

2ana kaanu ˈmfakkriin 2inn-i mish Taay2o
people thought I couldn't stand him

You may have noticed that none of the examples so far have featured إنو *2inno* or any other word corresponding to the word "that" even though many of the English sentences are "that" clauses. The term إنو *2inno* can and does appear in zero-imperfective clauses, but its distribution is more complicated than in indicative clauses and is subject to a lot of regional and personal variation. Imitate those around you!

Difference between Zero-Imperfective and Indicative

How do we know whether a structure is likely to combine with a zero-imperfective or an indicative clause? Language rarely follows precise semantic distinctions—there is obviously an element of established usage here too—but we might say that the difference is between indicative and zero-imperfective clauses:

- **Indicative:** An event that has actually happened or will happen, independently of the main verb. This includes main verbs expressing:
  - Knowledge of an event ("know," "am aware that"), belief ("think," "believe") or conjecture about how likely it is ("doubt," "expect")
  - Reported speech ("say," "told me")
- **Zero-imperfective:** An event in the abstract, the idea of an event, a possible event that is in some way contingent on the main verb.

This distinction will become clearer as we look at some actual zero-imperfective constructions.

Object Subordination

In this unit we will look at *object* subordinations. Remember the parallel between simple and complex sentences we noted above. The underlined subordinate clauses (verbal structures) on the right have the same role in the sentence as the underlined noun objects on the left:

Complex		Simple
بحب اركض	←	بحب فستانك
b7ibb <u>2irkoD</u>		b7ibb <u>*fistaanek*</u>
I like <u>running</u>		I like <u>your dress</u>
حكالك إنو جاي؟	←	حكالك إشي؟
7akaalak <u>2inno jaay</u>?		7akaalak <u>2ishi</u>?
did he say <u>that he was coming</u>?		did he say <u>anything</u> to you?
بتعرف تحكي عربي	←	بتعرف اسمك
bti3raf <u>ti7ki 3arabi</u>		bti3raf <u>2ismak</u>
she knows <u>how to speak Arabic</u>		she knows <u>your name</u>

As noted above, there is a distinction here between zero-imperfective and indicative constructions. Which construction is used depends on the main verb: some verbs take a zero-imperfective clause and some an indicative clause. We will begin by looking at indicatives, which are less complicated for an English speaker, and then move on to zero-imperfectives.

Indicative Constructions

A relatively small number of verbs take an indicative construction. A comprehensive list would be difficult, but it is possible to identify a few groups defined by meaning:

- Verbs of knowledge: عرف *3iref* "know," "find out," دري *diri* "find out," عندو خبر *3indo khabar* and معو خبر *ma3o khabar* "be aware."
- Verbs of opinion and belief and judgments of likelihood: اقتنع *iqtana3* "be convinced," ظن *Zann* "think," اعتقد *i3taqad* "think," شك *shakk* "suspect," فكر *fakkar* "think."
- Verbs of telling and saying: قال *2aal* "say," حكى *7aka* "say," "talk," خبر *khabbar* "tell," "inform," أعلن *2a3lan* "announce."
- Verbs of perception: شاف *shaaf* "see," سمع *sime3* "hear."

The indicative construction has the same basic structure whether the subject of the two verbs is the same or not. Other than the point made above about the lack of tense-shifting (see unit 58), the indicative construction should present few problems for English speakers:

بعرف إنو ما رح ينجح

ba3ref 2inno maa ra7 yinja7

I know he isn't going to pass

متوقعة إنو ما رح يجي

mitwaqq3a 2inno maa ra7 yiji

I expect he won't come

سمعت إنو فاتح دكانة

smi3ᵉt 2inno faate7 dikkaane

I heard he'd opened a shop

بظنلك إنو هون

baZunnillak 2inno hoon

I think he's here

خبرتو إنو في مشكلة

khabbarto 2inno fii mishᵢkle

I told him there was a problem

معك خبر إنو رجع؟

ma3ak khabar 2inno rije3?

did you know that he's come back?

Like the English word "that," many speakers can drop إنو *2inno* with some or all verbs. This is particularly common with قال *2aal* "say":

بقللك ما عندي!

b2illak maa 3indi!

I'm telling you I don't have any!

قلتلو فش حد

2ultillo fish 7add

I told him there wasn't anyone there

Complement Constructions ("I Saw Him Leaving")

Many of the verbs that can take indicative clauses can also form a slightly different structure that parallels the "complement object" (see unit 54) discussed in earlier units. In this structure the *topic* (see unit 48) of the subordinate clause becomes the *object* of the main verb. When the topic is a noun, this looks more or less like a normal indicative clause without *2inno*:

شفت نور طالعة

shufᵉt nuur Taal3a

I saw Nour leaving

بعرف أحمد ما رح يجي

ba3ref 2a7mad maa ra7 yiji

I know Ahmad isn't going to come

سمعت حدا عم يدق الباب
smi3^{e}t 7ada 3am ydi22 ^{i}lbaab
I heard someone knock on the door

فكرت سامي ما بحبني
fakkar^{e}t saami maa bi7ibbni
I thought Sami didn't love me

When the topic is a pronoun, however, the difference becomes more obvious:

شفتها طالع
shuftha Taal3a
I saw her leaving

بعرفو ما رح يجي
ba3^{i}rfo maa ra7 yiji
I know he isn't going to come

سمعتهم عم يدقو الباب
smi3thom 3am ydi22u ^{i}lbaab
I heard them knock on the door

فكرتو ما بحبني
fakkarto maa bi7ibbni
I thought he didn't like me

With verbs of perception, this construction is often equivalent to "small clauses" in English such as "I saw him leave/leaving."

Zero-Imperfectives

Now let's look at zero-imperfectives. There are so many verbs and structures that trigger zero-imperfective that listing them all would be impractical. More or less any verb that does not fall into one of the categories listed for the indicative above will take a zero-imperfective object clause.

As we have already seen in unit 58, zero-imperfective structures are generally more complicated and less intuitive for English speakers than their indicative counterparts, particularly with respect to tense. In the case of object zero-imperfectives, there is an additional complication: the structure differs depending on whether the subject of the main verb is the same as the subject of the zero-imperfective verb.

Same Subject

When the subject of the main verb and the zero-imperfective verb is the same, the construction is relatively straightforward:

رح اضطر شوفها
ra7 2iDTarr shuufa
I'm going to have to see her

بتعرف تحكي عربي
bti3raf ti7ki 3arabi
she knows how to speak Arabic

جربت أتعلم
jarrab^{e}t 2at3allam
I've tried to learn

حابب تمشي؟
7aabeb timshi?
would you like to leave?

Verbs that would require a preposition in order to take a noun object (see unit 52) usually do not take a preposition with a zero-imperfective object:

Complex		Simple
تعودت أدرس كل يوم ←		تعودت ع الجو
t3awwad^et 2adros kull yoom		*t3awwad^et 3 ajjaww*
I've got used to studying every day		I've got used to the weather
عم يفكر يرجع بكير ←		عم يفكر بمشروع جديد
3am yfakker yirja3 bakkiir		*3am yfakker bmashruu3 ʾjdiid*
he's thinking about going back early		he's thinking about a new project
منعوني أشوفك ←		منعوني من كل إشي
mana3uuni 2ashuufak		*mana3uuni min kull 2ishi*
they banned me from seeing you		they banned me from everything

> A rare alternative is to use the preposition plus إنو *2inno*, paralleling the fuS7a structure with أن *2an*: اضطررت على أن أعود *ʾDTarartu 3ala 2an 2a3uuda* "I was obliged to return."

Note that these structures allow flexible word order. All the following word orders are possible:

بحب سامي يمشي	سامي بحب يمشي	بحب يمشي سامي
bi7ibb saami yimshi	*saami bi7ibb yimshi*	*bi7ibb yimshi saami*
Sami wants to leave	Sami wants to leave	Sami wants to leave

When the main verb is imperative (see unit 43), the other verb is also placed in the imperative, producing a structure similar to a double-verb construction (see unit 62):

جرب امشي! ←		بجرب أمشي
jarreb 2imshi!		*bajarreb 2amshi*
try to walk!		I'll try to walk

Note the use of this structure with passive participles (see unit 30):

أنا مجبور أحكي معاها	إنت مسمحلك تساوي هيك؟
2ana majbuur 2a7ki ma3aaha	*2inte masmi7lak ʾtsaawi heek?*
I have to speak to her	are you allowed to do that?

Different Subject

When the subject of the main verb is *different* from the subject of the zero-imperfective verb, there are two slightly different patterns. Consider the following examples:

خايف سامي ما يجي

khaayef saami maa yiji

I'm scared Sami won't come

بساعد مروا تتعلم

basaa3ed marwa tit3allam

I help Marwa learn

بتمنى ديبة تجي

bitmanna diibe tiji

I hope Dibeh comes

تارك بديعة تطلع

taarek badii3a tiTla3

I've let Badia go out

These look like they all have the same structure. But when we replace the zero-imperfective verb's subject with a pronoun, it becomes clear that we are dealing with slightly different constructions. In the examples on the left the subject disappears, exactly like a normal subject or topic in a simple sentence (see units 48 and 51). In the examples on the right, it appears as an object pronoun on the main verb (see unit 18)

خايف ما يجي

khaayef maa yiji

I'm scared he won't come

بساعدها تتعلم

basaa3idha tit3allam

I help her learn

بتمنى تجي

bitmanna tiji

I hope she comes

تاركها تطلع

taarikha tiTla3

I've let her go

The bad news is that this is another situation where there are two possible constructions depending on the main verb. The two constructions are triggered by different main verbs. That is, a verb such as خاف *khaaf* "be afraid" always takes one construction, while a verb such as منع *mana3* "stop, forbid" always takes the other construction, and which is which must be learned on a verb-by-verb basis.

The good news, however, is that this distinction largely corresponds to a similar distinction in the English structures. Most verbs that take an infinitive structure in English will correspond to the structure on the right. This is only a rule of thumb, but it is a solid one.

Many speakers, particularly North Levantine speakers, can use إنو *2inno* in at least some of these structures without changing the meaning: بساعدها إنو تتعلم *bsaa3idha 2inno tit3allam* "I help her learn," نسيت إنو تقللو *nisyet 2inno t2illo* "she forgot to tell him," بتقدر إنو تفتح حساب *bti2der 2inno tifta7 7saab* "you can open an account."

Many speakers, particularly North Levantine speakers, can use the conjunction إنو *2inno* "that" in all the structures we have seen so far:

بساعدها إنو تتعلم

basaa3idha 2inno tit3allam

I help her learn

خايف إنو ما يجي

khaayef 2inno maa yiji

I'm scared he won't come

نسيت إنو تقللو

nisyet 2inno t2illo

she forgot to tell him

بتقدر إنو تفتح حساب

bti2der 2inno tifta7 i7saab

you can open an account

Nonobject Subordination

In unit 59 we looked at subordination constructions that took the place of *objects*. These are both the most common and the most complicated subordination constructions. In this unit we will look at a range of other similar constructions that occupy different positions: topics of "to be" sentences (see unit 49), subjects (see unit 51), objects of prepositions (see unit 22), and the second noun in *2iDaafe* (see unit 15).

Adjective Constructions

A second very common subordination construction combines an *adjective* with a subordinate clause. Once again, both indicatives and zero-imperfectives are possible, with different meanings. The zero-imperfective typically translates "it's X [for Y] to . . . ," while the indicative typically translates "it's X that . . ."; the former refers to abstract actions and the latter to more concrete actions. Note that there is no equivalent to the English "dummy 'it'" in either of these constructions:

Indicative Clause	Zero-Imperfective Clause
منيح إنو تعلمت شي جديد	منيح تتعلم شي جديد
mnii7 2inno t3allamᵉt shii jdiid	*mnii7 tit3allam shii jdiid*
it's good that you've learnt something new	it's good to learn something new
المهم بساعدك	المهم يساعدك
ⁱlmuhimm bisaa3dak	*ⁱlmuhimm ysaa3dak*
the important thing is he's helping you	the important thing is for him to help you
غريب إنو ما اتصل	غريب ما يتصل
ghariib 2inno maa TTaSal	*ghariib maa yiTTiSel*
it's weird that he hasn't rung	it's weird for him not to ring

Note that these structures often serve as a comment in a topic sentence (see unit 48):

سامي منيح يتعلم شي جديد

saami mnii7 yit3allam shii jdiid

it's good for Sami to learn something
new

سامي منيح إنو تعلم شي جديد

saami mnii7 2inno t3allam shii jdiid

it's good that Sami's learnt something
new

جودة غريب ما يتصل

juude ghariib maa yiTTiSel

it's weird for Joudeh not to ring

جودة غريب إنو ما اتصل

juude ghariib 2inno maa TTaSal

it's weird that Joudeh hasn't rung

Zero-Imperfectives

Beyond the general comments on indicatives above (see unit 58), there isn't much more to say about indicative structures of this kind. There is more to say about zero-imperfectives, however. The zero-imperfective structure is very common:

مش سهل آجي

mish sahᵉl 2aaji

it won't be easy for me to come

صعب تتعلم إنجليزي

Sa3b tit3allam 2ingliizi

it's hard [for you] to learn English

حرام يروح لحالو

7araam yruu7 la7aalo

it would be unfair for him to go alone

مو حلو تساوي هيك

muu 7ilw tsaawi heek

it's not right for you to do that

Many phrases that express, among other things, likelihood or possibility (see unit 46)—the equivalent of English auxiliary verbs—use this construction:

يمكن أروح

yimken 2aruu7

I might go

لازم تشوفيه!

laazem ᶦtshuufii!

you have to see it!

Comparatives and superlatives (see units 79–80) are also commonly used in this construction:

أحسنلك تروح معاها

2a7sanlak ᶦtruu7 ma3aaha

you'd be better off going with her

أريحلو يبقى بالبيت

2arya7lo yib2a bilbeet

it'd be more convenient for him to stay
at home

أحسن شي تضلك ماشية

2a7san shii TDallek maashye

the best thing is for you to keep
going

أسوأ شي بالكون تسمح لحدا يذلك

2aswa2 shii bilkawn tisma7 la7ada yzillak

it's the worst thing in the universe to let
someone humiliate you

Note that there are two meanings of "it's X to" in English. In the examples above, the "it" is a "dummy" pronoun that refers to the action ("learning," "coming," "doing," "going"). In some cases, however, the "it" refers to a noun, and the "X to" is a *trait* or *quality* of that noun. In these examples the noun will be the topic (explicit or implicit; see unit 48), and there will be a pronoun referring back to it:

صعب تشوفيه

منيح تتعلمها

Sa3b ˈtshufii

mnii7 tit3allamha

it [the mountain] is hard to see

it [Arabic] is good to learn

As we would expect, structures of this kind generally require a form of كان *kaan* (see unit 38) or another framing verb (see units 39–41) to put them in a nonpresent tense. The framing verb is always third-person singular masculine:

كان ممكن احكي معها

مكنش سهل آجي

kaan mumken 2i7ki ma3ha

makansh sahᵉl 2aaji

I could have talked to her

it wasn't easy for me to come

صار مستحيل تفوت

Saar musta7iil ˈtfuut

nowadays it's impossible to get in

Note that like the *b*-imperfective (see unit 34), however, these structures can also have conditional meaning ("would be") on their own. The only way of knowing which is meant is from context. The following translations may also work:

صعب تشوفيه

منيح تتعلمها

Sa3b ˈtshufii

mnii7 tit3allamha

it would be difficult to see

it would be good to learn

As with other zero-imperfective structures, there is considerable individual and regional variation in the use of إنو *2inno* "that" in this sort of structure. Some speakers treat it as relatively meaningless and can add it everywhere:

صعب إنو تشوفيه

منيح إنو تتعلمها

Sa3b 2inno ˈtshufii

mnii7 2inno tit3allamha

it would be difficult to see

it would be good to learn

For the most part, however, it is relatively marked and tends to be used only in more complicated or lengthy constructions such as the following:

صعب مثلا ع اللي ما بيعرف حدا إنو يتعرف ع ناس جديدة

Sa3ᵉb masalan 3a lli maa bya3ref 7ada 2inno yit3arraf 3a naas ᵢjdiide

it's difficult for example for someone who doesn't know anyone to meet new people

Subject Constructions

In the examples above the subordinate clauses corresponded to the object (see unit 52) of a simple verbal sentence (see unit 47). There is a parallel set of constructions, however, in which the subordinate clause technically corresponds to the subject:

عجبني إنو قال هيك

3ajabni 2inno 2aal heek

I liked that he said that

[= it pleased me that he said that]

عجبني وشو

3ajabni wishsho

I liked his face

[= his face pleased me]

صعب عليي أخلصها

Si3eb 3aleyy 2akhalliSha

it's too hard for me to finish it

صعبت علي النكتة

Si3bat 3aleyy ᵢnnukte

the joke was too hard for me [was lost on me]

Note that in English we can't straightforwardly make a subordinate clause the subject of a main verb; we have to use a meaningless ("dummy") "it" as the subject and shift to the end the subordinate clause that is *actually* the subject. The two Arabic structures are more straightforwardly parallel.

Structures of this kind are considerably less common than other kinds of subordination, and it is particularly difficult to come up with verbs that can take both normal (noun) subjects and complex subjects such as this. But there are quite a few examples of idiomatic structures that take this sort of complex subject:

صحلي شوفها قبل ما تسافر

Sa77illi shuufha 2abᵉl ma tsaafer

I got the chance to see her before she left

[= it happened to be possible

for me to see]

ما بيفرق معي إنو يروح

maa byifro2 ma3i 2inno yruu7

it makes no difference if he goes

[= it makes no difference to me

for him to go]

With Prepositions

It is possible for a subordinate clause to correspond to a noun following a preposition. In most such cases, however, we use a special conjunction counterpart of the preposition, often formed with *-ma* (for more on this, see unit 68 and appendix C):

بعد الحلفة   ←   بعد ما تجي سامية

ba3ᵈd ᵢl7afle   *ba3ᵉd ma tiji saamya*

after the party   after Samia comes

There are a couple of cases, however, in which prepositions can be followed by zero-imperfective constructions introduced by إنو *2inno*. The most common is in the following structures meaning "to be against" or "to be in favour of," where—as in other cases—the zero-imperfective corresponds to an English gerund:

أنا مش ضد إنو يصير غني   أنا مو مع إنو هاي تصير مهنتك

2ana mish Didd 2inno ySiir ghani   *2ana muu ma3 2inno haay ᵢtSiir mihᵢntak*

I'm not against him becoming rich   I'm not in favour of it becoming your career

A similar construction is used with من *min* "than" in certain comparative constructions, for which see unit 79.

> For some speakers this *2inno* can be dropped: أنا مش ضد يصير غني *2ana mish Didd ySiir ghani* "I'm not against him becoming rich."

In *2iDaafe*

Finally, subordinate clauses—generally introduced by إنو *2inno*—can be used in *2iDaafe* (see unit 15). With the indicative, this is largely limited to structures meaning something like "a matter of" and "an issue of" and as usual refers to concrete events or states:

مش مسألة إنو الشباب حياتهم أسهل   مو قصة إنو أصعب

mish mas2alet 2inno 7ayaathom 2ashal   *muu 2iSSet 2inno 2aS3ab*

it's not that they have it easier   it's not that it's harder

Zero-imperfectives, on the other hand, are used in the same constructions to talk about abstracts or hypotheticals:

مسألة إنو يروح لحالو شي تاني   قصة إنو تقعدي بالبيت شي غريب

mas2alet 2inno yruu7 la7aalo shii taani   *2iSSet 2inno ti2ᵢ3di bilbeet shii ghariib*

him going on his own is something else   this whole thing about you

whether he should go on his own is   sitting around at home is weird

another question

Clauses of this kind are also used with structures such as فكرة إنو *fikret 2inno* "the idea of." Here again, the zero-imperfective corresponds to a gerund and refers to an abstract idea:

فكرة إنو تصير غني

fikret 2inno tSiir ghani
the idea of you getting rich

Sometimes this structure occurs with the *maSdar* (see unit 31) of a main verb that takes a zero-imperfective clause as object, and in this sense these constructions are simply the complex equivalent of the *maSdar* object constructions we have already seen:

خوفي إنو ينضحك عليي

khoofi 2inno yinDi7ek 3aliyyi
my fear of being laughed at

إصرارو إنو ما نرجع

2iSraaro 2inno maa nirja3
his insistence that we not go back

Special Zero-Imperfectives

In this unit we will look at two final types of zero-imperfective construction. These types are used to express *purpose* and *simultaneous action* and have no indicative equivalent. While they appear only with a limited set of verbs, they are very common.

Zero-Imperfectives of Purpose

The first of these two constructions expresses *purpose*. Here the zero-imperfective clause corresponds not to a direct object but instead to a complement (see unit 54). Like complements, this construction is restricted to a small selection of main verbs, generally those expressing movement from one place to another ("go," "come," etc.) or else movement from one "pose" to another ("stand up," "sit down," "lie down," "stop," etc.). The best translation generally uses the English infinitive ("to X"):

أنا فايتة أنام

2ana faayte 2anaam

I'm going [into my room] to bed

نزلت اشتري غراض

nzilt 2ishtiri ghraaD

I went out to buy groceries

جاي أسلم عليكي

jaay 2asallem 3aleeki

I've come to talk to you

رحت احكي معو

ri7ᵉt 2i7ki ma3o

I went to talk to him

Less commonly a purpose zero-imperfective acts like an object complement (see unit 54). This means that its subject is the same as the *object* of the main verb, as in the different-subject constructions we examined in unit 59. Again, this only works with verbs that can take a complement object, often those that express a kind of movement:

حطوه بالصف يراقبنا

7aTTuu biSSaff yraa2ibna

they put him in the class

to keep an eye on us

ترکوني لحالي غني الليالي

tarakuuni la7aali ghanni llayaali

they left me alone

to sing the nights away

ببعتلك ياهم تقراهم

bab3atlak yaahom ti2raahom

I'll send them to you to read

بعتوها ع السوق تشتري أغراض

ba3atuuha 3 assuu2 tishtiri ghraaD

they sent her to the market to buy groceries

In a handful of cases it is possible to use a different subject entirely:

تعال أحكي معك كلمتين

ta3aal 2a7ki ma3ak kil'mteen

I want to have a word with you

[= come so I can . . .]

شو رأيك تجي ربيك؟

shuu ra2yak tiji rabbiik?

how about you come here

and I'll teach you some manners?

The same-subject construction is very similar both in structure and meaning to the double-verb construction we will look at in unit 62. There is a difference in meaning, however. The complement form expresses only the *purpose* of the action, not whether it was successful. Compare the following translations:

Double-Verb Structure	**Zero-Imperfective Structure**
نزلت اشتريت غراض	نزلت اشتري غراض
nzilt 'shtareet 'ghraaD	*nzilt 2ishtiri ghraaD*
I went [out] and bought groceries	I went [out] to buy groceries

For the usual purpose construction, see appendix C.

Zero-Imperfectives of Simultaneous Action

A zero-imperfective clause can also express ongoing simultaneous action: an action going on at the same time as the action described by the main verb. Like the purpose structure, this is only possible with certain main verbs (the catchall construction for expressing simultaneous action is the *7aal*, for which see unit 65). The range of possible main verbs here includes all verbs that can take a noun object describing the subject (see unit 54):

قاعدة تكتب مذكراتها

2aa3de tuktob muzakkaraatha

she's sitting writing her memoirs

لف البلد يسلم ع العالم

laff 'lbalad ysallem 3 al3aalam

he went all over town saying hi to people

واقف يتفرج علينا

waa2ef yitfarraj 3aleena

he's standing there watching us

خلقت احكي

khli2ᵉt 2i7ki

I was born talking

> This range generally corresponds to verbs that can take a subject complement
> in English, although this won't help most native speakers much. A good rule
> of thumb is that a verb that can be followed by an "-ing" participle without a
> comma will be able to appear in this structure in Arabic: "die laughing" and
> "go crying to your mum" but not "he wrote, laughing."

This construction is structurally identical to the "purpose" zero-imperfective described
above. It is often only possible to work out which of the two meanings—purpose or state—
is intended from context, although the simultaneous action use is rarer. Note that for many
North Levantine speakers, however, it is possible or even preferable to use the continuous
particle عم *3am* in these structures, which makes them unambiguous:

قاعدة عم تكتب مذكراتها

2aa3de 3am tiktob muzakkiraatha

she's sitting writing her memoirs

لف البلد عم يسلم ع العالم

laffᵢlbalad 3am ysallem 3 al3aalam

he went around the town saying "hi"
to people

واقف عم يتفرج علينا

waa2ef 3am yitfarraj 3aleena

he's standing there watching us

خلقت عم احكي

khli2ᵉt 3am 2i7ki

I was born talking

Note that this structure is the obvious origin of the use of قاعد *2aa3ed* "sitting" as a continuous marker, discussed in unit 35.

Double-Verb Construction

In this unit we will look at a very common Arabic structure: the *double-verb construction*. This structure has no straightforward parallel in English, although expressions like "go see" and "come look" show some similarities. There are three common kinds of double-verb construction: movement structures, quotation structures, and "taking" structures. After familiarising ourselves with the points that all three have in common, we will consider how each works in practice.

Basic Structure

A double-verb construction consists of two identically conjugated verbs placed directly alongside one another without an "and" to connect them. The closest equivalent in English is the following structure with "come" or "go":

Tell him to come see me ("come and see me")
Go get him ("go and get him")

Arabic uses a far broader range of structures of this kind. As in English, however, the two verbs must have the same subject and have exactly the same prefixes and suffixes:

رحت جبت المصاري

ليش ما يجي يشوفني؟

ru7^et jibt ʾlmaSaari

leesh maa yiji yshuufni?

I went and got the money

why doesn't he come see me?

Subjects and short adverbial expressions can appear between the two words:

راح محمد جاب المصاري

رجعت ع البيت جبت الموبايل

raa7 ʾm7ammad jaab ʾlmaSaari

rji3^et 3 albeet jibt ʾlmobaayl

Muhammad went and got the money

I went back home and got the phone

The whole structure is negated by a single negative particle/affix (see unit 76) attached to the first word:

ما نزلت اشتريت غراض؟

maa nzilt ⁱshtareet ⁱghraaD?

didn't you go and buy groceries?

مرحتش جبت القهوة

maru7t^esh jibt ⁱl2ahwe

I didn't go and get the coffee

There are three basic types of double-verb construction: the *movement* structure, the *quotation* structure, and the *taking* structure.

> A similar construction appears when a zero-imperfective is attached to an imperative (see unit 28). This assimilation of zero-imperfectives to double verb constructions also happens elsewhere in some parts of Lebanon and coastal Syria. You may hear forms like ما قدرو اجو *maa 2idru 2iju* for the more widespread ما قدرو يجو *maa 2idru yiju*.

Movement Structure

The movement structure closely resembles the "come see" construction in English. Of the two verbs, the first must either express movement from one place to another ("go," "come," "walk [to]," "swim [to]," etc.) or movement from one "pose" to another ("stand up," "sit down," "lie down," "stop," etc.). The second verb then expresses the "end point" of that action: the purpose *and* immediate consequence:

رحت جبت المصاري

ru7^et jibt ⁱlmaSaari

I went and got the money

قعود احكيلك كلمة

3ood 2i7kiilak kilme

sit back down and say something

برجع بسكر الباب

barja3 basakker ⁱlbaab

I'll go back and close the door

سبحت رجعتلهم الطابة

saba7^et rajja3tilhom ⁱTTaabe

I swam out and gave them the ball back

We have to be careful to distinguish this from the similar structure described in unit 61, which only expresses purpose. Although their meanings are similar and they can sometimes be used in the same situation, they are not the same. Compare the translations on the left and right:

نزلت اشتريت غراض

nzilt ⁱshtareet ⁱghraaD

I went and bought groceries

نزلت اشتري غراض

nzilt 2ishtiri ghraaD

I went to buy groceries

As we would expect, *shtareet* means that you *did* buy groceries, whereas *2ishtiri* expresses only that this was your *purpose* in going out.

A handful of verbs used in this structure have additional idiomatic uses. The construction قام *2aam* "get up" can be used literally but is often used in narratives to move them a long in a more dynamic way, giving a meaning something like "so then …" and "and then …":

قام رجع ع البيت

2aam rije3 3 albeet

so then he went home

قامت اتصلت علي

2aamat ⁱttaSlat 3aleyy

then she rang me up

> Some speakers treat *2aam* as invariable in this meaning: قام رجعت *2aam raj3et* "she came back."

The verb رجع *rije3* "go back," "come back" gives the nuance that someone has *resumed* or *repeated* an action. Although the meaning should be clear, there is no single English translation that will always fit; "back," "re-," "again," and so on are all possible in different contexts. Note that many North Levantine speakers have رد *radd* as an alternative:

رجعت دقيتلو مرة تانية

rji3ᵉt da22eetillo marra taanye

I rang him again

رجعت كتبتها

rij3at katbatha

she wrote it again

ايش رجعت نمت؟

2eesh, ⁱrji3ᵉt nimᵉt?

what, have you gone back to sleep?

برجع بحاكيك

barja3 ba7akiik

I'll call you back

شو رديت نمت؟

shuu, raddeet nimᵉt?

what, have you gone back to sleep?

برد بحاكيك

bridd ⁱb7aakiik

I'll call you back

Note that often this form is used where the repetition is either obvious from the context or explicitly stated using an adverb, in which case any direct translation into English would be unidiomatic:

رجع عمل نفس العملة

rije3 3imel nafs ⁱl3amle

he's done the same thing again

بردو بيرجعو

biriddu byirja3u

they'll be back

Sometimes *rije3* implies that you have reconsidered or changed your mind. Sometimes this can be conveyed by the English "went back and." In this sense *radd* is not possible:

رجع عملها مقالة

rije3 3imilha maqaale

He went back and turned it
into an article [after writing
it as a chapter]

بالأخير رجعت اشتريتو

bil2akhiir rji3t ˈshtareeto

then I changed my mind and
bought it anyway [after thinking
it was too pricey]

Quotation Structure

In the quotation structure, the *second* verb is always either قال *2aal* or (for some speakers) حكى *7aka*, both of which mean "say" and introduce direct speech. Sometimes this is the "end point" of the action described by the first verb:

دقلي قللي إنو

da22illi 2alli 2inno

he rang me and said that

اتصلت فيه قلتلو

TTaSalt fii 2iltillo

I rang him and told him

A common variant, however, is to combine a verb describing *how* you conveyed the information with a verb introducing direct or indirect speech expressing that information:

انفجرت فيه قلتلو انت واحد جحش

nfajarᵉt fii 2iltillo 2inte waa7ed ja7ᵉsh

I screamed at him that he was an idiot
[= I exploded, said "you're a donkey"]

بعتلو حكيتلو إنو

ba3attillo 7aketillo 2inno

I sent him a message saying

"Taking" Structure

The final type, the "taking" structure, is relatively unusual. In this case, the first verb must be a verb expressing the action of "taking," normally the straightforward أخد *2akhad* "take," but occasionally a synonym (e.g., مسك *misek* "pick up"). The meaning here is very similar to the first type: the second verb expresses both the *purpose* and *immediate consequence* of the picking up or taking. But in this case the structure is more restrictive. The object of the two verbs has to be the same, and both verbs have to be in the imperative. The first verb adds very little to the meaning and is often not worth translating literally:

مسكي عدي المصاري

msiki 3iddi lmaSaari

[take and] count the money

خود كول خبزة

khood kool khubze

[take and] have a piece of bread

Note that although both verbs have the same object, if the noun is replaced by a pronoun it only appears on the second verb:

خود كلو   امسكي عديهم

khood kilo   *2im'ski 3iddiihom*

[take and] eat it   [take and] count them

Basic Relative Clauses

In this unit we will look at how to form *relative clauses*. The subordination structures we have looked at so far have largely corresponded to *nouns* in simple sentences: to objects, subjects, topics, and so on. Relative clauses are different; they correspond to *adjectives*. We will start by exploring exactly what this means before looking at the structure of relative clauses in Arabic.

Basics

In English a *relative* clause is a specific kind of "that" clause. If the other kinds of subordinate clauses we have looked at so far take the place of nouns, a relative clause acts like an adjective, providing descriptive information about a noun:

the <u>tall</u> man	the man <u>who you saw</u>
the <u>little</u> cat	the cat <u>that was under the table</u>
a <u>red</u> bottle	a bottle <u>that you left in the fridge</u>

The parallel in English is not immediately obvious, since relative clauses follow the noun (rather than preceding it like an adjective) and are introduced by "that," which is a word with a whole range of functions. In Arabic, however, the parallel is more obvious. Not only do relative clauses appear in the same position as adjectives, they also "agree" for definiteness with their noun, with definite clauses introduced by a word, *'lli*, that looks quite like the definite article:

الشب الطويل ← الشب اللي شفتيه

'shshabb 'lli shuftii   *'shshabb 'TTawiil*

the guy who you saw   the tall man

قنينة حمرا ← قنينة تركتها بالبراد

2anniine taraktha bilbarraad   *2anniine 7amra*

a bottle that you left in the fridge   a red bottle

Similarly, just like definite adjectives, definite relative clauses can stand alone in the meaning "the one that":

اللي شفتيه   ←   الشب اللي شفتيه

ʾlli shuftii   *ʾshshabb ʾlli shuftii*

the one who you saw   the guy you saw

We will look first at the basic structure of a relative clause and then look more closely at idiomatic uses.

Structure

A relative clause is the subordinate clause equivalent to an adjective. Arabic relative clauses have two features that set them apart from their English equivalents:

- They agree in definiteness with the head noun, just like an adjective. A definite relative clause is introduced by the particle اللي *ʾlli*, while indefinite relative clauses have no introducing word at all.
- A pronoun generally appears within the relative clause to show the role of the noun it refers to (the "head noun") within that clause.

The definiteness point is straightforward enough. Although اللي *ʾlli* is sometimes glossed as "that," it is compulsory when the head noun is definite—just like the definite article *ʾl-* is on adjectives in this position (see unit 13)—and cannot appear when the head noun is indefinite:

شب أجا معاكي   الشب اللي أجا معاكي

shabb 2aja ma3aaki   *ʾshshabb ʾlli 2aja ma3aaki*

a guy who came with you   the guy who came with you

مادة درستها بالجامعة   المادة اللي درستها بالجامعة

maadde darastha biljaam3a   *ʾlmaadde lli darastha biljaam3a*

a subject you studied at university   the subject you studied at university

---

اللي *ʾlli* has many regional variants, with the most common being يلي *yalli*. You may also hear contracted forms such as الـ *ʾl-* and يلـ *yal-*. Note that although these look even more like the definite article, the *l-* does not assimilate: الشب الشفتيه *ʾshshabb ʾl-shiftii* "the guy that you saw."

The second point poses more problems for a native speaker of English. There are no issues when the head noun is the subject of the relative clause. Here the verb in the relative clause simply agrees with the head noun, as we would expect:

الشب اللي أجا معاكي

ˈshshabb ˈlli 2aja ma3aaki

the guy who came with you

الصبية اللي أجت معاكي

ˈSSabiyye lli 2ajat ma3aaki

the girl who came with you

> In "to be" structures (see unit 49), the agreement is not always quite as straight-forward. In structures such as انتي البنت اللي رحتي معو ع العرس *2inti lbint ˈlli ru7ti ma3o 3 al3urᵒs* "you're the girl who went with him to the wedding" and انت شب بتساعد الناس *2inte shabb bitsaa3ed ˈnnaas* "you're a guy who helps people", the verb in the relative clause tends to agree with the topic of the "to be" structure. Since *ˈlbint* and *shabb* both refer to the addressee, the verbs attached to them take second-person agreement. There are other examples for other persons too.

But consider the following sentences:

الشب اللي شفتو

ˈshshabb ˈlli shuft-o

the guy who you saw [him]

صبية شفتها

Sabiyye shuft-ha

a girl who you saw [her]

The head noun in both cases is the direct object of the verb in the relative clause; the answer to the question "who did you see" is, respectively, "a girl" and "the guy." In English, we know that this is the case because there is no other object explicitly present in the relative clause. In Arabic, however, we have to use a pronoun to refer back to the head noun and signal its role. The same applies to both animate and inanimate nouns:

البيت اللي سكنو

ˈlbeet ˈlli sakan-o

the house [M] that he moved into [it]

المكتبة اللي ركبها

ˈlmaktabe lli rakkab-ha

the bookcase [F] that he put [it] up

This rule also applies when the head noun is the object of a preposition in the relative clause:

التلفزيون اللي عم نتفرج عليه

ˈttilivizyoon ˈlli 3am nitfarraj 3alee-ʰ

the TV we're watching [it]

الغرفة اللي بتنام فيها

ˈlghurfe lli bitnaam fii-ha

the room that you sleep in [it]

In English, a head noun that occupies a possessor role in the relative clause requires a special structure with "whose." In Arabic, structures of this kind follow the same rule as all other relative clauses: a pronoun stands in for the head noun by attaching to the possessed noun:

الزلمة اللي بيتو حد بيتك

ᵎzzalame lli beet-o 7add beetak

the guy whose house is next to yours

[= that his house is by your house]

الولد اللي بتعرفي إمو

ᵎlwalad ᵎlli bti3rafi 2imm-o

the kid whose mum you know

[= that you know his mother]

With *la-* constructions, the corresponding form usually uses an *-l-* suffix (see unit 19). Compare the two examples below:

بعتت المصاري للصبايا

ba3att ᵎlmaSaari laSSabaaya

I sent the money to the girls

الصبايا اللي بعتلهن المصاري

ᵎSSabaaya lli ba3att-ᵎlhon ᵎlmaSaari

the girls I gave the money to [them]

Relative Clauses with "To Be" Sentences

Basic present tense "to be" sentences with an adjective or noun (see unit 49) are not usually used in relative clauses. For an indefinite clause, the best option is simply to place them alongside one another:

شب رفيقي

shabb ᵎrfii2i

a guy [who is] my friend

واحد كذاب

waa7ed kazzaab

a guy [who is] a liar

For a definite clause, it is possible to form a relative clause by using اللي *ᵎlli* plus a third-person pronoun that agrees with the head noun (see unit 18):

الشب اللي هو رفيقي

ᵎshshabb ᵎlli huwwe rfii2i

the guy who is my friend

الصبية اللي هي بنتك

ᵎSSabiyye ᵎlli hiyye bintak

the girl who is your daughter

It is common as well in what are called in English nonrestrictive relative clauses (separated with commas), which add supplementary or parenthetical information:

الصبية اللي هي بنتك ع فكرة

ᵎSSabiyye, ᵎlli hiyye bintak 3a fikra

the girl, who's your daughter by the way

With locational expressions (see unit 81), however, relative clauses do not require any pronoun:

الشب اللي ع الباب   البنت يلي جوا

'shshabb 'lli 3 albaab   *'lbint lli juwwa*

the guy [who is] at the door   the girl [who is] inside

These clauses are much more common than in English. In English we like to attach expressions of location to the noun directly, without a relative clause structure. In Arabic, however, a nonrelative prepositional expression of this kind is more likely to be attached in the listener's head to other parts of the sentence. Consider the following:

شراب المي ع الطاولة   شراب المي اللي عالطاولة

shraab 'lmayy 3 aTTaawle   *shraab 'lmayy 'lli 3 aTTaawle*

drink the water [while] on the table   drink the water [that's] on the table

In English, the listener will automatically understand "on the table" as referring to the noun. In Arabic, the absence of a relative clause marker means that it will probably be understood as the location in which you should drink!

Outside the present tense, where a form of *kaan* (see unit 38) is required, the structure is much more straightforward and looks more or less like any other relative clause:

الشب اللي كان معك   الصبية اللي كانت معلمة

'shshabb 'lli kaan ma3ak   *'SSabiyye lli kaanat 'm3allme*

'the guy who was with you   *'the girl who was a teacher*

In sentences such as the following, *kaan* even takes a pronoun referring back to the head noun, as though the thing that you "are" was a straightforward object:

إنت مو الشخص اللي كنتو قبل كم سنة

2inte muu shshakhS 'lli kinto 2abᵉl kamm sine

you're not the person you were [him] a few years ago

UNIT 64

More Complicated Relative Clauses

In unit 63 we looked at how to form Arabic relative clauses. The examples given there corresponded quite nicely with their English counterparts. In this unit we will look at some more specifically Arabic uses of relative clauses. We will start by discussing so-called headless relatives, relative clauses that have no head noun. We will then look at relative clauses with zero-imperfective verbs, which express the purpose of their head noun. Finally, we will consider idiomatic structures formed with *miin* "who."

Headless Relative Clauses

A "headless" relative clause is one that has no head noun. These are very common in Arabic. Just as with adjectives, definite relative clauses can stand alone with the meaning "the one who." Their structure is nearly identical to relative clauses with head nouns, as you can see by comparing them with the full relative clauses on the left:

البنت اللي بتحب الحلو *^{i}lbint ^{i}lli bit7ibb ^{i}l7ilu* the girl who loves sweets	اللي بتحب الحلو *^{i}lli bit7ibb ^{i}l7ilu* the one [F] who loves sweets
الشب اللي بتعرفوه *^{i}shshabb ^{i}lli bti3rafuu* the guy you know	اللي بتعرفوه *^{i}lli bti3rafuu* the one you know
الولاد للي كنت تلعب معاهم *l^{i}wlaad ^{i}lli kunt til3ab ma3aahom* the kids you used to play with	اللي كنت تلعب معاهم *^{i}lli kunt til3ab ma3aahom* the ones you used to play with

In the examples above the appropriate translation is "the one [who/that]." But this structure also very commonly translates the English "what" in the sense of "the thing/event/choice [that]":

آسفة ع اللي صار امبارح

2aasfe 3a lli Saar mbaare7

I'm sorry for what happened yesterday

اعمل اللي بدك ياه

2i3mel ᵢlli biddak ᵢyyaa

do what you want

اللي عملتو مش هين

ᵢlli 3milto mish hayyen

what you've done is not insignificant

اللي عاجبني فيه فكرتو الأساسية

ᵢlli 3aajibni fii fikᵢrto l2asaasiyye

what I like about it is its basic idea

In line with the general use of the definite article to mark generics (see unit 13), these structures are commonly used in a generic sense. The meaning here is something like "one who" and "anyone who":

اللي بيدرس منيح بينجح

ᵢlli byidros ᵢmnii7 byinja7

if you study hard, you'll pass

[= he who studies well, succeeds]

اللي بشوفك بقول إنك خايف

ᵢlli bishuufak bi2uul 2innak khaayef

if I didn't know better, I'd say you were scared

[= he who sees you would say . . .]

زي اللي انكب عليه سطل الزبالة

zayy ᵢlli nkabb 3alee saTl ᵢzzbaale

like someone who's had a rubbish bin emptied on them

[= like one on whom . . .]

اللي عندو مشروع براسو يحكي

ᵢlli 3indo mashruu3 ᵢbraaso yi7ki

anyone who has a project in mind should say something

[= he who has a project . . .]

Similarly, plural forms can be used to mean "those who":

قلال اللي بيعرفو عربي منيح

2alaal ᵢlli bya3ᵢrfu 3arabi mnii7

there aren't many people who know Arabic well

[= few are those who know . . .]

Note that headless relative clauses can appear in *2iDaafe* (see unit 15):

كل اللي عملتو إني

kill ᵢlli 3milto 2inni

all I've done is

نص اللي جايين لهون

nuSS ᵢlli jaayiin lahoon

half the people coming here

It is not possible to use an indefinite relative clause on its own in this way. Instead, as with indefinite adjectives (see unit 16), the word واحد *waa7ed/waa7ad* "one" and its feminine counterpart وحدة *wa7de* has to stand in for the head noun:

واحد تعرفت عليه بالجامعة
waa7ad ^{i}t3arraf^{e}t 3alee biljaam3a
one [guy] I met at university

وحدة ركبوها امبارح
wa7de rakkabuuha mbaare7
one they put up yesterday

Zero-Imperfective Relative Clauses

It is possible for an *indefinite* relative clause—not generally a definite one—to have a zero-imperfective verb. All the other points of structure discussed above apply here too. Nine times out of ten the meaning of the clause will then be to express purpose, translating "to X" in English:

فتاحة نفتح فيها القنينة
fattaa7a nifta7 fiiha l2anniine
an opener to open the bottle with
[= an opener we (can) open . . .]

شباك اهرب منو
shibbaak 2ihrob minno
a window to escape through
[= a window I (can) escape . . .]

فش إشي نعملو
fish 2ishi ni3^{i}mlo
there's nothing to do

حدا يصلحلي التلفزيون
7ada ySalli7li ttilivizyoon
someone to fix the TV for me

The same meaning is present here, although the English translation is different:

وحدة أصاحبها
wa7de 2aSaa7ibha
a girl I could go out with
a girl for me to go out with

شب تزوجني أخوه
shabb ^{i}tzawwijni 2akhuu
a guy whose brother you could set me up with

Occasionally, a zero-imperfective relative clause attaches to an indefinite noun in a context such as the following. Here it indicates a condition or desired quality of the main verb's object. Note that this construction is optional, and in both cases a relative clause without a zero imperfective verb would work just as well:

خليه محل نكون نعرفو
khallii ma7all ^{i}nkuun na3^{i}rfo
choose a place we'll know

بدنا حدا يكون شاطر
biddna 7ada ykuun shaaTer
we want someone clever

The usual points on the tense characteristics of the zero-imperfective apply.

Relative Clauses with *miin*

It is possible to form an indefinite relative clause with the pronoun مين *miin* "who" as the head noun. In this case *miin* means something like "some(one) who." There are only a handful of structures where this is common. One is في مين *fii miin* "there are some who," which is generally followed by a verb marked for tense:

في مين بقول إنو . . .

fii miin bi2uul 2inno . . .

there are those who say that . . .

there are some who say that . . .

في مين بحب يكون هيك

fii miin bi7ibb ykuun heek

there are those who like to be like that

there are some who like it to be like that

Almost all other examples are zero-imperfective, with the zero-imperfective clause playing its usual role as the equivalent of a "to" clause in English:

عندها مين يدافع عنها

3indha miin ydaafe3 3anha

she has people to defend her

بدي مين يساعدني

baddi miin ysaa3idni

I want someone to help me

For the more general use of *miin* and other question words in embedded questions ("I want to know *who you saw*"), see unit 75.

The *7aal*

In this unit we will be looking at a characteristically Arabic construction: the *7aal* حال, sometimes called the "circumstantial clause." The *7aal* has two main uses: it can express both background information and simultaneous action. Although these two meanings are related, they are distinct. The easiest way to capture this distinction is through the English translation:

Simultaneous	Background
لف البلد وهو عم يسلم ع العالم	مأجاش وأنا بالبيت
laff ᵢlbalad w huwwe 3am ysallem 3 al3aalam	*ma2ajaash w 2ana bilbeet*
he went all over town <u>saying hi to people</u>	he didn't come <u>while I was at home</u>

In the sentence on the left, the *7aal* corresponds to an English conjunction: "while," "as," or "when." In the sentence on the right, it corresponds to an English "-ing" form. We will begin by looking at the overall structure of a *7aal* clause, focusing on its "background" use. We will then look at simultaneous and other idiomatic uses of this construction.

Background *7aal*

A background *7aal* consists of a topic sentence (see unit 48), with a noun or pronoun topic, introduced by the word و *w* "and" and translates as "while," "as," or "when":

بيتعلم وهو عم يشتغل

byit3allam w huwwe 3am yishtighel

he learns while working

he learns as he works

بغني وأنا سايقة

baghanni w 2ana saay2a

I sing while driving

I sing as I drive

بلشت اتعلم وأنا صغيرة

ballasht 2it3allam w 2ana zghiire

I started learning when I was young

ما تشتغل وإنت زعلان

maa tishtighel w 2inte za3laan

don't work when you're upset

> In North Levantine, the *w* often appears after a pronoun topic: أنا وسايقة *2ana w saay2a* "while I'm driving," هي وصغيرة *hiyye w ʾzghiire* "when she was young."

Note that the subject can be different from the subject of the main verb:

شغلت المكنسة وأنا لسا مو مخلصة حكي!

shaghhal⁽ᵉ⁾t l⁽ᵉ⁾mik⁽ᵉ⁾nse w 2ana lissa muu mkhallSa 7aki!

you started hoovering when I still hadn't finished talking!

In all these examples, the *7aal* has followed the main sentence. But the *7aal* can also precede the main sentence, giving an effect similar to the same process in English:

وهو عم يشتغل سمع صوت	وهي عم تمشي شافت صاحبتها
w huwwe 3am yishtghel sime3 Soot	*w hiyye 3am timshi shaafat Saa7bitha*
as he was working, he heard a noise	as she was walking, she saw her friend

Note that the *7aal* can also be brought forward to the special "emphasis position" (see unit 66):

بربك إنت وسحابتك مفتوحة بدك تنقذ العالم؟

brabbak 2inte w sa77aabtak maftuu7a biddak tinqez ⁽ᵉ⁾l3aalam?

do you really think you're going to save the world *with your zipper undone?*

The *7aal* can follow من *min* "from" (see appendix B) in the sense "since X":

بعرفو من ونحنا صغار	كنت أقرا كتير من وأنا ولد
ba3⁽ᵉ⁾rfo min w ni7na zghaar	*kunt 2a2ra ktiir min w 2ana walad*
I've known him since we were small	I'd been reading a lot since I was a child

For the tense form here, see unit 34.

Simultaneous *7aal*

In all the examples above the *7aal* corresponded to an English conjunction clause of some sort. But the *7aal* is also the most universally workable way of expressing simultaneous actions or states. This corresponds, generally, to an English "X-ing" form or a simple adjective:

تعب وهو يشتغل	ضليت سنة وإنت عم تتعب فيها
ti3eb w huwwe yishtghel	*Dalleet sine w 2inte 3am tit3ab fiyya*
he got tired working	you've been working hard on it for a year

رجعت وهي مش مبسوطة

rij3et w hiyye mish mabsuuTa

she came back unhappy

رحت ورجعت وإنت زعلان

ru7ᵉt w ⁱrji3ᵉt w 2inte za3laan

you left annoyed and came back annoyed

With existential sentences (see unit 49) this form generally translates a specific sense of the English "with." The meaning is the same as the other sentences above, but the translation is different. Note that here, exceptionally, no noun or pronoun is needed after *w*:

رجعت ومعاها ولد

rij3at w ma3aaha walad

she came back with a kid

[= and she has a kid]

إجا وببالو أفكار جديدة

2ija w bbaalo 2afkaar ⁱjdiide

he came with new ideas on his mind

[= and he has new ideas in his mind]

Note that this meaning overlaps closely with the special object (see unit 54) and simultaneous zero-imperfective (see unit 61) constructions. The following sentences have exactly the same meaning:

بتطلع من هون مبسوط   =   بتطلع من هون وإنت مبسوط

btiTla3 min hoon mabsuuT   =   *btiTla3 min hoon w 2inte mabsuuT*

you'll leave here happy   you'll leave here happy

رجع ع بيتو يضحك   =   رجع ع بيتو وهو عم يضحك

rije3 3 abeeto yiD7ak   =   *rije3 3 abeeto w huwwe 3am yiD7ak*

he went home laughing   he went home laughing

Note as well that not all uses of the English "X-ing" form here correspond idiomatically to a *7aal* construction. For another construction used for "saying," see unit 62.

Tense in *7aals*

A *7aal* almost invariably looks like a present tense structure (it will have an imperfective verb, a continuous form, or a participle, or otherwise it will be a "to be" sentence). Like other subordinate clauses, however, the *7aal* takes its overall tense from the main verb (see unit 58). Since English subordinate clauses tend to tense-shift to agree with the main clause, a single *7aal* can have a range of translations depending on the main verb to which it is attached:

With Future Main Verb	With Past Main Verb
رح يسمع صوت وهو عم يمشي *ra7 yisma3 Soot w huwwe 3am yimshi* he'll hear a sound as he's walking along	سمع صوت وهو عم يمشي *sime3 Soot w huwwe 3am yimshi* he heard a sound as he was walking along

With Future Main Verb	**With Past Main Verb**
بشرب سيكارة وهو واقف برا	شربت سيكارة وهو واقف برا
bishrab sigaara w huwwe waa2ef barra	*shrib^et sigaara w huwwe waa2ef barra*
I'll have a cigarette	I had a cigarette
while he's standing outside	while he was standing outside

Note that sometimes a zero-imperfective form is used with continuous meaning, especially in South Levantine. The following structures have identical meanings:

بتعلم وهو يشتغل	=	بتعلم وهو عم يشتغل
bit3allam w huwwe yishtghel		*bit3allam w huwwe 3am yishtghel*
he learns while working		he learns while working

بتحكي القصة وهي تطبخ	=	بتحكي القصة وهي عم تطبخ
bti7ki l2uSSa w hiyye tuTbokh		*bti7ki l2uSSa w hiyye 3am tuTbokh*
she'll tell [you] the story as she cooks		she'll tell [you] the story as she cooks

The resultative participle (see unit 37) can be used in a *7aal* clause. This expresses an event that took place *before* the main clause:

فوتوها وأنا مو منضف البيت	كل الأخطاء ارتكبتها وأنا مش ماكلة
fawwatuuha w 2ana muu mnaDDefⁱlbeet	*kull ⁱl2akhTaa2 ⁱrtakabtha w 2ana mish maakle*
they let her in when I hadn't cleaned the house	all the mistakes I've made [have been] when I haven't eaten

While we might reasonably expect to be able to use the perfective here in the same meaning, we cannot. Perfective verbs never occur in normal *7aal* structures, although they do occur in a special idiomatic construction, the "rhetorical" *7aal*.

Rhetorical *7aal*

Something resembling the *7aal* structure can also be used for rhetorical purposes. The implication is usually that someone has suggested something that is impossible given the situation expressed by the *7aal*. The translation in English is generally "when":

كيف بدك تدفع عني وإنت معكش توكل؟

kiif biddak tidfa3 3anni w 2inta ma3aksh tookel?

how are you going to pay for me when you don't even have enough money to feed yourself?

Note that this *7aal* is unique in that it can be followed by perfective forms:

كيف بدي أعطيك وراتبي خلص من يومين؟

kiif biddi 2a3Tiik w raatbi khileS min yoomeen?

how am I supposed to give you [money] when I spent the last of my salary two days ago?

Changes to Word Order and Emphasis

Most of the examples in this book have demonstrated a default word order. But word order in Arabic is fairly free, and there are several ways of drawing attention to—or putting the "focus" on—specific elements in a sentence. In this unit we will look briefly at five ways of doing this: fronting, repeated pronouns, relative clauses, trailing, and using *nafs* ("itself") and *7atta* ("even").

Fronting

One of the most common ways of emphasising a particular word or phrase is to "front" it (i.e., bring it to the front of the sentence) and to pronounce it with stress. The rules for this are similar to those for topicalisation (see unit 48). A fronted subject, adverb, prepositional clause, or indefinite object will move straightforwardly, with no additional change needed. A fronted definite noun (not a subject) will leave a pronoun behind, and an indefinite object will leave nothing. All of these structures also involve a change in intonation to emphasise the fronted noun:

سامي إجا	إجا سامي
saami 2ija	*2ija saami*
Sami, he came	Sami came
عليه ما رح سلم!	ما رح سلم عليه!
3alee maa ra7 sallem!	*maa ra7 sallem 3alee!*
I won't say hi *to him!*	I won't say hi to him!
قهوة بشرب	بشرب قهوة
2ahwe bashrab	*bashrab 2ahwe*
coffee, I'll drink	I'll drink coffee

الغسالة ما شغلتها

ⁱlghassaale maa shaghghalt-ha

the washing machine, I didn't turn it on

ما شغلت الغسالة

maa shaghghalt ⁱlghassaale

I didn't turn on the washing machine

These structures obviously closely resemble the topic structures we have already seen. But they are not the same. For one thing, as we have seen, it is possible to front indefinite nouns, and we generally can't have an indefinite topic (see unit 48). More significantly, a sentence can have both a topic and a fronted phrase, in which case the topic comes first:

إلياس ع أصحابو ما بسلم

2ilyaas 3a 2aS7aabo maa bisallem

Ilyas doesn't say hi even to his friends

أنا قهوة بشربش

2ana 2ahwe bashrabᵉsh

I don't drink *coffee*

Still, many (but not all) structures of this kind are only distinguished from normal topic sentences by intonation.

What semantic effect does fronting have? Most examples are similar to spoken English sentences such as the following:

سلافة ما حكيت معاها

sulaafa maa 7akeet ma3aaha

Sulafa I didn't speak to

أنا قهوة بشربش

2ana 2ahwe bashrabᵉsh

coffee I don't drink

Often there is an explicit or implicit contrast with some other alternative. If you offer me tea and I turn it down and then you offer me coffee, I could say:

قهوة اي بشرب

2ahwe 2ee bishrab

sure, I'll have some coffee [but not tea]

Or similarly:

أنا قهوة بشرب بس شاي لأ

2ana 2ahwe bishrab bass shaay la2

I drink *coffee* but not tea

With negative verbs, the meaning is often "not even." This requires a rising intonation on the fronted word. For example:

أصحابي بحكيش معاهم!

2aS7aabi ba7kiish ma3aahom!

I don't even talk to my friends!

[and you expect me to talk to strangers?]

أنا عربي ما بعرف اكتب!

2ana 3arabi maa ba3ref 2iktob!

I don't even know how to write
in Arabic!

[and you expect me to write
English?]

Fronting in this meaning is closely associated with the use of حتى *7atta/7itta* "even" but often occurs without it.

Independent and Emphatic Pronouns

The independent pronouns (see unit 18) are often used for emphasis by placing the pronoun after its attached counterpart:

بحكي معك إنت!

bi7ki ma3ak 2inte!

I'm talking to *you!*

بحبني أنا!

bi7ibbni 2ana!

he loves *me!*

أخوكي إنتي!

2akhuuki 2inti!

he's *your* brother!

بيتي أنا!

beeti 2ana!

it's *my* house!

Note that for North Levantine speakers—but not for South Levantine speakers—it is also possible to use a form with إلـ *2il-* here:

عم بحكيلك إلك!

3am bi7kiilak 2ilak!

I'm talking *to you!*

بحبني إلي!

bi7ibbni 2ili!

he loves me!

Emphasis with *ˈlli*

As in English, it is possible to use a relative clause structure (see unit 63) to emphasise a particular phrase. Note that if the element before *ˈlli* is the subject, the verb has to agree, unlike in English:

هي اللي لازم تفهم!

hiyye lli laazem tifham!

it's her who needs to understand!

إنت اللي كسرتو!

2inte lli kasarto!

it was you who broke it!

سامية هي اللي لازم تفهم!

saamya hiyye lli laazem tifham!

it's Samia who needs to understand!

أحمد يللي رح يندم!

2a7mad yalli ra7 yindam!

it's Ahmad who's going to regret it!

In the examples so far, the *ʾlli* structure has been almost exactly equivalent to "it's X that" or "it's Y who." But the *ʾlli* structure can (optionally) be used in more contexts than its English counterpart, including contexts where a normal relative clause probably wouldn't work. With imperatives, for example:

إنت اللي روح من هون!

2inta lli ruu7 min hoon!

you get out of here!

إنتي اللي فهمي!

2inti lli fhami!

no *you* get this into your head!

Or in more complex sentences:

وهلق بدك ياني أنا اللي اطلع من البيت؟

w halla2 biddek yaani 2ana lli 2iTla3 mn ʾlbeet?

and now you want *me* to leave the house?

Trailing

Topics are regularly delayed to the very end of the sentence. We have already seen some examples of this in unit 48:

بالبيت أحمد

bilbeet 2a7mad

Ahmad's at home

بفوتو ناس كتير هدوله

bifawwtu naas ʾktiir hadoole

they let a lot of people in

Quite frequently, framing structures are similarly delayed until the end of the sentence (note that the *b-* is not dropped even where it would be if the verb was in the default position):

بحكي مع حالي كنت

ba7ki ma3 7aali kunᵉt

I was talking to myself

أنا مبسوط صرت

2ana mabsuuT Sirᵉt

I'm happy now

إنت صغير بعدك

2inte zghiir ba3dak

you're still young

هي عم تروح لساتها

hiyye 3am ʾtruu7 lissaatha

she's still going

They may also be delayed with لإنو *la2inno* "because," كإنو *ka2inno* and *kinno* "as if, seems like," باينتو *baayinto* "clearly," and عشنو *3ashanno* "because":

بدو يجي كإنو

biddo yiji ka2inno

it seems like he wants to come

ما شفتها لإني

maa shiftha la2inni

because I didn't see her

مشفتهاش عشني

mashufthaash 3ashanni

because I didn't see her

The effect of this varies. Occasionally, accompanied by a change in intonation, delaying the framing structure may stress the element brought to the front: "I was *talking to myself.*" More typically, however, the effect is to make the delayed item seem like more of an afterthought.

nafs, zaat "Itself," "the Exact"

The word نفس *nafs* can be combined with suffixed pronouns to produce an "emphatic" pronoun with the same meaning as the English "self":

أنا نفسي ما عندي مانع

2ana nafsi ma3 3indi maane3

I myself don't have a problem

إنت نفسك قلتها

2inte nafsak 2ulta

you said it yourself

There are many idiomatic expressions using this structure:

جيت بنفسي

jiit ᶦbnafsi

I came of my own accord

بذات نفسو!

ᶦbzaat nafso!

the man himself!

The words نفس *nafs* and ذات *zaat* can be combined with definite nouns to mean "the X itself":

البيت نفسو

ᶦlbeet nafso

the house itself

العمارة ذاتها

ᶦl3imaara zaatha

the building itself

Note that these words can also mean "the same," for which see unit 84.

7atta/7itta "Even"

The word حتى *7atta/7itta* means "even" and can precede or follow its noun or occur at the end or beginning of a sentence:

حتى أنا   سامية حتى!

7atta 2ana   *saamya 7itta!*

even me   even Samia!

حتى رحت معاهم!   شفتو بالبيت حتى!

7atta ru7ᵉt ma3aahom!   *shifto bilbeet 7atta!*

I even went with them!   I even saw him at home!

7atta/7itta is often combined, as you might expect from its meaning, with the emphasis position described above:

أسعد حتى معي ما عم يحكي   إختي خبز حتى ما بتاكل

2as3ad 7atta ma3i maa 3am yi7ki   *2ikhti khibᵉz 7atta maa btaakol*

Asad isn't even talking *to me*   my sister doesn't even eat bread

PART 6

Conjunction Constructions

Coordinating Conjunctions

In this unit we will look at *coordinating conjunctions*. Coordinating conjunctions are used to connect (or "coordinate," in linguistics jargon) different sentences or sentence elements in various kinds of relationship: "and," "or," "but." For the most part, these words work similarly in Arabic and in English, and as a result, this will be a relatively short unit. We will go through the various relationships expressed by English conjunctions and explain how to express those relationships in Arabic. We will then look at one conjunction that has no obvious counterpart in English.

"And"

"And" is translated as و *w*. This can connect both whole sentences and parts of sentences:

شاي وقهوة

shaay w 2ahwe

tea and coffee

حاج تلف وتدور

7aaj ᶦtliff w ᶦtduur

stop beating about the bush

[= turning and spinning]

Note that with coordinated pronouns, for many speakers the second pronoun is placed on the carrier *yaa*, producing structures such as the following:

أنا وياكي

2ana wiyyaaki

me and you

إنتي وياه

2inti wiyyaa

you and him

Note that in lists, *w* generally precedes all elements:

شاي وقهوة ومي وكل شي

shaay w 2ahwe w mayy w kill shii

tea, coffee, water, everything

Note that repeating a verb or participle with an intervening *w* expresses "anyway":

بما إنك جيت وجيت

bima 2innak jiit w jiit

since you're here anyway

أنا طالعة وطالعة

2ana Taal3a w Taal3a

I'm going out anyway

Similarly, note the following idiomatic constructions:

غلطة وغلطناها!

ghalTa w ghalaTnaaha!

it was a mistake, I admit it!

[now stop going on about it]

مصاري وعطيناك، هدايا وعطيناك . . .

maSaari w 3aTeenaak, hadaaya w 3aTeenaak . . .

we gave you money, we gave you gifts . . .

[you can't accuse us of falling short]

For *w* introducing *7aals*, see unit 65.

"Or"

Most speakers distinguish between two kinds of "or." The first, ولا *willa* or *walla* (North Levantine), offers two mutually exclusive alternatives:

شاي ولا قهوة؟

shaay walla 2ahwe?

tea or coffee?

[you can't drink both]

بدك تاكلي ولا بدك تحكي؟

biddek taakli willa biddek ti7ki?

do you want to eat or do you want to talk?

[you can't do both]

The second, أو *2aw*, connects multiple nonexclusive options and is the more generic word for "or":

أو خلينا نقول . . .

2aw khalliina n2uul . . .

or rather, let's say . . .

بدك شاي أو قهوة؟

biddak shaay 2aw 2ahwe?

do you want some tea or coffee?

For some speakers, *2aw* can often replace *willa* even in exclusive contexts. For "or" in negative structures ("not . . . or"), see "neither . . . nor" below.

"Either . . . or"

Levantine Arabic has a wealth of constructions available for presenting two different options. All of them consist of two elements, just like "either . . . or." Probably the most universal is يا . . . يا *yaa . . . yaa*:

إنت يا معي يا ضدي

2inte yaa ma3i yaa Diddi

you're either with me or against me

يا بتجي معي يا ما بتجي معي

yaa btiji ma3i yaa maa btiji ma3i

either you come with me or you don't

Alternatives include يا إما *yaa2imma,* إما *2imma,* أو *2aw,* and ولا *willa*:

يا إما هون يا إما هونيك

yaa2imma hoon yaa2imma huniik

either here or there

أو بتساعدنا أو منساعدك

2aw bitsaa3idna 2aw minsaa3dak

either you help us or we help you

إما بتجوزها إما ما عاد تشوفها

2imma btitjawwazha 2imma maa 3aad ᵻtshuufha

you either marry her or you never see her again

ولا بتروح ولا بتروحش

willa bitruu7 willa bitru7ᵉsh

you either go or you don't

"Neither . . . nor"

The negative counterpart to "either . . . or" is ولا . . . لا *laa . . . wala,* which replaces normal negators. Note that while structures with "neither . . . nor" are usually restricted in English to nouns and otherwise sound clumsy, in Arabic they commonly replace any pair of negatives connected by "and" and are in any case far more common:

لا هاي ولا هديك

laa haay wala hadiik

neither this one nor that one

لا هو أخوك ولا أنا صاحبك

laa huwwa 2akhuuk wala 2ana Saa7bak

he's not your brother and I'm not your friend

For more on this construction, see unit 78.

"But," "Though"

"But" is most commonly expressed with بس *bass,* which also means "only" (see unit 84):

ما بدي ياك بس ما بدي ياك تنساني

maa biddi yaak bass maa biddi yaak tinsaani

I don't want you, but I don't want you to forget me

شفتو بس ما قلتلو شي

shifto bass maa 2iltillo shii

I saw him but I didn't say anything to him

A higher-register equivalent is لكن *laaken*:

لكن ما توقعت أبدا إنو يساوي هيك

laaken maa twaqqa3ᵉt 2abadan 2inno ysaawi heek

but I never expected he'd do this

shii … shii and *2ishi … 2ishi* "Sometimes … Sometimes," "Some … Some"

The only major coordinating conjunction in this list that has no direct equivalent in English is formed with شي *shii* (North Levantine) or إشي *2ishi* (South Levantine), both literally meaning "thing." This conjunction expresses two exclusive and alternative but related situations:

إشي عندو شهادة إشي عندو دكتوراة

2ishi 3indo shahaade 2ishi 3indo dukturaa

some of them have degrees,
some of them have PhDs

هنه شي بحلب شي بالشام

hinne shii b7alab shii bishshaam

they're sometimes in Aleppo,
sometimes in Damascus

ma "You See," "After All"

The conjunction ما *ma* is used to link together two sentences with a kind of causal relationship (this should not be mistaken for the occasional use of *maa*, with a long vowel, in various negative meanings):

نايمين فوق. ما هنن ما نامو من امبارح

naaymiin foo2. ma hinnen maa naamu mn ᶦmbaare7

they're asleep upstairs. I mean/after all, they hadn't slept since yesterday

بعرف المنطقة. ما هو ساكن هون من زمان

bi3raf ᶦlmanTi2a. ma huwwe saaken hoon min zamaan

He knows the area. After all, he's been living here for a while

Here *ma* adds the nuance that the listener and the speaker both understand the obvious intuitive causal connection between what was said before and the sentence prefixed with *ma*. The same applies in the following sentence, although here it can be translated with "but":

مش صايم؟ ما الدنيا رمضان!

mish Saayem? ma ddinya ramaDaan!

you're not fasting? but [you know] it's Ramadan!

Subordinating Conjunctions

Subordinating conjunctions are conjunctions that (intuitively enough) subordinate the following clause, making it serve as part of a larger sentence. If the sorts of subordination we saw above largely make a clause act like a core part of another sentence—subjects, objects, etc.—then subordinating conjunctions generally make the clause act like an adverbial part, above all prepositional structures:

Subordination		Simple
إجو عشان قلتلن يجو	←	إجو عشانك
2iju 3ashaan 2iltillon yiju		*2iju 3ashaanak*
they came because you told them to come		they came because of you

Appropriately, many conjunctions are derived directly from prepositions. In unusual cases—such as عشان *3ashaan* "because of" and "because"—they are identical. In most cases, however, they are derived using the particle *-ma*. This often results in a distinction where English uses the same conjunction:

Subordination		Simple
سافر من دون ما يودعني	←	سافر من دون شطنة
saafar min duun ma ywaddi3ni		*saafar min duun shanTa*
he left without saying good-bye to me		he left without a bag
حاكيني قبل ما تروحي	←	حاكيني قبل الحفلة
7aakiini 2ab^el ma truu7i		*7aakiini 2abl ^i l7afle*
call me before you go		call me before the party

Subordination		Simple
بحكيش قد ما بحكي	←	بحكيش قدو
ba7kiish 2add ma bi7ki		*ba7kiish 2add-o*
I don't talk as much as he does		I don't talk as much as him

In the sections below, we will briefly discuss how subordinating conjunctions work in general before moving onto groups and types of conjunctions that require extra attention. For a noncomprehensive list of the most common subordinating conjunctions, see appendix C.

General Points

Clauses introduced by subordinating conjunctions generally behave very similarly to other types of subordinate clause (and in fact إنو *2inno* is itself a subordinating conjunction, although one that we have already looked at exhaustively and will not be considering here). There is a broad division between indicative and zero-imperfective clauses, as with more straightforward kinds of subordination (see unit 58). Some conjunctions are typically followed by indicative clauses, which can be any kind of sentence with any kind of verb form or no verb whatsoever:

ع أساس الزلمة مبسوط

3 a2asaas ᵢzzalame mabsuuT

on the assumption that the guy is happy

لإنو إجا امبارح

la2inno 2ija mbaare7

because he came yesterday

كإنو ما في شي

ka2inno maa fii shi

as though there wasn't a problem

مع إنو مش موجودة

ma3 2inno mish mawjuude

even though she isn't here

These sorts of conjunction are more or less straightforward, and the only significant point to bear in mind is that they are commonly "framed" by their main clause (see unit 58), which means that there is usually no tense-shifting as in English:

أجا يتركلها المصاري مع إنو مش موجودة

2aja yitrikᵢlha ᵢlmaSaari ma3 2innha mish mawjuude

he came to drop off the money even though she wasn't there

Other types of conjunction are always followed by zero-imperfective clauses. It goes without saying that these are also "framed" by their main clauses:

أحسن ما تجي تشوفني

2a7san ma tiji tshuufni

so she doesn't come and see me

lest she come and see me

مشان ما يضطر

mishaan maa yiDTarr

so he wouldn't have to

A few conjunctions can be followed by different types of structure depending on the meaning:

بعد ما إجا

ba3ᵉd ma 2ija

after he got here

بعد ما يجي

ba3ᵉd ma yiji

after he gets here

قبل ما حكت

2abᵉl ma 7akat

before she talked

قبل ما تحكي

2abᵉl ma ti7ki

before she talks

Those conjunctions that are followed straightforwardly and universally by indicative clauses should pose no problems for a learner. In what follows we will focus on unusual types of conjunction, those that trigger zero-imperfectives, and those that show exceptional behaviour of other kinds.

-nno Forms

The conjunctions كإنو *ka2inno* "as if" (for some speakers كنو *kinno*), لإنو *la2inno* "because," and عشنو *3ashanno* "because" appear by default at the beginning of the clause. The *-o* can—optionally—be replaced by another attached pronoun:

كإنهم مش مبسوطين

ka2innhom mish mabsuuTiin

as if they weren't happy

لإنو البنت مبسوطة

la2inno lbint mabsuuTa

because the girl is happy

عشني أحسن منهم

3ashanni 2a7san minhom

because I'm better than them

لإني مبسوطة

la2inni mabsuuTa

because I'm happy

Unlike other conjunctions, however, the *-nno* forms can move around in the clause (see unit 66):

مبسوطة لإني!

mabsuuTa la2inni!

because I'm happy!

بابا جاي بكرا عشنو

baaba jaay bukra 3ashanno

because dad's coming tomorrow

ما في فايدة كإنو

maa fii faayde ka2inno

it's as if there's no use

For the framing use of *ka2inno* and *kinno*, see unit 45.

Conjunctions of Purpose ("in Order to")

Conjunctions of purpose ("in order to") are invariably followed by a zero-imperfective clause. There are many ways of expressing "in order to," but the most common are منشان *minshaan,* عشان *3ashaan* (South Levantine and Lebanese), and كرمال *kirmaal* (Lebanese):

عشان تتفرج ع الفيديو

3ashaan titfarraj 3 alvidyo

soe she [can] watch the video

مشان تعرف شو الفرق

mishaan ta3ref shuu lfarᶜ2

so you understand the difference

كرمال شوفك

kirmaal shuufak

so I [can] see you

منشان ما تزعل

mishaan maa tiz3al

so you don't get upset

The term أحسن ما *2a7san ma* "lest" (so that . . . not) is a negative conjunction of purpose that behaves in the same way:

أحسن ما توقع

2a7san ma tuu2a3

so you don't fall over

أحسن ما يضحكو عليك

2a7san ma yiD7aku 3aleek

so they don't cheat you

The only exception is the conjunction بلكي *balki,* or بركي *birki* (North Levantine), "so that . . . maybe," which tends to be followed by a normal clause:

جبت بسبور بلكي بزورهم

jibᶜt basboor belki bazuurhom

I got a passport so I might be able to visit them

"Without"

Conjunctions meaning "without" are invariably followed by zero-imperfectives:

من دون ما يساوي شي

min duun ma ysaawi shii

without [him] doing anything

بلا ما تسلم عليي

bala ma tsallem 3aleyy

without [you] saying hi

For the idiomatic use of *bala ma,* see unit 43.

Conjunctions of Time ("When," "as Soon as," "After," "Before")

Conjunctions of time behave differently depending on the context. When they refer to a future action, they are invariably followed by a zero-imperfective clause:

قبل ما يجي حاكيني

2abᵉl ma yiji 7aakiini

call me before he gets there

بستنى لبين ما ترجع

bistanna labeen ma tirja3

I'll wait until she gets back

بقللو لما أشوفو

ba2ullo lamma 2ashuufo

I'll tell him when I see him

بس تشوفيه سلمي عليه

bass ᴵtshuufii sallmi 3alee

as soon as you see him, say hi

When conjunctions of time refer to a general or habitual action, some speakers use a *b*-imperfective, and some use a zero-imperfective:

قبل ما يجي بحاكيني = قبل ما بجي بحاكيني

2abᵉl ma yiji bi7aakiini   *2abᵉl ma biji bi7aakiini*

[every day] before he gets here, he calls me   [every day] before he gets here, he calls me

بوكل بعد ما يرجع = بوكل بعد ما برجع

bookol ba3ᵉd ma yirja3   *bookol ba3ᵉd ma birja3*

[every day] he eats after he gets back   [every day] he eats after he gets back

When conjunctions of time refer to a past single action, they are typically followed by a perfective.

قبل ما إجا

2abᵉl ma 2ija

before he got back

بعد ما إجا

ba3d ma 2ija

after he got back

Note, however, that قبل ما *2abᵉl ma* "before" can be followed by a zero-imperfective even in this sense:

حكالي قبل ما إجا   =   حكالي قبل ما يجي

7akaali 2abᵉl ma 2ija   =   *7akaali 2abᵉl ma yiji*

he phoned me before he got back   =   he phoned me before he got back

"Instead of"

Conjunctions meaning "instead of" exhibit unusual behaviour. They commonly are followed by a zero-imperfective clause:

عواض ما تكتبو خزعبلات   بدال ما تلعبو طابة

3awaaD ma tik'tbu khuza3balaat   *badaal ma til3abu Taabe*

instead of writing nonsense   instead of playing football

However, when the clause after "instead of" refers to a situation that is actually ongoing, these conjunctions can be followed by an indicative sentence. For example, if my friend is upstairs playing Xbox while I'm cleaning the kitchen, I can shout up to him:

انزل اتعبلك شوي بدال ما إنت قاعد فوق

2inzel 2it3ablak shwayy badaal ma 2inte 2aa3ed foo2

come down and do some work instead of sitting around upstairs

Note that here *-ma* must either be followed by a pronoun (in South Levantine) or have an attached pronoun (in North Levantine).

Other Structures with *-ma*

Other structures with *-ma*—that is, those that do not fall into the categories above—are generally followed by indicative clauses:

مطرح ما جينا   بشتغل قد ما فيني

maTra7 maa jiina   *bishtighel 2add ma fiini*

at the place we came from   I work as much as I can

متل ما بقولو اللبنانيين   فوق ما أحمد بساعدنيش

mitᵉl maa bi2uulu llibnaaniyyiin   *foo2 ma 2a7mad bisaa3idniish*

as the Lebanese say   not only does Ahmad not help me

[= on top of Ahmad not helping me]

The only anomaly is that when the subject of the sentence is a pronoun, the pronoun must be explicitly stated. This can simply mean using an independent pronoun (see unit 18) straight after *-ma*. For North Levantine speakers, however, the pronoun can also be suffixed to the *-ma*, producing a form that parallels their special negative "to be" structure (see unit 76). As there, Lebanese speakers generally use *mann-*, while Syrian speakers use *maan-*:

طول ما أنا موجود   طول ماني موجود

Tuul ma 2ana mawjuud   *Tuul maani mawjuud*

so long as I'm here   so long as I'm here

محل ما إنتي ساكنة   محل منك ساكنة

ma7all ma 2inti saakne   *ma7all mannek saakne*

the place where you live   the place where you live

زي ما إنت عارف   متل مانك عرفان

zayy ma 2inta 3aaref   *mit\u1d49l maanak 3arfaan*

as you know   as you know

la- Type of Conjunctions

The conjunctions لـ *la-* and حتى *7atta* have a broad range of possible meanings and, as a result, of behaviours. As conjunctions of time meaning "until" and "when," they trigger zero-imperfective or indicative as with other conjunctions of time:

استنيت لإجو   لييجو الجماعة

stanneet la2iju   *layiiju jjamaa3a*

I waited until they came   when the guys get here

The same is true of structures such as the following, which combine a fronted expression of time with a verb marked with *la-*:

بالصدفة لشوفو   لهلق لفهمت

biSSudfe lashuufo   *lahalla2 lafhim\u1d49t*

I only see him rarely   I've only just understood

[= by chance for me to see him]   [= until now until I understood]

In the sense used in the following sentences, they can be followed by a zero-imperfective. But if the clause refers to something that has actually happened or is currently true, indicatives can be used as well:

ايش عامل حتى شعراتو فازين هيك؟

2eesh 3aamel 7atta sha3raato faazziin heek?

what's he done to get his hair standing up like that?

مين إنت لحتى تحكي معي هيك؟

miin 2inte la7atta ti7ki ma3i heek?

who are you to talk to me like that?

The following regional forms pattern with *la-*:

تنو

tanno

(Palestinian)

تـ

ta-

(Lebanese, Palestinian)

لحتى

la7atta

(North Levantine)

PART 7

Conditional Structures

Open Conditionals

In this and the following units, we will be looking at conditional structures, structures that consist of a condition ("if . . .") and a consequence of that condition being fulfilled ("then . . ."). There are several different kinds of conditional structures. In English they are often divided up into "open" (or "possible"), "hypothetical," and "counterfactual," distinguished primarily by the form of the verb used:

Open	Hypothetical	Counterfactual
If you come, I'll give you the money.	If he came, I'd give him the money.	If he'd come, I'd have given him the money.
If she arrives early, you'll let her in.	If she arrived early, you'd let her in.	If she'd arrived early, you'd have let her in.

The basic distinction here is that a speaker will generally use the open conditional for situations where it seems possible or likely that the condition will be fulfilled and the hypothetical and counterfactual for imaginary scenarios in which fulfilment is unlikely (or unimportant) or impossible. There are many other nuances that we could discuss, but since Arabic makes the same basic distinction, our focus here will be on *how* these distinctions are made: how to form conditional structures of different kinds and how to recognise them.

In this unit, we will be looking specifically at open conditionals, usually formed with the particle إذا *2iza* "if," as well as some common alternatives.

Structures with *2iza*

The most common way of forming an open conditional is to use the word إذا *2iza* "if." This can be followed by a range of structures. When the condition is a possible future event—in which case the English sentence will be a simple "if" plus a present verb—it is normally followed by a perfective:

إذا شفتو   ←   بتشوفو

2iza shufto   *bitshuufo*

if you see him   you see him

إذا حكيتي معها   ←   بتحكي معها

2iza 7akeeti ma3ha   *bti7ki ma3ha*

if you speak to her   you speak to her

> There is some fuzziness with this rule. Some speakers also accept verbs appearing in the imperfective after *2iza*, but others do not.

As we know, however, the perfective cannot have state meaning (see unit 33). For states and descriptions, we thus use the normal form of the imperfective:

إذا منقدر نمشي   ←   منقدر نمشي

2iza mni2der nimshi   *mni2der nimshi*

if we can walk   we can walk

إذا بتغني كتير   ←   بتغني كتير

2iza bitghanni ktiir   *bitghanni ktiir*

if she sings a lot [characteristically]   she sings a lot [characteristically]

As usual, this produces contrasts with verbs that have both state and "beginning-state" meanings (see unit 33):

Imperfective	Perfective
إذا بتعرف شو الفرق	إذا عرفت شو الفرق
2iza bta3ref shuu lfarᵉ2	*2iza 3rifᵉt shuu lfarᵉ2*
if you know what the difference is	if you find out what the difference is

Note that occasionally, the condition itself is an event in the past. In this case, the perfective form is used. Note that although the English translation looks like a hypothetical ("if she left"), it isn't; it is a normal "possible" conditional, with past meaning:

إذا طلعت امبارح بتكون وصلت   ←   طلعت امبارح

2iza Til3at ᵢmbaare7 bitkuun wiSlet   *Til3at ᵢmbaare7*

if she left yesterday, she'll have [already] arrived   she left yesterday

Otherwise, most types of sentences can occur after *2iza* straightforwardly. This includes other verbal structures, such as future-marked forms (with the meaning "going to") and participles:

كتير دارسة   →   إذا كتير دارسة مو مشكلة

2iza ktiir daarse muu mish^ikle   *ktiir daarse*

if she's studied a lot, there's no problem   she's studied a lot

رح تشوفو   →   إذا رح تشوفو خبرني

2iza ra7 ^itshuufo khabbirni   *ra7 ^itshuufo*

if you're going to see him, tell me   you're going to see him

The same applies to "to be" sentences:

عسكري   →   إذا عسكري بيتحمل

2iza 3askari byit7ammal   *3askari*

if he's a soldier, he'll manage   [he's] a soldier

إنت اللي عم تدور   →   إذا إنت اللي عم تدور أكلنا هوا

2iza 2inte lli 3am ^itdawwer 2akalna hawa   *2inte lli 3am ^itdawwer*

if it's you who's looking, we're screwed   it's you who's looking

Note rhetorical constructions such as the following, which cast doubt on the certainty of the event:

هيدا إذا فوتونا أساسا!   هادا إذا عرفك!

hayda 2iza fawwatuuna 2asaasan!   *haada 2iza 3irfak!*

that's if they let us in to start with!   that's if he recognises you!

Less commonly, the result clause may likewise take a perfective form even when the meaning is not past. The general effect here is usually to emphasise a fact:

إذا شوب ارتفعت الأسعار   بترتفع الأسعار

2iza shoob ^irtaf3at ^il2as3aar   *btirtife3 ^il2as3aar*

if it's hot, prices go up   prices go up

إذا ما بتقللي أكلت هوا ها!   بتاكل هوا

2iza maa bit2illi 2akal^et hawa haa!   *btaakol hawa*

if you don't tell me, you're screwed!   you're screwed

Note that like English "if," *2iza* is the normal way of expressing a choice between two alternatives (i.e., the equivalent of "whether"). For more, see unit 75.

Alternatives to *2iza*

Although *2iza* is the most common way of forming open conditionals, there are a few alternative constructions that you may encounter. By far the most common uses the particle إن *2in-*, sometimes contracted to *n-*. This always triggers a past tense form in the condition clause and has to be combined with *kaan* in order to modify other types of sentences:

إن كان غيري سكن قلبك

2in kaan gheeri sakan 2albak

if someone else has taken up residence in your heart

إن شفتها خبرني

2in shuftha khabbirni

if you see her, tell me

Although generally less frequent than *2iza*, *2in* and *n-* do appear very commonly in a handful of set expressions:

إن صح التعبير

2in Sa77ʾtta3biir

so to speak

إن شاء الله

2in shaa2 2aLLaa

God willing

> The more common form is *nshaLLa*. The form *2inshaLLa* is also used in South Levantine.

The variants إنكان *2inkaan*, إذا كان *2iza kaan*, and إذكان *2izkaan* also occur very occasionally, especially in set expressions:[1]

نحنا مطلقين إذكان نسيت!

ni7na mTalla2iin 2izkaan ʾnsiit!

we're divorced, in case you've forgotten!

Possible Conditions and Suggestions with *wiza* and *barki/balki*

The particle وإذا *w2iza* expresses "what if X happens" and is always combined with a perfective form:

وإذا مسكوك؟

w2iza masakuuk?

what if they catch you?

وإذا معرفنش ترجع؟

w2iza ma3riftᵉsh tirja3?

what if you can't get back?

w2iza can also mean "so what?"

وإذا انمسكت!

w2iza nmasakᵉt!

so what if I get caught?

وإذا!

w2iza!

so what?

In North Levantine, the particle بلكي *balki* (also بركي *birki* in North Levantine) can also mean "what if...?" and is followed by a perfective:

بلكي معرفتش ترجع؟

balki ma3rift^esh tirja3?

what if you can't get back?

بركي مسكوك؟

birki masakuuk?

what if they catch you?

For "even if," see unit 70.

Note

1. These forms used to be much more common. They appear frequently in corpuses from the 1920s and 1960s cited in Jalonen and in Cowell's data and are given as the default forms in a turn-of-the-century textbook. However, they have been gradually displaced by the more fuS7a *2iza*. See Jënni Jalonen, "Conditional Constructions in Damascus Arabic" (bachelor thesis, Uppsala University, 2017); Mark Cowell, *A Reference Grammar of Syrian Arabic* (Georgetown University Press, 1964); and Francis Edward Crow, *Arabic Manual: A Colloquial Handbook in the Syrian Dialect* (University of California Press, 1901).

UNIT 70

Hypothetical Conditionals

In unit 69 we looked at so-called open conditionals, those whose fulfilment seems reasonably plausible. In this unit we will look at the other major kinds of conditionals: *hypothetical* and *counterfactual*. These are both formed primarily with the word لو *law* "if."

The formation of hypothetical conditionals is subject to a great deal of regional and individual variation, perhaps more than any other syntactic phenomenon. In order to keep the content manageable, I will begin by outlining how the most basic structure works, ignoring as much as possible the many alternative phrasings. We will then look at some of these alternatives in more detail before ending with some idiomatic uses of conditional structures and of *law*.

Basic Structure

The most straightforward way of forming a hypothetical conditional is to use the word لو *law* "if." A *law* clause is ambiguous with regard to tense and can be either a hypothetical present/future ("if you talked to her") or a hypothetical past ("if you *had* talked to her"), depending on context. Note that while *law* generally forces verbs into the perfective (see unit 33), "state" or "description" meanings of the verb have to appear in the imperfective:

بيشتري بيت *byishtiri beet* he buys a house	←	لو اشترى بيت *law shtara beet* if he bought a house
بتعرف تحكي عربي *bti3raf ti7ki 3arabi* she knows how to speak Arabic	←	لو بتعرف تحكي عربي *law* [i]*bti3raf ti7ki 3arabi* if she knew how to speak Arabic

Other kinds of structure—participles (see unit 37), pseudoverbs, and "to be" sentences (see unit 49)—all follow *law* directly:

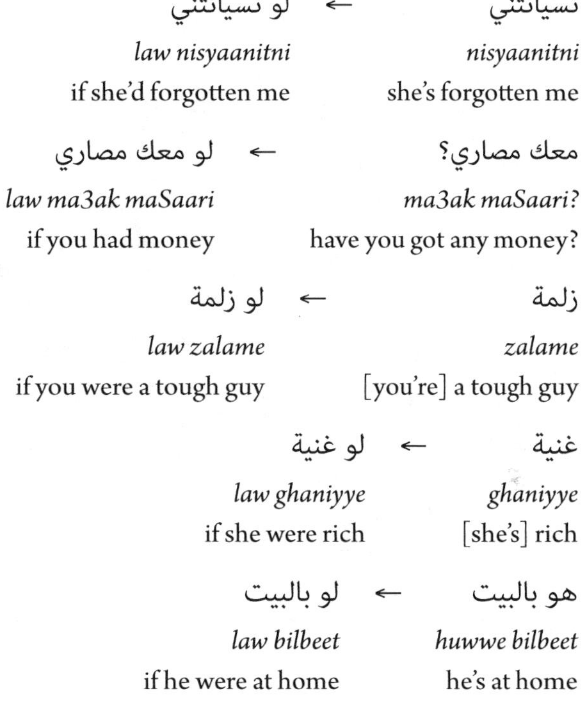

نسيانتني → لو نسيانتني

nisyaanitni → *law nisyaanitni*

she's forgotten me → if she'd forgotten me

معك مصاري؟ → لو معك مصاري

ma3ak maSaari? → *law ma3ak maSaari*

have you got any money? → if you had money

زلمة → لو زلمة

zalame → *law zalame*

[you're] a tough guy → if you were a tough guy

غنية → لو غنية

ghaniyye → *law ghaniyye*

[she's] rich → if she were rich

هو بالبيت → لو بالبيت

huwwe bilbeet → *law bilbeet*

he's at home → if he were at home

While the *law* clause is ambiguous as to tense, the main clause that follows it is not and distinguishes between hypotheticals ("would X") and counterfactuals ("would have Xed"). Hypotheticals are expressed with the *b*-imperfective:

لو درس منيح بينجح

law daras ᵢmnii7 ᵢbyinja7

if he studied properly he'd pass
[in theory, he still could]

لو جديدة مبتخربش

law ᵢjdiide mabtikhrabᵉsh

if it was new it wouldn't break
[in theory]

> As in English, the distinction between the two types of conditional is slightly murkier in practice. You may encounter apparently hypothetical forms in contexts that seem to require counterfactuals, for example.

Counterfactuals, meanwhile, are expressed with a form of كان *kaan* plus a perfective. For North Levantine speakers, this *kaan* acts normally, but for South Levantine speakers it is generally invariable and always takes the form *kaan* irrespective of the subject:

North Levantine	**South Levantine**
لو درست منيح كانت نجحت	لو درست منيح كان نجحت
law darset ˈmnii7 kaanet nij7et	*law darsat ˈmnii7 kaan nij7at*
if she'd studied properly	if she'd studied properly
she would've passed	she would've passed
كنت حكيت	كان حكيت
kint 7akeet	*kaan 7akeet*
I would've said	I would've said

For some speakers, especially North Levantine speakers, this *kaan* can be combined with hypotheticals as well: كان بحكيني *kaan bi7kiini* "he would tell me," كنت بعرف *kint ba3ref* "I would know." For others, it can be dropped in counterfactual clauses: لو درست منيح نجحت *law darset ˈmnii7 nij7et* "if she'd studied properly, she'd have passed."

When the result clause has no verb, a *b*-imperfective form of *kaan* (or some other framing verb) is generally required to give it conditional meaning:

لو دفعت ما بكون معي مصاري هلق ← معي مصاري

law dafa3ᵉt maa bikuun ma3i maSaari halla2   *ma3i maSaari*

if I'd paid, I wouldn't have money now   I have money

لو مو هون بكون بالشغل ← بالشغل

*law muu hoon bikuun bishshigh*ᵉ*l*   *bishshigh*ᵉ*l*

if he wasn't here, he'd be at work   [he's] at work

لو مش كاتب كان صرت مطرب ← أنا مطرب

*law mish kaateb kaan Sur*ᵉ*t muTreb*   *2ana muTreb*

if I wasn't a writer, I'd be a singer   I'm a singer

A handful of set phrases referring to the situation as a whole do not use *bikuun*:

لو مكبيتوش الباقي كان نص مصيبة

law makabbituush ˈlbaa2i kaan nuSS ˈmSiibe

if you hadn't thrown out the rest it wouldn't have been so bad

[= half a problem]

لو طلعنا بعد كمان ساعة كان رواق

law ⁱTli3na ba3ᵉd kamaan saa3a kaan rawaa2

if we'd left an hour later it would've been chill

Note that sometimes past hypotheticals carry the meaning "could have." This is determined by context:

لو خبرتني كنا تغدينا سوا!

law khabbartni kinna tghaddeena sawa!

if you'd told me we could have had lunch together!

Alternatives for the "If" Clause: *lawinno*

law can be combined with إنو *2inno* "that" to produce the compound form لو انو *lawinno*, which can take pronoun suffixes (لو اني *lawinn-i,* لو انك *lawinn-ak,* etc.). This neutralises the tense effects of *law* and allows the following structure to express tense normally. A past tense verb after *lawinno* thus has unambiguous past meaning:

<table>
<tr><td align="center">لو سرقتن</td><td align="center">لو اني سرقتن</td></tr>
<tr><td align="center">law sara2ton</td><td align="center">lawinni sara2ton</td></tr>
<tr><td align="center">if I stole them</td><td align="center">if I had stolen them</td></tr>
<tr><td align="center">if I had stolen them</td><td align="center"></td></tr>
</table>

<table>
<tr><td align="center">لو راح جابها</td><td align="center">لو انو راح جابها</td></tr>
<tr><td align="center">law raa7 jaabha</td><td align="center">lawinno raa7 jaabha</td></tr>
<tr><td align="center">if he went and got her</td><td align="center">if he had gone and got her</td></tr>
<tr><td align="center">if he had gone and got her</td><td align="center"></td></tr>
</table>

Similarly, a present tense clause after لو انو *lawinno* has unambiguously present meaning and requires a framing verb (see unit 38) to make it past. Note the difference between the literal meaning of the form with *kaan* and the correct English counterpart:

lawinno (Present)	*lawinno kaan* (Past)
لو انو معي مصاري	لو انو كان معي مصاري
lawinno ma3i maSaari	*lawinno kaan ma3i maSaari*
if I had money [now]	if I'd had money [then]
لو انو ما بيعرف يطبخ	لو انو ما كان يعرف يطبخ
lawinno maa bya3ref yiTbokh	*lawinno maa kaan ya3ref yiTbokh*
if he couldn't cook [now]	if he hadn't been able to cook [then]

lawinno (Present)	*lawinno kaan* (Past)
لو انو بالبيت *lawinno bilbeet* if he were at home	لو انو كان بالبيت *lawinno kaan bilbeet* if he had been at home

In general, *lawinno* forms are preferred whenever speakers feel a need to reduce ambiguity, although this varies from sentence to sentence and speaker to speaker. *lawinno* can also come across as less brusque and for many speakers is also strongly preferred with nonverbal clauses.

Alternatives for the "If" Clause: *law kaan*

In place of *lawinno*, some North Levantine speakers can insert كان *kaan* between *law* and any nonperfective structure. This does not affect the meaning or structure:

لو كان معي مصاري   =   لو معي مصاري

law ma3i maSaari   *law kaan ma3i maSaari*

if I had money   if I had money

if I'd had money   If I'd had money

لو ما بيعرف يطبخ   =   لو ما كان بيعرف يطبخ

law maa bya3ref yiTbokh   *law maa kaan bya3ref yiTbokh*

if he couldn't cook   if he couldn't cook

لو بالبيت   =   لو كانت بالبيت

law bilbeet   *law kaanet bilbeet*

if she was at home   if she was at home

if she'd been at home   if she'd been at home

Alternatives for the "Then" Clause: Future Marking

As well as the options discussed above, counterfactual "then" clauses can also be formed with *kaan* plus a future form of some kind. Both the future marker رح *ra7* (see unit 36) and its variants and the future formed with بد *bidd/badd-* work here. As usual, conditional *kaan* is invariable for South Levantine speakers:

North Levantine	South Levantine
كنتي رح تنجحي *kinti ra7 tinja7i* you would've succeeded	كان رح تنجحي *kaan ra7 tinja7i* you would've succeeded
كان بدك تنجحي *kaan biddak tinja7i* you would've succeeded	كان بدك تنجحي *kaan biddek tinja7i* you would've succeeded

For some speakers, especially North Levantine speakers, *kaan* can be dropped in these constructions too.

Idiomatic Uses of the Counterfactual

The counterfactual can be used to chastise people for a failure to do something:

كان حكيتلك كلمة!

kaan 7akeetlak kilme!

you could have said something!

كنت قلتلي!

kint 2iltilli!

you could have told me!

kaan can also be combined with the imperative (see unit 28) to give the same meaning:

كان احكيلك كلمة!

kaan 2i7kiilak kilme!

you could have said something!

كنت قللي!

kint 2illi!

you could have told me!

Note as well that *kaan* can be used to chastise someone for bad behaviour:

كان كسرت الشباك!

kaan kasart ⁱshshubbaak!

you could have broken the window!

كنت قتلتني!

kint 2ataltni!

you could have killed me!

Nonhypothetical Uses of *law*

law is not only a hypothetical "if." On its own or combined with another word (ولو *wlaw*, حتى ولو *7atta/7itta wlaw*, حتى لو *7atta/7itta law*) it can mean "even if." Although the resulting structures look identical to counterfactuals, the meaning is not necessarily counterfactual:

ولو ما درس بينجح

wlaw maa daras byinja7

even if he didn't study, he'd still succeed

صامدين لو بدنا نموت من الجوع

Saamdiin law biddna nmuut mn ⁱjjoo3

we're staying here, even if we're going to starve

ولو ألحيت عليي ماني رايحة!

wlaw 2ala77eet 3aliyyi maani raay7a!

even if you beg, I'm not coming!

law is also used to mean "if only" and to introduce wishes, for which see unit 44.

Other Conditional Constructions

In units 69 and 70 we looked at how to form conditional structures with two distinct words for "if": إذا *2iza* and لو *law*. These sorts of constructions are generally what people think of when "conditional sentences" are mentioned. But they are not the only kinds of conditional structure. There are various other ways of expressing conditions that a main clause might be dependent on. In this unit we will look at the most common examples: "ever" expressions, "the more . . . the more," "whether . . . or," and "so long as."

"Ever" Structures (*-ma*)

The basic equivalents to "whatever," "whoever," and "wherever" are typically formed by attaching *-ma* (or for some speakers *-man* or *-min*) to the question word (see units 73–74). These structures are typically followed by a perfective where possible and an imperfective where a perfective does not work, just like *law* (see unit 70).

كيف ما حسبتها بتطلع معك نفس الإشي	كيف ما
kiif ma 7assabtha btiTla3 ma3ak nafs ˈl2ishi	*kiif ma*
however you work it out, it amounts to the same thing	however
شو ما ساويت مش رح تزبط معك	شو ما
shuu ma saaweet mish ra7 tiZbaT ma3ak	*shuu ma*
whatever you do it won't work out	whatever
ايش ما سويت مش رح تزبط معاك	ايش ما
2eesh ma sawweet mish ra7 tuZboT ma3aak	*2eesh ma*
whatever you do it won't work out	whatever
	(South Levantine)

قد ما دورت هيدا أهبل حدا بالعالم	قد ما
2add ma dawwarᵉt hayda 2ahbal 7ada bil3aalam	*2add ma*
however much you search, this is the stupidest guy [you'll ever encounter]	however much
وين ما رحتي بتلاقي نفس الإشي	وين ما
ween ma ru7ti bitlaa2i nafs ᶦl2ishi	*ween ma*
wherever you go it's the same thing	wherever
مين ما كانت تكون ما رح ساعدها	مين ما
miin ma kaanet ᶦtkuun ma ra7 saa3idha	*miin ma*
whoever she is, I'm not going to help her	whoever
ايمتى ما بدكن شرفو لعندي	ايمتى ما
2eemta ma biddkon sharrfu la3indi	*2eemta ma*
whenever you want, just come by	whenever

Note as well the regional variants وينتا ما شلون ما *shloon ma* "however" (Syrian), وينتا ما *weenta ma* "whenever" (Palestinian), and ايمت ما *2eemat ma* "whenever."

Note the irregular form مهما *mahma* "whatever." Perhaps because it is originally fuS7a, it can only be followed by a perfective:

مهما ساويت مش رح تزبط معك	مهما
mahma saaweet mish ra7 tiZboT ma3ak	*mahma*
whatever you do it won't work out	whatever

Note that *shuu ma* and *mahma* can also mean "however much." This is related to the exclamation meaning of *shuu* (see unit 73):

شو ما درسو مش حينجحو	شو ما
shuu ma darasu mish 7ayinja7u	*shuu ma*
however much they study they won't pass	however much
مهما اعتذر منّي مساحمتو	مهما
mahma 3tazar manni msaami7to	*mahma*
no matter how much he apologises, I'll never forgive him	however much

These forms can be prefixed with لو *law* for extra effect:

لو شو ما سويت مش رح تزبط معاك

law shuu ma sawweet mish ra7 tuZboT ma3aak

whatever you do it won't work out for you

لو قد ما درست ما رح تنجح

*law 2add ma daras*ᵗ *maa ra7 tinja7*

no matter how hard you study, you won't pass

A handful of other nouns also combine with *-ma* to create similar structures. These structures are not always conditional in meaning but can be:

بصحى وقت ما بدي   وقت ما

biS7a wa2ᵉt ma biddi   *wa2ᵉt ma*

I get up whenever I want   whenever

منلتقي محل ما بدو   محل ما

*mnil*ᵗ*2i ma7all ma biddo*   *ma7all ma*

we'll meet wherever he wants   wherever

كل ما بصلي بحس هيك   كل ما

kull ma biSalli bi7iss heek   *kill/kull ma*

he feels like that whenever he prays   whenever

> You may occasionally encounter structures such as مدينة ما بدك *mdiine ma biddak* "whatever city you want" and بسعر ما بدو *bsi3ᵉr ma biddo* "whatever price he wants," with *-ma* used more productively with nouns.

The More . . . the More

As well as meaning "whenever," كل ما *kill/kull ma* is also used to translate "the more . . . the more." As with the English structure, *kill/kull ma* itself is repeated. Both clauses must be in either the perfective (see unit 33) or the *b*-imperfective:

السيارة كل ما صغر حجمها كل ما كانت أحسن

ᵢ*ssayyaara kill ma Sigher 7ajmha kill ma kaanet 2a7san*

the smaller the car, the better it is

أنا كل ما بشتغل أكتر كل ما بتعب أكتر

2ana kull ma bashtghel 2aktar kull ma bat3ab 2aktar

the harder I work, the more exhausted I feel

Whether . . . Or

"Whether . . . or" gives two possible outcomes or realities and emphasises that the main clause will be true regardless of which is true. There are various ways of expressing this in Arabic, but the most common is simply to juxtapose a positive and a negative verb separated by ولا *willa/walla* "or." As in structures with *law*, verbs are typically in the perfective (see unit 33), with the exact meaning provided by context:

قلت ولا ما قلت ما بتفرق معي!

رحت ولا مرحتش مش رح أزعل

2ilt walla maa 2ilt maa btifro2 ma3i!

ru7^et willa maru7t^esh mish ra7 2az3al

whether you said [something] or not, I don't care!

whether you go or not, I won't be upset

As usual, "descriptive" or "state" verbs (see unit 24) are an exception to the perfective rule:

بيحكي ولا ما بيحكي بضلو حيوان

بتعرف ولا بتعرفش ايش بهمني؟

byi7ki walla maa byi7ki biDallo 7aywaan

bti3raf willa bti3raf^esh 2eesh bihimmni?

whether it can talk or not, it's still an animal

whether you know or not, what do I care?

> Some speakers use إن *2in* or *n-* before a verb in this meaning: إن قلت ولا ما قلت *'n-2ilt willa maa 2ilt* "whether you say it or not."

So Long As

"So long as" (in the sense of "as long as you do X, Y will happen") is expressed with طالما *Taalama*, which is generally followed by a perfective:

طالما راضيتني بصير خير

Taalama raaDeetni biSiir kheer

so long as you keep me happy, everything will be good

The word مادام *maadaam*, which takes pronoun endings, can be used to mean "seeing as how" or "if [X thing that you have said is true]":

مادام كان بدك ياها كل هالقد، ليش ما تجوزتو؟

maadaam kaan biddak yaaha kill hal2add, leesh maa tjawwaztu?

if you were so keen on her, why didn't you get married?

مادامك برات البيت في مجال تجبلي معك قنينة مي؟

maadaamak barraat 'lbeet fii majaal 'tjibli ma3ak 2anniinet mayy?

since you're already out, could you bring me a bottle of water?

PART 8

Questions

Closed Questions

In this unit we will look at how to form the most basic kind of question: a "closed" question, one that allows for only a small number of predefined responses. The most common kind of closed question is a "yes/no" question. In English these generally involve a change in word order, often accompanied by a structure with "do":

I am happy	Am I happy?
You were there	Were you there?
I went	Did I go?

Closed questions in Arabic are much more straightforward. We will look first at how to transform normal sentences into closed questions. We will then look at how we offer two or three choices ("did you X or Y"). We will then consider the use of the negative particles مش *mish* and مو *muu* in forming special rhetorical questions as well as tag questions. Finally, we will see how closed questions are subordinated with "if/whether."

Basic Question Formation ("Yes/No")

In Levantine Arabic the most basic way of forming a yes-no question is simply by changing intonation. Various word orders are possible, just as in nonquestions. Topic and nontopic sentences (see unit 48) of all kinds can be made into questions using this method:

أبو محمد موجود؟ ← أبو محمد موجود

2abu m7ammad mawjuud?   *2abu m7ammad mawjuud*
is Abu Muhammad here?   Abu Muhammad is here

بروح ع الستة؟ ← بروح ع الستة

birawwe7 3 assitte?   *birawwe7 3 assitte*
does he go home at six?   he goes home at six

النمر بياكل بشر؟   ←   النمر بياكل بشر

ᵢnnimr ᵢbyaakol bashar?   ᵢnnimr ᵢbyaakol bashar

do tigers eat people?   tigers eat people

North Levantine speakers have a question particle شي *shii* that appears either directly after a verb or at the end of a sentence. Sometimes this particle simply indicates a question, while at times it has a meaning closer to "at all" or "even a little bit":

أبو محمد موجود شي؟   ودرست شي؟

2abu m7ammad mawjuud shii?   w darasᵉt shii?

Is Abu Muhammad here?   and did you do any studying?

In higher-register contexts, the fuS7a particle هل *hal* is sometimes used with "yes/no" questions:

هل بدك تشارك بالانتخابات؟   هل في علاقة بين هالفكرتين؟

hal biddak ᵢtshaarek bil2intikhaabaat?   hal fii 3alaaqa been halfikᵢrteen?

are you going to take part in the   is there a relationship between these

election?   two ideas?

Choices

A slight variation on the closed question offers someone the choice between different alternatives. The options are invariably separated by ولا *walla*/*willa* (see unit 67):

قهوة ولا شاي؟   درست أدب ولا حقوق؟

2ahwe walla shaay?   darasᵉt 2adab willa 7uquuq?

coffee or tea?   did you study literature or law?

We can of course offer someone the choice between a "yes" and a "no." In English we do this by saying "or not," and in Arabic we use لا *la2* in its role as a sentence stand-in (see unit 78):

النمر بياكل بشر ولا لأ؟   درست أدب ولا لأ؟

ᵢnnimr ᵢbyaakol bashar walla la2?   darasᵉt 2adab walla la2?

do tigers eat people or not?   did you study literature or not?

Rhetorical Questions with *mish*/*muu*

A more marked kind of closed question is introduced with the negative particle مش *mish* or مو *muu* (see unit 76), with the latter being Syrian. This creates a loaded question, heavily implying that you think that the answer is "no, you're right":

مو على أساس جوعانة؟

muu 3ala 2asaas joo3aane?

I thought you were supposed
to be hungry?

مش إنتي رحتي معاه؟

mish 2inti ru7ti ma3aa?

Didn't you go with him?

But I thought you'd gone with him?

مش كان معك مصاري كتير؟

mish kaan ma3ek maSaari ktiir?

I thought you had loads of money?

مش بدك تسافر؟

mish biddak ᵗtsaafer?

Didn't you say you wanted to travel?

I thought you wanted to travel?

Sometimes the negative participle is used to try to remind someone of important context they've forgotten:

مش كان في دكانة جنب بيتنا؟

mish kaan fii dukkaane jamb beetna?

don't you remember there was a shop
by our house?

مو رحتي إنتي وياها كمان؟

muu ri7ti 2inti wiyyaaha kamaan?

you and her went too, remember?

Tag Questions

One final kind of question that it is important to be aware of is the tag question. A tag question is a request for confirmation attached to the end of a nonquestion sentence. There are many possible tag question structures in Arabic, with a great deal of regional variation. Some of the most common, used in different areas, are مش هيك *mish heek* and مو هيك *muu heek* "isn't it so?"; صح *Sa77?* "right?"; فهمت كيف؟ *fhimᵉt kiif?* "you get me?"; and عرفت كيف *3rifᵉt kiif?* "you know?" (and variations thereof):

إنتي ساكنة بالأشرفية، مش هيك؟

2inti saakne bil2ashrafiyye, mish heek?

you live in Achrafieh, right?

وكان معي مصاري، عرفت كيف؟

w kaan ma3i maSaari, 3rifᵉt kiif?

and I had money with me, you know?

مش رح أروح، فهمتي علي كيف؟

mish ra7 2aruu7, fhimti 3alayy kiif?

I'm not going, you get me?

بدكش تروح، صح؟

biddaksh ᵗtruu7, Sa77?

you don't want to go, right?

Open Questions: Core Questions

In unit 72 we looked at how to form so-called closed questions, questions that offer a limited set of answers to choose from. In this unit and in unit 74, we will be talking about open questions. These allow for a much broader range of answers and are generally formed with question words.

We can divide open questions (and their associated question words) into two broad categories—core and adverbial—depending on their exact relationship to the rest of the sentence. In this unit we will look at core questions: those formed with "what," "which," "who," and "how much." I will begin by explaining exactly what "core" means in this context and exploring some of the behaviour that is common to all these words. We will then examine the individual question words one at a time.

Core Question Words

What do I mean by "core" question words? Question words fill a particular slot in a sentence; in this respect, they are a bit like pronouns. By "core," I mean a question word that can take the place of a normal noun—a topic (see unit 48), a subject (see unit 51), an object (see unit 52), or an object of a preposition (see unit 52)—as opposed to a whole location or manner expression (we will look at question words of this kind in more detail in later units).

To understand what I mean by "taking the place of," consider the following examples:

مين واقف برا؟   ←   رامي واقف برا

miin waa2ef barra?   *raami waa2ef barra*

<u>who</u>'s standing outside?   <u>Rami</u> is standing outside

شو بتحب؟   ←   بتحب القهوة

shuu bit7ibb?   *bit7ibb ᵢl2ahwe*

<u>what</u> does she love?   she loves <u>coffee</u>

بأيا ورقة عم تطلعو؟   ←   عم تطلعو بالورقة

b2ayya wara2a 3am tiTTil3u?   *3am tiTTil3u bilwara2a*

<u>what paper</u> are you looking at?   you're looking at <u>the paper</u>

The underlined sentence portions on the right clearly have the same function as those on the left. In both English and Arabic, however, they appear in different positions in the sentence. This is the first important point about the behaviour of core question words. They typically appear toward the beginning of the sentence, regardless of their formal role in the sentence:

مين شايفة؟   ←   شايفة الشب؟

miin shaayfe?   *shaayfe shshabb?*

who can you see?   can you see the guy?

ايش علمتهم؟   ←   علمتهم عربي

2eesh 3allamthom?   *3allamthom 3arabi*

what did I teach them?   I taught them Arabic

أني واحدة اشتريت؟   ←   اشتريت هاي الموزة

2ani wa7de shtareet?   *shtareet haay ᵢlmooze*

which one did you buy?   I bought this banana

In a topic sentence, however, the question word will generally *follow* and not precede the topic:

أبو محمود مين بحب؟   ←   أبو محمود بحبك

2abu ma7muud miin bi7ibb?   *2abu ma7muud bi7ibbak*

who does Abu Mahmoud love?   Abu Mahmoud loves you

النمر شو بياكل؟   ←   النمر بياكل بشر

ᵢnnimr shuu byaakol?   *ᵢnnimr ᵢbyaakol bashar*

what do tigers eat?   tigers eat people

Sometimes the inverted comment-topic order (see unit 48) is used instead of the topic-comment order. In this case, as we'd expect, the topic ends up toward the end of the sentence. This should not be mistaken for the English order:

مين بحب أبو محمود؟   ←   أبو محمود بحبك

miin bi7ibb 2abu ma7muud?   *2abu ma7muud bi7ibbak*

who does Abu Mahmoud love?   Abu Mahmoud loves you

شو بياكل النمر؟   ←   النمر بياكل بشر

shuu byaakol ᵢnnimr?   *ᵢnnimr ᵢbyaakol bashar*

what do tigers eat?   tigers eat people

Occasionally, question words will appear before topics: شو النمر بياكل؟ *shuu nnimr ʰbyaakol?* "what do tigers eat?" This is less common, however.

As in English, a question word that refers to part of a subordinate clause (see unit 58) will generally move to the beginning of the *main* clause:

مين قولتك رح يفوز؟   ←   قولتك أحمد رح يفوز؟

miin 2ooltak ra7 yfuuz?   *2ooltak 2a7mad ra7 yfuuz?*

who do you think will win?   do you think Ahmad will win?

ايش كان بدو ياها تشتري؟   ←   كان بدو ياها تشتري موز

2eesh kaan biddo yyaaha tishtri?   *kaan biddo yyaaha tishtri mooz*

what did he want her to buy?   he wanted her to buy bananas

شو قالت إنو ما عاد أكلو؟   ←   قالت إنو ما عاد أكلو شاورما

shuu 2aalet 2inno maa 3aad 2akalu?   *2aalet 2inno maa 3aad 2akalu shaawerma*

what did she say they don't eat any   she said they didn't eat shawarma any

more?   more

A question word replacing a prepositional object will take the preposition with it. This is possible in English but is usually quite stilted or formal. In Arabic it is obligatory:

مع مين عم تحكي؟   ←   عم تحكي مع أخوكي

ma3 miin 3am ti7ki?   *3am ti7ki ma3 2akhuuki*

who are you talking to?   you're talking to your brother

[= to whom . . .]

ع ايش عم تدور؟   ←   عم تدور ع المفتاح

3a 2eesh 3am ʰtdawwer?   *3am ʰtdawwer 3a lmuftaa7*

what are you looking for?   she's looking for the key

[= for what . . .]

من مين زعلت؟   ←   زعلت مني

min miin ʰz3ilᵉt?   *z3ilᵉt minni*

who did you get upset with?   you're upset with me

[= with whom . . .]

We will now look at the core question words themselves and how they are used.

shuu and *2eesh*

The word شو *shuu* is Pan-Levantine, while ايش *2eesh* is specifically South Levantine. Both mean "what":

<table>
<tr><td align="center">

شو معنى هالكلمة؟

shuu ma3na halkilme?

what does this word mean?

</td><td align="center">

ايش بتسوي؟

2eesh bitsawwi?

what are you doing?

</td></tr>
<tr><td align="center">

شو بتدرس؟

shuu btidros?

what do you study?

</td><td align="center">

ايش جنسيتك؟

2eesh jinsiyytek?

what nationality are you?

</td></tr>
<tr><td align="center">

عن شو الكتاب؟

3an shuu lᵢktaab?

what's the book about?

</td><td align="center">

الرز بايش بيتاكل؟

ᵢrruzz ᵢb2eesh byittaakal?

what do you eat rice with?

</td></tr>
</table>

In English it is possible to attach "what" directly to a noun: "what sweets do you have." This is not possible in Arabic. What is possible is to use a second "specifying" object (see unit 54), which occurs later in the sentence:

<table>
<tr><td align="center">

شو في عندك حلو؟

shuu fii 3indak 7ilw?

what sweets do you have?

what do you have in the way of sweets?

</td><td align="center">

ايش بتعرفي لغات؟

2eesh bti3rafi lughaat?

what languages do you know?

what do you know in the way of languages?

</td></tr>
</table>

> It is possible to have these words *occur* next to another noun: شو اسمك؟ *shuu 2ismak?* "what's your name." But some thought reveals that this is not the same as "what sweets." In "what's your name," "what" is taking the place of the comment, and "your name" is the topic. In "what sweets do you have," the whole phrase "what sweets" is the object.

Note the idiomatic use with a noun or an adjective in the sense "what do you mean X":

شو متأخرة؟ أنا هون من الصبح!

shuu mit2akhkhra? 2ana hoon mn ᵢSSibᶜ7!

what do you mean I'm late? I've been here all day!

Note as well that *shuu* is also a discourse marker often used before a question:

شو ما إلك مصلحة؟	شو طالع؟
shuu, maa 2ilak maSla7a?	*shuu Taale3?*
so you're not interested?	are you heading off?

For the use of *shuu* in exclamations ("you're so X!"), see unit 44.

miin "Who"

The term مين *miin* translates as "who":

مين قللك إني مش مبسوط؟	مع مين عم تحكي؟
miin 2allak 2inni mish mabsuuT?	*ma3 miin 3am ti7ki?*
who says I'm not happy?	who are you talking to?
محمود مين؟	مين محمود؟
ma7muud miin?	*miin ma7muud?*
Mahmoud who?	who's Mahmoud?

Like *shuu* and *2eesh*, a secondary object (see unit 54) can be added to a sentence with *miin*, specifying the category you are asking about:

مين عندك متعلم؟	مين بتعرف أجانب؟
miin 3indek mit3allem?	*miin ⁱbta3ref 2ajaaneb?*
who do you know who's educated?	what foreigners do you know?
[= who do you have educated?]	[= who do you know foreigners?]

For the use of *miin* with relative clauses, see unit 64.

2anu/2ani, 2anuu/2anii, 2ayya "Which"

The way of expressing "which" varies from region to region:

	Syrian	Palestinian	Lebanese and Jordanian
Masculine	أنو *2anu*	أنو *2anuu*	أيا *2ayya*
Feminine	أني *2ani*	أني *2anii*	

	Syrian	**Palestinian**	**Lebanese and Jordanian**
Plural	أنن *2anon*	أنمه، أننه *2anumme, 2aninne*	

> Note that in modern usage Syrian speakers often treat *2anu* and *2ani* as interchangeable and use them both for both masculine and feminine nouns: أني واحد *2ani waa7ed* "which one [M]," أنو وحدة *2anu wa7de* "which one [F]."

"Which" is slightly more complicated than "what" and "who" because it tends to form a unit with an indefinite noun rather than standing on its own. "Which" drags its noun with it to the front of the sentence, just like its English counterpart:

بأنو بيت ساكن؟

b2anu beet saaken?

which house are you living in?

أني طبعة اشتريتي؟

2anii Tab3a shtareeti?

which edition did you buy?

بأيا بيت ساكن؟

b2ayya beet saaken?

which house are you living in?

أيا طبعة اشتريتي؟

2ayya Tab3a shtareeti?

which edition did you buy?

Of course, it is possible to use "which" without a noun. In English, this most commonly (but not exclusively) triggers the form "which one." In Arabic, similarly, the word for "which" is most commonly combined with واحد *waa7ed/waa7ad* or وحدة *wa7de* "one," with gender agreement:

بأنو واحد ساكن؟

b2anu waa7ed saaken?

which one [M] are you living in?

أني وحدة اشتريتي؟

2ani wa7de shtareeti?

which one [F] did you buy?

أيا واحد بدك؟

2ayya waa7ad biddak?

which one [M] do you want?

ع أيا وحدة بتدوري؟

3a 2ayya wa7de bitdawwri?

which one [F] are you looking for?

It is also possible to use *2anu* and *2ani* on their own, although this is less common:

بأنمه ساكنين؟

b2anumme saakniin?

which ones do they live in?

أنون هنن يلي بدك ياهون؟

2anon hinnen yalli biddek iyyaahon?

which were the ones that you want?

> Some speakers use *2anu* to express derision: أنو بيت هادا؟ بيت؟ *beet? 2anu beet haada?* "house? What kind of house is this?"

The fuS7a word for "which," أي *2ayy*, occurs in a few set phrases:

بأي حق؟

b2ayy 7a22?

by what right?

أي ساعة بدك تجي؟

2ayy saa3a baddak tiji?

what time are you going to come?

For *2ayy* as a quantifier "any," see unit 84.

> For some speakers, أي *2ayy* is a normal word for "which."

2addeesh/2addee "How Much" and *kamm/2akamm/2akammen* "How Many"

The term قديش *2addeesh* and its variant قديه *2addee* mean "how much":

قديش كلفك هالقميص؟

2addeesh kallafak hal2amiiS?

how much did this shirt cost you?

قديش اشترى؟

2addeesh 2ishtara?

how much did he buy?

قديه بقي؟

2addee bi2i?

how much is there left?

بقديش جبتها؟

b2addeesh jibtha?

how much did you get it for?

> These words also have a noncore use, "for how long" (see unit 74).

Note that while English regularly uses "what" to ask about quantities and doesn't accept "how much," *2addeesh* can be used to ask about almost any number:

قديش عدد سكانو ؟

2addeesh 3adad sukkaano?

what's the population?

قديش رقم تليفونو؟

2addeesh ra2am tilifoono?

what's his phone number?

Note that unlike the English "how much," *2addeesh* cannot directly attach to a noun. Like the other question words we have looked at, however, a sentence with *2addeesh* can take a second object (see unit 54) specifying the scope of the question word:

قديش معك مصاري؟

2addeesh ma3ak maSaari?
how much money have you got?

قديش عندك أمل لسنة الألفين؟

2addeesh 3indak 2amal lasant ⁱl2alfeen?
how much hope do you have for the year 2000?

> This works in the same way as the structure with *shuu* above.

The word كم *kamm* (sometimes in South Levantine أكم *2akamm* or أكمن *2akammen*) most commonly translates as "how many" and is followed by a singular noun, although note that the agreement is often plural:

كم شخص بتعرف هونيك؟

kamm shakhS ⁱbta3ref huniik?
how many people do you know there?

أكم مرة قايللك؟

2akamm marra 2aayillak?
how many times have I told you?

كم واحد راحو؟

kamm waa7ed raa7u?
how many people went?

طاولة لكم شخص؟

Taawle lakamm shakhᵉS?
a table for how many?

> For some speakers, كم *kamm* can also be used for "how much," making it a full synonym of *2addeesh*: كم كلفك هالقميص *kamm kallafak hal2amiiS?* "how much did this shirt cost you?"

For the use of *2addeesh* and *kamm* in exclamations, see unit 44. For *kamm* as a quantifier meaning "a few," see unit 84.

Open Questions: Noncore Questions

In unit 73 we looked at "core" question words, those that replace nouns. In this unit we will look at the remainder of the Arabic question word set, what I call "noncore" question words. As before, we will first look at the definition and general behaviour of this sort of question word before moving onto the various uses of the words themselves.

Noncore Questions

If a core question word replaces (asks about) a noun, a noncore question word replaces (asks about) something bigger, usually a preposition or conjunction phrase. This is easiest to demonstrate with examples:

ساكنة جنبنا   ←   وين ساكنة؟

ween saakne?   saakne *jambna*

<u>where</u> does she live?   she lives <u>next to us</u>

جيت مشان شوفك   ←   ليش جيت؟

leesh jiit?   jiit *mishaan shuufak*

<u>why</u> did I come?   I came <u>so I could see you</u>

قطعتهم بالسكينة   ←   كيف قطعتهم؟

kiif 2aTTa3thom?   2aTTa3thom *bissikkiine*

<u>how</u> did you cut them?   you cut them <u>with a knife</u>

For the most part, these question words behave very similarly to core words. As you can see, they tend to shift to the beginning of the sentence, just like their core counterparts (and just like their English translations). They typically follow the topic in topic sentences (see unit 48):

المصاري راحو   ←   المصاري وين راحو؟

'lmaSaari raa7u   'lmaSaari ween raa7u?

the money is gone   where's the money gone?

رفيقك خلص القهوة   ←   رفيقك كيف خلص القهوة؟

rfii2ak khallaS 'l2ahwe   rfii2ak kiif khallaS 'l2ahwe?

your friend finished the coffee   how did your friend finish the coffee?

> As with core question words, it is possible for these words to appear before the topic, although this is a less common order: وين المصاري راحو؟ *ween 'lmaSaari raa7u?* "where's the money gone?" and كيف رفيقك خلص القهوة؟ *kiif rfii2ak khallaS 'l2ahwe?* "how did your friend finish the coffee?" This order might be more common with noncore than core question words.

For some reason, structures meaning "everyone" and "all of the" *cannot* appear before non-core question words:

الكل بقولو هيك   ←   ليش الكل بقولو هيك؟

'lkull bi2uulu heek   leesh 'lkull bi2uulu heek?

everyone says that   why does everyone say that?

كل الناس راحو   ←   وين كل الناس راحو؟

kill 'nnaas raa7u   ween kill 'nnaas raa7u?

all the people went   where did all the people go?

Otherwise, noncore questions behave as expected.

leesh/lee, shmi3na "Why"

The normal word for "why" is ليش *leesh*, occasionally ليه *lee*:

ليش تعلمت عربي؟   سامي ليش زعل كل هالقد؟

leesh 't3allamti 3arabi?   *saami leesh zi3el kill hal2add?*

why did you learn Arabic?   why did Sami get so upset?

ليه تارك كل شي؟   ليش أنا؟

lee taarek kill shii?   *leesh 2ana?*

why have you left everything?   why me?

leesh is unusual in that it can be tagged onto other questions. The effect is similar to opening a question with "why?" in English, but *leesh* attaches to the question as a particle:

بدو يشوفك ليش؟

baddo yshuufak leesh?

why, does he want to see you?

قديش أخد منك ليش؟

2addeesh 2akhad minnak leesh?

why, how much did he take from you?

The word شمعنى *shmi3na* also means "why," but its use is far more specific. It means something like "why . . . specifically" and carries a tone of defiance or suspicion. It is always followed by another word that it questions directly, as in these examples:

شمعنى أنا؟

shmi3na 2ana?

but why *me* [and not someone else]?

شمعنى هلق؟

shmi3na halla2?

but why *now* [and not some other time]?

2eemta / 2eemat / weenta "When," *2ayy saa3a* "What Time"

The most common word for "when" is ايمتى *2eemta* or its variant ايمت *2eemat*:

ايمتى راجعة؟

2eemta raaj3a?

when will you be back?

بديعة ايمتى طلعت؟

badii3a 2eemta Til3at?

when did Badia leave?

ايمتى بدنا نوصل؟

2eemta biddna niwSal?

when will we get there?

ايمت ناوي تسافر؟

2eemat naawi tsaafer?

when are you planning on leaving?

وينتا *weenta* is an exclusively Palestinian form:

وينتا راجعة؟

weenta raaj3a?

when will you be back?

بديعة وينتا طلعت؟

badii3a weenta Til3at?

when did Badia leave?

Note the forms من ايمتى *min 2eemta* "since when" and لإيمتى *la2eemta* "when . . . until":

لإيمتى بدنا نضل هيك؟

la2eemta biddna nDall heek?

how long are we going to go on like this?

أنا من ايمتى بعرف إنجليزي؟

2ana min 2eemta ba3ref 2ingliizi?

since when do I know English?

To ask for a specific clock time we use أي ساعة *2ayy saa3a* "what time":

بديعة أي ساعة طلعت؟   أي ساعة راجعة؟

badii3a 2ayy saa3a Til3at?   *2ayy saa3a raaj3a?*

what time did Badia leave?   what time are you coming back?

> Note the common Palestinian pronunciation *see3a*.

ween / feen "Where," *min ween / mneen* "Where . . . from"

وين *ween* is the usual form for "where," and فين *feen* is a less common variant:

وين كاتبين هالحكي؟   وين كنت لهلق؟

ween kaatbiin hal7aki?   *ween kunt lahalla2?*

where've they written that?   where've you been 'til now?

وين أخوكي؟   وين درستو؟

ween 2akhuuki?   *ween darastu?*

where's your brother?   where did you study?

In a "to be" sentence expressing location, *ween* can take attached pronouns (see unit 18), allowing it to "agree" with the topic:

وينو أخوكي؟   وينك؟

weeno 2akhuuki?   *weenek?*

where's your brother?   where are you?

Like the English "where," *ween* can express the end point of a motion (i.e., "where to") with the verb راح *raa7* "go":

وين رحتو؟   وين رايح؟

ween ru7tu?   *ween raaye7?*

where did you go?   where are you going?

For some speakers, however—the same ones who use the forms لهون *lahoon* "[to] here," لعند *la3ind-* "[to] by" (see unit 81), etc.—لوين *laween* is often used in this sense. Some South Levantine speakers prefer ع وين *3aween* or على وين *3ala ween*:

ع وين رايح؟   لوين رايح؟

3a ween raaye7?   *laween raaye7?*

where are you going?   where are you going?

laween is also used idiomatically alone by all speakers to mean "where are you going?" as in the following common expression:

لوين؟ قاعدين يا زلمة!

laween? 2aa3diin yaa zalame!

where are you going? We're having a good time here!

ween can also combine with من *min* "from" (see appendix B). Sometimes this translates "where . . . from":

من وين جبت المصاري؟

min ween jibt ˈlmaSaari?

where did you get the money from?

إنتي من وين؟

2inti min ween?

where are you from?

Note, however, that *min* can also express motion through or via a place (see unit 81), and in this sense *min ween* can translate as "which way" or "how":

من وين إجا ومن وين مشي؟

min ween 2ija w min ween mishi?

where did he come from and which way did he go?

من وين ساويت تلاتة أربعة؟

min ween saaweet ˈtlaate 2arba3a?

how have you made three four?

North Levantine speakers have an alternative to *min ween* in منين *mneen*:

منين جبت المصاري؟

mneen jibt ˈlmaSaari?

where did you get the money from?

إنتي منين؟

2inti mneen?

where are you from?

Note the idiomatic use of a contracted form of this with *-l-* pronouns (see unit 19), used to ask a suspicious or incredulous question about the origin of some possession or quality:

مننلك كل هالمصاري؟

mnallak kill halmaSaari?

where'd you get all this money?

مننلو كل هالثقة بالنفس؟

mnallo kull haththiqa binnafs?

how is he so self-confident?

The fuS7aism من أين لك هذا *min 2ayna laka haadha* is also used ironically in this meaning.

kiif/shloon "How"

The term كيف *kiif* is used throughout the Levantine area, while شلون *shloon* is specifically Syrian. Both typically correspond to the English "how" and are used to ask about means and methods:

كيف جيتي كل هالمسافة؟

kiif jiiti kull halmasaafe?

how did you come so far?

إنتو شلون بتروحو ع المدرسة؟

2intu shloon bitruu7u 3a lmadrase?

how do you get to school?

المنسف كيف بنعمل؟

ⁱlmansaf kiif binⁱ3mel?

how is mansaf made?

كيف بدنا نبلش؟

kiif baddna nballesh?

how should we begin?

In simple "to be" sentences (see unit 48) with the meaning "how are," "how is," and so on, كيف *kiif* and شلون *shloon* can take an attached pronoun (see unit 18):

كيفو أخوكي؟

kiifo 2akhuuki?

how is your brother?

شلونك؟

shloonak?

how are you?

The words كيف *kiif* and شلون *shloon* are the usual idiomatic equivalent to the English structure "what . . . like":

كيف شكلو أخوكي؟

kiif shiklo 2akhuuki?

what does your brother look like?

شلون كانت باريس؟

shloon kaanet baariis?

what was Paris like?

The words كيف *kiif* and شلون *shloon* are also the usual polite way of indicating that you haven't heard or understood, in which case the English equivalent is usually "sorry":

كيف؟ ما فهمت عليك

kiif? maa fhimt 3aleek

sorry? I didn't understand what you said

2addeesh, kamm "How Long"

The words قديش *2addeesh* and كم *kamm* "how long" are most commonly used in core questions (see unit 73), replacing or attaching to nouns, respectively. But they can also, less commonly, be used in a noncore sense of "for how long" (replacing time expressions). As you might expect, قديش *2addeesh* is more common in this meaning:

قديش بقي بألمانيا؟

2addeesh bi2i b2almaanya?

how long did he stay in Germany?

قديش لازم تدرسي تتتخرجي؟

2addeesh laazem tid'rsi tatitkharraji?

how long do you have to study to graduate?

The word كم *kamm* is only used in this sense by those speakers who also use it as an all-purpose synonym of *2addeesh,* meaning "how much."

Subordinated Questions

In units 72, 73, and 74, we looked at how to form normal question structures of various kinds. In this final unit of part 8 we will discuss how these question structures can be "subordinated." In an inversion of the order followed in previous units, I will start by setting out how *open* questions work—those with question words—before moving on to *closed* questions. This may seem counterintuitive but reflects the fact that subordination of closed questions is more complicated from a learner's perspective.

Open Questions (Question Words)

An open question is one that cannot be answered with a simple "yes" or "no." In practical terms, this is all questions beginning with a "question word" ("what," "who," "how," etc.). We looked at how these questions are structured in the last two units. Here we will be concentrating on how they operate as a kind of subordinate clause (see unit 58).

What do we mean when we say "subordinated questions"? Like other kinds of subordination, we are talking about something that could act as a full sentence in its own right—in this case a question—acting as the object, subject, or some other constituent of another sentence. This is probably easiest to demonstrate with examples:

بدي أعرف هالمشوار قديش بكلفني ← بدي أعرف المبلغ

biddi 2a3ref halmishwaar 2addeesh bikallifni   *biddi 2a3ref ⁱlmablagh*

I want to know <u>how much this trip would cost me</u>   I want to know <u>the amount</u>

استغربت كيف حكى معي ← استغربت من تصرفاتو

staghrabᵉt kiif 7aka ma3i   *staghrabᵉt min taSarrufaato*

I was surprised by <u>how he talked to me</u>   I was surprised <u>by his behaviour</u>

As in our other subordination examples above, the underlined sections in the sentences on the left and right are obviously serving the same function: they are both objects of the main verb. The difference is that in the sentences on the right, the object is a question. The question has been *subordinated* to the rest of the sentence.

You probably produce sentences like this all the time in English. And for the most part, the way Arabic handles these sorts of sentences is very similar. If anything, it is simpler in many respects. In English, subordinate questions have a different word order from nonsubordinate questions. In Arabic, the word order is identical in the two constructions. Compare the Arabic and the translation in the examples below:

بدي أعرف هالمشوار قديش بكلفني   ←   هالمشوار قديش بكلفني؟

biddi 2a3ref halmishwaar 2addeesh bikallifni   *halmishwaar 2addeesh bikallifni?*
I want to know how much this trip would   how much would this trip cost me?
cost me

استغربت كيف حكى معي   ←   كيف حكى معي؟

*staghrab*ᵉ*t kiif 7aka ma3i*   *kiif 7aka ma3i?*
I was surprised by how he talked to me   how did he talk to me?

بدي أعرف وين ساكنة   ←   وين ساكنة؟

baddi 2a3ref ween saakne   *ween saakne?*
I want to know where she lives   where does she live?

Similarly—like other subordination structures (see unit 58) and in line with how Arabic behaves generally (see unit 32)—there is no tense-shifting forced on the question by the main verb. Again, compare the Arabic and the translation:

سألتو ليش أجا   ←   ليش أجا؟

sa2alto leesh 2aja   *leesh 2aja?*
I asked him why he'd come   why did he come?

قلتلو شو بدي ساوي   ←   شو بدي ساوي؟

2iltillo shuu baddi saawi   *shuu baddi saawi?*
I told him what I was going to do   what am I going to do?

Verbs like عرف *3iref* "know," فكر *fakkar* "think," and شاف *shaaf* "see" that commonly take a complement construction (see unit 59) with other subordinate clauses can form the same type of structure with questions. Again, the effect of this is to turn the topic of the sentence into a direct object attached to the main verb:

إنت بتعرفو شو مسوي   إنت بتعرفو جاي

2inta bti3raf-o shuu msawwi   *2inta bti3raf-o jaay*
you know what he's done   you know he's coming
[= you know him what he's done]

شفتهن وين ساكنين؟

shift-hon ween saakniin?

have you seen where they're living?

[= have you seen them where they're living]

شفتهن طالعين

shift-hon Taal3iin

I saw them leaving

Occasionally subordinated questions with شو *shuu* will have the slightly different meaning of "what(ever)" (although constructions with -*ma* or *ᵗlli* are more common in this meaning, for which see units 68 and 64, respectively):

منساوي شو بدك   ←   شو بدك؟

minsaawi shuu baddak   *shuu baddak?*

we'll do what(ever) you want   what do you want?

Note, however, that the expanded subordinating use of "where" (= "in the same place as") and "how" (= "in the same way as") in English generally cannot be translated with a question word in Arabic. Instead, a different conjunction is required (see appendix C):

ساكنين محل ما إنتو كنتو ساكنين

saakniin ma7all ma 2intu kuntu saakniin

we live where you used to live

عايشين متل ما إنتو كنتو تعيشو

3aayshiin mitᵉl ma 2intu kintu 3aayshiin

we live how you used to live

Closed Questions ("If" and "Whether")

As we saw in unit 72, a closed question is one that can be answered with a simple "yes" or "no." In English these structures are typically formed by changes in word order and/or using auxiliaries such as "do" ("do you . . ."). Like open questions, closed questions can be made to stand in for another component of a sentence. Yet subordination is slightly more complicated for closed questions.

Closed questions are most straightforwardly subordinated using إذا *2iza* "if." Like open questions—but unlike their English counterparts—they do not involve any tense-shifting (see unit 58) or word order changes. Compare the Arabic and the translation in these examples:

سألتو إذا بدو ييجي   ←   بدو ييجي؟

sa2alto 2iza biddo yiiji   *biddo yiiji?*

I asked him if he wanted to come   does he want to come?

بتعرف إذا أبو سامي موجود؟   ←   أبو سامي موجود؟

bti3raf 2iza 2abu saami mawjuud?   *2abu saami mawjuud?*

do you know if Abu Sami's here?   is Abu Sami here?

إختي آكلة ولا لأ؟   ←   كان بدي أعرف إذا إختي آكلة ولا لأ

2ikhti 2aakle willa la2?   *kaan biddi 2a3ref 2iza 2ikhti 2aakle willa la2*

has my sister eaten or not?   I wanted to find out if my sister had eaten or not

This should be straightforward for an English speaker, since the overall strategy (using "if") parallels English. But if ولا *willa/walla* (see unit 67) is present, clearly signalling that the clause is a subordinated question, *2iza* is not compulsory. You may encounter structures such as the following:

بدو ييجي؟   ←   سألتو بدو ييجي ولا لأ؟

biddo yiiji?   *sa2alto biddo yiiji walla la2*

does he want to come?   I asked him if he wanted to come or not

أبو سامي موجود؟   ←   بتعرف أبو سامي موجود ولا لأ؟

2abu saami mawjuud?   *bti3raf 2abu saami mawjuud willa la2?*

is Abu Sami here?   do you know if Abu Sami's here or not?

ابنك فتح كتاب؟   ←   سآل ابنك فتح كتاب ولا لأ!

2ibnak fata7 ᵢktaab?   *s2aal 2ibnak fata7 ᵢktaab willa la2!*

has your son opened a book?   ask your son if he's opened a book or not!

For many speakers, *2iza* can be dropped even when *walla/willa* is not present:

بدو ييجي؟   ←   سألتو بدو ييجي ؟

biddo yiiji?   *sa2alto biddo yiiji*

does he want to come?   I asked him if he wanted to come [or not]

أبو سامي موجود؟   ←   بتعرف أبو سامي موجود؟

2abu saami mawjuud?   *bti3raf 2abu saami mawjuud?*

is Abu Sami here?   do you know if Abu Sami's here [or not]?

ابنك فتح كتاب؟   ←   سآل ابنك فتح كتاب!

2ibnak fata7 ᵢktaab?   *s2aal 2ibnak fata7 ᵢktaab!*

has your son opened a book?   ask your son if he's opened a book!

Where *2iza* is not present, verbs that take the complement construction (see unit 59) often have the same effect on a subordinate question as they do on other subordinate clauses: the topic of the subordinated question is treated as the object of the main verb. This is most obvious when the topic is replaced by a pronoun:

فاتت ولا لأ؟   ←   شفتها فاتت ولا لأ؟

faatet willa la2?   *shift-ha faatet willa la2?*

did she go in or not?   did you see if she went in or not?

Questions with the fuS7a particle هل *hal* can also be subordinated straightforwardly:

هل في علاقة؟   ←   بدي أعرف هل في علاقة؟

hal fii 3alaaqa?   *biddi 2a3raf hal fii 3alaaqa?*

is there a relationship?   I want to know whether there's a relationship

PART 9

Negation

Basic Negation

Negation is a difficult topic in Arabic, particularly when you are trying to describe multiple dialects at once. There are many possible ways of negating different types of sentences, and the systems in the different regions as well as the exact forms used do not necessarily map perfectly onto one another.

In order to simplify this complex topic as much as possible, in this unit we will look mainly at the distinction between the "verbal negators" *maa* (North Levantine) and *(ma)-sh* (South Levantine) and the "noun/adjective negators" *mish* (Palestinian, Jordanian, Lebanese) and *muu* (Syrian). These names are not entirely precise, since a number of verbal constructions are also negated with *mish*. But as we will see, they are reasonably accurate.

We will start by reviewing the negators themselves. We will then look at constructions that always take one or the other before considering those constructions that vary from region to region and speaker to speaker.

The Main Negators: *maa/(ma)-sh* and *mish/muu*

As noted above, there are many different negative constructions in Arabic, and the picture is further complicated by extensive regional variation. The two most important structures, however, are the "noun negator" *mish/muu* and the "verbal negator" *maa/(ma)-sh*. The different forms aside, these two negators are largely used in similar ways in all four regions.

Of these two, مش *mish* and مو *muu* are simpler structurally. They always retain the same form and are simply placed before whatever it is they are negating:

هادا مو منيح   ←   هادا منيح

haada muu mnii7   *haada mnii7*

this one isn't good   this one's good

مش غريبة؟   ←   غريبة

mish ghariibe?   *ghariibe*

isn't it weird?   it's weird

The verbal negators ما *maa* and ـش‌ـم *(ma)-sh* are a bit more complicated. The word *maa*, which is characteristic of North Levantine and poses few problems, is placed directly before the verb:

عجبني البيت   ←   ما عجبني البيت

maa 3ajabni lbeet   *3ajabni lbeet*
I didn't like the house   I liked the house

بتتعلم عربي   ←   ما بتتعلم عربي

maa btit3allam 3arabi   *btit3allam 3arabi*
she won't learn Arabic   she'll learn Arabic

In South Levantine, the form *(ma)-sh* is more common. This form consists of a prefix and a suffix, which attach on either side of the verb to be negated. In some contexts—we will look at which contexts in more detail below—the *ma-* can be dropped, leaving only the *-sh*:

عجبني البيت   ←   معجبنيش البيت

ma-3ajabnii-sh lbeet   *3ajabni lbeet*
I didn't like the house   I liked the house

بتتعلمش عربي   OR   متتعلمش عربي   ←   بتتعلم عربي

btit3allam-ᶜsh 3arabi   *ma-btit3allam-ᶜsh 3arabi*   *btit3allam 3arabi*
she won't learn Arabic   she won't learn Arabic   she'll learn Arabic

For the most part, *-sh* behaves as you would expect from a suffix (see unit 4). Note, however, that it interacts in an unexpected way with the masculine ("him") pronoun ـه, which normally manifests simply as lengthening of the previous vowel and a stress shift (see unit 18). A combination of these two suffixes manifests as ـهوش *-hoo-sh*:

بشوفوه   ←   مبشوفوهوش

ma-bishufuhoo-sh   *bishufuu*
they don't see him   they see him

عليه ديون   ←   معليهوش ديون

ma-3alihoo-sh ⁱdyuun   *3alee dyuun*
he hasn't got debts   he's got debts

While this shift is obligatory, there are also other pronouns with optional irregular forms:

ك   ←   ـكش   OR   ـكاش

-ak   *-ak-sh*   *-kaa-sh*
you [M]

كيش   OR   ـكش   ←   ـك

-kii-sh   -ek-sh   -ek

"you [F]"

ـهمش   OR   ـهمش   ←   ـهم

-humm-ᵉsh   -hum-sh   -hom

"them"

ـهنش   OR   ـهنش   ←   ـهن

-hinn-ᵉsh   -hin-sh   -hen

"them"

ـهنش   OR   ـهنش   ←   ـهن

-hunn-ᵉsh   -hun-sh   -hon

"them"

Constructions That Always Take *maa* or (*ma*)-*sh*

Perfective and *b*-imperfective constructions take *maa* or (*ma*)-*sh* straightforwardly. Note that *b*-imperfective forms can drop the *ma*- in (*ma*)-*sh*, but perfective forms cannot:

ما شفتها   ←   شفتها

maa shifta   *shifta*

I didn't see her   I saw her

ما بحكي معك   ←   بحكي معك

maa bi7ki ma3ak   *bi7ki ma3ak*

I don't talk to you   I talk to you

مشفتهاش   ←   شفتها

ma-shufthaa-sh   *shuftha*

I didn't see her   I saw her

بحكيش معاك   OR   مبحكيش معاك   ←   بحكي معاك

ba7kii-sh ma3aak   *ma-ba7kii-sh ma3aak*   *ba7ki ma3aak*

I don't talk to you   I don't talk to you   I talk to you

The verbs of zero-imperfective clauses (see unit 58) are negated in the same way. Note, however, that Southern Levantine speakers cannot drop the *ma*- here:

قللي احكي معك → قللي ما احكي معك

2alli 2i7ki ma3ak / 2alli maa 2i7ki ma3ak

he told me to talk to you / he told me not to talk to you

قللي أحكي معاك → قللي مأحكيش معاك

2alli 2a7ki ma3aak / 2alli ma-2a7kii-sh ma3aak

he told me to talk to you / he told me not to talk to you

Constructions That Always Take *mish* or *muu*

"To be" sentences are always negated with *mish* or *muu*:

هادا منيح → هادا مو منيح

haada mnii7 / haada muu mnii7

this one's good / this one isn't good

أسماء دكتورة → أسماء مش دكتورة

2asma duktoora / 2asma muu duktoora

Asma is a doctor / Asma isn't a doctor

أبو محمد بالبيت → أبو محمد مش بالبيت

2abu m7ammad bilbeet / 2abu m7ammad mish bilbeet

Abu Muhammad is at home / Abu Muhammad isn't at home

Participles are negated in the same way:

كاتبة كل شي → مش كاتبة كل شي

kaatbe kill shii / mish kaatbe kill shii

she's written everything / she hasn't written everything

أحمد وسامي متعلمين → أحمد وسامي مو متعلمين

2a7mad w saami mit3allmiin / 2a7mad w saami muu mit3allmiin

Ahmad and Sami are educated / Ahmad and Sami aren't educated

> Some North Levantine speakers may allow *maa* to take the place of *muu* or *mish* in some of these structures.

3am and ra7

Constructions with the preverbal particles عم *3am* (see unit 35) and رح *ra7* and حـ *7a-* (see unit 36) are negated differently in different regions. The most common pattern across the Levantine area—normal in Palestine, Jordan, and Lebanon—is to use the noun/adjective negator مش *mish*:

مش عم بحكي معاك   ←   عم بحكي معاك

mish 3am ba7ki ma3aak   *3am ba7ki ma3aak*

I'm not talking to you   I'm talking to you

مش رح شوفها   ←   رح شوفها

mish ra7 shuufa   *ra7 shuufa*

I'm not going to see her   I'm going to see her

مش حتغير!   ←   حتغير

mish 7atghayyar!   *7atghayyar*

I won't change!   I'll change

The alternative is to negate these forms with *maa*. This occurs to some extent across the Levantine region but is more or less the rule in Syria:

ما عم بحكي معك   ←   عم بحكي معك

maa 3am bi7ki ma3ak   *3am bi7ki ma3ak*

I'm not talking to you   I'm talking to you

ما رح شوفها   ←   رح شوفها

maa ra7 shuufa   *ra7 shuufa*

I'm not going to see her   I'm going to see her

ما حتغير!   ←   حتغير

maa 7atghayyar!   *7atghayyar*

I won't change!   I'll change

Imperatives and Independent Zero-Imperfectives

The negative imperative is more complicated than the other negative forms we have seen so far. The dedicated imperative form itself (see unit 28) cannot be straightforwardly negated. Instead, a zero-imperfective form is used. The simplest structure uses *maa* or (for South Levantine speakers) *(ma)-sh*, just like perfectives and imperfectives. Note that the *ma-* can be dropped:

احكي   →   ما تحكي

2i7ki   maa ti7ki

say something!   don't say anything!

متحكيش   →   OR   تحكيش

ma-ti7kii-sh   ti7kii-sh

don't say anything!   don't say anything!

جربي   →   ما تجربي

jarrbi   maa tjarrbi

try!   don't try!

متجربيش   →   OR   تجربيش

ma-tjarrbii-sh   jarrbii-sh

don't try   don't try!

For some North Levantine speakers, لا *laa* can be used to negate the imperative:

احكي   →   لا تحكي

2i7ki   laa ti7ki

say something!   don't say anything!

جربي   →   لا تجربي

jarrbi   laa tjarrbi

try!   don't try!

Independent zero-imperfectives (see units 43–44) can also be negated with *maa* or *ma-sh*:

بس يجي!   →   بس ما يجي!

bass yiji!   bass maa yiji!

just let him come!   just don't let him come!

بس ييجي!   →   بس ميجيش!

bass yiiji!   bass ma-yijii-sh!

just let him come!   just don't let him come!

Many set phrases with independent zero-imperfectives—generally taking the form of prayers or invocations of God—are negated with *laa*:

الله لا يردك!   الله لا يعطيكي عافية!

2aLLa laa yriddak!   *2aLLa laa ya3Tiiki 3aafye!*

good riddance!   screw you!

[= may God not bring you back]   [= may God not give you health]

For some North Levantine speakers, *laa* is more widely used to negate independent zero-imperfectives:

أي لا يجي، شو فيها؟   ←   أي يجي، شو فيها؟

2ee laa yiji, shuu fiyya?   *2ee yiji, shuu fiyya?*

so what if he doesn't come?   so what if he comes?

[= let him not come]   [= let him come]

Pseudoverbs

The last construction that we need to look at is pseudoverbs. This class of words is negated exactly like verbs, with *maa* or (*ma*)-*sh*:

ما بدك   ←   بدك

maa biddak   *biddak*

you don't want any   you want some

معليهوش ديون   ←   عليه ديون

ma-3alihoo-sh ⁱdyuun   *3alee dyuun*

he's not in debt   he's in debt

الاوضة ما فيها تخت   ←   الاوضة فيها تخت

ⁱl2ooDa maa fiiha takhᵉt   *ⁱl2ooDa fiiha takhᵉt*

the room doesn't have a bed   the room has a bed

There are various irregular forms, however. For North Levantine speakers, إلـ *2il-* "have" has an (optional) irregular negative:

مالك مصلحة   OR   ما إلك مصلحة   ←   إلك مصلحة

maa-lak maSla7a   *maa 2ilak maSla7a*   *2ilak maSla7a?*

you're not interested   you're not interested   are you interested?

For South Levantine speakers, بد *bidd-* "want" and فيـ *fii-* "have in it" can drop the *ma-*:

بدك   ←   بدكش

biddak-sh ← *biddak*

you don't want any ← you want some

الاوضة فيها تخت   ←   الاوضة فيهاش تخت

'l2ooDa fihaa-sh takh^et ← *'l2ooDa fiiha takh^et*

the room doesn't have a bed in it ← the room has a bed in it

For South Levantine speakers, في *fii* "there is" (see unit 49) has an irregular negative with a short vowel:

في حدا برا   ←   فش حدا برا

fi-sh 7ada barra ← *fii 7ada barra*

there isn't anyone outside ← there's someone outside

في مي بالبراد   ←   مفش مي بالبراد

ma-fi-sh mayy bilbarraad ← *fii mayy bilbarraad*

there isn't water in the fridge ← there's water in the fridge

maal/maan/mann- (North Levantine)

Before concluding this unit, it is worth noting the following forms, which are exclusively North Levantine (*mann-* is Lebanese, while the other two are Syrian):

مال ‍	مان ‍	من ‍
maal-	*maan-*	*mann-*
مالي	ماني	مني
maal-i	*maan-i*	*mann-i*
I'm not	I'm not	I'm not
مالك	مانك	منك
maal-ak	*maan-ak*	*mann-ak*
you're [M] not	you're [M] not	you're [M] not
مالك	مانك	منك
maal-ek	*maan-ek*	*mann-ek*
you're [F] not	you're [F] not	you're [F] not

مالـ	مانـ	منـ
maal-	*maan-*	*mann-*
مالو	مانو	منو
maal-o	*maan-o*	*mann-o*
he's not	he's not	he's not
مالها	مانها	منها
maal-a	*maan-a*	*mann-a*
she's not	she's not	she's not
مالنا	ماننا	مننا
maal-na	*maan-na*	*man-na*
we're not	we're not	we're not
مالكن	مانكن	منكن
maal-kon	*maan-kon*	*mann-kon*
you're [P] not	you're [P] not	you're [P] not
مالهن	مانهن	منهن
maal-on	*maan-on*	*mann-on*
they're not	they're not	they're not

These structures are effectively dedicated negatives for use in "to be" sentences. They can be used wherever *mish* or *muu* would be used:

منا دكاترة

manna dakaatra

we're not doctors

مانو ذكي

maano zaki

he's not clever

سامية منا كاتبة شي

saamiya manna kaatbe shii

Samia hasn't written anything

مالي عم اكذب

maali 3am 2ikzob

I'm not lying

Other Common Negatives

In unit 76 we looked at basic sentence negation: how to negate verbs, existential sentences, and "to be" sentences straightforwardly. In this unit we will be looking at two other very common negative structures: secondary uses of *mish* and *muu* and constructions with *wala*. We will also consider how to form the equivalents of English negative pronouns ("nobody," "anybody," etc.).

Other Uses of *mish* and *muu*

The noun and adjective negators مش *mish* and مو *muu* have a range of other uses. Essentially, they are the default way of saying "not" and can be used to negate all sorts of things. For example, they are sometimes prefixed to adjectives or nouns—appearing after the definite article (see unit 13)—to mean "non-," "un-," and so on:

<table>
<tr><td>المش منيح إنو . . .</td><td>لأ سامي المو تركي</td></tr>
<tr><td>'lmish 'mnii7 2inno . . .</td><td>la2, saami lmuu tirki</td></tr>
<tr><td>the not so good thing is . . .</td><td>no, non-Turkish Sami</td></tr>
</table>

This could also be interpreted as a contraction of اللي *'lli* (see unit 63).

More broadly, *mish* and *muu* are used to negate individual concepts, words and structures such as the following. Note that in the following sentences they work exactly like the English "not" followed by a phrase:

<table>
<tr><td>مش بيت</td><td>مو أكبر واحد</td></tr>
<tr><td>*mish beet*</td><td>*muu 2akbar waa7ed*</td></tr>
<tr><td>no, not a *house*</td><td>no, not *the biggest one*</td></tr>
</table>

مش هالدرجة!

mish lahaddaraje!

it's not *that* bad!

[= not to this degree]

مو بإسبانيا

muu b2isbaanya

not in Spain

مش لإنو بيعرفني

mish la2inno byi3rafni

not because he knows me

مو مشان شي

muu mishaan shii

not for any particular reason

Note that *mish* or *muu* must always appear at the beginning of a sentence; the only thing that can come before it is a topic (see unit 48). This means that to negate individual elements within a larger sentence, we have to bring them into the emphatic position just before the verb (see unit 66):

مو اليوم وصلت

muu lyoom waSSal͒t

it wasn't today I arrived

لأ مش بكرا طالع

la2 mish bukra Taale3

no, it's not tomorrow that he's leaving

The same is true for emphatic relative clauses (see unit 66):

مش أنا الصغير

mish 2ana l͒zghiir

it's not me who's the youngest

مو هو يلي بدا

muu huwwe yalli bada

he wasn't the one who started it

mish and *muu* can also be used to negate whole sentences. Here the meaning is usually close to the English structure "it's not that" (and إنو *2inno* "that" can in fact be added). As with the examples we have already seen, the negative word appears before the thing it negates. Compare the following examples of normal negatives and "whole-sentence" negations:

مش بحبها . . .

mish bi7ibbha . . .

it's not that he *loves* her . . .

ما بحبها

maa bi7ibbha

he doesn't love her

مش رحت معاها . . .

mish ru7t͒ ma3aaha . . .

it's not that I *went with* her . . .

مرحتش معاها

maru7t͒sh ma3aaha

I didn't go with her

مو البندورة غالية . . .

muu lbanadoora ghaalye . . .

it's not that tomatoes are expensive . . .

البندورة مو غالية

͒lbanadoora muu ghaalye

tomatoes aren't expensive

It may seem that in the verbal examples above *mish* and *muu* are replacing normal verbal negation. As the following examples show, however, that's not what's happening. In fact, *muu* and *mish* can negate sentences that are already negative, just like "it's not that" can in English:

مش مرحتش معاها . . .

mish maru7t^esh ma3aaha . . .

it's not that I didn't go with her . . .

مرحتش معاها

maru7t^esh ma3aaha

I didn't go with her

مو البندورة مو غالية . . .

muu lbanadoora muu ghaalye . . .

it's not that tomatoes aren't expensive . . .

البندورة مو غالية

ʾlbanadoora muu ghaalye

tomatoes aren't expensive

This structure is commonly used in rhetorical questions such as the following (for more examples see, unit 72):

مو عندك أخ؟

muu 3indak 2akh?

I thought you had a brother?

don't you have a brother?

مش رحت معاها؟

mish ru7^et ma3aaha?

I thought you said you went with her?

you went with her, remember?

It is also possible to combine *muu* or *mish* with a zero-imperfective (see unit 58) or negative imperative (see unit 76). Although this construction is probably related to the one we've just been looking at, it is distinct insofar as it isn't the direct negative counterpart of a positive sentence. With an imperative meaning the nuance is similar to the English "don't go X-ing" or "don't you . . .":

بس مش توسخ البيت متل العادة!

bass mish ʾtwassekh ʾlbeet mitl ʾl3aade!

but don't go messing the house up like usual!

مو ترجعلي صندويشتك وتقللي مو جوعان!

muu trajji3li Sandwiishtak w ʾt2illi muu joo3aan!

don't go bringing your sandwich back and saying you weren't hungry!

With other forms the construction expresses something along the lines of "I didn't expect X to . . ." or "X shouldn't just . . .":

يقعد عندي أسبوع بس مش يوسخ البيت ومينضفش وراه

yu23od 3indi 2usbuu3 bass mish ywassekh ʾlbeet w maynaDDif^esh waraa

he can stay at mine for a week, but he shouldn't just get the house dirty

and not clean up after himself

wala "Any," "No"

The word ولا *wala* has a wide range of uses. Most commonly, it combines with an indefinite subject (see unit 51) or object (see unit 52) in a verbal sentence or existential structure (see unit 49). In these contexts it means "any," "no," or "a single," depending on stress. Note that the main verb must be negative already:

ما شفت ولا شي

maa shif^et wala shii

I didn't see anything

مدرستش ولا مادة

madarast^esh wala maadde

I didn't study for a single subject

بعجبوش ولا إشي

bi3jiboosh wala 2ishi

nothing pleases him

ما بحبو ولا واحد فيهن

maa bi7ibbo wala waa7ed fiyyon

not a single one of them likes him

This structure is particularly common with شي *shii/*إشي *2ishi* "thing" and *7ada* "someone" and its variants. *wala shii/2ishi* and *wala 7ada/7adan/7add* are the normal translations for "nothing" and "nobody, no-one," for more on which see the next section below.

Adverbials can also be combined with *wala*:

ما رحت ولا مرة

maa ri7^et wala marra

I didn't go even once

ما شفت هيك شي ولا بعمري!

maa shif^et heek shii wala b3imri!

I've never in my life seen such a thing!

The same applies to indefinite prepositional objects (see unit 22). In these cases, *wala* most commonly comes *before* the preposition, although North Levantine speakers also allow it to come between the preposition and the noun:

مرحناش ولا ع محل

maru7naash wala 3a ma7all

we didn't go anywhere

ما حكينا مع ولا حدا

maa 7akeena ma3 wala 7ada

we didn't speak to anyone

Indefinite nouns with *wala* are often brought into initial position for emphasis (see unit 66). In this case *wala* makes the whole sentence negative, and the verb or existential will *not* have negative marking:

ولا شي شفت!

wala shii shif^et!

I didn't see a *single thing*!

ولا مادة درست!

wala maadde daras^et!

I didn't study for a *single subject*!

wala as a Sentence Negator

wala can also negate whole sentences, taking the place of verbal negation or "to be" sentence negation (see unit 76). This is comparatively unusual and strong. Compare the alternatives:

مش ممكن	ولا ممكن!
mish mumken	*wala mumken!*
it's not possible	it's just not possible!
مرحناش	ولا رحنا!
maru7naash	*wala ru7na!*
we didn't go	we didn't go even once!

Often *wala* expresses, with or without حتى *7atta* "even," "didn't even":

ولا رحنا أصلا	ولا حتى انخدش
wala ru7na 2aSlan	*wala 7atta nkhadash*
we didn't even go	it didn't even get scratched

wala can also be combined with comparative forms (see unit 79) in a similarly emphatic meaning:

ولا أحسن!	ولا أضرب من شركة الكهربا!
wala 2a7san!	*wala 2aDrab min shirket ^{i}lkahraba!*
there's nothing better!	there's nothing worse the electricity company!

For *wala* meaning "or," "nor," see unit 78. For the (identically written) word *willa* "or," see unit 67.

wala Meaning "Better . . . Than," "Rather . . . Than"

The construction "X *wala* Y" is distinct from the meanings above although probably related. "X *wala* Y" means something like "X, even though it's bad, is still better than Y." Consider the following (somewhat dramatic) examples:

الموت ولا الإذلال!	كل شي ولا هاد!
^{i}lmoot wala l2izlaal!	*kill shii wala haad!*
better death than humiliation!	anything but that!
	better anything than that!

Wala is often preceded by an imperative (see unit 28) and is followed by a zero-imperfective:

زقوني ولا تنسوني

zu22uuni wala tinsuuni

I'd rather be forcibly included than
have everyone forget about me

لا تحكي ولا تعلق هيك تعليقات!

laa ti7ki wala t3alle2 heek ta3li2aat!

better not talk at all than make
those sorts of comments!

Negative Pronouns ("Anybody," "Nobody," "Nothing," "Nowhere," etc.)

As noted in unit 18 on pronouns, Arabic generally has no distinct equivalent to the English pronouns "somewhere," "anything," etc. This is not to say that Arabic has no way of expressing the idea, just that usually the equivalent will be a straightforward noun, sometimes combined with the word *wala* that we have already seen.

For "something," "anything," and "nothing," شي *shii* (North Levantine) or إشي *2ishi* (South Levantine) "a thing" is the usual choice:

ما طلع منها شي

maa Tile3 minna shii

nothing came of it

مشفناش إشي

mashufnaash 2ishi

we didn't see anything

For "somewhere," "anywhere," and "nowhere," the most common options are محل *ma7all* or مطرح *maTra7*, with the appropriate prepositions:

ما رحتو ولا على محل؟

maa ri7tu wala 3ala ma7all?

you didn't go anywhere?

ما شفناه بمطرح

maa shufnaa bmaTra7

we didn't see him anywhere

Note that Arabic does have a distinct form for "someone," "anyone," and "no one," which is حدا *7ada* and its regional variants حد *7add* (South Levantine) or حدن *7adan* (Lebanese, Palestinian):

ما إجا حدا

maa 2ija 7ada

no one came

ما شفت ولا حدن

maa shif⁰t wala 7adan

I didn't see anyone

The term *7ada* is unusual. If it is the subject of a verb (see unit 51) and occupies the topic position (see unit 48)—that is, *precedes* the verb—then the verbal negation, whether *maa* or *ma-sh* (see unit 76), will attach to it and not to the verb:

محدش شافني

ma7add⁰sh shaafni

nobody saw me

ما حدا رح يقول شي

maa 7ada ra7 y2uul shii

nobody will say anything

> For some speakers the future particle رح *ra7* (see unit 36) can also move: ما رح حدا يشوفك *maa ra7 7ada yshuufak* "no one will see you."

In the examples above, the choice of "any-" or "no-" in English is determined by the structure of the sentence around it. Of course, "nothing," "no one," and so on. can also be used as stand-alone words. The equivalent in Arabic always uses *wala*. Consider the following examples:

مين إنت؟   ولا حدا

miin 2inte?   *wala 7ada*

who are you?   no one

شو بتعرف عن لبنان؟   ولا شي

shuu bta3ref 3an libnaan?   *wala shii*

what do you know about Lebanon?   nothing

Note that in sentences such as the following where English allows "any" to act as an object on its own, Arabic simply drops the object entirely:

مأكلتش   ما لقيت

*ma2akalt*ᵉ*sh*   *maa l2iit*

I didn't eat any   I didn't find any

Other Negative Structures

In this unit we will look at some miscellaneous negation structures: عمرو ما *3imro/3umro maa* "never," ما عاد *maa 3aad* "not anymore," لا . . . ولا *laa . . . wala* "neither . . . nor," لأ *la2* "no, not," and structures with إلا *2illa* and غير *gheer* "except."

3imro/3umro maa, ma3umroosh "Never"

The word عمرو ما *3imro/3umro maa* means "never." The *-o* is an attached pronoun (see unit 18) that agrees with the subject. Note that even speakers who use *-sh* forms elsewhere do not use it here:

<table>
<tr><td align="right">عمرها ما بتكذب عليك</td><td align="right">هدوله عمرن ما بيمسكوه</td></tr>
<tr><td align="right">3um^urha maa btikzeb 3aleek</td><td align="right">hadoole 3imron maa byimⁱskuu</td></tr>
<tr><td align="right">she'd never lie to you</td><td align="right">these guys'll never catch him</td></tr>
</table>

<table>
<tr><td align="right">التلفزيون عمرو ما اشتغل</td><td align="right">هالسنة عمرها ما حتخلص!</td></tr>
<tr><td align="right">'ttilfizyoon 3umro maa shtaghal</td><td align="right">hassine 3imrha maa 7atikhloS!</td></tr>
<tr><td align="right">the TV's never worked</td><td align="right">this year is never gonna finish!</td></tr>
</table>

عمر عمرو ما بروح ع الجيم

3umar 3umro maa biruu7 3 aljimm

Omar never goes to the gym

An alternative form is ما عمرو *maa 3imro/3umro* or معمروش *ma3umroosh* (in South Levantine). This only works with the past tense:

<table>
<tr><td align="right">هادا ما عمرو راح</td><td align="right">معمرهاش كذبت عليك</td></tr>
<tr><td align="right">haada maa 3imro raa7</td><td align="right">ma3um^urhaash kazbat 3aleek</td></tr>
<tr><td align="right">this guy's never been</td><td align="right">she's never lied to you</td></tr>
</table>

maa ba2a, maa 3aad "Not . . . Anymore" (North Levantine)

The words *maa 3aad* and *maa ba2a* are largely normal framing verbs (see unit 38) expressing "no longer," "not again," and so on. Like other framing verbs, they can be used with comments of all kinds (see unit 48), including nouns and adjectives and verbal sentences (for more examples of this straightforward usage, see unit 39):

ما عاد يجي

maa 3aad yiji

he doesn't come around anymore

هو ما بقى مبسوط

huwwe maba2a mabsuuT

he's not happy anymore

Note, however, that when the meaning is past—"I've never done it since," "I didn't do it again," or "[since then] I haven't smoked"—*maa 3aad* and *maa ba2a* can be followed by a perfective form:

من وقتها ما عاد دخنت

min wa2ta maa 3aad dakhkhan^et

since then I haven't smoked

Similarly, they quite commonly have future or imperative meaning:

ما بقى تشوفو!

maa ba2a tshuufo!

don't see him again!

من اليوم ورايح ما عاد أشوفو!

min ⁱlyoom wraaye7 maa 3aad 2ashuufo!

I won't see him again!

These forms are barely used in South Levantine. Although some southern speakers do occasionally use the form معدش *ma3adsh*, they are more likely to opt for the framing verb بطل *baTTal*, for which see unit 39.

laa . . . wala "Neither . . . nor"

The construction ولا . . . لا *laa . . . wala* replaces the negators we saw above. It is considerably more common than "neither . . . nor" in English and is used almost anywhere that "X and Y" would be in a nonnegative context. The construction can be used to negate all kinds of sentences and replaces both *mish/muu* and *maa/(ma)-sh*:

لا بعرفها ولا بدي أعرفها!

laa ba3rifha wala biddi 2a3rifha!

I don't know her and I don't want

to get to know her!

لا رحت ولا رجعت

laa ru7^et wala rji3^et

I didn't go and I didn't come back either

[= I never went]

هو لا أحمد ولا سامي

huwwe laa 2a7mad wala saami

he's not Ahmad and he's not Sami either

أنا لا دكتورة ولا ممرضة

2ana laa diktoora wala mumarriDa

I'm neither a doctor or a nurse

An alternative is to negate the first sentence normally and then negate the second with *wala*. This often doesn't have quite the same effect:

أنا متعلمتش ولا جربت أصلا

2ana mat3allamt^esh wala jarrab^et 2aSlan

I didn't learn—actually, I didn't even try

أنا مش بديعة ولا بعرف بديعة

2ana mish badii3a wala ba3ref badii3a

I'm not Badia and I don't know who she is

Like the use of *wala* described above, *laa ... wala* can coordinate two subjects (see unit 51), two objects (see unit 52), two adverbials, or two subordinate clauses (see unit 58). When these appear *after* the verb, the verb must be negated normally:

ما بحب لا الشاي ولا القهوة

maa ba7ibb laa shshaay wala l2ahwe

I don't like tea *or* coffee

مأجوش لا سامي ولا مرتو

ma2ajuush laa saami wala marato

neither Sami nor his wife came

ما بدو لا يروح ولا يجي

maa biddo laa yruu7 wala yiiji

he doesn't want to come or go

For agreement patterns with this sort of subject, see unit 50.

Wala is the natural equivalent to "neither" in structures such as the following:

ولا أنا

wala 2ana

me neither

ولا أنا رحت

wala 2ana ru7et

I didn't go either

North Levantine speakers who use the special *maal/maan/mann-* construction (see unit 76) can produce a parallel form with *laa-*:

أنا لاني ضد هالفكرة ولا معها

2ana laani DiDD halfikra wala ma3a

I'm neither for or against this idea

لنك رئيس ولا نائب

lannak ra2iis wala naa2eb

you're not a president and you're not an MP

la2 "No," "Not"

The word لأ *la2* is the normal word for "no." Note that it is often more idiomatic (or at the very least less abrupt and impolite) to combine *la2* with a negative verb form when answering a question:

رحتي؟ لأ مرحتش

ru7ti? *la2 maru7t^esh*

did you go? no, I didn't

حضرتك سوري؟ لأ مش سوري

7aDⁱrtak suuri? *la2 mish suuri*

are you Syrian? no, I'm not

For more examples, see the section on answering yes-no questions in unit 72.

la2 can also stand in for a negative clause in complex sentences; that is, it translates "not" in sentences such as the following:

بدك تجي ولا لأ؟ بتمنى لأ

biddak tiji willa la2? *batmanna la2*

do you want to come or not? I hope not

Note the use in contrast sentences such as the following:

أحمد جايه بس سامي لأ أنا بحبك بس هو لأ

2a7mad jaaye bass saami la2 *2ana b7ibbak bass huwwe la2*

Ahmad is coming but Sami isn't I love you but he doesn't

Note also لأى *la2aa* and لا *laa* "no way!"

Sentences with "Except" and "Only"

One special kind of negative sentence that is worth briefly discussing occurs with words for "except" and "only." Spoken Arabic has two very common words for "except": إلا *2illa* and غير *gheer*:

إلا إنت غير البيت

2illa 2inte *gheer ⁱlbeet*

except you other than the house

These words are typically combined with a negative main sentence in a way that is often best translated with "only." They can precede objects (see unit 52):

ما كتبت غير اسم واحد

maa katab^et gheer 2is^em waa7ad

I only wrote a single name

[= I didn't write (anything)

except one name]

ما قلت إلا الحقيقة

maa 2ilt 2illa l7a2ii2a

I only told the truth

[= I didn't say (anything)

except the truth]

Adverbial and locational expressions:

مشفتوش غير مرة

mashuftoosh gheer marra

I only saw him once

ما بيرتاح إلا بالبيت

maa byirtaa7 2illa bilbeet

he only relaxes when he's at home

And conjunction expressions:

ما بيهتمو فيك غير وقت ما بدك تترك

maa byihtammu fiik gheer wa2^et ma biddak titrok

they're only interested when you want to leave

Occasionally *2illa* and *gheer* precede subjects, in which case the verb sometimes defaults to masculine singular:

ما إجا غير سامي

maa 2ija gheer saami

only Sami came

[= no one came except Sami]

ما إجا إلا سامية

maa 2ija 2illa saamya

only Samia came

Note that *gheer* can take pronoun suffixes, while *2illa* has to be followed by an independent pronoun:

ما شفت حدا غيرك

maa shuf^et 7ada gheerak

I only saw you

ما شفت حدا إلا إنت

maa shif^et 7ada 2illa 2inte

I only saw you

These structures are generally fairly synonymous with other more familiar structures with بس *bass* (see unit 84) or (in more elevated language) فقط *faqaT*. But they also have idiomatic uses. First, it is quite common in narrative to use a structure such as the following for dramatic effect:

وما شفتلك غير كلب كبير!

w maa shiftillak gheer kalb ᵉkbiir!

and what did I see but a massive dog!

Second, إلا *2illa* is commonly used in a range of structures meaning "barely":

ما وصلت ع البيت إلا ودق ع الباب

maa waSSalt 3albeet 2illa w da22 3 albaab
I'd barely got home when he knocked on the door

يا دوب خلصت أكل إلا وهي حاطة كمان!

yaa doob khallaS^et 2ak^el 2illa w hiyye 7aaTTa kamaan!
I'd barely finished eating [the first lot] when she put even more [on the table]!

PART 10

Comparatives

Comparisons

In this unit we will be looking at how to express comparisons between two nouns, structures such as "bigger than" and "more intelligent than." At root, the Arabic strategy should be quite straightforward and intuitive for an English speaker: a special form of the adjective is used plus a word for "than," with slight variations depending on the exact nature of the comparison. Because of all these slight variations, this unit features an unusual number of subsections. But at its core the construction is more or less the same.

We will begin with the basic comparison structure before looking at more complicated types of comparative (with adjectives of colour and quality, with nouns, with adverbs, etc.). We will then consider complex comparisons, that is, comparisons involving subordination. Finally, we will see how to express that something is not "more" or "less" than but rather "as X as" something else.

Basic Comparisons

A comparative structure expresses a comparison between two nouns with regard to a particular quality. The most straightforward comparative structure in English uses the "-er" form of the adjective—or, for longer adjectives, a phrase with "more"—plus the word "than": "he is bigger than me," "you're more intelligent than her."

The structures used in Arabic are not all that different. All Arabic comparatives are formed with a comparative adjective on the shape *2af3al* (see unit 17); unlike most adjectives, comparative adjectives are invariable (i.e., do not agree with their noun for gender or number). Some adjectives have a simple comparative equivalent, while others simply add أكتر *2aktar* "more," similar to the English distinction between words that take "-er" and words that take "more." The object of the comparison is introduced with من *min*, which translates English "than":

أسعد أصغر من جودة ← أسعد صغير

2as3ad 2azghar min juude   *2as3ad ˈzghiir*

Asad's younger than Joudeh   Asad is young

هادا أحسن من هداك   ←   هادا منيح

haada 2a7san min hadaak   *haada mnii7*

this one's better than that one   this one's good

ستي أكبر من ستك   ←   ستي كبيرة

sitti 2akbar min sittek   *sitti kbiire*

my grandma's older than yours   my grandma's old

جدك محترم أكتر من جدي   ←   جدي محترم

jiddak mu7taram 2aktar min jiddi   *jiddi mu7taram*

your granddad's more respectable than mine   my granddad's respectable

أسعد مهتم فيك أكتر من جودة   ←   أسعد مهتم فيك

2as3ad mihtamm fiik 2aktar min juude   *2as3ad mihtamm fiik*

Asad cares more about you than Joudeh   Asad cares about you

Note that منيح *mnii7* "good" has an irregular comparative, أحسن *2a7san* or أفضل *2afDal* (just as English "good" has an irregular comparative in "better"). Whether an adjective has an *2af3al* comparative or not is largely arbitrary. Nonparticiples are more likely to have them, as are shorter more common adjectives. But many participles do in fact have *2af3al* equivalents: مناسب *munaaseb* "appropriate, convenient" > أنسب *2ansab* "more appropriate, more convenient"; مشهور *mashhuur* "famous" > أشهر *2ashhar* "more famous." Some adjectives are used with both *2af3al* forms and the *2aktar* construction.

Note the use of *heek* (see unit 14) translating "that" or "this" in comparisons of situations:

شو بدك أحسن من هيك   حظو أتعس من هيك بكتير

shuu biddak 2a7san min heek?   *7aZZo 2at3as min heek b[i]ktiir*

what more could you want?   his luck is much worse than that

[= what could you want that's

better than this?]

Note as well comparisons of time with قبل *2ab[e]l* and الأول *[i]l2awwal* "before":

كل شي أحسن من قبل   صار أصعب من الأول

kill shi 2a7san min 2ab[e]l   *Saar 2aS3ab mn [i]l2awwal*

everything's better than before   these days it's harder than it was

Comparisons with Adjectives of Colour and Quality

Adjectives of colour and quality (see unit 17) can also form *2af3als* straightforwardly. Since their normal masculine singular form itself has the shape *2af3al*, this means that there is no change in form:

هادا أبيض من التاني   ←   هادا أبيض

haada 2abyaD min ⁱttaani   *haada 2abyaD*

this one's whiter than the other one   this one is white

هادا لسا أهبل مني   ←   هادا أهبل

haada lissa 2ahbal minni   *haada 2ahbal*

this guy's even sillier than me   this guy's silly

In the feminine and plural, however, the difference is clear. A normal adjective will agree for gender and number, but a comparative will remain invariable:

هاي أبيض من التانية   ←   هاي بيضا

haay 2abyaD min ⁱttaanye   *haay beeDa*

this one's whiter than the other one   this one is white

هاي لسا أهبل مني   ←   هاي هبلا

haay lissa 2ahbal minni   *haay habla*

this girl's even sillier than me   this girl's silly

هدول أبيض من التاني   ←   هدول بيض

hadool 2abyaD min ⁱttaani   *hadool biiD*

these ones are whiter than the other one   these ones are white

هدول لسا أهبل مني   ←   هدول أهابل

hadool lissa 2ahbal minni   *hadool 2ahaabel*

these guys are even sillier than me   these guys are silly

Comparisons with Nouns

It is also possible to compare the "X-ness" of two nouns where X is *the quality of being the noun itself,* again using an *2af3al* or an *2aktar* structure. The English equivalent is usually "more of a(n) X than":

أنا سوري أكتر منك   ←   أنا سوري

2ana suuri 2aktar minnak   *2ana suuri*

I'm more of a Syrian than you   I'm a Syrian

أنا أحيون منك   ←   أنا حيوان

2ana 2a7aywan minnak   *2ana 7ayawaan*

I'm more of a jerk than you   I'm a jerk

Comparative Adverbs

If an adjective can be used adverbially, its comparative can also be used adverbially:

بحكي أحسن منك ← بحكي منيح

bi7ki 2a7san minnak ← *bi7ki mnii7*

he speaks better than you — he speaks well

بيشتغل أكتر من أخوه ← بيشتغل كتير

byishtighel 2aktar min 2akhuu ← *byishtighel ᶦktiir*

he works more than his brother — he works a lot

As noted in the section on adverbs, many Arabic adverbial expressions actually consist of a preposition and a noun (see unit 20). Nonetheless, some of these expressions can form comparatives using *2af3al*:

بركض أسرع منك ← بركض بسرعة

barkoD 2asra2 minnek ← *barkoD ᶦbsur3a*

I run faster than you — I run quickly

Definite Comparisons

Like other adjectives (see unit 16), a comparative attached to a noun agrees in definiteness (see unit 13):

المشكلة الأكبر هي الغلا

ᶦlmishᶦkle l2akbar hiyye lghala

the bigger problem is the high prices

أنا ما بتحمل الشب الأطول مني

2ana maa bit7ammal ᶦshshabb ᶦl2aTwal minni

I can't deal with guys [who are] taller than me

Also like other adjectives (see unit 16), definite comparatives can stand alone in the meaning "the X-er one":

بدي الأكبر

biddi l2akbar

I want the bigger one

الأغرب من هيك إنو تاني يوم رجع ع البيت!

ᶦl2aghrab min heek 2inno taani yoom rije3 3 albeet!

even weirder, the next day he came home!

> For some speakers, الأحسن *ᶦl2a7san* and الأفضل *ᶦl2afDal* are used to refer to situations: الأفضل تضل بالبيت *ᶦl2afDal ᶦtDall bilbeet* "the best thing is for you to stay at home."

Overall, though, definite comparatives are fairly infrequent in Levantine; they appear most commonly in high-register structures mimicking fuS7a. It is much more common to use a normal adjective:

بدي الكبيرة

biddi lʳkbiire

I want the big(ger) one

أخوي هو الكبير

2akhuuy huwwe lʳkbiir

my brother is the old(est) one

Idiomatic Use: Comparisons Attached to Other Sentences

Comparative adjectives commonly appear tacked onto other sentences, often with a *-l-* pronoun attached (see unit 19). This asserts an opinion about the outcome of the action described by the verb. Again, this is easier to demonstrate with examples:

خليك هون أحسنلك

khalliik hoon 2a7sanlak

stay here, it'll be better that way
[for you]

احكي لغتك أريحلك

2i7ki lughatek 2arya7lek

speak your language, it'll be easier
for you

بدفع تلاتين بوند أريحلي!

badfa3 tlaatiin boond 2arya7li!

I'd rather pay thirty pounds!
[I'll pay thirty pounds, that'd be
less trouble for me!]

كنت سويتو بالبيت أوفرلي!

kunt sawweeto bilbeet 2awfarli!

I could have made it at home and saved
myself some money!
[= it would have been more economical
for me]

Complex Comparisons (Subordination)

In all the examples above the object of the comparison has been a noun or a pronoun. But just as in English, it is possible to make the object a *full sentence*. This is a type of subordination and makes the sentence a complex sentence by our definition (see unit 58). There are two different structures here, distinguished both in English and in Arabic albeit in different ways.

The first structure compares the "quality" of two *actions*: how I *speak* versus how I *understand*, how I *write* versus how you *read*, how much it *hurts* versus how much it *helps*. In both Arabic and English, we use a word for "than" followed by a full sentence. The Arabic word that is used, منما *minma*, is the normal *min* plus the conjunction suffix *-ma* discussed in more detail below (see appendix C):

بحكي أحسن منما بفهم

ba7ki 2a7san minma bafham

I speak better than I understand

بتضر أكتر منما بتنفع

bitDurr 2aktar minma btinfa3

it hurts more than it helps

بكتب أسرع منما بتقرا

biktob 2asra3 minma bti2ra

I write faster than you read

The second structure compares two *situations*: the (current or imaginary) situation as compared with what it *would* be like *if* she misunderstood you, *if* you read it one page at a time, and so on. To express this idea in English we use a gerund ("misunderstanding," "reading," "helping"). In Arabic we use a zero-imperfective clause (see unit 58) introduced by *2inno* "that":

أصعب من إنو تقراها صفحة صفحة

2aS3ab min 2inno ti2raaha Saf7a Saf7a

it's harder than reading it one
page at a time

أحسن من إنو تفهمك غلط

2a7san min 2inno tifhamak ghalaT

it's better than her
misunderstanding you

For many speakers—particularly North Levantine speakers—some very common comparatives (particularly أحسن *2a7san* "better," أفضل *2afDal* "better," أكتر *2aktar* "more") can be followed directly by *-ma* in both constructions, replacing *minma* and *min 2inno*, respectively. In this case the distinction is made only by the zero-imperfective marking on the verb in "situation" comparisons:

أحسن ما تفهمك غلط

2a7san ma tifhamak ghalaT

it's better than her misunderstanding you

بحكي أحسن ما بفهم

bi7ki 2a7san ma bifham

I speak better than I understand

For constructions such as "it's better for you to . . . ," see the section in unit 60 on subordination with adjectives.

Equative ("as X as")

If superlative constructions express that something is "the X-est" and comparative constructions express that something is "X-er than something else," equative constructions express that something is "as X as something else." The most precise equivalent in Arabic is to use قد *2add* "as much as" (see appendix B):

أنا شاطر قدك

2ana shaaTer 2addak

I'm as clever as you

ما في حدا قدك

maa fii 7ada 2addek

there's no one as good as you

إنتي مرحتيش قدي

2inti maru7tiish 2addi

you haven't been as often as me

هدول أغنيا قدكم

hadool 2aghniya 2addkom

these guys are as rich as you

For a few adjectives a structure such as the following is available:

أنا طولي طولو

2ana Tuuli Tuulo

I'm the same height as him

[= my height is his height]

إنت وزنك وزنهم

2inta waznak waz'nhom

you're the same weight as them

[= your weight is their weight]

Often a construction with متل *mit'l* or زي *zayy* "like" is also a (less precise) idiomatic equivalent:

أنا شاطر متلك

2ana shaaTer mitlak

I'm as clever as you

هدول أغنيا زيكن

hadool 2aghniya zayykom

these guys are as rich as you

Another structure, slightly more elevated, uses the preposition بـ *b-* plus an abstract noun corresponding to the adjective. Consider these examples taken from interviews:

بدي ياه ما يكون بحساسيتي

baddi yyaa maa ykuun b7assassiyyti

I don't want him to be as sensitive as me

طريقة الشب مو بصعوبة طريقة المرأة

Tarii2t 'shshabb muu b'S3uubet Tarii2t 'lmar2a

it's not as difficult for guys as for women

Superlative Constructions

In unit 79, we looked at comparisons of various kinds. In this unit, we will look at a related but distinct construction: the superlative, which expresses that something is the "X-est" or "most X" of its kind. This naturally implies a comparison with all other members of the word's class, and Arabic uses the comparative adjective for this sort of structure. But there is no explicit comparison of the kind we saw in the previous unit, and the structure is syntactically quite distinct.

We will start by looking at how we form basic superlative constructions. We will then move on to superlative adverbs, "complex" superlatives (superlatives involving subordination), and superlative constructions with definite nouns.

Basic Superlative Construction

A superlative expresses that a noun is the "most X" of a particular category. In English, it is expressed either with the "-est" form of the adjective or by adding "most": "the biggest cat," "the most respectable bank."

Like comparatives, Arabic superlatives are formed with comparative adjectives on the form *2af3al* (see unit 17). Those adjectives that have simple *2af3al* forms place them before a bare noun, while those adjectives that take أكتر *2aktar* in the comparative place *2aktar* before the noun and the adjective after it:

<table>
<tr><td align="center">أطول شب بالصف</td><td align="center">أحسن إم بالعالم</td></tr>
<tr><td align="center">2aTwal shabb biSSaff</td><td align="center">2a7san 2imm bil3aalam</td></tr>
<tr><td align="center">the tallest guy in the class</td><td align="center">the best mum in the world</td></tr>
<tr><td align="center">أجمل شخص بالكون</td><td align="center">أكبر بنت بالمدرسة</td></tr>
<tr><td align="center">2ajmal shakh^eS bilkawn</td><td align="center">2akbar bin^et bilmadrase</td></tr>
<tr><td align="center">the most beautiful person in the universe</td><td align="center">the oldest girl in the school</td></tr>
</table>

أكتر شخص مهتم

2aktar shakh^eS mihtamm

the most interested person

أكتر بنك محترم

2aktar bank mu7taram

the most respectable bank

For the most part, superlatives cannot stand on their own in the meaning "the X-est one." Instead, Arabic uses واحد *waa7ed/waa7ad* (feminine وحدة *wa7de*) in the normal superlative construction. There is no all-purpose plural, although for people ناس *naas* works:

هي أكبر وحدة بالمدرسة

hiyye 2akbar wa7de bilmadrase

she's the oldest one in the school

هو أطول واحد بالصف

huwwe 2aTwal waa7ed biSSaff

he's the tallest guy in the class

هنه أكتر ناس مهتمين

hinne 2aktar naas mihtammiin

they're the most interested ones

أكتر واحد محترم

2aktar waa7ed mu7taram

the most respectable one

Superlative Adverbs

An adverb can also be superlative: "he writes the most," "he runs the fastest." These constructions are slightly complicated in Arabic. The first option is to use the *2af3al* plus شي *shii* (North Levantine) or إشي *2ishi* (South Levantine), which sits where the adverb would normally sit:

هي بتركض أسرع إشي

hiyye btirkoD 2asra3 2ishi

she runs the fastest

مين شرب أكتر شي؟

miin shireb 2aktar shii?

who drank the most?

أحمد درس أكتر شي

2a7mad daras 2aktar shii

Ahmad studied the most

هدول غنو أحسن إشي

hadool ghannu 2a7san 2ishi

these guys sang the best

الكيميا اجتهدت فيها أكتر شي

ⁱlkiimya jtahad^et fiyya 2aktar shii

I worked hardest at chemistry

ميسي حاولت افهمو أكتر شي

mesi 7aawalt 2ifhamo 2aktar shii

Messi [is the person] I've tried hardest to understand

Some people also accept واحد *waa7ed/waa7ad* and وحدة *wa7de* in this construction, as with ordinal numbers (see unit 83): أنا درست أكتر واحد *2ana dara-s^et 2aktar waa7ed* "I studied the most."

However, there is another very common construction that is less intuitive to an English speaker but is usually the go-to structure for an Arabic speaker. In this construction, the *2af3al* is prefixed to a noun—often a placeholder word such as *waa7ed/waa7ad*—and the rest of the sentence takes the form of a relative clause (see unit 63).

مين أكتر واحد شرب؟

miin 2aktar waa7ad shireb?

who drank the most?

هدوله أحسن ناس غنو

hadoole 2a7san naas ghannu

these guys sang the best

ميسي أكتر واحد حاولت افهمو

mesi 2aktar waa7ed 7aawalt 2ifhamo

Messi is the person I've tried hardest to understand

هي أسرع وحدة بتركض

hiyye 2asra3 wa7de btirkeD

she runs the fastest

أحمد أكتر واحد درس

2a7mad 2aktar waa7ad daras

Ahmad studied the most

الكيميا أكتر مادة اجتهدت فيها

ᵢlkiimya 2aktar maadde jtahadᵉt fiyya

I worked hardest at chemistry

The difference between the two constructions is a matter of nuance. They make the same basic point. The relative clause construction perhaps makes more of an assertion about the topic (see unit 48).

Complex Superlatives with *-ma*

Superlatives can be suffixed with the "conjunction particle" *-ma* (see unit 68) and followed by a subordinate clause (see unit 58). The most common use is with an expression of ability to mean "as X as":

انزلو أسرع ما بتقدرو

2inzilu 2asra3 ma bti2daru

get off as fast as you can

شد أقوى ما عندك

shidd 2a2wa ma 3indak

pull as hard as you can

مشيت أبعد ما قدرت

ᵢmshiit 2ab3ad ma 2dirᵉt

I walked as far as I could

Although common, this construction can only be used in a limited number of contexts. It is always adverbial; it can't be an object (see unit 59). More importantly, despite its translation, it can't be used as a catchall equivalent to the "as X as" structure in English (for ways of expressing this idea, see unit 79).

With a Definite Noun

With a definite noun, the superlative takes on the meaning "the X-est of" and can have a
singular or a plural meaning:

بدي شوفو أحسن الناس!

biddi shuufo 2a7san 'nnaas!

I want him to really shine!

[= I want to see him the best
of the people]

من أحلى الكتب اللي قريتهم

min 2a7la lkutob 'lli 2areethom

this is among the best books I've read

PART 11

Location and Destination

Location and Destination

In this unit we will look briefly at how Arabic expresses relationships of place. A longer (although by no means comprehensive) list of prepositions and their meanings is given in appendix B. Here we will focus on the specific behaviour of various expressions of *location*—static location, that is—and *movement* (toward a destination or away from an origin point).

Location

There are various basic prepositions (see unit 22) used to express location. The word ـب *b-* or *bi-* (فيـ *fii-* when pronouns are attached) expresses "in":

إنتي بالبيت؟

2inti bilbeet?

are you at home?

ملاقي فيو إشي؟

mlaa2i fiyyo 2ishi?

did you find anything in there?

The word على *3ala* or ع *3a-* expresses "on" (in the meaning of "attached to") or "at":

راسمين شي ع الحيط

raasmiin shii 3 al7eeT

they've drawn something on the wall

في حدا ع الباب

fii 7ada 3 albaab

there's someone at the door

The word عند *3ind* or *3and* (North Levantine) expresses "by," "near," or "at X's house" (French *chez*, German *bei*):

أنا عند الإشارة

2ana 3ind ᵎl2ishaara

I'm by the traffic light

إنت عند سمير؟

2inte 3and samiir?

are you at Samir's house?

The word جنب *jamb* and حد *7add* express "next to":

أنا حد بيتك

2ana 7add beetek

I'm by your house

قاعد جنبي

2aa3ed jambi

he's sitting next to me

The word حولين *7awaleen* expresses "around" (note that it loses its -*n* when pronouns are attached):

في سور حولين الجنينة

fii suur 7awaleen l'jneene

there's a fence around the garden

في ناس حوليكي

fii naas 7awaleeki

there are people around you

The word قبال *2baal,* مقابيل *m2abiil* and مقابل *m2aabel* all express "across from," "opposite":

نزلني مقابيل المطعم

nazzilni m2abiil 'lmaT3am

let me out opposite the restaurant

قبالها في شجرة كبيرة

'2baalha fii shajara kbiire

there's a big tree across from it

The words وسط *wisT/wusT* (North Levantine) and بنص *bniSS/bnuSS* express "in the middle of":

أنا وسط العجقة

2ana wisT 'l3aj2a

I'm in the middle of the traffic jam

بنص البيت

bnuSS 'lbeet

in the middle of the house

The word بقلب *b2alb* expresses "inside," "within." Note that it is much more neutral than the literal English equivalent "in the heart of":

كان بقلب الظرف

kaan b2alb 'ZZar³f

it was in the envelope

نحنا بقلب السفارة

ni7na b2alb 'ssafaara

we're inside the embassy

The word بين *been* (often بينات *beenaat,* especially with pronouns) expresses "between" or "among":

بين المحلين في بنك

been 'lma7alleen fii bank

between the shops there's a bank

في بيناتهم ناس غريبة

fii benaathom naas ghariibe

some of them are strange people

[= there are among them ...]

The word تحت *ta7ᵉt* expresses "below," "underneath":

تحت الأرض في نفط

ta7t ⁱl2arD fii nifᵉT

there's oil under the ground

اللي ساكنين تحتو

ⁱlli saakniin ta7to

the ones living underneath him

The word فوق *foo2* expresses "on top of," "above," "up in," and "over":

القنينة فوق الطاولة

ⁱl2anniine foo2 ⁱTTaawle

the bottle's on [above] the table

شفت الشمس فوق الجبل؟

shift ⁱshshams foo2 ⁱjjabal?

did you see the sun over the mountains?

The word قدام *2iddaam/2uddaam* expresses "in front of":

واقف قدام البيت

waa2ef 2uddaam ⁱlbeet

I'm standing in front of the house

واقف قدامو

waa2ef 2uddaamo

I'm standing in front of it

The word ورا *wara* expresses "behind," "beyond," or "on the other side of":

ورا العمارة في جنينة

wara l3imaara fii jneene

behind the building there's a garden

وراها في جنينة

waraaha fii jneene

behind it there's a garden

> Some speakers have قفا *2afa* as an alternative to *wara* and قبال *2baal* as an alternative to *2iddaam/2uddaam* (see appendix B).

The word جوا *juwwa* (often جوات *juwwaat*) expresses "inside":

شفتو جوات البيت

shufto juwwaat ⁱlbeet

I saw him in the house

جواها فش إشي

juwwaaha fish 2ishi

there's nothing inside it

The word برا *barra* (often براتـ *barraat-*) expresses "outside":

أنا برات البيت

2ana barraat ⁱlbeet

I'm not at home

أنا برات المحل

2ana barraat ⁱlma7all

I'm outside the shop

Prepositions That Can Stand Alone

A small subset of these locational words can be used on their own without a pronoun or noun object. Note that there are far more of these in English—where most prepositions have a corresponding stand-alone form—than in Arabic, and not all English expressions have a direct Arabic equivalent.

The word *wara* expresses "behind," "out [the] back," or "in [the] back":

في جنينة ورا

fii jneene wara

there's a garden out [the] back

قعدي ورا

23idi wara

sit in the back [of the car]

The word *2iddaam/2uddaam* expresses "out [the] front," "in front":

في جنينة قدام

fii jneene 2uddaam

there's a garden out [the] front

عدي قدام

3idi 2iddaam

sit in the front [of the car]

The word *barra* expresses "outside":

في جنينة برا

fii jneene barra

there's a garden outside

نقعد برا؟

nu23od barra?

shall we sit outside?

The word *juwwa* expresses "inside":

القعدة حلوة جوا

ⁱl2a3de 7ilwe juwwa

it's a nice atmosphere inside

نقعد جوا؟

nu23od juwwa?

shall we sit inside?

The word *foo2* expresses "on top," "above," "upstairs," or "farther up":

أنا بنام فوق

2ana banaam foo2

I sleep on the top [bunk]

I sleep upstairs

في حدا فوق

fii 7ada foo2

there's someone upstairs

there's someone up there

The word *ta7ᵉt* expresses "on the bottom," "below," "downstairs," or "farther down":

أنا بنام تحت

2ana banaam ta7ᵉt

I sleep on the bottom [bunk]

I sleep downstairs

المحل تحت

ᵢlma7all ta7ᵉt

the shop is down there

the shop is downstairs

Optionally these forms can be preceded by من *min* in the same meaning: من تحت *min ta7ᵉt* "below," for example. But the forms with *min* also have other motion-related meanings, and they are not always acceptable in the locational meaning, particularly in the more specific senses of, for example, "in the front [of a car]," "downstairs," and "upstairs." It is safer to stick with the forms without *min*.

Note as well that these forms can be preceded by لـ *la-* "to." This is primarily an expression of destination but can also express location with a strong implied sense of (imagined or actual) movement:

مكتبي لورا

maktabi lawara

my office is *toward the back*

المحل لقدام شوي

ᵢlma7all la2iddaam ᵢshwayy

the shop is *a bit further on*

Note بالوسط *bilwasaT* and بالنص *binniSS/binnuSS* "in the middle," "in between":

في محل بالوسط

fii ma7all bilwasaT

there's a shop in between

في حد بالنص

fii 7add binnuSS

there's someone in the middle

Also بالوجه *bilwishsh/bilwijᵉh* "on the other side," "opposite":

في محل بالوجه

fii ma7all bilwishsh

there's a shop just over the road

Motion

As a general rule, بـ *b/bi-* (فيـ *fii-* with pronouns) is used to express motion into something:

في إشي فات بعيني

fii 2ishi faat ᵢb3eeni

something's gone in my eye

حطو بالصندوق

7iTTo bissanduu2

put it in the box

The word على *3ala* or ع *3a*, on the other hand, is the default for motion "to" or "at" something:

رحنا على ميلانو

ru7na 3ala milaano

we went to Milan

راجعة ع البيت

raaj3a 3 albeet

I'm going home

The word باتجاه *bittijaah* and صوب *Soob* express "toward," "in the direction of":

روح باتجاه باب توما

ruu7 bittijaah baab tuuma

go toward Bab Touma

[= go in the direction of Bab Touma]

قربنا صوب البيت

2arrabna Soob ⁱlbeet

we went toward the house

With a handful of verbs, عن *3an* expresses "past":

طلاع عنو

Tlaa3 3anno

go past him

مرقت عنو وأنا مش حاسس

mara2ᵉt 3anno w 2ana mish 7aases

I walked past it without noticing

The word من *min* expresses "from" and "away from" and also "through," and "by way of":

جاي من مصر

jaay min maSᵉr

I've just come from Egypt

جينا من المعبر

jiina min ⁱlma3bar

we came via the crossing

Note that *min* combines with many of the expressions of location in both these senses:

"From" Meaning	"Via" Meaning
نزل من فوق الحيط *nizel min foo2 ⁱl7eeT* he came down off the wall [from atop]	نط من فوق الحيط *naTT min foo2 ⁱl7eeT* he jumped over the wall [via the space above]
طلع من تحت الأرض *Tile3 min ta7t ⁱl2arD* he came up out of the ground [from under]	روح من تحت الجسر *ruu7 min ta7t ⁱjjisᵉr* go under the bridge [via the space under]

"From" Meaning	**"Via" Meaning**
مسكني من قدام *misikni min 2iddaam* he grabbed me from the front	مرقنا من قدام البيت *mara2na min 2uddaam ⁱlbeet* we passed by the house [via the space in front of]
ضربني من ورا *Darabni min wara* he hit me from behind	مرقنا من ورا البيت *mara2na min wara ⁱlbeet* we passed the house from behind we went around the back of the house [via the space behind]
نزل من على الحصان *nizel min l ⁱ7Saan* he came down off the horse	

Similarly, many expressions of location can combine with ل *la-* to indicate destination. Note that South Levantine speakers often use these structures without *la-* in the same meaning:

la-	**Without *la-*** **(South Levantine)**
تعال لعندي! *ta3aal la3indi!* come here!	تعال عندي! *ta3aal 3indi!* come here!
طلاع لبرا! *Tlaa3 labarra!* get out!	اطلع برا! *2iTla3 barra!* get out!

These expressions can be used to express location as well.

PART 12

Numbers and Quantity Expressions

Numbers

This unit discusses the Arabic number system. Numbers in written Arabic are infamously difficult to master. The Levantine system too is more complicated than English:

- The numbers one and two are most commonly expressed by a singular or dual noun alone. They can be reinforced by adjective forms, which also double as the stand-alone forms for "one" and "two."
- Three to ten have two sets of forms, one used with nouns and the other (largely) standing alone. They are followed by plural nouns.
- Eleven to nineteen similarly have two sets of forms (with considerable regional variation). They are followed by singular nouns.
- From twenty upward, numbers have only one form and are followed by a singular noun.

In what follows we will look at the different numbers in more detail.

One

"One" is واحد *waa7ad* or *waa7ed* (Syrian). It has a feminine form وحدة *wa7de*. In Arabic the singular is often used to express "one" where English would use a number:

رحت مرة بس   مقالة مقالتين

ru7et marra bass   *maqaale maqaalteen*

I only went one time/once   one or two articles

The number itself is used before mass nouns, such as foodstuffs and currencies. Recall that most foods are mass nouns (see unit 11) and otherwise don't have a normal singular:

عطيني وحدة بيتسا   بكلفك واحد بوند

3aTiini wa7de biitsa   *bikallfak waa7ed boond*

give me one pizza   it'll cost you one pound

waa7ed/waa7ad is also used, as an adjective, to stress "one":

كلمة وحدة محكاش

kilme wa7de ma7akaash

he didn't say *a single word*

سؤال واحد بس

su2aal waa7ad bass

just *one question*

And like all other numbers, it can be used on its own:

وحدة منون كذابة

wa7de minnon kazzaabe

one of them is a liar

كام شخص معك؟ واحد

kamm shakhᵉS ma3ak? waa7ed

how many people are with you? one

For the use of *waa7ed/waa7ad* as a pronoun, see unit 57. For its use with adjectives, see unit 16. For its use with superlatives and ordinal numbers, see units 80 and 83.

Two

The dual form, generated by adding *-een*, is almost always used where we would use the number "two" in English. Dual nouns generally take plural adjectives:

في شخصين مهمين

fii shakhSeen muhimmiin

there are two important people

مقالة مقالتين

maqaale maqaalteen

one or two articles

Like "one," there is a distinct adjective form for "two," تنين *tneen*, with its own feminine form, تنتين *tinteen*. These forms are used to emphasise "two":

بعيوني التنتين

bᶦ3yuuni ttinteen

with my two eyes

في نقطتين تنتين

fii nuqTiteen tinteen

there are two points

> Note that North Levantine speakers often treat gender agreement in "two" as optional, using تنين *tneen* even for feminine nouns.

They are also used before nouns, similar to larger numbers. This is most common with mass nouns (foods and so on):

تنين شاي

tneen shaay

two teas

تنتين بيتسا

tinteen biitsa

two pizzas

And, of course, they can always be used on their own:

تنتين

tinteen

there's two of us

إنتو كام شخص؟

2intu kamm shakhᵉS?

how many of you are there?

Three to Nineteen

The numbers from three to nineteen have two sets of distinct forms:

- The "quantifying" set is used to quantify nouns: خمستعشر سوري *khamⁱsTa3shar suuri* "fifteen Syrians," تلت أشخاص *tlett 2ashkhaaS* "three people," عشر نسوان *3ashar niswaan* "ten women."
- The "independent" set is used when numbers stand alone: هن تلاتة *hinne ⁱtlaate* "there are three of them," رقم عشرة *raqam 3ashara* "number ten," واحد تنين تلاتة *waa7ad tneen tlaate* "one, two, three."

The independent form is also used, as an exception to this general rule, in the following cases:

- With mass nouns (see unit 11): تلاتة بيرة *tlaate biira* "three beers," خمستعش مشكل *khamⁱsTa3sh mshakkal* "fifteen mixed meats."
- As an extension, with currencies and units of measurement, especially foreign ones or ones that don't have obvious plurals: سبعة بوند *sab3a boond* "seven pounds [sterling]," خمسة لتر *khamse litᵉr* "five litres," سبعتعش جنيه *sabⁱ3Ta3sh ginee* "seventeen [Egyptian] pounds."
- With the plurals of some demonyms and ethnicities: تلاتة عرب *tlaate 3arab* "three Arabs," اربعة لبنانية *2arba3a libnaaniyye* "four Lebanese people."
- As an adjective in this less common counting structure: الرجال التلاتة *lⁱrjaal lⁱtlaate* "the three men."

Three to Ten

Forms for the numbers three to ten are given in the table below:

Independent		Quantifying		
تلاتة	تلاتة	تلت	تلت	3
tlaate	*talaate*	*tlett*	*talatt*	
(North)	(South)	(North)	(South)	

Independent		Quantifying		
أربعة 2arba3a		أربع 2arba3		4
خمسة khamse		خمس khams		5
ستة sitte		ست sitt		6
سبعة sab3a		سبع sabᵉ3		7
تماني tmaani (North)	تمانية tamanye (South)	تمن tmin (North)	تمن taman (South)	8
تسعة tis3a		تسع tisᵉ3		9
عشرة 3ashara		عشر 3ashar		10

The quantifying forms are combined with a plural noun:

أربع بيوت
2arba3 ⁱbyuut
four houses

تلت أشخاص
tlett 2ashkhaaS
three people

Note that for some speakers, these numbers cause a *ti-* to be prefixed to some plural forms. This happens for almost all speakers with the following common words:

ربع
rubᵒ3
quarters

تلت ترباع
tlett tirbaa3
three-quarters

آلاف
2aalaaf
thousands

أربع تالاف
2arba3 taalaaf
four thousand

شهور
shhuur
months

عشر تشهر
3ashar tishhor
ten months

ايام
2iyyaam
days

خمس تيام
khamᵉs tiyyaam
five days

For some speakers, this phenomenon is more widespread, potentially applying to any word beginning with a consonant cluster or an *2i-*. You may encounter forms such as خمس تلتورة *kham͡s ti-ltuura* "five litres" and عشر ترغفة *3ashar tu-rᵘghfe* "ten loaves."

Eleven to Nineteen

Like the numerals up to ten, eleven to nineteen have distinct independent and quantifying forms, although this time the quantifying forms are longer and distinguished by the addition of *-ar*:

NORTH LEVANTINE		SOUTH LEVANTINE		
Independent	**Quantifying**	**Independent**	**Quantifying**	
احدعش *7Da3sh*	احدعشر *7Da3shar*	احدعش *7Da3sh*	احدعشر *7Da3shar*	11
تنعش *Tna3sh*	تنعشر *Tna3shar*	تنعش *Tna3sh*	تنعشر *Tna3shar*	12
تلتعش *tlaTTa3sh*	تلتعشر *tlaTTa3shar*	تلتعش *tlaTTa3sh*	تلتعشر *tlaTTa3shar*	13
أربعتعش *2arba3Ta3sh*	أربعتعشر *2arba3Ta3shar*	أربعتعش *2arba3Ta3sh*	أربعتعشر *2arba3Ta3shar*	14
خمستعش *khamⁱsTa3sh*	خمستعشر *khamⁱsTa3shar*	خمستعش *khamⁱsTa3sh*	خمستعشر *khamⁱsTa3shar*	15
شتعش *siTTa3sh*	شتعشر *siTTa3shar*	شتعش *siTTa3sh*	ستعشر *siTTa3shar*	16
سبعتعش *sabⁱ3Ta3sh*	سبعتعشر *sabⁱ3Ta3shar*	سبعتعش *sabᵃ3Ta3sh*	سبعتعشر *sabᵃ3Ta3shar*	17
تمنتعش *tminTa3sh*	تمنتعشر *tminTa3shar*	تمنتعش *tamanTa3sh*	تمنتعشر *tamanTa3shar*	18
تسعتعش *tisⁱ3Ta3sh*	تسعتعشر *tisⁱ3Ta3shar*	تسعتعش *tisⁱ3Ta3sh*	تسعتعشر *tisⁱ3Ta3shar*	19

For some North Levantine speakers, the 3 in تعش is often dropped, and the structure is pronounced *-Taash*. Similarly, northern speakers may treat the quantifying forms as optional and use the independent forms everywhere.

These forms are always followed by singular nouns:

خمستعشر رغيف

khamⁱsTa3shar ⁱrghiif

fifteen loaves

سبعتعشر رجال

saba3Ta3shar rijjaal

seventeen men

Twenty to Ninety-nine

The round numbers twenty to ninety are as follows:

North Levantine	South Levantine	
عشرين *3ishriin*		20
تلاتين *tlaatiin*	تلتين *talatiin*	30
أربعين *2arb3iin*		40
خمسين *khamsiin*		50
ستين *sittiin*		60
سبعين *sab3iin*		70
تمانين *tmaaniin*	تمنين *tamaniin*	80
تسعين *tis3iin*		90

Units are prefixed to tens, giving forms with a literal structure like the archaic English "four-and-twenty." The simplest system involves no changes to either set of numbers. Note that there are no distinct gender or counting forms here:

واحد وعشرين *waa7ed w 3ishriin*	21	واحد و *waa7ed/waa7ad w*	X1
تنين وخمسين *tneen w khamsiin*	52	تنين و *tneen w*	X2
تلاتة وتلاتين *tlaate w tlaatiin*	33	تلاتة و *tlaate w*	X3
أربعة وستين *2arba3a w sittiin*	64	أربعة و *2arba3a w*	X4
خمسة وتسعين *khamse w tis3iin*	95	خمسة و *khamse w*	X5
ستة وأربعين *sitte w 2arba3iin*	46	ستة و *sitte w*	X6
سبعة وتمانين *sab3a w tmaaniin*	87	سبعة و *sab3a w*	X7
تماني وتسعين *tmaani w tis3iin*	98	تماني و *tmaani w* / تمانية و *tamanye w*	X8
تسعة وسبعين *tis3a w sab3iin*	79	تسعة و *tis3a w*	X9

These forms are all followed by singulars:

تسعة وسبعين رغيف
tis3a w sab3iin ʾrghiif
seventy-nine loaves

خمسة وخمسين رجال
khamse w khamsiin rijjaal
fifty-five men

Covering all the possible regional variations here would be difficult, but some common variations include pronouncing all ة as *-a* in compound numbers even when they are normally pronounced as *-e* (تلاتة وتلاتين *tlaata w tlaatiin* "thirty-three"), sometimes with lengthening (*tlaataa w tlaatiin*), and various other small contractions (واحد وعشرين *wa7d w 3ishriin* "twenty-one").

One Hundred and Above

Numbers one hundred and above are followed by singulars. They are formed straightforwardly.

The word for "one hundred" is مية *miyye,* which becomes ميت *miit* before nouns and has no distinct plural form when preceded by other numbers:

تلت ميت شخص

tlett miit shakhᵉS

three hundred people

ميت شخص

miit shakhᵉS

one hundred people

The word for "one thousand" is ألف *2alf.* It has a plural, آلاف *2aalaaf,* which generally becomes *taalaaf* when preceded by numbers from three to ten:

تلت تالاف كرسي

tlett taalaaf kursi

three thousand chairs

ألف كرسي

2alf kursi

one thousand chairs

Note the expression "thousands of," however, which is followed by a definite plural:

آلاف الدولارات

2aalaaf ᶦddolaaraat

thousands of dollars

آلاف الأشخاص

2aalaaf ᶦl2ashkhaaS

thousands of people

"Million" and "billion" are مليون *malyoon* and مليار *milyaar,* respectively. These tend to be combined with the independent forms of smaller numbers:

أربعة مليون مكتب

2arba3a malyoon maktab

four million offices

مليون مكتب

malyoon maktab

a million offices

"Millions of" and "billions of," however, do have distinct forms and, like *2aalaaf,* are followed by definite plurals:

ملايين الدولارات

malayiin ᶦddolaaraat

millions of dollars

مليارات الدولارات

milyaaraat ᶦddolaaraat

billions of dollars

All four of these words have dual forms:

ألفين طاولة

2alfeen Taawle

two thousand tables

ميتين سوري

miiteen suuri

two hundred Syrians

More complex numbers are formed straightforwardly using و *w* "and":

تلت مليون وخمسين ألف وتلت مية وستة وستين

tlett milyoon w khamsiin 2alf w tlett miyye w sitte w sittiin
three million fifty thousand three hundred sixty-six

مية وخمسة وخمسين

miyye w khamse w khamsiin
one hundred fifty-five

Ordinal Numbers and Fractions

In this unit we will look at ordinal numbers and fractions.

Ordinal Numbers

The ordinal numbers are those used to describe where something sits in an order: first, second, third, and so on. These are formed predictably using the pattern *faa3el* except for "first," which, as in English, is irregular, and "sixth," which is formed from a different root from the counting number:

Feminine	Masculine	
أولى *2uula* OR *2awle*	أول *2awwal*	first
تانية *taanye*	تاني *taani*	second
تالتة *taalte*	تالت *taalet*	third
رابعة *raab3a*	رابع *raabe3*	fourth
خامسة *khaamse*	خامس *khaames*	fifth
سادسة *saadse*	سادس *saades*	sixth
سابعة *saab3a*	سابع *saabe3*	seventh

Feminine	Masculine	
تامنة *taamne*	تامن *taamen*	eighth
تاسعة *taas3a*	تاسع *taase3*	ninth
عاشرة *3aashra*	عاشر *3aasher*	tenth

Note also how "last" is formed:

آخر

2aakher

last

These forms are most commonly used in a structure resembling the superlative (see unit 80). In this case, only the masculine is used and is followed by an indefinite noun:

<table>
<tr><td>أول واحد</td><td>تاني مرة</td></tr>
<tr><td>2awwal waa7ad</td><td>taani marra</td></tr>
<tr><td>the first one</td><td>the second time</td></tr>
</table>

Occasionally, however, they are used as adjectives, in which case they agree in gender and follow a definite noun:

<table>
<tr><td>المرة التاسعة</td><td>الشخص الأول</td></tr>
<tr><td>ˈlmarra ttaas3a</td><td>ˈshshakhS ˈl2awwal</td></tr>
<tr><td>the second time</td><td>the first person</td></tr>
</table>

For numbers larger than ten, the strategy is simply to use the normal independent form of the number as an adjective, complete with definite article:

<table>
<tr><td>المرة المية وخمسة وخمسين</td><td>الغرفة الاحداش</td></tr>
<tr><td>ˈlmarra lmiyye w khamse wkhamsiin</td><td>ˈlghurfe lˈ7Da3sh</td></tr>
<tr><td>the 155th time</td><td>the eleventh room</td></tr>
</table>

Fractions

Fractions up to ten are formed on *fi3l* (North Levantine) or *fu3l* (South Levantine). The resulting forms have normal plurals formed on *2af3aal*:

Plural	Singular	
أنصاص *(2a)nSaaS*	نص *niSS/nuSS*	half
أتلات *2atlaat*	تلت *tilt/tult*	third
أرباع *(2a)rbaa3*	ربع *rib^e3/rub^o3*	quarter
أخماس *2akhmaas*	خمس *khims/khums*	fifth
أسداس *2asdaas*	سدس *sids/suds*	sixth
أسباع *2asbaa3*	سبع *sib^e3/sub^o3*	seventh
أتمان *2atmaan*	تمن *tim^en/tum^en*	eighth
أتساع *2atsaa3*	تسع *tis^e3/tus^o3*	ninth
أعشار *2a3shaar*	عشر *3ish^er/3ush^or*	tenth

Smaller fractions are expressed using على *3ala* "on" (i.e., "divided between"):

واحد على خمسين	تنين على احداش
waa7ad 3ala khamsiin	*tneen 3ala 7Daash*
one-fiftieth	two-elevenths

Fractions are combined with indefinite nouns just like other kinds of quantity expression:

نص رغيف	ربع ساعة
nuSS ⁱrghiif	*rib^e3 saa3a*
half a loaf	quarter of an hour

Quantifiers and Other Quantity Expressions

A quantifier is a word that combines with a noun to provide more information about how much of that noun there is:

<u>a lot of</u> water   <u>a few</u> people
<u>many</u> writers   <u>a couple of</u> books

In this unit we will look at some quantifier expressions as well as a few related expressions that seem appropriate to discuss here, since their behaviour is similar.

ba3ᵉD "Some"

This word is generally followed by a definite article. It is slightly elevated and is not common in everyday speech:

بعض الناس   بعض اللي إجو

ba3D ᶦnnaas   *ba3D ᶦlli 2iju*

some people   some of the ones who came

Exceptionally, in the pointed expression مش متل بعض ناس *mish mitᵉl ba3ᵉD naas* "not like *some* people," it is followed by an indefinite noun.

> Some North Levantine speakers use هونيك *huniik* in this expression: مش متل هونيك ناس *mish mitᵉl huniik naas.*

bass "Just," "Only"

Bass can either precede or follow a noun:

بدي بس هدولا   بدي هدولا بس

biddi bass hadoola   *biddi hadoola bass*

I only want these ones   I only want these ones

hal2add, hal2adde "So Much," "So Many"

The words هالقد *hal2add* and هالقدة *hal2adde* (South Levantine) literally mean "this amount" and express "this much," "so much," and "as much." They can precede or follow indefinite nouns:

هالقد ناس   ناس هالقد

hal2add naas   *naas hal2add*

so many people   so many people

هالقدة مصاري   مصاري هالقده

hal2adde maSaari   *maSaari hal2adde*

so much money   so much money

Note that *hal2add* and *hal2adde* can also combine with adjectives and verbs:

درستي هالقدة   هالقد منيح

darasti hal2adde   *hal2add ᵢmnii7*

you studied so much   so good

gheer "Another"

This precedes indefinite nouns:

غير كتب   غير مكاتب

gheer kutob   *gheer makaateb*

other books   other offices

غير ناس   غير مرة

gheer naas   *gheer marra*

other people   another time

For *gheer* meaning "not," see unit 78. Note that *gheer* also sometimes means "other," "different" on its own: الحياة هون غير *ᵢl7ayaa hoon gheer* "life here is different."

kill/kull "the Whole," "All," "Every"

Combined with an indefinite singular noun, كل *kill/kull* means "every" or "each":

كل شي	كل مرة	من كل مدينة	بكل علبة
kill shii	*kull marra*	*min kull madiine*	*'bkill 3ilbe*
everything	every time	from every city	in every box

Combined with a definite plural noun or a mass noun (see unit 11), *kill/kull* means "all [the]." Of course, the definite can have a generic meaning (see unit 13):

كل النسوان	كل التفاح
kill 'nniswaan	*kull 'ttuffaa7*
all [the] women	all [the] apples

kill/kull can of course also be combined with a pronoun in the meaning "all of." For North Levantine speakers *kill/kull* often takes the form كلياتـ *killiyyaat-* in this case:

North Levantine Forms		**South Levantine Forms**	
كلياتها	كلياتهن	كلها	كلهم
killiyyaatha	*killiyyaathon*	*kullha*	*kullhom*
all of it	all of them	all of it	all of them

A suffixed form can also follow a definite noun. This can be used for emphasis—*all* the lessons—but is often simply another alternative to the basic *kill/kull* plus definite:

النسوان كلياتهن	التفاح كلو
'nniswaan killiyyaathon	*'ttuffaa7 kullo*
all the women	all the apples

الناس كلها	الدروس كلها
'nnaas killha	*'ddruus kullha*
all the people	all the lessons

With a singular definite count noun (see unit 11), *kill/kull* means "the whole":

كل الحارة	القنينة كلها
kull 'l7aara	*'l2anniine killha*
the whole neighbourhood	the whole bottle

Note as well that *kill/kull* usually take the object suffix ـني *-ni* (see unit 18) instead of *-i*:

صرت كلني عرق!

Sir^et killni 3ara2!

I'm drenched in sweat now!

Note that الكل *ⁱlkill/ⁱlkull* and كلو *killo/kullo* can also mean "everyone."

kamaan "More"

The word كمان *kamaan* means "more," "another," "an additional" in contexts such as the following:

كمان مي   كمان سؤال

kamaan mayy   *kamaan su2aal*

some more water   another question

The word كمان *kamaan* can also be used on its own:

صبلي كمان   كمان شوي

Sibbilli kamaan   *kamaan ⁱshwayy*

pour me some more   just a bit more

kamm, 2akamm(en) "a Few," *kaza* "Several"

The words كم *kamm,* أكم *2akamm,* and أكمن *2akammen* (the latter forms are South Levantine) mean "a few," while كذا *kaza* means "several." All of these structures are followed by a singular indefinite noun:

كام واحد   كذا سؤال   أكمن مشكلة

kamm waa7ad   *kaza su2aal*   *2akammen mushkile*

a few people   several questions   a few problems

Although the noun itself is singular, the whole expression is usually (although not invariably) treated as plural for the purposes of agreement (see unit 50):

كام واحد ظراف   كذا سؤال صغار

kamm waa7ad ⁱZraaf   *kaza su2aal ⁱzghaar*

a few nice people   a few small questions

ktiir "a Lot of," *2aliil* "Few"

The words *ktiir* "a lot of" and *2aliil* "few" are very common expressions. They can precede or
follow the noun. If preceding the noun, they are invariable:

قليل ناس

2aliil naas

not many people

كتير ناس

ktiir naas

lots of people

ناس قلال

naas 2laal

not many people

ناس كتار

naas ⁱktaar

lots of people

> For many speakers, ملیان *milyaan/malyaan* or ملان *malaan* can also be used
> before nouns, meaning "loads": ملان ناس *malaan naas* "loads of people."

The words *ktiir* and *2aliil* have the unusual property of being able to be fronted (see unit 66)
for emphasis while leaving their noun behind:

قليل في ناس

2aliil fii naas

there aren't many people

كتير في ناس

ktiir fii naas

there are lots of people

nafs, zaat "the Same"

The words نفس *nafs* and ذات *zaat* (mostly Lebanese) precede definite nouns. They mean
either "the same" or "the exact":

نفس المدينة

nafs ⁱlmadiine

the same city

ذات الشي

zaat ⁱshshi

the same thing

نفس الشي

nafs ⁱshshi

the same thing

نفس الشخص

nafs ⁱshshakhᵉS

the same person

nafs and *zaat* can of course be combined with pronouns, in which case the meaning is usually
"the same (one) as":

هاي نفسها

haay nafsha

this is the same one

نفسو ذاتو

nafso zaato

the same exact one

A definite noun followed by *nafs* or *zaat* with a pronoun has the same meaning as *nafs ⁱl-*:

الشي ذاتو   المدينة نفسها

<table>
<tr><td align="center">ⁱlmadiine nafsha</td><td align="center">ⁱshshi zaato</td></tr>
<tr><td align="center">the same city</td><td align="center">the same thing</td></tr>
</table>

الشخص نفسو   الشي نفسو

<table>
<tr><td align="center">ⁱshshi nafso</td><td align="center">ⁱshshakhᵉS nafso</td></tr>
<tr><td align="center">the same thing</td><td align="center">the same person</td></tr>
</table>

For *nafs* and *zaat* meaning "itself," "exactly," see unit 66. For their occasional use as a reflexive pronoun, see unit 55.

shwayyet "a Few," "a Bit of," "a Little," "Some"

The word شوية *shwayye* forms an *2iDaafe* with the following word (see unit 15), which by default will be indefinite and, if it is a count noun (see unit 11), plural:

شوية مي   شوية أخطاء

<table>
<tr><td align="center">shwayyet mayy</td><td align="center">shwayyet 2akhTaa2</td></tr>
<tr><td align="center">a bit of water</td><td align="center">a few mistakes</td></tr>
</table>

Note, however, that the whole expression can be made definite by making the noun definite:

شوية المي   شوية الأخطاء

<table>
<tr><td align="center">shwayyet ⁱlmayy</td><td align="center">shwayyt ⁱl2akhTaa2</td></tr>
<tr><td align="center">the little water</td><td align="center">the few mistakes</td></tr>
<tr><td align="center">[that I have got]</td><td align="center">[that you made]</td></tr>
</table>

zyaade "Extra," *zyaade 3an ⁱlluzuum* "Too Much"

This structure usually follows the noun:

عننا مصاري زيادة   معي أكل زيادة عن اللزوم

<table>
<tr><td align="center">3anna maSaari zyaade</td><td align="center">ma3i 2akᵉl zyaade 3an ⁱlluzuum</td></tr>
<tr><td align="center">we've got money left over</td><td align="center">I've got more food than I need</td></tr>
</table>

wala "Not a Single"

The word ولا *wala* means "no" or, with emphasis, "not a single." It is followed by a singular indefinite noun:

ولا إشي	ولا فرانك
wala 2ishi	*wala frank*
nothing	not a single franc

This word is discussed in more detail at unit 77.

"Both of," "All Three of"

There are two ways of expressing "both of," "all three of," "all four of," and so on. The most straightforward way is to use the independent number with a definite article:

التلاتة	التنين
ʾttlaate	lʾtneen
all three of them	both of them

The second option, which is exclusively North Levantine, is to attach a pronoun to the number. Note that *tneen* has an irregular form with *-aat*:

تلاتتهن	تنيناتهن
tlaatithon	*tneenaathon*
all three of them	both of them

In context, "both X-es" is sometimes expressed with a dual:

بس بالحالتين . . .

bass bil7aalteen . . .

but in both cases . . .

Container Expressions ("a Cup of," "a Bottle of")

The examples above are all specifically quantifier words. But Arabic also has a way of expressing things such as "four tons of wheat" and "a cup of water" with more normal nouns. Normally these structures use a sort of *2iDaafe* (see unit 15), with the first noun undergoing all the changes we would expect (see unit 4).Some examples with containers:

كمشة تراب

kamshet ⁱtraab

a handful of dirt

قنينة كولا

2anniinet koola

a bottle of cola

كيس زبالة

kiis ⁱzbaale

a bag of rubbish

كاسة مي

kaaset mayy

a cup of water

Some examples with units of measurement:

ألف طن شمينتو

2alf Tan shminto

a thousand tons of cement

سنة زمان

sinet zamaan

a year's time

[= a year of time]

كيلوين دهب

kiloween dahab

two kilos of gold

كيلو عدس

kiilo 3adas

a kilogram of lentils

To make these forms definite, we make the main noun definite, just as with other *2iDaafes*:

سنة الزمان

sint ⁱzzamaan

the year['s time]

كيلو العدس

kiilo l3adas

the kilo of lentils

كمشة التراب

kamshet lⁱtraab

the handful of dirt

كاسة المي

kaaset ⁱlmayy

the cup of water

For their behaviour with demonstrative "this," see unit 14.

Appendices

APPENDIX A: VERB TABLES

In this appendix I provide full verb tables, in both dialects, for all the (major) verb types that occur in Levantine. You do not need to memorise all fifty-one tables. The rules that are applied in producing these forms are set out (taking far less space) in units 25–30. These tables are intended to provide a convenient reference, particularly in more complex cases.

For a summary of the different types of roots and stems, see unit 5.

Given the variation that exists within the Levantine area, it will come as no surprise that these tables are not intended to be comprehensive or universal. The example verbs given have been chosen because they are in relatively wide use, but this is not to say that they are used—or used with the exact conjugation given here—in every region. Many Lebanese speakers, for example, have no perfectives in *fa3a*, replacing them with *fi3i* (حكي *7iki* for حكى *7aka* "spoke," طفي *Tifi* for طفى *Tafa* "turned off," etc.). This means that the existence of a paradigm for طفى *Tafa* below—to take one example—should not be taken to imply that everyone uses this form specifically. I have included it because all those speakers who do have perfectives on the shape *fa3a* will conjugate those perfectives as *Tafa* is conjugated here.

It is also worth noting again that there are many variants on these paradigms, explored in the main body of the book. Some South Levantine speakers say *byi-*, not *bi-*, just like North Levantine speakers. Some speakers have *bn-* instead of *mn-*. And *maSdar*s and passive participles vary dramatically. Including all these variations in the tables would be impossible, so I've stuck to what should be relatively representative forms. As always, imitate what you hear around you!

katab "Write" (*faʒal, -fʒol*, Sound)

NORTH LEVANTINE								
Noun of Instance		**maSdar**		**Passive Participle**		**Active Participle**		
N/A		*ktaabe* كتابة		*maktuub* مكتوب		*kaateb* كاتب		
Imperative		**Perfective**		**b-Imperfective**		**Zero-Imperfective**		
		katabᵉt	كتبت	*biktob*	بكتب	*2iktob*	اكتب	I
ktoob	كتوب	*katabᵉt*	كتبت	*btiktob*	بتكتب	*tiktob*	تكتب	you [M]
ktibi	كتبي	*katabti*	كتبتي	*btikⁱtbi*	بتكتبي	*tikⁱtbi*	تكتبي	you [F]
		katab	كتب	*byiktob*	بيكتب	*yiktob*	يكتب	he
		katbet	كتبت	*btiktob*	بتكتب	*tiktob*	تكتب	she
		katabna	كتبنا	*mniktob*	منكتب	*niktob*	نكتب	we
ktibu	كتبو	*katabtu*	كتبتو	*btikⁱtbu*	بتكتبو	*tikⁱtbu*	تكتبو	you [P]
		katabu	كتبو	*byikⁱtbu*	بيكتبو	*yikⁱtbu*	يكتبو	they

SOUTH LEVANTINE								
Noun of Instance		**maSdar**		**Passive Participle**		**Active Participle**		
N/A		*ktaabe* كتابة		*maktuub* مكتوب		*kaateb* كاتب		
Imperative		**Perfective**		**b-Imperfective**		**Zero-Imperfective**		
		katabᵉt	كتبت	*baktob*	بكتب	*2aktob*	أكتب	I
2uktob	اكتب	*katabᵉt*	كتبت	*btuktob*	بتكتب	*tuktob*	تكتب	you [M]
2ukᵘtbi	اكتبي	*katabti*	كتبتي	*btukᵘtbi*	بتكتبي	*tukᵘtbi*	تكتبي	you [F]
		katab	كتب	*buktob*	بكتب	*yuktob*	يكتب	he
		katbat	كتبت	*btuktob*	بتكتب	*tuktob*	تكتب	she
		katabna	كتبنا	*mnuktob*	منكتب	*nuktob*	نكتب	we
2ukᵘtbu	اكتبو	*katabtu*	كتبتو	*btukᵘtbu*	بتكتبو	*tukᵘtbu*	تكتبو	you [P]
		katabu	كتبو	*bukᵘtbu*	بيكتبو	*yukᵘtbu*	يكتبو	they

misek "Take" (*fi3el, -f3el*, Sound)

	NORTH LEVANTINE							
Noun of Instance		**maSdar**		**Passive Participle**		**Active Participle**		
maske مسكة		*masek* مسك		*mamsuuk* ممسوك		*maasek* ماسك		
Imperative		**Perfective**		***b-* Imperfective**		**Zero-Imperfective**		
		msik^et	مسكت	*bimsek*	بمسك	*2imsek*	امسك	I
mseek	مسيك	*msik^et*	مسكت	*btimsek*	بتمسك	*timsek*	تمسك	you [M]
msiki	مسكي	*msikti*	مسكتي	*btim'ski*	بتمسكي	*tim'ski*	تمسكي	you [F]
		misek	مسك	*byimsek*	بيمسك	*yimsek*	يمسك	he
		misket	مسكت	*btimsek*	بتمسك	*timsek*	تمسك	she
		msikna	مسكنا	*mnimsek*	منمسك	*nimsek*	نمسك	we
msiku	مسكو	*msiktu*	مسكتو	*btim'sku*	بتمسكو	*tim'sku*	تمسكو	you [P]
		misku	مسكو	*byim'sku*	بيمسكو	*yim'sku*	يمسكو	they

	SOUTH LEVANTINE							
Noun of Instance		**maSdar**		**Passive Participle**		**Active Participle**		
maske مسكة		*masek* مسك		*mamsuuk* ممسوك		*maasek* ماسك		
Imperative		**Perfective**		***b-* Imperfective**		**Zero-Imperfective**		
		msik^et	مسكت	*bamsek*	بمسك	*2amsek*	أمسك	I
2imsek	امسك	*msik^et*	مسكت	*btimsek*	بتمسك	*timsek*	تمسك	you [M]
2imiski	امسكي	*msikti*	مسكتي	*btim'ski*	بتمسكي	*tim'ski*	تمسكي	you [F]
		misek	مسك	*bimsek*	بمسك	*yimsek*	يمسك	he
		miskat	مسكت	*btimsek*	بتمسك	*timsek*	تمسك	she
		msikna	مسكنا	*mnimsek*	منمسك	*nimsek*	نمسك	we
2imisku	امسكو	*msiktu*	مسكتو	*btim'sku*	بتمسكو	*tim'sku*	تمسكو	you [P]
		misku	مسكو	*bim'sku*	بمسكو	*yim'sku*	يمسكو	they

tiʒeb "Get Tired" (*fiʒel, -fʒal*, Sound)

NORTH LEVANTINE							
Noun of Instance		**maSdar**		**Passive Participle**		**Active Participle**	
N/A		*ta3ab* تعب		N/A		*ta3baan* تعبان	
Imperative		**Perfective**		***b-* Imperfective**		**Zero- Imperfective**	
		t3ibᵉt	تعبت	*bit3ab*	بتعب	*2it3ab*	اتعب	I
t3aab	تعاب	*t3ibᵉt*	تعبت	*btit3ab*	بتتعب	*tit3ab*	تتعب	you [M]
t3abi	تعبي	*t3ibti*	تعبتي	*btit3abi*	بتتعبي	*tit3abi*	تتعبي	you [F]
		ti3eb	تعب	*byit3ab*	بيتعب	*yit3ab*	يتعب	he
		ti3bet	تعبت	*btit3ab*	بتتعب	*tit3ab*	تتعب	she
		t3ibna	تعبنا	*mnit3ab*	منتعب	*nit3ab*	نتعب	we
t3abu	تعبو	*t3ibtu*	تعبتو	*btit3abu*	بتتعبو	*tit3abu*	تتعبو	you [P]
		ti3bu	تعبو	*byit3abu*	بيتعبو	*yit3abu*	يتعبو	they

SOUTH LEVANTINE							
Noun of Instance		**maSdar**		**Passive Participle**		**Active Participle**	
N/A		*ta3ab* تعب		N/A		*ta3baan* تعبان	
Imperative		**Perfective**		***b-* Imperfective**		**Zero- Imperfective**	
		t3ibᵉt	تعبت	*bat3ab*	بتعب	*2at3ab*	أتعب	I
2it3ab	اتعب	*t3ibᵉt*	تعبت	*btit3ab*	بتتعب	*tit3ab*	تتعب	you [M]
2it3abi	اتعبي	*t3ibti*	تعبتي	*btit3abi*	بتتعبي	*tit3abi*	تتعبي	you [F]
		ti3eb	تعب	*bit3ab*	بتعب	*yit3ab*	يتعب	he
		ti3bat	تعبت	*btit3ab*	بتتعب	*tit3ab*	تتعب	she
		t3ibna	تعبنا	*mnit3ab*	منتعب	*nit3ab*	نتعب	we
2it3abu	اتعبو	*t3ibtu*	تعبتو	*btit3abu*	بتتعبو	*tit3abu*	تتعبو	you [P]
		ti3bu	تعبو	*bit3abu*	بتعبو	*yit3abu*	يتعبو	they

wiSel "Arrive" (*wiʒel, -wʒal*, Weak-Initial)

NORTH LEVANTINE								
Noun of Instance		**maSdar**		**Passive Participle**		**Active Participle**		
waSle وصلة		*wSuul* وصول		N/A		*waaSel* واصل		
Imperative		**Perfective**		**b-Imperfective**		**Zero-Imperfective**		
		wSilᵉt	وصلت	*buuSal*	بوصل	*2uuSal*	أوصل	I
wSaal	وصال	*wSilᵉt*	وصلت	*btuuSal*	بتوصل	*tuuSal*	توصل	you [M]
wSali	وصلي	*wSilti*	وصلتي	*btuuSali*	بتوصلي	*tuuSali*	توصلي	you [F]
		wiSel	وصل	*byuuSal*	بيوصل	*yuuSal*	يوصل	he
		wiSlet	وصلت	*btuuSal*	بتوصل	*tuuSal*	توصل	she
		wSilna	وصلنا	*mnuuSal*	منوصل	*nuuSal*	نوصل	we
wSalu	وصلو	*wSiltu*	وصلتو	*btuuSalu*	بتوصلو	*tuuSalu*	توصلو	you [P]
		wiSlu	وصلو	*byuuSalu*	بيوصلو	*yuuSalu*	يوصلو	they

> Note that for some speakers, an alternative imperfective form is available for some verbs in which the initial *w* drops: بتصل *bti-Sal*. See unit 26.

SOUTH LEVANTINE								
Noun of Instance		**maSdar**		**Passive Participle**		**Active Participle**		
waSle وصلة		*wSuul* وصول		N/A		*waaSel* واصل		
Imperative		**Perfective**		**b-Imperfective**		**Zero-Imperfective**		
		wSilᵉt	وصلت	*bawSal*	بوصل	*2awSal*	أوصل	I
2iwSal	اوصل	*wSilᵉt*	وصلت	*btiwSal*	بتوصل	*tiwSal*	توصل	you [M]
2iwSali	اوصلي	*wSilti*	وصلتي	*btiwSali*	بتوصلي	*tiwSali*	توصلي	you [F]
		wiSel	وصل	*biwSal*	بوصل	*yiwSal*	يوصل	he
		wiSlat	وصلت	*btiwSal*	بتوصل	*tiwSal*	توصل	she

			SOUTH LEVANTINE				
Imperative		**Perfective**		**b-Imperfective**		**Zero-Imperfective**	
		wSilna	وصلنا	mniwSal	منوصل	niwSal	نوصل	we
2iwSalu	اوصلو	wSiltu	وصلتو	btiwSalu	بتوصلو	tiwSalu	توصلو	you [P]
		wiSlu	وصلو	biwSalu	بوصلو	yiwSalu	يوصلو	they

naam "Sleep" (*faa3, -faa3*, Hollow)

NORTH LEVANTINE							
Noun of Instance		**maSdar**		**Passive Participle**		**Active Participle**	
noome نومة		noom نوم		N/A		naayem نايم	
Imperative		**Perfective**		**b-Imperfective**		**Zero-Imperfective**	
		nimᵉt	نمت	bnaam	بنام	naam	نام	I
naam	نام	nimᵉt	نمت	bitnaam	بتنام	tnaam	تنام	you [M]
naami	نامي	nimti	نمتي	bitnaami	بتنامي	tnaami	تنامي	you [F]
		naam	نام	binaam	بنام	ynaam	ينام	he
		naamet	نامت	bitnaam	بتنام	tnaam	تنام	she
		nimna	نمنا	minnaam	منام	nnaam	ننام	we
naamu	نامو	nimtu	نمتو	bitnaamu	بتنامو	tnaamu	تنامو	you [P]
		naamu	نامو	binaamu	بنامو	ynaamu	ينامو	they

SOUTH LEVANTINE							
Noun of Instance		**maSdar**		**Passive Participle**		**Active Participle**	
noome نومة		noom نوم		N/A		naayem نايم	
Imperative		**Perfective**		**b-Imperfective**		**Zero-Imperfective**	
		nimᵉt	نمت	banaam	بنام	2anaam	أنام	I

SOUTH LEVANTINE									
Imperative		Perfective		*b-* Imperfective		Zero- Imperfective		
naam	نام	*nimᵉt*	نمت	*bitnaam*	بتنام	*tnaam*	تنام	you [M]
naami	نامي	*nimti*	نمتي	*bitnaami*	بتنامي	*tnaami*	تنامي	you [F]
		naam	نام	*binaam*	بنام	*ynaam*	ينام	he
		naamat	نامت	*bitnaam*	بتنام	*tnaam*	تنام	she
		nimna	نمنا	*minnaam*	منام	*nnaam*	نام	we
naamu	نامو	*nimtu*	نمتو	*bitnaamu*	بتنامو	*tnaamu*	تنامو	you [P]
		naamu	نامو	*binaamu*	بنامو	*ynaamu*	ينامو	they

daa2 "Taste" (*faa3, -fuu3*, Hollow)

NORTH LEVANTINE								
Noun of Instance		*maSdar*		Passive Participle		Active Participle		
doo2a دوقة		*doo2* دوق		N/A		*daaye2* دايق		
Imperative		Perfective		*b-* Imperfective		Zero- Imperfective		
		di2ᵉt	دقت	*bduu2*	بدوق	*duu2*	دوق	I
duu2	دوق	*di2ᵉt*	دقت	*bitduu2*	بتدوق	*tduu2*	تدوق	you [M]
duu2i	دوقي	*di2ti*	دقتي	*bitduu2i*	بتدوقي	*tduu2i*	تدوقي	you [F]
		daa2	داق	*biduu2*	بدوق	*yduu2*	يدوق	he
		daa2et	داقت	*bitduu2*	بتدوق	*tduu2*	تدوق	she
		di2na	دقنا	*minduu2*	مندوق	*nduu2*	ندوق	we
duu2u	دوقو	*di2tu*	دقتو	*bitduu2u*	بتدوقو	*tduu2u*	تدوقو	you [P]
		daa2u	داقو	*biduu2u*	بدوقو	*yduu2u*	يدوقو	they

SOUTH LEVANTINE								
Noun of Instance		*maSdar*		Passive Participle		Active Participle		
doo2a دوقة		*doo2* دوق		N/A		*daaye2* دايق		
Imperative		Perfective		*b-* Imperfective		Zero- Imperfective		
		du2ᵉt	دقت	*baduu2*	بدوق	*2aduu2*	أدوق	I
duu2	دوق	*du2ᵉt*	دقت	*bitduu2*	بتدوق	*tduu2*	تدوق	you [M]
duu2i	دوقي	*du2ti*	دقتي	*bitduu2i*	بتدوقي	*tduu2i*	تدوقي	you [F]
		daa2	داق	*biduu2*	بدوق	*yduu2*	يدوق	he
		daa2at	داقت	*bitduu2*	بتدوق	*tduu2*	تدوق	she
		du2na	دقنا	*minduu2*	مندوق	*nduu2*	ندوق	we
duu2u	دوقو	*du2tu*	دقتو	*bitduu2u*	بتدوقو	*tduu2u*	تدوقو	you [P]
		daa2u	داقو	*biduu2u*	بدوقو	*yduu2u*	يدوقو	they

jaab "Bring" (*faa3, -fii3*, Hollow)

NORTH LEVANTINE								
Noun of Instance		*maSdar*		Passive Participle		Active Participle		
jeebe جيبة		*jayabaan* جيبان		*majyuub* مجيوب		*jaayeb* جايب		
Imperative		Perfective		*b-* Imperfective		Zero- Imperfective		
		jibᵉt	جبت	*bjiib*	بجيب	*jiib*	جيب	I
jiib	جيب	*jibᵉt*	جبت	*bitjiib*	بتجيب	*tjiib*	تجيب	you [M]
jiibi	جيبي	*jibti*	جبتي	*bitjiibi*	بتجيبي	*tjiibi*	تجيبي	you [F]
		jaab	جاب	*bijiib*	بجيب	*yjiib*	يجيب	he

NORTH LEVANTINE							
Imperative		**Perfective**		**b-Imperfective**		**Zero-Imperfective**	
		jaabet	جابت	*bitjiib*	بتجيب	*tjiib*	تجيب	she
		jibna	جبنا	*minjiib*	منجيب	*njiib*	نجيب	we
jiibu	جيبو	*jibtu*	جبتو	*bitjiibu*	بتجيبو	*tjiibu*	تجيبو	you [P]
		jaabu	جابو	*bijiibu*	بجيبو	*yjiibu*	يجيبو	they

For many North Levantine speakers, these verbs cannot form a regular passive participle. They rely on the *nfa3al* form instead: منجاب *minjaab*.

SOUTH LEVANTINE							
Noun of Instance		**maSdar**		**Passive Participle**		**Active Participle**	
jeebe جيبة		*jayabaan* جيبان		*majyuub* مجيوب		*jaayeb* جايب	
Imperative		**Perfective**		**b-Imperfective**		**Zero-Imperfective**	
		jibᵉt	جبت	*bajiib*	بجيب	*2ajiib*	أجيب	I
jiib	جيب	*jibᵉt*	جبت	*bitjiib*	بتجيب	*tjiib*	تجيب	you [M]
jiibi	جيبي	*jibti*	جبتي	*bitjiibi*	بتجيبي	*tjiibi*	تجيبي	you [F]
		jaab	جاب	*bijiib*	بجيب	*yjiib*	يجيب	he
		jaabat	جابت	*bitjiib*	بتجيب	*tjiib*	تجيب	she
		jibna	جبنا	*minjiib*	منجيب	*njiib*	نجيب	we
jiibu	جيبو	*jibtu*	جبتو	*bitjiibu*	بتجيبو	*tjiibu*	تجيبو	you [P]
		jaabu	جابو	*bijiibu*	بجيبو	*yjiibu*	يجيبو	they

madd "Stretch" (*fa33, -fi33*, Doubled)

		NORTH LEVANTINE						
Noun of Instance		*maSdar*		Passive Participle		Active Participle		
madde مدة		*madd* مد		*mamduud* ممدود		*maaded* مادد		
Imperative		Perfective		*b-*Imperfective		Zero-Imperfective		
		maddeet	مديت	*bmidd*	بمد	*midd*	مد	I
midd	مد	*maddeet*	مديت	*bitmidd*	بتمد	*tmidd*	تمد	you [M]
middi	مدي	*maddeeti*	مديتي	*bitmiddi*	بتمدي	*tmiddi*	تمدي	you [F]
		madd	مد	*bimidd*	بمد	*ymidd*	يمد	he
		maddet	مدت	*bitmidd*	بتمد	*tmidd*	تمد	she
		maddeena	مدينا	*minmidd*	منمد	*nmidd*	نمد	we
middu	مدو	*maddeetu*	مديتو	*bitmiddu*	بتمدو	*tmiddu*	تمدو	you [P]
		maddu	مدو	*bimiddu*	بمدو	*ymiddu*	يمدو	they

		SOUTH LEVANTINE						
Noun of Instance		*maSdar*		Passive Participle		Active Participle		
madde مدة		*madd* مد		*mamduud* ممدود		*maaded* مادد		
Imperative		Perfective		*b-*Imperfective		Zero-Imperfective		
		maddeet	مديت	*bamidd*	بمد	*2amidd*	أمد	I
midd	مد	*maddeet*	مديت	*bitmidd*	بتمد	*tmidd*	تمد	you [M]
middi	مدي	*maddeeti*	مديتي	*bitmiddi*	بتمدي	*tmiddi*	تمدي	you [F]
		madd	مد	*bimidd*	بمد	*ymidd*	يمد	he
		maddat	مدت	*bitmidd*	بتمد	*tmidd*	تمد	she

		SOUTH LEVANTINE						
Imperative		**Perfective**		***b-*** **Imperfective**		**Zero-** **Imperfective**		
		maddeena	مدينا	*minmidd*	منمد	*nmidd*	نمد	we
middu	مدو	*maddeetu*	مديتو	*bitmiddu*	بتمدو	*tmiddu*	تمدو	you [P]
		maddu	مدو	*bimiddu*	بمدو	*ymiddu*	يمدو	they

da22 "Tap" (*ʃa33, -ʃu33*, Doubled, South Levantine)

Note that for North Levantine speakers, *da22* conjugates identically to *madd* above.

		SOUTH LEVANTINE						
Noun **of Instance**		***maSdar***		**Passive** **Participle**		**Active** **Participle**		
da22a دقة		*da22* دق		*mad2uu2* مدقوق		*daa2e2* داقق		
Imperative		**Perfective**		***b-*** **Imperfective**		**Zero-** **Imperfective**		
		da22eet	دقيت	*badu22*	بدق	*2adu22*	أدق	I
du22	دق	*da22eet*	دقيت	*bitdu22*	بتدق	*tdu22*	تدق	you [M]
du22i	دقي	*da22eeti*	دقيتي	*bitdu22i*	بتدقي	*tdu22i*	تدقي	you [F]
		da22	دق	*bidu22*	بدق	*ydu22*	يدق	he
		da22at	دقت	*bitdu22*	بتدق	*tdu22*	تدق	she
		da22eena	دقينا	*mindu22*	مندق	*ndu22*	ندق	we
du22u	دقو	*da22eetu*	دقيتو	*bitdu22u*	بتدقو	*tdu22u*	تدقو	you [P]
		da22u	دقو	*bidu22u*	بدقو	*ydu22u*	يدقو	they

tamm "Stay" (*ʃa33, -ʃa33*, Doubled)

NORTH LEVANTINE								
Noun of Instance		**maSdar**		**Passive Participle**		**Active Participle**		
N/A		*tamm* تم		N/A		*taamem* تامم		
Imperative		**Perfective**		***b-*Imperfective**		**Zero-Imperfective**		
		tammeet	تميت	*btamm*	بتم	*tamm*	تم	I
tamm	تم	*tammeet*	تميت	*bittamm*	بتتم	*ttamm*	تتم	you [M]
tammi	تمي	*tammeeti*	تميتي	*bittammi*	بتتمي	*ttammi*	تتمي	you [F]
		tamm	تم	*bitamm*	بتم	*ytamm*	يتم	he
		tammet	تمت	*bittamm*	بتتم	*ttamm*	تتم	she
		tammeena	تمينا	*mintamm*	منتم	*ntamm*	نتم	we
tammu	تمو	*tammeetu*	تميتو	*bittammu*	بتتمو	*ttammu*	تتمو	you [P]
		tammu	تمو	*bitammu*	بتمو	*ytammu*	يتمو	they

SOUTH LEVANTINE								
Noun of Instance		**maSdar**		**Passive Participle**		**Active Participle**		
N/A		*tamm* تم		N/A		*taamem* تامم		
Imperative		**Perfective**		***b-*Imperfective**		**Zero-Imperfective**		
		tammeet	تميت	*batamm*	بتم	*2atamm*	أتم	I
tamm	تم	*tammeet*	تميت	*bittamm*	بتتم	*ttamm*	تتم	you [M]
tammi	تمي	*tammeeti*	تميتي	*bittammi*	بتتمي	*ttammi*	تتمي	you [F]
		tamm	تم	*bitamm*	بتم	*ytamm*	يتم	he
		tammat	تمت	*bittamm*	بتتم	*ttamm*	تتم	she
		tammeena	تمينا	*mintamm*	منتم	*ntamm*	نتم	we
tammu	تمو	*tammeetu*	تميتو	*bittammu*	بتتمو	*ttammu*	تتمو	you [P]
		tammu	تمو	*bitammu*	بتمو	*ytammu*	يتمو	they

Tafa "Turn Off" (*fa3a, -f3i*, Defective)

For some North Levantine speakers, especially Lebanese speakers, many or all verbs of this category have a perfective in *fi3i*, which conjugates like *nisi* below.

NORTH LEVANTINE									
Noun of Instance		*maSdar*			Passive Participle		Active Participle		
Tafye طفية		*Tafi* طفي		*miTfi* مطفي		*Taafi* طافي			
Imperative		Perfective		*b-* Imperfective		Zero- Imperfective			
		Tafeet	طفيت	*biTfi*	بطفي	*2iTfi*	اطفي	I	
Tfii	طفي	*Tafeet*	طفيت	*btiTfi*	بتطفي	*tiTfi*	تطفي	you [M]	
Tfii	طفي	*Tafeeti*	طفيتي	*btiTfi*	بتطفي	*tiTfi*	تطفي	you [F]	
		Tafa	طفى	*byiTfi*	بيطفي	*yiTfi*	يطفي	he	
		Tafet	طفت	*btiTfi*	بتطفي	*tiTfi*	تطفي	she	
		Tafeena	طفينا	*mniTfi*	منطفي	*niTfi*	نطفي	we	
Tfuu	طفو	*Tafeetu*	طفيتو	*btiTfu*	بتطفو	*tiTfu*	تطفو	you [P]	
		Tafu	طفو	*byiTfu*	بيطفو	*yiTfu*	يطفو	they	

SOUTH LEVANTINE									
Noun of Instance		*maSdar*			Passive Participle		Active Participle		
Tafye طفية		*Tafi* طفي		*maTfi* مطفي		*Taafi* طافي			
Imperative		Perfective		*b-* Imperfective		Zero- Imperfective			
		Tafeet	طفيت	*baTfi*	بطفي	*2aTfi*	أطفي	I	
2iTfi	اطفي	*Tafeet*	طفيت	*btiTfi*	بتطفي	*tiTfi*	تطفي	you [M]	
2iTfi	اطفي	*Tafeeti*	طفيتي	*btiTfi*	بتطفي	*tiTfi*	تطفي	you [F]	
		Tafa	طفى	*biTfi*	بطفي	*yiTfi*	يطفي	he	
		Tafat	طفت	*btiTfi*	بتطفي	*tiTfi*	تطفي	she	

				SOUTH LEVANTINE				
Imperative		Perfective		*b-* Imperfective		Zero- Imperfective		
		Tafeena	طفينا	*mniTfi*	منطفي	*niTfi*	نطفي	we
2iTfu	اطفو	*Tafeetu*	طفيتو	*btiTfu*	بتطفو	*tiTfu*	تطفو	you [P]
		Tafu	طفو	*biTfu*	بطفو	*yiTfu*	يطفو	they

nisi "Forget" (*fi3i, -f3a,* Defective)

			NORTH LEVANTINE				
Noun of Instance		*maSdar*		Passive Participle		Active Participle	
naswe نسوة		*nisyaan* نسيان		*minsi* منسي		*nisyaan* نسيان *naasi* ناسي	
Imperative		Perfective		*b-* Imperfective		Zero- Imperfective	
		nsiit	نسيت	*binsa*	بنسى	*2insa*	انسى	I
nsii	نسي	*nsiit*	نسيت	*btinsa*	بتنسى	*tinsa*	تنسى	you [M]
nsii	نسي	*nsiiti*	نسيتي	*btinsi*	بتنسي	*tinsi*	تنسي	you [F]
		nisi	نسي	*byinsa*	بينسى	*yinsa*	ينسى	he
		nisyet	نسيت	*btinsa*	بتنسى	*tinsa*	تنسى	she
		nsiina	نسينا	*mninsa*	مننسى	*ninsa*	ننسى	we
nsuu	نسو	*nsiitu*	نسيتو	*btinsu*	بتنسو	*tinsu*	تنسو	you [P]
		nisyu	نسيو	*byinsu*	بينسو	*yinsu*	ينسو	they

			SOUTH LEVANTINE				
Noun of Instance		*maSdar*		Passive Participle		Active Participle	
naswe نسوة		*nisyaan* نسيان		*mansi* منسي		*naasi* ناسي	
Imperative		Perfective		*b-* Imperfective		Zero- Imperfective	
		nsiit	نسيت	*bansa*	بنسى	*2ansa*	أنسى	I

SOUTH LEVANTINE								
Imperative		**Perfective**		**b-Imperfective**		**Zero-Imperfective**		
2insa	انسى	*nsiit*	نسيت	*btinsa*	بتنسى	*tinsa*	تنسى	you [M]
2insi	انسي	*nsiiti*	نسيتي	*btinsi*	بتنسي	*tinsi*	تنسي	you [F]
		nisi	نسي	*binsa*	بنسى	*yinsa*	ينسى	he
		nisyat	نسيت	*btinsa*	بتنسى	*tinsa*	تنسى	she
		nsiina	نسينا	*mninsa*	مننسى	*ninsa*	ننسى	we
2insu	انسو	*nsiitu*	نسيتو	*btinsu*	بتنسو	*tinsu*	تنسو	you [P]
		nisyu	نسيو	*binsu*	بنسو	*yinsu*	ينسو	they

naja "Survive" (*faʒa, -fʒu*, Defective)

This form occurs only with *fuS7aisms*. Many examples have synonyms on *-fʒi*.

NORTH LEVANTINE								
Noun of Instance		**maSdar**		**Passive Participle**		**Active Participle**		
najwe نجوة		*najaa* نجاة		N/A		*naaji* ناجي		
Imperative		**Perfective**		**b-Imperfective**		**Zero-Imperfective**		
		najeet	نجيت	*binju*	بنجو	*2inju*	انجو	I
2inju	انجو	*najeet*	نجيت	*btinju*	بتنجو	*tinju*	تنجو	you [M]
2inji	انجي	*najeeti*	نجيتي	*btinji*	بتنجي	*tinji*	تنجي	you [F]
		naja	نجا	*byinju*	بينجو	*yinju*	ينجو	he
		najet	نجت	*btinju*	بتنجو	*tinju*	تنجو	she
		najeena	نجينا	*mninju*	مننجو	*ninju*	ننجو	we
2inju	انجو	*najeetu*	نجيتو	*btinju*	بتنجو	*tinju*	تنجو	you [P]
		naju	نجو	*byinju*	بينجو	*yinju*	ينجو	they

<table>
<thead>
<tr><th colspan="9" align="center">SOUTH LEVANTINE</th></tr>
<tr><th colspan="2" align="center">Noun
of Instance</th><th colspan="2" align="center">*maSdar*</th><th colspan="2" align="center">Passive
Participle</th><th colspan="2" align="center">Active
Participle</th><th></th></tr>
<tr><td colspan="2" align="center">*najwe* نجوة</td><td colspan="2" align="center">*najaa* نجاة</td><td colspan="2" align="center">N/A</td><td colspan="2" align="center">*naaji* ناجي</td><td></td></tr>
<tr><th colspan="2" align="center">Imperative</th><th colspan="2" align="center">Perfective</th><th colspan="2" align="center">*b-*
Imperfective</th><th colspan="2" align="center">Zero-
Imperfective</th><th></th></tr>
</thead>
<tbody>
<tr><td></td><td></td><td>*najeet*</td><td>نجيت</td><td>*banju*</td><td>بنجو</td><td>*2anju*</td><td>أنجو</td><td>I</td></tr>
<tr><td>*2inju*</td><td>انجو</td><td>*najeet*</td><td>نجيت</td><td>*btinju*</td><td>بتنجو</td><td>*tinju*</td><td>تنجو</td><td>you [M]</td></tr>
<tr><td>*2inji*</td><td>انجي</td><td>*najeeti*</td><td>نجيتي</td><td>*btinji*</td><td>بتنجي</td><td>*tinji*</td><td>تنجي</td><td>you [F]</td></tr>
<tr><td></td><td></td><td>*naja*</td><td>نجا</td><td>*binju*</td><td>بنجو</td><td>*yinju*</td><td>ينجو</td><td>he</td></tr>
<tr><td></td><td></td><td>*najat*</td><td>نجت</td><td>*btinju*</td><td>بتنجو</td><td>*tinju*</td><td>تنجو</td><td>she</td></tr>
<tr><td></td><td></td><td>*najeena*</td><td>نجينا</td><td>*mninju*</td><td>مننجو</td><td>*ninju*</td><td>ننجو</td><td>we</td></tr>
<tr><td>*2inju*</td><td>انجو</td><td>*najeetu*</td><td>نجيتو</td><td>*btinju*</td><td>بتنجو</td><td>*tinju*</td><td>تنجو</td><td>you [P]</td></tr>
<tr><td></td><td></td><td>*naju*</td><td>نجو</td><td>*binju*</td><td>بنجو</td><td>*yinju*</td><td>ينجو</td><td>they</td></tr>
</tbody>
</table>

3aTa, 2a3Ta "Give" (Irregular)

<table>
<thead>
<tr><th colspan="9" align="center">NORTH LEVANTINE</th></tr>
<tr><th colspan="2" align="center">Noun
of Instance</th><th colspan="2" align="center">*maSdar*</th><th colspan="2" align="center">Passive
Participle</th><th colspan="2" align="center">Active
Participle</th><th></th></tr>
<tr><td colspan="2" align="center">*3aTwe* عطوة</td><td colspan="2" align="center">*3aTa* عطا</td><td colspan="2" align="center">N/A</td><td colspan="2" align="center">*3aaTi* عاطي</td><td></td></tr>
<tr><th colspan="2" align="center">Imperative</th><th colspan="2" align="center">Perfective</th><th colspan="2" align="center">*b-*
Imperfective</th><th colspan="2" align="center">Zero-
Imperfective</th><th></th></tr>
</thead>
<tbody>
<tr><td></td><td></td><td>*3aTeet*</td><td>عطيت</td><td>*ba3Ti*</td><td>بعطي</td><td>*2a3Ti*</td><td>أعطي</td><td>I</td></tr>
<tr><td>*3aTi*</td><td>عطي</td><td>*3aTeet*</td><td>عطيت</td><td>*bta3Ti*</td><td>بتعطي</td><td>*ta3Ti*</td><td>تعطي</td><td>you [M]</td></tr>
<tr><td>*3aTi*</td><td>عطي</td><td>*3aTeeti*</td><td>عطيتي</td><td>*bta3Ti*</td><td>بتعطي</td><td>*ta3Ti*</td><td>تعطي</td><td>you [F]</td></tr>
<tr><td></td><td></td><td>*3aTa*</td><td>عطى</td><td>*bya3Ti*</td><td>بيعطي</td><td>*ya3Ti*</td><td>يعطي</td><td>he</td></tr>
</tbody>
</table>

NORTH LEVANTINE								
Imperative		Perfective		*b-* Imperfective		Zero- Imperfective		
		3aTet	عطت	bta3Ti	بتعطي	ta3Ti	تعطي	she
		3aTeena	عطينا	mna3Ti	منعطي	na3Ti	نعطي	we
3aTu	عطو	3aTeetu	عطيتو	bta3Tu	بتعطو	ta3Tu	تعطو	you [P]
		3aTu	عطو	bya3Tu	بيعطو	ya3Tu	يعطو	they

For many Lebanese speakers, the perfective is عطي *3iTi*, which conjugates like *nisi* above.

SOUTH LEVANTINE								
Noun of Instance		*maSdar*		Passive Participle		Active Participle		
3aTwe عطوة		3aTa عطا		N/A		ma3Ti معطي		
Imperative		Perfective		*b-* Imperfective		Zero- Imperfective		
		2a3Teet	أعطيت	ba3Ti	بعطي	2a3Ti	أعطي	I
2a3Ti	أعطي	2a3Teet	أعطيت	bta3Ti	بتعطي	ta3Ti	تعطي	you [M]
2a3Ti	أعطي	2a3Teeti	أعطيتي	bta3Ti	بتعطي	ta3Ti	تعطي	you [F]
		2a3Ta	أعطى	ba3Ti	بعطي	ya3Ti	يعطي	he
		2a3Tat	أعطت	bta3Ti	بتعطي	ta3Ti	تعطي	she
		2a3Teena	أعطينا	mna3Ti	منعطي	na3Ti	نعطي	we
2a3Tu	أعطو	2a3Teetu	أعطيتو	bta3Tu	بتعطو	ta3Tu	تعطو	you [P]
		2a3Tu	أعطو	ba3Tu	بعطو	ya3Tu	يعطو	they

3iref "Know" (Irregular, Patterns with *3imel*)

	NORTH LEVANTINE							
Noun of Instance		**maSdar**		**Passive Participle**		**Active Participle**		
N/A		ma3rife معرفة		ma3ruuf معروف		3arfaan عرفان 3aaref عارف		
Imperative		**Perfective**		**b-Imperfective**		**Zero-Imperfective**		
		3rif[e]t	عرفت	ba3ref	بعرف	2a3ref	أعرف	I
3reef	عريف	3rif[e]t	عرفت	bta3ref	بتعرف	ta3ref	تعرف	you [M]
3rifi	عرفي	3rifti	عرفتي	bta3[i]rfi	بتعرفي	ta3[i]rfi	تعرفي	you [F]
		3iref	عرف	bya3ref	بيعرف	ya3ref	يعرف	he
		3irfet	عرفت	bta3ref	بتعرف	ta3ref	تعرف	she
		3rifna	عرفنا	mna3ref	منعرف	na3ref	نعرف	we
3rifu	عرفو	3riftu	عرفتو	bta3[i]rfu	بتعرفو	ta3[i]rfu	تعرفو	you [P]
		3irfu	عرفو	bya3[i]rfu	بيعرفو	ya3[i]rfu	يعرفو	they

Note that this paradigm is also used for عمل *3imel* "do." Its main quality is the use of *a* in the imperfective prefix, for which see unit 34.

	SOUTH LEVANTINE							
Noun of Instance		**maSdar**		**Passive Participle**		**Active Participle**		
N/A		ma3rife معرفة		ma3ruuf معروف		3aaref عارف		
Imperative		**Perfective**		**b-Imperfective**		**Zero-Imperfective**		
		3rif[e]t	عرفت	ba3raf	بعرف	2a3raf	أعرف	I
2i3raf	اعرف	3rif[e]t	عرفت	bti3raf	بتعرف	ti3raf	تعرف	you [M]
2i3rafi	اعرفي	3rifti	عرفتي	bti3rafi	بتعرفي	ti3rafi	تعرفي	you [F]

SOUTH LEVANTINE								
Imperative		Perfective		*b-* Imperfective		Zero- Imperfective		
		3iref	عرف	bi3raf	بعرف	yi3raf	يعرف	he
		3irfat	عرفت	bti3raf	بتعرف	ti3raf	تعرف	she
		3rifna	عرفنا	mni3raf	منعرف	ni3raf	نعرف	we
2i3rafu	اعرفو	3riftu	عرفتو	bti3rafu	بتعرفو	ti3rafu	تعرفو	you [P]
		3irfu	عرفو	bi3rafu	بعرفو	yi3rafu	يعرفو	they

2akhad "Take" (Irregular, Patterns with *2akal*)

Only two verbs follow this pattern: أكل *2akal* "eat" and أخد *2akhad* "take." Note the differences between North Levantine and South Levantine in the imperfective. The northern forms (e.g., *btaakhod*) also occur for some South Levantine speakers.

NORTH LEVANTINE								
Noun of Instance		*maSdar*		Passive Participle		Active Participle		
2akhde أخدة		2akhed أخد		ma2khuud مأخود		2aakhed آخد		
Imperative		Perfective		*b-* Imperfective		Zero- Imperfective		
		2akhad^et	أخدت	baakhod	باخد	2aakhod	آخد	I
khood	خود	2akhad^et	أخدت	btaakhod	بتاخد	taakhod	تاخد	you [M]
khidi	خدي	2akhadti	أخدتي	btaakhdi	بتاخدي	taakhdi	تاخدي	you [F]
		2akhad	أخد	byaakhod	بياخد	yaakhod	ياخد	he
		2akhdet	أخدت	btaakhod	بتاخد	taakhod	تاخد	she
		2akhadna	أخدنا	mnaakhod	مناخد	naakhod	ناخد	we
khidu	خدو	2akhadtu	أخدتو	btaakhdu	بتاخدو	taakhdu	تاخدو	you [P]
		2akhadu	أخدو	byaakhdu	بياخدو	yaakhdu	ياخدو	they

			SOUTH LEVANTINE				
Noun of Instance		**maSdar**		**Passive Participle**		**Active Participle**	
2akhde أخدة		*2akhed* أخد		*ma2khuud* مأخود		*maakhed* ماخد	
Imperative		**Perfective**		**b-Imperfective**		**Zero-Imperfective**	
		2akhad^et	أخدت	*baakhod*	باخد	*2aakhod*	آخد	I
khood	خود	*2akhad^et*	أخدت	*btookhod*	بتوخد	*tookhod*	توخد	you [M]
khudi	خدي	*2akhadti*	أخدتي	*btookhdi*	بتوخدي	*tookhdi*	توخدي	you [F]
		2akhad	أخد	*bookhod*	بوخد	*yookhod*	يوخد	he
		2akhdat	أخدت	*btookhod*	بتوخد	*tookhod*	توخد	she
		2akhadna	أخدنا	*mnookhod*	منوخد	*nookhod*	نوخد	we
khudu	خدو	*2akhadtu*	أخدتو	*btookhdu*	بتوخدو	*tookhdu*	توخدو	you [P]
		2akhadu	أخدو	*bookhdu*	بوخدو	*yookhdu*	يوخدو	they

2ija, 2aja "Come" (Irregular)

			NORTH LEVANTINE				
Noun of Instance		**maSdar**		**Passive Participle**		**Active Participle**	
jiyye جية *majye* مجية		*jayaan* جيان *majye* مجية		N/A		*jaaye* جايه	
Imperative		**Perfective**		**b-Imperfective**		**Zero-Imperfective**	
		jiit	جيت	*biji*	بجي	*2iji*	اجي	I
ta3aal	تعال	*jiit*	جيت	*btiji*	بتجي	*tiji*	تجي	you [M]
ta3aali	تعالي	*jiiti*	جيتي	*btiji*	بتجي	*tiji*	تجي	you [F]
		2ija	إجا	*biji*	بجي	*yiji*	يجي	he
		2ijet	إجت	*btiji*	بتجي	*tiji*	تجي	she
		jiina	جينا	*mniji*	منجي	*niji*	نجي	we
ta3aalu	تعالو	*jiitu*	جيتو	*btiju*	بتجو	*tiju*	تجو	you [P]

NORTH LEVANTINE							
Imperative		Perfective		*b-* Imperfective		Zero- Imperfective	
		2iju	إجو	*biju*	بجو	*yiju*	يجو	they

SOUTH LEVANTINE							
Noun of Instance		*maSdar*		Passive Participle		Active Participle	
jayye جية		*jayye* جية		N/A		*jaay* جاي	
Imperative		Perfective		*b-* Imperfective		Zero- Imperfective	
		jiit	جيت	*baaji*	باجي	*2aaji*	آجي	I
ta3aal	تعال	*jiit*	جيت	*btiiji*	بتيجي	*tiiji*	تيجي	you [M]
ta3aali	تعالي	*jiiti*	جيتي	*btiiji*	بتيجي	*tiiji*	تيجي	you [F]
		2aja	أجا	*biiji*	بيجي	*yiiji*	ييجي	he
		2ajat	أجت	*btiiji*	بتيجي	*tiiji*	تيجي	she
		jiina	جينا	*mniiji*	منيجي	*niiji*	نيجي	we
ta3aalu	تعالو	*jiitu*	جيتو	*btiiju*	بتيجو	*tiiju*	تيجو	you [P]
		2aju	أجو	*biiju*	بيجو	*yiiju*	ييجو	they

The alternative form تعال *ta3* (feminine and plural تعي *ta3i* and تعو *ta3u*) is also common in the imperative.

zabbaT "Fix" (*fa33al*)

NORTH LEVANTINE							
Noun of Instance		*maSdar*		Passive Participle		Active Participle	
tazbiiTe تزبيطة		*tazbiiT* تزبيط		*mzabbaT* مزبط		*mzabbeT* مزبط	
Imperative		Perfective		*b-* Imperfective		Zero- Imperfective	
		zabbaTet	زبطت	*bzabbeT*	بزبط	*zabbeT*	زبط	I

NORTH LEVANTINE								
Imperative		**Perfective**		*b-***Imperfective**		**Zero-Imperfective**		
zabbeT	زبط	*zabbaTet*	زبطت	*bitzabbeT*	بتزبط	*tzabbeT*	تزبط	you [M]
zabbTi	زبطي	*zabbaTti*	زبطتي	*bitzabbTi*	بتزبطي	*tzabbTi*	تزبطي	you [F]
		zabbaT	زبط	*bizabbeT*	بزبط	*yzabbeT*	يزبط	he
		zabbaTet	زبطت	*bitzabbeT*	بتزبط	*tzabbeT*	تزبط	she
		zabbaTna	زبطنا	*minzabbeT*	منزبط	*nzabbeT*	نزبط	we
zabbTu	زبطو	*zabbaTtu*	زبطتو	*bitzabbTu*	بتزبطو	*tzabbTu*	تزبطو	you [P]
		zabbaTu	زبطو	*bizabbTu*	بزبطو	*yzabbTu*	يزبطو	they

SOUTH LEVANTINE								
Noun of Instance		*maSdar*		**Passive Participle**		**Active Participle**		
tazbiiTe تزبيطة		*tazbiiT* تزبيط		*mzabbaT* مزبط		*mzabbeT* مزبط		
Imperative		**Perfective**		*b-***Imperfective**		**Zero-Imperfective**		
		zabbaTet	زبطت	*bazabbeT*	بزبط	*2azabbeT*	أزبط	I
zabbeT	زبط	*zabbaTet*	زبطت	*bitzabbeT*	بتزبط	*tzabbeT*	تزبط	you [M]
zabbTi	زبطي	*zabbaTti*	زبطتي	*bitzabbTi*	بتزبطي	*tzabbTi*	تزبطي	you [F]
		zabbaT	زبط	*bizabbeT*	بزبط	*yzabbeT*	يزبط	he
		zabbaTat	زبطت	*bitzabbeT*	بتزبط	*tzabbeT*	تزبط	she
		zabbaTna	زبطنا	*minzabbeT*	منزبط	*nzabbeT*	نزبط	we
zabbTu	زبطو	*zabbaTtu*	زبطتو	*bitzabbTu*	بتزبطو	*tzabbTu*	تزبطو	you [P]
		zabbaTu	زبطو	*bizabbTu*	بزبطو	*yzabbTu*	يزبطو	they

3abba "Fill" (*faʒʒa*)

NORTH LEVANTINE							
Noun of Instance		***maSdar***		**Passive Participle**		**Active Participle**	
N/A		*ti3baaye* تعباية		*m3abba* معبى		*m3abbi* معبي	
Imperative		**Perfective**		**b- Imperfective**		**Zero- Imperfective**	
		3abbeet	عبيت	*b3abbi*	بعبي	*3abbi*	عبي	I
3abbi	عبي	*3abbeet*	عبيت	*bit3abbi*	بتعبي	*t3abbi*	تعبي	you [M]
3abbi	عبي	*3abbeeti*	عبيتي	*bit3abbi*	بتعبي	*t3abbi*	تعبي	you [F]
		3abba	عبى	*bi3abbi*	بعبي	*y3abbi*	يعبي	he
		3abbet	عبت	*bit3abbi*	بتعبي	*t3abbi*	تعبي	she
		3abbeena	عبينا	*min3abbi*	منعبي	*n3abbi*	نعبي	we
3abbu	عبو	*3abbeetu*	عبيتو	*bit3abbu*	بتعبو	*t3abbu*	تعبو	you [P]
		3abbu	عبو	*bi3abbu*	بعبو	*y3abbu*	يعبو	they

SOUTH LEVANTINE							
Noun of Instance		***maSdar***		**Passive Participle**		**Active Participle**	
N/A		*ti3baay* تعباي		*m3abba* معبى		*m3abbi* معبي	
Imperative		**Perfective**		**b- Imperfective**		**Zero- Imperfective**	
		3abbeet	عبيت	*ba3abbi*	بعبي	*2a3abbi*	أعبي	I
3abbi	عبي	*3abbeet*	عبيت	*bit3abbi*	بتعبي	*t3abbi*	تعبي	you [M]
3abbi	عبي	*3abbeeti*	عبيتي	*bit3abbi*	بتعبي	*t3abbi*	تعبي	you [F]
		3abba	عبى	*bi3abbi*	بعبي	*y3abbi*	يعبي	he
		3abbat	عبت	*bit3abbi*	بتعبي	*t3abbi*	تعبي	she
		3abbeena	عبينا	*min3abbi*	منعبي	*n3abbi*	نعبي	we
3abbu	عبو	*3abbeetu*	عبيتو	*bit3abbu*	بتعبو	*t3abbu*	تعبو	you [P]
		3abbu	عبو	*bi3abbu*	بعبو	*y3abbu*	يعبو	they

jaakar "Spite" (*faaʒal*)

NORTH LEVANTINE							
Noun of Instance		**maSdar**		**Passive Participle**		**Active Participle**	
N/A		*mjaakara* مجاكرة		*mjaakar* مجاكر		*mjaaker* مجاكر	
Imperative		**Perfective**		**b-Imperfective**		**Zero-Imperfective**	
		jaakaret جاكرت		*bjaaker* بجاكر		*jaaker* جاكر	I
jaaker جاكر		*jaakaret* جاكرت		*bitjaaker* بتجاكر		*tjaaker* تجاكر	you [M]
jaakri جاكري		*jaakarti* جاكرتي		*bitjaakri* بتجاكري		*tjaakri* تجاكري	you [F]
		jaakar جاكر		*bijaaker* بجاكر		*yjaaker* يجاكر	he
		jaakaret جاكرت		*bitjaaker* بتجاكر		*tjaaker* تجاكر	she
		jaakarna جاكرنا		*minjaaker* منجاكر		*njaaker* نجاكر	we
jaakru جاكرو		*jaakartu* جاكرتو		*bitjaakru* بتجاكرو		*tjaakru* تجاكرو	you [P]
		jaakaru جاكرو		*bijaakru* بجاكرو		*yjaakru* يجاكرو	they

SOUTH LEVANTINE							
Noun of Instance		**maSdar**		**Passive Participle**		**Active Participle**	
N/A		*mjaakara* مجاكرة *jakaar* جكار		*mjaakar* مجاكر		*mjaaker* مجاكر	
Imperative		**Perfective**		**b-Imperfective**		**Zero-Imperfective**	
		jaakaret جاكرت		*bajaaker* بجاكر		*2ajaaker* أجاكر	I
jaaker جاكر		*jaakaret* جاكرت		*bitjaaker* بتجاكر		*tjaaker* تجاكر	you [M]
jaakri جاكري		*jaakarti* جاكرتي		*bitjaakri* بتجاكري		*tjaakri* تجاكري	you [F]
		jaakar جاكر		*bijaaker* بجاكر		*yjaaker* يجاكر	he
		jaakarat جاكرت		*bitjaaker* بتجاكر		*tjaaker* تجاكر	she
		jaakarna جاكرنا		*minjaaker* منجاكر		*njaaker* نجاكر	we
jaakru جاكرو		*jaakartu* جاكرتو		*bitjaakru* بتجاكرو		*tjaakru* تجاكرو	you [P]
		jaakaru جاكرو		*bijaakru* بجاكرو		*yjaakru* يجاكرو	they

daawa "Treat (Medicinally)" (*faaʒa*)

NORTH LEVANTINE							
Noun of Instance		**maSdar**		**Passive Participle**		**Active Participle**	
N/A		*mdaawaa* مداواة		*mdaawa* مداوى		*mdaawi* مداوي	
Imperative		**Perfective**		***b-* Imperfective**		**Zero- Imperfective**	
		daaweet داويت		*bdaawi* بداوي		*daawi* داوي	I
daawi داوي		*daaweet* داويت		*bitdaawi* بتداوي		*tdaawi* تداوي	you [M]
daawi داوي		*daaweeti* داويتي		*bitdaawi* بتداوي		*tdaawi* تداوي	you [F]
		daawa داوى		*bidaawi* بداوي		*ydaawi* يداوي	he
		daawet داوت		*bitdaawi* بتداوي		*tdaawi* تداوي	she
		daaweena داوينا		*mindaawi* منداوي		*ndaawi* نداوي	we
daawu داوو		*daaweetu* داويتو		*bitdaawu* بتداوو		*tdaawu* تداوو	you [P]
		daawu داوو		*bidaawu* بداوو		*ydaawu* يداوو	they

SOUTH LEVANTINE							
Noun of Instance		**maSdar**		**Passive Participle**		**Active Participle**	
N/A		*mdawaa* مداواة		*mdaawa* مداوى		*mdaawi* مداوي	
Imperative		**Perfective**		***b-* Imperfective**		**Zero- Imperfective**	
		daweet داويت		*badaawi* بداوي		*2adaawi* أداوي	I
daawi داوي		*daweet* داويت		*bitdaawi* بتداوي		*tdaawi* تداوي	you [M]
daawi داوي		*daweeti* داويتي		*bitdaawi* بتداوي		*tdaawi* تداوي	you [F]
		daawa داوى		*bidaawi* بداوي		*ydaawi* يداوي	he
		daawat داوت		*bitdaawi* بتداوي		*tdaawi* تداوي	she
		daweena داوينا		*mindaawi* منداوي		*ndaawi* نداوي	we
daawu داوو		*daweetu* داويتو		*bitdaawu* بتداوو		*tdaawu* تداوو	you [P]
		daawu داوو		*bidaawu* بداوو		*ydaawu* يداوو	they

2a3lan "Announce" (*2af3al*)

NORTH LEVANTINE								
Noun of Instance		**maSdar**		**Passive Participle**		**Active Participle**		
N/A		2i3laan إعلان		mi3lan معلن		mi3len معلن		
Imperative		**Perfective**		**b- Imperfective**		**Zero- Imperfective**		
		2a3lanᵉt	أعلنت	bi3len	بعلن	2i3len	اعلن	I
3leen	علين	2a3lanᵉt	أعلنت	bti3len	بتعلن	ti3len	تعلن	you [M]
3lini	علني	2a3lanti	أعلنتي	bti3ⁱlni	بتعلني	ti3ⁱlni	تعلني	you [F]
		2a3lan	أعلن	byi3len	بيعلن	yi3len	يعلن	he
		2a3lanet	أعلنت	bti3len	بتعلن	ti3len	تعلن	she
		2a3lanna	أعلننا	mni3len	منعلن	ni3len	نعلن	we
3linu	علنو	2a3lantu	أعلنتو	bti3ⁱlnu	بتعلنو	ti3ⁱlnu	تعلنو	you [P]
		2a3lanu	أعلنو	byi3ⁱlnu	بيعلنو	yi3ⁱlnu	يعلنو	they

SOUTH LEVANTINE								
Noun of Instance		**maSdar**		**Passive Participle**		**Active Participle**		
N/A		2i3laan إعلان		mu3lan معلن		mi3len معلن		
Imperative		**Perfective**		**b- Imperfective**		**Zero- Imperfective**		
		2a3lanᵉt	أعلنت	ba3len	بعلن	2a3len	أعلن	I
2i3len	اعلن	2a3lanᵉt	أعلنت	bti3len	بتعلن	ti3len	تعلن	you [M]
2i3ⁱlni	اعلني	2a3lanti	أعلنتي	bti3ⁱlni	بتعلني	ti3ⁱlni	تعلني	you [F]
		2a3lan	أعلن	bi3len	بعلن	yi3len	يعلن	he
		2a3lanat	أعلنت	bti3len	بتعلن	ti3len	تعلن	she
		2a3lanna	أعلننا	mni3len	منعلن	ni3len	نعلن	we
2i3ⁱlnu	اعلنو	2a3lantu	أعلنتو	bti3ⁱlnu	بتعلنو	ti3ⁱlnu	تعلنو	you [P]
		2a3lanu	أعلنو	bi3ⁱlnu	بعلنو	yi3ⁱlnu	يعلنو	they

2aSarr "Insist" (*2afa33*)

NORTH LEVANTINE									
Noun of Instance		*maSdar*			Passive Participle		Active Participle		
N/A		*2iSraar* إصرار			N/A		*muSirr* مصر		
Imperative		Perfective		*b-* Imperfective		Zero-Imperfective			
		2aSarreet	أصريت	*bSirr*	بصر	*Sirr*	صر	I	
Sirr	صر	*2aSarreet*	أصريت	*bitSirr*	بتصر	*tSirr*	تصر	you [M]	
Sirri	صري	*2aSarreeti*	أصريتي	*bitSirri*	بتصري	*tSirri*	تصري	you [F]	
		2aSarr	أصر	*biSirr*	بصر	*ySirr*	يصر	he	
		2aSarret	أصرت	*bitSirr*	بتصر	*tSirr*	تصر	she	
		2aSarreena	أصرينا	*minSirr*	منصر	*nSirr*	نصر	we	
Sirru	صرو	*2aSarreetu*	أصريتو	*bitSirru*	بتصرو	*tSirru*	تصرو	you [P]	
		2aSarru	أصرو	*biSirru*	بصرو	*ySirru*	يصرو	they	

SOUTH LEVANTINE									
Noun of Instance		*maSdar*			Passive Participle		Active Participle		
N/A		*2iSraar* إصرار			N/A		*muSirr* مصر		
Imperative		Perfective		*b-* Imperfective		Zero-Imperfective			
		2aSarreet	أصريت	*baSirr*	بصر	*2aSirr*	أصر	I	
Sirr	صر	*2aSarreet*	أصريت	*bitSirr*	بتصر	*tSirr*	تصر	you [M]	
Sirri	صري	*2aSarreeti*	أصريتي	*bitSirri*	بتصري	*tSirri*	تصري	you [F]	
		2aSarr	أصر	*biSirr*	بصر	*ySirr*	يصر	he	
		2aSarrat	أصرت	*bitSirr*	بتصر	*tSirr*	تصر	she	
		2aSarreena	أصرينا	*minSirr*	منصر	*nSirr*	نصر	we	
Sirru	صرو	*2aSarreetu*	أصريتو	*bitSirru*	بتصرو	*tSirru*	تصرو	you [P]	
		2aSarru	أصرو	*biSirru*	بصرو	*ySirru*	يصرو	they	

2ahda "Dedicate" (2af3a)

NORTH LEVANTINE								
Noun of Instance		**maSdar**		**Passive Participle**		**Active Participle**		
N/A		2ihdaa2 إهداء		mihdi مهدي		mihdi مهدي		
Imperative		**Perfective**		**b- Imperfective**		**Zero- Imperfective**		
		2ahdeet	أهديت	bihdi	بهدي	2ihdi	اهدي	I
2ihdi	اهدي	2ahdeet	أهديت	btihdi	بتهدي	tihdi	تهدي	you [M]
2ihdi	اهدي	2ahdeeti	أهديتي	btihdi	بتهدي	tihdi	تهدي	you [F]
		2ahda	أهدى	byihdi	بيهدي	yihdi	يهدي	he
		2ahdet	أهدت	btihdi	بتهدي	tihdi	تهدي	she
		2ahdeena	أهدينا	mnihdi	منهدي	nihdi	نهدي	we
2ihdu	اهدو	2ahdeetu	أهديتو	btihdu	بتهدو	tihdu	تهدو	you [P]
		2ahdu	أهدو	byihdu	بيهدو	yihdu	يهدو	they

SOUTH LEVANTINE								
Noun of Instance		**maSdar**		**Passive Participle**		**Active Participle**		
N/A		2ihdaa2 إهداء		mahdi مهدي		mihdi مهدي		
Imperative		**Perfective**		**b- Imperfective**		**Zero- Imperfective**		
		2ahdeet	أهديت	bahdi	بهدي	2ahdi	أهدي	I
2ihdi	اهدي	2ahdeet	أهديت	btihdi	بتهدي	tihdi	تهدي	you [M]
2ihdi	اهدي	2ahdeeti	أهديتي	btihdi	بتهدي	tihdi	تهدي	you [F]
		2ahda	أهدى	bihdi	بهدي	yihdi	يهدي	he
		2ahdat	أهدت	btihdi	بتهدي	tihdi	تهدي	she
		2ahdeena	أهدينا	mnihdi	منهدي	nihdi	نهدي	we
2ihdu	اهدو	2ahdeetu	أهديتو	btihdu	بتهدو	tihdu	تهدو	you [P]
		2ahdu	أهدو	bihdu	بهدو	yihdu	يهدو	they

t3allam "Learn" (*tfa33al*)

NORTH LEVANTINE							
Noun of Instance		**maSdar**		**Passive Participle**		**Active Participle**	
N/A		*ta3allom* تعلم		N/A		*mit3allem* متعلم	
Imperative		**Perfective**		***b-* Imperfective**		**Zero- Imperfective**	
		t3allam^et	تعلمت	*bit3allam*	بتعلم	*2it3allam*	اتعلم	I
t3allam	اتعلم	*t3allam^et*	تعلمت	*btit3allam*	بتتعلم	*tit3allam*	تتعلم	you [M]
t3allami	اتعلمي	*t3allamti*	تعلمتي	*btit3allami*	بتتعلمي	*tit3allam*	تتعلمي	you [F]
		t3allam	تعلم	*byit3allam*	بيتعلم	*yit3allam*	يتعلم	he
		t3allamet	تعلمت	*btit3allam*	بتتعلم	*tit3allam*	تتعلم	she
		t3allamna	تعلمنا	*mnit3allam*	منتعلم	*nit3allam*	نتعلم	we
t3allamu	اتعلمو	*t3allamtu*	تعلمتو	*btit3allamu*	بتتعلمو	*tit3allamu*	تتعلمو	you [P]
		t3allamu	تعلمو	*byit3allamu*	بيتعلمو	*yit3allamu*	يتعلمو	they

SOUTH LEVANTINE							
Noun of Instance		**maSdar**		**Passive Participle**		**Active Participle**	
N/A		*ta3allom* تعلم		N/A		*mit3allem* متعلم	
Imperative		**Perfective**		***b-* Imperfective**		**Zero- Imperfective**	
		t3allam^et	تعلمت	*bat3allam*	بتعلم	*2at3allam*	أتعلم	I
t3allam	اتعلم	*t3allam^et*	تعلمت	*btit3allam*	بتتعلم	*tit3allam*	تتعلم	you [M]
t3allami	اتعلمي	*t3allamti*	تعلمتي	*btit3allami*	بتتعلمي	*tit3allami*	تتعلمي	you [F]
		t3allam	تعلم	*bit3allam*	بتعلم	*yit3allam*	يتعلم	he
		t3allamat	تعلمت	*btit3allam*	بتتعلم	*tit3allam*	تتعلم	she
		t3allamna	تعلمنا	*mnit3allam*	منتعلم	*nit3allam*	نتعلم	we
t3allamu	اتعلمو	*t3allamtu*	تعلمتو	*btit3allamu*	بتتعلمو	*tit3allamu*	تتعلمو	you [P]
		t3allamu	تعلمو	*bit3allamu*	بتعلمو	*yit3allamu*	يتعلمو	they

tkhabba "Hide" (*tfa33a*)

	NORTH LEVANTINE						
Noun of Instance		*maSdar*		Passive Participle		Active Participle	
N/A		*tkhibbi* تخبي		N/A		*mitkhabbi* متخبي	
Imperative		Perfective		*b-*Imperfective		Zero-Imperfective	
		tkhabbeet	تخبيت	*bitkhabba*	بتخبى	*2itkhabba*	اتخبى	I
tkhabba	تخبى	*tkhabbeet*	تخبيت	*btitkhabba*	بتتخبى	*titkhabba*	تتخبى	you [M]
tkhabbi	تخبي	*tkhabbeeti*	تخبيتي	*btitkhabbi*	بتتخبي	*titkhabbi*	تتخبي	you [F]
		tkhabba	تخبى	*byitkhabba*	بيتخبى	*yitkhabba*	يتخبى	he
		tkhabbet	تخبت	*btitkhabba*	بتتخبى	*titkhabba*	تتخبى	she
		tkhabbeena	تخبينا	*mnitkhabba*	منتخبى	*nitkhabba*	نتخبى	we
tkhabbu	تخبو	*tkhabbeetu*	تخبيتو	*btitkhabbu*	بتتخبو	*titkhabbu*	تتخبو	you [P]
		tkhabbu	تخبو	*byitkhabbu*	بيتخبو	*yitkhabbu*	يتخبو	they

	SOUTH LEVANTINE						
Noun of Instance		*maSdar*		Passive Participle		Active Participle	
N/A		*tkhibbi* تخبي		N/A		*mitkhabbi* متخبي	
Imperative		Perfective		*b-*Imperfective		Zero-Imperfective	
		tkhabbeet	تخبيت	*batkhabba*	بتخبى	*2atkhabba*	أتخبى	I
tkhabba	تخبى	*tkhabbeet*	تخبيت	*btitkhabba*	بتتخبى	*titkhabba*	تتخبى	you [M]
tkhabbi	تخبي	*tkhabbeeti*	تخبيتي	*btitkhabbi*	بتتخبي	*titkhabbi*	تتخبي	*you [F]*
		tkhabba	تخبى	*bitkhabba*	بتخبى	*yitkhabba*	يتخبى	he
		tkhabbat	تخبت	*btitkhabba*	بتتخبى	*titkhabba*	تتخبى	she
		tkhabbeena	تخبينا	*mnitkhabba*	منتخبى	*nitkhabba*	نتخبى	we
tkhabbu	تخبو	*tkhabbeetu*	تخبيتو	*btitkhabbu*	بتتخبو	*titkhabbu*	تتخبو	you [P]
		tkhabbu	تخبو	*bitkhabbu*	بتخبو	*yitkhabbu*	يتخبو	they

tjaawab "Respond" (*tfaaȝal*)

NORTH LEVANTINE							
Noun of Instance		maSdar		Passive Participle		Active Participle	
N/A		*tajaawob* تجاوب		N/A		*mitjaaweb* متجاوب	
Imperative		Perfective		b-Imperfective		Zero-Imperfective	
		tjaawab‹t	تجاوبت	*bitjaawab*	بتجاوب	*2itjaawab*	اتجاوب	I
tjaawab	تجاوب	*tjaawab‹t*	تجاوبت	*btitjaawab*	بتتجاوب	*titjaawab*	تتجاوب	you [M]
tjaawabi	تجاوبي	*tjaawabti*	تجاوبتي	*btitjaawabi*	بتتجاوبي	*titjaawabi*	تتجاوبي	you [F]
		tjaawab	تجاوب	*byitjaawab*	بيتجاوب	*yitjaawab*	يتجاوب	he
		tjaawabet	تجاوبت	*btitjaawab*	بتتجاوب	*titjaawab*	تتجاوب	she
		tjaawabna	تجاوبنا	*mnitjaawab*	منتجاوب	*nitjaawab*	نتجاوب	we
tjaawabu	تجاوبو	*tjaawabtu*	تجاوبتو	*btitjaawabu*	بتتجاوبو	*titjaawabu*	تتجاوبو	you [P]
		tjaawabu	تجاوبو	*byitjaawabu*	بيتجاوبو	*yitjaawabu*	يتجاوبو	they

SOUTH LEVANTINE							
Noun of Instance		maSdar		Passive Participle		Active Participle	
N/A		*tajaawob* تجاوب		N/A		*mitjaaweb* متجاوب	
Imperative		Perfective		b-Imperfective		Zero-Imperfective	
		tjaawab‹t	تجاوبت	*batjaawab*	بتجاوب	*2atjaawab*	أتجاوب	I
tjaawab	تجاوب	*tjaawab‹t*	تجاوبت	*btitjaawab*	بتتجاوب	*titjaawab*	تتجاوب	you [M]
tjaawabi	تجاوبي	*tjaawabti*	تجاوبتي	*btitjaawabi*	بتتجاوبي	*titjaawabi*	تتجاوبي	you [F]
		tjaawab	تجاوب	*bitjaawab*	بتجاوب	*yitjaawab*	يتجاوب	he
		tjaawabat	تجاوبت	*btitjaawab*	بتتجاوب	*titjaawab*	تتجاوب	she
		tjaawabna	تجاوبنا	*mnitjaawab*	منتجاوب	*nitjaawab*	نتجاوب	we
tjaawabu	تجاوبو	*tjaawabtu*	تجاوبتو	*btitjaawabu*	بتتجاوبو	*titjaawabu*	تتجاوبو	you [P]
		tjaawabu	تجاوبو	*bitjaawabu*	بتجاوبو	*yitjaawabu*	يتجاوبو	they

tdaawa "Get Treated (Medicinally)" (*tfaa3a*)

NORTH LEVANTINE								
Noun of Instance		**maSdar**		**Passive Participle**		**Active Participle**		
N/A		*tadaawi* تداوي		N/A		*mitdaawi* متداوي		
Imperative		**Perfective**		***b-* Imperfective**		**Zero- Imperfective**		
		tdaaweet	تداويت	*bitdaawa*	بتداوى	*2itdaawa*	اتداوى	I
tdaawa	تداوى	*tdaaweet*	تداويت	*btitdaawa*	بتتداوى	*titdaawa*	تتداوى	you [M]
tdaawi	تداوي	*tdaaweeti*	تداويتي	*btitdaawi*	بتتداوي	*titdaawi*	تتداوي	you [F]
		tdaawa	تداوى	*byitdaawa*	بيتداوى	*yitdaawa*	يتداوى	he
		tdaawet	تداوت	*btitdaawa*	بتتداوى	*titdaawa*	تتداوى	she
		tdaaweena	تداوينا	*mnitdaawa*	منتداوى	*nitdaawa*	نتداوى	we
tdaawu	تداوو	*tdaaweetu*	تداويتو	*btitdaawu*	بتتداوو	*titdaawu*	تتداوو	you [P]
		tdaawu	تداوو	*byitdaawu*	بيتداوو	*yitdaawu*	يتداوو	they

SOUTH LEVANTINE								
Noun of Instance		**maSdar**		**Passive Participle**		**Active Participle**		
N/A		*tadaawi* تداوي		N/A		*mitdaawi* متداوي		
Imperative		**Perfective**		***b-* Imperfective**		**Zero- Imperfective**		
		tdaweet	تداويت	*batdaawa*	بتداوى	*2atdaawa*	أتداوى	I
tdaawa	تداوى	*tdaweet*	تداويت	*btitdaawa*	بتتداوى	*titdaawa*	تتداوى	you [M]
tdaawi	تداوي	*tdaweeti*	تداويتي	*btitdaawi*	بتتداوي	*titdaawi*	تتداوي	you [F]
		tdaawa	تداوى	*bitdaawa*	بتداوى	*yitdaawa*	يتداوى	he
		tdaawat	تداوت	*btitdaawa*	بتتداوى	*titdaawa*	تتداوى	she
		tdaweena	تداوينا	*mnitdaawa*	منتداوى	*nitdaawa*	نتداوى	we
tdaawu	تداوو	*tdaweetu*	تداويتو	*btitdaawu*	بتتداوو	*titdaawu*	تتداوو	you [P]
		tdaawu	تداوو	*bitdaawu*	بتداوو	*yitdaawu*	يتداوو	they

nmasak "Get Caught" (*nfaʒal*)

Note that the North Levantine forms have irregular stress on the middle syllable in the imperfective (see unit 27), while the South Levantine forms delete the middle vowel where possible.

NORTH LEVANTINE							
Noun of Instance		*maSdar*		**Passive Participle**		**Active Participle**	
N/A		N/A		N/A		*minmisek* منمسك	
Imperative		**Perfective**		***b-* Imperfective**		**Zero-Imperfective**	
		nmasakᵉt	انمسكت	*binmisek*	بنمسك	*2inmisek*	انمسك	I
nmisek	انمسك	*nmasakᵉt*	انمسكت	*btinmisek*	بتنمسك	*tinmisek*	تنمسك	you [M]
nmiski	انمسكي	*nmasakti*	انمسكتي	*btinmiski*	بتنمسكي	*tinmiski*	تنمسكي	you [F]
		nmasak	انمسك	*byinmisek*	بينمسك	*yinmisek*	ينمسك	he
		nmasket	انمسكت	*btinmisek*	بتنمسك	*tinmisek*	تنمسك	she
		nmasakna	انمسكنا	*mninmisek*	منمسك	*ninmisek*	ننمسك	we
nmisku	انمسكو	*nmasaktu*	انمسكتو	*btinmisku*	بتنمسكو	*tinmisku*	تنمسكو	you [P]
		nmasaku	انمسكو	*byinmisku*	بينمسكو	*yinmisku*	ينمسكو	they

SOUTH LEVANTINE							
Noun of Instance		*maSdar*		**Passive Participle**		**Active Participle**	
N/A		N/A		N/A		*minimsek* منمسك	
Imperative		**Perfective**		***b-* Imperfective**		**Zero-Imperfective**	
		nmasakᵉt	انمسكت	*banˈmsek*	بنمسك	*2anˈmsek*	أنمسك	I
2inˈmsek	انمسك	*nmasakᵉt*	انمسكت	*btinˈmsek*	بتنمسك	*tinˈmsek*	تنمسك	you [M]
2inmiski	انمسكي	*nmasakti*	انمسكتي	*btinmiski*	بتنمسكي	*tinmiski*	تنمسكي	you [F]
		nmasak	انمسك	*binˈmsek*	بنمسك	*yinˈmsek*	ينمسك	he

SOUTH LEVANTINE								
Imperative		**Perfective**		*b-* **Imperfective**		**Zero- Imperfective**		
		nmaskat	انمسكت	*btin'msek*	بتنمسك	*tin'msek*	تنمسك	she
		nmasakna	انمسكنا	*mnin'msek*	مننمسك	*nin'msek*	ننمسك	we
2inmisku	انمسكو	*nmasaktu*	انمسكتو	*btinmisku*	بتنمسكو	*tinmisku*	تنمسكو	you [P]
		nmasaku	انمسكو	*binmisku*	بنمسكو	*yinmisku*	ينمسكو	they

This is an alternative to the forms with *i-e*, much more common in Lebanon although occurring with some verbs for Syrian speakers as well.

NORTH LEVANTINE								
Noun of Instance		*maSdar*		**Passive Participle**		**Active Participle**		
N/A		N/A		N/A		*minmisek* منمسك		
Imperative		**Perfective**		*b-* **Imperfective**		**Zero- Imperfective**		
		nmasak^et	انمسكت	*binmasak*	بنمسك	*2inmasak*	انمسك	I
nmasak	انمسك	*nmasak^et*	انمسكت	*btinmasak*	بتنمسك	*tinmasak*	تنمسك	you [M]
nmasaki	انمسكي	*nmasakti*	انمسكتي	*btinmasaki*	بتنمسكي	*tinmasaki*	تنمسكي	you [F]
		nmasak	انمسك	*byinmasak*	بينمسك	*yinmasak*	ينمسك	he
		nmasket	انمسكت	*btinmasak*	بتنمسك	*tinmasak*	تنمسك	she
		nmasakna	انمسكنا	*mninmasak*	مننمسك	*ninmasak*	ننمسك	we
nmasaku	انمسكو	*nmasaktu*	انمسكتو	*btinmasaku*	بتنمسكو	*tinmasaku*	تنمسكو	you [P]
		nmasaku	انمسكو	*byinmasaku*	بينمسكو	*yinmasaku*	ينمسكو	they

nshaaf "Be Seen" (*nfaal*)

NORTH LEVANTINE								
Noun of Instance		**maSdar**		**Passive Participle**		**Active Participle**		
N/A		N/A		N/A		*minshaaf* منشاف		
Imperative		**Perfective**		**b- Imperfective**		**Zero- Imperfective**		
		nshifᵉt	انشفت	*binshaaf*	بنشاف	*2inshaaf*	انشاف	I
nshaaf	انشاف	*nshifᵉt*	انشفت	*btinshaaf*	بتنشاف	*tinshaaf*	تنشاف	you [M]
nshaafi	انشافي	*nshifti*	انشفتي	*btinshaafi*	بتنشافي	*tinshaafi*	تنشافي	you [F]
		nshaaf	انشاف	*byinshaaf*	بينشاف	*yinshaaf*	ينشاف	he
		nshaafet	انشافت	*btinshaaf*	بتنشاف	*tinshaaf*	تنشاف	she
		nshifna	انشفنا	*mninshaaf*	مننشاف	*ninshaaf*	ننشاف	we
nshaafu	انشافو	*nshiftu*	انشفتو	*btinshaafu*	بتنشافو	*tinshaafu*	تنشافو	you [P]
		nshaafu	انشافو	*byinshaafu*	بينشافو	*yinshaafu*	ينشافو	they

SOUTH LEVANTINE								
Noun of Instance		**maSdar**		**Passive Participle**		**Active Participle**		
N/A		N/A		N/A		*minshaaf* منشاف		
Imperative		**Perfective**		**b- Imperfective**		**Zero- Imperfective**		
		nshafᵉt	انشفت	*banshaaf*	بنشاف	*2anshaaf*	أنشاف	I
2inshaaf	انشاف	*nshafᵉt*	انشفت	*btinshaaf*	بتنشاف	*tinshaaf*	تنشاف	you [M]
2inshaafi	انشافي	*nshafti*	انشفتي	*btinshaafi*	بتنشافي	*tinshaafi*	تنشافي	you [F]
		nshaaf	انشاف	*binshaaf*	بنشاف	*yinshaaf*	ينشاف	he
		nshaafat	انشافت	*btinshaaf*	بتنشاف	*tinshaaf*	تنشاف	she
		nshafna	انشفنا	*mninshaaf*	مننشاف	*ninshaaf*	ننشاف	we
2inshaafu	انشافو	*nshaftu*	انشفتو	*btinshaafu*	بتنشافو	*tinshaafu*	تنشافو	you [P]
		nshaafu	انشافو	*binshaafu*	بنشافو	*yinshaafu*	ينشافو	they

The non–third-person perfective forms (i.e., those that require a shortened vowel) are not very common, and some speakers find them to be unnatural.

nkabb "Be Poured Out" (*nfa33*)

NORTH LEVANTINE								
Noun of Instance		**maSdar**		**Passive Participle**		**Active Participle**		
N/A		N/A		N/A		*minkabb* منكب		
Imperative		**Perfective**		**b-Imperfective**		**Zero-Imperfective**		
		nkabbeet	انكبيت	*binkabb*	بنكب	*2inkabb*	انكب	I
nkabb	انكب	*nkabbeet*	انكبيت	*btinkabb*	بتنكب	*tinkabb*	تنكب	you [M]
nkabbi	انكبي	*nkabbeeti*	انكبيتي	*btinkabbi*	بتنكبي	*tinkabbi*	تنكبي	you [F]
		nkabb	انكب	*byinkabb*	بينكب	*yinkabb*	ينكب	he
		nkabbet	انكبت	*btinkabb*	بتنكب	*tinkabb*	تنكب	she
		nkabbeena	انكبينا	*mninkabb*	مننكب	*ninkabb*	ننكب	we
nkabbu	انكبو	*nkabbeetu*	انكبيتو	*btinkabbu*	بتنكبو	*tinkabbu*	تنكبو	you [P]
		nkabbu	انكبو	*byinkabbu*	بينكبو	*yinkabbu*	ينكبو	they

SOUTH LEVANTINE								
Noun of Instance		**maSdar**		**Passive Participle**		**Active Participle**		
N/A		N/A		N/A		*minkabb* منكب		
Imperative		**Perfective**		**b-Imperfective**		**Zero-Imperfective**		
		nkabbeet	انكبيت	*bankabb*	بنكب	*2ankabb*	أنكب	I
2inkabb	انكب	*nkabbeet*	انكبيت	*btinkabb*	بتنكب	*tinkabb*	تنكب	you [M]
2inkabbi	انكبي	*nkabbeeti*	انكبيتي	*btinkabbi*	بتنكبي	*tinkabbi*	تنكبي	you [F]
		nkabb	انكب	*binkabb*	بنكب	*yinkabb*	ينكب	he

SOUTH LEVANTINE								
Imperative		**Perfective**		***b*- Imperfective**		**Zero- Imperfective**		
		nkabbat	انكبت	*btinkabb*	بتنكب	*tinkabb*	تنكب	she
		nkabbeena	انكبينا	*mninkabb*	مننكب	*ninkabb*	ننكب	we
2inkabbu	انكبو	*nkabbeetu*	انكبيتو	*btinkabbu*	بتنكبو	*tinkabbu*	تنكبو	you [P]
		nkabbu	انكبو	*binkabbu*	بنكبو	*yinkabbu*	ينكبو	they

n3ama "Be Blinded" (*nfa3a*)

Note that the North Levantine forms have irregular stress on the middle syllable in the imperfective (see unit 27), while the South Levantine forms delete the middle vowel where possible.

NORTH LEVANTINE								
Noun of Instance		***maSdar***		**Passive Participle**		**Active Participle**		
N/A		N/A		N/A		*min3imi* منعمي		
Imperative		**Perfective**		***b*- Imperfective**		**Zero- Imperfective**		
		n3ameet	انعميت	*bin**3i**mi*	بنعمي	*2in**3i**mi*	انعمي	I
n3imi	انعمي	*n3ameet*	انعميت	*btin**3i**mi*	بتنعمي	*tin**3i**mi*	تنعمي	you [M]
n3imi	انعمي	*n3ameeti*	انعميتي	*btin**3i**mi*	بتنعمي	*tin**3i**mi*	تنعمي	you [F]
		n3ama	انعمى	*byin**3i**mi*	بينعمي	*yin**3i**mi*	ينعمي	he
		n3amet	انعمت	*btin**3i**mi*	بتنعمي	*tin**3i**mi*	تنعمي	she
		n3ameena	انعمينا	*mnin**3i**mi*	مننعمي	*nin**3i**mi*	ننعمي	we
n3imu	انعمو	*n3ameetu*	انعميتو	*btin**3i**mu*	بتنعمو	*tin**3i**mu*	تنعمو	you [P]
		n3amu	انعمو	*byin**3i**mu*	بينعمو	*yin**3i**mu*	ينعمو	they

SOUTH LEVANTINE								
Noun of Instance		**maSdar**		**Passive Participle**		**Active Participle**		
N/A		N/A		N/A		*mini3mi* منعمي		
Imperative		**Perfective**		**b-Imperfective**		**Zero-Imperfective**		
		n3ameet	انعميت	*ban3imi*	بنعمي	*2an3imi*	أنعمي	I
n3imi	انعمي	*n3ameet*	انعميت	*btin3imi*	بتنعمي	*tin3imi*	تنعمي	you [M]
n3imi	انعمي	*n3ameeti*	انعميتي	*btin3imi*	بتنعمي	*tin3imi*	تنعيي	you [F]
		n3ama	انعمى	*bin3imi*	بنعمي	*yin3imi*	ينعمي	he
		n3amat	انعمت	*btin3imi*	بتنعمي	*tin3imi*	تنعمي	she
		n3ameena	انعمينا	*mnin3imi*	منعمي	*nin3imi*	ننعمي	we
n3imu	انعمو	*n3ameetu*	انعميتو	*btin3imu*	بتنعمو	*tin3imu*	تنعمو	you [P]
		n3amu	انعمو	*bin3imu*	بنعمو	*yin3imu*	ينعمو	they

n3aTa "Be Given" (Irregular)

NORTH LEVANTINE								
Noun of Instance		**maSdar**		**Passive Participle**		**Active Participle**		
N/A		N/A		N/A		*min3iTi* منعطي		
Imperative		**Perfective**		**b-Imperfective**		**Zero-Imperfective**		
		n3aTeet	انعطيت	*bin3aTa*	بنعطى	*2in3aTa*	انعطى	I
n3aTa	انعطى	*n3aTeet*	انعطيت	*btin3aTa*	بتنعطى	*tin3aTa*	تنعطى	you [M]
n3aTi	انعطي	*n3aTeeti*	انعطيتي	*btin3aTi*	بتنعطي	*tin3aTi*	تنعطي	you [F]
		n3aTa	انعطى	*byin3aTa*	بينعطى	*yin3aTa*	ينعطى	he
		n3aTet	انعطت	*btin3aTa*	بتنعطى	*tin3aTa*	تنعطى	she
		n3aTeena	انعطينا	*mnin3aTa*	منعطى	*nin3aTa*	ننعطى	we
n3aTu	انعطو	*n3aTeetu*	انعطيتو	*btin3aTu*	بتنعطو	*tin3aTu*	تنعطو	you [P]
		n3aTu	انعطو	*byin3aTu*	بينعطو	*yin3aTu*	ينعطو	they

		maSdar		Passive Participle		Active Participle		
SOUTH LEVANTINE								
Noun of Instance		*maSdar*		**Passive Participle**		**Active Participle**		
N/A		N/A		N/A		*mini3Ti* منعطي		
Imperative		**Perfective**		*b-* **Imperfective**		**Zero- Imperfective**		
		n3aTeet	انعطيت	*ban3aTa*	بنعطى	*2an3aTa*	أنعطى	I
N/A		*n3aTeet*	انعطيت	*btin3aTa*	بتنعطى	*tin3aTa*	تنعطى	you [M]
N/A		*n3aTeeti*	انعطيتي	*btin3aTi*	بتنعطي	*tin3aTi*	تنعطي	you [F]
		n3aTa	انعطى	*bin3aTa*	بنعطى	*yin3aTa*	ينعطى	he
		n3aTat	انعطت	*btin3aTa*	بتنعطى	*tin3aTa*	تنعطى	she
		n3aTeena	انعطينا	*mnin3aTa*	مننعطى	*nin3aTa*	ننعطى	we
N/A		*n3aTeetu*	انعطيتو	*btin3aTu*	بتنعطو	*tin3aTu*	تنعطو	you [P]
		n3aTu	انعطو	*bin3aTu*	بنعطو	*yin3aTu*	ينعطو	they

shtaghal "Work" (*fta3al*)

Note that the North Levantine forms have irregular stress on the middle syllable in the imperfective (see unit 27), while the South Levantine forms delete the middle vowel where possible.

		maSdar		Passive Participle		Active Participle		
NORTH LEVANTINE								
Noun of Instance		*maSdar*		**Passive Participle**		**Active Participle**		
N/A		*shighel* شغل		N/A		*mishtighel* مشتغل		
Imperative		**Perfective**		*b-* **Imperfective**		**Zero- Imperfective**		
		shtaghalᵉt	اشتغلت	*bishtighel*	بشتغل	*2ishtighel*	اشتغل	I
shtighel	اشتغل	*shtaghalᵉt*	اشتغلت	*btishtighel*	بتشتغل	*tishtighel*	تشتغل	you [M]
shtighli	اشتغلي	*shtaghalti*	اشتغلتي	*btishtighli*	بتشتغلي	*tishtighli*	تشتغلي	you [F]

NORTH LEVANTINE								
Imperative		**Perfective**		**b-Imperfective**		**Zero-Imperfective**		
		shtaghal	اشتغل	*byishtighel*	بيشتغل	*yishtighel*	يشتغل	he
		shtaghlet	اشتغلت	*btishtighel*	بتشتغل	*tishtighel*	تشتغل	she
		shtaghalna	اشتغلنا	*mnishtighel*	منشتغل	*nishtighel*	نشتغل	we
shtighlu	اشتغلو	*shtaghaltu*	اشتغلتو	*btishtighlu*	بتشتغلو	*tishtighlu*	تشتغلو	you [P]
		shtaghalu	اشتغلو	*byishtighlu*	بيشتغلو	*yishtighlu*	يشتغلو	they

SOUTH LEVANTINE								
Noun of Instance		**maSdar**		**Passive Participle**		**Active Participle**		
N/A		*shughol* شغل		N/A		*mishtghel* مشتغل		
Imperative		**Perfective**		**b-Imperfective**		**Zero-Imperfective**		
		shtaghal^{e}t	اشتغلت	*bashtghel*	بشتغل	*2ashtghel*	أشتغل	I
2ishtghel	اشتغل	*shtaghal^{e}t*	اشتغلت	*btishtghel*	بتشتغل	*tishtghel*	تشتغل	you [M]
2ishtighli	اشتغلي	*shtaghalti*	اشتغلتي	*btishtighli*	بتشتغلي	*tishtighli*	تشتغلي	you [F]
		shtaghal	اشتغل	*bishtghel*	بشتغل	*yishtghel*	يشتغل	he
		shtaghlat	اشتغلت	*btishtghel*	بتشتغل	*tishtghel*	تشتغل	she
		shtaghalna	اشتغلنا	*mnishtghel*	منشتغل	*nishtghel*	نشتغل	we
2ishtighlu	اشتغلو	*shtaghaltu*	اشتغلتو	*btishtighlu*	بتشتغلو	*tishtighlu*	تشتغلو	you [P]
		shtaghalu	اشتغلو	*bishtighlu*	بشتغلو	*yishtighlu*	يشتغلو	they

ttaSal "Get Connected" (*ttaʒal*)

Note that the North Levantine forms have irregular stress on the middle syllable in the imperfective (see unit 27), while the South Levantine forms delete the middle vowel where possible.

NORTH LEVANTINE							
Noun of Instance		**maSdar**		**Passive Participle**		**Active Participle**	
N/A		*2ittiSaal* اتصال		N/A		*mittiSel* متصل	
Imperative		**Perfective**		**b- Imperfective**		**Zero- Imperfective**	
		ttaSalᵉt اتصلت		*bittiSel* بتصل		*2ittiSel* اتصل	I
ttiSel	اتصل	*ttaSalᵉt* اتصلت		*btittiSel* بتتصل		*tittiSel* تتصل	you [M]
ttiSli	اتصلي	*ttaSalti* اتصلتي		*btittiSli* بتتصلي		*tittiSli* تتصلي	you [F]
		ttaSal اتصل		*byittiSel* بيتصل		*yittiSel* يتصل	he
		ttaSlet اتصلت		*btittiSel* بتتصل		*tittiSel* تتصل	she
		ttaSalna اتصلنا		*mnittiSel* منتصل		*nittiSel* نتصل	we
ttiSlu	اتصلو	*ttaSaltu* اتصلتو		*btittiSlu* بتتصلو		*tittiSlu* تتصلو	you [P]
		ttaSalu اتصلو		*byittiSlu* بيتصلو		*yittiSlu* يتصلو	they

SOUTH LEVANTINE							
Noun of Instance		**maSdar**		**Passive Participle**		**Active Participle**	
N/A		*2ittiSaal* اتصال		N/A		*mittSel* متصل	
Imperative		**Perfective**		**b- Imperfective**		**Zero- Imperfective**	
		ttaSalᵉt اتصلت		*battSel* بتصل		*2attSel* أتصل	I
2ittSel	اتصل	*ttaSalᵉt* اتصلت		*btittSel* بتتصل		*tittSel* تتصل	you [M]
2ittiSli	اتصلي	*ttaSalti* اتصلتي		*btittiSli* بتتصلي		*tittiSli* تتصلي	you [F]
		ttaSal اتصل		*bittSel* بتصل		*yittSel* يتصل	he
		ttaSlat اتصلت		*btittSel* بتتصل		*tittSel* تتصل	she
		ttaSalna اتصلنا		*mnittSel* منتصل		*nittSel* نتصل	we
2ittiSlu	اتصلو	*ttaSaltu* اتصلتو		*btittiSlu* بتتصلو		*tittiSlu* تتصلو	you [P]
		ttaSalu اتصلو		*bittiSlu* بتصلو		*yittiSlu* يتصلو	they

rtaa7 "Rest" (*ftaal*)

NORTH LEVANTINE								
Noun of Instance		**maSdar**		**Passive Participle**		**Active Participle**		
N/A		*2irtiyaa7* ارتياح		N/A		*mirtaa7* مرتاح		
Imperative		**Perfective**		**b-Imperfective**		**Zero-Imperfective**		
		rta7^et ارتحت		*birtaa7* برتاح		*2irtaa7* ارتاح		I
rtaa7 ارتاح		*rta7^et* ارتحت		*btirtaa7* بترتاح		*tirtaa7* ترتاح		you [M]
rtaa7i ارتاحي		*rta7ti* ارتحتي		*btirtaa7i* بترتاحي		*tirtaa7i* ترتاحي		you [F]
		rtaa7 ارتاح		*byirtaa7* بيرتاح		*yirtaa7* يرتاح		he
		rtaa7at ارتاحت		*btirtaa7* بترتاح		*tirtaa7* ترتاح		she
		rta7na ارتحنا		*mnirtaa7* منرتاح		*nirtaa7* نرتاح		we
rtaa7u ارتاحو		*rta7tu* ارتحتو		*btirtaa7u* بترتاحو		*tirtaa7u* ترتاحو		you [P]
		rtaa7u ارتاحو		*byirtaa7u* بيرتاحو		*yirtaa7u* يرتاحو		they

Note that many Syrian speakers have *i* as the short vowel in the perfective (see unit 33).

SOUTH LEVANTINE								
Noun of Instance		**maSdar**		**Passive Participle**		**Active Participle**		
N/A		*2irtiyaa7* ارتياح		N/A		*mirtaa7* مرتاح		
Imperative		**Perfective**		**b-Imperfective**		**Zero-Imperfective**		
		rta7^et ارتحت		*bartaa7* برتاح		*2artaa7* أرتاح		I
2irtaa7 ارتاح		*rta7^et* ارتحت		*btirtaa7* بترتاح		*tirtaa7* ترتاح		you [M]
2irtaa7i ارتاحي		*rta7ti* ارتحتي		*btirtaa7i* بترتاحي		*tirtaa7i* ترتاحي		you [F]
		rtaa7 ارتاح		*birtaa7* برتاح		*yirtaa7* يرتاح		he
		rtaa7at ارتاحت		*btirtaa7* بترتاح		*tirtaa7* ترتاح		she
		rta7na ارتحنا		*mnirtaa7* منرتاح		*nirtaa7* نرتاح		we

SOUTH LEVANTINE							
Imperative		**Perfective**		**b-Imperfective**		**Zero-Imperfective**	
2irtaa7u	ارتاحو	rta7tu	ارتحتو	btirtaa7u	بترتاحو	tirtaa7u	ترتاحو	you [P]
		rtaa7u	ارتاحو	birtaa7u	برتاحو	yirtaa7u	يرتاحو	they

DTarr "Have to" (*fta33*)

NORTH LEVANTINE							
Noun of Instance		**maSdar**		**Passive Participle**		**Active Participle**	
N/A		2iDTiraar اضطرار		N/A		miDTarr مضطر	
Imperative		**Perfective**		**b-Imperfective**		**Zero-Imperfective**	
		DTarreet	اضطريت	biDTarr	بضطر	2iDTarr	اضطر	I
DTarr	اضطر	DTarreet	اضطريت	btiDTarr	بتضطر	tiDTarr	تضطر	you [M]
DTarri	اضطري	DTarreeti	اضطريتي	btiDTarri	بتضطري	tiDTarri	تضطري	you [F]
		DTarr	اضطر	byiDTarr	بيضطر	yiDTarr	يضطر	he
		DTarret	اضطرت	btiDTarr	بتضطر	tiDTarr	تضطر	she
		DTarreena	اضطرينا	mniDTarr	منضطر	niDTarr	نضطر	we
DTarru	اضطرو	DTarreetu	اضطريتو	btiDTarru	بتضطرو	tiDTarru	تضطرو	you [P]
		DTarru	اضطرو	byiDTarru	بيضطرو	yiDTarru	يضطرو	they

SOUTH LEVANTINE							
Noun of Instance		**maSdar**		**Passive Participle**		**Active Participle**	
N/A		2iDTiraar اضطرار		N/A		miDTarr مضطر	
Imperative		**Perfective**		**b-Imperfective**		**Zero-Imperfective**	
		DTarreet	اضطريت	baDTarr	بضطر	2aDTarr	أضطر	I
DTarr	اضطر	DTarreet	اضطريت	btiDTarr	بتضطر	tiDTarr	تضطر	you [M]

SOUTH LEVANTINE								
Imperative		**Perfective**		***b-*Imperfective**		**Zero-Imperfective**		
DTarri	اضطري	DTarreeti	اضطريتي	btiDTarri	بتضطر	tiDTarri	تضطر	you [F]
		DTarr	اضطر	biDTarr	بضطر	yiDTarr	يضطر	he
		DTarrt	اضطرت	btiDTarr	بتضطر	tiDTarr	تضطر	she
		DTarreena	اضطرينا	mniDTarr	منضطر	niDTarr	نضطر	we
DTarru	اضطرو	DTarreetu	اضطريتو	btiDTarru	بتضطرو	tiDTarru	تضطرو	you [P]
		DTarru	اضطرو	biDTarru	بضطرو	yiDTarru	يضطرو	they

lta2a "Meet Up" (*fta3a*)

> Note that the North Levantine forms have irregular stress on the middle syllable in the imperfective (see unit 27), while the South Levantine forms delete the middle vowel where possible.

NORTH LEVANTINE								
Noun of Instance		***maSdar***		**Passive Participle**		**Active Participle**		
N/A		N/A		N/A		milti2i ملتقي		
Imperative		**Perfective**		***b-*Imperfective**		**Zero-Imperfective**		
		lta2eet	التقيت	bilti2i	بلتقي	2ilti2i	التقي	I
lti2i	التقي	lta2eet	التقيت	btilti2i	بتلتقي	tilti2i	تلتقي	you [M]
lti2i	التقي	lta2eeti	التقيتي	btilti2i	بتلتقي	tilti2i	تلتقي	you [F]
		lta2a	التقى	byilti2i	بيلتقي	yilti2i	يلتقي	he
		lta2et	التقت	btilti2i	بتلتقي	tilti2i	تلتقي	she
		lta2eena	التقينا	mnilti2i	منلتقي	nilti2i	نلتقي	we
lti2u	التقو	lta2eetu	التقيتو	btilti2u	بتلتقو	tilti2u	تلتقو	you [P]
		lta2u	التقو	byilti2u	بيلتقو	yilti2u	يلتقو	they

Noun of Instance		maSdar		Passive Participle		Active Participle		
SOUTH LEVANTINE								
N/A		N/A		N/A		milt2i ملتقي		
Imperative		**Perfective**		**b-Imperfective**		**Zero-Imperfective**		
		lta2eet التقيت		balt2i بلتقي		2alt2i ألتقي		I
2ilt2i التقي		lta2eet التقيت		btilt2i بتلتقي		tilt2i تلتقي		you [M]
2ilt2i التقي		lta2eeti التقيتي		btilt2i بتلتقي		tilt2i تلتقي		you [F]
		lta2a التقى		bilt2i بلتقي		yilt2i يلتقي		he
		lta2at التقت		btilt2i بتلتقي		tilt2i تلتقي		she
		lta2eena التقينا		mnilt2i منلتقي		nilt2i نلتقي		we
2ilt2u التقو		lta2eetu التقيتو		btilt2u بتلتقو		tilt2u تلتقو		you [P]
		lta2u التقو		bilt2u بلتقو		yilt2u يلتقو		they

byaDD "Turn White" (*fʒall*)

Noun of Instance		maSdar		Passive Participle		Active Participle		
NORTH LEVANTINE								
N/A		N/A		N/A		mibyaDD مبيض		
Imperative		**Perfective**		**b-Imperfective**		**Zero-Imperfective**		
		byaDDeet ابيضيت		bibyaDD ببيض		2ibyaDD ابيض		I
byaDD ابيض		byaDDeet ابيضيت		btibyaDD بتبيض		tibyaDD تبيض		you [M]
byaDDi ابيضي		byaDDeeti ابيضيتي		btibyaDDi بتبيضي		tibyaDDi تبيضي		you [F]
		byaDD ابيض		byibyaDD ببيض		yibyaDD ييبيض		he
		byaDDet ابيضت		btibyaDD بتبيض		tibyaDD تبيض		she
		byaDDeena ابيضينا		mnibyaDD منبيض		nibyaDD نبيض		we
byaDDu ابيضو		byaDDeetu ابيضيتو		btibyaDDu بتبيضو		tibyaDDu تبيضو		you [P]

NORTH LEVANTINE						
Imperative		Perfective		*b-* Imperfective		Zero- Imperfective	
		byaDDu	ابيضو	*byibyaDDu*	بيبيضو	*yibyaDDu*	يبيضو	they

SOUTH LEVANTINE						
Noun of Instance		*maSdar*		Passive Participle		Active Participle	
N/A		N/A		N/A		*mibyaDD* مبيض	
Imperative		Perfective		*b-* Imperfective		Zero- Imperfective	
		byaDDeet	ابيضيت	*babyaDD*	ببيض	*2abyaDD*	أبيض	I
2ibyaDD	ابيض	*byaDDeet*	ابيضيت	*btibyaDD*	بتبيض	*tibyaDD*	تبيض	you [M]
2ibyaDDi	ابيضي	*byaDDeeti*	ابيضيتي	*btibyaDDi*	بتبيضي	*tibyaDDi*	تبيض	you [F]
		byaDD	ابيض	*bibyaDD*	ببيض	*yibyaDD*	يبيض	he
		byaDDat	ابيضت	*btibyaDD*	بتبيض	*tibyaDD*	تبيض	she
		byaDDeena	ابيضينا	*mnibyaDD*	منبيض	*nibyaDD*	نبيض	we
2ibyaDDu	ابيضو	*byaDDeetu*	ابيضيتو	*btibyaDDu*	بتبيضو	*tibyaDDu*	تبيضو	you [P]
		byaDDu	ابيضو	*bibyaDDu*	ببيضو	*yibyaDDu*	يبيضو	they

staghrab "Find Strange" (*staf3al*)

NORTH LEVANTINE						
Noun of Instance		*maSdar*		Passive Participle		Active Participle	
N/A		*2istighraab* استغراب		*mistaghrab* مستغرب		*mistaghreb* مستغرب	
Imperative		Perfective		*b-* Imperfective		Zero- Imperfective	
		staghrab^et	استغربت	*bistaghreb*	بستغرب	*2istaghreb*	استغرب	I

NORTH LEVANTINE								
Imperative		**Perfective**		***b-*** **Imperfective**		**Zero- Imperfective**		
staghreb	استغرب	*staghrabᵉt*	استغربت	*btistaghreb*	بتستغرب	*tistaghreb*	تستغرب	you [M]
staghⁱrbi	استغربي	*staghrabti*	استغربتي	*btistaghⁱrbi*	بتستغربي	*tistaghⁱrbi*	تستغربي	you [F]
		staghrab	استغرب	*byistaghreb*	بيستغرب	*yistaghreb*	يستغرب	he
		staghrabet	استغربت	*btistaghreb*	بتستغرب	*tistaghreb*	تستغرب	she
		staghrabna	استغربنا	*mnistaghreb*	منستغرب	*nistaghreb*	نستغرب	we
staghⁱrbu	استغربو	*staghrabtu*	استغربتو	*btistaghⁱrbu*	بتستغربو	*tistaghⁱrbu*	تستغربو	you [P]
		staghrabu	استغربو	*byistaghⁱrbu*	بيستغربو	*yistaghⁱrbu*	يستغربو	they

SOUTH LEVANTINE								
Noun of Instance		***maSdar***		**Passive Participle**		**Active Participle**		
N/A		*2istighraab* استغراب		*mustaghrab* مستغرب		*mistaghreb* مستغرب		
Imperative		**Perfective**		***b-*** **Imperfective**		**Zero- Imperfective**		
		staghrabᵉt	استغربت	*bastaghreb*	بستغرب	*2astaghreb*	أستغرب	I
2istaghreb	استغرب	*staghrabᵉt*	استغربت	*btistaghreb*	بتستغرب	*tistaghreb*	تستغرب	you [M]
2istaghⁱrbi	استغربي	*staghrabti*	استغربتي	*btistaghⁱrbi*	بتستغربي	*tistaghⁱrbi*	تستغربي	you [F]
		staghrab	استغرب	*bistaghreb*	بستغرب	*yistaghreb*	يستغرب	he
		staghrabat	استغربت	*btistaghreb*	بتستغرب	*tistaghreb*	تستغرب	she
		staghrabna	استغربنا	*mnistaghreb*	منستغرب	*nistaghreb*	نستغرب	we
2istaghⁱrbu	استغربو	*staghrabtu*	استغربتو	*btistaghⁱrbu*	بتستغربو	*tistaghⁱrbu*	تستغربو	you [P]
		staghrabu	استغربو	*bistaghⁱrbu*	بستغربو	*yistaghⁱrbu*	يستغربو	they

staqaal "Resign" (*stafaal*)

NORTH LEVANTINE								
Noun of Instance		**maSdar**		**Passive Participle**		**Active Participle**		
N/A		*2istiqaale* استقالة		N/A		*mistaqiil* مستقيل		
Imperative		**Perfective**		**b-Imperfective**		**Zero-Imperfective**		
		staqal^et	استقلت	*bistaqiil*	بستقيل	*2istaqiil*	استقيل	I
staqiil	استقيل	*staqal^et*	استقلت	*btistaqiil*	بتستقيل	*tistaqiil*	تستقيل	you [M]
staqiili	استقيلي	*staqalti*	استقلتي	*btistaqiili*	بتستقيلي	*tistaqiili*	تستقيلي	you [F]
		staqaal	استقال	*byistaqiil*	بيستقيل	*yistaqiil*	يستقيل	he
		staqaalet	استقالت	*btistaqiil*	بتستقيل	*tistaqiil*	تستقيل	she
		staqalna	استقلنا	*mnistaqiil*	منستقيل	*nistaqiil*	نستقيل	we
staqiilu	استقيلو	*staqaltu*	استقلتو	*btistaqiilu*	بتستقيلو	*tistaqiilu*	تستقيلو	you [P]
		staqaalu	استقالو	*byistaqiilu*	بيستقيلو	*yistaqiilu*	يستقيلو	they

SOUTH LEVANTINE								
Noun of Instance		**maSdar**		**Passive Participle**		**Active Participle**		
N/A		*2istiqaale* استقالة		N/A		*mistaqiil* مستقيل		
Imperative		**Perfective**		**b-Imperfective**		**Zero-Imperfective**		
		staqal^et	استقلت	*bastaqiil*	بستقيل	*2astaqiil*	أستقيل	I
2istaqiil	استقيل	*staqal^et*	استقلت	*btistaqiil*	بتستقيل	*tistaqiil*	تستقيل	you [M]
2istaqiili	استقيلي	*staqalti*	استقلتي	*btistaqiili*	بتستقيلي	*tistaqiili*	تستقيلي	you [F]
		staqaal	استقال	*bistaqiil*	بستقيل	*yistaqiil*	يستقيل	he
		staqaalat	استقالت	*btistaqiil*	بتستقيل	*tistaqiil*	تستقيل	she
		staqalna	استقلنا	*mnistaqiil*	منستقيل	*nistaqiil*	نستقيل	we
2istaqiilu	استقيلو	*staqaltu*	استقلتو	*btistaqiilu*	بتستقيلو	*tistaqiilu*	تستقيلو	you [P]
		staqaalu	استقالو	*bistaqiilu*	بستقيلو	*yistaqiilu*	يستقيلو	they

Many high-frequency verbs on this pattern can drop the *a* in the imperfective: تستريح *tistrii7* "you get some rest."

staghall "Take Advantage of" (*stafa33*)

NORTH LEVANTINE							
Noun of Instance		**maSdar**		**Passive Participle**		**Active Participle**	
N/A		*2istighlaal* استغلال		*mistaghall* مستغل		*mistaghill* مستغل	
Imperative		**Perfective**		**b-Imperfective**		**Zero-Imperfective**	
		staghalleet	استغليت	*bistaghill*	بستغل	*2istaghill*	استغل	I
staghill	استغل	*staghalleet*	استغليت	*btistaghill*	بتستغل	*tistaghill*	تستغل	you [M]
staghilli	استغلي	*staghalleeti*	استغليتي	*btistaghilli*	بتستغلي	*tistaghilli*	تستغلي	you [F]
		staghall	استغل	*byistaghill*	بيستغل	*yistaghill*	يستغل	he
		staghallet	استغلت	*btistaghill*	بتستغل	*tistaghill*	تستغل	she
		staghalleena	استغلينا	*mnistaghill*	منستغل	*nistaghill*	نستغل	we
staghillu	استغلو	*staghalleetu*	استغليتو	*btistaghillu*	بتستغلو	*tistaghillu*	تستغلو	you [P]
		staghallu	استغلو	*byistaghillu*	بيستغلو	*yistaghillu*	يستغلو	they

SOUTH LEVANTINE							
Noun of Instance		**maSdar**		**Passive Participle**		**Active Participle**	
N/A		*2istighlaal* استغلال		*mustaghall* مستغل		*mistaghill* مستغل	
Imperative		**Perfective**		**b-Imperfective**		**Zero-Imperfective**	
		staghalleet	استغليت	*bastaghill*	بستغل	*2astaghill*	أستغل	I
staghill	استغل	*staghalleet*	استغليت	*btistaghill*	بتستغل	*tistaghill*	تستغل	you [M]
staghilli	استغلي	*staghalleeti*	استغليتي	*btistaghilli*	بتستغلي	*tistaghilli*	تستغلي	you [F]
		staghall	استغل	*bistaghill*	بستغل	*yistaghill*	يستغل	he
		staghallt	استغلت	*btistaghill*	بتستغل	*tistaghill*	تستغل	she

SOUTH LEVANTINE

Imperative		Perfective		b- Imperfective		Zero- Imperfective		
		staghalleena استغلينا		*mnistaghill* منستغل		*nistaghill* نستغل	we
staghillu استغلو		*staghalleetu* استغليتو		*btistaghillu* بتستغلو		*tistaghillu* تستغلو	you [P]
		staghallu استغلو		*bistaghillu* بستغلو		*yistaghillu* يستغلو	they

Many high-frequency verbs on this pattern can drop the *a* in the imperfective: تستغل *tistghill* "you take advantage."

staghla "Find Too Expensive" (*staf3a*)

NORTH LEVANTINE

Noun of Instance		*maSdar*		Passive Participle		Active Participle	
N/A		*stighli* استغلي		N/A		*mistaghli* مستغلي	

Imperative		Perfective		b- Imperfective		Zero- Imperfective		
		staghleet استغليت		*bistaghli* بستغلي		*2istaghli* استغلي	I
staghli استغلي		*staghleet* استغليت		*btistaghli* بتستغلي		*tistaghli* تستغلي	you [M]
staghli استغلي		*staghleeti* استغليتي		*btistaghli* بتستغلي		*tistaghli* تستغلي	you [F]
		staghla استغلى		*byistaghli* بيستغلي		*yistaghli* يستغلي	he
		staghlet استغلت		*btistaghli* بتستغلي		*tistaghli* تستغلي	she
		staghleena استغلينا		*mnistaghli* منستغلي		*nistaghli* نستغلي	we
staghlu استغلو		*staghleetu* استغليتو		*btistaghlu* بتستغلو		*tistaghlu* تستغلو	you [P]
		staghlu استغلو		*byistaghlu* بيستغلو		*yistaghlu* يستغلو	they

		SOUTH LEVANTINE					
Noun of Instance		**maSdar**		**Passive Participle**		**Active Participle**	
N/A		*stighli* استغلي		N/A		*mistaghli* مستغلي	
Imperative		**Perfective**		**b-Imperfective**		**Zero-Imperfective**	
		staghleet	استغليت	*bastaghli*	بستغلي	*2astaghli*	أستغلي	I
2istaghli	استغلي	*staghleet*	استغليت	*btistaghli*	بتستغلي	*tistaghli*	تستغلي	you [M]
2istaghli	استغلي	*staghleeti*	استغليتي	*btistaghli*	بتستغلي	*tistaghli*	تستغلي	you [F]
		staghla	استغلى	*bistaghli*	بستغلي	*yistaghli*	يستغلي	he
		staghlat	استغلت	*btistaghli*	بتستغلي	*tistaghli*	تستغلي	she
		staghleena	استغلينا	*mnistaghli*	منستغلي	*nistaghli*	نستغلي	we
2istaghlu	استغلو	*staghleetu*	استغليتو	*btistaghlu*	بتستغلو	*tistaghlu*	تستغلو	you [P]
		staghlu	استغلو	*bistaghlu*	بستغلو	*yistaghlu*	يستغلو	they

sashwar "Blow-Dry" (*fa3lal*)

		NORTH LEVANTINE					
Noun of Instance		**maSdar**		**Passive Participle**		**Active Participle**	
N/A		*sashwara* شورة *tsishwer* تسشور		*msashwar* مسشور		*msashwer* مسشور	
Imperative		**Perfective**		**b-Imperfective**		**Zero-Imperfective**	
		sashwaret	سشورت	*bsashwer*	بسشور	*sashwer*	سشور	I
sashwer	سشور	*sashwaret*	سشورت	*bitsashwer*	بتسشور	*tsashwer*	تسشور	you [M]
sash'wri	سشوري	*sashwarti*	سشورتي	*bitsash'wri*	بتسشوري	*tsash'wri*	تسشوري	you [F]
		sashwar	سشور	*bisashwer*	بسشور	*ysashwer*	يسشور	he
		sashwaret	سشورت	*bitsashwer*	بتسشور	*tsashwer*	تسشور	she

NORTH LEVANTINE								
Imperative		**Perfective**		**b-Imperfective**		**Zero-Imperfective**		
		sashwarna	سشورنا	*minsashwer*	منسشور	*nsashwer*	نسشور	we
sashⁱwru	سشورو	*sashwartu*	سشورتو	*bitsashⁱwru*	بتسشورو	*tsashⁱwru*	تسشورو	you [P]
		sashwaru	سشورو	*bisashⁱwru*	بسشورو	*ysashⁱwru*	يسشورو	they

SOUTH LEVANTINE								
Noun of Instance		*maSdar*		**Passive Participle**		**Active Participle**		
N/A		*sashwara* سشورة *tsishwer* تسشور		*msashwar* مسشور		*msashwer* مسشور		
Imperative		**Perfective**		**b-Imperfective**		**Zero-Imperfective**		
		sashwaret	سشورت	*basashwer*	بسشور	*2asashwer*	أسشور	I
sashwer	سشور	*sashwaret*	سشورت	*bitsashwer*	بتسشور	*tsashwer*	تسشور	you [M]
sashⁱwri	سشوري	*sashwarti*	سشورتي	*bitsashⁱwri*	بتسشوري	*tsashⁱwri*	تسشوري	you [F]
		sashwar	سشور	*bisashwer*	بسشور	*ysashwer*	يسشور	he
		sashwarat	سشورت	*bitsashwer*	بتسشور	*tsashwer*	تسشور	she
		sashwarna	سشورنا	*minsashwer*	منسشور	*nsashwer*	نسشور	we
sashⁱwru	سشورو	*sashwartu*	سشورتو	*bitsashⁱwru*	بتسشورو	*tsashⁱwru*	تسشورو	you [P]
		sashwaru	سشورو	*bisashⁱwru*	بسشورو	*ysashⁱwru*	يسشورو	they

farsha "Brush" (*faʒla*)

NORTH LEVANTINE								
Noun of Instance		*maSdar*		**Passive Participle**		**Active Participle**		
N/A		*tfirshi* تفرشي		*mfarsha* مفرشى		*mfarshi* مفرشي		
Imperative		**Perfective**		**b-Imperfective**		**Zero-Imperfective**		
		farsheet	فرشيت	*bfarshi*	بفرشي	*farshi*	فرشي	I

NORTH LEVANTINE							
Imperative		Perfective		b- Imperfective		Zero- Imperfective	
farshi	فرشي	*farsheet*	فرشيت	*bitfarshi*	بتفرشي	*tfarshi*	تفرشي	you [M]
farshi	فرشي	*farsheeti*	فرشيتي	*bitfarshi*	بتفرشي	*tfarshi*	تفرشي	you [F]
		farsha	فرشى	*bifarshi*	بفرشي	*yfarshi*	يفرشي	he
		farshet	فرشت	*bitfarshi*	بتفرشي	*tfarshi*	تفرشي	she
		farsheena	فرشينا	*minfarshi*	منفرشي	*nfarshi*	نفرشي	we
farshu	فرشو	*farsheetu*	فرشيتو	*bitfarshu*	بتفرشو	*tfarshu*	تفرشو	you [P]
		farshu	فرشو	*bifarshu*	بفرشو	*yfarshu*	يفرشو	they

SOUTH LEVANTINE							
Noun of Instance		maSdar		Passive Participle		Active Participle	
N/A		*tfirshi* تفرشي		*mfarsha* مفرشى		*mfarshi* مفرشي	
Imperative		Perfective		b- Imperfective		Zero- Imperfective	
		farsheet	فرشيت	*bafarshi*	بفرشي	*2afarshi*	أفرشي	I
farshi	فرشي	*farsheet*	فرشيت	*bitfarshi*	بتفرشي	*tfarshi*	تفرشي	you [M]
farshi	فرشي	*farsheeti*	فرشيتي	*bitfarshi*	بتفرشي	*tfarshi*	تفرشي	you [F]
		farsha	فرشى	*bifarshi*	بفرشي	*yfarshi*	يفرشي	he
		farshat	فرشت	*bitfarshi*	بتفرشي	*tfarshi*	تفرشي	she
		farsheena	فرشينا	*minfarshi*	منفرشي	*nfarshi*	نفرشي	we
farshu	فرشو	*farsheetu*	فرشيتو	*bitfarshu*	بتفرشو	*tfarshu*	تفرشو	you [P]
		farshu	فرشو	*bifarshu*	بفرشو	*yfarshu*	يفرشو	they

tkarkab "Get Messed Up" (*tfaʒlal*)

	NORTH LEVANTINE							
Noun of Instance		**maSdar**		**Passive Participle**		**Active Participle**		
N/A		*karkabe* كركبة		N/A		*mitkarkeb* متكركب		
Imperative		**Perfective**		**b-Imperfective**		**Zero-Imperfective**		
		tkarkabᵉt	تكركبت	*bitkarkab*	بتكركب	*2itkarkab*	اتكركب	I
tkarkab	اتكركب	*tkarkabᵉt*	تكركبت	*btitkarkab*	بتتكركب	*titkarkab*	تتكركب	you [M]
tkarkabi	اتكركبي	*tkarkabti*	تكركبتي	*btitkarkabi*	بتتكركبي	*titkarkabi*	تتكركبي	you [F]
		tkarkab	تكركب	*byitkarkab*	بيتكركب	*yitkarkab*	يتكركب	he
		tkarkabet	تكركبت	*btitkarkab*	بتتكركب	*titkarkab*	تتكركب	she
		tkarkabna	تكركبنا	*mnitkarkab*	منتكركب	*nitkarkab*	نتكركب	we
tkarkabu	اتكركبو	*tkarkabtu*	تكركبتو	*btitkarkabu*	بتتكركبو	*titkarkabu*	تتكركبو	you [P]
		tkarkabu	تكركبو	*byitkarkabu*	بيتكركبو	*yitkarkabu*	يتكركبو	they

	SOUTH LEVANTINE							
Noun of Instance		**maSdar**		**Passive Participle**		**Active Participle**		
N/A		*karkabe* كركبة		N/A		*mitkarkeb* متكركب		
Imperative		**Perfective**		**b-Imperfective**		**Zero-Imperfective**		
		tkarkabᵉt	تكركبت	*batkarkab*	بتكركب	*2atkarkab*	أتكركب	I
tkarkab	اتكركب	*tkarkabᵉt*	تكركبت	*btitkarkab*	بتتكركب	*titkarkab*	تتكركب	you [M]
tkarkabi	اتكركبي	*tkarkabti*	تكركبتي	*btitkarkabi*	بتتكركبي	*titkarkabi*	تتكركبي	you [F]
		tkarkab	تكركب	*bitkarkab*	بتكركب	*yitkarkab*	يتكركب	he
		tkarkabat	تكركبت	*btitkarkab*	بتتكركب	*titkarkab*	تتكركب	she
		tkarkabna	تكركبنا	*mnitkarkab*	منتكركب	*nitkarkab*	نتكركب	we
tkarkabu	اتكركبو	*tkarkabtu*	تكركبتو	*btitkarkabu*	بتتكركبو	*titkarkabu*	تتكركبو	you [P]
		tkarkabu	تكركبو	*bitkarkabu*	بتكركبو	*yitkarkabu*	يتكركبو	they

tfarsha "Be Brushed" (*tfaʒlal*)

NORTH LEVANTINE								
Noun of Instance		*maSdar*		Passive Participle		Active Participle		
N/A		*tfirshi* تفرشي		N/A		*mitfarshi* متفرشي		
Imperative		Perfective		*b-* Imperfective		Zero- Imperfective		
		tfarsheet	تفرشيت	*bitfarsha*	بتفرشى	*2itfarsha*	اتفرشى	I
tfarsha	تفرشى	*tfarsheet*	تفرشيت	*btitfarsha*	بتتفرشى	*titfarsha*	تتفرشى	you [M]
tfarshi	تفرشي	*tfarsheeti*	تفرشيتي	*btitfarshi*	بتتفرشي	*titfarshi*	تتفرشي	you [F]
		tfarsha	تفرشى	*byitfarsha*	بيتفرشى	*yitfarsha*	يتفرشى	he
		tfarshet	تفرشت	*btitfarsha*	بتتفرشى	*titfarsha*	تتفرشى	she
		tfarsheena	تفرشينا	*mnitfarsha*	منتفرشى	*nitfarsha*	نتفرشى	we
tfarshu	تفرشو	*tfarsheetu*	تفرشيتو	*btitfarshu*	بتتفرشو	*titfarshu*	تتفرشو	you [P]
		tfarshu	تفرشو	*byitfarshu*	بيتفرشو	*yitfarshu*	يتفرشو	they

SOUTH LEVANTINE								
Noun of Instance		*maSdar*		Passive Participle		Active Participle		
N/A		*tfirshi* تفرشي		N/A		*mitfarshi* متفرشي		
Imperative		Perfective		*b-* Imperfective		Zero- Imperfective		
		tfarsheet	تفرشيت	*batfarsha*	بتفرشى	*2atfarsha*	أتفرشى	I
tfarsha	تفرشى	*tfarsheet*	تفرشيت	*btitfarsha*	بتتفرشى	*titfarsha*	تتفرشى	you [M]
tfarshi	تفرشي	*tfarsheeti*	تفرشيتي	*btitfarshi*	بتتفرشي	*titfarshi*	تتفرشي	you [F]
		tfarsha	تفرشى	*bitfarsha*	بتفرشى	*yitfarsha*	يتفرشى	he
		tfarshat	تفرشت	*btitfarsha*	بتتفرشى	*titfarsha*	تتفرشى	she
		tfarsheena	تفرشينا	*mnitfarsha*	منتفرشى	*nitfarsha*	نتفرشى	we
tfarshu	تفرشو	*tfarsheetu*	تفرشيتو	*btitfarshu*	بتتفرشو	*titfarshu*	تتفرشو	you [P]
		tfarshu	تفرشو	*bitfarshu*	بتفرشو	*yitfarshu*	يتفرشو	they

shma2azz "Be Repulsed" (*f3alall*)

NORTH LEVANTINE							
Noun of Instance		**maSdar**		**Passive Participle**		**Active Participle**	
N/A		2ishmi2zaaz اشمئزاز		N/A		mishma2izz مشمئز	
Imperative		**Perfective**		**b- Imperfective**		**Zero- Imperfective**	
		shma2azzeet	اشمأزيت	bishma2izz	بشمئز	2ishma2izz	اشمئز	I
shma2izz	اشمئز	shma2azzeet	اشمأزيت	btishma2izz	بتشمئز	tishma2izz	تشمئز	you [M]
shma2izzi	اشمئزي	shma2azzeeti	اشمأزيتي	btishma2izzi	بتشمئزي	tishma2izzi	تشمئزي	you [F]
		shma2azz	اشمأز	byishma2izz	بيشمئز	yishma2izz	يشمئز	he
		shma2azzet	اشمأزت	btishma2izz	بتشمئز	tishma2izz	تشمئز	she
		shma2azzeena	اشمأزينا	mnishma2izz	منشمئز	nishma2izz	نشمئز	we
shma2izzu	اشمئزو	shma2azzeetu	اشمأزيتو	btishma2izzu	بتشمئزو	tishma2izzu	تشمئزو	you [P]
		shma2azzu	اشمأزو	byishma2izzu	بيشمئزو	yishma2izzu	يشمئزو	they

SOUTH LEVANTINE							
Noun of Instance		**maSdar**		**Passive Participle**		**Active Participle**	
N/A		2ishmi2zaaz اشمئزاز		N/A		mishma2izz مشمئز	
Imperative		**Perfective**		**b- Imperfective**		**Zero- Imperfective**	
		shma2azzeet	اشمأزيت	bashma2izz	بشمئز	2ashma2izz	أشمئز	I
shma2izz	اشمئز	shma2azzeet	اشمأزيت	btishma2izz	بتشمئز	tishma2izz	تشمئز	you [M]
shma2izzi	اشمئزي	shma2azzeeti	اشمأزيتي	btishma2izzi	بتشمئزي	tishma2izzi	تشمئز	you [F]
		shma2azz	اشمأز	bishma2izz	بشمئز	yishma2izz	يشمئز	he
		shma2azzat	اشمأزت	btishma2izz	بتشمئز	tishma2izz	تشمئز	she
		shma2azzeena	اشمأزينا	mnishma2izz	منشمئز	nishma2izz	نشمئز	we
shma2izzu	اشمئزو	shma2azzeetu	اشمأزيتو	btishma2izzu	بتشمئزو	tishma2izzu	تشمئزو	you [P]
		shma2azzu	اشمأزو	bishma2izzu	بشمئزو	yishma2izzu	يشمئزو	they

APPENDIX B: PREPOSITIONS

In the introduction to this book I promised that I would stay firmly away from dictionary work. But given the shortage of good dictionaries for spoken Arabic, how important prepositions are, and how (relatively) small a class they are, it seems remiss to completely avoid giving any definitions for them whatsoever. In this appendix we will look at the various prepositions used in Levantine Arabic and briefly discuss their meanings. Neither the list as a whole nor the definitions given are intended to be comprehensive, but they should provide a decent foundation and allow you to understand the majority of sentences. We will begin with the most high-frequency and irregular prepositions: *3ala, 3an, 3and/3ind, b-, min, la-,* and *ka-*. We will then give a survey of the other prepositions.

Note that since there is a whole unit on expressing direction and location (see unit 81), I have not gone into too much detail on this particular point. For details on the general functioning of prepositions, see unit 22.

3ala

The word *3ala* is the most versatile preposition. It is often contracted to ع *3a*, especially before the definite article. When combined with pronouns it takes the form علي‍ـ *3alee-*:

North Levantine		South Levantine	
عليي *3aliyyi* on me		علي *3alayy* on me	
عليكي *3aleeki* on you [F]	عليك *3aleek* on you [M]	عليكي *3aleeki* on you [F]	عليك *3aleek* on you [M]

North Levantine		South Levantine	
عليها	عليه	عليها	عليه
3aleyya	*3alee*	*3aleeha*	*3alee*
on her	on him	on her	on him
علينا		علينا	
3aleena		*3aleena*	
on us		on us	
عليكن		عليكم	
3aleekon		*3aleekom*	
on you [P]		on you [P]	
عليهن		عليهم	
3aleyyon		*3aleehom*	
on them		on them	

It can mean "on" or "at" (in the sense of "by" or "next to") when expressing location and "to" or "onto" when expressing direction (see unit 81):

نايمة ع التخت

naayme 3 attakh[e]t

lying on the bed

رايح على ألمانيا

raaye7 3ala 2almaanya

going to Germany

في حدا ع الباب

fii 7ada 3a lbaab

there's someone at the door

علقوه ع الحيط

3all2uu 3 al7eeT

hang it on the wall

As well as these basic uses, *3ala* can add an extra dimension of movement or destination to verbs that don't inherently express movement (see unit 53) or else add a second simultaneous destination:

تجوزت على أميركا

tjawwazet 3ala 2ameerka

she got married [and through marriage moved] to America

رحت عندو ع البيت

ru7[e]t 3indo 3 albeet

I went round to his house [= to him to his house]

As we saw in unit 53, *3ala* can also add an extra object to a verb with the implication that that person was negatively affected by the verb:

طلع عليي إشاعات

Talla3 3aliyyi 2ishaa3aat

he started rumours about me

راح عليك الباص

raa7 3aleek ⁱlbaaS

you missed the bus

Note the idiomatic use on its own:

شو يا عبود، علينا؟

shuu yaa 3abbuud, 3aleena?

come on, Abboud, trying to pull a fast one
on me?

ع مين؟

3a miin?

do you know who you're messing
with?

Followed by a definite number, *3ala* expresses "at" in clock time:

ع الستة

3 assitte

at six

ع التلاتة ونص

3 attlaate w nuSS

at three-thirty

With certain adjectives *3ala* translates "to," expressing personal feeling:

عزيز عليي

3aziiz 3aliyyi

he's dear to me

الساعة غالية علي

ⁱssaa3a ghaalye 3aleyy

the watch is worth a lot to me

With many other adjectives, however, *3aala* implies "(too) X for":

تقيلة علينا

t2iile 3aleena

[too] heavy for us

صغير عليك

zghiir 3aleek

[too] small for you

قليل عليك

2aliil 3aleek

it doesn't do you justice
[= too little for you]

كتير عليي

ktiir 3aliyy

[too] much for me

Like the English "on," *3ala* can also express that someone will pay for something:

العرس علي

ⁱl3urºs 3alayy

the wedding's on me

خليها عليي!

khalliiha 3aliyyi!

it's on me!

3ala often means something like "in accordance with," "operating according to":

خلاهم يغنو ع الدور

khallaahom yghannu 3 addoor

he had them take turns singing

[= sing on the turn]

أغلبهم ماشيين ع النظام

2aghlabhom maashyiin 3 anniZaam

most of them operate according to the rules

[= on the system]

الزلمة على دينو

ⁱzzalame 3ala diino

the guy is a committed Muslim

[= on his religion]

قديش صارلها على هالحالة؟

2addeesh SaLLa 3ala hal7aale?

how long has she been in this state?

[= on this state]

In a related meaning, *3ala* forms many adverbial expressions (see unit 20):

ع الماشي

3 almaashi

in passing

[= on the walking]

ع السريع

3 assarii3

quickly

[= on the quick]

It also occasionally expresses duration (e.g., of a contract):

العقد على سنة

ⁱl3aqd 3ala sine

the contract is for a year

[= on a year]

Note expressions such as the following used by South Levantine speakers (the North Levantine equivalent is with *3ind*):

ايش بدك على هالصبح؟

2eesh biddak 3ala haSSubᵒ7?

why are you bothering me like this in the morning?

[= what do you want on this morning?]

In more elevated language, *3ala* plus a noun can mean "must":

على الطرف التاني يوقع

3ala TTaraf ⁱttaani ywaqqe3

the second party must sign

عليكي توقعي

3aleeki twaqq3i

you must sign

Finally, for North Levantine speakers, *3ala* can mean "in spite of" in limited contexts such as the following:

بحبو على عيبو

b7ibbo 3ala 3eebo

I love him despite his flaws

3and/3ind

The word عند *3ind* or (for some North Levantine speakers) عند *3and* combines with pronouns straightforwardly except the "we" form, where for many speakers it becomes *3in/3an-*:

North Levantine		South Levantine	
عندي *3andi* by me		عندي *3indi* by me	
عندك *3andek* by you [F]	عندك *3andak* by you [M]	عندك *3indek* by you [F]	عندك *3indak* by you [M]
عندها *3anda* by her	عندو *3ando* by him	عندها *3indha* by her	عندو *3indo* by him
عننا *3anna* by us		عننا *3inna* by us	
عندكن *3andkon* by you [P]		عندكم *3indkom* by you [P]	
عندهن *3andon* by them		عندهم *3indhom* by them	

3and/3ind is largely locational in meaning and expresses "by," "at X's house," or "where X is":

عند المدخل

3ind ᶦlmadkhal

by the entrance

عند الكازية

3and ᶦlkaaziyye

by the petrol station

عند خالد

3ind khaaled

at Khaled's

المشكلة عندك

ᶦlmishᶦkle 3andak

the problem's at your end

Note that for South Levantine speakers *3and/3ind* can also have a "destination" meaning, whereas for North Levantine speakers ل *la-* must be added:

North Levantine	South Levantine
رحت لعندو	رحت عندو
ri7ᵉt la3ando	*ru7ᵉt 3indo*
I went to his house	I went to his house

Note the following use for North Levantine speakers (South Levantine speakers use *3ala* here):

شو بدك مني عند هالصبح؟

shuu biddak minni 3ind haSSibᵉ7?

why are you bothering me this early in the morning?

b-

The word *b-* is a versatile preposition with no one single translation. When pronouns are attached, it takes the form ـفي *fii*:

North Levantine		South Levantine	
فيي OR فيني		في	
fiyyi OR *fiini*		*fiyyi*	
in me		in me	
فيكي	فيك	فيكي	فيك
fiiki	*fiik*	*fiiki*	*fiik*
in you [F]	in you [M]	in you [F]	in you [M]

North Levantine		South Levantine	
فيها *fiyya* in her	فيه *fii* in him	فيها *fiiha* in her	فيو *fiyyo* in him
فينا *fiina* in us		فينا *fiina* in us	
فيكن *fiikon* in you [P]		فيكم *fiikom* in you [P]	
فيهن *fiyyon* in them		فيهم *fiihom* in them	

b- commonly expresses static location, largely corresponding to "in" although also "at" with certain institutions (church, mosque, school, university):

الخريطة بالسيارة

'lkhariiTa bissayyaara

the map's in the car

أبو محمد بالبيت؟

2abu m7ammad bilbeet?

is Abu Muhammad at home?

أخوكي بغرفتو

2akhuuki bghur"fto

your brother's in his room

بنتي بالجامعة

binti bijjaam3a

my daughter's at university

It also often expresses motion into something:

فات بعينو

faat 'b3eeno

it went in his eye

حطو بالكيس

7uTTo bilkiis

put it in the bag

b- is used to express the means by which you do something. Here it usually corresponds to the English "with" and is often followed by a definite noun (see unit 13):

جيت بالتاكسي

jiit bittaaksi

I came by taxi

قطعتو بالسكينة

2aTa3to bissikkiine

I cut it with a knife

ما بحب سافر بالطيارة

maa b7ibb saafer biTTayyaara

I don't like going places by plane

كنت أكتب بالقلم

kunt 2akteb bil2alam

I used to write with a pen

With verbs expressing emotion, *b-* often shows the source of the emotion in a way that sometimes cannot be nicely translated into English:

شايف حالو فيكي

shaayef 7aalo fiiki

he's big-headed because of [being related to] you

فخورة فيك

fakhuura fiik

I'm proud of you

b- expresses "for" in the sense of price:

بقديش جبتها؟

b2addeesh jibtha?

how much did you get it for?

قديش طالب فيها؟

2addeesh Taaleb fiiha?

how much is he asking for it?

b- can also be used with verbs of motion. This expresses that the subject is "taking" or "bringing" the object of *b-* along as they go. Consider the following examples:

رح سوق فيكن لفوق

ra7 suu2 fiikon lafoo2

I'm going to drive you up

غرقت السفينة بكل اللي فيها

ghir2at 'ssafiine bkull 'lli fiiha

the ship sank [together] with everything on it

b- can be used with pronouns (but not with nouns) in the meaning "among" or "of," as in the following:

ما حدا فينا منيح

maa 7ada fiina mnii7

none of us is a good person

بحبك أكتر وحدة فيكن

bi7ibbek 2aktar wa7de fiikon

he loves you the most of all [of you]

It is also used idiomatically to replace normal direct objects in a way that adds a nuance of long, continuous action:

قديش صارلك عم تترجم بالكتاب؟

2addeesh SaLLak 3am ⁱttarjem bilⁱktaab?

how long have you been translating [away at] the book?

ضلو يضرب فيه زي المجنون

Dallo yuDrob fii zayy ⁱlmajnuun

he kept beating [away at] him like a madman

Note the expression *killo/kullo* X-*b*-X "it's all...":

الحياة كلها مشاكل بمشاكل

ⁱl7ayaa kullha mashaakel ⁱbmashaakel

life is nothing but problems

كلو أبيض بأبيض

killo 2abyaD ⁱb2abyaD

it's all white

b- forms many adverbial expressions (see unit 20):

بسرعة

bsir3a/bsur3a

quickly

بأمن وأمان

b2amn w 2amaan

safely

For the North Levantine use of فيـ *fii-* as a pseudoverb meaning "can," see unit 46.

la-

The word لـ *la-* most commonly translates as "for" or "to." Combinations of *la-* with a pronoun are often replaced by the special *-l-* suffixes on a verb (see unit 19). In those cases where a normal preposition-pronoun combination *is* used, however, the pronouns are usually attached to the stem إلـ *2il-*:

North Levantine		South Levantine	
إلي *2ili* for me		إلي *2ili* for me	
إلك *2ilek* for you [F]	إلك *2ilak* for you [M]	إلك *2ilek* for you [F]	إلك *2ilak* for you [M]
إلها *2ila* for her	إلو *2ilo* for him	إلها *2ilha* for her	إلو *2ilo* for him

North Levantine	South Levantine
إلنا	إلنا
2ilna	*2ilna*
for us	for us
إلكن	إلكم
2ilkon	*2ilkom*
for you [P]	for you [P]
إلهن	إلهم
2ilon	*2ilhom*
for them	for them

> Many speakers attach an additional *la-* to the beginning of these forms: لإلك
> *la2ilak* "for you," لإلها *la2ila* "for her." You may also encounter forms derived
> from the stem *lee-*.

The most common translation of *la-* is "for":

هدية لمرتي   كتاب لابني

hdiyye lamarti   *ktaab la2ibni*

a present for my wife   a book for my son

la- sometimes means "until":

لهلق سهران؟   سهران للصبح!

lahalla2 sahraan?   *sahraan laSSub°7!*

you're still awake?   I'm staying up till morning!

[= until now you're awake (at night)?]

Especially in North Levantine, *la-* combines with various expressions of location to express
destination or movement (see unit 81). Consider the following:

لهون   لعندو   لوين؟   هونيك

lahoon   *la3indo*   *laween?*   *lahuniik*

[to] here   to his house   where to?   [to] there

For the noun-introducing use of *la-* in so-called repeated object constructions, see unit 53.

ma3

The word مع *ma3* means "with" and can be combined with pronouns regularly for all speakers, but South Levantine speakers also have an alternative stem, معا *ma3aa-*:

North Levantine		South Levantine	
معي *ma3i* with me		معاي *ma3aay* with me	
معك *ma3ek* with you [F]	معك *ma3ak* with you [M]	معاكي *ma3aaki* by you [F]	معاك *ma3aak* by you [M]
معها *ma3a* with her	معو *ma3o* with him	معاها *ma3aaha* by her	معاه *ma3aa* by him
معنا *ma3na* with us		معانا *ma3aana* with us	
معكن *ma3kon* with you [P]		معاكم *ma3aakom* with you [P]	
معهن *ma3on* with them		معاهم *ma3aahom* with them	

ma3 is used to mean "with" ("in company with" or "along with"), occasionally in the metaphorical sense of "standing with" or "being with (and not against)":

رحت معو
ru7^et ma3o
I went with him

بحكي معاك!
ba7ki ma3aak!
I'm talking to you!

إنت مع سامية؟
2inte ma3 saamya?
are you with Samia?

إنت معنا ولا معهن؟
2inte ma3na willa ma3on?
are you with (for) us or them?

Note that *ma3* does not mean "with" in the sense of "using," which is expressed by بـ *b-*. Like the English "with," *ma3* can express "in favour of":

إنتي مع هالفكرة؟

2inti ma3 halfikra?

are you in favour of this idea?

أنا مع إنو تقرر لحالها

2ana ma3 2inno tqarrer la7aala

I'm in favour of her deciding for herself

For use with "distancing" expressions, see unit 57.

3an

The word *3an* has a range of uses, although it perhaps most commonly means "about." When suffixes are attached, *3an* takes the form *3ann-*:

North Levantine		South Levantine	
عني *3anni* about me		عني *3anni* about me	
عنك *3annek* about you [F]	عنك *3annak* about you [M]	عنك *3annek* about you [F]	عنك *3annak* about you [M]
عنها *3anna* about her	عنو *3anno* about him	عنها *3annha* about her	عنو *3anno* about him
عننا *3anna* OR *3annᵢna* about us		عننا *3anna* about us	
عنكن *3annkon* about you [P]		عنكم *3annkom* about you [P]	
عنهن *3annon* about them		عنهم *3annhom* about them	

3an commonly expresses distance or movement away/separation from something. In this context it is partially interchangeable with *min*:

أنجيلينا انفصلت عن براد

2anjiliina nfaSlet 3an ᵢbraad
Angelina broke up with Brad
[= separated from]

قديش بتبعد عن البيت؟

2addeesh ᵢbtub3od 3an ᵢlbeet?
how far is it from the house?

مرقت عنو

mara2ᵉt 3anno
I went past him

متقدمين عني

mit2addmiin 3anni
they're ahead of me

3an also commonly means "about." In this sense *3an* is partially interchangeable with *3ala*:

هيدا اللي قلتلك عنو

hayda lli 2iltillak 3anno
the one I told you about

الكتاب بحكي عن لبنان بالقرون الوسطى

lᵢktaab bi7ki 3an lubnaan bilquruun ᵢlwusTa
the book talks about Lebanon in the Middle Ages

3an also expresses "instead of" and "on behalf of":

أنا بدفع عنك

2ana bidfa3 3annek
I'll pay for you

أحمل عنك؟

2a7mel 3annak?
should I carry it for you?

Occasionally *3an* also expresses duration (e.g., of a contract):

العقد عن سنة

ᵢl3aqd 3an sine
the contract is for a year

3an forms many adverbial expressions:

عن حقد

3an 7i2ᵉd
maliciously
[= out of malice]

عن جد؟

3an jadd?
seriously?
[= out of seriousness?]

min

The word من *min* is most commonly translated as "from." Like *3an*, the *n* in *min* is doubled when pronouns are attached, but it is otherwise regular:

North Levantine		South Levantine	
مني *minni* from me		مني *minni* from me	
منك *minnek* from you [F]	منك *minnak* from you [M]	منك *minnek* from you [F]	منك *minnak* from you [M]
منها *minna* from her	منو *minno* from him	منها *minnha* from her	منو *minno* from him
مننا *minna* OR *minn'na* from us		مننا *minna* from us	
منكن *minnkon* from you [P]		منكم *minnkom* from you [P]	
منهن *minnon* from them		منهم *minnhom* from them	

min most commonly expresses point of origin ("from") or movement via ("through"):

من بيروت	من الباب التاني	من هون	من سوريا
min beyruut	*min 'lbaab 'ttaani*	*min hoon*	*min suurya*
from Beirut	through the door	this way [= from here]	from Syria

In both senses *min* can be combined with other prepositions (see unit 81):

نطت من فوق البيت	جبتها من ع النيت
naTTet min foo2 'lbeet	*jibtha min 3a nnet*
it jumped over the house	I got it [from] online

min also very commonly expresses cause:

من غير شي متضايق

min gheer shii mitdaaye2

I'm bothered about something else

[= from something else]

ما عم شوف من هالعتمات

maa 3am shuuf min hal3itmaat

I can't see because it's dark

[= from the darkness]

With time, *min* expresses "since" or (for North Levantine speakers) "ago":

من تلت سنين

min tlett ⁱsniin

three years ago

من وقت ما فات

min wa2ᵉt ma faat

since he came in

min can also mean "starting from":

من هلق مبسوط

min halla2 mabsuuT

I'm already [= from now] happy

من هون ورايح لا تحكي شي

min hoon w raaye7 laa ti7ki shii

from now on, don't say anything

ka-

The word ك *ka-* is relatively rare and has no forms with attached pronouns. *ka-* generally translates "as" in contexts such as the following:

أنا كعربي . . .

2ana ka3arabi . . .

as an Arab, I . . .

عم بحكي معاك كصديق

3am ba7ki ma3aak kaSadiiq

I'm talking to you as a friend

Relatedly, *ka-* occasionally occurs in a sense similar to the English "-wise." Note the use with the independent pronoun in the second example:

إذا قصدك أنا كأنا مش عارفة

2iza 2azdak 2ana ka2ana, mish 3aarfe

if you mean me as in *me*, I dunno

أنا كوضعي المالي تمام

2ana kawaD3i lmaali tamaam

money-wise I'm fine

Note that many instances of the English "as" are translated with a secondary object (see unit 54).

2ab^el and ba3^ed

Both *2ab^el* "before and *ba3^ed* "after" can be used in a way that corresponds with their English counterparts:

بعد الحفلة

ba3d ⁱl7afle

after the party

قبل العرس

2abl ⁱl3ur^os

before the wedding

A structure with *b-* can be used to introduce a specific period of time:

قبل العرس بيومين

2abl ⁱl3ur^os byoomeen

two days before the wedding

بعد الحفلة بساعة

ba3d ⁱl7afle bsaa3a

an hour after the party

It is also possible to use *2ab^el* and *ba3^ed* directly with a time period, in which case they correspond to English words such as "ago," "prior," and "later":

أنا مسافر بعد ساعة

2ana msaafer ba3d saa3a

I'm leaving in an hour

قبل سنتين كنت قدس

2ab^el santeen kunt bil2uds

two years ago I was in Jerusalem

For North Levantine speakers and most South Levantine speakers, pronouns are attached straightforwardly. For some South Levantine speakers, pronouns beginning with consonants are combined with the stems قبلي *2ablii-* and بعدي *ba3dii-*: قبليها *2abliiha* "before her," قبلينا *2abliina* "before us."

2add

The word *2add* literally means "the size of" or "the extent of" and often corresponds to "as much as" in English (for more examples of this, see unit 79). It also has some idiomatic uses:

في كرسي قدي؟

fii kursi 2addi?

is there a chair big enough for me?

[= a chair my size?]

مين بحبك قدي؟

miin bi7ibbak 2addi?

who loves you as much as me?

بحبك قد الدنيا

ba7ibbak 2add ˈddinya

I love you to the moon and back

[= as much as the world]

أنا قدها

2ana 2addha

I'm up to the task

[= I am its size]

The word على قد *3ala 2add* or قد ع *3a 2add* has its own uses. Idiomatic translations will vary; some more or less literal equivalents would be "commensurate with," "in the same number as," and "according to the size of," as demonstrated in the examples below:

الكراسي على قد الضيوف

ˈlkaraasi 3ala 2add ˈD-Dyuuf

there are as many chairs as guests

[= the chairs are in the same number as the guests]

أحلامي على قدي

2a7laami 3ala 2addi

my dreams aren't too big for me

[= my dreams are commensurate with me]

بدك تاخدو على قد عقلاتو

biddak taakhdo 3ala 2add 3a2laato

you have to meet him where he is (mentally)

[= take him according to the size of his brains]

badaal, 3awaaD, badalan min

These three expressions—*badaal* is definitely the most common and *badalan min* is higher register—express "instead of":

في حدا بدو يروح بدالي؟

fii 7ada baddo yruu7 badaali?

does anyone want to go instead of me?

بدال الحزن والبكى

badaal ˈl7uzᵒn w ˈlbuka

instead of sadness and crying

بياكلو كاتو عواض الخبز

byaaklu gaatto 3awaaD ˈlkhibᵉz

they eat cake instead of bread

بدلا من تضييع الوقت هيك روح اقرا

badalan min taDyii3 ˈlwa2ᵉt heek ruu7 i2ra

instead of wasting time like this, go and read

bala, min duun, biduun

The words *bala*, *min duun*, and *biduun* mean "without" and are straightforward:

حضرتوه من دوني؟

7aDartuu min duuni?

did you watch it without me?

رحت بلاه

ru7ᵉt balaa

I went without him

بشرب القهوة بدون سكر

bashrab ّl2ahwe biduun sukkar

I drink coffee without sugar

Note the following two idioms with *bala* (often *balaash* in South Levantine):

أحسن من بلا

2a7san min bala

better than nothing

[= better than without]

يا هيك الكتب يا بلا!

yaa heek ّlkitob yaa bala!

Now that's what I call a real book!

[= books are either like this, or without]

bala has a number of additional idiomatic uses, for which see unit 43.

been

The word بين *been* means "between" and "among":

بين الشجر

been ّshshajar

among the trees

بين المحلين

been ّlma7alleen

between the two shops

Note that when one of the two elements is a pronoun, *been* must be repeated:

بيني وبين البيت

beeni w been ّlbeet

between me and the house

بيني وبينك

beeni w beenak

between you and me

With plural pronouns, *been-* often becomes بيناتـ *beenaat-*:

مش بيناتنا

mish beenaatna

This won't come between us

[= not between us]

Note the common usage meaning "one of":

المجرم بين هالتلاتة

ّlmujrem been halّtlaate

one of these three is the criminal

Soob, naa7, Tarii2, 2ittijaah, bittijaah

The words *Soob*, *naa7*, *Tarii2*, *2ittijaah*, and *bittijaah* all mean "toward" and have different regional distributions. The term صوب *Soob* is predominantly North Levantine, while ناح *naa7* is exclusively Syrian, and *2ittijaah* and *bittijaah* are higher register:

<table>
<tr><td align="center">رايحين طريق سوريا</td><td align="center">ما تقرب صوبي</td></tr>
<tr><td align="center">raay7iin Tarii2 suuriya</td><td align="center">maa t2arreb Soobi</td></tr>
<tr><td align="center">they're going toward Syria</td><td align="center">don't come near me</td></tr>
<tr><td align="center">[= in the direction of Syria]</td><td align="center">[= in my direction]</td></tr>
</table>

mitᵉl, zayy

The words *mitᵉl* and *zayy* mean "like." *mitᵉl* is used everywhere but relatively uncommon among Jordanian speakers, while *zayy* is used throughout South Levantine:

<table>
<tr><td align="center">زي أخوي</td><td align="center">متل رامي</td></tr>
<tr><td align="center">zayy 2akhuuy</td><td align="center">mitᵉl raami</td></tr>
<tr><td align="center">like my brother</td><td align="center">like Rami</td></tr>
</table>

With similes these words are often followed by definites (see unit 13), unlike their English counterparts:

<table>
<tr><td align="center">زي اللي بعرفش إشي</td><td align="center">متل الولاد الصغار</td></tr>
<tr><td align="center">zayy ⁱlli bi3rafsh 2ishi</td><td align="center">mitᵉl lⁱwlaad ⁱzzghaar</td></tr>
<tr><td align="center">like someone who doesn't know anything</td><td align="center">like little kids</td></tr>
</table>

Note the idiomatic repetition:

<table>
<tr><td align="center">زيو زي اللي مراحوش</td><td align="center">أنا متلي متلك</td></tr>
<tr><td align="center">zayyo zayy ⁱlli mara7uush</td><td align="center">2ana mitli mitlak</td></tr>
<tr><td align="center">he's exactly like the ones who didn't go</td><td align="center">I'm just like you</td></tr>
<tr><td align="center">[= like him like the ones that didn't go]</td><td align="center">[= I'm like you like me]</td></tr>
</table>

7awaleen, daayer

The word *7awaleen* is used everywhere, while *daayer* is exclusively North Levantine. Both express "around":

<table>
<tr><td align="center">داير البيت</td><td align="center">حولين الجنينة في سور</td></tr>
<tr><td align="center">daayer ⁱlbeet</td><td align="center">7awaleen lⁱjneene fii suur</td></tr>
<tr><td align="center">around the house</td><td align="center">there's a wall around the garden</td></tr>
</table>

Note that *3ala daayer*, which is used everywhere, means "around the perimeter of." Note as well that *7awaleen* loses its *-n* when pronouns are attached, patterning with على *3ala*:

يللي حواليك مجانين

yalli 7awaleek majaniin

the people around you are crazy

Note also the following idiomatic use:

حواليك مواسرجي؟

7awaleek mawasirji?

do you know of a plumber around here?

[= is there a plumber around you?]

foo2 and *ta7ᵉt*

As we have seen, *foo2* can mean "above" and "on top of"; *ta7ᵉt* means "below" and "under":

<table>
<tr><td align="center">فوق الشجرة</td><td align="center">فوق التلاجة</td></tr>
<tr><td align="center">foo2 ˈshshajara</td><td align="center">foo2 ˈttallaaje</td></tr>
<tr><td align="center">up in the tree</td><td align="center">on top of the fridge</td></tr>
<tr><td align="center">تحت الأرض</td><td align="center">تحت الطاولة</td></tr>
<tr><td align="center">ta7t ˈl2arᵉD</td><td align="center">ta7t ˈTTaawle</td></tr>
<tr><td align="center">under the ground</td><td align="center">under the table</td></tr>
</table>

foo2 also has the metaphorical meaning "on top of":

فوق كل هاد بدك تتجوزي؟

foo2 kull haad biddek titjawwazi?

on top of all this you want to get married?

For North Levantine speakers and most South Levantine speakers, pronouns attach straightforwardly. For some South Levantine speakers, an *-ii* is added with pronouns beginning with consonants: فوقينا *fo2iina* "above us," تحتيها *ta7tiiha* "under it." For the independent use of *foo2* and *ta7ᵉt*, see unit 81.

jamb, 7add

The words *jamb* and *7add*, meaning "next to," are straightforward:

جنب البيت

jamb ⁱlbeet

next to the house

واقف حدي

waa2ef 7addi

standing next to me

قاعد جنبي

2aa3ed jambi

sitting next to me

البيت حد المطعم

ⁱlbeet 7add ⁱlmaT3am

the house is next to the restaurant

For North Levantine speakers and most South Levantine speakers, pronouns attach straightforwardly. For some South Levantine speakers, however, an *-ii* is added with pronouns beginning with consonants: جنبينا *jambiina* "next to us."

juwwa(*at*) and *barra*(*at*)

juwwa(*at*), "inside," and *barra*(*at*), "outside," each have two forms, yet those with *-aat* are more common:

جوا البيت

juwwa lbeet

inside the house

برا البيت

barra lbeet

outside the house

جوات البيت

juwwaat ⁱlbeet

inside the house

برات البيت

barraat ⁱlbeet

outside the house

This is particularly true with pronouns, which almost invariably attach to the *-aat* forms. For the independent use of *juwwa* and *barra*, see unit 81.

b2alb

Although *b2alb* literally translates as "in the heart of," it is a neutral way of saying "inside":

بقلب السفارة

b2alb ⁱssafaara

inside the embassy

بقلب الظرف

b2alb ⁱZZarᵉf

inside the envelope

2baal, mwaajiih, mwaajeh, bwijj/bwishh

These words all express "across from" and "opposite." *2baal* is used in South Levantine. The other forms are predominantly North Levantine, with *mwaajiih* being the most common:

مواجه المطعم

قبال المكتبة

mwaajeh ⁱlmaT3am

2baal ⁱlmaktabe

across from the restaurant

across from the library

بيتو بوجه بيتي

مواجيه الدكان

beeto bwijj beeti

mwaajiih ⁱddikkaan

his house faces mine

across from the shop

m2aabiil, m2aabel

The forms *m2aabiil* and *m2aabel* can express "opposite" and "across from":

مقابل بيتك

مقابيل المحل

m2aabel beetak

m2aabiil ⁱlma7all

across from your house

opposite the place

m2aabiil and *m2aabel* can also mean "in exchange for":

باع البيت مقابيل هالمصاري

baa3 ⁱlbeet ⁱm2aabiil halmaSaari

he sold the house in exchange for this money

2iddaam / 2uddaam and wara

The word *2iddaam / 2uddaam* "in front of" is straightforward:

ورا العمارة

قدام المحل

wara l3imaara

2uddaam ⁱlma7all

behind the building

in front of the shop

Note that *wara* "behind" has many idiomatic uses. In particular, it often translates as "after" in contexts such as the following:

بنضفش وراه

سنة ورا سنة

binaDDifᵉsh waraa

sane wara sane

he doesn't clean up after himself

year after year

وراي شغل

waraay shughᵒl

I've got work to do

[= is after me work]

For the independent use of *wara*, see unit 81.

la-, la7add

The forms *la-* and *la7add* mean "until":

لحد بكرا

la7add bukra

until tomorrow

سهران للصبح

sahraan laSSub°7

staying up till the morning

The form *la7add* sometimes becomes لحديت *la7addiit* before nouns.

bZarf, khilaal

The words *bZarf* and *khilaal* "within" both refer to time. *ᵢbZarf* is perhaps more dramatic, while *khilaal* is more elevated:

خلال ساعة

khilaal saa3a

within an hour

بظرف دقيقة

bZarf da2ii2a

in the space of a minute

Tuul, 3aTuul

Tuul and *3aTuul* "all along" are straightforward. They can refer both to space and to time:

طول السنة

Tuul ᵢssine

all year long

ع طول الشارع في شجر

3a Tuul ᵢshshaare3 fii shajar

all the way along the street there are trees

min wara

The structure *min wara* can be a straightforward combination of *min* and *wara*, for which see unit 81. However, *min wara* can also express "because of" and "as a result of," in which case it is usually used for bad events:

كل الناس خسرت من ورا هالشركة

kill ᵢnnaas khisret min wara hashshirke

everyone has lost [money] thanks to this company

كلو من ورا تصرفاتك الغبية!

kullo min wara taSarrufaatak ᵢlghabiyye!

it's all because of your stupid behaviour!

bniSS/bnuSS

The term بنص *bniSS/bnuSS* (literally "in the half of") means "in the middle of":

<table>
<tr><td align="center">بنص الشارع</td><td align="center">بنص البيت!</td></tr>
<tr><td align="center">*bniSS ّshshaare3*</td><td align="center">*bnuSS ّlbeet!*</td></tr>
<tr><td align="center">in the middle of the street</td><td align="center">in the middle of the house!</td></tr>
</table>

3ashaan, minshaan, mishaan

These words can express "because of," "for," and "for the sake of." Although all forms occur across the Levantine area, عشان *3ashaan* is probably the most common choice in Lebanon, Palestine, and Jordan, while منشان *minshaan* is most common in Syria:

<table>
<tr><td align="center">منشان الله!</td><td align="center">عشانك بروح</td></tr>
<tr><td align="center">*minshaan 2aLLa!*</td><td align="center">*3ashaanek baruu7*</td></tr>
<tr><td align="center">for God's sake!</td><td align="center">for you I'll go</td></tr>
<tr><td align="center">عشان هيك مرحتش</td><td align="center">مرحتش عشان الولاد</td></tr>
<tr><td align="center">*3ashaan heek maru7t^esh*</td><td align="center">*maru7t^esh 3ashaan lⁱwlaad*</td></tr>
<tr><td align="center">that's why I didn't go</td><td align="center">I didn't go for the kids' sake</td></tr>
<tr><td align="center">[= that's why I didn't go for that]</td><td align="center"></td></tr>
</table>

There are many other variants, including بشان *bshaan*.

kirmaal/kurmaal

The word كرمال *kirmaal/kurmaal* is used in all regions to mean "for the sake of," and in this sense it is a partial synonym of *3ashaan*:

<table>
<tr><td align="center">كرمال الولاد</td><td align="center">كرمال أهلي</td></tr>
<tr><td align="center">*kurmaal lⁱwlaad*</td><td align="center">*kurmaal 2ahli*</td></tr>
<tr><td align="center">for the kids' sake</td><td align="center">for my parents' sake</td></tr>
</table>

But Lebanese speakers in particular are inclined to use *kirmaal* as a full synonym of *3ashaan*, allowing it to mean "because of" as well:

<table>
<tr><td align="center">جيت كرمال المصاري</td><td align="center">كرمال هيك . . .</td></tr>
<tr><td align="center">*jiit kirmaal ّlmaSaari*</td><td align="center">*kirmaal heek . . .*</td></tr>
<tr><td align="center">I came because of the money</td><td align="center">that's why . . .</td></tr>
</table>

APPENDIX C: CONJUNCTIONS

In this appendix we will look very briefly at the most common subordinating conjunctions in Arabic. As with appendix B on prepositions, this overlaps with some of the content of the main book, specifically unit 68 on subordinating conjunctions. For that reason, we will not focus much here on the behaviours of the different conjunctions or on whether they trigger zero-imperfectives or indicatives. Instead, we will review—very briefly and not at all comprehensively—their uses and meanings.

Because

The most universal way of expressing "because" is لإنو *la2inno*:

لإنو بدي احكي معها

la2inno baddi 2i7ki ma3ha

because I want to talk to her

لإنو مشفنيش

la2inno mashafniish

because he didn't see me

For South Levantine and Lebanese speakers, عشان *3ashaan* and عشنو *3ashanno* are also commonly used:

عشني بدي احكي معها

3ashanni biddi 2i7ki ma3ha

because I want to talk to her

عشان مشفنيش

3ashaan mashafniish

because he didn't see me

As If

The phrase "as if" is expressed with كإنو *ka2inno* or (for some speakers) كنو *kinno*. Note that unlike its English counterpart, it does not require any syntactic changes to the clause that follows:

كإنو ما في شي

ka2inno maa fii shii

as if nothing was wrong

كإني مو موجود

ka2inni muu mawjuud

as if I wasn't there

These structures can be combined with ولا *wala* (see unit 77). This gives a negative meaning, usually a surprised or emphatic negative:

ولا كإنو صار شي

wala ka2inno Saar shii

as if nothing at all had happened

ولا كنو شافني

wala kinno shaafni

as if he'd not seen me

> Some speakers have *kinno* available, but it is only a partial synonym of *ka2inno* and is used mainly in the framing use, for which see unit 45.

"Since," "Although"

The words مادام *maadaam* and بما إنو *bima 2inno* both mean "since" and "given that":

مادامك برات البيت

madaamak barraat 'lbeet

since you're not at home

بما إنك جيت وجيت

bima 2innak jiit w jiit

since you're here anyway

The word مع إنو *ma3 2inno* means "although":

مع إنو ما بدك

ma3 2inno maa biddak

although you don't want to

مع إنك مش هون

ma3 2innek mish hoon

although you're not here

The word غير إنو *gheer 2inno* usually means "on top of the fact that":

غير إنو ما عننا مصاري

gheer 2inno maa 3inna maSaari

on top of us not having money

Conjunctions of Purpose

The conjunctions of purpose vary from region to region. The most common are عشان *3ashaan* (used everywhere but Syria) and منشان *minshaan*:

منشان ما تسبي عليي

عشان أشوفك

minshaan maa tsibbi 3aliyyi

3ashaan 2ashuufek

so you don't swear at me

to see you

so I can see you

The words دِشان *mishaan*, كرمال *kirmaal* (Lebanese), and بشان *bshaan* (Jordanian) are also used:

بشان أشوفك

كرمال ما تسبي عليي

bshaan 2ashuufek

kirmaal maa tsibbi 3aliyyi

to see you

so you don't swear at me

so I can see you

The word لـ *la-* and its various synonyms (تـ *ta-*, لحتى *la7atta*) can also be used:

لحتى ما تسبي عليي

تأشوفك

la7atta maa tsibbi 3aliyyi

ta2ashuufek

so you don't swear at me

to see you

The word أحسن ما *2a7san ma* is a sort of negative conjunction of purpose "so that X doesn't" (or "lest"):

أحسن ما تحترقي

أحسن ما يشوفني

2a7san ma ti7t'r2i

2a7san ma yshuufni

so you don't burn yourself

so he doesn't see me

For *2a7san ma* in comparisons, see unit 79.

Conjunctions of Time

"As soon as" is expressed with أول ما *2awwal ma*:

أول ما توصل حاكيني

2awwal ma TuuSal 7aakiini

call me as soon as you get there

"Before" and "after" are expressed with بعد ما *ba3ᵉd ma* and قبل ما *2abᵉl ma*:

قبل ما يجي حاكيني

بوكل بعد ما يرجع

2abᵉl ma yiji 7aakiini

bookol ba3ᵉd ma yirja3

call me before he gets there

he'll eat after he gets back

"Once" is expressed with بس *bass*:

بس تجي منطلع

bass tiji mniTla3

as soon as she gets here we'll set off

بس أخلص بحكي معاك

bass 2akhalleS ba7ki ma3aak

once I finish I'll tell you

"Every time that" is expressed with كل ما *kill ma/kull ma*:

كل ما آجي أسلم عليه

kull ma 2aaji 2asallem 3alee

every time that I'm about to say hi to him

كل ما بروحو

kill ma biruu7u

every time they go

"When" is most commonly expressed with لما *lamma* (variants لمن *lamman* and *limmen*) or, in North Levantine, وقت *wa2ᵉt* or وقت ما *wa2ᵉt ma*. Note as well the *7aal* construction (see unit 65):

كل يوم لما يجي

kull yoom lamma yiji

every day when he arrives

لما يجي بحكي معاه

lamma yiji ba7ki ma3aa

when he gets here, I'll tell him

وقت ما بجي احكي

wa2ᵉt ma biji 2i7ki

when I'm about to say something

وقت كنا بالمدرسة

wa2ᵉt kinna bilmadrase

when we were in school

"Since" is expressed with some combination of the preposition من *min* plus another time expression:

من وقت ما جيت عننا

min wa2ᵉt ma jiit 3inna

since you came to our house

من لما شفتك

min lamma shiftek

since I saw you

من أنا وصغير

min 2ana w ᵢzghiir

since I was small

من قبل ما تعرفيها

min 2abᵉl ma ti3rafii

since before you knew her

"Until" is expressed using لحد ما *la7add ma,* على ما *3ala ma,* لـ *la-,* حتى (لحتى) *7atta* *la7atta,* تـ *ta-,* etc.):

عود هون ليرجع

3ood hoon layirja3

sit here until he comes back

بستنى تتخلصي

bastanna tatkhallSi

I'll wait until you finish

بسنتى على ما تخلصي

bistanna 3ala ma tkhallSi

I'll wait until you finish

عود هون لحد ما يرجع

3ood hoon la7add ma yirja3

sit here until he comes back

The words لبين ما *labeen ma* (North Levantine) and عبين/عبيل ما *3abeen/3abeel ma* (South Levantine) mean both "until" and "by the time that":

لبين ما نخلص بكون استوى الأكل

labeen ma nkhalleS bikuun stawa l2ak^el

by the time we finish, the food will be ready

بقرا كتاب عبيل ما تخلصي

ba2ra katab 3abeel ma tkhallSi

I'll read a book until you finish
[while you're working]

"The whole time that" and "so long as" are both expressed with طول ما *Tuul ma* and طول الوقت و *Tuul ^ilwa2^et w*:

طول الوقت وأنا بالبيت

Tuul ^ilwa2^et w 2ana bilbeet

the whole time I was at home

طول ما كنت بالمكتبة

Tuul ma kint bilmaktabe

the whole time I was in the library

Miscellaneous Conjunctions

The words بدال ما *badaal ma,* بدل ما *badal ma,* and عواض ما *3awaaD ma* are used to express "instead of." The first is far more common:

بدل ما يروح لحالو

badal ma yruu7 la7aalo

instead of going on his own

بدال ما تقعد فوق

badaal ma tu23od foo2

instead of sitting upstairs

The words بدون ما *biduun ma,* بلا ما *bala ma,* and من دون ما *min duun ma* all mean "without":

نزلت من دون ما أمشط

nzil^et min duun ma 2amashsheT

I went downstairs without combing my hair

روح بلا ما يقللي

rawwa7 bala ma y2ulli

he went home without telling me

The words متل ما *mit^el ma* and زي ما *zayy ma* are the counterparts of the prepositions متل *mit^el* (used everywhere but less so in Jordan) and زي *zayy* (South Levantine). The translation is usually "as" in the sense of "similar to" or "the way that":

خدني زي ما أنا

khudni zayy ma 2ana

take me as I am

متل ما بقولو اللبنانيين

mit^el maa bi2uulu llibnaaniyyiin

as the Lebanese say

Like their prepositional counterparts, they can be doubled in contexts like the following:

متل ما رحتي متل ما جيتي

mit^el ma ri7ti mit^el ma jiiti

things are just the way they've always been

[= as you went, as you came back]

The word فوق ما *foo2 ma* is the counterpart of the preposition فوق *foo2* "on top of" in its metaphorical meaning of "in addition to (all these other problems)":

فوق ما بدي أساعدك . . .

foo2 ma biddi 2asaa3dak . . .

here I was trying to

help you . . .

فوق ما أحمد بساعدنيش بالبيت . . .

foo2 ma 2a7mad bisaa3idniish bilbeet . . .

on top of Ahmad not helping me

around the house . . .

The word قد ما *2add ma* is the conjunction equivalent of the preposition قد *2add* "as much as" and has the same meaning but is followed by a sentence rather than a noun:

بشتغل قد ما فيني

bishtighel 2add ma fiini

I work as much as I can

ادفع قد ما بدك

2idfa3 2add ma biddak

pay as much as you want

The word حسب ما *7asab ma* is the counterpart of the preposition حسب *7asab* "according to." Its idiomatic translation is often "as," but it has a different meaning than *mit^el ma* and *zayy ma*:

حسب ما قالولي

7asab ma 2aluuli

according to what they told me

حسب ما فهمت

7asab ma fhim^et

as I understand it

The forms من كتر ما *min kit^er ma* and من قد ما *min 2add ma* literally mean something like "from/due to the [great] amount that." They are used in sentences such as the following:

من كتر ماني مبسوط مو شايف قدامي

min kit^er maani mabsuuT muu shaayef 2iddaami

I'm so happy I'm in a total daze

[= I can't see in front of me]

حفظت شكلهم ع الآخر من قد ما بصورهم

7f^eZet shik^elhom 3 al2aakher min 2add ma baSawwirhom

I've totally memorised their shape I take so many photos of them

Some North Levantine speakers use ع كتر ما *3a kitᵉr ma* and ع قد ما *3a 2add ma* instead.

The words مطرح ما *maTra7 ma* and محل ما *ma7all ma* all mean "where," in the sense "the place where." These expressions often carry an implied preposition, such as "at," "from," "to," or "via," which has to be understood from context:

رجعنا محل ما طلعتنا

rajji3na ma7all ma Talla3tna

take us back [to] the place where
you picked us up

مطرح ما جينا

maTra7 maa jiina

the place we came [from]
[at] the place we came in

Although the phrase itself can be preceded by *min* meaning "from," when it means "([at] the place) where" or "to the place where" it generally appears alone:

خلينا نرجع مطرح ما كنا

khalliina nirja3 maTra7 ma kunna

let's go back [to] where we were

The word لدرجة إنو *ladarajet 2inno*, sometimes pronounced *ladaraje 2inno*, literally means "to the degree that" and connects two sentences straightforwardly:

نفسيتي تعبانة لدرجة إنو بدي قص شعري

nafsiyyti ta3baane ladarajet 2inno baddi 2iSS sha3ri

I'm so down (mentally) I want to cut my hair
[= my mental state is exhausted to the point that . . .]

la- and Its Synonyms

The words لـ *la-* and حتى *7atta*—and their regional variants تـ *ta-* (Lebanese/Palestinian), تنو *tanno* (Palestinian), and لحتى *la7atta* (North Levantine)—have a range of possible meanings. They can act as purpose conjunctions or time conjunctions meaning "until":

خلينا نستنى ليجي

khalliina nistanna layiji

let's wait till he comes back

بدي مصاري تادفع

baddi maSaari ta2idfa3

I need money to pay

Note the idiomatic use "I had to X before I could":

نكشت البيت لحتى جبتها

nakasht ⁱlbeet la7atta jibtha

I had to turn the house
upside down to get it
[= I rifled through the house until . . .]

تعبت كتير للقيتها

t3ibt ⁱktiir lal2iitha

I had to work really hard to find it
[= I worked a lot until . . .]

They can be combined with *leesh* to mean "why would," "why should":

وليش تإزعل؟

w leesh ta2iz3al?

why would I be upset?

They are also idiomatically used to express a different kind of causal relationship:

مين إنت لحتى تحكي معي هيك؟

miin 2inte la7atta ti7ki ma3i heek?

Who are you to talk to me like that?

ايش صار معك تنو صفيتي هون؟

2eesh Saar ma3ek tinno Saffeeti hoon?

what happened to you that you ended up here?

شو حاطط ع شواربو تفازين هيك؟

shuu 7aaTeT 3a shwaarbo tafaazziin heek?

what's he put on his moustache to make it puff out like that?

They sometimes express "when" or implicitly "I'm just waiting for":

تتفتح الإشارة

tatifta7 ⁱl2ishaara

just as soon as the light turns green

بس لتخلص وراقها

bass latkhalleS wraa2a

just until she finishes her paperwork

They can also be used, following an expression of time, to introduce the rest of the sentence. Note that in the sentence on the left the first *la-* is part of the time expression and the second *la-* introduces the main verb:

للأسبوع الجاي لأحكي معاه

lal2usbuu3 ⁱjjaay la2a7ki ma3aa

I won't speak to him until next week
[= until next week for me to speak to him]

بالصدفة لشوفو

biSSudfe lashuufo

I only see him rarely
[= by chance for me to see him]

In North Levantine, *la-* can be combined with مو *muu* or مش *mish* to give the meaning "supposed to," as in the following:

مو لنحكي بعد نص ساعة؟

muu lani7ki ba3ᵉd niSS saa3a?
weren't we supposed to be speaking in half an hour?

For these particles' use in oaths, see unit 44. For their independent use with first-person imperatives, see unit 43.

APPENDIX D: POLITENESS, IMPOLITENESS, AND TERMS OF ADDRESS

In this appendix, we will look very briefly at some of the words and phrases that can be used to express politeness or affection as well as some generic terms of address. This is obviously a large topic that is beyond the scope of this book, extending into the sociolinguistics of the individual dialects, individual speakers' preferences, and dictionary making. This unit is thus meant largely as a quick guide to help you get your linguistic bearings in this area and not as a comprehensive list or detailed cultural discussion. We will look at three broad categories of language use:

- Language for being polite,
- Language for expressing affection, and
- Language for being rude.

All three categories, especially the last one, come with usage warnings. Being overly polite may come across as cold or sarcastic, and being overly affectionate may seem as forward (or even romantically aggressive). Using a rude turn of phrase to a friend may be taken as a joke or interpreted as overfamiliarity or even hostility. Be careful.

Politeness

None of the four dialects of Levantine Arabic has a particularly highly developed system of expressing respect grammatically. As in English, being polite is mostly a matter of phrasing. However, there are a few elements of polite address that are worth discussing here briefly.

2abu and 2imm/2umm

Names using أبو *2abu* "father of" and إم/أم *2imm/2umm* (*2umm* is a specifically Jordanian form) "mother of" are given to parents based on the name of their oldest (or only) son or, failing that, oldest daughter: أبو محمد *2abu m7ammad* in this schema will have at least one son named Muhammad who is either the only son or the eldest. Someone called أبو زينب *2abu zaynab* will have no sons but will have at least one daughter, named Zeinab, who is either the only daughter or the eldest. While *2abu m7ammad*'s name will not change, *2abu zaynab*'s might if he subsequently has a boy. Traditionally, people with children are almost invariably referred to by these names in polite and even fairly informal contexts.

> Fake names formed on this pattern are also fairly often used as pseudonyms or noms de guerre. In this case, obviously, any actual child's name will not be used.

Reference to nuclear family units is typically not by surname/family name but instead by بيت *beet* or in South Levantine دار *daar* "house of" plus the father's *2abu* nickname. A man whose full name is سليم عمار السلايمة *saliim 3ammaar 'ssalaayme*, for example, might be referred to as أبو زينب *2abu zeynab* and his family (the Salaymehs) as بيت أبو زينب *beet 2abu zeenab*.

Use of Titles

One of the most common ways of showing respect is to use a title alongside or instead of a someone's name. Native titles and those borrowed from European languages precede someone's first name rather than their surname as in English. The most common title is probably استاذ *2istaaz/2ustaaz*, with the feminine استاذة *2istaaze/2ustaaze*. This can be used in almost any professional context to be polite, either accompanying a name (in which case it is similar to Mr or Mrs) or on its own as a form of address.

The word دكتور *doktoor* is properly used for medical and academic doctors, although some people extend it to highly educated professionals in general (this is stigmatised as uneducated).

The word آنسة *2aanse* "miss" may be used in some regions for unmarried women and for schoolteachers; the borrowing مس *miss* is also used everywhere in the latter sense.

The word معلم *m3allem* "boss" is commonly used as a term of address between friends and also to address shopkeepers, waiters, and other workers in less formal establishments, although this may come across as overly familiar and is not advisable in a posh restaurant.

The word سيدي *siidi/sayyidi* "sir" is generally used in the military or similar contexts (with policemen, for example).

The words أخي *2akhi* "my brother" and especially أختي *2ukhti* "my sister" are particularly common among conservative religious speakers (especially where *2akhi* is a fuS7aism, that is, outside Syria; see unit 15). The more colloquial forms أخوي *2akhuuy* (South Levantine), خيو *khayyo* (Syria), خيا *khayya* (Palestinian), and خيي *khayyi* (Lebanese) are more akin to the English "bro," "mate," "pal," and so on.

The Turkish titles أفندي *2afandi* "Efendi," بيك *beek* "Bey," باشا *baasha* "Pasha," خواجة *kha-waaja* "Khawaja," and خانم *khaanom* "Hanim" all follow the name rather than preceding it. None of them are today particularly common as titles: *beek* is occasionally used for important dignitaries in some regions, and *khaanom* is used to some extent in North Levantine to mean "miss." *Baasha* and *2afandi* are generally used ironically.

Other Polite/Affectionate Forms of Address

When addressing considerably older men in fairly informal contexts (e.g., on public transport or when greeting someone in the neighbourhood), it is often polite to use the word عمو *3ammo* "uncle." For older women too, a variant on "auntie" is used, variously خالتو *khaalto*, طانط *TaanT* (from French *tante*) or أنتي *2aanti* (from English "auntie").

For older people, Muslims often use the words حج *7ajj* and حجي *7ajji* for men and حجة *7ajje* for women. These literally refer to someone who has completed the pilgrimage to Mecca (although in practice they are used simply for older people) and are not typically used by non-Muslims.

Plural for Politeness

Many European languages, most famously French, use the second-person plural to express politeness. Although this feature does exist marginally in Levantine Arabic—perhaps originally influenced by a similar convention in Ottoman Turkish—its usage is limited to the most elevated contexts: addressing royalty and government ministers, for example. It is very unlikely that you will ever encounter it in a real-life situation except perhaps ironically.

When it is used, plural marking often co-occurs with one of various unusual formal pseudopronouns: سيادتك *siyaadtak* "your sovereignty," سعادتك *sa3aadtak* "your felicity," جنابك *janaabak* "your honour." These can be combined with *7aDret*: حضرة جنابك *7aDret janaabak* "your most esteemed honour." These are more frequently used sarcastically.

Of all the various formal constructions, *7aDret* (usually followed by a second-person pronoun, حضرتك *7aD'rtak, 7aD'rtek,* حضرتكم *7aDritkom,* حضرتكن *7aDritkon,* etc.) is by far the most common. Nonetheless, its use is far more limited than the *vous, Sie,* or *usted* forms it is usually compared to. There are two main contexts in which it is likely to be used:

- When asking questions of someone you have just met or don't know, in particular whether they're the person you're looking for: حضرتك الإستاذ مجيد؟ *7aD'rtak 'l2istaaz majiid?* "Are you Mr. Majid?," ايش بتشتغل حضرتك؟ *2eesh btishtghel 7aD'rtak?* "What do you do for a living?"
- By adults working in service industries addressing people of assumed higher social status, such as a taxi driver speaking to a university professor.

It is also universally available for ironic or sarcastic use. A mother might say to her son who stayed out late:

ملاقية حضرتك راجع بنص الليل!

mlaa2ye 7aD ͥrtak raaje3 bniSS ͥlleel!
I see you've finally graced us with your
presence at midnight, Esteemed Sir!

The intention here is obviously not respectful.

In all uses *7aDret* typically occurs alongside the simple use of a second-person pronoun; that is, from sentence to sentence one or the other will be used. In this sense it is more like a word of address in English, used alongside "you" to indicate respect rather than replacing it.

Other Forms of Indirect Politeness

In some contexts, particularly masculine and traditional ones, there is a bit of a convention of avoiding direct address. You are likely to hear questions such as the following:

من وين الأخ؟

min ween ͥl2akh?
where are you from?
[= where is the brother from?]

الشباب من هون؟

ͥshshabaab min hoon?
are you [P] from here?
[= are the guys from here?]

Note as well the occasional use of *bikuun* (see unit 49) for distancing:

مين بتكون حضرتك؟

miin bitkuun 7aD ͥrtak?
who are you, if you don't mind me asking?

Family Members

The terms of address for family members are mostly straightforward. Many of these terms are derived using the suffix *-o* (also used in forming nicknames) or using the possessive; some speakers may also use the unmodified terms (*yaa khaal* "uncle"). As in English, the exact terms of address used differ from region to region and family to family, and since this is not a dictionary, these examples should not be taken as comprehensive but rather as representative:

سيدو *siido* جدي *jiddi* جدو *jiddo*	←	"grandfather" *jidd* جد
ستي *sitti* ستو *sitto* تاتا *taata* تيتا *teeta*	←	"grandmother" *sitt* ست
عمي *3ammi* عمو *3ammo*	←	"uncle" *3amm* عم
خالي *khaali* خالو *khaalo*	←	"uncle" *khaal* خال
عمتي *3ammti* عمتو *3ammto*	←	"auntie" *3amme* عمة
خالتي *khaalti* خالتو *khaalto*	←	"auntie" *khaale* خالة

The words for parents are slightly more complicated. Middle-class and educated and urban families in particular typically use the European (perhaps originally Turkish?) style ماما *maama* and بابا *baaba*. More traditional forms such as ياما *yaama,* يما *yamma,* and يابا *yaaba* are common but in some areas are stigmatised as uneducated or rural.

> In some regions, members of the family are also addressed literally with, for example, "my brother," "my wife," and "my nephew" in a way that would be quite unnatural in English.

Unlike most dialects of English, it is common when talking to your siblings to use possessive pronouns where in English this would sound strange and imply a lack of shared parentage (we would use simply "mum" or "dad" instead). I might say to my awful brother:

بدك تجلطها لإمك؟

biddak 'tjalliTha la2immak?

are you trying to give mum a heart attack?

There is one final point about family terms that needs to be underlined because of how strange it seems to native English speakers. Most Arabic terms of this kind are reciprocal; that is, uncles call their nephews and nieces *3ammo* or *khaalo,* mothers call their sons and daughters *maama,* granddads call their grandchildren *jiddo,* and so on.

Other Affectionate Forms of Address

Nicknames or affectionate ways of addressing close friends, siblings, and the like are far more common in Levantine Arabic than in English. The words usually used for this phenomenon are دلع *dalᵃ3* (Jordanian, Syrian, Palestinian; verbal form دلّع *dalla3,* literally "to spoil") and تغنيج *taghniij* (Lebanese; literally "being cute").

One common kind of nickname uses *2abu* or *2imm/2umm.* There are three different possibilities here:

- The word *2abu* or *2imm/2umm* can be combined with a name even for a childless person. For a male who is the only son or the eldest son, this is sometimes his father's name (and thus the assumed name of his first male child according to naming traditions). Sometimes it is a common nickname associated with the person's first name or place of origin: a man called *3ali* may be nicknamed أبو حسن *2abu 7asan* because Ali bin Abi Talib's son was called Hasan, for example.
- The broader use of *2abu* and *2imm/2umm* to mean approximately "the one with" (see unit 15) can be used to produce a nickname: ابو النضارة *2abu nnaDDaara* "glasses guy,"

إم الأحمر *2imm ˈl2a7mar* "the one in the red," أبو حلب *2abu 7alab* "Aleppo guy," أبو الأمتال *2abu l2amtaal* "Mr. Proverbs."

- The person's first name can be modified using root-and-pattern morphology to produce a single syllable to which *2abu* or *2imm/2umm* is then prefixed (sometimes with a definite article): لؤي *lu2ayy* > أبو اللول *2abu lluul,* زينب *zaynab* > إم الزوز *2imm ˈzzuuz,* مصطفى *muSTafa* > أبو صطيف *2abu STeef.*

Another sort of nickname uses the suffix *-o.* This can be attached to names either directly or to a shortened version: مجيدو *majiido* "Majeed," جملو *jamlo* "Jameel." This can be used for both men and women, but some female names have a variant with *-a*: ريما *riima* "Reem."

Finally, speakers may also derive nicknames using patterns. Some patterns, such as *fa33uul(e)* and *fa33aal(e),* can keep the root consonants of the original intact. Note that the addition of the feminine suffix here, although sometimes read as "cutesy," is equally applicable to boys' and girls' names:

صطيف	←	مصطفى		حمودة	←	محمد
Steef		*muSTafa*		*7ammuude*		*m7ammad*
		Mustafa				Muhammad

But there are also various different shortened forms that involve the removal or doubling of certain root consonants:

جوج	←	جمانة		زوزو	←	زينب
juuj		*jumaana*		*zuuzu*		*zaynab*
		Jomana				Zeinab

علوش	←	علي		دندون	←	دانا
3alluush		*3ali*		*danduun*		*daana*
		Ali				Dana

These are perhaps more common with women and children's names and are less likely to be used with adult men's names on their own.

yaa

The particle يا *yaa* is sometimes used with names and titles. This is mostly dramatic or exasperated or else part of set expressions, although in a few cases—notably with oaths formed with والله *waLLa* (see unit 44)—it is more or less compulsory:

يا بابا، فهام عليي	والله العظيم يا سيدي ما بعرف
yaa baaba, fhaam 3aliyyi	*waLLaahi l3aZiim yaa siidi maa ba3ref*
dad, *please* try to understand	I swear to God, sir, I don't know

Aggressiveness, Rudeness

Just as with politeness, aggressiveness and rudeness are more a matter of word choice and tone than of strictly grammatical phenomena. But there is a set of particles, varying slightly between countries, that can be used to add a distinctly aggressive or rude tone. The most common forms are ولا *wala* (masculine) and ولي *wale* (feminine) in South Levantine and ولا *wlaa* (masculine) and ولي *wlee* (feminine) in North Levantine:

شو قلت ولا؟   بدك ترد حكي ولا؟

shuu 2ult wlaa?   *biddak ʾtridd 7aki wala?*

what did you just say?   are you talking back to me?

> Note that for many Lebanese speakers, ولي *wlee* is used for both masculine and feminine.

These should be used with extreme caution or ideally not at all by a learner. As is the case more generally with impolite language, however, it is sometimes possible to use these sorts of rude expressions with close friends in a way that expresses closeness or playfulness.

ABOUT THE AUTHORS

Chris Hitchcock is a translator, interpreter, and Arabic teacher who has always loved languages. As well as this book, he is the translator of several major works of sociology and political science, including Azmi Bishara's *On Sects*. Hitchcock currently lives in London.

Elias Shakkour directs the Translator and Interpreter Corps at DePaul University and is a certified translator of Arabic, Dutch, French, German, Italian, Portuguese, and Spanish.